UNIVERSITY OF NORTH CAROLINA AT CHAPEL HILL
DEPARTMENT OF ROMANCE LANGUAGES

NORTH CAROLINA STUDIES IN THE ROMANCE LANGUAGES AND LITERATURES

Founder: URBAN TIGNER HOLMES

Distributed by:

UNIVERSITY OF NORTH CAROLINA PRESS

CHAPEL HILL

North Carolina 27514

U.S.A.

NORTH CAROLINA STUDIES IN THE
ROMANCE LANGUAGES AND LITERATURES
Number 193

MARCEL PROUST'S GRASSET PROOFS
Commentary and Variants

MARCEL PROUST'S GRASSET PROOFS

Commentary and Variants

BY

DOUGLAS ALDEN

CHAPEL HILL

NORTH CAROLINA STUDIES IN THE ROMANCE LANGUAGES AND LITERATURES

U.N.C. DEPARTMENT OF ROMANCE LANGUAGES

1978

Library of Congress Cataloging in Publication Data

Alden, Douglas.
Marcel Proust's Grasset proofs.

(North Carolina studies in the Romance languages and literatures; 193)
1. Proust, Marcel, 1871-1922—Criticism, Textual. I. Proust, Marcel, 1871-1922. A la recherche du temps perdu. II. Title. III. Series.

PQ2631.R63Z46174 843'.9'12 77-28650
ISBN 0-8078-9193-2

I.S.B.N. 0-8078-9193-2

DEPÓSITO LEGAL: V. 1.337 - 1978 I.S.B.N. 84-399-8335-2

ARTES GRÁFICAS SOLER, S. A. - JÁVEA, 28 - VALENCIA (8) - 1978

PUBLISHER'S NOTE

All texts from the Grasset Proofs, *published here for the first time, remain the property of Madame Gérard Mante Proust who, through her agent, the Editions Gallimard, has graciously authorized this publication. None of these unpublished texts may be reproduced, translated or paraphrased in French without the permission of the Editions Gallimard. The passages from the* Grasset Proofs *reproduced herein are keyed to the "Pléiade edition" of Marcel Proust's* A la recherche du temps perdu *(3 vol., Paris, Editions Gallimard, 1954).*

TABLE OF CONTENTS

*The asterisk will be used henceforth in the function of *sic*.

Part I

COMMENTARY

> ... mais la vérité subsiste dans la progression des rapports, sans qu'un mot ait l'importance que lui attribuent les amateurs de "variantes"...
>
> Marcel Proust (in 1911 version of *Le Temps retrouvé,* Cahier 57, Folio 37)

The *Grasset Proofs* [1] of *A la recherche du temps perdu* present the only consecutive pre-original version of Proust's masterpiece known to exist. Like the early Spanish explorers looking for the fabulous city of Cibola, Proust scholars have dreamed of discovering one day the Ur-Proust, that continuous first version which supposedly underlies the entire *Recherche.* The first scholar ever to study Proust with a scientific method, Professor Albert Feuillerat of Yale, who wrote his *Comment Marcel Proust a composé son roman* in 1934, believed fervently in this Ur-Proust which he claimed to detect as a palimpsest, but most Proust specialists soon rejected his findings. Maurice Bardèche, the only specialist to make a thorough study of the unpublished manuscripts in the Fonds Proust of the Bibliothèque Nationale, expressed the opinion in his *Marcel Proust romancier* (1971) that

[1] In the reference system of this commentary, we shall distinguish *levels* of text in this manner: references to the *Grasset Proofs* will be given either as variants (example 263:32) to be found in the compendium of variants hereinafter or as italicized page numbers referring to the Pléiade edition (example: *p. 237*) in cases where the texts of the *Grasset Proofs* and of the Pléiade edition are identical; "new text" from the Pléiade edition will be identified by a simple page reference (example: p. 238).

Proust first composed fragmentary episodes in his *cahiers* and that by 1913 the assembling of this raw material into a continuous narrative had probably progressed no further than the first *Grasset Proofs* which were put in type that year. Of course, more recently, Proust's former *gouvernante,* Céleste Albaret, in her *Monsieur Proust* (1973), has appeared to contradict Barrère by asserting that the *cahiers,* which she was known to have destroyed on Proust's orders, were not simply some of the workbooks, similar to those which have survived, but rather a special set of thirty-two *cahiers noirs,* as Proust called them, written in a very legible hand which must have dated from a time when Proust did not write in bed. It is her opinion that the *cahiers noirs* were an earlier continuous version, and the inference is that this version went through the *Temps retrouvé.* No longer needing the *cahiers noirs,* she says, Proust had her destroy them systematically in 1916 and 1917 as he progressed in his writing. If there was an Ur-Proust, which still has to be proved, this holocaust placed it far beyond the reach of Proust scholars whose only available continuous text is still the *Grasset Proofs.*

In the Fonds Proust of the Bibliothèque Nationale there are two sets of *Grasset Proofs,* one dated 1913 and the other 1914. We shall discuss the second set later. Corresponding to the first set, there are two typescripts with many interpolations, some in Proust's often illegible handwriting and others in the very legible handwriting of a copyist. [2] Curiously, it was the less legible "original" typescript which was used in the manufacturing process, as marginal instructions to the printers indicate. It is probable that the second typescript, in which most of the interpolations were made by a copyist, was prepared so that Proust might retain his own copy of the text given to the printers. Although the text of the two typescripts is almost identical (in the *variants* we call attention to one case where this is not true), one typescript is not a copy of the other in the usual sense of the word, that is to

[2] In the manuscripts of *Grasset A* there is this somewhat desperate note from the typist (presumably the English one who worked for Proust at Cabourg): "Monsieur Proust—Monsieur, Je vous envoie le travail de copie. Malheureusement je ne peux pas lire la suite de la page 54 (l'intercalation). Si vous voulez bien me le faire remettre demain matin j'essayerai de le finir, mais ce soir la lumière ne permet pas que je le lise. Stenographer."

say that, except for one or two pages of original typing, both manuscripts are composed from carbon copies of a missing original and sometimes the contrasting carbon copies do not even derive from the same original. It is quite clear that this is not a *static* manuscript, one which is ostensibly finished at one point and then copied continuously by a typist or typists. Bardèche assumes that this typescript corresponding to the *Grasset Proofs* was the same manuscript which Proust began to peddle from publisher to publisher in 1912, only to meet with rejections. He fails to note that the text of the *Grasset Proofs* already differs considerably from an earlier version which is quite visible in the worked over and crossed out typed text itself. [3] If the manuscript which Proust took to publishers in 1912 was identical with, or anything like, the manuscript of the *Grasset Proofs*, replete with typographical errors and containing many unfinished and illegible interpolations, it is understandable that Proust had such a hard time getting a publisher and that Gide, in the name of the Nouvelle Revue Française, threw up his hands in disgust. [4] Grasset apparently did not bother to look at the manuscript since

---

[3] We have surveyed this problem only in a superficial manner, for any other approach would have added a second volume to the present study. It would be difficult to establish with certainty the text of this earlier version. There would be pages missing from the typescript since it is clear, from the original typed page number subsequently replaced by a handwritten number, that Proust moved many pages from their original place and that some of them completely disappeared (although sometimes they reappear as scrap paper on the back of which Proust wrote some of his interpolations). Furthermore, because the typist had such a difficult time copying from some other handwritten manuscript, the typescript is so full of mistakes and blanks that it would often be hazardous to reestablish the original text as distinguished from Proust's subsequent corrections and stylistic improvements. The immediate usefulness of this search for an earlier text would be in a further study of the structure of Proust's work. Because of the state of the manuscripts, partially typed and partially handwritten, it is immediately possible to observe which passages were additions to the earlier version. Likewise the moving about of the original pages would be a clue to structural changes. Fortunately, when he crossed out a passage in the typescript, Proust did not render it illegible, and he even left fully crossed out pages in the manuscripts of the *Grasset Proofs*. We have made a few observations in footnotes. This material must ultimately be collated with the texts contained in the *cahiers* and in *Dossier 21: Manuscrit contenant des fragments autographes*.

[4] Our example may be ill-chosen, for Céleste Albaret, in her *Monsieur Proust,* insists that Gide did not even untie the package.

Proust was paying all of the printing costs himself. As their correspondence shows, Proust had ultimately to pay handsome sums for the corrections.

The *Grasset Proofs* of 1913, as well as the corresponding typescripts, bear the title *Les Intermittences du cœur* and cover the equivalent of what is now called *Du côté de chez Swann* and *A l'ombre des jeunes filles en fleurs*. Typesetting began on May 31, 1913, according to the printer's rubber stamp on the proofs. Henceforth we shall refer to this first set of *Grasset Proofs* as *Grasset A*.

Léon Pierre-Quint's *Comment parut "Du côté de chez Swann"* (originally published in 1930, it was reissued in 1954 as *Proust et la stratégie littéraire*), quoting from the then unpublished letters of Proust, contains the record of what happened to *Les Intermittences du cœur*. Proust had envisioned a two-volume work but had not yet submitted the entire text for the first volume when Grasset objected that there was already too much type to make one marketable volume and insisted that Proust would have to cut. He did, and to the first volume of what was now presumably to be a three-volume work he gave the title *Du côté de chez Swann*, while rebaptizing the entire work *A la recherche du temps perdu*. Proust not only cut, he rewrote; and this extensive rewriting is, of course, the fascinating thing about the *Grasset Proofs*.

Just before the outbreak of the First World War, Grasset began to set type for a continuation of Proust's work. The new proofs, bearing the printer's stamp of June 6, 1914, were entitled *Le Côté des* Guermantes*.[5] Once again Proust was using his printer as a less affluent mortal would use his typist, that is to say, to make a clear copy from which he could work better. The first part of these proofs was new text, coming after the end of *Grasset A*. In the typescript and subsequent proofs the narrative stops at the point where Charlus drives off in the cab after Madame de Villeparisis's tea party. According to the announcement "pour paraître en 1914" on the back of the "faux titre" of

---

[5] This might have been a printer's error, for Proust, in the correspondence of this period and in the 1913 edition of *Du côté de chez Swann*, definitely refers to the volume as *Le Côté de Guermantes*.

the 1913 edition of *Du côté de chez Swann,* the second volume of *A la recherche du temps perdu* was to have been entitled *Le Côté de Guermantes* and was to have included all of the text now called *A l'ombre des jeunes filles en fleurs* plus the narrative going through "Le Salon de Mme de Villeparisis." [6] After this new material which corresponds to *Le Côté de Guermantes* in terms of the Pléiade edition, the 1914 proofs also reprinted completely the unutilized portions of *Grasset A* but with certain corrections and interpolated material which must have come from a partially corrected set of *Grasset A* proofs now lost. In the new printing this old material lacks a title, whereas it bore in *Grasset A* the title "Noms de pays." These second *Grasset Proofs* we shall designate henceforth as *Grasset B.*

We present hereinafter the variants from *Grasset A,* the variants from *Grasset B* in relation to *Grasset A* where the two texts overlap, and subsequently the remaining variants from *Grasset B.* It is regrettable that we cannot juxtapose in the same volume the definitive text and this earlier version, but the cost of publishing even the earlier text in extenso with a critical apparatus would have been prohibitive. The method which we have adopted has the advantage of pointing out immediately the differences between the earlier version and the final text. All variants are keyed to the corresponding sections of the Pléiade text. [7] Where the *Grasset Proofs* are essentially identical with the Pléiade edition, the passage of the original text is clearly delineated on the final text. Thus, by passing from the variant to the delineated section of the Pléiade and back again, one can read consecutively the entire text of the earlier version. Our primary purpose has been to make this *instrument de travail* available to devotees of Proust, after a delay of well on to forty years.

It was, in truth, Albert Feuillerat who, seeking the Ur-Proust, came upon the 1914 proofs which we designate as *Grasset B.* Although he described his *Grasset Proofs,* he never published any

[6] Feuillerat reproduces all of this information in an appendix to his *Comment Marcel Proust a composé son roman* (p. 273).

[7] Before utilizing the compendium of variants, the reader would be well advised to prepare himself a kind of ruler made with the edge of an envelope on which he has ticked off and numbered the 43 lines of a Pléiade page.

of the text so that even the most scientific part of his demonstration remained a matter of hearsay. In the intervening years, these *Grasset Proofs* became as legendary as the Ur-Proust itself and few scholars took seriously Feuillerat's controversial conclusions. It is our intention to reassess these conclusions only when they apply to the material covered by *Grasset A* and *Grasset B*; that will bring us to the mid-point of Feuillerat's book, the remainder being outside our domain.

The *Grasset Proofs,* as we present them hereinafter in the form of variants and delineated passages in the Pléiade edition, contain some interesting secondary information about characters and events but, more importantly, they register in the case of *Du côté de chez Swann* the transition from a still imperfect text to a masterpiece. [8] In the case of *A l'ombre des jeunes filles en fleurs* and the first part of *Le Côté de Guermantes,* the *Grasset Proofs* [9] reveal simultaneously with technical progress some of the fundamental flaws in Proust's method which he overcame in *Du côté de chez Swann* but never had time to overcome in the remainder of his work, even in those parts which appeared during his lifetime. Although we shall now try to summarize our tentative conclusions regarding these texts, our primary purpose is to make them available to Proust scholars. Only when all of the extant texts, such as these, are published will we be able to master the problem of a total textual criticism of *A la recherche du temps perdu.*

Combray

What a close study of the *Grasset Proofs* first reveals is a structural pattern serving to order materials probably composed

[8] As to imperfections in the original *Grasset Proofs,* they of course abound. It may seem rather fastidious to have reproduced so many of them in the compendium of variants, but our purpose has been to make it possible to read the Grasset text as it actually appeared in print. Any other method seemed to lead to too many arbitrary decisions.

[9] In the parlance of the Bibliothèque Nationale, only *Grasset B* is designated as *Epreuves Grasset.* What we call *Grasset A* is erroneously labeled as proofs of *Du côté de chez Swann. Grasset A* is more exactly the proofs of *Les Intermittences du cœur* and there are no proofs extant for *Du côté de chez Swann,* properly so-called.

originally in a haphazard manner. In rechecking Feuillerat in *Grasset B,* being then unaware that *Grasset A* had any unusual interest, we discovered that in the part corresponding to *A l'ombre des jeunes filles en fleurs* the material subdivided naturally into a certain number of *basic narratives.* Sometimes this was the story of one specific event such as the Norpois dinner which began, developed and ended in a very coherent manner which was more visible than in the final text because of the absence of the later interpolations. However, in the case of the carriage trip with Madame de Villeparisis and also the dinner with Saint-Loup at Rivebelle, both of which episodes had visibly a beginning, a middle, and an end, it was not really a matter of one single event but rather of an indeterminate number of superimposed similar events. In other words, they were *composite basic narratives.* If now we look at *Du côté de chez Swann* with the perspective of *Grasset B,* we perceive that "Combray" is precisely a succession of composite basic narratives. Take the very first scene. The narrator is in bed and is awakening from a troubled sleep, undoubtedly drug-induced, as we gather from several passages later omitted; he remembers other rooms which superimpose themselves until the "story" becomes a composite basic narrative, in which are mingled various generalizations on the central theme further disrupting whatever narrative there is; yet the scene ends neatly with a return to the narrator in his original room (which *Grasset A* identifies as "ma chambre de Paris" in the passage at the end of "Combray" where this bedchamber is evoked a final time [186:11]). It is obvious that this technique is the stylistic equivalent of the theory of involuntary memory; it is the very essence of Proust's style.

The next episode in *Du côté de chez Swann* has two introductions before settling down into a basic narrative; the first introduction is more subjective, being the story of the magic lantern; the second, as is characteristic of *Du côté de chez Swann,* belongs to the Balzacian tradition, for it is a quick series of realistic sketches of life at Combray. In fact, the presence of the Balzacian text makes one speculate whether this is not an interpolation which disrupted a more simplified narrative belonging to some earlier state of the manuscript.[10] Be that as it may, the real basic narrative at this point is the story of the good night kiss. In the beginning the composite nature of this narrative is immediately apparent: "Ma seule consolation, quand je montais me coucher.... Quelquefois quand, après m'avoir embrassé, elle ouvrait ma porte..." Innumerable commentators have called attention to Proust's unusual use of the imperfect, which is inevitably the tense for these composite events. In the Pléiade text of this episode, after the "Balzacian" biography of Swann which interrupts the narrative for several pages, the imperfect suddenly yields to a *passé simple:* "Elles furent plus intéressées quand la veille du jour où Swann devait venir dîner..." (p. 22).[11] A little further on: "Nous étions tous au jardin quand retentirent les deux coups..." (p. 23). The composite narrative has now become a precise event. In *Grasset A,* the first *passé simple* occurs six pages later (in terms of the Pléiade edition) and it slips unobtrusively into a dense paragraph of imperfects. All of the conversation in the garden comes before the *passé simple;* it presumably occurred at another time and not on the night of the *dramatic* good night kiss. The complete episode of the good night kiss was considerably rewritten in the final text, pages were moved about, minor episodes reappeared in different contexts, and all such changes were for greater clarity. The result came much closer to being a traditional realistic novel; in the rewriting process Proust had done violence to his method to heighten the novelistic qualities of his work. Much later, in "Noms de pays: le nom," we are reminded again that he originally viewed the entire good night kiss as a composite event by this remark from *Grasset A* which has survived in the Pléiade text: "je m'étais si souvent, le soir, rendu ridicule en envoyant demander à maman

---

[10] It would seem to be dangerous, however, to consider all "Balzacian" passages as additions to an originally more lyrical text, as Feuillerat was inclined to do, because *Jean Santeuil* belonged in so many respects to the realistic tradition. *Cf.* our discussion of this point in "The Break with Realism," in Larkin B. Price, *ed., Marcel Proust, a Critical Panorama.*

[11] Crossed out in the typescript of *Grasset A* there is a long development on Swann's mother whose social ascension, despite, and partially because of, being Jewish, prepares the way for her son's social achievements.

de monter dans ma chambre me dire bonsoir, pendant qu'elle prenait le café avec lui" *(p. 408)*.

To the casual reader the remainder of *Du côté de chez Swann* may seem discursive. Not so at all. Despite the presence of realistic episodes, dialogues and anecdotes, all of which are already in *Grasset A*, the structure is henceforth a sequence of basic narratives. These are so attentuated as to become almost leitmotifs and yet they are what holds this part of the novel together in neat patterns. After a "Balzacian" description of Combray and after some "Balzacian" dialogue on the part of the Combray characters, the narrator leaves for mass, attends mass and returns home. It is the same kind of *déplacement* which provides most of the structure of *A l'ombre des jeunes filles en fleurs*. This "Sunday" theme then continues; the narrator's mother tells him to take a breath of air before settling down to read, as is his "Sunday" custom. From then on the leitmotif is "reading." The narrator is reading not on one particular Sunday but on many Sundays; his age will vacillate in a somewhat disconcerting manner and his reading will get more profound until it culminates in a discussion of Bergotte's esthetic. Then the "asymmetrical Saturday" takes over, subdivided into various walks, one of them in the direction of Méséglise and the other in the direction of Guermantes.

The cuts and rearrangements of texts which Proust made in *Grasset A* reveal an unusual sense of style and of artistic appropriateness. Some passages were omitted or altered because the tone was wrong. Thus, in the opening paragraphs, where the narrator is turning over in bed, the "lit de fer" (6:26) becomes a "lit à baldaquin" and the narrator no longer worries about so prosaic a thing as his unfinished homework. Not necessarily because he wants to hide anything but probably because he feels that the intrusion of an adult omniscient author in these early stages is bothersome, he eliminates allusions (of which there are several) to "ces autres hosties où le pharmacien enferme du sommeil" (13:32) and that curious aside about himself belonging to the "catégorie des monstres" (15:29) as well as the long paragraph on the danger of being killed by a carriage ending with the remark: "Mais bientôt viendra la nuit où l'on ne peut plus peindre et après laquelle le jour ne se relève pas" (44:19).[12] Feuillerat objected further on to such intrusions of Proust's old-age fatigue and used them as a means of dating passages. Little did he realize that this disabused Proust was present in his so-called "première version." It is noteworthy that Proust also cut out some references to religion: the crucifix over the bed at Combray (6:35), a discussion of the immortality of the soul (64:36), and a long badly written passage in which the curé spoke with admiration about his bishop (106:31). A passage which included the description of the "petite pièce sentant l'iris" *(p. 12)* where the narrator indulged in onanism for the first time, is greatly reduced so as to omit mention of the "Collines du Calvaire" and the "souffrances de ma grand'mère à la Passion du Sauveur" (12:31), all of which is rather meaningless in context, although it may have had a particular symbolism, of course, for the author.

Proust also sacrificed many passages and allusions because he placed them too soon. An allusion, in the introduction, to "l'heure d'aller dormir" (6:35) appeared redundant in anticipation of the episode of the good night kiss. The same was true of the long passage ending: "les bras fermés à tout jamais qui seuls savent me guérir" (10:38).[13] A casual reference to the "Vertus et... Vices de Giotto" (18:21), coming too early, would have spoiled the subsequent development of the same subject.[14]

---

[12] Even before sending *Grasset A* to the printer, Proust crossed out the first two sentences in his text which contained the statement: "j'étais déjà malade."

[13] In view of the fact that the mother is still alive in *Le Temps retrouvé* (Pléiade III, p. 931), it is noteworthy that Proust omitted two allusions to her death in *Grasset A* (the reference given above and 13:32). On the other hand, the allusion to the father's death in *Grasset A* (37:8) remains in the Pléiade edition.

[14] This process of pruning anticipatory passages which might ultimately have lessened the impact of future events in the novel had already begun in the typescript of *Grasset A.* Situated at 8:33 in terms of the Pléiade text, there was a long crossed out passage beginning with the subject of the fear of sleeping in an unknown room, continuing with the subject of the obliteration of past friendships by new ones, and ending in the theme of resistance to death. The passage obviously anticipated the development on the fear of strange rooms with which "Noms de pays" begins. Apropos of the obliteration of friendships, it contained the remark: "Partez pour les îles délicieuses de l'Océanie...;" later on, in *Grasset A,* this remark is

That Proust had a propensity for generalizations is quite obvious in *Jean Santeuil.* Feuillerat insisted that generalizations were characteristic of what he called Proust's second manner. In arriving at such a conclusion he totally overlooked the innumerable generalizations in *Du côté de chez Swann* where we still read: "Un homme qui dort... tient en cercle autour de lui le fil des heures, l'ordre des années et des mondes" (5:12). Or: "Peut-être l'immobilité des choses autour de nous est-elle imposée par notre certitude que ce sont elles et non pas d'autres..." *(p. 6).* Long generalizations still remaining in "Combray" treat "notre personnalité sociale" *(p. 19)* and "l'ingéniosité du premier romancier" *(p. 85).* Also there is a strange shift of point of view from Swann to a generalized "nous" in that curious and much rewritten passage, about which we will have more to say later, where the narrator's amorous anxiety for his mother is compared to the amorous anxiety of Swann. Whereas, by the very nature of the subject which required analysis and justified generalization, "Un Amour de Swann" contains a large number of generalizations, "Combray" on the other hand had more of them in the original text than it does now. Proust seemed to realize here that they were a disruptive force in fiction. One long generalization having to do with flowers versus painting he eliminated altogether (139:8). Another on the effect of art on the imagination of children he reduced in size and transformed

---

ascribed to Swann (670:38), but here it is ascribed to "M. de Penhoët" who is never again mentioned in *Grasset A.* It seems likely that Penhoët was an earlier name for Silaria and that Proust here anticipated more of an affair between Mademoiselle de Silaria and the narrator than actually occurred. Another passage (Pléiade 46:40), eliminated from the "madeleine" episode, looked forward explicitly to the uneven paving stones of the baptistry of Saint Mark's, an episode now occurring, of course, in *Le Temps retrouvé.* Corresponding to 82:24 of the Pléiade, in the midst of an already long development on Giotto, there was originally a long passage describing the narrator's later visit to the Giotto chapel, and to this was appended a curious page-long footnote about painting, beginning with a comment on Gustave Moreau. In connection with the discussion of the "deux côtés," Méséglise and Guermantes, there was originally an anecdote (located Pléiade 134:33) about the narrator, on an automobile trip, seeing an unknown castle at the end of an avenue and then being told that it was Guermantes; this turns out to be the proof that one can get to Guermantes via Méséglise, an observation which would obviously ruin the later development on the same subject in *Le Temps retrouvé.*

into a remark by the grandmother's sisters (146:25): A long development on sadism became a psychological analysis of Mademoiselle Vinteuil (163:24).

Practically all of the realistic descriptions of the setting were already present in the original text; in minor alterations, the church at Combray acquired another window (60:42) but lost a door (63:3). But other kinds of realism received considerable attention, particularly dialogue. The loquacious curé was deprived of his stupid monologue in which he tried to talk simultaneously about the view from the Combray church tower and his visit to the bishop (106:31) but he acquired a new monologue on etymologies, much longer and equally boring perhaps, for his interlocutors (p. 105).[15] This time Proust was indulging himself. In another case, however, he paid far more attention to the reality of his conversations. The original dialogue in which Swann and the narrator's parents and other relatives engaged was trivial and amounted only to some miscellaneous remarks about the "jeune institutrice suédoise" (p. 25) and about Swann's readings in Saint-Simon. The introduction of the "vin d'Asti" plus the allusions to the article about Swann in *Le Figaro* incorporate and submerge these banalities which, now thoroughly integrated, constitute one of the most amusing realistic conversations in the novel.

The "vin d'Asti" does not involve only one addition but rather a sequence of additions which weave through various episodes until they reach what might loosely be termed a dramatic conclusion. This is an interesting example of how Proust reworked his text in a conscious effort to introduce a semblance of plot.

[15] This is the first example of a peculiar technique of *parallel construction* found several times in *Grasset A* and *Grasset B*. Three other cases should be noted: Madame de Villeparisis talking simultaneously about fruit and books (697:26); Fleurus-Charlus talking simultaneously about the château of the Montmorency and his "cousine Avaray" (764:16); a minor application of the technique when both Saint-Loup and Françoise go to the post office (785:4). Somewhat similar is the blending of superimposed images as in the lyrical overture to "Noms de pays" where the narrator thinks alternately of Bricquebec-Balbec and Florence, a phenomenon which is frequent in Proust's work. In fact, this superimposing of images seems to be a psychological trait and may be the explanation of the peculiar confusion about the geographical location of Bricquebec-Balbec (whether it is in Brittany or in Normandy).

Already, in this same section of *Grasset A*, there were two other sequences similar to the "vin d'Asti." One dealt with Legrandin and led up to the final revelation of his character. Whether these bits and pieces were added at an earlier stage to enliven a languishing story can only be a matter of conjecture but their arrangement was not haphazard, as is indicated by the fact that Proust, revising his proofs before publication, gave the Legrandin sequence a wider spread by moving the first encounter with him from the Saturday walks to the earlier return from Sunday mass. The third sequence dealt with a character named Vington in *Grasset A* who was replaced by quite a different character, the composer Vinteuil, in the final text. The Vington sequence went through a curious evolution before assuming its final form. Vington was a naturalist who lived at La Combe and he was first mentioned in *Grasset A* as a frequent visitor to the narrator's family, on a par with Swann. At the point in the Grasset text where he was first mentioned, the corresponding Pléiade text now reads: "Le monde se bornait habituellement à M. Swann qui, en dehors de quelques étrangers de passage, était à peu près la seule personne..." (p. 13). Returning to the Grasset text we read: "Le 'monde' se bornait habituellement à M. Vington et à M. Swann" (13:37). But the remainder of the Pléiade sentence is to be found at the very end of the long variant: "En dehors de quelques étrangers de passage... M. Swann était à peu près..." It is evident that this first Vington passage has been unsuccessfully inserted into an earlier text, since this arrangement causes two biographies (Swann's being already there) to interrupt further the episode of the good night kiss and since the boy narrator in the Vington passage is psychologically older than the boy narrator who is the hero of the good night kiss.[16] Obviously Proust shared our opinion about the passage since he excised it

[16] We have subsequently confirmed these deductions about the insertion of the Vington episode in an earlier text by a more attentive examination of the manuscripts for *Grasset A*. The first and second Vington episodes (the second occurring in connection with the walk to mass) are handwritten interpolations but, curiously, the final profanation scene is part of a continuous typewritten text. This last fact may prove nothing other than that the final episode had been added already to an earlier manuscript which the typist was then copying.

altogether in correcting the proofs. In the excised passage the narrator was a *voyeur* peering through a window of La Combe. In a second *Grasset A* passage, more successfully integrated into the narrative of the Sunday mass, the narrator encounters Vington and there is a development on the masculinity of his daughter. All of this is a logical, albeit somewhat artificial, preparation for a third *Grasset A* passage where the narrator looks again through the window of La Combe and sees the Lesbians cavorting. When (as we shall see presently) Berget, the composer of "Un Amour de Swann," became Vinteuil and assumed far greater importance in the novel, Proust decided to merge the musical and the Lesbian themes by transforming Vington also into Vinteuil. While excising the first Vington passage, he still needed the first *voyeur* (being concerned about the plausibility of his second *voyeur* scene), so he transplanted him to the Sunday mass where he is now to be found in the Pléiade text.

The scene of the profanation by the Lesbians obviously looks forward to something but, whatever that is at this stage of the development of the *Recherche*, it is outside the text of *Grasset A*. In a letter to René Blum at this time, Proust speaks of "pages indécentes" leading to "d'autres qui le sont encore plus." [17] In the E.-J. Bois interview of 1913, Proust insisted on the importance of these *preparations* as a structural device. [18] This is essentially the same technique as in the plot sequences just described, only on a much larger scale and with less concern for plot interest. The ambiguous gesture of Gilberte at La Frapelière-Tansonville is in the Grasset text but its interpretation is somewhere beyond *Grasset B*. On the other hand, some of the *preparations* already have a destination within the proofs. All allusions to the Guermantes obviously anticipate the narrator's one-way love affair with the Duchesse de Guermantes in *Grasset B*. [19] When the

---

[17] Léon Pierre-Quint, *Proust et la stratégie littéraire*, p. 32.

[18] *Textes retrouvés*, ed. Philip Kolb and L. B. Price, pp. 215-220.

[19] The first reference to the Guermantes occurs in precisely the same spot in *Grasset A* (60:42) and in the Pléiade text. However, much earlier in *Grasset A*, Madame de Villeparisis says to the narrator's grandmother: "Je crois que vous connaissez beaucoup M. Swann qui est un grand ami de mes neveux Villebon" (20:25). This is obviously an old passage dating from the time when the Guermantes were Villebons (see P.-L. Larcher: "Le

narrator's parents question Legrandin *(p. 129)* on the subject of Balbec (here called Brilquebec and Querqueville in *Grasset A*), it is necessarily with a view to the narrator's future trip in "Nom de pays: le pays." Gurcy-Charlus (142:20) as the supposed lover of Madame Swann ties in with the allusions to his virility in the Querqueville-Balbec episodes. The awkward passage, added in the rewriting of *Grasset A* (p. 149), where Swann tries to remember the question that he wanted to ask about Vinteuil, has an only too obvious link with "Un Amour de Swann." The Villeparisis sequence is a little more difficult to unravel. In *Grasset A*, when the narrator's grandmother goes to call on her former convent friend, the latter urges her to rent an apartment in the same house. Yet this house does not seem to be Hôtel de Guermantes but rather one house in a series of "rowhouses" with uniform façades (19:37). Nevertheless, when the narrator's parents do move to the Hôtel de Guermantes in *Grasset B*, there will be a common denominator between the two episodes, the *fleuriste* of the distinguished manners. Curiously enough it is not the *fleuriste* but rather an "ouvrière en journée" (20:25) who quotes Madame de Sévigné. If the *fleuriste*, who becomes Jupien in the revisions, does not yet have a distinct personality, the allusion to Madame de Sévigné already prepares us for the grandmother's interest in this writer. Thus these passages are already interrelated in the *Grasset Proofs* although the relationships may vary somewhat from those in the final text.

Finally there is the problem of the Saint-André-des-Champs sequence, which lingers on as a leitmotif through the entire *Recherche*. In the revised text published as *Du côté de chez Swann*, the narrator and his parents, during one of their Méséglise walks, take refuge in the "porche" of the Gothic church of Saint-André-des-Champs which the narrator enthusiastically describes in

---

château de Villebon ou le château de Guermantes révélé," *Bulletin de la Société des Amis de Marcel Proust*, no. 17, 1967). In the final version, Proust corrected this to read: "mes neveux des Laumes." This is clearly an error for, although the future Duc de Guermantes bore the title of Prince des Laumes in *Du côté de chez Swann*, it is hardly likely that Palamède and Gilbert bore that name. Of course, it is possible that Laumes was an intermediate choice between Villebon and Guermantes, but we know of no evidence to support such a theory.

detail, particularly since he thinks that he finds in one of the Medieval figures a representation of Théodore, "le garçon de chez Camus" (p. 151). The question is whether this passage existed in some embryonic form in *Grasset A,* in which there is an unfortunate lacuna at this point. In the margin of one of the manuscripts only there are some undecipherable additions concerning Saint-André-des-Champs; we conjecture that, if the missing fragments of *Grasset A* are ever found, these scribblings will not have been reproduced.[20] In any event, there is no mention of this church elsewhere in the *Grasset Proofs* until we get to the Elstir episode in the section corresponding to *A l'ombre des jeunes filles en fleurs.* Here the narrator discusses with Elstir *(p. 840)* the "porche" of the Balbec church and compares it to Saint-André-des-Champs, which Elstir knows only from photographs. Since the Elstir episode occurs only in *Grasset B* in a somewhat rudimentary form, it seems likely that, when making this addition to *Grasset A,* Proust also decided to add Saint-André-des-Champs to "Combray." Not exactly a *preparation,* the "Combray" passage unquestionably has a relationship with the later episode.

In *Grasset A* there was an earlier appearance of Madame de Villeparisis in an obtrusive *flash-forward* which describes the narrator many years later preparing to go down to dinner in her château (6:35). The original passage seems to have the exclusive purpose of accustoming the reader to the name of this character who will eventually play a prominent role in *Grasset A.* Transformed into an allusion to Gilberte de Saint-Loup at Tansonville,[21] the passage in the final text anticipates, as Proust says

---

[20] In a letter to Gaston Gallimard in 1919, Proust writes: "Cher ami et éditeur, vous paraissez me reprocher mon système de retouches. Je reconnais qu'il complique tout . . . Mais quand vous m'avez demandé de quitter Grasset pour venir chez vous, vous le connaissiez, car vous êtes venu avec Copeau qui devant les épreuves remaniées de Grasset s'est écrié: 'Mais c'est un nouveau livre!' " (*Choix de lettres,* publiées et datées par Philip Kolb, p. 244). The rewriting of *Grasset A,* in order to make *Du côté de chez Swann,* took place on the proofs and, in fact, a fragmentary set of these corrected proofs has survived (see our explication preceding the compendium of variants). It is definitely an anomaly to find therefore, in one of the manuscripts of *Grasset A,* what appears to be an addition to *Grasset A.*

[21] In *Le Temps retrouvé,* Tansonville is occupied by the Germans and Combray is the scene of a battle. Except for the problem of dates of

in the Bois interview of 1913, "tel mariage entre deux personnes qui dans le premier volume appartiennent à des mondes bien différents . . ."[22]

Feuillerat objected to Proust's disregard for the age of his narrator in the corrections to *Grasset B*. He had only to look at *Du côté de chez Swann* to see that Proust was already showing the same disregard because of his technique of the *composite basic narrative*. When correcting *Grasset A*, Proust succeeded in eliminating some inconsistencies in the age of his narrator but he left many others. In the original version of the good night kiss, when guests arrived the narrator was habitually sent to bed but then allowed to return to the "petit salon," far from the guests, until nine o'clock. There he meditated on the beauties of nature: "Je mettais devant la mienne [ma pensée] la beauté de ce jardin, les vers que j'aimais le mieux, les pensées philosophiques . . ." (28:21). If the narrator was supposed, psychologically, to be approximately seven years of age, as Proust's biographers have assumed, then this precociousness is disturbing. Also disturbing is the allusion to reading *Quentin Durward* and other novels just before the scene where the narrator's mother initiates him to literature by reading *François le Champi.* Near the end of the Pléiade version of "Combray," in a passage beginning "cette année-là," thus making it contemporaneous with the encounter with Gilberte, there is a surprising reversal of the psychological age of the narrator when, saying adieu to the hawthorns, he is wearing a "douillette de velours" *(p. 145).* In the original text he is also wearing "bigoudis" (145:7). Proust did not accomplish much by removing the curlers since he left the velvet coat. A similar confusion of the narrator's psychological age occurs in the Uncle Adolphe episode where the narrator's tongue-tied and naive behavior is that of a very small boy and yet we are told that this same small boy discusses art with a

---

composition, one might logically suppose a connection between the destruction of Combray and the statement in *Du côté de chez Swann*: "La muraille de l'escalier . . . n'existe plus" (p. 37). George D. Painter (*Marcel Proust: The Early Years,* p. 15) argues that this is an inadvertency which proves that the good night kiss took place at Auteuil and not at Illiers. It may be worth noting that the inadvertency existed in *Grasset A.*

[22] *Textes retrouvés,* p. 217.

capital "A" with his school friends. It only confuses the issue when, in a *flash-forward,* he says: "Plus tard, quand je fus au collège . . ." *(p. 74)* and then goes on to report his discussion of the leading actors of the day. It is evident that "plus tard" was already mixed up with the small boy's present before the words were used in the text. One similar confusion, however, which Proust managed to eliminate, had to do with Gilberte. In the 1913 text Swann's daughter is mentioned much earlier when his "unfortunate" marriage is alluded to; at that point the narrator's mother feels very sorry for Swann and, despite the family attitude, often brings the conversation around to the daughter when she is alone with him. This daughter is as precocious as the narrator sometimes is, for she knows Reims and Chartres by heart and has been promised a visit to Bourges. This episode is moved out of Swann's biography and into the conversation in the garden preceding the narrator's departure for bed; only an inconsequential fragment remains which reduces Gilberte's precociousness to the mother's remark that Gilberte must have "le goût des belles œuvres comme son papa" (p. 24). When Gilberte is a few years older, Swann tells the narrator, in an addition to *Grasset A,* that his daughter is a good friend of Bergotte and that they go together to visit "les vieilles villes, les cathédrales, les châteaux" (p. 99). On the ground that he, too, is old enough, we can perhaps accept without protest the Leconte de Lisle jargon of Bloch but there is no doubt that it has always jarred readers of Proust at this early point in the novel. Already precocious in everything he says and does, the insufferable Bloch becomes even more advanced for his age when, in an addition to the *Grasset A* passage in which he got himself expelled by the narrator's parents for having cast aspersions on the virtue of the great-aunt, he assured the narrator privately that "toutes les femmes ne pensaient qu'à l'amour et qu'il n'y en a pas dont on ne pût vaincre les résistances" (p. 93). [23]

[23] Except for this sensuous addition, the character portrait of Bloch passed without significant alteration from *Grasset A* to the Pléiade text. The narrator's anti-Semitic grandfather, it will be recalled, was accustomed to make the family uncomfortable by humming or singing passages of *La Juive* whenever a Jewish friend of the narrator was present. It is very

The esthetic system of "Combray" was already essentially complete in the Grasset text, going from Bloch's revelation of the originality of Bergotte, to the *aubépines,* to the inadequacy of language in the "zut" episode, and ending in the prose poem on the belltowers of Martinville. In the passages on Bergotte the original idea seems to have been that the new author interested the narrator because of his archaic style and his "philosophie idéaliste" *(p. 94).* The narrator of *Grasset A* says: "J'aurais voulu que tous ses livres fussent une suite de morceaux et posséder son opinion, c'est-à-dire la Vérité, sur toutes les grandes questions" (95:23). He looked forward with eager anticipation to the time when he would be "dans la classe appelée Philosophie" (97:8). Whereas he has astute observations to make about Bergotte's use of language, he does not attempt to define the term idealist philosophy and regrets that, on almost all questions, "son opinion m'était inconnue" (95:23). In the process of expanding these passages significantly, Proust rewrote the sentence just quoted in this manner: "Aussi sentant combien il y avait de parties de l'univers que ma perception infirme ne distinguerait pas s'il ne les rapprochait de moi, j'aurais voulu posséder une opinion de lui, une métaphore de lui, sur toutes choses..." (p. 95). Also he rewrote the sentence preceding this one in such a way that the word "image," which had accidentally crept into the original text, became the important idea. This rewording seems to make Bergotte a Proustian *avant la lettre* and one therefore finds the new material which follows very enigmatic. A rather long addition tells how "quand je commençai de composer un livre, certaines phrases dont la qualité ne suffit pas pour me décider à le continuer, j'en retrouvai l'équivalent dans Bergotte" (p. 96). One cannot avoid seeing here an allusion to *Les Plaisirs et les jours.* Is the fault to be construed as the narrator's or as Bergotte's? If Proust had not just inserted these remarks about metaphors and images, we would readily interpret this as a condemnation of

---

curious to note that, although Proust had already transferred this material to its present position in *Grasset A,* the typescript contains, in the middle of Swann's biography, a crossed out passage which states that, even though the Jew, Swann, was his friend, the grandfather hummed the passages of *La Juive* when other Jews were visiting. The narrator comments that these were "préjugés absurdes."

Bergotte's style. All of these ambiguities have somewhat muddled a text which was originally brilliant in its literary insights, however precocious they might seem in the mind of a young boy, and which carried a message for the future of the narrator's esthetic: "Il me sembla soudain que mon humble vie et les royaumes du vrai n'étaient pas aussi séparés que j'avais cru" *(p. 96).* In the backwash of these esthetic considerations, Swann suffers somewhat as the whipping boy of the narrator (in "Un Amour de Swann" [p. 193] the old text already says: "je commençai à m'intéresser à son caractère à cause des ressemblances qu'en de tout autres parties il offrait avec le mien"), for a long new passage, which is perhaps the crucial analysis of his character in the entire *Recherche,* criticizes his ironical manner of speaking and his lack of purpose in life: "Pour quelle autre vie réservait-il de dire enfin sérieusement ce qu'il pensait des choses, de formuler des jugements qu'il pût ne pas mettre entre guillemets, et de ne plus se livrer avec une politesse pointilleuse à des occupations dont il professait en même temps qu'elles sont ridicules?" (p. 98).[24]

Proust's effort, in rewriting the "Combray" section, was directed towards polishing the style, eliminating banalities in the narrative, fitting pieces more logically together, and, above all, improving those characteristics which are germane to the novel: character presentation, setting and action. The introductory section, doubtless already the most rewritten Proustian text, required a further rewriting before it came out as the poetic masterpiece which we know today. The capital scene of the good night kiss went through a complete recasting to remove banalities and to introduce more life and action; in the process a long digression on Françoise's independence of her masters almost completely vanished, but another equally digressive passage on the narrator's adult love affairs survived in an altered form (we shall return to it later in discussing similarities between Odette and Albertine). The long poetic description of the church of Saint-Hilaire, which

[24] In a suppressed passage in the typescript of *Grasset A* (situated Pléiade 353:16), Swann also seems to have asthma; at least he cannot stand the odor of chrysanthemums. Another suppressed passage (358:40) made him particularly sensitive to the death of his mother.

had originally been related for no good reason to the curé's visit, moved from page 106 to page 59, which places it on the way to mass, a much more logical position, not too far from the initial description of Combray. And, of course, Legrandin moved from page 111 to page 67. While the changes introduced technical improvements, they did not alter the basic pattern of the novel which continued to oscillate between the subjective narrative of "je" and the objective recounting of an omniscient author. In fact, Proust did not adhere to a particular novelistic technique, so that commentators have continued to distinguish various "voix narratives." In *Jean Santeuil* there were numerous shifts of optics; that is to say, the focus of the central intelligence shifted from one character to another. In the final text of the "Combray" section, two examples of this shift survive from the original, once when Swann's father remembers his deceased wife *(p. 15)* and once when "ma mère" reflects on the sad life of Vington-Vinteuil (159:37). A more striking passage, in which "ma grand'mère" reflects on the tower of Saint-Hilaire (64:36), occurs only in *Grasset A*. Although the "Combray" section was still in many ways an anti-novel in this confusion of manners of writing and narrating, it was clear that Proust was still measuring his performance against the standard of his predecessors. His improvements were designed to make a better novel rather than a more iconoclastic anti-novel.

Un Amour de Swann

"Un Amour de Swann," which follows "Combray," shifting from the first person to the third person, imposes an almost totally new pattern on the novel which Proust was writing. In *Grasset A* the narrator was concerned about the verisimilitude of this third person narrative, for he says: "J'en avais connu l'histoire avec une précision qui paraîtra peu vraisembable, mais seulement parce qu'on ne s'avise pas du moyen par lequel j'ai pu l'apprendre. Combien d'inventions de la science, de résurrections de l'archéologie, ou de découvertes de la police, qui auraient pu paraître impossibles, tant qu'on ignorait le biais par lequel cette impossibilité a été tournée" (186:11). The same preoccupation remains in the final text but it is still an article of faith as to how the narrator gained his intimate knowledge of Swann's life. The prevailing opinion is that "Un Amour de Swann" is not, as a text discovered by André Maurois once suggested, a crypt beneath the cathedral, but rather an addition composed in one piece and inserted between the already written "Combray" section and the Querqueville-Balbec section which was eventually to become *A l'ombre des jeunes filles en fleurs.* Bardèche seems to have proved this point conclusively by reference to Proust's *cahiers.* A further argument in support of this view can be made on the basis of a difference in styles. As we have already said, the Querqueville-Balbec section is structured according to the principle of the *composite basic narrative.* Starting "Un Amour de Swann," Proust continued to write in this lyrical manner and launched into a preposterous comparison between the Verdurins and certain squares of Venice (he reused the Venice part in *Albertine disparue*), but, after this lyrical introduction, he suddenly switched into a linear narrative conceived in the tradition of the French "psychological novel." There is only one subject, Swann in love, and this subject is pursued relentlessly from beginning to end. The story has a perfect structure which can be represented as a curve ascending from Swann's disinterest in Odette, through the identification with "Zéphora" and the first crystallization (the Maison Dorée episode), and leveling off in a brief plateau of happiness; [25] then descending through separation by action of the Verdurins, through jealousy of Forcheville, reaching finally emotional indifference, due to the action of space and time, and tapering off in a dream. The whole tone of "Un Amour de Swann" remains prosaic and Proust breaks into his characteristic lyricism only once when he describes the grooms on the stairway of Madame de Saint-Euverte's townhouse and then the monocles of the guests. Even these passages are carefully rewritten in the final version to tighten the style.

---

25 This plateau is more visible in *Grasset A* since the added passages amplify Swann's anxiety about the durability of love. However, this sentence is in both texts: "qu'importait qu'elle lui dît que l'amour est si fragile, le sien était si fort" (236:21 and p. 237). Also the lovers' games of the original text survive and Proust even added some more kissing (p. 238).

In the transition from *Grasset A* to the published text, very little of the original text of "Un Amour de Swann" was suppressed. Aside from the Venetian introduction,[26] which totally disappeared, the only noteworthy elimination was the inept passage on Madame Verdurin's "aquarelle de fruits" (207:19a) which shows that lady in a sentimental light to which we are unaccustomed.[27] The "aquarelle" is related to another passage which might be entitled: "ces raisins-là me purgent" *(p. 208).*[28] Both passages seem to have survived from a time when the character of Madame Verdurin was not firmly established in Proust's mind and when he confused triviality with realism. At any rate, Proust seemed to feel that two such stories were too much; he kept the more grotesque one, perhaps to show up the vulgarity of Madame Verdurin, and sacrificed the more naive one. Usually the additions were so carefully integrated that the reader does not sense that they are new material. An exception to this statement will be found on page 214 of the Pléiade where there is a confusing coming and going between omniscient remarks concerning the "peintre" knowing that Vinteuil is ill and a bantering conversation between Madame Verdurin and Cottard about Dr. Dieulafoy-Potain. The confusion is entirely the result of the insertion of new material. There is also one example of the kind of addition in which Proust later indulged most indiscriminately, a *flash-forward* in which, "that evening," Oriane discusses Swann with her husband (p. 343).

A curious suppression was the removal of four references to Swann's characteristic gesture of stroking his "brosse."[29] These

---

26 It will be noted that the new introduction is manufactured from the old text but with changes in the order of paragraphs.

27 The Verdurins were originally "cousins des Vington" (199:25).

28 Reexamination of the manuscript of *Grasset A* discloses that the "aquarelle de fruits" was a handwritten interpolation in the margin of the typescript. Page 254 of the Pléiade text still refers to the "exposition d'un artiste, ami de Mme Verdurin, qui était mort récemment..." This must have been the person who painted the "aquarelle de fruits."

29 In "Combray," in both texts, Swann had "un haut front entouré de cheveux blonds presque roux" *(p. 14).* In "Un Amour de Swann," both texts mention "la brosse de ses cheveux roux" *(p. 195).* There is a new text which mentions a visit to the hairdresser "par lequel il se faisait relever sa 'brosse'" (p. 345) and this seems to be related to a final allusion to the

cuts were obviously made in a spirit of antirealism, for such *tics* were traditionally an aspect of character presentation among the realists. The only concession to outward forms of realism in "Un Amour de Swann" was the detailed description of Odette's apartment which was already in *Grasset A*. All of the original "Balzacian" characters, from Brichot to Saniette, were in the original text, but two of the most amusing anecdotes are new material, Saniette's story about the duc de la Trémoïlle (p. 261) and the "serpent à sonates" (p. 264). But now Proust's attention was fully absorbed by problems of "psychological realism" as he analyzed his main character Swann. His additions to the original text do not significantly change any aspect of this already extensive analysis but they add depth. For example, Swann's identification of Odette with Botticelli's "Zéphora" *(p. 222)* is in the original but a page and a half of further analysis are added here. The frantic search for Odette in nocturnal Paris is also in the older text but there are two new analyses, the second of which includes a paragraph of typical Proustian generalization on "ce grand souffle d'agitation qui parfois passe sur nous" (p. 230).[30] The "petite ouvrière fraîche et bouffie comme une rose" *(p. 218)*, whom Swann originally preferred to Odette, is evoked thrice in added passages (pp. 226, 246, 325).

As in "Combray," Proust sometimes made sequential retouchings according to the system of *preparations*. Thus he added a passage on Chopin (p. 335) in which the real purpose was to demonstrate Oriane's eagerness to speak to Swann so as to prepare better the variant where they do speak (p. 340). As though looking forward to the appearance of Saint-Loup in *Grasset A* (it is well-known that Proust likes identical psychological situations), he added a very brief passage in which Swann travels in the South with Odette and has the same jealousy reactions as Saint-Loup

"brosse" and the visit of the hairdresser, which was in both texts (p. 381). However, all allusions to stroking the "brosse" have vanished.

[30] In fact, Feuillerat notwithstanding, generalizations are not infrequent in "Un Amour de Swann." *Grasset A* contains the following generalizations: love has its "propres lois inconnues et fatales" *(p. 196)*; "un plaisir nouveau s'il s'agit de femmes assez difficiles" *(p. 234)*. New generalizations are: "ce grand souffle d'agitation qui parfois passe sur nous" (p. 230); "premières apparitions que fait dans notre vie un être destiné plus tard à nous plaire" (p. 381).

when he appears in public with his mistress. In another retouching, designed to motivate better Swann's disgrace at the hands of the Verdurins, which was due in the original text only to his snobbish attitude with regard to "Mme La Trémoïlle" *(p. 265)*, Proust added some unpleasant remarks by Swann concerning Brichot. To tie in with the anecdote of Swann being impelled to bring in the name of La Pérouse in his conversation with General de Froberville *(p. 343)*, which was new material, he changed Odette's street address from "Pauquet" to "La Pérouse" (321:14), identified Odette's apartment as being not only "derrière l'Arc de Triomphe" but also on "rue La Pérouse" (p. 219), and then kept referring to the rue La Pérouse in new texts to strengthen the association between Odette's name and her address (pp. 266, 322, 364, 372). He also made the Lapérouse restaurant Swann's favorite haunt (p. 296).

The most important sequential alterations concern what might be called the Maison Dorée "plot" which assumed much greater importance when Proust decided to introduce more system into Odette's deceitfulness. It will be recalled that one of her most startling admissions was that she had not been at the Maison Dorée at all when Swann had sought her frantically throughout Paris. Evidently Proust had not originally anticipated this development, for the admission was in a new text and, to prepare it carefully, he made the Maison Dorée into a leitmotif. In the old text the restaurant where Odette claimed to have been was called "chez Larue" (231:26) and it was never mentioned again. In the revisions it became the "Maison Dorée" and sometimes the "Maison d'Or" (Odette uses both names on p. 371). In the passage in which Odette sent Swann a letter saying "ma main tremble si fort" *(p. 225)*, which was in both versions, Proust added the information that this letter was written from the "Maison Dorée" on the day of the "fête de Paris-Murcie donnée pour les inondés de Murcie." In rewriting another passage he added a recall of the letter and again mentioned the Maison Dorée (p. 345). The *dénouement* of all this was a new text in which Odette alluded accidentally to the fact she had dinner with Forcheville "le jour de la fête de Paris-Murcie" (p. 370). At that point Swann realized that she had penned on that very same day the letter which he had kept as his most cherished possession. When she swore that he was mistaken, he brought up, in a threatening manner, the name of the "Maison d'Or," as he called it this time, and Odette readily confessed that she had not been there, as she once claimed, that other night when Swann had sought her everywhere. The *dénouement* of the Paris-Murcie sequence also set up a relationship with another passage inserted earlier (p. 217) in which Odette proposed to Swann that she might tell a white lie to Madame Verdurin.

In the Grasset text there was already a sequential relationship with another letter from Odette to Swann in which she said in the original wording: "Vous avez laissé chez moi vos cigarettes, que n'y avez-vous laissé aussi votre cœur, je ne vous l'aurais pas rendu" (234:41). This other letter was part of another sequence leading to one of the more dramatic episodes of the book where Swann opens Odette's letter to Forcheville and finds her using the same words with him (p. 282). The "cigarette" letter was originally the second letter from Odette to Swann but Proust moved it back thirteen pages so that it became the first letter. With the letter in the new position it now appeared that Odette was taking the initiative in this amorous maneuvering. The cigarette letter, occasionally juxtaposed with the trembling hand letter, carries on as a leitmotif to the end of the novelette.

Probably the most extensive additions of all concerned the character and behavior of Odette. Although these additions emphasize more than ever the unpleasant sides of her character, it would be unwarranted to say that they are added in a spirit of vilification, for they only dramatize what had already been said about her in the original text. An example of such dramatization is the new passage in which Swann thinks that she has hidden in the apartment someone "dont elle avait voulu faire souffrir la jalousie ou allumer les sens" (p. 373). From the outset, Odette lies, as we have just said. But Swann himself is partly to blame, for on one occasion in *Grasset A* he not only condones but encourages another white lie on Odette's part; when she sees Madame Verdurin again she blushes and stammers (p. 239). She is a poor liar, as we note again in that long passage in *Grasset A* where Swann pities Odette, but says nothing, as she tries to lie her way out of the difficult situation created by her failure to answer the doorbell an hour earlier (p. 278). Ultimately Swann takes a more active role and lectures her on the danger of lying (p. 291), but that does not prevent her from lying about her time of arrival in Paris each time she takes a trip (p. 295). That Odette was ignorant and superstitious was not new either. In the old text the Verdurins say that "ce n'est pas une vertu ni une intelligence" *(p. 228)* and Swann also realized "qu'elle n'était pas intelligente" *(p. 240)*. Her superstitiousness was mentioned only once in the original text when Swann, in his bitter interrogation of her near the end, told her to swear on her "médaille" (362:29). This was in the old text but it had crept in without explanation; therefore Proust added allusions to her "médaille de Notre-Dame de Laghet" (pp. 221, 362).

Particularly in respect to lying, but also in many other ways, the behavior of Odette and Swann towards each other anticipates similar behavior on the part of the narrator and Albertine. For example, Swann is as much a liar as the narrator and uses lies to provoke responses. Because of Swann's lie in a letter, Odette replies with the trembling hand letter. But the most striking similarity between Odette and Albertine is that they are both accused of Lesbianism. The old text already contained the long development on the "Filles de Marbre" *(p. 360)* which made Swann suspect a Lesbian relationship between Odette and Madame Verdurin. Whereas the narrator seeks, but never finds, the absolute truth concerning Albertine's Lesbianism, Swann does not pursue the matter because he is more interested in Odette's heterosexual relationships. Since the anonymous letter accused her, in the old text, not only of Lesbianism but also of being at the beck and call of an "entremetteuse" (p. 369), Swann interrogated her on this latter point but in vain. When (still in *Grasset A*) he eventually learns *(p. 378)*, under circumstances which are not explained because they are now unimportant, that she was Forcheville's mistress, the news does not affect him in the least. The law of forgetting has become operative, as it will later in the case of the narrator. Moreover, the entire story of Swann revolved around the theory of the subjectivity of love, beginning with the Botticelli identification which has no counterpart in the narrator-Albertine story. But where the two stories particularly come together is in emphasizing the disparity between the flesh and blood mistress and the imaginary creature who causes such emotion. Like the narrator later, Swann, in the old text, is astonished by "sa chair qui devenait d'ailleurs plus flasque" (308:14); in moments of lucidity, he too is aware of the disparity. In general, Swann's love for Odette appears to be more intense than the narrator's for Albertine, but his love also vacillates like the narrator's. At one point in the old text, Swann "ne voyait plus aucun inconvénient à ajourner un essai de séparation" *(p. 307)*; at another, he found himself hoping "qu'elle mourrait sans souffrances dans un accident" *(p. 355)*, which has an analogy in the narrator wishing for Albertine's death.

In adding lengthy new texts to expand the basic premises of the Swann-Odette relationship, Proust heightened the resemblance to the narrator-Albertine relationship. When Odette returns from traveling, she hides out for a day or two, then pretends that she has just arrived (p. 296); Albertine does the same thing but with more complications. Some additions introduce contradictory evidence about Odette's physical appearance, so that she keeps changing as much as Albertine does later; at one point the new text records that she "épaississait" (p. 291); eight pages later a new passage made her beautiful again (p. 298), but this is contradicted somewhat later by the old passage on her "chair flasque," already noted, which was the pretext for another new text on the disparity between the "figure de chair" and the "trouble douloureux" (p. 308).

As to be expected, several important additions concerned Swann's suspicion that Odette was a Lesbian. In the original text, Swann forced her to confess that she had done this kind of thing "peut-être deux ou trois fois" *(p. 363)*; but then, pressing his advantage, he failed to get further when, contradicting herself, Odette said that she had made everything up so that he would stop bothering her (365:36). The first expansion occurred after the word "fois" where Proust introduced a long analysis of the emotional repercussions of this news on Swann. The second expansion was a new admission by Odette that she had done it one evening in the Bois de Boulogne "dans l'île" (p. 365). In the new text Proust reintroduced her retraction of the whole thing but added another long analysis of the effect of this on Swann. In the course of this interior monologue in indirect discourse, Swann remembered that Odette "avait éte livrée, presque enfant, à Nice, à un riche Anglais" (p. 367). This referred back to another new text in which Swann regretted his break with the narrator's Uncle Adolphe (in the old text Odette had said that Uncle Charles "venait d'essayer de la prendre de force") because he wanted to "tirer au clair certains bruits relatifs à la vie qu'Odette avait menée autrefois à Nice" (p. 312). It will be recalled that Albertine also had a past related to Nice.

Now it is a curious fact that, whereas the essential elements of the Lesbian interrogation scene were already in the old text, the Paris-Murcie scene, in which Odette inadvertently disclosed that she had been with Forcheville on that day in the past, was a later addition. It is as though Proust had originally forgotten the main point of his story, namely that Swann was jealous of Forcheville and not of any Lesbian. Since the source of the Lesbian interrogation was already in *Jean Santeuil* and also in the earlier short story "Avant la nuit," without a doubt it was part of the repertory of indispensable scenes either in Proust's mind or in his *cahiers*. Rereading his text, he must have realized that he had given undue prominence to this passage which was so charged with personal meaning. Although he expanded it, he still placed it therefore in a subordinate position in relation to the structurally more important Paris-Murcie scene, the technique of which was obviously suggested by the already written Lesbian interrogation scene.

To finish with the resemblances between Odette and Albertine, we note that included in the Paris-Murcie scene was a visit by Swann to a brothel in search of some trace of Odette. The narrator makes a similar visit to a brothel in search of news of Albertine. And finally we note that Odette is also a "prisoner" like Albertine since Charlus-Fleurus is appointed to take her out and in general to report her comings and goings (pp. 315, 322).

In his 1934 account of *Grasset B,* Feuillerat stated (quite correctly, as we shall see later) that Albertine does not appear as a character, although she is, of course, in the final text. Robert Vigneron's discoveries in 1937 concerning Agostinelli led to a general acceptance of the hypothesis that Albertine did not exist until Proust began rewriting *Grasset B.* [31] Bardèche says, for ex-

[31] Robert Vigneron: "Genèse de Swann," *Revue d'Histoire de la*

ample (op. cit. II, p. 33): "Il semble donc évident que le personnage d'Albertine et les engagements profonds que l'insertion de ce personnage va provoquer dans le plan de la *Recherche* ont pour origine la liaison de Proust en 1913 avec Alfred Agostinelli . . ." Later Bardèche modifies this categorial statement when he says (ibid., p. 191): "Je préfère croire que Proust suivait en lui-même . . . une piste inscrite depuis beaucoup plus longtemps dans son imagination, depuis le temps où, bien avant de connaître Agostinelli, il inventa la scène de Montjouvain . . ." [32] Proust himself said very explicitly in a sentence added to the La Combe-Montjouvain scene: "On verra plus tard que, pour de tout autres raisons, le souvenir de cette impression devait jouer un rôle important dans ma vie" (p. 159). He seems to state unequivocally now that this apparently gratuitous scene has a definite plot function.

The *Grasset Proofs* yield some additional evidence that Proust was thinking of *an* Albertine long before he gave her a name. In one variant in "Combray" he says: ". . . je pressentais déjà ce que je devais connaître plus tard dans l'amour non partagé" (43:17). But the capital passage is a long one in "Combray" still standing somewhat obtrusively in the midst of the scene of the good night kiss (p. 30). In the final version it is a condensed preview of "Un Amour de Swann" in which the narrator compares his childhood anguish to the mature anguish of Swann. In the original text this has nothing to do with Swann but is rather a generalization which purports to come from the mature experience of the narrator. A little further along there is a lengthy variant which has left no trace in "Combray." It is another generalization, this time on the subject of "la bienveillance d'un tiers" (31:35). As the generalization develops it becomes anecdotal and an "editorial we" intervenes to tell a story of going to a ball, of expecting "our" mistress to object to being spied upon, and of having her say on the contrary: "Vous ne voudriez pas m'attendre

Philosophie et d'Histoire Générale de la Civilisation, Jan. 15, 1937. Feuillerat hypothesizes, however, that the additions which Proust made in writing *A l'ombre* were primarily parts of the Ur-Proust which were moved backwards.

[32] Bardèche merely echoes Painter's view in the matter. Cf. Painter, op. cit., p. 209.

cinq minutes, je vais partir, nous reviendrions ensemble, vous me ramèneriez chez moi." The anecdote has a familiar ring because it is transported elsewhere and becomes an episode of "Un Amour de Swann" (p. 298). However, the original passage continues and, as the narrator returns to the story of the good night kiss, he slips back naturally into the first person singular but then, when he alludes once more to his future love affairs, he forgets to change to a less personal pronoun. Thus we find him saying: "Même dans les amours les plus mêlées de jalousie, je réussissais habituellement à ne pas penser à ce que ma maîtresse pouvait faire pendant le jour. Mais le soir, pour avoir cette paix, cette paix mêlée de trouble, la seule que peut donner une maîtresse puisqu'au moment même où on croit en elle on doute d'elle encore, et qu'on ne possède jamais son cœur comme l'enfant reçoit dans un baiser le cœur de sa mère . . . il fallait qu'elle m'eût dit: 'Bonne nuit, je vais me coucher', pour que je pusse m'endormir" (31:35). Whatever else this may tell us (for example, it suggests a parallel with the passage in which Albertine confers on her lover the good night kiss), it states without question that the narrator is to have a mistress and that the leitmotif of their affair will be jealousy. All of this has disappeared from "Combray" except for the fragment already mentioned which was altered so as to refer to Swann and except for a curious passage in which, in the original, the anxiety of the narrator is suddenly transferred to the abandoned mistress who, fraternizing with the doorman, receives in answer to her letter the message "qu'il n'y avait pas de réponse." In the final text this anecdote becomes a device for dramatizing the narrator's anxiety when Françoise reports: "Il n'y a pas de réponse" (p. 32).

On one hand, it could be argued that these vague allusions to the narrator's mistress antedate the decision to write "Un Amour de Swann" and that, therefore, in writing about Swann and Odette, Proust, at that stage at least, had abolished the mistress originally projected. Of course, the opposite view is just as tenable, namely that "Un Amour de Swann" was intended, as it is in the final text, to be a preview of the affair with Albertine. However, certain facts are incontrovertible. As we have seen, the La Combe-Montjouvain scene was a late addition, even though it is in *Grasset A*. At that time Proust must have decided to reintroduce, or to plan more carefully to introduce, *an* Albertine into his story. Furthermore, when he rewrote "Un Amour de Swann," previous to its publication in 1913, he was so preoccupied with his future Albertine that he made Odette resemble her even more.

Originally the arts in "Un Amour de Swann" had only a psychological function. In the case of painting, despite additions, there was no fundamental change in approach. To the original brief statement that Swann saw a resemblance between Odette and Botticelli's "Zéphora," Proust added a long passage telling how Swann identified his coachman Rémi with Rizzo's "Lorédan," M. de Palancy's nose with a Ghirlandajo, and Dr. du Boulbon with a Tintoretto, all of which only heightened the psychological function. Even the long poetic digression on the grooms at Madame de Saint-Euverte's reception had no abstract esthetic purpose but, as the old text said, was an example of Swann's "disposition particulière qu'il avait toujours eue à chercher des analogies entre les êtres vivants et les portraits des musées" (p. 323). In fact, this passage was so explicit in underlining the psychological function that the addition one hundred pages earlier was quite unnecessary. Likewise Swann's interest in Vermeer, unchanged from the original version, had no esthetic implications but was merely an example of his inability to be profound or productive, which ultimately elicited unkind comments from Odette.

There is, of course, a character whom the old text calls simply "le peintre," but whom two additions identify as " 'monsieur' Biche" (p. 203) and "M. Biche" (p. 213). As every reader of the final text of the *Recherche* knows, Biche is a nickname for Elstir. However, returning to this point later, we shall discover that Elstir does not appear in *Grasset A*, that he was added in *Grasset B*, but that the passage identifying Biche with Elstir was an even later addition. Hence it cannot be argued with absolute certainty that Proust identified his anonymous "peintre" as Biche with a view to future use in connection with Elstir, but it does seem likely. However, the introduction of the name Biche on two occasions only does not have any effect on the character who was clearly not conceived as Elstir (that is to say, as the exemplar of all modern painting) in the beginning and who was not in any way altered by the magic name of Biche. The "peintre" has no esthetic function and no esthetic depth. He is rather a Balzacian character on a level with Cottard or Brichot. His only distinguishing characteristic is his vulgarity which he uses on the painting of his contemporaries in order to achieve the same social success as Cottard does by his puns or Saniette by his apocryphal anecdotes. Proust kept all of the original passages and never once did he replace the designation "le peintre" with "Biche," the name, as we said, being used only in two totally new passages. The original text gives us no information about his painting (the "aquarelle de fruits" is not by him but by a "maître mort récemment" [199:30]). The second addition in which Biche is mentioned identifies our painter as a member of the avant-garde who, to the disgust of the Cottards, paints women with "les cheveux mauves" (p. 213). Whether this is good or bad is not explained; only the guaranteed stupidity of the Cottards seems to imply that it is perhaps good.

Music, in the original text of "Un Amour de Swann," was also assigned exclusively a psychological function. After much comment on Madame Verdurin's physiological reaction to music, it is announced that the "sonate de Berget" (206:9) will be played, not the "andante" as the final text says but rather the "scherzo." At this point the old text becomes confused and the same confusion survives in the final text. First, with no comment having been made on the music, we are told that the playing is over ("quand le pianiste eut joué") and that Swann is particularly gracious with the pianist *(p. 208)*. Then, in both versions, occurs the flashback to "l'année précédente" when Swann had heard the sonata for the first time, but subsequently the text continues with the rendition of the sonata at the Verdurins' soirée, after which Swann again *(p. 212)* goes through the motions of thanking the pianist ("quand le pianiste eut fini"). Usually this kind of repetition occurs when material has been added; it is possible that the flashback was an insertion at an earlier stage of the text but this hypothesis is hard to defend because the psychological principle of recall is so fundamental to the whole demonstration. However, we note already in the original text a curious inverse amplification of the material; whereas the sonata at the Verdurins' is played only by a pianist, the earlier rendition involved a violinist who seemed to be indispensable for a proper artistic effect. If the earlier rendition was more complex, the old text still does not dwell on the music but rather on its effect on Swann. Proust is here propounding a psychological theory of musical appreciation. According to the old text (and the rewritten text incorporates this idea), Swann had a distinct advantage the first time in that "il ne savait pas la musique" (208:32). His first impression is one of pleasure and confusion because the music does not give him time to reflect but gradually, as he listens, his memory stores up certain sensations so that, when an identical sensation is created by the music, he begins to distinguish the parts which give him pleasure. After the music is over he wishes to have the opportunity of hearing it again, but a "deuil" in the family of his hosts makes it impossible to go back to them with questions and he never learns the name of his composer. When he hears this music a second time at the Verdurins', his memory again identifies certain characteristic sensations and particularly "la phrase aérienne et odorante qu'il aimait" (p. 211). Although Swann is enjoying music in a pure state, that is to say without emotional associations, Proust's approach to the problem is still essentially psychological rather than esthetic. In fact, it is even asserted that Swann was in love with the "petite phrase" and that he transferred this love to Odette. Somewhat inconsistently, Swann steps out of his role of ignorant amateur by explaining to Odette, not yet knowing her lack of intelligence, that "une phrase musicale est un être invisible... elle est vêtue de son..." (212:26). Although he eliminated this passage, Proust inadvertently left in a recall of the passage when Verdurin says: "Je ne sais si tu as entendu ce qu'il lui débitait l'autre soir sur la sonate de Vinteuil; j'aime Odette de tout mon cœur, mais pour lui faire des théories d'esthétique, il faut tout de même être un fameux jobard!" (p. 228).

Henceforth the old text emphasized only the emotional significance of Berget's music which had become recognized by everyone at the Verdurins' as "l'hymne national de leur amour" (218:18). So unimportant does the esthetic value of the music become that Swann, at Odette's suggestion, gives up all idea of having the entire sonata played and regrets that it has "une beauté intrinsèque et fixe, étrangère à eux" *(p. 219)*. The sonata even becomes mingled with their amorous games so that art is readily interrupted by trivialities. Even though the Verdurins are about to ostracize Swann, they accede to Odette's request and arrange at a restaurant for a surprise rendition of the sonata in Swann's honor (in the revised text they even have this idea themselves). Finally, when the sonata appears a last time at the Saint-Euverte reception, it is the impetus for a whole catalogue of past events as Swann remembers the principal episodes of his affair with Odette.[33] In fact, the original catalogue is quite prosaic as he remembers "le soir où il avait buté contre elle rue Royale, où dans la voiture il l'avait enfin embrassée et possédée" (345:35); in the rewriting it becomes less precise and far more poetic. Shades of Musset then descend on the scene: "Et Swann aperçut, immobile en face de ce bonheur revécu, un malheureux qui lui fit pitié parce qu'il ne le reconnut pas tout de suite..." *(p. 347).* Even in the original text, this last passage is lengthy and rises above the emotional level in describing the sound of the violin *(p. 347)* and in generalizing the role of the subconscious in the mnemonic process *(p. 350).* At last Proust is expressing himself in the language which he will adopt for his revisions when he writes, for example: "ce n'est pas un clavier mesquin de sept notes, qui est ouvert à l'invention du musicien, c'est un clavier incommensurable, encore inconnu, comme inexistant..." (349:13).

The revisions of the sonata passages are extensive and, in all cases but one, thoroughly integrated. Having been renamed Vinteuil and being the same Vinteuil whom we met in the revisions of "Combray," the musician now has a personality of his own for the reader although he still remains essentially anonymous for Swann who refuses to believe that he was the "professeur de piano des sœurs de ma grand'mère" (p. 214). The only information about Berget furnished by the old text was that the "peintre" knew that he was "très malade et que le docteur Dieulafoy craignait de ne pouvoir le sauver" (214:21). The new text added that Vinteuil was "menacé d'aliénation mentale" and "qu'on pouvait s'en apercevoir à certains passages de sa sonate"

[33] In the typescript of *Grasset A* it was the reception of the Princesse de Parme but Proust changed the name to Saint-Euverte before sending the manuscript to the printer.

(p. 214), remarks which perplexed Swann in his musical interpretation. Rising, at the Saint-Euverte reception, to esthetic heights, Swann invokes the genius Vinteuil who has become "ce frère inconnu et sublime qui lui aussi avait dû tant souffrir" (p. 348). In the beginning, for some unaccountable reason, Proust momentarily places an aura of mystery around this name of Vinteuil. Whereas, in the original text, Madame Verdurin announces that her pianist is about to play Berget's sonata, in the new text Swann learns the name of his musician only after the rendition. In the very first revision which describes his initial encounter with the sonata, Swann, although allegedly ignorant of music, has an amazing depth of perception "quand, au-dessous de la petite ligne du violon, mince, résistante, dense et directrice, il avait vu tout d'un coup chercher à s'élever en un clapotement liquide, la masse de la partie de piano, multiforme, indivise, plane et entrechoquée comme la mauve agitation des flots que charme et bémolise le clair de lune" (p. 208). This time the music has an imperceptible message and conveys "la présence d'une de ces réalités invisibles auxquelles il avait cessé de croire" (p. 211) which distinctly gave him the feeling of a "possibilité d'une sorte de rajeunissement" (p. 210). However, the original idea was that, beginning on a pinnacle of appreciation, Swann gradually lost the ability to hear the message because his love for the abstract music blended with his love for Odette, and this idea was not lost because the old text remained. Yet each addition insured the continuing artistic presence of music even though Swann heard the music less well. Thus, when Odette played the sonata, the music now reserved space for "une jouissance qui elle non plus ne correspondait à aucun objet extérieur et qui pourtant, au lieu d'être purement individuelle comme celle de l'amour, s'imposait à Swann comme une réalité supérieure aux choses concrètes" (p. 237). Whereas the old text left Swann with only a physical enjoyment of music, now Swann found himself "transformé en une créature étrangère à l'humanité" (ibid.). As to be expected, it was the Saint-Euverte concert which received the most painstaking rewriting. This time Proust makes a more technical description of the music and attributes the impression which it created "au faible écart entre les cinq notes qui la composaient et au rappel constant de deux d'entre elles" (p. 349), a passage which has subsequently enabled musicologists to identify the piece. In a final addition, which this time is badly glued in place (it begins with the statement that Swann knew that the little phrase "reparaîtrait à la fin du dernier mouvement" [p. 351] and ends with the same statement that he "savait qu'elle allait parler une fois encore" [p. 352]), Swann has become an accomplished musicologist; it would appear that he had forgotten Odette's admonition not to study the work of Vinteuil. In the last analysis, all that he learned from the experience was that "le sentiment qu'Odette avait pour lui eu ne renaîtrait jamais, que ses espérances de bonheur ne se réaliseraient plus" (p. 353).

Noms de pays: le nom

The next "partie" after "Un Amour de Swann" was entitled simply "Noms de pays "and this designation applied to everything up to the end of *Grasset A*. In the Pléiade edition, of course, there are three subtitles in this section: "Noms de pays: le nom," "Autour de Mme Swann," and "Noms de pays: le pays." [34] The first two subtitles resulted from Proust's decision to finish *Du côté de chez Swann* with a return to his hero, the narrator, and this produced a very artificial break in his text. From the structure of the original "Noms de pays," it is evident that Proust first thought of this part as one unit since it began (and, in fact, the Pléiade version still begins) with an overture on the theme of Querqueville-Brilquebec-Bricquebec-Bolbec-Balbec which does not really become the subject until the second half of "Noms de pays." [35] However, in spite of the absence of any

[34] Feuillerat (op. cit., p. 273) reproduces in facsimile the announcement "pour paraître en 1914" which assigns to the two remaining volumes the titles *Le Côté de Guermantes* and *Le Temps retrouvé*. The following subdivisions are indicated for *Le Côté de Guermantes*: "Chez Mme Swann. —Noms de pays: le pays.—Premiers crayons du baron de Charlus et de Robert de Saint-Loup.—Noms de personnes; la duchesse de Guermantes. —Le salon de Mme de Villeparisis." However, *Grasset B*, although put in type after the publication of *Du côté de chez Swann*, contains no subtitles.

[35] In the original typescript of *Grasset A*, before correction, the name Bolene is also found for Balbec (*Ire Dactylographie*, p. 261, according to Proust's numbering system). The narrator comments in *Grasset A* on "l'ornementation presque persane" of the name Bricquebec (658:24). In the Pléiade

break whatever in the printed text of *Grasset A*, there is still a logical break in *Grasset A* since that text includes, in the middle (that is to say where "Autour de Mme Swann" now ends), the elaborate conclusion to the Madame Swann theme. For the sake of convenience, we shall therefore adopt for this remaining portion of *Grasset A* the designations "Noms de pays: le nom" and "Noms de pays: le pays," although nothing in Proust's text authorizes such appellations.

In tone and structure "Noms de pays: le nom" returns essentially to the inspiration of "Combray." The narrator has come back to his childhood reminiscences and has no intention of imposing any particular plot on them. There is a slight difference, however: whereas "Combray" seemed to condense a block of time in the narrator's past, obliterating chronology, there will be henceforth an essential narrative following the chronological order of events.

If "Noms de pays: le nom" can be said to have a subject, it must be the narrator's love for Gilberte. In the original story, this love recedes into the background when the narrator turns all of his attention, if not his affection, on Madame Swann. The mother eventually eclipses the daughter. Thus Madame Swann, rather than Gilberte, is the subject of the "finale" which we now find subdivided in the Pléiade text between the end of the "partie" now called "Autour de Mme Swann" and the end of *Du côté de chez Swann*. In order to comply with Grasset's request, Proust did not write a new conclusion to *Du côté de chez Swann* (if we exclude from this remark the last three sentences on p. 427, which are new), as has often been said; rather he moved two paragraphs, which had originally preceded the long transition to the Montfort-Norpois dinner (they moved from p. 413 to p. 416), and placed immediately after them the second half of the material on Madame Swann in the Bois which concluded the original "Noms de pays" (the section displaced originally fitted after variant 637:40). Although this deft work with the scissors pro-

text this same comparison applies to Balbec. The name having evolved to "Bolbec," which was the name of a town near Le Havre, Proust must have decided to go all of the way and make it sound like "Balbek," a city which, although not in Persia, is vaguely over in that direction.

duced an artistically integrated result, this arrangement seemed to cut off the story of Gilberte in mid-air, inevitably leaving the reader perplexed. Perhaps some future editor of Proust will have the temerity to override this unfortunate decision and rearrange the texts in their natural order. Let us now return to our study of the text in this natural order.

The lyrical overture records the imaginings of a small boy who has been stimulated by Legrandin's remark that Bricquebec-Balbec is at the end of the world (130:39), in a spot more remote than Finistère itself *(p. 384)*, and by Swann's remark that its church is an example of "l'art persan" *(p. 385)*. To this fabulous place goes "le beau train généreux d'une heure vingt-deux." The fantastic itinerary of the train takes us through recognizably Norman cities, through "Bolbec" wherever it is, and finally seems to end at Quimperlé which is, according to most geography books, in Finistère.[36] A little further on in the text of *Grasset A*, the name of Bolbec definitely suggests to the young narrator a "poterie normande" *(p. 388)* but, a few lines further on, he seems to give us a choice between "l'architecture et les paysages de la Normandie ou de la Bretagne" as though still influenced by Legrandin's allusion to Finistère. Of course, the narrator really does know where Balbec is because he once told us, when he was still calling the place Querqueville, that Legrandin had a sister "mariée dans la Manche, près de Querqueville, avec un gentilhomme bas-normand" (68:8). The ephemeral qualities of this Norman-Breton geography persist, as we shall see, when the narrator eventually sets out for Balbec.

When the narrator's father proposed an Easter trip to Florence, a poetic image of this city, originally composed for the most part only of sun rays, blended with the images of Balbec. This led to observations on the evocative effect of the names of cities, the result being "des images confuses qui tirent d'eux la couleur dont elles sont peintes" (387:37). Because of reading *La Chartreuse de Parme*, the narrator brings Parma into his musings and then Venice infiltrates without warning. Parma vanishes but Florence and Venice, coupled together and occasionally mingled

---

[36] In Volume III of the Pléiade (p. 542), Quimperlé is identified as a station on the local railway near Balbec.

with Balbec, live on in his imagination until finally his father announces an imminent departure for sunlit Venice which contrasts with Paris whose chestnut trees are only beginning to show signs of spring. Shortly after the trip to Italy they are supposed to go to Balbec, according to the old text (389:19). All of this comes to an abrupt end when the narrator has a "mal de gorge" and the doctor condemns him to going no farther than the Champs-Elysées.

Although most of the first part of the overture survived with only stylistic improvements, the end changed considerably (beginning on p. 389). In describing Florence, Proust first suggested that the narrator imagined it through painting but then quickly substituted the notion that he was seeing it rather through the illustrations in guide books in which he was intrigued by "ce personnage minuscule que le dessinateur avait figuré se promenant en chapeau haut de forme, la canne à la main au pied du portail" (389:19). Guide books seeming out of keeping with this poetic purpose, Proust substituted at this point the notion that his narrator was seeing Venice through the paintings of Giotto "qui montrent à deux moments différents de l'action un même personnage" (p. 390). In his imagination the narrator did not have a total image of Florence but rather a fragmented one, as though he were seeing the city in a succession of paintings. Allusions to Giorgione and Titian, apropos of Venice, were already in the old text and they remained, but the personage of the guide book moved over to the imminent departure for Venice and, now in a photograph, became a minute character with a derby hat standing in front of St. Mark's.

The small boy condemned to the Champs-Elysées was accompanied by Françoise. Since Proust had neglected to explain how Françoise got there, he hastened to add that she had entered "notre service après la mort de ma tante Léonie" (p. 393). Another minor correction was less fortunate; in an unaltered old passage he had already explained that his parents had proposed an Easter trip to Florence *(p. 386)* but he inadvertently remarked in the rewritten part: "Quand mon père eut décidé, une année, que nous irions passer les vacances de Pâques à Florence et à Venise..." (p. 389). Being, in the long run, more preoccupied with infinite rather than finite time, he cut out altogether the interesting remark that the period of anticipation lasted two years after his father's first announcement about the trip to northern Italy and that it was only at the "carême de la troisième année" (389:19) that precise plans for departure were made. Also gone in the final text (but reappearing in the second volume of the Pléiade edition, p. 256) was the passing allusion to a trip really accomplished by Proust to a German watering place.

The final text of the overture contains the brief remark that the doctor also forbade the narrator to go to see La Berma. This now seems to be only a *preparation* for the La Berma scene to come later, but it was originally the pretext for introducing a very curious passage which stood in the same relationship to this second overture as the "madeleine" passage did to the first overture. As in the final text, but at greater length, the narrator states that he would not have minded too much going to the Champs-Elysées if only Bergotte had described it. The old text goes on to say that he did try to be artistic in a Parisian setting, that he went to the Pont de la Concorde and recited verses of Heredia in an attempt to transform the Seine into the Nile and the bateau-mouche into a "trirème," after which he remarks: "Ce n'est pas que je ne fusse capable d'éprouver de moi-même des plaisirs d'imagination." Then the curious passage begins. It is an anecdote which relates how, in the Champs-Elysées, he went to the "water-closets, où je dus attendre Françoise." Suddenly the mustiness envelops him with "une félicité qui semblait... me rendre plus vaste, m'étendre, m'appuyer à elle, si bien que je m'aventurais dans la zone aromatique avec une ivresse inexpliquée et tranquille, comme si j'avais traversé un monde soudain plus durable et plus vrai" (393:35). But his meditations are interrupted by "la tenancière de l'établissement, vieille dame à perruque rousse et à joues plâtrées" who invites him to make use of the facilities "gratis." He ventures to ask her what the smell is and she says it is the "humidité du bois ancien." Returning home, he drinks a little beer to prevent a "crise d'étouffement" and suddenly identifies the musty odor of the old "bureau d'octroi," in which the toilets had been installed, with that of "la petite pièce de mon oncle Charles à Combray." But the narrator goes on to say that this revelation was fruitless since he continued to turn for inspiration to works of art rather than recognizing that "un peu de poésie se trouvait parfois se produire en moi au contact de la réalité quotidienne." Finally the fact of having to drink beer requires a long explanation. Completely rewritten, all of this material, including the explanation of the beer, moves forward a hundred pages. The "tenancière" reappears in a Balzacian scene as the unforgettable Marquise de Saint-Ferréol and even rudiments of the W. C. episode remain (pp. 492 and 494) but they are so buried in the surrounding text that this olfactory "madeleine" loses completely its esthetic significance. The W. C. episode would seem to be a gross caricature of the original "madeleine" passage if it were not told in complete seriousness, as though it were even an indispensable event transposed from real life. In the artistic life of the narrator of the *Grasset Proofs* it appears to be an event of the utmost importance and one to which he will refer back several times.

The story of Gilberte in the Champs-Elysées is related in the same straightforward linear manner as "Un Amour de Swann," if one can call "linear" a narrative composed, most of the time, of composite scenes related in the imperfect. It is the result of one continuous inspiration whose integrity has been respected, for, contrary to his habit, the author did not subsequently graft on other materials. Since the passing of time is registered so frequently, one even has the impresison that the story covers more space than its actual nineteen pages. The pattern of the narrative is almost geometrical; a scene in the Champs-Elysées alternating with the narrator at home. The "plot" may be analyzed as follows: (A) First encounter when the narrator hears the name of Gilberte as he once heard it at Combray; [37] in the next few days he is invited to play with her and this continues, although she does not mind being absent when a matinee with a friend is more tempting. (B) At home, the nar-

[37] The narrator asserts that he has loved Gilberte "dès Combray" *(p. 410)*, which is perhaps only a slight exaggeration, given the intensity of his "amour" when he saw her for the first time *(p. 142)*. However, there is no need to take him too seriously, for he had also said of the Duchesse de Guermantes: "Et aussitôt je l'aimai" *(p. 177)*.

rator watches the weather. Will it prevent her coming? The vegetation changes and winter sets in. (A) One snowy day he goes to the park, sees the old lady of the *Débats,* is about to give up when Gilberte comes sliding in on the ice. Like "des moineaux hésitants," the other children appear and one of them identifies the narrator as belonging automatically to "le camp de Gilberte." (B) Believing in Amour with a capital "A", the narrator sees more and more evidence that Gilberte does not love him. He has trouble remembering what she really looks like; he subdivides her into two *moi,* the one who lives in his imagination and the one, so different, with whom he plays. (A) Gilberte gives him a talisman, the "bille d'agate," which might be construed as a token of affection, and lends him Bergotte's brochure on Racine to which Swann, in an addition, had referred years before at Combray (p. 99). She even asks him to call her Gilberte. (B) The disparity between the real and the imaginary Gilberte is still so great that her recent actions have no real meaning for him. (A) With the return of spring, after a somewhat circuitous walk from his college to the park (which is reduced slightly in the final text), the narrator arrives at his destination expecting Gilberte to burst in on the scene as she did on that other first day of the season. Only the old lady of the *Débats* is there, as she was on the snowy day. He gives up hope, drags Françoise off in the direction of the Arc-de-Triomphe, but then returns to find Gilberte at the park. Swann arrives to pick up Gilberte, appears not to recognize the narrator, and the narrator asks Gilberte to come early the next day, which she declines to do, for she has a series of engagements which will probably keep her occupied through the Christmas season. (B) The despairing narrator imagines an impossible letter in which Gilberte confesses her love, consoles himself by reading Bergotte on Racine, and then, by a process of dialectics, arrives at the conclusion that he is the only one in love. But he decides to make one last desperate effort by writing her, perhaps on New Year's Day, a letter asking her "de renoncer à notre amitié ancienne et de jeter les bases d'une nouvelle amitié" *(p. 412).* Seventy-four pages will intervene before this letter is actually written. Meanwhile the beautiful linear narrative, which was already so perfect in the original version that only minor stylistic retouching was necessary, would be interrupted by the transition to the dinner with Norpois and then the dinner itself.

If the transition and the Norpois dinner interrupt the linear development of the Gilberte story and disrupt its symmetry, they are not extraneous to the story, for, in spite of all of the digressions, we get back to the Swanns in the course of the dinner and then specifically to Gilberte. In fact, there is also a plot relationship with what follows. In the original text, the transitional section begins with the narrator's "pèlerinage" (416: 30) to the Swanns' house, to the Bois "où se promenait presque chaque jour Mme Swann" (417:11) and to the rue Duphot to spy on Swann going to the dentist. Alterations to this passage consist of the elimination of the allusion to the Bois because this is to be the subject of the conclusion of *Du côté de chez Swann* and of the addition of Odette's "confiance à des médailles" (p. 416) which ties in with the Notre-Dame de Laghet theme already identified in "Un Amour de Swann." After that come the amusing passages in which the narrator discusses Swann with his parents. Here the alterations involve a more lengthy development on the narrator's mania for repeating Swann's name and for talking continually about Gilberte; they also include two minor alterations which make the narrator pull his nose, in imitating Swann, instead of humping his back (414:25) and which replace Swann's "cravate à pois" (415:6) with a "manteau à pèlerine."

Before Montfort-Norpois actually gets there for dinner, we are served up his Balzacian biography in several courses. In the first part, there are two minor additions, the allusions to his service as "contrôleur de la Dette, en Egypte" (p. 434) and to the *Journal des Débats*. But another addition near the end is especially interesting because it clearly spells out Proust's reason for spending so much time on this character; he indicates that he is fascinated by the "formes surannées du langage particulières à une carrière" (p. 437). Later on we discover that this interest of the mature author is not shared by the youthful narrator.

Before the dinner can begin we are already off the subject. Because there has been no interruption in the *Grasset Proofs*, except for the ambassador's biography, the author can allude with impunity to "l'approche des vacances du jour de l'an pendant lesquelles... je ne devais pas voir Gilberte" (p. 439) and can explain that, "en voyant l'abattement" (439:1), his mother suddenly announced that he could go to see La Berma whom he had worshipped since "Combray." This change of heart on his parents' part was due to the recommendation of Montfort-Norpois, which explains how this long episode can intervene at this point.[38] In its original shape the La Berma episode is an uninterrupted linear narrative which begins with the mother's announcement, continues with the narrator's period of intense anticipation, takes him to the theatre where amazement at the art of play acting yields to disappointment when La Berma performs in the role of Phèdre, and causes him to applaud nonetheless when he shares "le vin grossier de [cet] enthousiasme populaire" (451:9).

The story of the La Berma matinee obviously had to be told somewhere since it had been anticipated by so many previous allusions and since it was indispensable to the esthetic and psychological patterns of the total work. Coming at this juncture and interrupting another narrative, it encouraged Proust in his own bad habits. In "Un Amour de Swann" and in the narrative of Gilberte up to the point to which we have just taken it, he had proved that he could not only tell a straightforward story but could structure it with unequaled artistry. However, in "Combray," he had also demonstrated that he could shape apparently shapeless material in the most artistic of patterns while avoiding a convention such as chronology and while juxtaposing the most disparate scenes gleaned from his notebooks. In truth, he was himself very much aware of a difference in techniques, for, at the time when he was negotiating an agreement with Grasset and when he was contemplating only two volumes, he wrote to René Blum: "ce premier volume est beaucoup moins narratif que le second."[39] Once the dam had been broken by

---

[38] It will be noted in the variants that Proust says "Norpois" about as frequently as "Montfort." The typescript shows that he kept changing the name back and forth as though he had not decided which name to use.

[39] Pierre-Quint, op. cit., p. 40.

the La Berma episode, it almost seemed that Proust set out consciously to disrupt the various narratives which held together, not necessarily the "second" volume, but the latter part of what he originally called the "first" volume. When he rewrote *Grasset B* to make a new volume entitled *A l'ombre des jeunes filles en fleurs,* he adopted the casual and matter-of-fact tone of the final version of the beginning of "Un Amour de Swann" and discoursed at random on various characters. After an allusion to the upcoming Norpois dinner, he immediately began a long discussion of Cottard and then of the new social-climbing Swann, following this with an announcement of things which were going to happen at La Raspelière a few volumes farther on in a part of the text which perhaps had not been written in 1914. In this circuitous fashion he then got back quite naturally to the biography of Norpois, carried over from the old text. Everything he says in this new introduction is going to prove to be repetitious; Swann's social climbing was already the subject of a long development farther on in *Grasset A* and was retained; Cottard was scheduled to reappear at La Raspelière and would have had nothing to do with *A l'ombre des jeunes filles en fleurs* (except for a passing allusion in *Grasset A*) if Proust had not contrived during the rewriting to bring him in briefly.

In *Grasset A,* the La Berma episode already contained the embryo of another digression where the focus suddenly shifts to La Berma herself as, presented through the optic of an omniscient author, she reigns over the personnel of her theatre and arrives before curtain time in her "calèche à deux chevaux à longue crinière" (446:24). When he reworked the La Berma episode, Proust did not hesitate to continue with his *roman à tiroir* technique and to introduce another long episode which might be entitled "Françoise et Michel-Ange, ou Bœuf à la gelée." Although logically tied in place by virtue of being a preparation for the Norpois dinner to come, it obviously disrupts the story of La Berma. The third long addition is a generalization about the concierge being the first to learn that a war is over (p. 450) which is placed before the already existing passage on the contagious effect of applause on the narrator. A few other minor alterations are worth noting: Proust changed the Racine quotation

(p. 441); "Bergotte," mentioned in the same breath with "Anatole France" (442:25), was crossed out; the anonymous domestic in the gallery became Françoise (p. 447); and the "attitude d'offrande" (449:24) of La Berma became "le bras levé à la hauteur du visage," to which was added "un artifice d'éclairage dans une lumière verdâtre" (p. 449). The passage on the opera glasses *(p. 449)* was shortened and that on the fact that "Phèdre* allait être pour un jour une pièce comme ces autres nouveautés" (442:25) was omitted altogether.

The Montfort-Norpois dinner, as a succession of conversations, is by definition entitled to be discursive. It is therefore surprising to note that, in the Grasset text, it is essentially unified and progresses towards a logical terminus. After describing in detail Montfort's diplomatic affability and his habit of scrutinizing his interlocutor intently, the narrator reports on the first subject of conversation, which is literature. As Montfort (who had recommended that the narrator be permitted to go to see La Berma and also to become a writer rather than a diplomat) discusses literature, the narrator realizes that the ambassador's view of that subject is repulsive to him, as is also the model whom Montfort advises him to imitate, the insufferable young man who writes on the "réforme du recrutement dans l'armée bulgare" (453:27) and who is destined to become a member of the "Académie des Sciences Morales." Quite naturally, the next step in showing off the young narrator is to have him fetch for Montfort the "petit poème en prose" *(p. 455)* written at Combray. When Montfort gives it back without comment, the adulating father brings up the subject of La Berma's performance that afternoon but the son fails him by being able to say only that he was "déçu," whereupon the ambassador is full of praise for the actress and this time the narrator hangs on his words. During all of this the author of the Grasset text had forgotten to seat his characters at the dinner table; however, we find that they are indeed at table when a triviality intentionally slips in as Montfort compliments his hostess for having "un chef de tout premier ordre" who prepares such excellent "poulet" (457:33). He does not appreciate the salad, however *(p. 459)*. Then the conversation, now become irrelevant to the main theme but justifiably so for once, turns political and the ambassador shines. It is again the host who passes the ball to him by asking about "le roi Théodose" *(p. 459)* and Montfort comments at length on the king's speech on "affinités." The host remarks that "M. de Norpois" must be pleased with the result (in the final text this character has become "Vaugoubert" and "Montfort" has become "Norpois"). Norpois-Vaugoubert is then the excuse for another verbal deluge from the garrulous ambassador who uses another page of language so highly diplomatic that one wonders what he has really said. The host suggests another subject, the "télégramme de l'empereur d'Allemagne" *(p. 464)*, but the ambassador's only reply is to glance skyward in disapproval. The timid hostess brings up a new subject, summer plans, and Spain and Bricquebec are mentioned. Trying something new, the host alludes to the "banquet des Affaires étrangères" and Montfort says that he could not go because he had to dine at the house of "la belle Madame Swann" *(p. 465)*. With that we are back on the main track. Goaded on by his hostess, who seems a little too curious about the notorious Madame Swann, Montfort comments at great length on Swann's social ambitions in the "monde républicain," an ironical situation, he says, in the light of his brilliant position among the aristocracy. Swann, he says, would only have to make the right sign to certain highborn ladies who would receive his wife, "auquel cas, vraisemblablement, plus d'un mouton de Panurge aurait suivi" *(p. 466)*. Although disapproving of Swann's misplaced social ambitions and although repeating gossip about infidelities on both sides, Montfort is unkind neither to Swann nor to Odette. Of Odette he asserts that "il est indéniable qu'elle semble avoir de l'affection pour lui" *(p. 467)* and later on, pressed again by his inquisitive hostess to summarize his impression, he says enthusiastically: "Elle est *charmante*" (472:34). At this point a major digression occurs (to which we will return presently) when the omniscient author interrupts Montfort to give his own account of the biography of Swann since "Un Amour de Swann." Once the Swanns have been mentioned, the narrator tries to keep the conversation going on this subject and inquires whether Swann is not the friend of the "Comte de Chambord" (472:10), to which Montfort gives an informed reply accompanied by an anecdote. Was Bergotte at the dinner? inquires the narrator. This time he has unleashed a diatribe and he hears his favorite author described as a "joueur de flûte" guilty of "maniérisme" and "afféterie" *(p. 473)*, a bad influence on the younger generation and particularly on the narrator (as the prose poem shows), pretentious and vulgar as a person. Stunned by these remarks, the narrator allows himself a justifiable digression to reflect on the meaning of this; in the course of these reflections, he remembers that, when reading Bergotte at Combray, he used to pass beside "cette pièce de mon oncle Charles" (474:39), the recollection of which gave him an esthetic pleasure, akin to the enjoyment of Bergotte, that other day in the Champs-Elysées. Meanwhile Montfort goes on to tell how, when ambassador at Vienna, he refused to receive the famous writer because the latter insisted on bringing his mistress. Restimulating the conversation, the narrator asks whether "la fille de Mme Swann" was also at the dinner. Struck by the narrator's enthusiasm for both mother and daughter, Montfort spontaneously promises to mention this the next time he dines with the Swanns but, when the narrator nearly kisses his hand in gratitude, Montfort's facial expression reveals that the promise will not be kept. Such is the *dénouement* of the Norpois episode which, in a way, had been carefully prepared and which will have a plot relationship with what follows. After this comes a "tapering off" conclusion (so frequently found in Proust) in which the father reads in the evening paper a critique of La Berma's performance that afternoon and then everyone indulges in a post mortem of the dinner, commenting on Montfort's ideas and mannerisms.

Except for the long biography of Swann intruding in the middle, the account of the Montfort-Norpois dinner in *Grasset A* was unified and logical. Whereas some of the numerous additions in the final text were improvements, many others introduced further elements of chaos which Proust, in his effort to finish his gigantic work, seemed inclined to ignore. The attention which he paid to the diplomat's language resulted in improvements. Here and there he replaced words or added sentences, such as: "En somme, sans pouvoir dire qu'il soit au pinacle, il a conquis de haute lutte une fort jolie position . . ." (p. 453). But the most amusing passage of all, a page-long catalogue of diplomatic locutions (such as: "Le Cabinet de Saint-James ne fut pas le dernier à sentir le péril" [p. 462]) which Norpois had in his repertory but could not seem to use on this occasion, was inserted in the already incredibly long discourse on "affinités." To confuse the structure further, Proust also inserted in the middle of this same discourse a page more of subtleties concerning Vaugoubert and his possibilities as ambassador to the Holy See. The result is that, in the final text, a question raised by the narrator's father is not answered until more than two pages later (on p. 460, the father asks whether Vaugoubert was "content" with the king's toast, and Norpois answers on p. 463: "Il s'attendait en effet à un toast correct . . ." Another example of disruption occurs in the midst of the original discussion on literature when the father, in a page-long addition, consults Norpois about the best stocks in which to invest the inheritance which his son has just received from Aunt Léonie (p. 454). This makes a non sequitur out of the father's subsequent order to his son to fetch the prose poem. In fact, the insertion of still another new passage immediately after the prose poem introduces a second non sequitur when we get back to La Berma who, in the Grasset text, had followed along very logically. To be sure, this addition has the effect of getting everyone to table, a practical necessity which Proust had originally overlooked, but the new passage also includes miscellaneous shop talk between the ambassador and his colleague on the Commission, shop talk which, in a more rudimentary form, had been apparently grafted onto the paragraph concerned with La Berma where it was like a cancerous excrescence in the *Grasset Proofs* (note that this variant 456:19 still leaves a trace in the final text although the original words are utilized on the preceding page). In the old text, as we observed, the discussion of La Berma ended when the guest complimented his hostess on the "poulet." In the new text, the "poulet" has metamorphosed into "bœuf froid aux carottes . . . couché par le Michel-Ange de notre cuisine sur d'énormes cristaux de gelée pareils à des blocs de quartz transparent" (p. 458). Hence we now understand that this simile suggested to the author the long digression on Françoise and Michelangelo which interfered with the departure of the narrator to see La Berma. The allusion to the beef is brief enough the second time but the new passage incites Norpois to some culinary hyperboles followed by anecdotes of the diplomatic service which are not reported but during which the narrator reflects that the ambassador's pompous style is not his kind of literature. This new diversion in the narrative interrupts the original diversion so that the "salade d'ananas," which should have followed the beef, gets lost on the next page. Françoise and Michelangelo will become a final diversion in the post mortem after the ambassador's departure where the guest's "compliments to the cook," a brief remark in the original text, expand to two and a half pages in which (preceded by a further diversion on the subject of a rabbit executed by Françoise) the narrator's cook and part-time nurse reacts to the ambassadorial praise and comments on the art of cooking (p. 484).

In discussing the original structure of the Montfort-Norpois dinner, we noted in the old text a major disruption when the omniscient author decided that Montfort's remarks were inadequate and that he would at last have to explain how it happened that Swann married Odette, as the reader had been told so many times in "Combray." In the original text, the narrator had the good grace to begin by saying: "J'ai su depuis..." (467:7) but, in the new version, he indulges in no such amenities. To reach a symmetrical conclusion, "Un Amour de Swann" had left the reader with the impression that, having wasted years of his life on a woman "qui n'était pas mon genre" *(p. 382)*, Swann would logically never see her again. On this score, Montfort's remarks in the Grasset text were not really inadequate (or at least were far better than the final text which gives no explanation), for, after insinuating certain skulduggery on both sides, he notes that, paradoxically, they both seem to be happy and that this strange marriage has a simple explanation: "Je crois tout simplement qu'ils se sont mariés parce qu'ils ne pouvaient se quitter" (467:7). It is precisely after this explanation that the omniscient author (or rather the omniscient narrator) interrupts and undertakes on his own a psychological study of Swann after "Un Amour de Swann." Making no comment on the fact that Swann continues to see Odette, although logically he should not have, the author notes that, no longer being in love with her nor she with him, Swann becomes aware of a certain affection on her part, which he now reciprocates. Meanwhile she continues to lead her "vie scandaleuse," but he is indifferent and does not even bother to "limer la brosse de ses cheveux." Nevertheless each takes pleasure "à retrouver dans l'autre sa vie passée" and Odette even becomes an expert on "Ver Meer" (as Proust always spells it). All of this leads to the psychological observation that "les vieilles liaisons ont quelque chose de la douceur et de la force des affections de famille" (468:38). However, this period of affection and calm does not last because they have had a daughter (we are never told when) and now Odette thinks that Swann ought to marry her "comme d'autres hommes du monde." Although Odette has no social ambition higher than that of frequenting the "bals de l'Elysée," Swann sometimes imagines that his marriage has taken place and that he is able at last to present his wife and daughter to the Princesse des Laumes, whereupon the author adds that that "se réalisa bien autrement qu'il l'avait esquissée.*" Now Swann goes through a period of "jalousie sans désir et sans amour" because Odette had meanwhile become "violente et disputeuse," since she was making no progress in getting him to marry her. Proust compares this jealousy without love, as he calls it, to "une curiosité . . . comme on en éprouve à l'égard d'une domestique par qui l'on se croit bafoué." He avenges himself by telling all his friends that he has no intention of marrying her, so that the news will reach her ears. Meanwhile Odette has changed maxims; whereas she once thought that a woman can do anything with a man in love, now she has decided that, once men have fallen out of love, they are capable of anything "parce qu'ils sont si mufles." And meanwhile Swann's attitude is not consistent. On occasion he thinks of her "bonté" and comes back to her, but just at that point she punishes him by depriving him of his daughter. On another occasion he imagines her to be an adventuress of the kind who have children with wealthy men in order to get themselves married and who then murder their husbands so as to inherit their fortunes. Even after his marriage to Odette (which is not pinpointed in time or explained further in any way), he continues to suspect her of murderous intentions but finally he is won over by her "bonté" and "tendresse," for she is really kind and was vicious only when upset by his refusal to marry her. Swann is now so well reconciled with her that he fosters her low-level mundane ambitions.

When this account is rewritten, Norpois' remarks become more malicious as he reports on the "vilaines manœuvres de chantage de la part de la femme" (p. 466). The omniscient biography, itself, is much shorter in the final version. It begins by recounting Swann's refusal to marry Odette and her bitter response. Her character became infernal but "one" should have been able to predict that this would not continue after marriage because she was not fundamentally vicious. So she got married but in unexplained circumstances. Here the new text picks up a fragment of the old one, an allusion to her interest in Swann's work and in Vermeer but this now falls after the marriage. There follows then a generality about "vieilles liaisons" which have "quelque chose de la douceur et de la force des affections de famille" (p. 468). Thus stage one of the original progress of Swann towards marriage is likewise placed now after the marriage. More than half of the omniscient intervention, the remaining half, is taken over by social considerations: what has happened to Swann's high social station and how he has a secret ambition (now that he is married) to present his wife and daughter to the Duchesse de Guermantes. Knowing better what will happen, the omniscient author refers even more explicitly to the future plot of his novel which will bring Odette and Gilberte together with the Duchess. Although more polished stylistically, the new version of the omniscient intervention explains much less. Proust evidently changed his mind about enlarging his theory of love to include affection and pointed now only to the paradox of this "bonheur après décès que ce mariage avec cette Odette qu'il avait passionnément aimée... et qu'il avait épousée quand il ne l'aimait plus, quand l'être qui, en Swann, avait tant souhaité et tant désespéré de vivre toute sa vie avec Odette, quand cet être-là était mort?" (p. 471).

There were some interesting alterations in the Bergotte passages of the Norpois dinner but nothing which changed the original vehemence of the ambassador's *éreintement*. It will be recalled that, in rewriting the Bergotte passage in "Combray,"

Proust seemed to make this favorite author of the narrator resemble somewhat an author named Marcel Proust. Assuming that Bergotte stands for Anatole France, Montfort's original barbs seem to be aimed at him. An addition to this text now says: "Jamais on ne trouve dans ses ouvrages sans muscles ce qu'on pourrait nommer la charpente. Pas d'action — ou si peu — mais surtout pas de portée. Ses livres pèchent par la base ou plutôt n'y a pas [sic] de base du tout" (p. 473). This time the remarks seem to apply less to Anatole France than to Proust himself. Another addition reads: "Je sais que c'est blasphémer contre la Sacro-Sainte Ecole de ce que ces messieurs appellent l'Art pour l'Art, mais à notre époque il y a des tâches plus urgentes que d'agencer des mots d'une façon harmonieuse" (ibid.). Once again, rather than being an allusion to France's Parnassian days, this might well be construed as a reference to Proust's own esthetic. A third and longer addition does not change any fundamental meanings; it merely says that Bergotte has written no great novel.

The final important addition was entirely new text, inserted, this time very logically, into the post mortem after Norpois' departure. It is an elaboration on the idea that Norpois was responsible for persuading the father to view differently his son's desire for a literary career. Rediscussing the issue, the mother is opposed to this renunciation of the "carrière," but the father defends his son's right to make his own decisions with such energy that the son is seized with a desire "d'embrasser au-dessus de sa barbe ses joues colorées" (p. 482). The father's remark that he is no longer a child gives the son for the first time a subjective appreciation of the fact that he too is subject to time with a capital "T."

A few more miscellaneous alterations are worthy of mention. Instead of replying with just a facial expression to his host's remark about the Emperor of Germany's telegram, which was a good excuse for the mother to pick up the conversation, the ambassador, apparently forgetting diplomatic protocol, makes a strong adverse comment but still does not say what the telegram was about. One wonders whether, in the new version, the mother had interrupted something important. When the mother gets the conversation onto Bricquebec and mentions the excellent new hotel, in an addition Norpois is made to remark that he must give this information to "certaine personne" (p. 464), which is, of course, a *preparation* for things to come.

Compared to the Norpois dinner, which did have a distinct form in the original version although it lost it in the revisions, the final section of "Noms de pays: le nom" in the original text, having started out with a certain momentum, becomes disjointed and purposeless after the narrator is admitted to the Swann household. The initial action does not differ particularly, going from the old version to the new, but it is nevertheless more skeletal and, curiously enough, seems less dramatic than in the final amplified version. On New Year's Day the narrator rushes immediately to the Champs-Elysées and entrusts to "notre marchande" (p. 486) the letter to Gilberte which he had imagined himself writing some seventy-four pages earlier. But his thoughts are diverted by the picture of La Berma, which he chances to buy, and he spends more time thinking about the love life of the great actress than he does about his desire to "refaire la connaissance de Gilberte comme au premier jour du monde" (487:26).[40] "Quelques jours plus tard" (490:27), Gilberte finally comes back to the park but she is not all sweetness and light. Assuming the "air vague" that she had on her bad days when she was overjoyed at the idea of not coming to the park, she informs the narrator, in answer to his question, that her parents "étaient loin de me rendre la sympathie que j'avais pour eux" (490:35). The next day she has "ce même regard 'en dessous', rêveur et fourbe que je lui avais vu la première fois à Combray" *(p. 493)* as she returns unopened to the narrator another letter which he had just sent to Swann protesting the honorability of his intentions. Suddenly "attiré par son corps," he invites her to wrestle to get the letter and in the struggle "je jetai comme quelques gouttes de sueur arrachées par l'effort, mon plaisir auquel je ne pus m'attarder même le temps de le goûter" (493:37). He wonders whether

40 In fact, in a passage crossed out in the typescript of *Grasset A*, the narrator is so concerned with the love life of La Berma that he imagines that he has sequestered her "dans une maison isolée" in order to enjoy exclusively "ces joies qu'elle prodiguait aux autres" (the suppressed text follows variant 488:31).

Gilberte is aware of what has happened. One morning he falls ill but still makes it to the Champs-Elysées; after that a long illness sets in and at one point his tearful grandmother gives him cognac, as the doctor once prescribed. Then the miracle happens: a letter comes from Gilberte inviting him to a "goûter." Forthwith the narrator explains how this could have happened; it must have been due to a lie by Bloch in the presence of Cottard, the "nouveau médecin de mon père" (502:21), who, thinking that the narrator was in the good graces of the Swanns, then spoke highly of him to them. Just the same, after this lengthy explanation, the narrator remarks that he is sure that his mother engineered the invitation.

The next episodes, such as they are, are built around the theme of the "goûter." Several times the text wanders: a first long paragraph drifts from Gilberte's correspondence paper to the murmur of the guests at the "goûter," to the appearance of Swann's apartment, to the narrator's parents' observations on the apartment. Then the "goûter" proper begins; Madame Swann takes part in the children's conversation; Swann enters. At this point there is a curious digression when, as on several occasions noted previously, the narrative shifts to an omniscient focus and we find Swann thinking about Forcheville. In the text something strange has happened; the passage begins: "Alors M. Swann entrait à son tour" but the next paragraph also begins: "Alors M. Swann entrait à son tour" (511:14). There can be no doubt that this passage, although it is in *Grasset A*, is a graft onto an earlier text (ultimately Proust moved it elsewhere, as we shall see later).[41] At the "goûter," Swann's conversation is entirely concerned with his wife's social success and the narrator surmises that he hopes that the news of these achievements will reach the ears of the narrator's parents. This is the excuse for a digression in which we hear the narrator's mother commenting on Madame Swann's social ambitions and the fact that she has brought in Madame Cottard to be a witness who will report these achievements to Madame Verdurin.

The "goûter" theme having come to an end, the "sortie" theme takes over but remains very rudimentary until expanded

---

[41] It is indeed a handwritten addition to the typescript of *Grasset A.*

in the rewriting. In a sequence of imperfect tenses, there are vague allusions to excursions to the Jardin d'Acclimatation, to the Eden, to the tombs of Saint-Denis, and, very awkwardly in the same sentence, there is an allusion to "les vertus vraiment rares de Gilberte" (525:42). This last point is illustrated by the "ouvrage" which she made for "la marchande des Champs-Elysées" (536:25), by her condemnation of Mademoiselle Vington who was not kind to her own father and by her solicitous attitude towards Swann when it is "l'anniversaire de la mort de son père" *(p. 537)*. There follows then a long generalization on the fact that "la pensée ne peut même pas reconstituer l'état ancien pour le confronter au nouveau" *(p. 537)*. This prepares Gilberte's comment that one would not have thought that all of these changes could take place. Then the narrator describes the Swanns' apartment equipped with things from the previous dwellings of both Swann and Odette. Finally, still under the heading "promenades," there is the "matinée théâtrale" *(p. 544)* apropos of which Gilberte engages in a dispute with the narrator because he shares her parents' opinion that she ought to stay home on the anniversary of her grandfather's death. Here the symmetrical relationship to the other allusion to the anniversary of the grandfather's death is obvious.

At this point the long Bergotte luncheon intervenes. It is the most important episode taking place while the narrator is at the Swanns'. Because of its complexity we shall postpone discussion.

A new theme, this time more distinctly a *basic narrative*, opens up after Bergotte has been disposed of when Madame Swann says to the narrator: "C'est très bien de venir voir Gilberte, mais j'aimerais aussi que vous veniez quelquefois pour *moi . . . (p. 592)*. Thus we find the narrator at one of Odette's teas which, with all of the additions subsequently made, will occupy twenty-three pages in the Pléiade edition. As in the case of the "goûter," the "thé" begins with a descriptive passage, the setting being this time Odette's "jardin d'hiver" *(p. 592)*. The "action" begins when Madame Cottard shows signs of leaving and Madame Swann restrains her. Nothing else happens except Madame Bontemps's conversation in which she complains of the stupidity of politicians' wives and tells how her daughter insulted a particular politician by claiming that his father was a "marmiton" (598:19). Then she shows signs of leaving again and Odette stops her (603:40), whereupon Madame Bontemps gushes on, mentioning the politician's wife who thought *Lohengrin* was a review at the Folies Bergère. Now the conversation wanders; Madame Cottard makes some inane remarks about her husband's passion, which turns out to be reading. Reading is bad for his sight and that brings up the subject of Madame Verdurin's intention to equip her new apartment with electric lights. From there Madame Cottard goes on to the telephone which a friend has installed, and then she rushes off, leaving the narrator with no choice but to go home since his hostess has all but said: "on ferme" *(p. 607)*.

Still Madame Cottard must have the last word and her parting shot is a remark about the furniture. This is the beginning of the theme on which "Noms de pays: le nom" will end and which is the theme of "Odette" herself. Again there is a long development on Odette's interior in which a taste for the Far East is yielding to one for the French Eighteenth Century. Now comes Odette's apotheosis; she has become elegant and has developed a kind of beauty which the narrator, in his enthusiasm, calls "une jeunesse immortelle" *(p. 617)*. Despite her elegance, she is still "mal élevée" (616:7), but Swann is so used to that that he even likes it. On the other hand, the narrator does not at all subscribe to the belief that Madame Swann is unintelligent and says that many people would be amazed, particularly the Belgian minister who is a frequent visitor, if they knew that in the Verdurin coterie they had this opinion about her. The next few pages are devoted to Odette's clothes: the "écossais" which she wears to go walking with the narrator and Gilberte at the Jardin d'Acclimatation (619:6); the velvet, crêpe de chine or satin dresses which she wears in the afternoon "pour venir assister un instant à notre goûter" (620:2). Then comes the final vision, the "finale" of what has become a symphony on Odette, as the narrator follows her to the Bois. She may be persona non grata to the Guermantes, but that is of little matter. "Toute une suite l'environnait; Gilberte, Swann, quatre ou cinq hommes de club qui étaient venus la voir le matin ou qu'elle venait de rencontrer . . ." (636:12). In the society of men Odette has been a success. Speaking to the narrator "sous un berceau de glycines," she sends in the direction of the passing horsemen "un bonjour de la main amical, conscient de leurs noms, notoires pour le public mais familiers pour elle, souverain, printanier, matinal, irisé, d'un reflet bleu" (637:40). The narrator wonders whether she recognizes in him "l'adolescent qui un ou deux ans plus tôt ne perdait pas une occasion de l'apercevoir" but he does not dare ask her. "Noms de pays: le nom" ends with the long flashback to the earlier period when, first being in love with Gilberte, he admired and saluted her mother walking in the Bois. Then comes the ultimate conclusion in which the mature narrator, years later, seeks the memory of Odette in the Bois and in which we find that the eternal Odette, though absent, is still with us: "Mme Swann m'eût répondu d'un château qu'elle ne rentrerait qu'en février . . ." *(p. 427).* We have already seen that Proust moved all of this material to *Du côté de chez Swann.*

What becomes of Gilberte? The fact that she has acquired a nasty disposition seems not to matter or perhaps it simply emphasizes the point which the narrator had already made concerning the dichotomy between imagination and reality. During the Bergotte dinner her presence is still alluded to from time to time. At one point, she ("à qui on avait déjà dit deux fois d'aller se préparer" [564:3]) seems slightly disobedient but she also might simply have been fascinated by the conversation. As she leans on her father's shoulder, the narrator is himself so fascinated by her that he describes her for more than a page, comparing her to her mother and calling her "cette mélusine*" (565:24). He even notes that "on voyait dans ses yeux ce regard incertain, dissimulé et triste qu'avait sa mère quand elle mentait" (565:5) but he goes on to explain that this is a conditioned reflex totally without significance. He also leaves us in doubt as to whether she was a blonde or a redhead since both descriptions are in the original text and persist in the Pléiade edition. At the conclusion of this same passage there is even a tender scene where she hides her head "entre les genoux de son père" (566:36); in the rewritten and expanded text she hides her head "sous le bras de son père" and all of the sentimentality remains. After the Bergotte luncheon, Gilberte seems to have been eclipsed by her mother. Nevertheless the eclipse is not total, for she is still there, as evidence already recorded proves. She goes to the Jardin d'Acclimatation with the narrator, she is serving her eternal "goûter" when her mother sweeps in in her beautiful dresses, and she is in the Bois when her mother is admired by the passing gentlemen.

So far we have not had occasion to refer to *Grasset B*, although it began with the Norpois dinner (in other words, the beginning of *A l'ombre des jeunes filles en fleurs*). That is because, up to page 508 in terms of the Pléiade edition, Proust had made only minor corrections, many of them being concerned only with typographical errors. Page 508 places us well along in the first "goûter." After that point, we shall take *Grasset B* into consideration.

In studying *Grasset B*, Feuillerat was so impressed with the frequency of generalizations in the additions that he concluded that the generalization was the most important principle for recognizing what he called Proust's second manner. While it is true that, commencing with the Norpois dinner, many of Proust's additions were long generalizations, Feuillerat not only disregarded the innumerable generalizations which we detected in *Du côté de chez Swann* but he failed to observe that there were three long generalizations already in the section of *Grasset B* with which we are now concerned (the passages in question were also in *Grasset A*). The first we have already noted; it asserted that "la pensée ne peut même pas reconstituer l'état ancien pour le confronter au nouveau" *(p. 537)*. The second generalization was: "Les êtres nerveux sont . . . ceux qui 's'écoutent' le moins . . ." (495:8). The third was: "Peut-être n'est-ce que dans des vies réellement vicieuses que le problème moral peut se poser . . ." *(p. 558)*.

Taking up now the changes which Proust made in this final section of "Noms de pays: le nom" (that is to say, going from New Year's Day to the scenes of Madame Swann in the Bois de Boulogne), we note that Proust was primarily concerned with amplifying his text rather than altering it. *Grasset A* had alluded to visits on New Year's Day but that was all. Since it was psychologically important to suggest more strongly the narrator's eagerness to rush to the Champs-Elysées, the author delayed him by a detailed list of the visits made. *Grasset A* finished the description of New Year's Day with the disappointment that this day had been just like any other day; a new paragraph goes on to describe it as "le Ier janvier des hommes vieux" (p. 488). Instead of saying too rapidly: "Quelques jours plus tard, Gilberte revint aux Champs-Elysées . . ." (490:27), Proust adds a paragraph to occupy the intervening time and describes the Place de la Concorde, essentially on the basis of a passage cut out of *Grasset A* (486:38). This is followed by still another new passage on the theme of waiting when the narrator was not far from believing that, "ne pouvant me rappeler les traits de Gilberte, je l'avais oubliée elle-même, je ne l'aimais plus" (p. 490).

Up to this point the additions have not been disruptive in the least, but now a major disruption occurs when Françoise interrupts the crucial discussion between Gilberte and the narrator concerning the letter to Swann. Françoise insists on taking the narrator to the water closets and thereupon ensues a scene with which we are already familiar because it originally occurred at the beginning of "Noms de pays: le nom." In the rewriting the scene becomes one of the most memorable Balzacian episodes in the book. After that the narrator returns to Gilberte and wrestles with her to obtain the letter; then he goes home and there, as in *Grasset A,* he suddenly remembers Uncle Adolphe's room at Combray. There is no mention of a further stimulation for this memory, and that is because the passage on stimulants has been moved. In the final version, it no longer has any relation with the W. C. episode but it has a more logical connection with the narrator's illness *(p. 496).*

The account of the narrator's illness is preceded by the long generalization, already noted, on "les êtres nerveux" (495:8); the old text also mentions that a doctor has been consulted and then, later, the grandmother notices her grandson's suffering and tearfully brings him cognac. By inserting between the doctor's visit and the grandmother's cognac the old passage on stimulants, Proust made this doctor number one responsible for prescribing the stimulants. But then, in the new text, he introduced a doctor number two who was none other than Cottard. It will be recalled that, in *Grasset A*, Cottard was accidentally present during the narrator's illness but was not brought in for consultation. In the new version he was brought in because the illness persisted (cognac was apparently the wrong remedy but we still find the narrator taking stimulants later) and it was to prepare this reentry that the portrait of Cottard was placed in the new introduction to *A l'ombre des jeunes filles en fleurs.* The new material on Cottard the great clinician is one of the memorable passages of the *Recherche.* The old material on Cottard also remains and it continues to be presented as a flashback. In the original text, this flashback followed immediately Gilberte's letter which it explained but, as we previously noted, the narrator also remarked at the end that probably his mother's intervention was more important than Cottard's in bringing about the Swann's invitation. The new version confuses the whole matter. After reproducing the text of the letter exactly as in *Grasset A,* Proust undertakes for nearly three pages an analysis of the effect of this letter on the narrator's sensibility; the result is the kind of passage which Feuillerat singled out as exemplifying Proust's new "analytical" style, particularly since it includes a lengthy generalization on "ces obstacles contre lesquels les amants ont à lutter" (p. 501). Embedded in this long analysis are the two explanations for the letter, but the mother explanation comes first so that when, after an interval, the Cottard explanation comes up it seems superfluous.

Gilberte's "goûter" is the pretext for embellishments of many kinds. The "gâteau de Savoie" becomes a "pâtisserie ninivite" (p. 506). The narrator is upset by drinking tea (p. 507). We learn that the Swanns belong to the "commen allez-vous" set (p. 504). Somewhat later we are told that they also affect a short "o" in "odieux" (p. 511). At the "goûter" Odette continually startles the narrator with English words such as "studio," "toast," "cake," and "nurse." In fact, Proust must have made rather early this decision to Anglicize Odette, for the "nurse" is the subject of a rather long new passage added at the stage of *Grasset B.* Later, when the "sorties" begin, Odette introduces "lunch" and the narrator himself takes up "Christmas," to the annoyance of his father (p. 526). In a tea shop, Madame Swann makes disobliging remarks in English to the narrator about the other customers, whereas the narrator is the only one in the place not understanding English. Finally, at the outset of the Bergotte dinner, there are lengthy comments on Odette's newest English habits, including that of engraving "Mr." on her husband's calling cards and of giving mysterious envelopes to her guests when they are about to go in to dinner table. Feuillerat attaches much importance to Odette's Anglomania and considers it to be part of her transformation from a "cocotte" to an elegant society lady. That is not our opinion. Let us remember that Odette spoke English from the very beginning of "Un Amour de Swann" and it was probably an oversight that she did not speak English in the Grasset version of "Noms de pays: le nom." When Proust decided to liven up the Bergotte dinner with the mysterious letter, he probably realized that he had missed an opportunity all along the line by not emphasizing Odette's original Anglomania.

Although related in the imperfect tense most of the time, which makes it a typical *composite basic narrative,* the "goûter," in the original text, appears to be the account of one particular episode. In his revisions Proust radically disrupts this basic chronology. In the original, this chronology is simple: Gilberte serves the "goûter," then Madame Swann enters and converses, after which Swann enters and converses. Between Madame Swann's entry and her husband's, in the new version, there are not only long comments on the English words "toast" and "nurse" (which do fit in logically, however), but also two entire pages describing other visits of the narrator when Gilberte was not there and when Swann received the narrator like the "fils d'un roi" (p. 509). In the process of working back to the original "goûter," a new transitional paragraph relates how Odette imitates the loud talking of Madame Verdurin and unconsciously uses expressions of the Guermantes clan which she has absorbed from her husband. This particular paragraph is part of the transformation of Odette into a society lady, most of which comes later, and it is slightly confusing when, getting back to the "goûter" at last, we see the original Odette surrounded by none but her bourgeois friends.

Because of the narrator's tendency to switch to an omniscient point of view when writing about Swann, this character continues to be a disruptive force throughout the remainder of "Noms de pays: le nom." It will be recalled that, in *Grasset A*, his entry for the first time at the "goûter" provoked an omniscient digression which was so badly grafted on to the surrounding text that Proust removed it. In *Grasset B* this digression has already been moved to its definitive position at the end of the "goûter" episode. The opening line in *Grasset B* reads: "Les jours où sa femme ne donnait pas de thé, Swann rentrait généralement plus tard" (523:10). The word "thé" at this point is confusing but it is obviously related to a variant from *Grasset A* which follows immediately: "Ce ne fut pas seulement à ces thés..." (525:37). Proust has momentarily forgotten that he is writing about a "goûter" and not a "thé," which will come later. The final text reads, in the first case: "De ses visites Swann rentrait souvent assez peu de temps avant le dîner" (p. 523); and in the second case: "Ce ne fut pas seulement à ces goûters..." (p. 525). With this later correction in mind, we may still say then that the disgression comes at the end of the "goûter" episode but it nevertheless has no real relation to it. *Grasset B* and the final text both incorporate the original *Grasset A* text with slight modifications but follow it up with extensive new developments. After emphasizing further how hard it was now for Swann to imagine that he had ever been upset by Odette, *Grasset B* goes on, in a *flash-forward,* to describe how Swann suffered the same torment apropos of another woman, this time a totally unjustified torment because the woman was faithful but Swann's affair with Odette had conditioned him to react forever in the same pattern. This particular version is intended to prove a basic psychological principle: "A partir d'un certain âge nous ne sommes plus amoureux d'une femme mais à propos d'une femme" (523:43). The narrator makes a point of telling us (since he says it twice) that Charlus, whom he knew somewhat later, was his informant. At the second mention of Charlus, the narrator states without further explanation that, according to his informant, Swann died of "angoisse" on account of this new mistress. At the end of this long development on the new mistress, the narrator remarks: "Comme il aurait souhaité quand il souffrait par Odette de pouvoir un jour lui laisser voir qu'il en aimait une autre" (523:43). But now he does his best to hide this from Odette. In the final version of this text it is the ending of the *Grasset B* variant which becomes the main point. The narrator's interest is no longer in a new Swann following an old pattern but rather in the somewhat threadbare theme of the "death of jealousy." The allusion to Forcheville in *Grasset A* now becomes the pretext for evoking the full Forcheville episode when "il avait sonné et frappé au carreau sans qu'on lui ouvrît" (p. 523). Now the new information is provided that, even after the demise of his jealousy, Swann continued "machinalement" to try to find out whether Forcheville was in bed with Odette on that memorable day. One is reminded of the narrator's behavior, volumes later, after Albertine's death. Perhaps he was already preoccupied with the story of Albertine. In a second paragraph, still on the theme of jealousy, the narrator (or more exactly the omniscient author) picks up the conclusion of *Grasset B* and develops the theme that, when he was jealous of Odette, Swann would have welcomed the chance to avenge himself by saying that he loved another woman. Now that he loves another woman he is no longer interested in revenge but is concerned with hiding things from his wife. Thus the "other woman" story is no longer the main point but is fully subordinated to the theme of "death of jealousy."

Later on, in what we have called the "sorties" subdivision, Swann is the subject of another long interpolation presented from the omniscient point of view. At the point where the narrator is discussing the unreality of his really being at the Swanns', he suddenly compares himself to Swann dreaming of "cet appartement commun à Odette et à lui qui lui était apparu si inaccessible" (p. 538).

During the "goûter" there is incidental conversation between Swann and Gilberte in the narrator's presence. From Swann's point of view the purpose is to impress the narrator with Odette's social position so that he will report on it to his parents but, from the reader's point of view, the purpose is to build up the image of this social position. For Swann the principal star in this bourgeois galaxy seems to be Madame Bontemps who is otherwise an inconsequential character in the original text. For some reason which is not apparent the name "Bontemps" becomes "Trombert" in the final revisions made in the passage in which the narrator's mother comments ironically on Madame Swann's social achievements (p. 515); Madame Trombert had also been mentioned at random by Madame Swann somewhat earlier in the original text *(p. 507)*. Some of the revisions in this part of the text continue to focus on Odette's bourgeois frequentations. When Swann remarks ostentatiously that M. Bontemps is a member of the Legion of Honor, Proust adds in *Grasset B* a totally superfluous description ending with the remark that Bontemps has "une voix nasale et un œil de verre" (512:15). In the final text this became "une voix nasale, l'haleine forte et un œil de verre" (p. 512). In another revision Swann gives more details about M. Bontemps and Gilberte volunteers the information that she knows his niece, Albertine, remarking: "Elle sera sûrement très 'fast', mais en attendant elle a une drôle de touche" (p. 512). This is the first allusion in the final text to Albertine.

Other very extensive revisions, however, are aimed at raising Odette to a higher social level. Feuillerat considered this to be a fundamental contradiction in the novel and we are inclined to share his opinion. If this evolution had been gradual, it might have been defensible but, having decided to transform Odette, Proust, as he did so frequently, retouched all down the line with the result that the new Odette cohabits with the old one. We are less inclined, however, to accept Feuillerat's explanation that Proust was merely following another model. We believe, rather, that, in revising the end of *Du côté de chez Swann*, he was impressed with the transformation which Odette had undergone and felt the need better to motivate this change. It is noteworthy that the revisions do not simply amount to imposing black on white or red on green but that Proust tries constantly to blend the two points of view with varying degrees of success. We have already noted a first meager step in this process of making Odette into a society lady; the principal effort in the revisions comes after Swann's conversation with Gilberte about the Bontemps. This two-page addition, while suggesting that Swann is acting like a fallen princess who now caters to "vieilles raseuses" (p. 513), emphasizes that Odette's real object now is to impress the Verdurins (the idea was in *Grasset A* and was expressed by the narrator's mother [516:7]) and that Swann is sincere in admiring Madame Bontemps since he had learned from the Guermantes to take a kindly interest in grand duchesses who are not the intellectual equal of the Guermantes coterie. The next six-page addition continues to develop the same ideas. Emphasizing once more that "les femmes élégantes n'allaient pas chez elle" (p. 516), Proust explains that society is not static and that, later on, the Dreyfus affair made radicals socially acceptable whereas they could not be invited in the days when the narrator visited the Swanns. This observation serves no purpose other than to introduce a Jewess, Lady Rufus Israëls, Swann's aunt (to prepare this development Proust added a remark earlier to Norpois' discourse on the Swanns [p. 466]) who uses her influence to prevent Odette from being received by the aristocracy. To our amazement we now discover that Odette is actually being received by the aristocracy since she visits a certain Madame de Marsantes who turns out later, of course, to be the mother of Saint-Loup. To be sure, this breakthrough is of short duration since Lady Israëls puts an end to it. To contrast with this incipient ascension, a collection of Odette's "hérésies mondaines" (p. 519) is now presented and we are informed that Swann is blind to the "médiocrité de son intelligence" (p. 519). Feuillerat is bothered by this last remark, for he considers that it contradicts the image of an elegant Odette which Proust is now attempting, more and more, to project. It should be pointed out that, contrary to what Feuillerat believes, this addition is not made necessarily in an attempt to denigrate Odette but rather to tie the Odette, who is on the verge of being elegant, back to the Odette of "Un Amour de Swann," who was frequently accused of a lack of intelligence. To finish with this long addition, we will now note that it meanders back to the subject of the state of society and to the fact that, at this particular time, "des femmes chez qui on allait en toute confiance avaient été reconnues être des filles publiques, des espionnes anglaises" (p. 520). Despite this one more reason for Odette's exclusion from society, the addition concludes with a description of how Swann enjoys making "des bouquets sociaux" (p. 521) by inviting on the same occasion Madame Bontemps and the Duchesse de Vendôme. Again there is no clear comment, and we must assume that the duchess is one of those high-born ladies whom the Guermantes did not receive at all or whom they received with a certain benevolent condescension. However, the fact is now firmly established that we are dealing with a new Odette who has already ascended to another rung of the social ladder.

In *Grasset A*, as we have already observed, the "sortie" theme was never fully developed, although various possible "sorties" were enumerated. In revising the text, directly after this old introduction, Proust supplied a long *composite basic narrative* which began with the preliminaries preceding the "sortie." In a burst of lyricism brought on by the anticipation of pleasures to come, the narrator describes at length his arrival at the Swanns' house, then Swann's cordial greeting and finally Odette's tardy return. On certain days the "sortie" did not take place and then everyone stayed home, during which time two events in particular took place: one was the "lingerie" episode when Swann showed the narrator the mysterious place to which Gilberte sometimes disappeared; the other was Odette's playing of the Sonate de Vinteuil. Feuillerat considers this piano playing to be further evidence of the transformation of Odette into an accomplished lady, but he forgets that Odette already played this music in "Un Amour de Swann." In this first encounter with the sonata, the narrator has somewhat the same physical reaction as Swann did the first time; he has difficulty perceiving the sounds individually and, in fact, he seems to make less progress than Swann in discerning the originality of the music, for he confesses: "même quand j'eus écouté la Sonate d'un bout à l'autre, elle me resta presque tout entière invisible" (p. 530). Implying that later he will understand, he develops a page-long generalization to prove that the time that it takes him to understand "n'est que le raccourci et comme le symbole des années, des siècles parfois, qui s'écoulent avant que le public puisse aimer un chef-d'œuvre vraiment nouveau" (p. 531). Then he goes on for another two pages to prove that Swann's current interpretation of the sonata is entirely false since the "feuillages nocturnes" which he perceives in it are only his recollection of the bowers in the suburban restaurants where he used to hear the sonata. This trivial conversation about music with Swann and Odette now shifts into more trivial conversation about Madame Blatin and the insult which she received from the "négro" at the Jardin d'Acclimatation. Thus we are back to the theme of the "sortie," but a specific "sortie" still does not take place because now the old text of *Grasset A* intervenes: the virtues of Gilberte, the description of the apartment, and finally the very brief allusion to a trip to the Jardin d'Acclimatation which was in the original text. At this point the new material resumes and the trip (or more exactly trips since this is also a composite narrative) to the Jardin d'Acclimatation takes place. The social ascension of Odette continues; she calls her husband's attention to Madame de Montmorency and this lady, "heureuse de faire à Mme Swann une politesse qui ne tirait pas à conséquence" (p. 541), actually stops and speaks to her. Odette has now become so elegant "qu'il eût été difficile de dire, de la femme de Swann ou de l'aristocratique passante, laquelle des deux était la grande dame" (p. 541). The next person they meet is none other than Princess Mathilde and Proust writes a memorable page to describe this historical character. Interrupting the Princess Mathilde episode there is a badly integrated episode consisting of an encounter with Bloch during the same trip. In this passage, which must antedate the Princess Mathilde passage since it occurs in *Grasset B*, Madame Swann seems to recognize Bloch but thinks that he is "M. d'Echebrune" (543:21). After a few more miscellaneous "sorties" condensed into one paragraph, this section ends with the original dispute between the narrator and Gilberte on the subject of the anniversary of her grandfather's death.

After an initial confusion between walks in the Jardin d'Acclimatation (from which Odette's floating cloak is detached and moved backwards five pages) and the luncheon with Bergotte, the luncheon finally settles down in the original text to a very clear narrative, beginning immediately with the unexpected presentation to the "doux chantre aux cheveux blancs" who turns out to be a youngish man with a "nez camard" and a "barbiche noire" (547:22). For the narrator the shock is so great that "la beauté d'une œuvre immense" *(p. 547)* crumbles forthwith. Even more so than the nose and the beard, the writer's "organe bizarre" absorbs the narrator's attention and logically, consistently and with deep penetration he analyzes the relationship between Bergotte's everyday speech and the style of his work. In so doing, he seems to become reconciled to the reality of Bergotte. He still calls Bergotte's work "livres divins" but observes that Bergotte himself does not seem to believe in the reality of the literature which he has produced. This, says the narrator, may be due to the fact that he has learned to "simuler la déférence envers des écrivains médiocres" *(p. 557)* so as to draw closer to a "fauteuil académique." As to the vices which Norpois attributed to him, the narrator seems to accept all the accusations, including that of an "amour incestueux" (558:8), as essentially true, but he seems to defend these vices as a necessary attribute of genius since all great writers "se servent de leurs vices pour arriver à concevoir la règle morale de tous" *(p. 558)*. After this systematic presentation of Bergotte there is a succession of miscellaneous bits and pieces: conversation on La Berma in which Bergotte displays his classical erudition; remarks on Gilberte's physical appearance (to which we have already referred); then more conversation on La Berma in which Swann participates. In answer to Bergotte's question: "Avez-vous été content?" (567:22), the narrator admits that he did not like La Berma and then worries for the length of a page that Bergotte would take him for an imbecile. He is reassured when Gilberte whispers in his ear: "vous avez fait la conquête de mon grand ami Bergotte" *(p. 569)*. On the way to the Jardin d'Acclimatation (for one of the "sorties" has slipped in again), when the narrator is traveling alone in the same carriage with Bergotte, the writer asks the narrator about his health and vaunts "les plaisirs de l'intelligence"; but the narrator has little confidence in his own ability since he has not understood the message of "les water-closets des Champs-Elysées" (569:31). Finally there comes the characteristic tapering off of the Bergotte episode when, back home, the narrator recounts to his parents his day with Bergotte; they become furious when the narrator informs them that Bergotte "ne goûtait pas du tout M. de Norpois" (573:7) but their attitude changes when they learn that Bergotte found their son intelligent.

In rewriting the story of the Bergotte luncheon, Proust immediately resorted to the same technique as in the "vin d'Asti" sequence in "Combray." To enliven the action, he introduced a sequence on the mysterious envelope which Madame Swann gave him before the guests went in to lunch. Since this was presumably an English custom, a long digression on Odette's Anglomania preceded the first mention of the envelope and all of this delayed considerably the presentation of the narrator to Bergotte. Another paragraph on the envelope and the related subjects of the bachelor's button and caviar followed the initial comments on Bergotte. At the very end of the entire Bergotte episode, as a neat conclusion to everything, the narrator finally opens the famous envelope and discovers too late that it contains the name of his luncheon partner. Other additions were not as symmetrical. After registering the narrator's disappointment on discovering the real Bergotte, Proust immediately repeated the same idea in a long addition originally introduced into *Grasset B* (547:33). In *Grasset B* he also made Bergotte's nose more complicated and it became a "nez rouge en forme de coquille de colimaçon" (p. 547). Rewriting later the *Grasset B* variant he expanded it further to include the amusing comparison with the "ingénieur pressé" (p. 548). After a further fragment of the original text which returns to the subject of the narrator's incredulity, there occurs a further addition to *Grasset B* which, by analogy with the engineer comparison, now compares Bergotte to someone engaged in the "commerce des perles" (p. 549). Next comes the second reference to the mysterious envelope, followed by the long *Grasset A* development on the originality of Bergotte's style, this being followed by a new generality: "Il en est ainsi pour tous les grands écrivains, la beauté de leurs phrases est imprévisible" (p. 551). Now there follows a passage of the old text developing the idea that Bergotte's style is based on a principle of paradox; in the middle of this discussion there is a new generality on "l'élimination préalable du poncif auquel nous étions habitués" (p. 552). Back to *Grasset A*, the discussion of style continues with reference to the consonants *v*, *d*, and g and then with the "hereditary" aspects of Bergotte's diction. This brings on a new paragraph of generalization affirming that genius comes less from intellectual elements than from "la faculté de les transformer" (p. 554). This passage makes use of some anachronistic metaphors involving motor cars and airplanes. Then *Grasset A* resumes by describing how Bergotte's style has influenced an entire generation of writers.

This very same *Grasset A* passage continues with the statement that the new generation, although unconsciously imitating Bergotte, claims to have no connection with him; "il n'était pas tout à fait de son temps," adds the narrator *(p. 556)*. At this point there is a revision to the effect that "il détestait Tolstoï, George Eliot, Ibsen et Dostoïevsky" (p. 556). Reminding us that these are Proust's favorite authors, Feuillerat argues that Proust is now demolishing Anatole France whom he once admired. He continues his argument by pointing out in the next paragraph, which is new text taking the form of a *flash-forward,* the remark that there came a time when Bergotte "n'eut plus de talent" (p. 556) and he says that he considers this remark by Proust to be due to the latter's dissatisfaction with Anatole France's conduct during the war. While all of this may be true, the argument does not altogether stand up in view of the fact that *Grasset A* already says that Bergotte is outmoded (to amplify this by saying that his talent subsequently diminished is logical enough) and in view of the fact that the next paragraph (p. 557), likewise new text, refers again to "le secret de sa force." [42] The next paragraph, found in *Grasset A,* emphasizes, as we previously noted, Bergotte's academical ambitions. In support of his argument for a denigration of Bergotte by Proust, Feuillerat might have pointed out an addition to this paragraph: "on entendait alterner avec les propos du vrai Bergotte ceux du Bergotte égoïste, ambitieux et qui ne pensait qu'à parler de tels gens puissants, nobles ou riches, pour se faire valoir" (p. 558). Again one could argue, however, that this addition is a logical amplification in view of the next paragraph, already in *Grasset A,* in which the narrator, as we have noted, repeats all of the accusations of Norpois.

The next addition comes after the initial discussion of La Berma. In this new text Madame Swann intervenes to refer to the opuscule which Bergotte had written on *Phèdre* and then the narrator goes on to remark on the "éclairage vert" (which ties back to an earlier addition when the narrator was at the theatre). Hearing Bergotte talk about *Phèdre,* the narrator now states in this new text that Bergotte's ideas on the subject are really no

---

[42] Feuillerat considers this passage, which he quotes in its entirety, to be ironical.

more valid than those of Norpois. This leads him to mention Norpois to Bergotte and immediately an avalanche of abuse is unloosed. Although *Grasset A* states that the narrator subsequently told his parents that Bergotte had spoken ill of Norpois, there was no corresponding scene in the original text. Manifestly Proust is making up for an omission but the violence of Bergotte's language gives further support to Feuillerat's denigration argument and is clearly related to the tone of another passage to which we shall soon come.

However, *Grasset A* now provides an interruption with the comparison of Gilberte to Mélusine. This provokes a new passage, a long paragraph consisting of a generality about heredity and a development on the three personalities of Gilberte. *Grasset A* intervening again, we are back to Gilberte but, in the middle of this passage, Swann, to hide his emotion concerning his daughter, mingles in the conversation about La Berma. This is the pretext for a short new text in which Odette joins the conversation. Unfortunately this new text replaces the part of *Grasset A* in which the narrator admits to Bergotte that he did not appreciate La Berma. Without this information, the rest of the *Grasset A* text, which has been retained and which continues to refer to the narrator's misgivings about his opinion of La Berma, loses its point, as does also the final reassuring remark from Gilberte.

In *Grasset A* the narrator now finds himself alone in a carriage with Bergotte en route to the Jardin d'Acclimatation. *Grasset B* changes the destination to St.-Cloud. [43] The final text simply explains that Bergotte drives the narrator home. A new passage is inserted before their departure to prepare for important events to come; it is an allusion to the scene in *Grasset A* in which Gilberte revealed the unpleasant side of her character on the occasion of the anniversary of her grandfather's death. The part of the conversation in the carriage between the narrator and

[43] On page 569 of the Pléiade the narrator asks Gilberte: "Où allons-nous?" At this point, *Grasset B* had said: "C'est à Saint-Cloud que nous allons avec lui n'est-ce pas?" (569:12). The corrected text makes no sense because the narrator and Gilberte are not going anywhere together, now that Saint-Cloud has been eliminated.

Bergotte which comes from *Grasset A* is pleasant enough since the illustrious writer dissipates some of the doubts of his young disciple concerning the latter's literary future. A long addition returns to the subject of the narrator's health in a noticeable non sequitur; Bergotte advises him to replace Cottard with Dr. du Boulbon who is better suited to treating a patient addicted to literature. Feuillerat notes that at this point Bergotte's manner of speaking is getting on the narrator's nerves: "Cette manière de parler me fatiguait beaucoup . . ." (p. 571). Momentarily the narrator becomes completely disgusted with Bergotte because of his malevolence toward Swann who, in Bergotte's words, "avale par jour cinquante couleuvres de femmes qui ne veulent pas recevoir la sienne, ou d'hommes qui ont couché avec elle" (p. 571). Feuillerat uses this passage as the crowning argument for his denigration thesis. He may well be right; yet it must also be pointed out that this addition is not gratuitous but that it is rather the result of a logical progression from the first disappointment when the image of the kindly old man with the white beard was shattered. Furthermore the narrator seems to accommodate himself very readily to the reality of Bergotte since, in the same new text, he goes on to register inwardly his pride at being "parmi les amis du grand écrivain" (p. 572). Being now reminded of the time which we were never told about) when, at Combray, his parents refused to allow him to accept Swann's invitation to dine with Bergotte, he now resolves to tell his parents about "cette faveur que m'avait faite Swann" (p. 573). Thus this passage attaches neatly to the tapering off episode in *Grasset A*. Despite the digressions introduced by so many generalizations, this account of the Bergotte luncheon has lost none of its cohesion in the portrait of the great writer; the portrait has only become more realistic and doubtless the function of the *Recherche* as a Bildungsroman has been heightened.

Between the Bergotte luncheon and the narrative of the "thé" we find in *Grasset B* the account of the narrator's first visit to a brothel under Bloch's tutelage. It is obviously a *preparation* for the episode in *Le Côté de Guermantes* (the part covered also by *Grasset B*) where the narrator discovers that Saint-Loup's mistress, who, up to that point, had not had a name, is "Rachel quand du Seigneur." Rachel is the amateur prostitute whose services the narrator keeps refusing in the brothel. The *Grasset B* version of the brothel scene suggests that this episode is to have some further relation with the narrator's life ("les maisons de passe que je fréquentais quelques années plus tard" [575:40]) but, although this allusion survives in the final text, there is, of course, no corresponding episode elsewhere in the *Recherche.* In rewriting the brothel episode, Proust was evidently aware that he had left the reader in doubt concerning the narrator's activities in the brothel. In the midst of a few piquant details, he now made it clear that he really did nothing except that, because of a peculiar liking for the "tenancière," he gave her most of the furniture inherited from Aunt Léonie, including a couch on which "j'avais connu pour la première fois les plaisirs de l'amour avec une de mes petites cousines" (p. 578). This is another example of how Proust refers back to episodes which are lacking in *Du côté de chez Swann* because he could not revise the already published text.

The brothel sequence is an intrusion in the surrounding text to which it bears no relationship. Psychologically it advances further the age of the narrator when the reader's credulity has already been overtaxed in this regard. Apropos of "Combray" we noted a similar problem and registered Feuillerat's objections to this lack of verisimilitude in the text of *Grasset B.* Innumerable commentators, including Feuillerat, have pointed out that when the narrator went to the Champs-Elysées, he was really a small boy since he was accompanied by his "bonne." An inadvertency in *Grasset A* ("contrairement à ce que j'avais cru quand j'étais enfant, si chacun a sa place, en revanche il n'y a qu'une seule scène" [568:25]) referring back to the La Berma performance, seems to make him an "enfant" at that time. Customarily, though, commentators of Proust, among them Feuillerat, have accepted Norpois's statement that Gilberte was "une jeune personne de quatorze à quinze ans" (p. 476), as *Grasset A* said. Hence the narrator must have been about the same age. Even if Proust really intended things to be this way, this does not in any way solve the problem of the discrepancy in ages between the children who play in the park and the adolescents who meet at the Swanns'. If it is somewhat startling to find this erstwhile young boy visiting a brothel not only once but becoming for a time a habitué, albeit somewhat inactive, this does not upset the chronology in terms of Norpois's remark. However, Feuillerat points out that further additions to this episode age the narrator even more and that he must be in his twenties if he is able to dispose of his aunt's furniture without consulting his parents. Feuillerat fails to note that the additions to the Gilberte plot (which we are about to examine) also age the narrator noticeably. While at times he makes himself out to be a young romantic (and hence we can suppose him to be fifteen or sixteen), at other times the narrator is psychologically older since he anticipates the time when he will love "une autre femme" (p. 611) and since he spends the money from the sale of Aunt Léonie's "potiche" to "pleurer dans les bras de femmes que je n'aimais pas" (p. 625).

After the brothel episode, the text of *Grasset A* comes in again with a transition to the "thé." Bergotte having recognized his intelligence, say the parents of the narrator, there is no reason why their son should not get to work, since he intends to be a writer, but the narrator lets himself be persuaded by Madame Swann that, if a great writer like Bergotte comes to her house, there is no reason why he should not emulate him. One day Odette, as though intentionally displacing her daughter, invites the narrator to come, whenever he wishes, to her grown-up tea parties. In this "transition to the tea party" there are now two additions. In one of them Odette has become so influential that she has been able to get Bergotte appointed to do "le *leader article*" in *Le Figaro* (p. 581). The other is a very long addition concerning Gilberte which is somewhat illogically placed because it refers to going to see Madame Swann before she had invited him to do so.

This long addition must now occupy our attention. It is part of a sequence of long additions by which Proust sought to compensate for the lack of a plot in this part of *Grasset A*. This new plot, fully centered on Gilberte, is the result of one continuous inspiration and can readily be compared to "Un Amour de Swann" both structurally and from the point of view of its subject. In asserting that the narrator's behavior now becomes too sophisticated, Feuillerat overlooks the fact that the narrator is familiar with the events of "Un Amour de Swann" by this time and that his precocious knowledge of love had not been acquired from experience bur rather from hearsay. It is as though he had learned about love in books and doubtless part of his knowledge had literary origins, although there is no indication of this. The narrator is a young romantic and in this regard he is inevitably lacking in sophistication; he has no experience of life and, retrospectively, he says of himself: "Je me rendais compte que c'était la seule manière de tuer un amour, et j'étais encore assez jeune, assez courageux pour entreprendre de le faire . . ." (p. 632).

As so frequently happened in the case of a new development, the seed for the new idea was already in the original text. The seed this time was the scene where Gilberte refused to stay home because of the anniversary of her grandfather's death. We have also noted a new passage in which the narrator was reminded of Gilberte's petulance on that occasion. Likewise we have remarked the "lingerie" scene which was also inserted with the new plot in mind. This new plot begins dramatically when this "douce vie où je pouvais voir Gilberte comme je voulais" (p. 581) is interrupted by circumstances beyond the narrator's control. He had already noticed signs of annoyance in Gilberte because her parents were now forcing the narrator on her and the inevitable outburst came when they forbade her to go to a dancing lesson so as to stay home and entertain the narrator. In the midst of saying: "C'est vous qui n'êtes pas gentil!" she also manages to slip in: "Je vous aimais vraiment, vous verrez cela un jour" (p. 584). The remark is introduced in such a way that the reader wonders if she really said she loved him (the narrator imagines so many things that one is never quite sure) but a later recall of the episode establishes the fact that she did say it, although the narrator doubts that she meant it (p. 614). Realizing that he has made a mistake in showing his sorrow, the narrator suddenly has the "courage" to resolve never to see her again. Back home, he writes Gilberte a letter filled with furious and then tender phrases but there is no indication that this particular letter ever got in the post. Likewise his resolution is of short duration, for he goes to the Swanns' the next day. Gilberte is not at home. Now he must prove to her that he can live without her, but he still expects her to write a letter of apology for her absence on the day of his visit. She never writes that particular letter and he makes a new resolution never to see her. His will is stronger this time and when she writes proposing various rendezvous, he accepts and then calls off the meeting at the last minute. Now he goes to see Madame Swann (who has not invited him yet) but always when he knows that Gilberte will not be there. Secretly he still hopes for a reconciliation, believing that she will eventually yield through a desire to see him. Henceforth, whenever the narrator is in Madame Swann's company elsewhere in the text of *Grasset A*, all mention of Gilberte's presence will be removed and a slight alteration in the text will remind us that the narrator has chosen to come precisely at a time when Gilberte is absent.

The second installment of the Gilberte plot is inserted at the end of Madame Swann's "thé" but also before Madame Cottard's parting remarks about the furniture. This creates an unusual structural problem, for the two events are proceeding at different rates: the tea party is presumably taking place within the limits of one afternoon whereas this new segment of the Gilberte plot, like the first one, encompasses blocks of time of unspecified duration. Now the narrator's attitude has changed; he tries to think that their separation is not definitive, but secretly he has come to believe that it will be. On a New Year's Day similar to the one of the preceding year he expects the miracle to happen, a letter from Gilberte saying: "je suis folle de vous" (p. 608). When the letter never comes, he decides to kill the "moi qui en moi-même aimait Gilberte" (p. 610). Knowing Swann's story (but he does not say so, of course), he realizes that his love will die in time and that he will certainly love another "woman." For the moment this thought only increases his sorrow and, realizing also the subjectivity of love and the impossibility of communication, he cannot warn Gilberte, if she loves him, of the danger for her in the demise of his love. On the other hand, a realistic trait in him makes him realize that if he shows any sign of yielding, Gilberte will simply conclude that "mon amour pour elle, le besoin que j'avais d'elle, étaient encore plus grands qu'elle n'avait cru" (p. 613). So he continues to write letters which indifferently say: "Je ne vous verrai probablement plus" (p. 614), while inwardly he continues to suffer.

The third installment of the Gilberte plot is inserted more or less at random in what we have previously called the "Odette" section with which "Noms de pays: le nom" ends. It comes after the long description of Odette's dresses to which it has no relation. Proust has exhausted the possibilities of a static, subjective plot; now he will again introduce action over which the narrator has no control. This time it is not the narrator who is imitating "Un Amour de Swann" but rather life which is following the pattern of the novelette. As it happened with Swann, the narrator's love is subsiding under the effects of time: "cette résistance me coûtait de moins en moins" (p. 621). However, when Madame Swann relays an invitation from Gilberte, the narrator is suddenly moved and resolves to visit Gilberte the next day. To buy her flowers, he sells Aunt Léonie's "potiche" and sets out, but, near the rue de Berri, he sees Gilberte walking with a young man.[44] Like Swann in the case of Forcheville, he is violently jealous. Of three things he is now certain: Gilberte does not love him; he can still see her if he wants to; if he does not see her he will forget her. He says that he would have gone back to see her if (like Swann) he had not had a dream in which a young man made him suffer through his perfidy, the young man being, he realized, Gilberte. He also had a feeling of guilt because of his conduct with her "derrière le massif de lauriers" (p. 630). Like Swann imagining all kinds of turpitude in Odette, he imagines Gilberte doing things in the "lingerie" with her young man. Meanwhile the correspondence with Gilberte continues and she also adopts the use of the past tense in referring to their friendship. Gradually "chaque refus de la voir me fit moins de peine" (p. 634). To hasten the process of forgetting he decides to see Madame Swann less often. This last provides an artificial graft, for what follows now is the final apotheosis of Odette from *Grasset A*. Analytical, logical, carefully structured but interrupted by frequent generalizations which were nevertheless to the point and sometimes brilliant in a metaphorical sense, the Gilberte plot was the antithesis of the lyrical narrative with which the story

[44] It is possible that Proust already intends this to be Léa since Odette certifies to the narrator that Gilberte has gone out with "une de ses amies" (p. 624).

of Gilberte began in the Champs-Elysées. It was apparently not too much to Feuillerat's liking since he considered it to be typical of Proust's "new" manner of writing. It is our opinion, on the contrary, that in these additions Proust merely recaptured the inspiration of "Un Amour de Swann" and that, in so doing, he saved the end of "Noms de pays: le nom" by making it into a novel.

Let us now dispose of the remaining additions to "Noms de pays: le nom." In the description of the "jardin d'hiver," there is a long interpolation explaining that Odette's taste for flowers is really the result of a "luxe secret" which is typical of a "cocotte" whose day begins not when she dresses, but when she undresses for a man. This addition shows that Proust was still very conscious of the double nature of Odette and that he was not forgetting the courtesan while building up the society lady. On the other side of this ledger, shortly further on, there is an addition making her "une espèce de Lespinasse" (p. 595). Since the *basic narrative* of this section was a tea party in which conversation was essential, Proust more than doubled the conversations, taking pains, although not always successfully, to make them haphazard and yet logically consecutive. At a point where Madame Cottard used the learned word "défensive," Proust had the idea of a long development, with illustrations, on her "langage noble" (p. 596). One change in Madame Bontemps's conversation was less fortunate; originally she called Odette "intelligente," but this idea being utilized in a new passage concerning the Prince d'Agrigente, the remark about Odette was cut with the result that the subsequent contrast with the stupid wives of bureaucrats was lost. In the rewriting Madame Bontemps's story about the "marmiton," originally attributed to her daughter, was now attributed to her niece Albertine. After this miscellaneous conversation from *Grasset A*, there are five new pages, largely composed of conversation, in which Proust introduced two new participants. One was the Prince d'Agrigente, obviously exemplifying Odette's social ascension; the other was Madame Verdurin come to spy on Odette and to seek recruits for her salon (there is already an indication that, despite her vehement statements to the contrary, she is looking forward to the day when she will become the Princesse de Guermantes). At this point

Proust seems to have forgotten that the tea party was essentially a *basic narrative* dealing with one particular day; for the new material he switches to a *composite basic narrative,* as he records in the imperfect tense and in the same dense paragraph, first Swann's intervention concerning the Prince d'Agrigente and then the visit of Madame Verdurin at an entirely different time when Swann would not have been there because he was avoiding the Patronne with whom his wife had his permission to exchange only two visits per year. In these new conversations Odette is even attempting to become witty as she picks up Madame Cottard's remark about deceiving her "fleuriste" (p. 603). After a return to *Grasset A* on the subject of *Lohengrin,* Madame Cottard and Madame Bontemps discuss their planned visit to Madame Verdurin as though Madame Verdurin's visit had occurred on the same day as *Lohengrin* was discussed. The same addition ends with a long generalization in which Swann's interest in Madame Bontemps is compared to the case of a great artist who prefers to "la société des gens originaux" the adulation of his "élèves" (p. 606). After this, with no visible logic, we return to Madame Cottard's witticism on her husband's passion which is part of the passage finally ending the tea party.

The final section, devoted exclusively to Odette, began in *Grasset A,* as we have noted, with Madame Cottard's parting remarks on furniture which led into a long report by the narrator on Odette's furnishings and then into a somewhat random discussion of Odette herself. At the point where he had mentioned Odette's "jeunesse immortelle" (p. 617), Proust added a passage on Swann and Botticelli which indicates that Odette objects to Swann's attempts to make her resemble the painting. After inserting the third installment of the Gilberte plot, Proust successfully worked back to the subject of Odette and picked up a long segment of the *Grasset A* text describing Odette in the Bois de Boulogne. The original text had a circular movement; having completely exhausted the subject, it began a second time: "Dès son arrivée, je la saluais . . ." (637:40). Proust did nothing to arrest this circular motion but began again with a completely rewritten section which still commenced: "Dès son arrivée, je saluais Mme Swann . . ." (p. 637). This new text includes a detailed description of Odette's "chemisette" (p. 638) made of fragments of a long passage in *Grasset A* which originally began: "je lui demandais quel était le nom de ces soutaches, de ces boutons, de cette cravate, comme j'aurais demandé à un musicien comment s'appelait cette sorte de finale, de trait, d'arpège..." (621:7). This amusing comparison was sacrificed to make way for the third installment of the Gilberte plot. After the "chemisette" Proust placed three pages of new text which did nothing to decrease the circular effect but which continued with a long description, once more, of Odette in the Bois de Boulogne. His purpose now is a last definition of the social role of Odette whom he describes as belonging to "cette classe intermédiaire, inférieure au faubourg Saint-Germain, et qui avait ceci de particulier que, déjà dégagée du monde des riches, elle était la richesse encore..." (p. 639). Predicting that Odette will one day frequent the Faubourg Saint-Germain, Proust describes her greeting the Prince de Sagan and waving to Antoine de Castellane and Adalbert de Montmorency who are riding by on horseback. It will be recalled that the gentlemen on horseback, though anonymous, were already in *Grasset A*, which indicates that in describing this social ascension of Odette, Proust was only filling out an idea which he had developed too incompletely in his original text. Also the new version presents a fitting conclusion for the Gilberte plot as Odette says to the narrator: "Alors... c'est fini? Vous ne viendrez plus jamais voir Gilberte. Je suis contente... que vous ne me 'dropiez' pas tout à fait" (p. 640).

Noms de pays: le pays

"Noms de pays: le pays," as we have already remarked, does not exist as a title in the *Grasset Proofs* and there is no break in the text. However, this account of the sojourn at Bricquebec-Balbec is a very distinct unit which begins with the narrator's departure and ends with his return to Paris. It bears no immediate relation to the text which precedes and, when Proust writes: "Quand nous partîmes cette année-lò pour Balbec [sic]..." (642:18), he has clearly embarked on a new subject. In the *Grasset Proofs* there is no overture to this section, as there was in "Combray" and in "Noms de pays: le nom." Proust plunges immediately into his subject, which is the narrator's anxiety about sleeping in an unfamiliar room, and then describes one after the other the events of the departure, the trip, and the arrival at Bricquebec-Balbec. Long before the end of the sojourn at Bricquebec, the Grasset version tapers towards a conclusion as the changes in the season announce at a distance the inevitable departure and this leads to a "finale" comparable in the complexity of its orchestration to the original end of "Noms de pays: le nom." Because this "finale," as we shall discover later, picks up not only the theme of Bricquebec, which is only logical under the circumstances, but also the theme of Florence which bears no relation to the actual events which precede and to nothing which follows (unless it be, in *La Fugitive,* the trip to Venice for which the detached fragment of the end of *Grasset A,* found in *Grasset B* [II, 148:28-148:42], might be regarded as a *preparation*), it is directly related to the overture of "Noms de pays" and must be the conclusion for the entire original section designated by that simpler title.

A close reading of the *Grasset Proofs* reveals what Proust originally intended to have happen to Gilberte. As the narrator leaves for Bricquebec, nothing has apparently changed; there has been no interval between the final events of "Noms de pays: le nom" and this beginning of "Noms de pays: le pays." In other words, the narrator still loves Gilberte and he still says so somewhat obliquely in a passage of the original text which reads: "... refus désespéré qu'opposent les choses qui constituent le meilleur de notre vie présente à ce que nous revêtions mentalement de notre acceptation la formule d'un avenir où elles ne figurent pas; refus qui était au fond de l'horreur que me faisait éprouver la pensée que mes parents mourraient un jour, que les nécessités de la vie pourraient m'obliger à vivre loin de Gilberte..." (670:22). In rewriting this passage, Proust changed one verb: "... l'horreur que m'avait fait si souvent éprouver la pensée..." (p. 670). By putting this verb in the pluperfect Proust signals that he has plunged into the remote past this assertion which originally applied to the simple past of his narrative. The meaning is clearly indicated by what follows. Swann "had told him" to leave for "ces îles délicieuses de l'Océanie," whereupon the narrator replied: "Mais alors je ne verrais plus votre fille" (670:38). But the narrator also says to himself: "Quand M. Swann te dit que tu ne reviendras pas, il entend par là que tu ne voudras pas revenir..." (p. 670). There follows then a long development on "l'habitude." Habit brings on forgetfulness if we are deprived of the presence of the things or persons which or whom we are to forget, "car alors notre moi serait changé: ce ne serait plus seulement le charme de nos parents, de notre maîtresse, de nos amis, qui ne serait plus autour de nous; notre affection pour eux aurait été si parfaitement arrachée de notre cœur dont elle est aujourd'hui une notable part, que nous pourrions nous plaire à cette vie séparée d'eux dont la pensée nous fait horreur aujourd'hui..." *(p. 671).* The narrator seems less concerned about forgetting Gilberte than he is about this separation from his parents, for that is the anxiety uppermost in his mind, but it is obvious that Gilberte is to be included in this general process of forgetting. However, in *Grasset A*, there is no further mention of Gilberte, so that we have no more evidence, other than these subtle hints, as to what became of her in the sentimental life of the narrator (in *A l'ombre des jeunes filles en fleurs,* on the contrary, the name of Gilberte continues to occur frequently, but always in new passages).

Another problem of which we shall make immediate disposition is that of the age of the narrator. As in the case of "Combray" and of "Noms de pays: le nom," there is no way in "Noms de pays: le pays" to reconcile the discrepancies in the psychological age of the narrator. The narrator seems a very small boy when the mother uses a kind of baby talk to him and says: "Eh bien, qu'est-ce que dirait l'église de Bricquebec si elle savait que c'est avec cet air malheureux qu'on s'apprête à aller la voir?" (648:43). But, in the next sentence, she says: "Est-ce cela, le voyageur ravi dont parle Ruskin?" Then there is, of course, the additional childish behavior when the grandmother undresses him and when he knocks on the wall of his bedroom, not to mention the total atmosphere of childish anxiety attendant on the departure for an unknown place and an unknown room. Whether or not there is an earlier text underlying this material, we cannot say with the evidence in the *Grasset Proofs.* We note, however, this remark embedded in this early material: "J'étais le même homme qui avait pris à la fin de l'après-midi le petit chemin de fer de Bricquebec" (665:40). In context, this remark does not necessarily make the narrator a "man," but it could. From a biographical point of view, we know, of course, that Proust compressed into his Bricquebec-Balbec narrative reminiscences of different sojourns on the Channel coast, but we are concerned only with the meaning of *Grasset A* as it presently stands. All we can say is that, although he occasionally acts like a child, the narrator of *Grasset A,* who attempts to pull the milkmaid into the railway car and who revels at Rivebelle, has to be psychologically in early manhood.

The beginning of "Noms de pays: le pays" is composed of materials which reappear in the final version but which are arranged so differently in the *Grasset Proofs* that there is little resemblance to the rewritten and expanded final version. The first subject treated is the narrator's anxiety about sleeping in a new room, which offsets the anticipated pleasure of seeing "l'église persane à côté de la tempête" (642:18). The "nouveau médecin" (who becomes in the final text "le docteur qui me soignait" [p. 646], making one wonder what happened to Cottard), lisping as he says "esquis," remarks: "Ça n'a pas l'air de vous amuser de partir" (642:18). The narrator goes on to explain that his desire to leave was really greater than the doctor's but that the obstacle to vanquish was greater than the desire, for the experience of La Berma and Gilberte had taught him not to expect too much from reality. Then he explains the details of plans: his mother will spend the summer in a rented house in St.-Cloud; his grandmother wanted to give him "de ce voyage une 'épreuve' ancienne" (646:14) by retracing the itinerary of Madame de Sévigné but, faced with the father's objections, she has resigned herself to taking the "train de une heure vingt-deux" *(p. 647).* Finally they get to the station, "ce lieu tragique et merveilleux" (648:19). At this point there is a digression comparing the advantages of train travel as opposed to the automobile travel of "today," to seeing 18th Century paintings on the nude walls of a museum as opposed to seeing them in an artificially composed 18th Century décor in a private house; Proust prefers the intellectual enjoyment of sudden contrast rather than the gradual approach. After this diversion, the narrator gets back to the departure and it is now that the childish behavior occurs. To divert her son's attention, as though he were still a very small boy, the mother comments on Françoise's hat and coat, which brings on another digression on the subject of Françoise and Anne de Bretagne. With no transition, the narrator is now in the train where, since he has an asthma attack caused by "le chagrin de quitter maman" (651:21), he asserts his right to get an alcoholic drink from the "buffet" or "wagon-bar" from which he returns slightly inebriated and is advised by his grandmother to stop talking and go to sleep. Later in the day, his grandmother suggests that he get off at Bayeux, leaving her to continue to her first destination, her friend's house, but the temptation to see "la tapisserie de la reine Mathilde" (652:17) is not as great as his desire to stay with his grandmother. So, as planned, after a short visit with the grandmother's friend in an unnamed place, he continues on alone over night to Bricquebec. Awakening in the morning in the moving train, he has an unusually poetic vision of the outside world and perceives the first of the sylphs who are haunting his imagination at this time. The narrator even points out that his desire for a complaisant maiden is related to the period when, in "Combray," "j'errais seul du côté de Méséglise, dans les bois de Troussinville" (655:26), an unproductive episode directly preceding the spying on Mademoiselle Vington and her friend. The sylph he sees from the train is a milkmaid selling milk to passengers at the station; in the original version the narrator tried unsuccessfully to pull her into the railway coach. When he arrives at Bricquebec-le-Vieux he discovers his Persian church preceded by tramway lines and surrounded by commercial signs, not at all enveloped in a sea tempest because it is five leagues from the shore. This is a surprise rather than a tragic disappointment; he is now adult enough to take a great interest in the Medieval sculpture. When he joins his grandmother at the station of the "petit chemin de fer d'intérêt local" (661:3), she is alone because Françoise has taken the wrong train and is speeding towards Bordeaux. As he approaches Bricquebec, he imagines in advance the cool reception of the director of the hotel and the embarrassment which his grandmother will cause him by haggling over prices. The imaginary scene takes place in real life exactly as he had anticipated. After a walk about town, followed by the amusing description of the "lift" and then the preparations for bed with the grandmother's assistance, this section ends with the generalization on habit.

The beginning of "Noms de pays: le pays" in *A l'ombre des jeunes filles en fleurs* is quite different. It commences "deux ans plus tard" (p. 642), that is to say after the cessation of relations with the Swanns, but the narrator has not quite forgotten Gilberte. Jumping ahead with a bound which shows Proust's disrespect for the unity of his narrative in the process of rewriting, the narrator tells how at Balbec he was emotionally disturbed by a remark by someone on the "digue" concerning "la famille du directeur du ministère des Postes" (p. 643) because it recalled a similar remark by Gilberte; of course, this is a *preparation* also for the eventual appearance of Albertine. Next comes a development on habit in which he says: "Le changement d'habitude, c'est-à-dire la cessation momentanée de l'Habitude, paracheva l'œuvre de l'Habitude quand je partis pour Balbec" (p. 644). The repetition of this idea (repetition because of the long passage on the same subject situated later both in the original and in the final text) proves that, in rereading the *Grasset Proofs*, Proust was impressed by the original explanation which he had given for the disappearance of Gilberte from the narrator's world; although meanwhile he had introduced a new and better explanation for this disappearance, the old one also served his purpose and he insisted on it more than ever. Immediately following the new passage on habit comes the old passage on automobile travel, followed by a passage added in *Grasset B* on the "antres fumeux" (644:42) of the station, a passage which picks up a few words from the allusion to the station originally occurring a few pages later (648:19). A slight allusion to Madame de Sévigné will have been noticed in the original text in connection with the proposed itinerary to Bricqueville. From this point on, in the new version, Madame de Sévigné becomes the leitmotif of the grandmother and frequent new allusions to the writer of epistles will occur almost without provocation. Immediately after Madame de Sévigné was mentioned for the first time, there is a new allusion (p. 646). Just after her daughter has invoked Ruskin, the grandmother slips in a comparison with her favorite author (p. 649). When the mother is citing the example of Regulus in beseeching her son to be brave, in the new text she also manages to quote

Madame de Sévigné (p. 650). When the grandson has returned inebriated from the "wagon-bar," a new passage is added, containing a second admonition to the grandson to rest; this time she passes him a volume of Madame de Sévigné but he prefers to contemplate the beauties of the "store bleu," whereupon he meditates for the length of a page on Madame de Sévigné in her connections with Elstir, the painter whom he says he will meet later, and with what he says he will call later "le côté Dostoïevsky des *Lettres*..." (p. 654).

The first addition on Madame de Sévigné also includes a mention of Legrandin who still, over the span of years from "Combray," has not produced that letter of introduction for his sister living near Balbec. This is a curious new tie-in with the earlier text which has frequently been noticed by the commentators of Proust and which is analogous to the plans, in "Combray," for the trip to Bricquebec which never materialized until "Noms de pays: le nom."

Getting back now to the additions in the sequence of their occurrence, we come, after the first allusion to Madame de Sévigné, to the episode of Françoise and her hat followed by a new passage which is a tribute to her "noble détachement d'un esprit d'élite" (p. 650). From that point on the episodes of *A l'ombre des jeunes filles en fleurs* follow the same order as in the *Grasset Proofs.* The next change worthy of note is the suppression of a rather long lyrical passage in which the sun is compared to an egg and which was originally attached to the paragraph describing the sunrise as seen from the train window (655:19). When he came to the passage on the milkmaid Proust replaced the sentence describing the narrator's attempt to pull her into the railway carriage by a sentence comparing her to a "vitrail illuminé" (p. 657). As he approached Balbec, Proust changed the names of all of the stations on the "petit chemin de fer" (661:21). When he got to the director of the Grand Hôtel, whom he had already described in the Balzacian manner, insisting repeatedly on his scars and pimples, he added a paragraph on his snobbery (p. 663) and, a little later, began what was subsequently to become a systematic study of his malapropisms, the first example being his assertion that he was "d'originalité roumaine" (p. 666).

The next section of "Noms de pays: le pays," which we may characterize as the *prise de contact* with the environment, is not as haphazard as we may have implied, for, in the original text, it is held together by a certain logical thread. After a poetic description of the sea which has often been cited as an unusual example of Proust's use of metaphor, there comes the luncheon scene where the grandmother surreptitiously opens a "carreau" of the "grande baie vitrée" causing a blast of sea air which carries off "menus, journaux, voiles et casquettes" (675:9) of everyone eating lunch. Then the narrator describes, in his best Balzacian manner including some dialogue, a group of provincial bourgeois patrons of the establishment, all members of the legal profession. They and the maître d'hôtel, Aimé, despise the two newcomers, the narrator and his grandmother, because they eat "œufs durs" in their salad. Next the narrator enumerates the other patrons of the hotel whom this particular group despises, the Frenchman who had proclaimed himself king "d'un petit îlot d'Océanie habité par quelques sauvages" (676:36), an actress from the Odéon accompanied by her lover and two aristocratic friends whom the bourgeois group had no chance to snub because they were never in the dining room, and finally a "vieille dame riche et titrée" (681:39) whom they considered an impostor and who had arrived with "femme de chambre, cocher, chevaux, voitures, et avait été précédée par un maître d'hôtel chargé de choisir les chambres et de les rendre, grâce à des bibelots, ... aussi peu différentes que possible de celles que sa maîtresse habitait à Paris" (681:39). Although this is not a composite narrative relating the events of the first day (as it might have been if Proust had followed his characteristic system), there are occasional allusions to events of the first day, and now we are told that the narrator and his grandmother did not see the noble Parisian lady on that day because she was in her room, but they did have a brush with another noble, M. de Silaria, who accused them of taking his reserved table. As though particularly fascinated by the actress and her companions, the narrator now interrupts his orderly presentation for the first time and comes back to them in a passage which is all the more digressive because of a brief shift of optics. Increasing the disorder, Proust introduced into the same paragraph an apparently irrelevant sentence on Swann "qui aurait cru en faisant venir de Paris sa maîtresse pour passer sur elle le désir qu'une inconnue lui avait inspirée*, ne pas croire à ce désir" (682:18), a text later cut. The paragraph concludes on the subject of Legrandin's brother-in-law, whose name in *Grasset A* is M. de Soulangy.[45] All of these people the narrator would like to meet, but especially M. de Silaria whose daughter attracts him. His grandmother has the key to this Pandora's box because the director has just leaned over to whisper into her ear that the noble lady from Paris is Madame de Villeparisis. When the narrator hears this name, he recognizes it as that of an old friend of his grandmother. If only his grandmother would give up the game of pretending that she does not know the Marquise, the narrator's social prestige would be greatly enhanced. At this point, as so often happened in "Combray," there is a change of pace as the barrister and the wife of the "premier président" engage in a Balzacian dialogue on the subject of the "comte de Soulangy" (688:7) and M. de Silaria. This brings the reader back to Mademoiselle de Silaria. One wonders how the narrator could be interested in her because of her "dureté foncière" *(p. 688)* but the real reason is that he perceives in her "le goût prédominant des plaisirs des sens" (p. 688), as a later change in the text says. The original text describes her in an imaginary feudal Breton décor hunting with her young cousins who "devaient avoir pris la douce habitude, le contact familier de son corps" (688:40).

Whatever happened to Monsieur and Mademoiselle de Silaria (or rather de Stermaria) we never learn in the final text, but the original text says that they went home, after which the grandmother and the Marquise de Villeparisis, with a feigned surprise worthy of Molière, as Proust points out, finally see each other. The Marquise overwhelms her new found friends with presents and kindness. One day, at the hotel, the narrator and his grandmother see "des fruits plus beaux que ceux que Mme de Villeparisis avait sur sa table" (698:12) and this mystery intrigues them until they discover that they are the gift of a newly arrived char-

---

[45] Of course, he became M. de Cambremer in the final text. Legrandin's sister was already called Madame de Cambremer in *Grasset A* when she appeared at Madame de Saint-Euverte's reception, but the typescript, at that point, originally called her Madame de Lenouves.

acter, the Princesse de Luxembourg. A few days later they attend the morning concert on the beach to hear a program of Wagner and Schumann. This is Bloch's doing because he had urged the narrator to go to this concert. This digression, which cuts abruptly into the story of the Princesse de Luxembourg, is a typical spore which, this time, was not allowed to develop, for it survives in such a vestigial form that one wonders what the brief sentence of comment really means. It will be recalled that Bloch was originally the catalyst for the narrator's interest in contemporary literature; now, judging by the space devoted to this episode in *Grasset A,* Proust intended to assign the same role to Bloch in contemporary music. Having described the program of the concert in some detail, enumerating the pieces played (all of this has disappeared from the final text), the narrator remarks: "Et persuadé que les œuvres que j'entendais exprimaient vraiment les vérités les plus hautes, je tâchais de m'élever aussi haut que je pouvais pour atteindre jusqu'à elles" (698:38). This is the kind of sentence which Proust would normally have expanded but this time he evidently thought better of this idea despite his personal preference for Wagner over Saint-Saëns, who, according to the commentators, [46] was the original for Vinteuil. Meanwhile the narrator had already mentioned that they met Madame de Villeparisis on leaving the concert; after the digression on the concert, he returns to Madame de Villeparisis and tells us that she now presented him and his grandmother to the Princesse de Luxembourg who, in an amusing scene greatly expanded and improved in the final version, treats them as though they were "des animaux étranges" (699:25) in the Jardin d'Acclimatation. After the departure of the Princess, Madame de Villeparisis reveals an intimate knowledge of the progress of the trip of Monsieur de Montfort and the narrator's father in Spain; this mystifies the narrator and only much later will he learn the explanation, the fact that Madame de Villeparisis is the mistress, or ex-mistress, of the ex-ambassador. Picking up again the theme of the beginning of this section, there is a kind of conclusion which returns the bourgeois patrons of the hotel to center stage; they are again

[46] See on this subject Georges Piroué: *Proust et la musique du devenir.*

sputtering about the effrontery of the mistress of the king of the savages but they now extend their indignation to include the Princesse de Luxembourg who, for them, "sentait l'horizontale d'une lieue" *(p. 702)*. In this passage they call her "une femme avec un nègre," but the "nègre" was not mentioned in the preceding text before the additions to the revised version of the earlier scene where the narrator and his grandmother are presented to the Princess.

In rewriting this section on the *prise de contact,* Proust was aware of the disorder created in his narrative by the fragmentation of the story of the actress and her friends. He therefore consolidated the two fragments but not altogether successfully. In *Grasset A* the second fragment began: "Et certes dans le désir d'isolement qui poussait le jeune homme riche, sa maîtresse et ses amis à ne voyager qu'ensemble, à ne prendre leurs repas qu'après tout le monde, il n'y avait aucun sentiment malveillant à l'endroit des autres . . ." (680:17). In the original, "Et certes" does not make too much sense but at least it can be defended as a locution serving to introduce a subject already treated; referring back to nothing in the text, this expression now serves only the more to highlight the digressive nature of the story of the actress. The first part of the final version of the "actress" text is rewritten from the variant (680:18) of *Grasset A* originally situated on page 677 in terms of the Pléiade edition and it retains the "observer" point of view when the narrator summarizes the "known" elements of their biography and describes the actress bursting forth from the elevator "comme d'une boîte de joujou*" (681:39). In the original version the second fragment referred to their Parisian existence and then shifted to an omniscient point of view as the optic followed them going down "la route bordée de pommiers qui part de Bricquebec" (681:14).

Between the two original fragments much rewritten, Proust introduced a further digression which has nothing to do with the actress and her friends. This new passage was grafted on the other material in a curious manner: "Et le soir ils ne dînaient pas à l'hôtel où . . ." (p. 681). The relative clause beginning with "où" goes on to describe the "population ouvrière de Balbec" watching through the great plate glass window of the dining room of the Grand Hôtel illuminated with electric lights. Feuillerat points out that this is a unique instance where Proust comments on the lower classes looking in on the idle rich: "...(une grande question sociale, de savoir si la paroi de verre protégera toujours le festin des bêtes merveilleuses et si les gens obscurs qui regardent avidement dans la nuit ne viendront pas les cueillir dans leur aquarium et les manger)" (p. 681). Feuillerat comments that this unusual remark may originate in a momentary fear of social revolution near the end of the First World War (but he forgets that the gardener in "Combray," watching the parading troops, said to Françoise: "la révolution vaudrait mieux" [*p. 89*]). The next addition is likewise curious, for it places in this crowd "quelque écrivain, quelque amateur d'ichtyologie humaine" (p. 681) watching the "vieux monstres féminins" of the Faubourg Saint-Germain in their aquarium eating their salad like fishes. Feuillerat does not comment on this identification of Proust himself with the critics of the upper class.

The great plate glass window was in *Grasset A* and we have already noted that, although it would presumably have been a solid piece, the narrator's grandmother managed to open a "carreau" and let in the sea breeze. The first addition made to the *prise de contact* section reversed the situation of the plate glass window and now we find the narrator, on his arrival at Balbec, looking out through it onto the passing heteroclite crowd but without any political or sociological implications (p. 674). Most other additions involved in some way or other the patrons of the hotel. In connection with the first mention of Legrandin's brother-in-law (shortly to be called the Marquis de Cambremer instead of the Comte de Soulangy), Proust added the anecdote of how the new director of the hotel had originally snubbed this provincial noble because he was not properly dressed for "la vie des Palaces" (p. 682). In commenting on how he would like to make the acquaintance of these people, the narrator in *Grasset A* had already mentioned that he would even be glad to know a "jeune tuberculeux" *(p. 683)*. Now, just preceding this entry, he mentioned some other characters he would likewise not mind knowing, "les fils du propriétaire véreux d'un magasin de nouveautés" (p. 683). A further comment on miscellaneous people was introduced just after the director "revealed" the identity of Madame de Villeparisis to the narrator's grandmother; it is an amusing passage inspired by the notion that "sous les traits d'une petite vieille" the narrator had discovered "la plus puissante des fées," a comparison which suggested three similar analogies: "il m'était arrivé de rencontrer Legrandin, le concierge de Swann et Mme Swann elle-même, devenus, le premier, un garçon de café, le second, un étranger de passage que je ne revis pas, et la dernière, un maître baigneur" (p. 685).

To the director and the maître d'hôtel, Aimé, Proust added, in his revised text, another member of the hotel profession, the Director General of the hotel chain, whose chief interest for the narrator is the fear that he inspires in others, particularly in the director of the hotel (p. 691). Feuillerat comments that Proust, in his additions, as in the case of the lower classes peering through the plate glass window, was now concerned more than ever before with the socially inferior and therefore hotel employees were of special interest to him.

Immediately following the new passage on the Director General, Proust inserted several new passages on Françoise in her role as a servant. We agree with Feuillerat that this new material about the "prolétaires," as Proust now says, is interconnected, but we do not subscribe to his opinion that there has been an abrupt change in Françoise. Even though he was unaware of the conclusive evidence in the digression on Françoise within the *Grasset A* version of the good night kiss, he should not have missed the surviving allusion to "l'entêtement qu'elle mettait à ne pas vouloir faire certaines commissions que nous lui donnions" (p. 29). To speak of a new vilification of Françoise also seems excessive in view of her epic persecution of the scullery maid whom Swann called "la Charité de Giotto" (p. 80).

The several new passages, to which we now refer, begin by describing Françoise's adherence to the rules of protocol among servants (pp. 692-4); this is one of the most amusing realistic scenes in the novel and can hardly be called unsympathetic. If we return to the comparison between Françoise and Anne de Bretagne, mentioned earlier, we note an addition in which the narrator describes, in the case of Françoise, her "regard intelligent et bon d'un chien" (p. 650) and suggests that beneath this apparent stupidity there may lie some real native intelligence which lacks only the varnish of education. Simultaneously, as Proust is critical of Françoise, he makes an effort to build her up and thus he mentions, near the end of this long new section concerning her, both "son amour excessif pour nous" and "le plaisir qu'elle avait à nous être désagréable" (p. 696), the contrasting remarks being in the same sentence. Like most Proustian characters, Françoise is merely ambivalent. In fact, it is difficult to pinpoint her basic social and political attitudes. After the Moliéresque scene of the meeting of the grandmother and Madame de Villeparisis, which has now become so embedded in this continuous text on Françoise that it almost seems to be an aside (the paragraph now begins: "A la fin, nous aussi, nous fîmes une relation..." [p. 694]), the transition back to Françoise is made by way of Aimé. Aimé's attitude changes abruptly when he learns that the grandmother is a friend of the Marquise, for Aimé likes no one better than titled personages. Strangely enough, the narrator does not consider Aimé to be a snob. Having come back to Françoise, we are told that she was not "de la race agréable et pleine de bonhomie dont Aimé faisait partie" (p. 695) and that she considered that "Mme de Villeparisis avait donc à se faire pardonner d'être noble" (p. 696). One is tempted to rise to her defense and say that, like the narrator's great aunt who would have retorted: "Si vous ne voulez pas que ce soit répété, pourquoi le dites-vous?" (p. 572), Françoise is of the angular race of Combray and will not tolerate false fronts; but Proust does not say it. However, Françoise does redeem herself by finally liking Madame de Villeparisis whom "elle préféra à toutes les personnes que nous connaissions" (p. 696). Nevertheless, in still another passage coming in between bits and pieces about Madame de Sévigné, Françoise's disdain of the upper classes again comes out when she refuses to believe that Madame de Villeparisis was ever beautiful because that was said by the grandmother who "mentait dans un intérêt de classe, les gens riches se soutenant les uns les autres" (p. 697). These seem to be echoes of a proletarian revolt and therefore it will be with no little surprise that we will discover, when we later return to this point apropos of Françoise's attitude towards Saint-Loup, that she is politically a conservative and perhaps a royalist.

We have noted that Madame de Sévigné was the subject of many additions; in the *prise de contact* section she was already in the original text but the material was rewritten, expanded and considerably rearranged. In *Grasset A*, after running into Madame de Villeparisis in the Molièresque scene, the grandmother was most anxious to know "comment elle faisait pour avoir des grillades à son repas et son courrier plutôt* que nous" (694:21). To the second question she got a reaction almost immediately (only one sentence intervened about Madame de Villeparisis's habit of coming to sit daily at their table) and it was: "Je dirai à ma femme de chambre d'aller prendre vos lettres en même temps que les miennes. Comment, vous vous écrivez *tous les jours* avec votre fille?" (696:39). She should have added: like Madame de Sévigné. When, resenting this invasion of her privacy, the grandmother did not deign to answer, Madame de Villeparisis continued: "Qu'est-ce que vous avez là! Ah! oui, je vous voyais toujours avec les lettres de Mme de Sévigné . . ." (697:12). The grandmother still said nothing and placed her handbag over her other volume, "les mémoires de Mme de Charlus" (697:26).[47] This is the end of Madame de Sévigné in the original and then there follows one of these typical "parallel" structures in which Madame de Villeparisis is simultaneously sending fruit and books to the grandmother. After that comes an isolated paragraph in which the grandmother says that she would like to ask Madame de Villeparisis whether she is a Guermantes, a suggestion which makes her grandson indignant. Then the episode of the Princesse de Luxembourg follows.

These texts occur in a very different order in the final version. In the first place, after the "grillades," Proust managed to insert an unattached Sévigné quotation (p. 694) and then he delayed Madame de Villeparisis's answer on the subject of the mail by the following passages: a sentence added in *Grasset B* on the "moment sordide" after a meal; a short passage on Balbec as the "pointe extrême de la terre" (p. 694); the long development on

[47] There is a Madame de Charlus in the *Mémoires* of Saint-Simon but we have no evidence that she, herself, wrote any memoirs. We therefore conclude that her memoirs are as apocryphal as the *Mémoires de Madame de Beausergent* which replace this allusion in the text.

Aimé and Françoise; the parallel passage on fruit and books; a paragraph added in *Grasset B* on eating oysters. When the old text containing the answer is finally in place, it is followed immediately by a new text registering the grandmother's disdainful silence while the narrator imagines all sorts of Sévigné quotations with which she might have replied. The grandmother then breaks her silence by talking about fruit but subsequently manages a quotation from Sévigné. This perhaps provides a slightly better motivation for the next remark than was the case in the original text, as Madame de Villeparisis says: "Ah, oui, vous lisez Madame de Sévigné. Je vous vois depuis le premier jour avec ses *Lettres* . . ." (p. 697). Under the circumstances, since she was the one who brought up Madame de Sévigné, the grandmother should have been more polite this time, but Proust continues with only a slightly modified version of the original text; the grandmother again looks upon this as an invasion of her privacy, says nothing, and places her handbag over the *Mémoires de Madame de Beausergent.* The new material continues with the passage on Françoise misquoting the messages of Madame de Villeparisis and refusing to believe that the latter was ever beautiful; then comes the Guermantes discussion and finally the Princesse de Luxembourg. Finally the neat little conclusion with which the *prise de contact* section originally ended is overrun by new material, some general observations suggested by this bourgeois incomprehension of the importance of the Princesse de Luxembourg, "nièce du roi d'Angleterre et de l'empereur d'Autriche" (p. 703). These remarks concern the separation of classes, the fact that the bourgeois consider the nobles of the Faubourg Saint-Germain as "des décavés crapuleux" and cannot understand how a noble who has made a financial success in the bourgeois world of business can still frequent a ruined marquis and even marry his daughter to him.

Because of the narrator's poor health, Madame de Villeparisis offers to take him and his grandmother driving. We have already cited this account of the "promenades en voiture" as the most typical *composite basic narrative,* for the episodes succeed each other in what resembles a linear narrative without ever departing from the convention that this is a mosaic composed of an unspecified number of "promenades."

It is never clear whether this composite narrative concerns a half day trip or a whole day trip. The narrator tells us first that, when he went on carriage trips with Madame de Villeparisis, he was required to rest until lunch time and that he lay in his bed watching the luminous column moving about his room like the one "qui précédait les Hébreux dans le désert" (704:21), for Françoise had pinned the curtains of his room but they still let in some light. Presently we discover that some trips took an entire day, but the narrator makes no comment on the routine on such days. On Sundays (but we no longer know whether it was early in the morning or after lunch) they see other carriages preparing to leave for the château of M. de Chimesey (the name of M. de Soulangy having meanwhile changed) and other carriages pointedly going elsewhere because their occupants were not invited by the count. Then they leave, going past the railway station and entering a country road bordered with apple trees. Here the narrator indulges in a *flash-forward* and tells how, the following year in May, he bought apple blossoms at the Paris florist's in memory of his sojourn at Bricqueville (which was not at apple blossom time, he points out). Then comes a seascape accompanied by quotations from Leconte de Lisle and Baudelaire. Then follows a forestscape which he appreciates "enchaîné à mon strapontin comme Prométhée sur son rocher" (720:12). Not knowing his way, the coachman asks directions and the narrator hears the name of the village of Blenpertuis about whose church he had read in his "Précis d'archéologie monumentale de l'ouest." Because it is not directly on their road, he does not dare ask his hostess to go there and Blenpertuis remains the symbol of the unattainable but necessary artistic goal: "Renoncer à Blenpertuis c'eût été le premier pas que je ne voulais pas faire vers cette déchéance où je tomberais peut-être un jour de ne plus considérer la vie comme la connaissance et la possession de ce que j'avais désiré, c'eût été de demander à la réalité ce dont mon imagination et mon intelligence avaient d'abord fixé le prix" (708:17). Knowing, somehow, that the narrator likes churches, Madame de Villeparisis takes him to Brissinville to see one covered with ivy. At this point the narrator drops that subject to discourse on Madame de Villeparisis' knowledge of architecture which comes from having been brought up in a Renaissance castle where Chopin played and Lamartine recited his poetry. This blends into actual conversation by the Marquise in which she mentions that she is wearing the same necklace as an ancestor wore in a painting by Titian. However, she continues to talk with modesty about "la reine des Belges en visite, Louis-Philippe entrant chez son père" and places birth and rank "bien après le talent et l'intelligence" (709:17). Whether or not this is all the same conversation is beside the point because this is a composite narrative; at any rate, in her conversation she expresses unusually liberal political attitudes: she is surprised that anyone is scandalized by the expulsion of the Jesuits, has a good word for the Republic, and announces: "Un homme qui ne travaille pas, pour moi ce n'est rien" (709:29). Other conversations, or the same one, record her opinions about great writers, Balzac, Hugo, Vigny, but here the narrator is surprised by her preference for the more urbane members of aristocratic society; she finds great writers vulgar and pretentious (this seems to contradict what she said about talent and intelligence).

Thereupon we get back to the fact that this is a trip; the carriage is crossing fields of "bleuets" which seem to the narrator to be "des champs miraculeusement vrais" that, since Combray, had come to symbolize "tout ce qui est dans notre pensée" (711:10). Now he begins to see sylphs, on foot, on bicycles, on carts or in carriages, and he remembers Bloch's revelation that they are all accessible; being ill, he knows that he cannot make love with them but he is like a child brought up in a prison or hospital who, knowing only bread or medicine, suddenly learns of the existence of peaches, apricots, and grapes. One passing "fillette" he would like to impress with his existence but she has already disappeared. Was she really beautiful or did she just seem that way? It was always his misfortune to be with "quelque grave personne" (712:38) on occasions like this. Now we get back to the "église couverte de lierre" (715:12); our author has evidently forgotten that he had already mentioned it and that it was at Brissinville, not at Briseville, as he now says. Briseville or Brissinville, he now encounters a "belle pêcheuse" to whom, in the hope of impinging more durably on her consciousness, he gives a five franc tip and has her take a message to the Marquise waiting in her carriage; but now, having broken the ring of mystery around his sylph, he no longer desires her. In fact, according to the old text, he does not have to wonder whether she is beautiful or not: "Il ne restait qu'une fille assez laide avec un grand corps et un joli nez, et par laquelle il me fut indifférent d'être contemplé..." (974:27). On another day (tense usage in the new version makes it the same day as the visit to Briseville-Carqueville), when they are going down the Couliville road, the narrator has the revelation of the three trees which he likens to what he once felt "en respirant l'odeur humide du petit pavillon des Champs-Elysées" (717:12). At no point, strangely enough, does the old text establish any relationship with the episode of the three steeples of Martinville in *Du côté de chez Swann* (although the final version does, of course, at the same time that it omits the reference to the Champs-Elysées). One might conjecture that the Briseville trees antedate the Martinville steeples but such a conclusion is unwarranted in terms of our texts since *Grasset A* includes the Martinville episode.

On other days, the sun having set before their return, the narrator recites Romantic poetry. Madame de Villeparisis comments: "Et vous trouvez cela beau?" *(p. 721).* Then she goes on to say that Stendhal would have been amazed by such admiration; she also tells the anecdote of Chateaubriand's stereotyped eloquence in the moonlight, objects to Vigny's pretentiousness and to Balzac's sociological inaccuracies, and relates how her father did not stay through the presentation of *Hernani.*

"Il fallait songer au retour" (719:41), now says the text of *Grasset A.* On one occasion they return by the "vieille route de Bricquebec" where even the prosaic Madame de Villeparisis seems to enjoy the "ormes séculaires" (719:41). On another occasion they return through the forest and are waved at by the Princesse de Luxembourg passing by rapidly in another carriage. Then follows a small dimensional symphonic conclusion as the narrator evokes many other such returns in later life, on all of which occasions he remembers the supreme return to Bricquebec. Even the hotel is hospitable when they get back to it; they are so famished that, instead of going up to their rooms, they wait for the dining room to open up. Noticing that the director of the hotel is insulted when she asks him to take their coats, the Marquise now tells the anecdote illustrating the simplicity of the Duc de Nemours but then she continues with a series of anecdotes which illustrate the exact opposite, the snobbishness of the nobility concerning rank and privilege. Her final anecdote, however, about the Duchesse de La Rochefoucauld gets back to a more simple tone. After that comes the typical post mortem as the grandmother and the narrator discuss Madame de Villeparisis together. Then they talk about themselves and the grandmother implies that she might not always be there. The grandson seems not to comprehend or to be indifferent, but the next day he discourses on the bankruptcy of materialism in philosophy, concluding that "le plus probable était encore l'éternité des âmes et leur future réunion" *(p. 728).* This final paragraph is very strange in view of the fact that later the narrator is supposed to have no premonition of the grandmother's fatal illness.

At this juncture one legitimately wonders what all these plotless promenades were about. For the narrator, Bricquebec seems to be retrospectively as enchanted a place as Combray. Although much of this unsophisticated enthusiasm has survived in the final text, Proust did make at least two attempts to tone it down. He reduced the dithyrambic passage on the "bleuets" to a few mutilated fragments, sacrificing even most of the final sentence which was particularly fortunate in the original: "Un bleuet exposant au bas d'un champ sa signature pour en certifier l'authenticité me semblait quelque chose de plus estimable que ces fleurettes par lesquelles certains maîtres anciens signaient leurs toiles" (711:10). He also shortened the passage on the political opinions of Madame de Villeparisis to the point where only an enumeration of these views remained, removed all reference to the enthusiastic reception of these "opinions d'une bourgeoise conservatrice" (709:29) by the narrator and his grandmother, and supplied a possible motivation which was not in the original text: "peut-être seulement parce qu'elle sentait ce qu'ils prenaient de piquant, de savoureux, de mémorable dans sa bouche" (p. 709). He also added a new remark: that socialism was her "bête noire." On the whole, Proust made little effort to reassess the character of Madame de Villeparisis. He had originally summarized her attitude as "l'horreur du snobisme dans ces éloges de la médiocrité, ces railleries de la noblesse, ces vues élevées, et le goût du snobisme, parce qu'en écoutant ce langage élevé on entrait plus avant dans l'aristocratique fréquentation de Mme de Villeparisis et ses interlocuteurs princiers" (709:29). And he went on to make an observation which has survived in about the same words: "A ces moments-là je n'étais pas loin de croire qu'en Mme de Villeparisis trônaient la mesure et le modèle de la vérité en toutes choses." In the post mortem, the narrator even restates this estimate more explicitly in the final text than in the original, speaking now of "les qualités qui nous charmaient chez Mme de Villeparisis, le tact, la finesse, la discrétion, l'effacement de soi-même" (p. 726). To be sure, both in the original and in the final text, the narrator still questions her opinion concerning certain great names of literary history and wonders whether literary geniuses, with all their vanity and bad judgment, are not more important for the progress of the world than the Molés and the Vitrolles (Loménies in the final text) with all their urbanity. We can write off this last observation as a *préjugé d'école.* More important is the fundamental nature of this aristocrat. At the end of his discussion with his grandmother, the narrator asks "si elle avait remarqué telle phrase que Mme de Villeparisis avait dite et dans laquelle se marquait la femme qui tenait plus à sa naissance qu'elle ne l'avouait" (p. 727). The narrator's final judgment on this point is lacking but at least the omniscient author (or is it the narrator? one seldom knows) had previously summarized the whole problem: Madame de Villeparisis hopes to continue social relations with the grandmother and the narrator even when she returns to Paris; but now, in Bricquebec, she is outdoing herself to be nice in order to "prendre l'avance d'un solde créditeur, qui lui permettra prochainement d'inscrire à son débit le dîner ou le raout où elle ne les invitera pas" (p. 724). Perhaps there is a certain amount of sham in her political views or perhaps some resentment at being ostracized by society (but there is no proof here that Proust anticipates this further revelation about her, which comes later). In any event, there still seems to be a contradiction between her political attitudes and her innate snobbery worthy (as the reader of the *Recherche* will later discover) of her nephew Charlus.

Proust made no changes in the fundamental significance of the "promenades" section. He did not make additions which "consistent presque exclusivement en des passages où le narrateur dit son désir des jolies filles rencontrées au cours des promenades dans la campagne," as Feuillerat misleadingly states (op. cit., p. 49). There are two such episodes taking place in the country and they have survived from *Grasset A* with no important changes. One thing which Proust did was to disturb the symmetry of the original presentation (a symmetry which was hardly perfect because of the repetition and confusion in connection with Brissinville-Briseville) by reversing the order of two similar blocks of text. One began: "Le jour tombait souvent avant que nous fussions de retour" (721:20); it followed originally the Couliville-Hudimesnil episode of the three trees and introduced the anecdotes on the Romantic poets. The second one began: "Il fallait songer au retour" (719:41); it followed the Romantic poets and began a description of the route home. Proust reversed these texts with the result that we suddenly jump from the Romantic poets to the arrival at the hotel, whereas the route home comes before the poets. Another change was to take the Stendhal passage out of its original context just preceding the Romantic poets and to attach it to the earlier discussion of writers who were boors in society (p. 710); whereas Madame de Villeparisis had originally said that Stendhal was "de bonne compagnie" (710:32), she now attributed to him a "vulgarité affreuse." For some unknown reason Prometheus on his rock emigrated from the first description of the forest of the Arbonne (708:16) to the drive home along the "vieille route" (p. 720).

Among miscellaneous cuts and additions, we note that the passage describing the "sourire approbatif" of Madame de Villeparisis's maître d'hôtel and Françoise leaning out of the window, contrary to orders, as the carriage trip begins (705:36), is replaced by a development on the "chasseurs" of the hotel, appropriate perhaps but so long and detailed as to be digressive. A major cut was the entire episode of Blenpertuis (708:17). The episode of the first sylph is greatly expanded; the original text having raised the question: "Etait-ce à cause du passage si rapide que je l'avais trouvée si belle?" (712:38), Proust now develops a page-long generalization on how the most deformed torso can be transformed into a thing of beauty provided the carriage goes fast enough, a discussion which is capped off by the new anecdote of the narrator pursuing Madame Verdurin on the darkened streets of Paris on the supposition that she was an unknown beautiful woman (p. 713). This long paragraph is followed by yet another new one which begins with the statement that the narrator asked to get out of the carriage, on the pretext that he had a headache, in order to try to find the first sylph (in *Grasset A* he thought of asking but did not). The same paragraph continues with a story of a new sylph, the "laitière" (p. 714) whom he saw at the Grand Hôtel and whom he thought to be the author of a letter which turned out, when he opened it, to come from Bergotte. Since it interferes with the account of the "promenades," this change of locale is disruptive; furthermore these sylphs within sylphs are very confusing. Finally, there was the addition of Musset to Madame de Villeparisis' remarks on the affectations of the Romantics, followed by some additional comments on Vigny who had already been mentioned.

In the next section of "Noms de pays: le pays," Proust returns essentially to a linear narrative to relate the arrival of two new characters at Bricquebec; one, bearing alternately, sometimes in the same passage, the names Beauvais and Montargis, will ultimately be renamed Saint-Loup, and the other, named Fleurus (earlier he was Gurcy), will become Charlus. In this part of the *Grasset Proofs*, incidentally, "Charlus" continues to be the name of a contemporary of Madame de Sévigné (cf. 735:19). Except that Beauvais has already entered Saint-Cyr (and is not a candidate for Saumur, as is the case with Saint-Loup, and is not garrisoned at Doncières, a place which is not mentioned in *Grasset A*), there are no fundamental differences between the Beauvais-Montargis narrative and the Saint-Loup narrative. The narrator anticipates the arrival of Madame de Villeparisis's nephew (actually she should have called him a grand-nephew because Fleurus was also her nephew at the same time that he was Beauvais's uncle) with the same enthusiasm in both texts, is sorely disappointed by his aristocratic disdain but then makes of him the perfect friend after the proper introductions have occurred. In rewriting the Beauvais narrative, Proust added some "omniscient" information concerning this character; whereas he was presented originally in terms of what Madame de Villeparisis said and in terms of what the narrator saw, the revised version referred to his having been a second for the "jeune duc d'Uzès" (p. 729), of having been pursued by "les plus jolies femmes du grand monde," and of having been considered virile in spite of his "air efféminé." Another example of careful and extensive rewriting can be observed in the case of the introduction scene in which, for example, the stiffly extended hand of the young noble now suggests to the narrator that he is being challenged to a duel. In the original version as well as in the final text, much stress is laid on the fact that this handsome and elegant noble is emotionally in revolt against his class, reads Proudhon (but not Nietzsche, as Saint-Loup does), and likes the company of "jeunes étudiants prétentieux et mal mis" *(p. 737)*. These observations about Beauvais-Montargis's social and political outlook lead in the original text to three illustrative anecdotes which are so widely dispersed in the final version that their illustrative function is no longer apparent. The first concerns Bloch whom the young noble already happens to know; mispronouncing the word "lift" (p. 739), Bloch causes Beauvais great embarrassment for fear that the arrogant student will perceive his error later and think that he has been despised for his mistake. In the original and in the final version, in a *flash-forward,* Bloch does indeed discover his error later but shrugs off his mistake with the remark: "Cela n'a d'ailleurs aucune espèce d'importance" (740:3). The second anecdote follows immediately in the original version and again presents Beauvais's social outlook but in a paradoxical form: he is not polite with his coachman because politeness to an inferior would be a sign of aristocratic superiority. This leads to a third illustration which has survived only in an abbreviated form in the final text; Beauvais-Montargis calls the Princesse de Luxembourg "une carpe" *(p. 780)* and adds: "C'est d'ailleurs un peu ma cousine." In the original, the narrator asks his friend to explain the genealogical relationship but the latter expresses contempt for all genealogies.

At this point comes the explanation for Beauvais's revolt against his class; it is due to the deplorable influence of a mistress whom the Grasset text had not mentioned yet (whereas, in the Pléiade text, Mme de Villeparisis had already revealed her existence when talking about her nephew before his arrival). Once again the story of this mistress does not undergo any fundamental changes; it begins with a long generalization on the relation of clubmen and their mistresses, then tells how Beauvais's mistress has been influenced, by her literary friends and by an unfortunate experience in presenting a symbolist play at the house of her lover's aunt, to despise her lover's intellect and to envisage a definitive break with him. In *Grasset B* this material received two long additions, the first dealing with Saint-Loup's refusal (for the name "Saint-Loup" occurs for the first time in these additions) to show the narrator a photograph of his mistress and to "constituer un capital" (783:16) for her; the second being a long development, later shortened, concerning Saint-Loup's suffering at the hands of his mistress (785:23).

The Beauvais-Montargis narrative ends in a long passage which has completely disappeared from the final text. The narrator goes in the evening with Montargis to dine at an "ancien moulin" (785:35) which is frequented by "sous-officiers" from the neighboring garrison and by "employés" seeking a change from the "sécheresse de leurs occupations." While waiting for their trout to be cooked, the two friends go boating on the mill pond. Once at table, the narrator asks his companion "s'il croyait qu'on pourrait facilement faire monter la servante dans la petite chambre qu'on louait en haut." Since Montargis does not think so, the narrator drops the matter but continues to question him "sur la légèreté certaine ou possible d'une femme ou d'une autre." Montargis says that he regrets that he had not been there to introduce the narrator to Mademoiselle de Silaria: "je vous aurais abouchés." Then the narrator questions him about one of his cousins, presently identified as Mademoiselle Claremonde, whom the narrator thought to be the radiant blonde whom he once encountered in a Paris street and who looked at him "avec une impudeur que n'aurait pas eue une cocotte." [48] Montargis assures him that Claremonde is "d'une vertu revêche" and would not look at anyone lower than a grand duke. But a few days later

[48] In the original typescript of *Grasset A* both Mademoiselle de Silaria and Claremonde were missing from the episode of the dinner at the old mill. They were added in a handwritten interpolation in the margin.

the narrator encounters Claremonde on a deserted part of the "digue" and she makes equivocal signs, perhaps intended for him or perhaps for someone else whom he could not see. This peculiar and inconclusive text finishes with the statement (having no relation with what precedes) that Montargis could not accompany the narrator to visit the painter Elstir "dont nous avions fait tous deux connaissance," because he wanted to spend the day with his uncle who was due to arrive.

The uncle is, of course, the Baron de Fleurus. In the new text the Baron de Charlus enters immediately after an expanded version of the Bloch anecdote (the one having to do with the word "lift"). It will be recalled that the original Bloch anecdote was intended as an explanation of Montargis's character and that there were two other anecdotes serving the same purpose. In the final text these two anecdotes are delayed for forty pages by the insertion of the Charlus narrative and an additional long text on Bloch to which we shall return later. Since the story of Montargis-Saint-Loup's mistress remains in the same relative position, that is to say after the two remaining anecdotes, this return to Saint-Loup in the new text seems arbitrary, whereas it was the continuation of a logical structure in the original text.

Although the Fleurus-Charlus narrative moves from the top of page 786 to page 748, in terms of the Pléiade edition, there are no radical changes in the essential elements of the story. In both versions, Fleurus-Charlus is "très adonné aux exercices physiques" (748:38) and arrives at Bricquebec-Balbec on foot, sleeping in farms as he goes. Even though it is obvious why the virility of this character has thus been emphasized, it is strange that Proust has retained this naively conceived detail which does not sit well with the subsequent description of his impeccable sartorial appearance. The other details coincide in both versions: the character's piercing glance and his equivocal manner which makes the narrator think that he is about to rob the hotel; his heterosexual amorous affairs (including the one which did not take place with Madame Swann at Combray) and his beating of the homosexual; his presentation by Madame de Villeparisis as the "baron de Guermantes" (p. 753); the invitation to tea; his literary conversation; the lending and then the gift of the Bergotte volume. In the original version, Montargis's description of his uncle so fires the imagination of the narrator that he says: "Il me donnait l'idée d'une puissance, non pas seulement plus grande que celle des autres hommes comme est celle des rois, mais d'une puissance autre, particulière au noble Palamède..." (749: 43). Thus the narrator's anticipation of Palamède's coming is analogous to his anticipation of La Berma and of Montargis-Saint-Loup himself. This anticipation explains how the narrator simply could not believe that the robber with the piercing glance was the noble Palamède and the suppression of this passage removes the motivation for the subsequent passage, retained in the final text with some alterations, in which the narrator could not get over his astonishment that "le visage et le corps de M. de Fleurus étaient semblables au visage et au corps de beaucoup de beaux hommes" (761:1). He even noticed on this occasion a "légère couche de poudre" on the Baron's cheek. In connection with the presentation of Fleurus as the "baron de Guermantes," Proust made another suppression; in the original text, Montargis not only comments on the battle cry of the Guermantes but, in response to a further question from the narrator, he asks the narrator whether he has been to Guermantes and then, responding to another question, comments on the paintings in the château. In the final text, Proust substitutes a lyrical passage on the Guermantes and the metamorphoses of Ovid for the first reply and he alters the second reply to replace Carolus Duran and Delacroix with an allusion to Carrière, Whistler and Vélasquez which is designed to show up the artistic ignorance of Saint-Loup. However, the lack of taste of Montargis-Saint-Loup is borne out in the original by the allusion to the wainscoting which Fleurus preserved and which Montargis would have destroyed (757:9). One change in the plot is particularly worthy of note, for it demonstrates again Proust's efforts to introduce action into his novel. In the original version, Madame de Villeparisis invites the narrator and his grandmother to tea with the Baron. In the new version, it is the Baron who issues the invitation but without telling his aunt, which leads to some subtle complications which bring this section to life. However, it should be noted that the remaining plot elements, concerned with the ambiguous conduct of Fleurus, are in the original: his visit to the narrator's room to give him a volume of Bergotte and his remark: "Mais on s'en fiche bien de sa vieille grand'mère, hein? petite fripouille!" *(p. 767)*. In the final text, there are some additions concerning a second Bergotte volume which Fleurus wants Aimé to get but which never arrives because Aimé is abed and refuses to get up. In both versions, Madame de Villeparisis begins the tea party with the request that the Baron describe for the grandmother a château where Madame de Sévigné resided. Although this leads to much discussion of Madame de Sévigné, La Fontaine, and even Racine, with some expansion in the rewriting, the château is forgotten in the final text, whereas it is elaborated on in the original. According to Fleurus, it belonged to the Montmorency family which is extinct. When Montargis protests that his uncle has a cousin called the Duc de Montmorency, Fleurus replies that the title has been usurped. In any event, the château passed into other hands and is about to be sold again. This leads to a typical Proustian parallel passage in which Fleurus, having pushed a protruding handkerchief back into his pocket "avec la mine effarouchée d'une femme pudibonde" (764:16), speaks simultaneously of "une belle cousine Avaray qui a mal tourné" and the château which has been compromised; of both of them he has photographs in his pocket. Then he brings up a second family castle which has fallen into the hands of the "Gebzeltern" (764:19). In the final text, the Gebzeltern have become the Israëls and their château has absorbed the first one along with the cousin, now called Clara de Chimay, and the embroidered handkerchief of the Baron. However, it is no longer clear that the château is being discussed in answer to Madame de Villeparisis' request two pages earlier.

The longest additions in this section concern Bloch and his Jewish entourage. In the original text, the name Bloch slips in unobtrusively and he commits his solecism with respect to the word "lift" only to illustrate Montargis' character. In the new text, Bloch and his entourage take over. Bloch now appears declaiming at length against his Jewish brethren at Balbec. "On se croirait rue d'Aboukir" (p. 738), he exclaims. After this introduction comes the original "lift" text but it is cut asunder by more than a page and a half of new text about the picturesqueness of the Jewish colony which forms "une phalange compacte" to combat the anti-Semitism of local society. Before getting back to the remainder of the "lift" text, Proust introduced an additional Bloch solecism, "les *Stones de Venaïce* de Lord John Ruskin" (p. 739). The fragment of original "lift" text is followed by eight more pages on Bloch, beginning with his accusing the narrator "de traverser une jolie crise de snobisme" (p. 740). Despite this accusation, the narrator is ready to forgive him since he thinks that Bloch's faults are the result of his "mauvaise éducation" and that he really intends to be kind. There follows then a three-page generalization purporting to prove that "ce n'est pas le bon sens qui est 'la chose du monde la plus répandue', c'est la bonté" (p. 741). After pointing out further aspects of Bloch's character, the unevenness of his literary opinions, his admiration for Legrandin, his malicious remarks to Saint-Loup about the narrator and vice versa, his exaggerated emotionalism on occasion, the narrator concludes that since "la race de Combray" (p. 746) is nearly extinct he will be satisfied to seek out "honnêtes brutes" like Bloch to be his friends. The eight new pages on Bloch end with an invitation to dinner for the narrator and Saint-Loup and, in the process, the omniscient author records the full conversation of Bloch *père* when he learns that his son has been able to invite the Marquis de Saint-Loup-en-Bray whose father was "président du Canal de Suez" (p. 748). However, because of the arrival of Charlus, the dinner does not take place at this point but rather nineteen pages later after Charlus has left. At the dinner the emphasis shifts to the Bloch family and the omniscient author analyzes and quotes Bloch *père* at length, for he is "enclavé en mon camarade Bloch" (p. 769). The elder Bloch is a name-dropper but he does not really know Bergotte, as he claims, and not even Sir Rufus Israëls whose cards, permitting him to ride free on the railways, he gets from an employee of the great man. In the Bloch entourage there is even a more caricatural version of Bloch *père* in the person of an uncle, Nissim Bernard, who, according to Bloch himself, is "plus menteur encore que l'Ithakèsien Odysseus" (p. 775). Feuillerat comments that these sketches of Jewish life and character arise from Proust's increased interest in social classes, already noted in the case of domestics and hotel employees. While this is undoubtedly true, it should also be noted that Proust is interested in the character of

Bloch himself and that the essential elements of this character are found in "Combray."

In order to provide a transition back to his original text, Proust added a paragraph of comment by Françoise on Bloch and then another one by her on Saint-Loup. To our amazement, this erstwhile enemy of the upper classes now turns out to be a royalist as she disapproves of Saint-Loup's republicanism. This is indeed paradoxical if the study of Bloch and his psychological backgrounds is to be interpreted as socially oriented. Is Proust so little concerned about social problems that he forgets that he recently made Françoise a symbol of revolt? Françoise finally concludes that Saint-Loup is a "hypocrite," to use her word, and that as a noble he cannot be a republican; hence she forgives him and considers that the proof of his real nature is that, while pretending to admire the common people, he mistreats his coachman. All of these subtleties seem to be a subterfuge to justify the retention of the original anecdote about Saint-Loup and his coachman. Françoise is all wrong about Saint-Loup, says the narrator, as he goes on with the original version of the anecdote.

After the departure of Fleurus in *Grasset A* but after the account of Saint-Loup's relations with his mistress in the final text, Saint-Loup offers to photograph the narrator's grandmother before he leaves; however, this "enfantillage" (786:7) so irritates the narrator that he is extremely unpleasant with his grandmother and deprives himself of her good night kiss. Although this episode is obviously a *preparation* for events which will occur in *Le Côté de Guermantes,* it seems at first to have no relation to the surrounding text. Yet it does have the function of opening up the general theme of "conclusion," for the departure of Saint-Loup, now announced for the first time, will be the signal for the actual conclusion of the *Grasset A* version. The section immediately following, "Rivebelle," also brings up again the theme of conclusion as the elevator boy says to the narrator: "Cela commence à devenir vide, on s'en va, les jours baissent" (799:25). In fact, the entire "Rivebelle" section converges on the real conclusion as it suggests in its numerous lyrical passages the atmospheric changes due to the inexorable march of the season. Ultimately Proust so expanded "Rivebelle" and his original "conclusion," that this convergence on a conclusion became even embarrassing, so that, for example, the narrator remarks in the new text, apropos of the elevator boy's statement: "Il disait cela, non que ce fût vrai, mais parce qu'ayant un engagement pour une partie plus chaude de la côte, il aurait voulu que nous partissions tous le plus tôt possible afin que l'hôtel fermât et qu'il eût quelques jours à lui, avant de 'rentrer' dans sa nouvelle place" (p. 799). Curiously, Proust left all of the original allusions to an impending departure of Saint-Loup but he also sought to negate them by referring several times to the fact that the narrator's friend, because of his military responsibilities, now commuted frequently between Balbec and Doncières (cf. pp. 770, 787, 807, 866).

"Rivebelle," as we have already had occasion to remark, is comparable in structure to the "promenades" with Madame de Villeparisis. It is a *composite basic narrative* relating the narrator's expeditions with Saint-Loup to the restaurant at Rivebelle. We have already observed a curious preview of this episode in the trip to the mill. Since the *Grasset A* version of "Rivebelle" emphasizes that the grandmother has at last given her permission for evening expeditions because she considers that Saint-Loup's influence is "salutaire" (798:34), this is clearly designated as the beginning of the evening expeditions and leads to the conclusion that Proust must have intended to remove the earlier passage from his manuscript. The superimposed expeditions to Rivebelle have been shaped in a characteristically Proustian manner and begin with an introduction: preparations for departure. Since the narrator is obliged to rest before leaving, he goes up to his room for his siesta and thus the basic patterns of the "promenades" text are repeated in the "Rivebelle" text, the poetic evocation of the hotel with its "cage thoracique mobile" (799:25) and the background of the sea, changing as the days get shorter (for this is not one siesta but many). At last the narrator gets up, saying: "Il est temps" (806:13). When the two friends arrive at the restaurant, in the beginning the sunset is still in progress but later it is quite dark. As the narrator enters this place of pleasure, he forgets all of his good intentions, "la nécessité de ne pas mourir, l'importance de travailler" *(p. 809)*. Gradually real intoxication adds to the intoxication of the setting, as he is lulled by the music. In the final text his vague amorous feelings are generalized around "une femme qui nous a aperçu" (812:23 and p. 812), but in the original version they are unexpectedly concentrated on Mademoiselle de Silariat* whom we had thought he had forgotten; this is because he hears a melody by Reynaldo Hahn, "Je sais un coin perdu de la grève Bretonne*" (812:23). On the return home, the narrator makes the coachman drive at breakneck speed, risking "ma vie à venir, mes livres à composer" *(p. 815).* This should logically have been the conclusion of the Rivebelle expeditions, but *Grasset A* included another episode tacked on at the end in which the women present, recognizing Saint-Loup, wonder whether he is still with his wench, about whose underclothing they have uncomplimentary things to say.

While making additions, Proust respected the original arrangement of his material; that is to say he left it in the illogical order which placed the return home before the scene of the women. As if to disprove Feuillerat's theory which divided him into a lyrical and then an analytical period, Proust made lengthy additions in both manners. At the point where the narrator went up to his room for his siesta, he added an amusing realistic conversation with the elevator boy which is both a linguistic and a sociological study. On the other hand, esteeming no doubt that he had not done justice to his real subject, Rivebelle, he added a marvelously lyrical description of the waiters and diners in the restaurant (pp. 810, 811, 813). Then he wrote a lyrical analysis of his sensations as the carriage careened down the Normandy road (p. 815) and finally a magnificently orchestrated four-page conclusion for the entire Rivebelle episode on the theme of sleep and forgetfulness, ending on the question of what is free will when one remembers in spite of oneself "la jeune blonde à l'air triste que j'avais vue à Rivebelle" (p. 822).

However, there are entirely foreign elements in the Rivebelle section and they are parts of a new plot sequence which at last, after 356 pages of Pléiade text, are going to justify the new title, *A l'ombre des jeunes filles en fleurs.* Just as he grafted onto the story of Gilberte a new plot which turned the languishing end of "Noms de pays: le nom" into a more dramatic novel, so he used the same procedure on the languishing end of "Noms de pays: le pays." In fact, in this second case, one wonders why he waited so long and introduced so much new material into a section of his novel which was already shaped as a conclusion. Counting from the photograph scene, the novel which was in the process of ending in *Grasset A* now has 169 pages to go in the Pléiade text.

Rigorously structured as though it had been written by the author of "Un Amour de Swann," the introductory passage of the new plot covers eleven pages and occurs directly after the "photograph" episode and thus directly before the beginning of the "Rivebelle" section. For the first time (or at least for the first time that it has so graphically come to our attention), Proust attaches importance to paragraphs. Usually the Proustian paragraph is a most arbitrary unit and the *alinéa* moves about with no visible logic as we go from one version to another; also the grafting of new material often destroys any unity of thought which the paragraph might have had. In the case of the introductory passage on the "jeunes filles" there are fifteen paragraphs, each a very carefully written separable unit, but also part of a logical pattern. The subjects of these paragraphs may be sketched as follows: *1.* The narrator is in a state of amorous vacancy. *2.* He sees "cinq ou six fillettes." *3.* They are wearing sporting clothes. *4.* There is a miscellaneous crowd on the "digue." *5.* The girls are mixed into the crowd and the narrator has a composite picture of them, the eyes of one and the cheeks of another. *6.* Yet they constitute a social collectivity. *7.* The social collectivity looks upon the rest of the crowd as the enemy and one of the girls expresses her contempt by jumping over a banker's head. *8.* The narrator has compressed all of the girls into one, "la grande" who jumped over the banker, but this one is composed of bits and pieces which, reinterpreted, makes them all mistresses of "coureurs cyclistes" and casts doubt on their virtue. *9.* At last they are individualized. *10.* Is the "brune aux grosses joues" aware of his existence? *11.* He will not possess this young cyclist unless he possesses what is in her eyes. *12.* The "brune" is no good because she does not resemble Gilberte, but she might introduce him to others. *13.* Are these girls like the fleeting sylphs seen from Madame de Villeparisis' carriage? At any rate, if available in a brothel, they would lose their charm. *14.* Their social standing is ambiguous because seaside resorts confer anonymity on individuals. *15.* The narrator can see them better now than he ever saw the sylphs, but nevertheless they are finally metamorphosed into flowers.

The narrator's contemplations are ended by the necessity of going to Rivebelle with Saint-Loup; thus we come back to the old text. The next piece of "jeune fille" text is somewhat arbitrarily inserted after the passage on the elevator boy. At last the narrator has a name for his composite young girl since he has heard people mention "la petite Simonet." Hence he asks the elevator boy to get him the list of new arrivals at the hotel, whereupon he steps out of the elevator and back into the old text. It will take him nearly five pages to get that list; what is more, an indefinite amount of time has elapsed as this isolated *passé simple*: "On frappa" (p. 806), cuts into these pages of timeless imperfects. Curiously, too, the inexorable march of time has just taken a new leap forward in a newly inserted passage, just preceding, in which the weather now gets so bad (the season having advanced so far) that the "vitres" of the dining room have to be clossed while the "essaim des pauvres et des curieux" (p. 806) still cling to the panes of plate glass. It is Aimé who finally brings the list, making in passing a remark about the Dreyfus affair which has been used by Proust commentators as a vantage point from which to date events of the *Recherche.* On this list is the name of Simonet; now the narrator knows that he is in love with Mademoiselle Simonet. The next passage on the "jeunes filles" is very successfully inserted in the midst of the intoxication scene at Rivebelle. So great is his intoxication that he becomes indifferent to Mademoiselle Simonet and all of her friends. The "de moins en moins existante Mlle Simonet" (p. 817) is replaced by a young blonde dining at Rivebelle, and this provides a good transition back to the old passage on the women of Rivebelle talking about Saint-Loup's affair.

If the narrator is in love with Mademoiselle Simonet, he still is not certain which girl she is. This hesitation about her identity will continue through the next episode which centers around Elstir, a character already mentioned twice in *Grasset A,* but only vaguely, as someone whom the narrator and Saint-Loup had already met and whom the narrator went once to visit. In *Grasset B* these two allusions survive but now there is also a long new section on Elstir which differs considerably from the final version, particularly in the respect that there are no "jeunes filles." Obviously the first two allusions to Elstir in *Grasset B* should have been removed (as they were later) to accommodate the new text.

As originally conceived in *Grasset B,* the Elstir episode is another caboose to the Rivebelle section, following directly the other caboose containing the women who talk about Saint-Loup. That the "jeunes filles" have not been thought of yet is quite clear from the attempts to include this text in the notion of a conclusion. When the narrator, after seeing Elstir's painting, wishes he could himself look at the scenes which the master had painted, he remarks that "il était trop tard dans la saison" (842:29). Likewise the entire Elstir passage in *Grasset B* tapers off to a conclusion, as the narrator runs around the darkened railway car shouting the praises of Elstir while the conductor also shouts: "Appolloville*, Briseville, Transville, tous les noms de stations que j'avais entendus une première fois dans des dispositions bien différentes, quand j'avais fais* avec ma grand'mère, le jour de l'arrivée à Bolbec* le même petit chemin de fer d'intérêt local" [syntax sic] (842:29).

In *Grasset B* and in the final text, the narrator and Saint-Loup meet Elstir at Rivebelle in precisely the same circumstances; when they notice the tall and athletic stranger (he annexes a "barbe grisonnante" in the new text), they ask the restaurant keeper who he is and are told that he is the famous painter Elstir. Although they have never seen any of his paintings and although the narrator might be mistaken in thinking that he is a friend of Swann (the new text loses some of the subtlety of the original on this point), they send a letter to the great man's table. Just as the painter seems to have ignored their letter and to be heading for the door, he changes his mind and comes back to talk to them. In *Grasset B* the author's omniscient remarks on Elstir's biography and reputation precede the sending of the letter, whereas in the final text they follow. In both texts, the next paragraph registers the unbounded admiration of the narrator for Elstir whose complete sincerity contrasts with Saint-Loup's manner: "Saint-Loup cherchait à plaire, Elstir aimait à donner, à se donner" *(p. 827).* The symbolism of the white beard in the new text is obvious: Elstir succeeds, where Bergotte failed, in conforming to the narrator's idea of the great artist. Already one can detect, especially in the light of subsequent remarks, an identification of Proust himself with Elstir as he commends the painter's "sauvagerie" and his desire to "produire en vue de quelques personnes" *(p. 828).* When the narrator goes to visit Elstir in his studio, he first spends several pages in *Grasset B* discussing with Elstir the Medieval sculpture on the portal of the Balbec church. In the artistic anthology which one could make from the *Recherche,* these brilliant pages would be a first choice; yet it is strange to make a painter discourse on another art form, even though, as the narrator points out, it displays the tremendous erudition of which he will make a *tabula rasa* when starting to paint. In *Grasset B,* the discussion of painting comes next. This long passage records in embryonic form many of the ideas which are fundamental to Proust's own esthetic as propounded in the totally rewritten version of these same pages; but there is a difference of emphasis in that the whole idea in *Grasset B* is art appreciation. A man of taste, says the narrator, laid in him the foundations for a new appreciation of art and later "cet homme de goût je n'ai pas eu besoin d'aller le consulter dans un atelier, à Balbec, car peu à peu il s'en est développé un en moi-même" (842:29). Not only has this visionary taught him to understand the sculpture of the church portal, but, through his painting, he has taught him to look at reality from a new perspective. By his paintings of provincial scenes, Elstir has shown him that it matters little that there is a sign saying "Billard" in front of the church of Balbec if the artist has chosen to reinterpret this scene with his own vision, billiard sign or not. He makes the point clearer in speaking of Elstir's seascapes: the painter had the courage to forget his preconceived notions "afin de prendre les choses comme elles apparaissent." Thus it is difficult to distinguish the sky from the sea in some of his paintings. Some people say, continues the narrator, that Elstir is too close to the impressionists whose mistake is "de ne faire que des effets." Evidently Proust is not quite an impressionist though he is obviously close to being one.

For this discarded text Proust substituted a much longer and now famous text in which he creates the painting of the port of

Carquethuit which is comparable in his esthetic scheme to the sonata of Vinteuil. In fact, this text goes far beyond the sonata because it defines Proust's use of metaphor. In the revised version of the Elstir episode, the description of the port of Carquethuit and others of this artist's paintings precedes the discussion of the portal of the Balbec church, with the result that this conversation no longer has the revelatory function which it had in *Grasset B*; it is merely brilliant improvisation by an erudite artist. Another new passage, isolated from the first one, has only an anecdotal interest when it mentions the portrait of *Miss Sacripant* but acquires a broader, though repetitious, meaning by telling how a common looking woman like Madame Elstir is transfigured by art.

The "jeunes filles" plot in the final text continues straight through the Elstir episode and, in the new version, Elstir contributes to it. As was the case with other portions of this plot, the time remains finite, so that the Elstir episode, set apart by a blank space in the new text, begins: "Ce jour-là était justement le lendemain de celui où j'avais vu défiler devant la mer le beau cortège de jeunes filles" (p. 823). In spite of this localization in time, what follows immediately has an implication of timelessness as the author describes how, later, he came into possession of photographs of the "jeunes filles" as children (this makes one wonder whether the "jeunes filles" in real life dated from a childhood sojourn at Cabourg or were rather, as Marcel Plantevignes says in his book of reminiscences, *Avec Marcel Proust*, a transposition of Plantevignes's own success with adolescent girls when Proust was composing an early version of this text at Cabourg). Immediately thereafter the passage on Rivebelle, where the two friends meet Elstir, begins thus: "Bientôt le séjour de Saint-Loup toucha à sa fin" (p. 825). This line is totally out of context, for it belongs on page 866 of the Pléiade edition. A meaningless remark here, it serves only to bring in again the name of Saint-Loup whom the narrator, for some unclear reason, was expecting to introduce him to the girls. The "jeunes filles" come up again in a transitional text establishing an interval between the meeting with Elstir and the visit to his studio; in this interval, rejecting his grandmother's admonitions to profit by Elstir's invitation, the narrator continues to observe the girls, perceives one with golf clubs, prefers her to "la grande," and presumes that she is Mademoiselle Simonet. After the discussion of the portal of the Balbec church, Proust introduced two new paragraphs on "les joies intellectuelles que je goûtais dans cet atelier" (p. 842) and the fact that the narrator made Elstir sad by using the word "gloire" because the painter knew that glory would come to him only after death (one should remember that there are allusions to the narrator's own death elsewhere in *Grasset A*); then he returned to the "jeunes filles" and described how a passing girl on a bicycle greeted Elstir by the customary French handshake and then went on her way. Asking her name, the narrator is told that she is Albertine Simonet, but there is no indication at this point that he identifies her as the niece of Madame Bontemps although later (p. 873) he definitely knows that she is. Now, at last, he is assured of his introductions and he immediately arranges to have Elstir accompany him on a walk; but Elstir keeps him waiting in order to finish a painting, during which time the narrator discovers the canvas depicting *Miss Sacripant*. Gradually the narrator seems to be getting annoyed at being kept waiting, but his annoyance takes a peculiar form: a discourse on how people, if they have "la nature de ma grand'mère" (p. 852), sacrifice themselves for others, after which come curious observations about himself, his "total égoïsme" compared to his grandmother and also his own courage in the face of danger which still might be construed as the desire to impress others. When at last, on the "digue," the narrator has the opportunity to be introduced to the girls, he loses his chance because of his coyness. Then the narrator and Elstir converse on the port of Carquethuit and on the original of the painting of *Miss Sacripant* which turns out to be an early portrait of Odette de Crécy in a theatrical costume. Suddenly the narrator asks Elstir whether he was not once known as Monsieur Biche. Elstir, "en vrai maître" (p. 863), forgives the narrator for dredging up a past of which he is not proud and, in a long discourse, summarizes his basic morality: "On ne reçoit pas la sagesse, il faut la découvrir soi-même après un trajet que personne ne peut faire pour nous..." (p. 864). In the presence of this Proustian (or even Gidian) wisdom, it is even more difficult to accept Feuillerat's theory that a disabused Proust was the author of this new text.

After these generalizations, the final text returns to what appears to be a random narrative when it relates that the grandmother, because of the "préparatifs du départ de Saint-Loup" (p. 866), now decides to give the narrator's friend "de nombreuses lettres autographes" by Proudhon. The sophisticated young noble unexpectedly acts like an embarrassed adolescent: "il devint écarlate comme un enfant qu'on vient de punir" *(p. 866)*. This is all in *Grasset A* where it began with the remark: "Le séjour de Montargis à Bricquebec toucha à sa fin" (866:2), which, as we have already noted, was the fragment of text that unaccountably became detached and that turned up forty-one pages earlier. In *Grasset A* this sentence does indeed introduce the conclusion, which begins with Saint-Loup's departure. In both the new and the old versions, Saint-Loup is so touched by the grandmother's present that he thanks the narrator again through the train window and then writes a thank-you letter which is the beginning of an extensive correspondence with the narrator whom he addresses in the most affectionate terms. In the new version, because Saint-Loup had already commuted so much between Doncières and Balbec, Proust felt obliged to comment on this departure, so he explained that Saint-Loup was now leaving for good and was taking the steam tramway because he had to transport so much baggage. He also introduced another segment of the Bloch sequence which is more a "theme" than a "plot," although momentarily it takes on more the characteristics of a plot. Bloch having gone with the narrator to see Saint-Loup off, Saint-Loup is obliged to include Bloch in an invitation to come to Doncières and Bloch will continue to pop up now and then during the rest of the "jeunes filles" text to remind the narrator about the trip to Doncières. In *Grasset A*, it is never clear where Montargis went; somewhat as in the final text, he says: "me voici revenu . . . au milieu de cette vie grossière que vous méprisez sans doute et qui n'est pourtant pas sans charme" (868:21). He also says that he has been to Paris and has told his mistress about his friendship with the narrator. It is not at all certain in the original whether the remark about "vie grossière" referred to Paris or to Saint-Cyr (if we assume that he returned there in due course). The final text brings the mistress briefly to Doncières and there is no doubt that "vie grossière" describes life in that garrison town.

Before discussing further the original conclusion of *Grasset A*, it will be more expedient to examine the solid block of eighty-three pages of new text that Proust now inserted before reutilizing the next fragment of *Grasset A.* Although this new text focuses on the single subject of the "jeunes filles," it appears most unlikely that Proust wrote these pages in the burning heat of one continuous inspiration because there are so many asides and generalizations. Undoubtedly this text evolved in the characteristic manner with many graftings of new material coming in to interrupt a more symmetrical basic plot. However, lacking the documentation, we shall not attempt to distinguish various levels of text in this material. What holds it all together is a linear plot that moves slowly but systematically towards a *point culminant.*

The new material begins with a diversion, a description of the dinner table at the hotel when the meal is over and when the objects left at random form a still life worthy of the brush of an Elstir; the spore for this passage seems to be a few lines added to the final pages of *Grasset B* but then removed (952:10). Then we return to the "jeunes filles" plot. The narrator has now contrived to persuade Elstir, in spite of his previous boorishness, to give a most elegant reception with buffet, flowers in one's buttonhole and fancy dresses, so that the narrator may meet Albertine. Characteristically, he is no longer interested in her but he goes to the reception anyway and ascertains that she is not "trop peu différente de tout ce que je connaissais" (p. 876). Furthermore, like the duchesse de Guermantes with her pimple at Combray, she has a "tempe assez enflammée et peu agréable à voir." The text is dense and highly analytical. Then there follows a series of miscellaneous encounters on the beach: Albertine who appears quite different, the inflammation on her forehead having gone down or having been dissimulated; and then the individuals whom he meets while in Albertine's company, the young sportsman Octave, Bloch whom Albertine calls an "ostrogoth." As usual, Proust shows a tendency to disgress and to allow the narrative to run slightly ahead of itself. That is what happens when he comments at length on Albertine's reactions to Bloch and on Bloch's character in general; then, again characteristically (whether he does this intentionally or accidentally when making an addition one cannot say without the evidence), he brings the reader suddenly out of a nest of imperfect tenses by announcing: "Nous nous quittâmes, Albertine et moi . . ." (p. 881). They have agreed to make some excursions together. "Cette fois-là (continues the narrator) nous rencontrâmes presque tout de suite la grande, Andrée . . ." (p. 882). On this occasion his finite time is a subterfuge. Which of the many times was it? Even though Proust is playing his usual game with tenses he is nevertheless telling a story according to a preconceived pattern. The next subject or event is meeting more specifically the other members of the "bande": Andrée, who is not an athlete but an intellectual and who tells some white lies of which the narrator does not approve; Gisèle who will not be there long because she must take an examination; then Andrée again who seems more "fine" than Albertine who, meanwhile, has come to resemble the unpleasant side of Gilberte in her search for pleasure. Having lost interest in Albertine, the narrator pursues the departing Gisèle to the station but misses her. On the pretext of Albertine's similarities to Gilberte, the narrator now indulges in a generalization on uniform patterns in love. On the subject of bicycle excursions, the narrator makes another deviation to register Françoise's annoyance at having to make lunches. Now the excursions bring an encounter with Elstir who talks about race tracks, yachting and women's styles, with allusions to Veronese and Carpaccio. All of this takes place on the Channel cliffs which, although the narrator had previously said that it was already too late in the season for the proper light effects, are now bathed in sunlight, producing the same impressionistic effects as in Elstir's painting. As the young people play games on the cliff, the narrator digresses to tell us about Saint-Loup and how he, the narrator, does not really believe in friendship: "Et l'amitié n'est pas seulement dénuée de vertu comme la conversation, elle est de plus funeste" (p. 907). This can be interpreted either as an evolution on the part of the narrator who has become egotistical because of his preoccupation with girls or as old age cynicism on the part of Proust.[49] Although nothing in particular has happened yet, it is safe to assume that the reader still expects something to happen; but the good will of the reader cannot be counted on indefinitely.

The time has manifestly come for action and Proust is enough of a novelist not to eschew his responsibility. He merely whets the reader's interest the first time by interrupting the succession of imperfect tenses long enough to allow Albertine to ask for a pencil and paper and to write surreptitiously to the narrator: "Je vous aime bien" (p. 911). Thereupon Andrée diverts the subject to an amusing critique of Gisèle's baccalaureate essay on "Sophocle écrit des Enfers à Racine pour le consoler de l'insuccès d'*Athalie*" (p. 911). Albertine's note seems to be taking effect, however, for the narrator decides that "c'était avec elle que j'aurais mon roman" (p. 915). Yet we judge that he is still not quite sure of himself since he now discourses on the difficulty of loving one person exclusively in the beginning: "nous nous souvenons . . . d'un paon et nous trouvons une pivoine" (p. 916). In the Stendhalian system something is needed to crystallize the narrator's love, a little obstacle perhaps. While playing the game of "furet,"[50] the narrator infuriates Albertine by his stupidity at the very moment that he is mooning about her. Now he talks to Andrée about Albertine in the hope that she will report their conversation, but nothing of the sort happens for Andrée is jealous, is condescending towards Albertine although ostensibly very kind to her, and considers her "immariable" (p. 924) because of her straitened circumstances. The narrator says: "Je savais maintenant que j'aimais Albertine, mais hélas! je ne me souciais pas de le lui apprendre" (p. 925). So he pretends to prefer Andrée.

[49] Feuillerat devotes several pages to Saint-Loup. He considers that, since "celui qui posa pour ce personnage était mort glorieusement" (op. cit., p. 49), Proust embellished the portrait of Saint-Loup. In spite of the extensive rewriting, it is difficult to detect any additions which significantly alter the character of Saint-Loup for better or for worse, except for the new suggestion (which Feuillerat also points out) that he is effeminate and except for this long diatribe against friendship which Feuillerat, curiously, does not mention.

[50] Commentators of Proust sometimes refer to the "furet" episode as further proof that Proust's "jeunes filles" are children, but he makes it quite clear in the text that they are young people being silly.

A month after the "furet" episode (obviously Proust has all of the time in the world to finish his story), Albertine announces that she will spend the night in the Grand-Hôtel in order to leave by the earliest train, that she has a cold making it necessary to go to bed early, and that the narrator may visit her in her room. This catches the narrator by surprise; he concludes that he was right the first time when he categorized her as the mistress of a bicycle racer and wrong when he later decided that she was a proper bourgeoise. Only Proust could describe the narrator's feelings as he approaches her door. When Albertine sees that he is about to kiss her, she threatens: "Finissez ou je sonne" (p. 933). He persists and she rings. While this is the *point culminant* towards which all this part of the novel has been converging, it is not a *dénouement* for nothing will be solved before *A l'ombre des jeunes filles* ends. The narrator will spend many pages analyzing his attitude (he had thought that his love was not founded on physical desire and yet?) and trying to explain Albertine's conduct (he sees her objectively and spends some time describing her curious "utilisation multiple d'une seule action" [p. 938] but still cannot decide whether she was really virtuous or only coquettish about some unpleasant body odor). *A l'ombre* comes to an end, instead of reaching a crisis. By all of the rules of Stendhalian and Proustian psychology, Albertine's resistance should have had a more violent effect but, of course, the real stimulus in this system is jealousy and that will not come until the still unwritten part of the *Recherche.* In any event, as happens characteristically in a Proustian conclusion, the end doubles back to the beginning, and we find the narrator hesitating again as to which girl he really loves. Albertine has become so fragmented that he no longer knows which is her real "moi" and he ends up in a profusion of imperfect tenses, "ces beaux corps bruns et blonds, de types si opposés, répandus autour de moi dans l'herbe" (p. 950).

Bad weather comes, the season ends, and the first to leave is Albertine. "Elle n'a dit ni quoi ni qu'est-ce et puis elle est partie" (p. 950), grumbles Françoise. Even the "chemin de fer d'intérêt local" stops running but the narrator lingers on because he has picked up again the weak parts of *Grasset A.*

In *Grasset A* the narrator finally makes the acquaintance of the "jeune homme riche," his mistress the actress and his companion the young noble, who invite him to dinner. In both *Grasset A* and in the final text, he declines but in a fragment added to *Grasset B* he seems to accept because he likes oysters (952:39). In *Grasset B*, Proust added two other passages which he later eliminated, one a conversation with the manager and the elevator boy and one a passage on the beauty of jellyfish on the beach (952:40). The rewritten version of this material, describing the gradual shutting down of the Grand-Hôtel after the departure of the "jeunes filles," is much more vivid; the narrator enjoys the emptiness, the bad weather, and the officiousness of the manager "qui revient hanter les ruines de ce qui fut jadis son palais" (p. 951) and even joins forces with "le premier président" and his coterie, as well as making the acquaintance of the "jeune homme riche" of *Grasset A*. Finally the cold in this heatless hotel drives the narrator and his grandmother away. As in *Grasset A*, the manager offers better rooms for next year but the narrator says he would prefer the one he has.

So, in all versions, the narrator leaves and, having left and having gone somewhere, presumably back to Paris, he looks back on Bricquebec-Balbec in a lyrical summation. In *Grasset A* and *B*, he is still in Bricquebec in his mind as he remembers how, in the last days, his friends wrote asking whether he intended to remain in Bricquebec forever whereas, on his part, he felt so firmly established there that the place name on a letter seemed to be the realization of his most cherished dreams (a fragment of this text survives but is situated in the new version before the departure). Still in Bricquebec in his mind, he looks out of the window and feels that the mountainous sea is now part of him. Then all his memories surge forth in a lyrical "finale": his original imaginings of an "église persanne*" in a tempest, then the more realistic memories of Madame de Villeparisis waving a greeting to the Princesse de Luxembourg or announcing that they would have "œufs à la crème et des soles frites" (952:41) for lunch; or memories of "une barque arrêtée au fil de l'eau devant l'ancien moulin." Now he wants to return to exactly the same mill and to exactly the same trout (note that there is no mention of Rivebelle but rather a return to what we have looked upon as an earlier version of the same events), but he realizes that things will never be the same, that Madame de Villeparisis may be too old to come the next time, that the Princesse de Luxembourg may be somewhere else, and that even the path leading to the beach will have changed. He concludes that these places, conventionally situated in space, are only in his mind and now they assume the idealized form which they once had before he went to Bricquebec. Sometimes the imaginary visions of pre-Bricquebec days drive away the church with the billiard sign, leaving only the Persian church in its pristine purity. This reversion to the pre-Bricquebec state brings back simultaneously his original longings for Florence. Spring comes again, as Françoise sees in the unseasonable weather "une preuve de la colère du bon Dieu," but the narrator is deep in the "anémones de la Porte* Vacchio.*" One wonders whether this ending, which picks up, as we have said, the themes of the original beginning of "Noms de pays," announces a new chapter never written or whether it is a leitmotif anticipating the trip to Venice, after the death of Albertine. The hypothesis of a new chapter would have little foundation because it is not mentioned in the list of chapters to come as announced in the first edition of *Du côté de chez Swann.*

The rewritten version of the *finale* is quite different. At first the narrator is still mentally back in Balbec, but, instead of remembering the more homely details, he has returned to the unreality of his hotel room as the sun, through the gaps in the curtains incompletely pinned back by Françoise, spreads "sur le tapis comme un écarlate effeuillement d'anémones parmi lesquelles je ne pouvais m'empêcher de venir un instant poser mes pieds nus" (p. 953). Françoise's pins were found in an earlier passage of *Grasset A*, now situated on page 704 of the Pléiade edition, where the light effects in the room are still described but where their primary cause, the pinned back curtains, is missing. Still imagining himself at Balbec, the narrator realizes that "mes amies étaient sur la digue" (p. 954) and later Albertine tells him that, his blinds having remained shut, they had not looked for him to go to the concert. With a slight allusion to the original imaginary Balbec "battu par la tempête et perdu dans les brumes," the narrator now remembers Françoise unpinning at last the wrappings of the "somptueuse et millénaire momie... embaumée dans sa robe d'or" (p. 955).

Le Côté de Guermantes

At this point *Grasset A* ends. However, *Grasset B* continues and the new section in the proofs bears the heading "Recherche du temps perdu pl. 1," followed by "Le Côté des* Guermantes" in larger type. The printers began to set this new material on June 6, 1914 but, having reached the equivalent of page 295 of the Pléiade edition, abruptly stopped. On June 12 they began to reset the unutilized portions of the *Grasset A* proofs. We can be certain that, on June 12, they were working from corrected proofs rather than from the old manuscript because *Grasset B* records, for a considerable distance, exactly the corrections needed to correct *Grasset A* and then reproduces accurately all of the misprints and omissions in the remainder of *Grasset A*. Since the *Nouvelle Revue Française* of July 1, 1914 published not only fragments of *Le Côté de Germantes* occurring in *Grasset B* but also four fragments which would occur after page 295 of the Pléiade edition, and since Proust himself wrote to Grasset: "quand j'ai voulu faire paraître des extraits dans la *N. R. F.*, je vous ai demandé de faire tirer des épreuves un peu plus loin," [51] it seems obvious that there was a continuous manuscript, perhaps still untyped, which went somewhere beyond the point where *Grasset B* ends.

The *Grasset B* continuation is not entirely contemporaneous with *Grasset A* since it contains passages on Elstir and "Rachel quand du Seigneur" who were introduced for the first time in the earlier portions of *Grasset B*. On the other hand, whereas *Grasset B* now uses the same proper nouns as the final text, there are occasional slips where earlier, now extinct, names occur. The only such name which definitely goes back to the level of *Grasset A* is Montargis. However, there are also Criquebec (for

[51] Pierre-Quint, op. cit., p. 154.

Balbec), Borniche (for Jupien), Clodion (for Aimé) and Madame de Saint-Loup (for Madame de Marsantes), which do not relate to *Grasset A* but which prove the existence of underlying texts. Whether the underlying text is a continuous manuscript is an unanswerable question in terms of the present evidence. Feuillerat points out that Proust makes only minor changes in the *Grasset B* section of *Le Côté de Guermantes* and it is our opinion that this is essentially a finished text, far more complete than the portion of *Grasset B* corresponding to *A l'ombre des jeunes filles en fleurs.* If there is a palimpsest on the level of *Grasset A* beneath *Le Côté de Guermantes,* it has been submerged in the extensive reworking which has already taken place. It is also possible that Proust was putting together this material for the first time and that he "enriched" it as he went along, inserting new paragraphs into sections already composed. This rewriting apparently continued uninterrupted in spite of the emotional impact on Proust of Agostinelli's death on May 30, 1914 (Painter and Céleste Albaret agree that there was no interruption but disagree on the extent of the emotional impact). It was the war which finally stopped publication and gave Proust the chance to rewrite more extensively than he might have done.

Grasset B contains no mention of the "jeunes filles en fleurs" and hence no mention either of Albertine. However, there is a mysterious passage which, like those which we discovered earlier in *Les Intermittences du cœur,* seems to allude to "an Albertine." This passage, which survives almost without change in the final text, is as follows: "Mais la première, Françoise me donna l'exemple (que je ne devais comprendre que plus tard quand il me fut donné de nouveau et plus douloureusement, comme on le verra dans le dernier volume de cet ouvrage, par une personne qui m'était plus chère), que la vérité n'a pas besoin d'être dite pour être manifestée . . ." (66:10). This time the proof appears conclusive that "an Albertine" will appear in the last volume (the final text makes the necessary correction to "les derniers volumes"). At this juncture, however, Proust has no plan to make her appear in the text so far composed. On the other hand, as Feuillerat was the first to point out, the "jeunes filles" were destined to appear almost immediately, according to the "table des matières" announced in *Du côté de chez Swann.* In the original plan, as revised after Grasset's intervention, volume 2, *Le Côté de Guermantes,* was supposed to end with "Le salon de Mme de Villeparisis," and volume 3, *Le Temps retrouvé,* was supposed to begin with "A l'ombre des jeunes filles en fleurs." Bardèche has recently published in his *Marcel Proust romancier* some early "à l'ombre" texts which give an idea of what this section would probably have been; the theme, to which all of the "sylphs" whom we have observed along the narrator's road would have contributed, would have been the narrator's sensual desire for young girls (Bardèche does not hesitate to call him a young ogre). There is no Albertine in these early texts. Because of the "table des matières" of *Du côté de chez Swann,* Feuillerat concluded that Proust merely excised his "jeunes filles" from the Ur-Proust corresponding to *Le Côté de Guermantes* and spread them through *A l'ombre des jeunes filles en fleurs.* Given the essential unity of each section and its relation to the surrounding original text, this explanation seems highly improbable. It appears more likely that, remembering his sketches in the *cahiers,* Proust composed new material in the same manner that he had previously improved the second half of the Gilberte plot.

Le Côté de Guermantes, at least as far as we shall be concerned with it, is held together by a loose plot structure which is essentially the same in *Grasset B* and in the final text. Even in the final text, the narrator seems to have forgotten Albertine and to have transferred his amorous attentions to the Duchesse de Guermantes. Later on, of course, Albertine will reappear without warning but in a part of the novel which comes after the end of *Grasset B.* The plot concerned with the Duchesse de Guermantes is as tenuous as the original Gilberte plot after the narrator began to frequent the Swanns. We have already seen how Proust found it necessary to introduce a new Gilberte plot to salvage that part of the novel and how he did precisely the same thing in *A l'ombre* by introducing Albertine. It is probable, on the other hand, that he did not dramatize the Duchesse de Guermantes plot because, being already committed to the Albertine plot in his revised text, he either felt that too much emphasis on the Duchess would exaggerate the illogicality of having inserted Albertine before this episode or that an eventual return to the Albertine plot would compensate for any lack of dramatic movement in this part of the novel. As a result, the Duchesse de Guermantes just fades out of the narrator's emotional life as Gilberte did in the *Grasset A* version. If the Duchesse de Guermantes plot leads nowhere, it does hold together the five episodes of the remaining *Grasset B* text: the move to the Hôtel de Guermantes, the return to La Berma, the encounters with the Duchess, the visit to Saint-Loup in his garrison town, and the reception of Madame de Villeparisis.

Characteristically, *Le Côté de Guermantes* begins with an overture which, although it survives in the final text, is preceded by a new text. No longer does the name of Guermantes carry with it the "reflet d'un verre de lanterne magique" *(p. 11),* although it is sometimes released by involuntary memory from its little oxygen ball. Montargis (as he is still called in this passage) has passed the plough over the crenelated towers of Guermantes, which in the narrator's imagination rose high above France long before the towers of Notre-Dame de Paris and of Notre-Dame de Chartres were erected, by informing the narrator that the Guermantes came to Combray only in the seventeenth century and that the village of Guermantes, a typical urbanization project of the period, derived its name from the castle. Assuring us that "la fée dépérit si nous nous approchons de la personne réelle" *(p. 11),* the narrator predicts in this overture the final outcome of the Duchesse de Guermantes plot. That imagination cannot survive the contact with reality is by now a familiar theme. At last Proust will treat it in a banal, realistic manner. For a short period he attempts to transfer his imaginings to the Paris dwelling of the Guermantes and to believe that they live in a Medieval enclave within the modern city. Then his own family becomes tenants of the Guermantes and, although the Guermantes residence is picturesque and contains Borniche's shop, somewhat as cathedrals are often covered with excrescences of this kind, he soon learns from Françoise that the Guermantes do not exercise immemorial rights on this spot but are themselves renters. However, the narrator manages to substitute a third dream when "un vieil ami de mon père" *(p. 28)* states that the Duchesse de Guermantes is the most exclusive lady of the entire Faubourg Saint-Germain.

It is noteworthy that the deglamorizing of the name of Guermantes is the original subject and that all passages on this subject, particularly Montargis's remarks on the history of Guermantes, are part of the original text. Throughout this section a realistic tone prevails as the narrator observes the Duc de Guermantes shaving at his window, inspecting his horse in the courtyard, or conversing with the narrator's father with the forced subservience of a descendant of a royal valet de chambre. However, it is particularly Françoise who sets the realistic tone of this section as she enters into contact with her new surroundings by conversing with the Duke's servants. So important has Françoise become in the rewritten text that Proust assigns to her the role of opening *Le Côté de Guermantes.* The seed for the new passage is a remark in *Grasset B* (19:30) that the narrator and Françoise have a common interest in their initial failure to adjust to the new surroundings. The new text, two pages long, presents the whole experience from Françoise's perspective, after which the unrevised original overture begins. Thus it is not news when the original text finally announces, after five more pages, that the narrator's family has actually moved into the dwelling of the fabulous Guermantes. A slight revision is necessary at this point to compensate for the statement in the new introduction that the family had moved on account of the grandmother's health; the original text restated the proposition in *Du côté de chez Swann* that Madame de Villeparisis urged the grandmother to move (15:36). This makes one wonder why Proust introduced the scene of the grandmother's photograph by Montargis into the Bricquebec section if he did not anticipate the grandmother's illness. Françoise was already important in the original text, not only because of her role as Guermantes informant but also because Proust included more long comments about her relations with her employers. The amusing episode of the servants' resistance to their masters' interference with their lunch hour is already in the original text; so likewise are the comments on Françoise's loyalty to her employers which takes the egotistical form of desiring proper respect from other servants. Françoise clearly was not the symbol of class revolt in the original version and she does not become so in the additions, at least not quite. In a new passage, when she becomes exasperated at her employer's insistence on having special "biscottes," the maître d'hôtel says that all of that will one day be over because the workers in Canada are striking. Françoise cannot see how strikes in Canada will have any effect on the need for "biscottes" and she opines: "Tant que le monde sera monde, voyez-vous, disait-elle, il y aura des maîtres pour nous faire trotter et des domestiques pour faire leurs caprices" (p. 27). At heart, she is still the political conservative that she was at Bricquebec, for, in another new passage, the valet de chambre seeks to enter into her good graces by denouncing "les mesures terribles que la République allait prendre contre le clergé" (p. 22). Another new passage presents her as a naive admirer of titles of nobility (p. 35). Françoise's conservatism is doubtless related to her peasant origins, but nothing is made of this point even though, in her conversations with the other servants, she keeps regretting the good old days at Combray. In this regard, although even in context it is relevant to nothing whatever, we note this curious remark in the original text: "Ce ton chantant révélait chez Françoise non moins que la pureté arlésienne de son visage une origine méridionale et que la patrie qu'elle regrettait n'était qu'une patrie d'adoption" (17:42). This Southern origin for the one character personifying Combray must have startled even Proust himself, for he altered the text later to make it a comparison rather than an affirmation. Proust's continuing interest in linguistic problems is indicated by two new paragraphs on Françoise's speech habits (pp. 23, 26).

Already in the old text the narrator's family has come up in the world, for they now have a maître d'hôtel and a valet de chambre, and Françoise is presently promoted by the valet de chambre, in a new text, to the rank of "gouvernante" (p. 24). The author of the index to the Pléiade edition points out that the valet de chambre is named Victor on page 22, but that on page 322 the same name has been transferred to the maître d'hôtel. It is noteworthy that the original use of the name Victor occurs in new text. Various domestics of the Guermantes household also appear episodically, but the miscellaneous character who receives the most attention is a "fleuriste" by the name of Borniche who occupies the shop in the courtyard and who pleases Françoise by saying that her masters could afford a carriage if they wanted one. The "fleuriste" we have already encountered in *Grasset A.*

By the time this character reappears to annoy the Duc de Guermantes by saying "M. Norpois" instead of "M. de Norpois," *Grasset B* has already given him the name of Jupien. In rewriting the "fleuriste" passage, Proust inserted the word "giletier" but also introduced a long biographical sketch in which he explained that Jupien was no longer a "giletier" but rather was employed "dans un ministère" (p. 20) and that his niece, although she made an occasional waistcoat, was using the shop for "la couture pour dames."

The next episode is the return to La Berma. Whereas the first La Berma episode, back in the days when the narrator still loved Gilberte, was a kind of hors-d'œuvre which further disrupted an already disorderly presentation, the new episode has a definite function in the plot concerning the Duchesse de Guermantes. About the only noteworthy difference between the old and new texts is that the gala performance takes place at the Opéra-Comique, rather than at the Opéra. The narrator goes to the gala only because a friend of his father had a spare ticket. He is in no mood to be receptive to Racine because his interest in Elstir and modern art forms has eclipsed his former orthodoxy and he notes, not without melancholy, that he is indifferent to La Berma. The fact that the old text brings in Elstir suggests that the entire La Berma episode is contemporaneous with the *Grasset B* additions in *A l'ombre des jeunes filles en fleurs*. Being indifferent to what happens on the stage, the narrator concentrates his attention on the distinguished audience which includes, so says someone sitting nearby, the Princesse de Guermantes. As the Princess and her entourage accomplish the rite of sharing a box of candy, they are transformed for the narrator, perhaps by semantic association (the word "baignoire"), into bearded Tritons and colorful goddesses perched on coral reefs. This is, of course, a celebrated passage. When the act from *Phèdre* begins (no commentator has ever explained why Proust approached Racine on both occasions in the context of a *morceaux choisis*), the narrator notes that the voices and muscles of the actors seem to obey orders but are otherwise uninspired. While La Berma is reciting her lines, a "petite femme" (46:36) cries out: "Mais elle est trop vieille." This little woman makes three short appearances in the original text and she obviously has the same structural function as those other animators whom Proust, in making corrections, frequently added to his text to give the appearance of action. But now the miracle happens; since he no longer comes at La Berma "avec un trop grand désir" *(p. 49)*, the narrator is at last able to perceive that "l'interprétation de la Berma était, autour de l'œuvre, une seconde œuvre vivifiée aussi par le génie." When La Berma acts in a modern play, the name of which is never mentioned, the narrator finds her to be just as sublime and spends nearly two pages analyzing her art. It is unfortunate that the point of reference continues to be a totally unidentified play and that Proust was not inspired to expand these pages as he did elsewhere in the case of Vinteuil and Elstir. Once the art of the stage has been disposed of, the narrator turns back to the Princess and the other aristocrats, applying a few more feeble bathtub metaphors to them. The center of his attention is now the Duchesse de Guermantes and her husband who entered just before the modern play began. At this point, however, the original as well as the final text contains a long digression, presented from the omniscient point of view, concerning Madame de Cambremer who is also in a box looking with envy at the exclusive Guermantes and calculating that it will take her five years to be accepted socially by them, during which time a mortal illness will probably have ended her life. When the Duchesse de Guermantes, recognizing the narrator as her neighbor, waves to him, we are back to the plot and this long diversion on La Berma has been more than justified.

Additions to the La Berma episode are not numerous. To the description of the entourage of the Princesse de Guermantes, Proust added a short scene, presumably taking place in another box, in which Madame d'Ambresac, in a fawning manner, insists on helping the royal Duc d'Aumale take off his coat. This irrelevant passage must be regarded as a *preparation* for a future event. In the midst of his comments on his indifference to Racine, the narrator goes on, in a new text, to record his lack of enthusiasm for anything artistic, even when he is going to see in some castle a painting by Elstir or a Gothic tapestry (this is a misplaced remark since the narrator is not accustomed yet to visit private castles and has not yet seen the Elstirs of the Duc de Guermantes). Another brief new text interrupts the cries of the "petite dame" to explain, omnisciently as always seems to be the case with La Berma, that she had no reason to be envious of the great actress who was riddled with debts. A further addition to this already disjointed paragraph introduced a comparison of the interpretive arts, acting and playing musical instruments. In this comparison Vinteuil steps out of his role of composer to become a pianist interpreting music.

In the third episode the narrator, emboldened by the Duchess's greeting at the theatre, posts himself on the street corner at a time when she is likely to pass. With this statement the episode begins but, immediately in the old version and presently in the new version, the narrator backtracks to explain that, before going to the theatre, he used to walk in the streets and encounter sylphs, "une pensionnaire suivie de son institutrice ou une laitière avec ses manches blanches" *(p. 59)*. For a time, before she finally won out, the Duchess had to take her place beside the sylphs in competing for the narrator's interest on these morning walks. Each time the sight of the Duchess produces something of a shock because she is not like the mental image which the narrator has of her and he cannot see beyond the "marques rouges, dont je ne savais si elles étaient dues au grand air ou à la couperose, sur un visage maussade" *(p. 61)*. Each time the Duchess appears annoyed by the narrator's greeting accompanied by a feigned air of surprise. Then, one day, he is really not paying attention when a grand lady greets him and, only too late, he realizes that it was the Duchess. It is Françoise, however, who, by her disapproving manners, communicates to the narrator the idea that the Duchess is annoyed by these encounters, for she has doubtless gotten the idea from that lady's servants. This is the excuse for a long digression on Françoise's intuitive powers; no one can hide anything from her. Conversely, the narrator is unable to fathom Françoise's true sentiments towards him. He is unaware yet that he is "quelquefois menteur et fourbe" but he does know that she has told Jupien "que je ne valais pas la corde pour me pendre" (p. 66). Getting back now to the main subject, the narrator concludes: "J'aimais vraiment Mme de Guermantes" (p. 67). His way of loving her is to hope that all the calamities in the world might descend on her head so that she would come to him for help. He is even afraid that his usual method of feigning indifference will not work and yet the idea of going away from her continues to take form until he finally decides that he might accomplish something by a visit to her nephew, Saint-Loup.

Revisions this time about doubled the size of the text but without making any fundamental changes. An addition at the very beginning of the episode gave more details about the narrator posting himself further along the street so as not to be seen by the concierge. After the sylphs and after the Duchess took her place beside them, another addition told how the narrator compared his mental image of the Duchess with his mental images of Gilberte, Albertine and Gisèle and how he concluded that his image of the Duchess was only "une petite étoile" (p. 60), being limited to his vision of her at the Opera. Shortly beyond the "marques rouges" and beyond a remark about the difficulty of perceiving the real Duchess because she changed her dress and hat so often, another insertion changed the Duchess into a bird by giving her a "bec d'oiseau" and the thick plumage of "certains vautours" (p. 62). After the encounter in which the narrator failed to return the Duchess's greeting, there is the first example of what will become a systematic defamation of the Duchess who is now presented as a despot in her dealings with servants. Two additions also doubled in size the commentary on Françoise. One was placed after the remarks about Françoise's source of information being the Duchess's servants; it was a long comment on the fundamental change taking place in the old family servant whose forthright Combray reflexes are vanishing under the evil influence of city life. Her slanderous remark to Jupien about the narrator inspired a generalization on the theme that "toute réalité est peut-être aussi dissemblable de celle que nous croyons percevoir directement" (p. 67). Finally a slightly inept addition came after the narrator's remark that he did not have the courage to leave Paris and the Duchess. The narrator adds here a correction and says: "J'y songeais quelquefois" (p. 68) and then he goes on to tell how he often had Françoise prepare his trunks while, in the language of Saint-Simon, she protested "que je 'balançais'."

The next section relates the narrator's visit to Saint-Loup in his garrison town. The name Doncières is not mentioned in *Grasset B* or in the 1913 edition of *Du côté de chez Swann*; its first occurrence is in the 1917 edition of the latter work (cf. Pléiade I, p. 959, note to p. 9). Furthermore there is no allusion to such a garrison town either in *Grasset A* or in the part of *Grasset B* corresponding to *A l'ombre des jeunes filles en fleurs.* Likewise no such episode is foreseen in the 1913 "table des matières" but there the entries are so brief that the failure to mention this particular episode is no proof of its non-existence. Where Montargis went after leaving Bricquebec was never clear; now the *Grasset B* version of *Le Côté de Guermantes* states that Saint-Loup wrote from a garrison town, which the narrator seems to take special pains not to mention by name, the letters that the narrator received while still at Bricquebec-Balbec. The nameless town of *Grasset B* is situated "dans le nord" (70:16) but not so far away from Paris as to make a round trip impossible in one day. In the final text Doncières is still accessible on a round trip but it is now moved so as to be "moins loin de Balbec que le paysage tout terrien ne l'aurait fait croire" (p. 70). It would have been awkward to move it any closer to the Channel because the landscape had already been described in some detail. Curiously, the anonymity of the garrison town is accidentally preserved for the first eleven pages (p. 81), although it had been mentioned frequently by name in the revisions of *A l'ombre des jeunes filles en fleurs.*

Since this episode is a *déplacement* like so many other units which we have studied, one would expect it to take the characteristic form of a *composite basic narrative.* It does indeed take this form to a certain extent but not altogether because the narrator never made more than one trip to the garrison town. Thus there are a precise arrival and a precise departure but between these two events are two time schemes which are both designed to produce an illusion rather than record a chronological reality. The more deceptive of these time schemes is the one which appears to be based on an exact chronology. Counting from the day of arrival, we know that the narrator spent the first night in Saint-Loup's room; in the original text there is then a gap of one day which is subsequently filled by a new text commencing "le lendemain matin" (p. 80); then the old text picks up to inform us that "dès le second jour, il me fallut coucher à l'hôtel" *(p. 82)*; next the old text refers to "le lendemain" (85:19), but at this point the second time scheme takes over. In spite of the fact that all precise time becomes illusory, there continue to be references to "le troisième jour" *(p. 96)*, "le troisième soir" *(p. 104)*, "une semaine plus tard" (p. 118), and "quatorze jours" (120:36). When the narrator wakes up in his hotel room on the third morning, what follows is a *composite basic narrative* in which all events, even though they repeat themselves on other occasions or are similar events arranged in sequence, fall into the pattern of one single day: an awakening by the regimental band; getting up only when the fire is lighted; an occasional visit from Saint-Loup who is about to go out on the day's maneuvers; following the troops on maneuvers (but this is an addition found only in the final text); a visit to the barracks if Saint-Loup is not out on maneuvers; return to the hotel to rest before dinner; walking from the hotel to the restaurant; then dinner and conversation with Saint-Loup's friends. It will be noted that all these conversations are grouped together and take place in the evening, in other words at the end of the stylized day.

The garrison city episode is the most realistic part of the *Recherche* so far, that is to say realistic first of all in the sense that the setting is described with a detail which is not characteristic of Proust. The decision to visit Saint-Loup has been sudden and nothing in this visit has had time to work on the narrator's imagination. The trip in itself is a necessary evil; he is even surprised when, like an automaton or rather just like any other traveler, he seems to know precisely what he wants as he orders the porter to carry his trunk and the cabby to take him to the "quartier de cavalerie" (70:35). For a time he sees things as they are. While he waits for Saint-Loup, he is aware of the soldiers around him "titubant comme s'ils descendaient à terre dans quelque port exotique" *(p. 71)*. Talking to Saint-Loup, he is aware of a "sous-officier" *(p. 72)* exercising a horse in the courtyard. He does not miss a detail when Saint-Loup salutes his captain. Once in Saint-Loup's room, he is as observant as Balzac in cataloguing every object, notes the fire on the hearth and the "tic tac" of Saint-Loup's watch which he cannot localize (the digression which comes in at this point is new text). Forced at last to move to his hotel room, he is amazed to find that the lachrymose "moi" of Balbec has not been reborn and that he is fascinated by this former XVIIIth century dwelling (which, surprisingly, is equipped with an elevator). Before going to bed, he explores his "féerique domaine" *(p. 84)* which is anything but fairylike since it has a precise topography and is filled with very tangible objects. On the days when he goes to see Saint-Loup at the barracks, he reports on the setting and on the passing soldiers and their conversations. Returning to his hotel at sunset, he is fully aware of the city through which he passes with the "poudrière du château" *(p. 95)* silhouetted against the sky, the fountains illuminated by the setting sun, the orangerie, the Caisse d'Epargne and the Corps d'armée.

When the narrator sets out again from his hotel to join Saint-Loup, however, real objects are transformed by the darkness pierced by occasional illuminations. Ever a peeping Tom, he looks into people's windows as he passes and, because of the light effects, imagines that he is looking at a Rembrandt. In the same manner the rubicund faces of the soldiers, lighted by the passing tram on which the narrator is riding, make him think of Breughel. When he finally reaches the restaurant, he seems to have stepped out of the real world into a painting: "c'était, pendant que je traversais directement la cour qui s'ouvrait sur de rougeoyantes cuisines où tournaient des poulets embrochés, où grillaient des porcs, où des homards encore vivants étaient jetés dans ce que l'hôtelier appelait le 'feu éternel', une affluence (digne de quelque 'Dénombrement devant Bethléem' comme en peignaient de vieux maîtres flamands) d'arrivants qui s'assemblaient par groupes dans la cour, demandant au patron ou à l'un de ses aides . . . s'ils pourraient être servis et logés, tandis qu'un garçon passait en tenant par le cou une volaille qui se débattait" *(p. 98)*. Inside the restaurant the diners seem to be acting out "un repas de l'Evangile." At this point Proust's real world seems to have been absorbed by art; one may legitimately question whether this restaurant ever existed anywhere except in a Flemish painting.

There is never any technical explanation as to what Saint-Loup is doing in this garrison town. Long ago the old text said that he was a Saint-Cyrien and the new that he was preparing for the cavalry school at Saumur. There is never any further explanation, although we might logically assume that he is preparing for Saumur since this is a cavalry regiment. For a brief period he seems like a commissioned officer since his quarters are so luxurious and since he has an "ordonnance" *(p. 78)*. Eventually the information comes out specifically that he is a "sous-officier" *(p. 93)* but there is no mention of an officer candidate program such as the one in which Proust was enrolled in real life.

The narrator makes it clear from the outset that his enthusiasm for Saint-Loup's friendship is not what it once was: "L'amitié, l'admiration que Saint-Loup avait pour moi, me semblaient imméritées et m'étaient restées indifférentes" *(p. 69)*. The self-interested attitude of the narrator contrasts therefore with the solicitude of Saint-Loup for the narrator's physical and moral well-being. Even Saint-Loup's exemplary friendship does not resist the machinations of the narrator in attempting to get Madame de Guermantes' photograph: "Je compris qu'il avait une arrière-pensée, qu'il m'en prêtait une, qu'il ne servirait mon amour qu'à moitié, sous la réserve de certains principes de moralité, et je le détestai" *(p. 103)*. The narrator has obviously gone too far and has only himself to blame, for Saint-Loup has just promised to get the narrator a dinner invitation with the Duchess. A second time, under cover of the same ruse of a hurried confidential conversation which other persons present must not overhear, the narrator asks his friend to get him invited to see the Duke's Elstirs and this Saint-Loup cheerfully promises to do *(p. 126)*. Though the narrator exploits Saint-Loup's friendship, he never questions Saint-Loup's own sincerity and is well aware of his "bonté" (p. 117). A long addition, coming immediately after the misunderstanding about the Duchess's photograph, assures us, apparently in spite of what has just happened, that his kindness was "involontaire et faite seulement de tout ce qu'il devait dire à mon sujet quand j'étais absent et qu'il taisait quand j'étais avec lui" (p. 103). He continues: "La mère d'une débutante ne suspend pas davantage son attention aux répliques de sa fille et à l'attitude du public." Then he tells some anecdotes to illustrate the point. This is an unusual document which ends: "Telle est l'amitié," and which contrasts with the diatribe against friendship in the new text of *A l'ombre des jeunes filles en fleurs* (I, p. 907). Since these are both new texts, it is impossible with the present evidence to deduce which was written first. When the narrator has finally decided to go home to Paris, he goes to say good-by to his friend but is apparently snubbed by him as the latter, speeding by in his carriage, gives only an icy salute as though he did not recognize the person crossing the street. This is one of those enigmatic episodes which have capital importance in the Proustian novelistic system; they are subject to only the most conjectural interpretations. It is certain that this episode has a structural function since it comes as the *dénouement* to a series of events illustrating the subject of friendship. Not only is the narrator unable to provide a rational interpretation (he is convinced that Saint-Loup is not as myopic as that) for Saint-Loup's action but he is also saddened by being unable to say good-by; he makes no further observations on the meaning of friendship or on human conduct in general.

In justifying to Saint-Loup his interest in the Duchess, the narrator claims that, in order to become a writer, he wants to observe her "à un point de vue balzacien" *(p. 100).* In spite of the lack of sincerity in this remark, Proust himself is registering officially, as it were, his awareness of being a historian of society. Feuillerat, as we have said, correctly pointed out the increasing concern with social classes in the additions to earlier parts of *Grasset B*; now we note that this sociological function, added to the preoccupation with external reality, makes the sojourn in the garrison town doubly Balzacian. One social category to which Proust pays particular attention is the common soldier. The army is a social melting pot which forces "le jeune licencié" *(p. 94),* not without pedantry, to adopt the linguistic patterns of his lower class comrades and which causes them to talk with envy, but not with malevolence, concerning the rich young non-commissioned officers serving in their regiment. When they reappear on the day of the narrator's departure, the sociological purpose of these soldiers is again emphasized by the presence of the young Breton peasant who speaks French as a foreign language.

The officer class is represented particularly by one individual, Saint-Loup's captain. For most of *Grasset B* he is nameless; the narrator admires his majestic bearing and remarks that he gets on his horse "avec une noblesse de gestes étudiée comme dans quelque tableau historique et s'il allait partir pour une bataille"

(74:6). He seems to be a kindly type as well since he allows the narrator to sleep for two nights in Saint-Loup's room. Much later, the narrator asks Saint-Loup to classify and rank all of the officers, just as he, himself, had once ranked the actors of the Théâtre Français, and they do so, mentioning Gallifet, Négrier, Pau and others; but the narrator inquires particularly about another one with whom he had dined: "Comme il avait été obligé d'avoir Saint-Loup à dîner dans un repas de corps il m'avait invité avec lui, c'était son capitaine, le Prince de Borodino" (128:33).[52] This is the first time that the captain's name has been mentioned in *Grasset B* and a totally different picture of him suddenly emerges. Although Saint-Loup is received socially by officers belonging to the legitimate nobility, he has only "rapports de service" with the Prince de Borodino who is not only a Bonapartist but, according to rumor, a direct descendant of Napoleon. Having only recently belonged to a ruling class, he has only disdain for the pretenders of the Faubourg Saint-Germain. Whereas Saint-Loup "prenait amicalement la main de n'importe quel bourgeois qu'on lui présentait" *(p. 130)*, Borodino disdains the bourgeois as well. It seems obvious that Proust suddenly invented the character of the Prince de Borodino quite independently of Saint-Loup's captain. In rewriting *Grasset B*, he had to make numerous changes to compensate for this tardy decision to combine the captain and the Prince. Unfortunately, he left the biography where it was, at the entire end of the sequence, so that, without the final explanation, his remarks along the way are enigmatic. At the first mention of the captain, he now calls him a "napoléonide" (p. 74) who finds it hard to have Place de la République as his address. After driving his unintellectual friends away the first night so that they will not disturb the narrator, Saint-Loup, in an addition, goes on to explain that not everything in military life is unintellectual and that a certain course on military history is particularly enlightening. It is given by a commandant who is a Free Mason

[52] Early in the manuscript of *Grasset A* (Pléiade 19:21), there is a crossed out passage which compares Swann's incognito in Combray society with that of the "Duc de Borodino" who was a frequent guest of the "médecin major du régiment de Montargis." The "medic" did not know the duke's real identity and considered him only "un bon garçon, un peu solennel, probablement ruiné."

and who is the antithesis of the Prince de Borodino "que vous 'adorez'" and who is really "le plus grand imbécile que la terre ait jamais porté" (p. 79). Never would the Prince receive this free-thinking commandant of bourgeois origin, says Saint-Loup, and the omniscient author adds that it is class prejudice on the part of Saint-Loup to disdain "la noblesse d'Empire." Even though this is fragmentary information, the full-length biography which comes later is somewhat redundant. The next new mention of Borodino is a lengthy and amusingly superficial anecdote about the captain consenting to give Saint-Loup a leave for Bruges when the barber intercedes in his behalf while holding a razor at Borodino's throat. Finally, the full-length biography has an additional paragraph which, in a *flash-forward,* tells how the Prince ungratefully severed relations with the families of certain bourgeois officers at Doncières when he was transferred to Beauvais. At the end of *Grasset B,* Borodino is still majestic: "Droit sur son cheval, le visage plein, l'œil lucide et résolu le capitaine de Borodino leva le bras et d'un beau geste tira son sabre, et avec la voix calme des suprêmes résolutions lança: "Face en arrière" (139:38). In the revised text this becomes: "Je vis le capitaine de Borodino passer majestueusement en faisant trotter son cheval, et semblant avoir l'illusion qu'il se trouvait à la bataille d'Austerlitz" (p. 139). The original captain seems to have survived somehow in spite of the new disparaging remarks.

Saint-Loup's personal friends are nobles with a few proper bourgeois mixed in. They are not the object of sociological study in themselves but it is apropos of discussions with them that the Dreyfus case, with all its sociological implications, comes up. There is a fundamental difference between *Grasset B* and the final text in that Saint-Loup was not originally a Dreyfusard. Originally the Dreyfusard was the individual first designated as "un de ses amis" *(p. 104).* He is the person with whom the narrator has such pleasure talking that Saint-Loup later seems jealous. The narrator exclaims that nothing is better than "ces sympathies entre hommes qui n'ayant pas d'attrait physique à leur base sont les seules qui soient tout à fait mystérieuses" (104:30). The original text continues: "Saint-Loup m'avait parlé de ce jeune homme; je savais que seul d'eux tous il était partisan de la révision du procès Dreyfus" (105:17). Saint-Loup is actually very critical of the young man and accuses him of too much prejudice in favor of Dreyfus when he questions the infallible judgment of General de Boisdeffre and General Saussier, to the despair of his aristocratic family. The narrator interjects that "On est l'homme de son idée" *(p. 106)* and that one cannot escape the influence of one's milieu. Then the omniscient author gives a long example, that of the very brother of this friend of Saint-Loup, a pupil at the Schola Cantorum, who does not think like his family on musical matters, and he adds a second example of "une jeune princesse d'Orient" who has succeeded in being Victor Hugo and Alfred de Vigny in spite of her family (an allusion in real life to Anna de Noailles). The final text gets very confused as to who is who among the Dreyfusards. According to the revised text, it is not the first friend ("un de ses amis"), who is the Dreyfusard, but rather "un autre de ses camarades" *(p. 105)* and Saint-Loup himself who are both Dreyfusards. The remarks critical of the Dreyfusard friend are taken out of the mouth of Saint-Loup and put in the mouth of the person designated as "un de ses amis" (this individual now tolerates Saint-Loup as a Dreyfusard but not "un autre de ses camarades"). Later we discover that "un de ses amis" is not so sure of himself, that his opinions "paraissaient assez flottantes" (p. 108). Dreyfus never serves as a particular bond between Saint-Loup and the narrator who consequently seems, in the final text, not to have made up his mind yet about Dreyfus. On the other hand, it is quite clear that the bond which originally joined the narrator and the young noble called "un de ses amis" was Dreyfus (this does not necessarily prove that the narrator had made up his mind in the old text either) and that, with that motivation removed, this friendship has no viable reason for existing. Another Dreyfus passage, occurring directly after the discussion of military strategy, became hopelessly muddled because of the reversal of roles. The original text read: "... me disait Saint-Loup. Dès que la conversation devint générale, comme lui était pour l'état-major on évitait de parler de Dreyfus de peur de froisser mon nouvel ami" (118:28). In the original, another comrade remarked, apropos of the first friend, how curious it was that, "leur camarade, vivant dans un milieu si militaire, fut* tellement Dreyfusard*" (118:28). When the narrator repeats his previous comment that "l'influence du milieu n'a pas grande importance," Saint-Loup picks up the idea as his own and plagiarizes the narrator. Actually the original text is somewhat bungled so that the idea of plagiarism comes out clearly only in the final text when Saint-Loup repeats the narrator's original aphorism: "On est l'homme de son idée" (p. 119, cf. p. 106). In spite of this improvement, the final text makes Saint-Loup comment on a statement which he could not have heard since it was now about him and must have been made behind his back.

When discussing the structure of the *composite basic narrative* in this section, we noted the insertion of a new text telling how the narrator followed Saint-Loup to maneuvers. Although this text is in its logical place in the stylized day, it does violence to a more fundamental logic. It comes after the narrator has awakened from a troubled sleep and has summoned Saint-Loup to his bedside; this did not necessarily happen on the narrator's first morning at the hotel since the event is being related in the imperfect tense. But it is nevertheless a *morning* text. The new text on maneuvers begins: "Mais un peu plus tard j'allai souvent voir le régiment faire du service en campagne, quand je commençai à m'intéresser aux théories militaires que développaient à dîner les amis de Saint-Loup . . ." (p. 91). By thus referring to an *evening* text, this addition, like all typical Proustian *flash-forwards*, constitutes a digression among the other *morning* texts. In reality this new text has little to do with military strategy and mentions rather the "bonnes fatigues" which remind the narrator of the good old Combray days. The *evening* texts on military strategy, all of them new, are conversations at table among Saint-Loup and his friends in the presence of the narrator who has raised the subject. The passage is part of the long addition which begins with the fluctuating opinions of "mon nouvel ami" (p. 108). It goes on to mention Saint-Loup's interest in one of his colonels who is beginning to have doubts about Dreyfus's guilt and who still esteems Picquart. Saint-Loup is in the habit of saying little about the Dreyfus case because he knows that others do not share his opinions; yet we suddenly find him talking openly about the colonel who is still blinded by his "cléricalisme." There is one person who is not blinded and who "marche à fond dans nos idées" (p. 109) and that is Commandant Duroc, continues Saint-Loup who appears to be talking as though in a tête-à-tête with the narrator, although they are manifestly seated at a table since the narrator states: "je demandai à mon voisin si c'était exact que ce commandant fît, de l'histoire militaire, une démonstration d'une véritable beauté esthétique." By saying "nos idées" it is obvious that Saint-Loup regards the narrator as a Dreyfusard but there is still no absolute proof that he is right in doing so. The "voisin" is Saint-Loup who gives the narrator a ten-page lecture on military strategy, as though no one else were present. It is a treatise of the utmost clarity which appeals to the philosophical sense of the narrator because "sous le particulier on me montrait le général" (p. 117). Feuillerat (op. cit., p. 79) observes: "Si ce professeur d'histoire militaire n'était pas radical-socialiste et franc-maçon, il ressemblerait étrangement à certain professeur de l'Ecole de guerre dont la réputation est aujourd'hui mondiale." He also points out that Proust probably got all of his ideas from the wartime articles of Henri Bidou. For our purposes we shall simply note that this abstract discussion is entirely in keeping with the essentially realistic tone of the sojourn at Doncières.

Since we have already had occasion to allude to the two ruses by the narrator, it is obvious that the Duchesse de Guermantes has not been altogether forgotten. That first night in Saint-Loup's room the narrator spent some time gazing at the photograph and an addition made at that point emphasized a physical resemblance between nephew and aunt, including "le nez en bec de faucon" (p. 80). On the night of the Rembrandt paintings, however, seized by the old Méséglise voluptuousness, the narrator pursues women "dans la ruelle noire qui passe devant la cathédrale" (97:19) and, on one occasion, tries to "refermer les bras sur la passante effrayée." At this point he remarks: "essayer d'oublier Mme de Guermantes me semblait affreux, mais raisonnable et, pour la première fois, possible, facile peut-être" *(p. 97)*. It is therefore with no little surprise that much later, in the same paragraph containing Saint-Loup's plagiarism and after a badly placed aphorism ("Un souvenir, un chagrin, sont choses mobiles"), the narrator states: "j'avais peine à marcher on aurait dit qu'une partie de ma poitrine avait été sectionnée par un anatomiste habile" (119:19). While this pain is due to an evocation of his two other great loves, Gilberte and his mother (the passage is almost untouched and the final text contains no mention of

Albertine), it also includes, we discover presently, Madame de Guermantes whom he has not seen for "quatorze jours." Since the aphorism had been so completely bungled, Proust removed it and reused it in the earlier paragraph in which he talked about forgetting the Duchess (p. 96). Then he not only started a new paragraph but also introduced a spacing in the printed text, so that he now silhouetted a new sentence: "je regrettais tellement Mme de Guermantes, que j'avais peine à respirer" (p. 119). Thus the contradiction, which existed in the original text (but which was intended as a "generalized" pain brought about by memories), was emphasized even more.

On arriving at the restaurant, the pain, whether generalized or particular, is still so great that the narrator asks whether Saint-Loup has any news from Paris. He means, of course, whether his friend has heard from the Duchess. Since he is so evasive, Saint-Loup fails to understand and begins to report on his latest quarrels with his mistress. As he did on other occasions when writing about Saint-Loup, Proust immediately shifted to an omniscient point of view, so that the general effect is that of a brief novelette interrupting the sojourn in the garrison city. The original version is much shorter. In a long exchange of letters, Saint-Loup entreats his mistress to explain what she reproaches him for. Then he accepts "sincèrement ou par feinte une rupture" (121:17) but continues to receive reports on his mistress from the "femme de chambre" by telegraph or by the newly installed telephone system. Communication has become more difficult because the mistress has moved to the suburbs as a result of her landlord's objections to her menagerie. Once, while napping in the narrator's room, Saint-Loup has a nightmare in the narrator's presence and, on awakening, reports that he has dreamed that a rich lieutenant was making love with his mistress while the "maréchal des logis" forcibly restrained him from interfering *(p. 123)*. Finally the mistress asks Saint-Loup to forgive her but, characteristically, "il vit tous les inconvénients d'une réconciliation" (124:21). The digression, which has been related entirely outside the time system of the surrounding text, ends with a return to the dinner table and a resumption of the conversation in which Saint-Loup is now saying that he will be unable to help the narrator out because he will not get to Paris before Easter on account of his difficulties with his mistress. Of course, one wonders whether this text, which we have called a digression, was an insertion in an earlier text or whether, this time, Proust wrote it this way.

Dissatisfied with this rather factual account of Saint-Loup's troubles, Proust rewrote it much more in the manner of "Un Amour de Swann" in order to express the depth of emotion by deeper analysis. In the new text, Saint-Loup more lucidly feigned a rupture. After the dream, in a new paragraph, Saint-Loup is so moved that he wants to telephone to his mistress immediately, an enterprise in which the narrator, even though his parents have just had a telephone installed, is reluctant to assist because of the impropriety of the situation. Could Saint-Loup have forgotten that his mistress moved to the suburbs or maybe she still spends time in Paris?

In a very arbitrarily placed addition, which chances to fall just after the discourse on friendship, the narrator suddenly asks Saint-Loup whether he intends to marry Mademoiselle d'Ambresac and gets a categorical denial accompanied by the statement "qu'il ne savait pas qui c'était" (p. 105). This is an undramatic ending for a plot theme which had been running through the new passages since Albertine picked up the rumor at Balbec (I, p. 884) and which probably explained the somewhat useless allusion to Madame d'Ambresac at the Opera, already mentioned.

The various remarks about telephones, in both the old and new text, lead to the closing episode in which the narrator has the experience of telephoning for the first time. Saint-Loup has had the idea and has already written to the narrator's grandmother to telephone at a quarter to four, at which time the narrator will be ready in the local post office. This *morceau d'anthologie* was carried over almost without change from *Grasset B*; Proust added a new dash of preciosity at the end on the "messagères de la parole" (p. 136). When the narrator arrives at dinner that evening, Saint-Loup understands that his friend's departure is imminent. At this point Proust added a new passage in which the narrator is summoned to the telephone by mistake; someone else with an almost identical name is being called by his grandmother.

In *Grasset B,* as we have seen, the account of the sojourn in the garrison town was structured and was, for Proust, unusually realistic in tone. Most of the original text survived in the final version, but there were a few exceptions. The first omitted text fits on page 96 at the point where the narrator sets out for the first time from his hotel to join Saint-Loup and his friends at dinner. It is clearly one of the earliest fragments of the sojourn in the garrison town since the name of Montargis is mentioned and it has that shapelessness which characterizes many of Proust's earliest texts. For that reason it was very justifiably eliminated. It is a meditation on the purposelessness of the narrator's life and includes a renewal of his resolutions to work; it ends in a generalization on how "nous rendons l'idée de la mort à peu près nulle en écartant du présent immédiat l'attente de sa réalisation" (96:16). Another omitted text was situated at the point where Saint-Loup consents to arrange for the narrator to see the Elstirs belonging to the Guermantes. It stressed the narrator's desire to have Elstir interpret all of the objects and localities which were dear to the narrator's childhood. The narrator was still at the stage of wanting to find again "les sensations mêmes que me donnait la vue de ces tableaux" (125:18). The new version, which replaces this older text, shifts the emphasis from the subject of the painting to the finished work. This time there is no attempt at lyricism but rather a prosaic statement that he wants to see the Guermantes collection because he has been reading magazine articles about Elstir, knows where the principal collections are and wants to see them rather than the places which Elstir painted. Finally, a rewriting of the last scene at Doncières, which originally included both Borodino and Saint-Loup giving orders to the troops, now eliminated Saint-Loup.

In stressing the realistic side of the sojourn in the garrison city, we have omitted so far all mention of two lengthy additions which are the most penetrating passages which Proust ever wrote on the sensations. As sound psychological observation, they are an aspect of what Feuillerat would call the analytical Proust, but, as usual, Proust has clothed these remarks in the most poetic language so that the frontier between analysis and lyricism certainly is ill-defined, to say the least. The first such passage fits perfectly into the original text because it is inspired by the allusion in *Grasset B* to hearing the "tic tac" *(p. 75)* of Saint-Loup's watch. For more than a page, Proust describes how, with "les boules qui ferment le conduit auditif" (p. 76) in which we recognize an autobiographical detail, one can control the flow of sound with astonishing effects. The second passage is a new episode in the hypothetical day in the garrison city. After the narrator has inspected his hotel room and hotel in every detail, without an *alinéa* the new text begins: "Je me couchai" (p. 84). This time Proust studies the physiological conditions of sleep. In due course, this new text picks up a fragment of *Grasset B* in which Proust had described his sensations on being awakened by the regimental band passing under his hotel windows. After this fragment of old text, the new text resumes and discusses the different forms of sleep, including nightmares and the proverbial "sommeil de plomb," from which one emerges "cherchant sa pensée, sa personnalité comme on cherche un objet perdu" (p. 88). There is also a brief addition on the subject of acoustics in the section on the evening walk from the hotel to the restaurant (p. 97).

The ultimate conclusion to the sojourn in the garrison city was a paragraph on the return to Paris. The telephone call had left the narrator with an uncontrollable desire to see his grandmother. The only thing that he sees on his arrival is she; for her, he is still absent since she does not know that he is there looking at her. She appears as in a photograph of "une vieille femme accablée que je ne connaissais pas" *(p. 141)*. With a few polishing touches, the final text is the same as in *Grasset B*.

Until the next major episode begins, there are a dozen pages of miscellaneous events which fit into no particular pattern. The narrator of *Grasset B* notes first that Saint-Loup's promise to open the doors of the Hôtel de Guermantes has come to naught and this leads to a generalization on one's usual lack of success in answering for others. Without any transition, there springs anew in the narrator a desire to return to Balbec-Criquebec (both names figure alternately in the text) where he would see again Madame de Villeparisis waving to the Princesse de Luxembourg and would eat again a "déjeuner des œufs à la crème et des soles frites" (142:23). Inevitably the original romanticized image of Balbec creeps in and one night the narrator has a dream of "une cité du moyen âge au milieu des flots immobiles comme sur un vitrail." Time passes and the approach of carnival makes him think of Venice and Florence. He still walks in the streets in the morning, at the urging of his parents, but he tries not to see the Duchesse de Guermantes when he encounters her. He is still thinking of her to such an extent that he forgets his obligations to meet certain friends at the Louvre or on the Avenue du Bois. Saint-Loup comes to Paris and suggests that the narrator substitute an invitation from "ma cousine Poictiers" *(p. 147)* for the missing one from the Duchess. The weather having become cold again, Françoise, as an adept of Aunt Léonie's theology, concludes: "C'est le restant de la colère de Dieu" (148:17). But meanwhile the narrator is thinking again of Fiesole and the Ponte-Vecchio, using precisely the same text as that which served as the original conclusion to *A l'ombre des jeunes filles en fleurs* (this means that *Grasset B* repeated the same passage since *Grasset B* picked up the entire conclusion of *Grasset A*). Finally, the narrator's father, who has been talking to the Duc de Guermantes and to Norpois, suggests that his son would do well to accept Madame de Villeparisis's invitation and profit by her "bureau d'esprit" *(p. 150)* in order to further his literary ambitions. The narrator keeps to himself his own doubts about the sincerity of his vocation. Thus the next major episode is prepared.

There were, however, many additions to this original sequence of events in *Grasset B*. After the first generality, Proust introduced a brief paragraph on how Jupien was offended because the narrator did not stop to see him as he went up the stairs on his return from Doncières (p. 142). Then there was a complete ablation of the original text on a return to Balbec. An allusion to Florence and Venice was inserted after the first mention of the weather (p. 143). After the encounters with Madame de Guermantes came a new text on sleep, justified by the afternoon naps which the narrator's parents insisted that he take after staying up all night. This really continues Proust's previous essay on the same subject and takes up the interrelation of the thoughts which precede sleep and the content of dreams. The passage contains a *flash-forward* in which the narrator is really in Venice and dreams of "une cité gothique au milieu d'une mer aux flots immobilisés comme sur un vitrail" (p. 146). This time the Gothic city is Venice, whereas, in the omitted passage, it was Balbec. In a second paragraph, Proust discusses dreams in which the patient is speechless and cannot move his limbs. After the mention of "ma cousine Poictiers," a further addition made this lady a tepid Dreyfusarde. Then, without interruption, comes a new passage on Françoise who is disturbed by the Duchess's arbitrary decisions regarding her servants and who is shirking her household responsibilities by going off to visit her relatives and her daughter (p. 147). At the very end comes a brief addition on the Grandmother's poor health and then a long explanation as to why the father is interested in Madame de Villeparisis. He wants to become a candidate for a seat in the Institute, cannot count on Norpois, and hopes that his son will say the right word at Madame de Villeparisis's reception. Rather than call this a new found cynicism on Proust's part we may regard it as unprejudiced observation on human nature. The final new paragraph, which is only obliquely concerned with the father, relates how Madame Sazerat has snubbed him because she knows of his anti-Dreyfusard persuasions. This new text also clarifies at last the narrator's stand on the matter by stating that the father refused to sign "une liste révisionniste" and then did not speak to his son for a week "quand il apprit que j'avais suivi une ligne de conduite différente" (p. 152).

The important event to come is the reception by Madame de Villeparisis, but the narrator will make a long detour to get there because Saint-Loup, who is taking him to the reception, wants first to pick up his mistress in her suburban retreat and then, after lunch, attend the performance at her theater. This is a long narrative which, in *Grasset B,* will present each event in its logical order. On the way to meet Saint-Loup, the narrator encounters Legrandin who makes fun of his "livrée" (the narrator, setting out in the morning, is already dressed for the reception) and vows that he will never be seen in the company of these aristocrats who should all have been beheaded. Some sixth sense seems to have told him where the narrator is going. The picturesque suburban village, reached by the belt railway, is bursting with fruit blossoms when Saint-Loup and the narrator arrive and they enchant the latter because they remind him of

Combray. On the way Saint-Loup indicates that he will sacrifice everything for his mistress, his career, his family, his social position, and will even make a rich marriage to have the money to keep her. But he will not marry her because "il lui fallait la tenir par l'attente du lendemain" (155:39). When the narrator finally meets the mistress, he is amazed to discover that she dates back to his brothel days and is none other than "Rachel quand du Seigneur." For a page and a half the narrator goes on expressing his amazement that his friend was ready to sacrifice millions for what anyone else could get for twenty francs (he repeats the price four times). Now, says the narrator, he really understands what is meant by "la puissance de l'imagination" (p. 160). They have chosen to go to a particular restaurant because the narrator, still obsessed with the idea of Balbec, wants to talk about the seaside resort with Aimé-Clodion who, in the winter, is a maître d'hôtel in Paris. Clodion is so handsome that Zézette, the erstwhile Rachel, keeps making eyes at him; this is a habit with her and she knows that it will make her lover furious. Apparently obeying previous orders from Saint-Loup, Zézette engages in a literary conversation for the narrator's benefit but, already knowing Madame de Villeparisis's opinion of her intellect, he has nothing but disdain for her. Turning to the theatre, she unexpectedly takes the defense of La Berma against Saint-Loup but also speaks of other well-known actors in an irritating manner. The narrator does not conceal his disregard for her but she is not offended because she has in her a "grand talent non reconnu encore" *(p. 168)*. Perhaps to get rid of Saint-Loup so that she may speak more freely to Clodion, she now makes eyes at a "jeune boursier" *(p. 168)* and this has the desired effect, for Saint-Loup marches off in a rage. Soon Saint-Loup sends a message that he wants her to come to a private room where the narrator subsequently joins them, after which they go to the theatre. The narrator has lost his interest in the art of the theatre but is intrigued by the actors themselves: "je voyais une autre pièce, muette et expressive, se jouer sous la pièce parlée" *(p. 172)*. When they are backstage, Saint-Loup, in response to a question from the narrator, says that he simply did not have time to stop on that day, in the garrison city, when he gave the narrator only an icy salute. The narrator concludes that Saint-Loup is two people; in one role "il était véritablement mon frère" (176:27) but in the other he was "un autre personnage qui ne me connaissait pas" *(p. 176).* His noble upbringing had taught him "un certain nombre de dissimulations de bienséance." There follows then another lengthy jealousy scene between Saint-Loup and Rachel in the form of a dramatic dialogue, at the end of which Saint-Loup threatens not to give his mistress the necklace which the jeweler Boucheron is holding for him *(p. 178).* Rachel threatens to find someone else to buy the necklace for her and, while she is pursuing the dancer again, Saint-Loup slaps a journalist because he will not put out a cigar which is bothering the narrator. The slap does not end in a duel because of the poltroonery of the journalist and his friends. Slightly upset by all of these events, Saint-Loup asks his friend to leave him and promises to join him later at the reception.

On this narrative Proust grafted many additions, all of them suggested by the original text. Near the beginning he placed another of these sequential plot motifs which we have noted frequently as a structural device in his work; this one is another reference to Françoise's concern about the Duchess's servants who are still at the mercy of the spying concierge. Further along Proust added a note saying that the narrator forgives Legrandin because they are still joined by the little bridge crossing the Vivonne. He also rewrote carefully Saint-Loup's remarks concerning his mistress, changing their order considerably. After the narrator discovers the real identity of Saint-Loup's mistress, Proust shifts to an omniscient point of view to relate some more lurid details of Rachel's career as a prostitute. After the narrator exclaims about the powers of the imagination, in another addition Rachel is accosted by some "vulgaires 'poules'" as they are getting on the train and, through these former friends of his mistress, Saint-Loup himself has a vision of the "other" Rachel similar to the twenty-franc prostitutes whom he has just seen. Switching again to the omniscient perspective (that happens particularly often in the case of Saint-Loup, we have observed), the author now shows us Saint-Loup imagining Rachel walking the sidewalks of the Place Pigalle. In the same addition, the narrator resumes his story, saying that Rachel "ne s'interrompit de me parler livres, art nouveau, tolstoïsme" (p. 164); this produces a contradiction with the old text which follows (p. 166) and in which Rachel is discussing literature for the first time. At this point, still in the same addition, the narrator happens to mention Dreyfus and Zézette begins to sob. At the point where the second literary conversation began (the first in terms of *Grasset B*), Proust introduced a characteristic linguistic observation about Saint-Loup's influence on Rachel's language (p. 167). In the same addition, the narrator also observes Rachel's awkwardness in eating and wonders how she can be a good actress. After the remark about Rachel's unrecognized talent, there comes a very confusing addition in which the narrator, although he is not yet at the theatre, thinks he is in a theatre foyer (p. 168). Having no compunctions about interrupting the argument between Zézette and Saint-Loup about the "jeune boursier," Proust inserted a passage in which Saint-Loup, looking out the window, sees Charlus speaking with Aimé and assumes that his family has sent this "vieux coureur de femmes" (p. 169) to spy on him. After joining Saint-Loup and his mistress in the private room, the narrator, in a new passage, becomes as intoxicated as at Rivebelle and, looking into a succession of concentric mirrors, sees himself as "hideux, inconnu" (p. 171). Proust also filled in the sketchy account of the dramatic representation. The original text, which was, of course, retained, said something about an "ingénue," a "jeune premier," and a "tirade amoureuse." However, the new version adds two new parts to the performance and the second part is not a play but rather a young woman making her début as a singer. This singer is the butt of sarcasms on the part of persons whom Rachel has planted in the audience to ruin the young lady's act; the narrator does not at all enjoy this "méchanceté" (p. 173). The addition continues by describing a play in which Rachel acts; the narrator, having heretofore seen only "les taches de rousseur et les boutons" on Rachel's face (p. 175), now understands that Saint-Loup has fallen in love with her because, on stage, she is a beautiful creature. When the narrator and Saint-Loup go backstage, in another addition, the narrator is disappointed to see again the real Rachel: "La forme, l'éclat de ce jeune astre si brillant tout à l'heure avaient disparu" (p. 177). In her argument with Saint-Loup about the necklace in the original text, Rachel had sought to insult him by saying:

"C'est bien ce qu'on dit: Marsantes, *Mater Semita,* ça sent la race" (179:1, with misprint corrected). In an addition, Proust explains that the anti-Dreyfusards are wrong and that *semita* signifies "sente" and not "Sémite." Finally there is a lengthy addition, at the end, in which Saint-Loup, like Charlus before him, chastises a homosexual who has made advances.

All of these additions in no way alter the structural pattern of this section but some of them obviously change the tone. The trip to the Paris suburb began rather joyously in a burst of fruit tree blossoms. Someday Proust scholars may tell us that Proust picked this lyrical text out of his *cahiers* and that it dates from an earlier period; however, we conjecture that Proust composed the present Rachel episode either simultaneously with, or after, the insertion of the brothel episode into the Gilberte narrative and that, since the brothel episode was added at the level of *Grasset B,* none of the present Rachel episode could have belonged to the level of *Grasset A.* In other words, it is our opinion that the *Grasset B* version of the present Rachel episode was composed more or less at one time and that this lyricism, whether it came accidentally from an earlier text or not, was quite intentional; it set the original lyrical tone of the entire episode.[58] Proust's subject in the original version is the power of the imagination. The Rachel of this original version may be realistic in her behavior but she is not repulsive; one even has the feeling that Saint-Loup is partly at fault and has brought these provocations upon himself. He is violently in love with Rachel and the emotion of love is somehow lyrical *per se.* The additions radically altered that lyrical tone. For once we are inclined to agree with Feuillerat that Proust is turning against his world and that, even though it was part of his plan to show ultimately some of the seamy sides of life, he has now begun to blacken things somewhat prematurely and arbitrarily. Was it necessary, in the interests of greater realism, to introduce a flashback showing Rachel plying her trade as a prostitute?

[58] In the manuscript of *Grasset B* the trip to the suburban town to see Rachel is a handwritten interpolation. Therefore, in reply to Feuillerat, it is particularly significant to note that Proust is still apparently writing lyrical passages (including one which he subsequently omitted [157:41]).

That point was taken care of long ago in an addition in the earlier stages of *Grasset B*. Would it not have been more Proustian to leave everything in Saint-Loup's imagination and not have him meet up with the "poules" at the railway station? It was quite sufficient, and perhaps useful, to have additional information on how he first met her when she was not a prostitute but an actress. What was gained by that scene in which Rachel wrecked the début of the young singer? Her behavior is too rational, whereas what appealed about her before was a kind of irrationality in the manner of Colette. This scene fails particularly because it seems to be a plagiarism of the scene in which the "petite femme" interrupted the performance of La Berma. Even more of a plagiarism is the episode of Saint-Loup beating up the homosexual since it is so obviously modeled on the other episode in which Charlus was the hero. Disruptive though it was for the surrounding text, Charlus's call on Aimé at the restaurant was much more subtle and ultimately just as effective (in fact, let us not forget a similar episode when, at Balbec, Charlus tried to get Aimé to bring the Bergotte volume). Perhaps what is lacking most of all in these additions is subtlety.

The tea party of Madame de Villeparisis, not a special occasion but only one of her "jours" to which people came at random, is the final episode of the *Grasset Proofs*. What Proust is now trying to depict is the complexity of a social gathering in which everyone is talking at once and seldom saying anything of consequence. Furthermore he is fully conscious now of his role as a historian of society and, for him, society is essentially a social gathering. Since a novel must always tell some kind of story, plot considerations are necessary accessories. The story still being told is the love affair, if one may call it that, with Madame de Guermantes, but it is a very tenuous thread which is not yet quite prepared to break. The love affair can hardly be said even to furnish the rudiments of a plot and what action there is has to come from other sources. The dominant theme is still the one announced in the overture to this section, that "la fée dépérit si nous approchons de la personne réelle" *(p. 11)*.

In their broadest outline the events of this section are as follows: conversation of Madame de Villeparisis with the historian of the Fronde and with Bloch, during which the Duchesse de Guermantes enters; gate-crashing by Legrandin who is then insulted by the narrator and whose sister is maligned by the Duchess; Bloch knocking over the vase; simultaneous conversation, in different places, between Bloch and Norpois about the Dreyfus affair, and between the Duchess and various other characters concerning Rachel's performance in *Les Sept Princesses* and then (the Duc de Guermantes now being involved) concerning Saint-Loup's Dreyfusism; arrival of Saint-Loup's mother, Madame de Marsantes, and then of Saint-Loup himself who tries unsuccessfully to get a conversation going between the Duchess and the narrator; arrival of the German prime minister and a long digression concerning him; pursuit by Charlus as the narrator is about to go off to discuss Rachel with Saint-Loup; in spite of Madame de Villeparisis' opposition, departure of the narrator with Charlus. In the final text, there are three essential changes; Charlus enters later than in *Grasset B;* the episode of Bloch's dismissal by Madame de Villeparisis is added; Madame Swann, who was not present at the tea party in *Grasset B,* is the subject of extensive additions.

Like the earlier Norpois dinner which was also structured around conversations, the tea party begins with the biography of Madame de Villeparisis. The point of view varies from omniscience on the part of the author to conjecture on the part of the narrator and to such an extent that it is difficult to say who is speaking. After the author has said that she was born into a "maison glorieuse" *(p. 183)* but that something happened to lower her social prestige, the narrator steps in to make his conjectures. The cause of her decline, he says, cannot be her twenty-year-old liaison with Norpois, for such affairs are acceptable among the aristocracy; it might therefore have been "d'autres aventures" *(p. 184)* in her past which made women hate her for what she had done to their men. The narrator seems to favor, however, another explanation: that, being intelligent but not too much so "ayant passé à côté des grandes choses sans les approfondir" *(p. 185),* she adulterated her salon with too many bourgeois intellectuals "avec une insistance qui la dépréciait peu à peu aux yeux des snobs habitués à coter un salon d'après les gens que la maîtresse de maison exclut" *(p. 187).* Now that she is trying to rebuild the social prestige of her salon, she particularly regrets her inability to attract a certain Madame Leroi who, in spite of her apparently plebeian name (about which Proust makes no comment), is a friend and almost a duplicate of the Duchesse de Guermantes in social behavior and prestige. Proust was not satisfied to leave the biography of Madame de Villeparisis in this conjectural form but added another paragraph in which he seemed to say more emphatically, but still not unequivocally, that she "mangea peut-être la fortune, d'hommes couchés depuis dans la tombe" (p. 187). A further addition stated that Madame Leroi might be cutting her but that she was still receiving visits from "la reine Marie-Amélie" (p. 188). As at Balbec, the narrator of *Grasset B* does not disapprove of her anecdotes showing off her noble origins and, curiously enough, these particular anecdotes, including the addition which made her family more noble than "les filles du roi de France" (p. 199), are told for the benefit of Bloch who likewise has no objection. She remains essentially a kind person and, even in the addition which causes her summarily to dismiss Bloch, she repents a few days later: "elle le reçut très bien parce qu'elle était bonne femme" (p. 249). Nevertheless, a further addition summarily disposes of her once and for all when Charlus tells the narrator that, in a second marriage, she became the wife of a certain Monsieur Thirion who later usurped the name of de Villeparisis and that she aided her husband in this enterprise by collecting "toutes les peintures se rapportant aux Villeparisis véritables" (p. 294).[54] This new information shatters all of the narrator's illusions concerning her and she becomes again "ce qu'elle m'avait paru être dans mon enfance, une personne qui n'avait rien d'aristocratique" (p. 294). This is not denigration, of course; it is merely the end of an illusion.

As though to corroborate the conjecture that Madame de Villeparisis was guilty of scandalous conduct when she was young and beautiful, Proust introduced in a lengthy addition the "trois

[54] It is doubtful whether Proust originally foresaw this disclosure concerning Madame de Villeparisis. In *Grasset A*, he does refer to her as a member of the "illustre maison de Bouillon" (19:37), but he also referred to "M. de Villeparisis son père" (722:43). In the Pléiade text this becomes "M. de Bouillon son père" (p. 723), obviously in anticipation of Charlus's remarks.

divinités déchues" who had lost their social standing because "ces trois Parques à cheveux blancs, bleus ou roses, avaient filé le mauvais coton d'un nombre incalculable de messieurs" (p. 197). The symmetry is almost anti-realistic: "Chacune de ces dames avait sa 'duchesse de Guermantes', sa nièce brillante qui venait lui rendre des devoirs, mais ne serait pas parvenue à attirer chez elle la 'duchesse de Guermantes' d'une des deux autres" (p. 196). One particularly objectionable member of the trio, Alix, pops up twice again, once when she claims that Madame de Villeparisis's painting is a copy (p. 199) and once when she engages in a back-biting scene with her (p. 202).

Although the essential Bloch was already present in *Grasset B,* Proust was so interested in this character that he made many additions to the already grossly caricatural portrait. The first addition, coming immediately after the first mention of Bloch's name, was a two-page commentary on the "kaléidoscope social" (p. 190) which was about to precipitate the Jews to the bottom of the social scale. Picking up an allusion in *Grasset B* to Bloch, with a glove in one hand, looking like an Assyrian scribe holding a roll of papyrus (193:30), Proust now wrote an almost lyrical description of Jewish physical traits which, coming down through the ages from the Assyrians themselves, made him feel that he was "en présence de créatures surnaturelles que la puissance du spiritisme aurait fait apparaître" (p. 191). For a time, in the old text, Bloch seems genuinely interested in what Madame de Villeparisis is saying about her noble past but soon he falls into one of the many traps which his own ignorance of society has set for him; when Madame de Villeparisis tells how Charlus announced himself as the Queen of Sweden, Bloch bursts into loud guffaws, only to be told that the Queen of Sweden was really a frequent visitor. When he upset the vase, Bloch's reply in *Grasset B* was in keeping with his character: "Cela ne présente aucune importance, dit-il, car je ne suis pas mouillé" *(p. 215).* Proust let that incident stand as it was but, at the point where Bloch got up to leave, he made an addition to explain that Bloch was furious and blamed the servants for having put the vase in an exposed position. The next addition turns out to be very maladroit from a structural point of view. It occurs after Madame de Villeparisis has rejected Bloch's suggestion to hire Rachel for a dramatic entertainment. Although the Marquise is telling the narrator in private what she thinks about Borodino for aiding her nephew in his love affair, suddenly and with no explanation as to how or why Bloch invades their privacy, we hear Bloch calling Saint-Loup a "mauvais chien, parce qu'il est extrêmement bien élevé" (p. 218), after which he tells his anecdote about Sir Rufus Israëls that no one understands. In the same addition, he goes on displaying his bad upbringing by asking the narrator how rich Saint-Loup is and then by insisting on opening the window although, as an earlier addition explained (p. 189), Madame de Villeparisis had a cold. When the Marquise asks Bloch whether he would like to meet Norpois, in an addition Bloch inquires whether he was not that slightly gaga old gentleman who aimed at his seat before sitting on it (p. 220). The next addition, structurally speaking, is even more maladroit. It is inserted in a conversation on Maeterlinck's *Sept Princesses* and Saint-Loup's affair and this conversation is so badly fragmented already that no one knows who is speaking to whom. In reality, it is a conversation taking place between Argencourt and the Duchess and, if the narrator overhears it, he is certainly not a party to it, for, although he was introduced to the duchess on her arrival, he has not dared to speak to her and she has not deigned to say anything to him. Hence it is totally inappropriate for this addition to begin: "entendant que nous parlions de Saint-Loup" (p. 228). This time Bloch speaks so much ill of Saint-Loup that "tout le monde en fut révolté." Then the same paragraph becomes a *flash-forward* in which Bloch says to someone, presumably to the narrator, that "il comptait déposer d'une façon mensongère et dont l'inculpé ne pourrait pas cependant prouver la fausseté" (p. 228). By contrast with all the *gaffes* in *Grasset B* and all of the more malicious remarks in the final text, Bloch is amazingly restrained and perceptive in discussing the Dreyfus affair with Norpois. When the discussion is over in *Grasset B*, Bloch turns to Argencourt for his opinion but is rebuffed, not so much by the words as by the tone of the reply of the Belgian chargé d'affaires. To this passage Proust made an addition in which Bloch turns for support to the young Duc de Châtellerault, whom he expected to be a friend, and is the object of an anti-Semitic insult. Bloch is an almost tragic figure as he mutters: "qui vous a dit?" (p. 247). It is now quite clear that Proust exaggerated Bloch's aggressiveness in order to express the revolt coming basically from insults like this. In a way, the new scene which follows is less a final defeat for Bloch than it is a final manifestation of his lack of savoir-faire as he fails to comprehend the insult which Madame de Villeparisis, in pretending to be asleep, aims at him. He is saved by his own ineptitude. It should be noted that *Grasset B* lacked a *dénouement* for the Bloch plot; in that respect the final text was a decided improvement.

Before Bloch can take Norpois aside to discuss the Dreyfus affair, the ex-ambassador has conversations with the narrator in two additions. In the first addition, Norpois alludes to his earlier conversation with the narrator about his writing and about Bergotte and the narrator dares to mention, but with disastrous results, the name of Elstir in the hope that Norpois can arrange for him to see the collection belonging to the Duc de Guermantes. In the second addition, the narrator remembers his promise to his father and talks about the latter's candidacy for the Institute but the ex-ambassador's opinion is that he should wait for ten or fifteen years. This addition makes the Faffenheim episode, which comes later, seem strangely redundant.

When at last the great conversation between Bloch and Norpois begins in *Grasset B,* the first exchanges are made not without humor; Bloch is flattered by Norpois's seeming regard for his literary talent and for excluding him from the general bankruptcy of society then taking place. Before Bloch can get Norpois on to the subject of Dreyfus, Proust intervenes with a new digression to describe (obviously a borrowing from *Jean Santeuil*) how Bloch had attended the Zola trial "avec une provision de sandwiches et une bouteille de café" (p. 234). At this point, returning to *Grasset B,* Norpois begins to talk about Henry and Picquart, but then the scene shifts and new characters, led by the Duc de Guermantes, are heard discussing Dreyfus in what might be considered a caricature of the serious conversation between Bloch and Norpois. The Duke asserts that Dreyfus is the "amant de la femme du ministre de la Guerre" (p. 238) and the Duchess gives birth to one of her witticisms: "Quel malheur pour eux qu'ils ne puissent pas changer d'innocent!" (p. 239). The scene now shifts abruptly again to Bloch and to Norpois who is speaking so diplomatically that Bloch thinks now that he is a Dreyfusard and now that he is an Anti. In the old text, the omniscient author begins to comment that Norpois "était tellement anti-dreyfusard que, trouvant que le gouvernement ne l'était pas assez, il en était l'ennemi tout autant qu'étaient les dreyfusards" *(p. 241)*. An addition continued the same paragraph by explaining that Bloch was fundamentally wrong in assuming that the government really knew the truth about Dreyfus and had a secret dossier on the subject. The remaining text in the original was brief and fragmentary; Proust filled it out but it said essentially the same thing: that Norpois would make no comment on the falsification of documents and that he did not approve of the "manifestations du Prince Henri d'Orléans" *(p. 242)*. At that point the original text had added: "d'avoir serré dans ses bras le Capitaine Esterhazy." In the considerably expanded final text, the same words occur but they are now so remote from the other half of the sentence that one remains in doubt as to what Henri d'Orléans did. When the conversation between Bloch and Norpois had come to an end because of Madame de Villeparisis's intervention, Proust added a paragraph on Bloch's manner of speaking and the fact that he had abandoned "la mode néo-homérique" (p. 243). It is therefore surprising to note an earlier addition (p. 234) causing Bloch to use his Homeric style, whereas, in *Grasset B,* he had ceased talking in this manner. Madame de Villeparisis intervened in the Dreyfus discussion on the pretext of bringing up the Princesse de Sagan's ball, apropos of which Bloch made a few more social errors. After this, the old text seemed to have made a mistake by starting the Bloch-Norpois discussion over again. Instead of eliminating this apparent error, Proust rewrote the passage to make it say that Bloch insisted on plying Norpois with more questions. Then he added two more pages of a soliloquy by Norpois which seemed to be an appeal to Bloch's patriotism: "Etes-vous prisonnier des fauteurs de désordre?" he asks (p. 246). "La France dans son immense majorité désire le travail dans l'ordre."

Although the paramount subject in terms of plot was the disillusionment of the narrator with Madame de Guermantes, there is no attempt to dramatize any of the activities concerning the

Duchess and she is lost among the other events. When she entered, Madame de Villeparisis introduced the narrator and the historian to her but the narrator was so convinced of the "nullité de l'impression" (p. 200) which they both produced on her that he was afraid to engage in conversation with her. He seems, however, to have been a silent participant in many conversations in which she was involved (in fact, the problem of who does or who can speak to whom is further complicated by an addition in which the Duchess, seemingly not otherwise present, cuts into a conversation between Norpois and the narrator to exclaim: "Ah! ne dites pas de mal de Bergotte" [p. 222]). Lacking any evidence to the contrary, we are inclined to conclude that, even though they were said "à mi-voix" (p. 202), he overheard the Duchess's expostulations concerning Madame de Cambremer. Evidently this outburst does not affect his judgment immediately concerning the Duchess, for there soon follows a long development on the Duchess being accompanied by her duchy: "la vie inconcevable que ce nom signifiait, ce corps la contenait bien" *(p. 205)*. The narrator has the feeling that, in her eyes, he is only a grease spot on one of the armchairs. In *Grasset B*, the next episode involving the Duchess seems to begin her gradual decline in the opinion of the narrator when she compares Madame Leroi to a pregnant frog. Although this remark may still be regarded as just an illustration of the Duchess's wit, it is obviously a malevolent wit usually exercised at the expense of others. When Madame de Villeparisis sends Bloch and Norpois off to talk about the Dreyfus case, the Duchess begins a long conversation on Saint-Loup and Rachel which is so fragmented by later additions that the reader does not realize that this was originally a connected text. While disapproving of Saint-Loup's affair, she is not unduly malicious and even admits that love does strange things. Her maliciousness is suddenly directed at Madame Swann (who, we repeat, is not a *figurante* in the Grasset version of the tea party) when Argencourt, to illustrate the strange course of love, alludes to the notorious case of Swann in love; the Duchess now calls Odette "immonde" (p. 228) although she was once ravishing. Whether the narrator has so far been affected by any of this he does not say. However, when the Duchess becomes very sarcastic about the play in which Rachel acted, he momentarily loses all respect for her intelligence: "Je trouvais une sorte d'âpre satisfaction à constater sa complète incompréhension de Maeterlinck" *(p. 229).* Yet his feeling of superiority is short-lived, for he quickly adds: "Tels étaient les mots que je me disais; ils étaient le contraire de ma pensée." Now the Duchess resumes her maliciousness, again apropos of Madame de Cambremer whom she calls a "troupeau de vaches" *(p. 232).* At the end of the first segment of the discussion of the Dreyfus affair between Bloch and Norpois, the Duc de Guermantes, with the Duchess as one of the interlocutors, begins to make his own comments on the Dreyfus affair; in the *Grasset B* version what she says is of no consequence. Later she has a brief comment to make on the ball of the Princesse de Sagan and ironically proclaims that she does not know what a "solennité mondaine" (p. 244) is, a remark which catches the unsophisticated Bloch unawares. When Argencourt, on the pretext of being Belgian, brings up *Les Sept Princesses,* the Duchess repeats herself on the subject but says nothing new and it is rather the chargé d'affaires who demolishes Maeterlinck. When Saint-Loup enters, the Duchess manages to place one of her witticisms: "quand on parle du Saint-Loup" (p. 254). It is shortly after this that the Duchess, because of Saint-Loup's insistence, actually speaks to the narrator. The next time we see Madame de Guermantes, she is offering the German prime minister a cup of tea and then she leaves abruptly because "je dîne chez Mme Leroi" *(p. 263).* Thus there is no particular structure in the account of Madame de Guermantes, not even progress beyond the narrator's first disillusionment concerning her opinion of *Les Sept Princesses.*

The additions merely underline some of the points already made concerning the Duchess and do not bring things into any better focus. However, in the midst of the essentially lyrical passage on the duchess and her duchy, the narrator, in an addition, does look ahead to the period "quand elle me fut devenue indifférente" (p. 204), which is a useful reminder of the real intent of all of this exposition. At this point he also gave her what seems to be a slightly whiskey voice: "une voix qu'on eût crue, aux premiers sons enroués, presque canaille, où traînait, comme sur les marches de l'église de Combray ou la pâtisserie de la place, l'or paresseux et gras d'un soleil de province" (p. 205).

Many of the additions were designed to emphasize further the Duchess's sarcasm or wit. Her first outburst on the subject of Madame de Cambremer is expanded on the subject of that lady's use of the word "plumatif" (p. 203). Discussing love and having just disposed of Madame Swann, the Duchess now brings in her witticism concerning Saint-Loup who may enjoy the "ivresse" but who lacked taste in the choice of his "flacon" (p. 229). An additional witticism is her remark about the dullness of Dreyfus's epistolary style (p. 239). With his increased interest in sociology, Proust picked up and expanded a brief remark in his original text: "tout le monde disait que c'était une femme très intelligente, d'une conversation spirituelle, vivant dans une petite coterie des plus intéressantes" (209:40). Directly after the original lyrical passage on the still magic effect of the name of Guermantes on the narrator, Proust introduced a digression on the entrance of "l'excellent écrivain G . . ." (p. 206) whom the Duchess greets cordially and who is the pretext for a long analytical development on the intellectual atmosphere of the Duchess's salon. The omniscient author explains that the Duchess receives great bourgeois intellectuals (note that *Grasset B* already said the same thing about the Duchess's social facsimile, Madame Leroi), always without their wives, never talks to them about anything but the most trivial matters but also regales them with her wit on these trivial subjects. Furthermore, she is also well educated and can quote Hugo and Lamartine, if need be. Other additions continue to emphasize the intellectual character of the Duchess's salon. By a somewhat artificial transition, after the remarks about the frog-like appearance of Madame Leroi, the Duchess has the opportunity to say that she wishes she knew Bergotte and the narrator realizes that he missed his chance on the occasion of La Berma's gala performance when he might have greeted the writer ostentatiously and thus might have made an impression on the Duchess (but nothing had previously been said about Bergotte being present). A further addition, placed at random (Madame de Villeparisis is talking about gentlemen's hats), has the Belgian chargé d'affaires exclaim that Madame de Guermantes is "vraiment étonnante" (p. 213) because she is always surrounded by the most interesting men in a social gathering, even by Pierre Loti and Edmond Rostand (p. 213). The last sociological addition is the Duchess's remark, apropos of Dreyfus, that she is tired of the whole thing and objects to having to frequent people just because they are anti-Dreyfusard (p. 238).

In *Grasset B,* the Duc de Guermantes wears no halo. The adjective "malicieux" (p. 223) is immediately applied to him. He enters with "un sourire permanent de bon roi d'Yvetot légèrement pompette" *(p. 224).* The additions change the nature of this comic opera character. On the same page with the King of Yvetot there is an addition in a totally different, and hence discordant, tone in which he is presented as being as proud of his riches and noble station as he is of his "succès de femmes, qui faisaient le malheur de la sienne" (p. 224). Other new passages referred to his brutality towards his wife (p. 235) and his neglect of her (p. 254). Another addition says that his "bizarre vocabulaire permettait à la fois aux gens du monde de dire qu'il n'était pas un sot et aux gens de lettres de le trouver le pire des imbéciles" (p. 227). In the old text, one of the Duke's principal functions was to stimulate his wife's repartee; thus it was he who goaded her on to produce the "troupeau de vaches." On the other hand, his own language is far from witty, as witness for example his repetition of the trite expression: "quand on s'appelle Saint-Loup, on n'est pas dreyfusard, que voulez-vous que je vous dise!" (235:21). This led Proust to introduce a new page of generalization on the laws of language which lead a duke to use bourgeois expressions that get into his speech "par un hasard comparable à celui qui fit germer en France une mauvaise herbe d'Amérique dont la graine prise après la peluche d'une couverture de voyage était tombée sur un talus de chemin de fer" (p. 236). On the other hand, the haughty duke will not take linguistic lessons from others when, in the old text, the archivist tries to teach him the word "mentalité." When the historian defends the word, saying that he has heard it used in his "cercle Volney" *(p. 237),* the Duke replies with a feigned humility, which deceives no one, that he is only a member of the Jockey and could not be expected to know the word. It is not quite certain whether the Duke is serious when he reports that Dreyfus is the lover of the wife of the Minister of War. It is also doubtful whether he really means it when he says that he is not a "féodal" like his brother Gilbert and that "je me promènerais avec un nègre s'il était de mes amis" *(p. 238).*

He comes back to his annoyance with Saint-Loup, repeats the *Mater Semita* accusation which is going the rounds of the Jockey Club, and proclaims that there is really no Jewish blood in his family. When, in new text, his wife interrupts to place the witticism about Dreyfus, the Duke makes sure that everyone has heard it, then finds it smart to say: "Je ne fais aucun cas de l'esprit" (p. 239). Aware that he has perhaps not made his point with the Duc de Guermantes, Proust puts in an addition the preposterous remarks by the narrator who says to Charlus apropos of Saint-Loup: "Il est en train de parler avec cet idiot de duc de Guermantes" (p. 278). Proust tries to compensate for the total awkwardness of this remark by explaining in a parenthesis that the narrator had forgotten that Saint-Loup had told him, at Balbec, that Charlus and the Duke were brothers. It is as though Bloch and the narrator had suddenly traded characters. As the narrator is leaving, in a new passage there is a final vision of the Duke in a superb Olympian pose: "Il me semblait voir cette statue de Jupiter Olympien que Phidias, dit-on, avait faite tout en or" (p. 284).

Saint-Loup appears only momentarily at his great-aunt's tea party. After he has made the effort to bring the narrator and the Duchess together, the narrator thanks him profusely. In the final text, these thanks are cut apart by a new passage in which Saint-Loup says that he must dine with Bloch because he is afraid that he has offended him. The passage seems to have the primary purpose of giving the narrator an opportunity to say a final word concerning Bloch: "Le dénigrement furieux était souvent chez Bloch l'effet d'une vive sympathie qu'il avait cru qu'on ne lui rendait pas" (p. 275). In the old text, Saint-Loup confides in the narrator that he has changed his mind and intends to get the necklace after all and to take it to Rachel. A new text then follows which is surprisingly unfinished since it contains twice, only five lines apart, the same words: "ignorait presque toutes ces infidélités" (p. 282). The passage itself is somewhat paradoxical because it begins with the statement that Rachel has refused the necklace after all and that she must be altruistic because she is capable of "charités insensées" (p. 282). However, the passage continues with a generalization on "cocottes" who ruin men having the misfortune to be in love with them. The passage ends with the remark that Saint-Loup avoids certain men in Paris: "c'est qu'ils avaient été ruinés par Rachel" (p. 283). This final remark seems to indicate clearly that Proust intends the entire passage to be a denigration of Rachel in keeping with the passages previously noted.

It is in his role as a son that a new aspect of Saint-Loup is revealed. Saint-Loup's mother, Madame de Marsantes (occasionally Madame de Saint-Loup in the old text), seems to resemble Madame de Villeparisis in that, although she is capable of aristocratic haughtiness, she is essentially a nice person. As soon as she enters, *Grasset B* refers to her as "un être supérieur, d'une bonté, d'une résignation angéliques" *(p. 250)*. This, says the narrator, is especially astonishing because she is the sister of the Duc de Guermantes and of Charlus, and he goes on at length to express his incredulity that someone bearing the same physical resemblance could be "un grand esprit sans aucune tare de sottise, une sainte sans aucune entrave de cette brutalité" (250:40). A lengthy addition repeated the same characterization but with some significant reservations. "Cette bonté s'accompagnait d'une feinte timidité" (p. 251), remarks the narrator concerning her behavior with him, and he goes on to imply that her exaggerated pronunciation of the word "*hon*-neur" is really an affectation. Likewise, after describing her charities to the poor around her château, he adds: "Elle tenait à faire un mariage colossalement riche à Robert" so as to "jouer à la grande dame, c'est-à-dire, pour une part, jouer la simplicité" (p. 252). The same addition, after an interruption to bring in Madame Swann (who figures in various pieces of new text), includes Madame de Marsantes's defense of Odette, who is attacked by the Duchess. However, the defense has little meaning for, in the next breath, Madame de Marsantes swears that she will never again frequent Lady Israëls (at whose house, we recall, she met Odette) or any other "personne de cette nation" (p. 253). In these additions, Proust has clearly reduced Madame de Marsantes from the rank of saint which she had in *Grasset B*. However, when he later returns to her in her role as a mother, the portrait is again sympathetic, both in the original version and in the additions. In *Grasset B*, Madame de Marsantes is all tenderness for her son who is annoyed by her attitude *(p. 271)*. Somewhat later the narrator is a third party to their conversations and is so aware of Saint-Loup's unkindness to his mother that he wants to tell her that her son "avait pour elle infiniment plus d'affection que pour moi" *(p. 277)*. When Saint-Loup is about to leave, there is an addition in which the narrator explains that Saint-Loup is not like so many sons who take pleasure in humiliating their mothers in public but that he is brutal with her because he is upset about his mistress. Then the text of *Grasset B* reappears and Saint-Loup does take brutal leave of his mother; when she says that it is not "gentil" of him not to give her any of his time, he replies: "gentil ou non, c'est ainsi" *(p. 280)*. In an addition following this, the narrator says that he would now have done anything to break up Saint-Loup's liaison (p. 281). Nevertheless, in a final revision, Proust does not forget that he has radically recast the character of Saint-Loup's mother and he tries to reconcile the conflicting points of view; she is completely sincere in all that she says about Robert, but, in taking leave, she loses her sincerity "pour redevenir grande dame" (p. 283).

Among the minor characters who underwent alterations, there was the historian, Monsieur Pierre, who acquired a piece of Proust's own biography in the form of "insomnies nerveuses" which prevented him from sleeping; when his research forced him to go out, he did so "en se campant artificiellement debout dans une redingote comme un homme de Wells" (p. 193). The first portion of the Legrandin story passed without alteration from *Grasset B* into the final text but the second portion, in which the narrator spoke to him, was expanded by a long comment on the "bête immonde et inconnue" (p. 204) which comes out when we are angry. There was also an alteration in the text: in the final text the narrator says that he had no intention of offending Legrandin, whereas the original suggests that he might have had such an intention.

Another minor character occupied an inordinate amount of space and, already in *Grasset B,* was the subject of a long digression. He was the Prince of Faffenheim-Munsterburg-Weinigen, the German prime minister, who announced his arrival just after the Duchesse de Guermantes had finally spoken to the narrator and whom Norpois went to escort in with suitable ceremony. Having nothing whatever to do with the action, the anecdote of the Prince's candidacy for the Institute fills eight pages and is totally outside the time pattern of the surrounding text. The anecdote, which reutilizes the brief allusion in *Grasset A* to the narrator's sojourn in Germany, begins with a lyrical introduction provoked by the similarity between the Prince's name and the "petite ville d'eaux" (p. 256) where the narrator went during his childhood. Over the years, the Prince made three attempts to persuade Norpois to support his candidacy; the first time he gave him the "cordon de Saint-André," the second time he wrote flattering remarks about him in the *Revue des deux mondes,* and the third time he simply said that he would be honored to be invited to tea by Madame de Villeparisis. Whether he ever succeeded in his candidacy will never be known. [55] In the middle of this long anecdote, Proust introduced two new pages of text. The first paragraph of the new text developed an amusing analogy between diplomats threatening war or peace, while seated on a bench of the Kurgarten, and similar strategy on the part of Faffenheim and Norpois. The second paragraph continued the analogy in the domain of "cocottes" and then went on with war and pacifism. In conclusion, Proust picked up a remark at the beginning of the *Grasset B* version and discoursed on the narrator's astonishment at hearing the prime minister say, with the accent of an Alsatian concierge: "Ponchour, Matame la marquise" (p. 263).

A curious leitmotif ran through the entire tea party. It began with Madame de Villeparisis's anecdote involving the wearing of one's hat on the occasion of a visit from the king. Still in *Grasset B*, Argencourt, Châtellerault and the Baron de Guermantes bring in their tall silk hats and put them on the floor beside their chairs. Even though no one seems to have asked her, Madame de Villeparisis explains: "c'est une nouvelle habitude qu'ont ces messieurs de poser leurs chapeaux à terre" *(p. 213).* Thereupon the historian reminds Madame de Villeparisis that she has just

---

[55] In a passage crossed out in the typescript of *Grasset B,* Norpois does assure the German statesman that he will soon be elected to the Institute (situated Pléiade 283:21). In this passage the German is referred to as "Prince Tchiguine."

told a story about hats, but no one tries to establish a connection between the historic and the contemporary custom. When Norpois, summoned by Madame de Villeparisis to talk to Bloch, enters, he picks up a hat in the antechamber and brings it in with him, to give the impression that he has arrived from the outside, whereas he really lives with the Marquise *(p. 221)*. Nothing happened to this particular hat in *Grasset B* but Proust corrected the text to read "que je crus reconnaître" (p. 221) and then, in the addition in which he made the narrator converse with Norpois, he arranged to have the narrator gently take away the hat from the ex-ambassador because "c'était le mien" (p. 222). In another addition much later, the narrator, while talking to Madame Swann, carefully keeps his eye on his hat "parmi tous ceux qui se trouvaient sur le tapis" (p. 271) and, while doing so, notes that one of the hats has the initial "G" surmounted by a ducal crown. This anticipates another addition six pages later where the narrator, being pursued by Charlus, notices that the latter has picked up the hat with the "G." When, a little further on, he accuses Charlus of taking the wrong hat, the latter says: "Vous voulez m'empêcher de prendre mon chapeau?" (p. 277). We will never have a reasonable explanation as to why Charlus had a "G" in his hat and can only guess. This hat game seems to have the purpose of introducing stage play where there is too much dialogue but it might also be a *preparation* for the dramatic scene, outside the limits of the Grasset text, where the narrator stamps on Charlus's hat.

If it was intended to enliven the action, as the "vin d'Asti" had succeeded in doing in "Combray," the hat game was no more effective than the introduction of a sequence of new episodes involving Madame Swann. There is no ongoing plot in these episodes which interest the reader only because Madame Swann is a familiar character. After two pages of new text on Madame de Marsantes, Proust suddenly, still in new text, switches back to Madame de Villeparisis who is warning the Duchesse de Guermantes that she has invited Madame Swann. The omniscient author then explains that, "craignant que les origines de son mari ne se tournassent contre elle" (p. 252), Madame Swann has become a violent anti-Semite and a nationalist, thanks to which she is now beginning to be received in society. In the remainder of this addition, the Duchess says that she does not want to meet Madame Swann and also expresses indignation that her aunt should think that she has anything to do with Lady Israëls. At this point, Madame de Marsantes makes the remark about Lady Israëls already noted. When Madame Swann finally enters ten pages later, the omnipotent author establishes a connection between her arrival and the Duchesse de Guermantes's departure. Saint-Loup also tells the narrator that he does not want to meet her because she is an "ancienne grue" (p. 264) and a nationalist. Again the omniscient author interrupts to say that, "à cause des conséquences qu'il [le fait] devait avoir beaucoup plus tard," he must tell about Morel, the son of his great-uncle's valet. The Morel digression relates to the surrounding text only because the valet's son brings the narrator a photograph of Elstir's *Miss Sacripant.* Getting back to Madame Swann, we see Monsieur de Charlus lavishing his attentions on her, as he is accustomed to do with beautiful women. Now another long digression informs us that Charlus is not on good terms with his aunt and the omniscient author tells the anecdote of the three thousand francs which his aunt borrowed from him and of which he demanded the return in a telegram. Now the narrator attempts to speak to Madame Swann but she is rather distant, not wishing to have to introduce the narrator to Madame de Marsantes and to Charlus. So the narrator greets Charlus on his own and, for a moment, the text picks up a segment of *Grasset B.* Then the narrator begins to converse with Madame Swann, who has gestured to him to come over. He now seems to have been infected by the pernicious habit, so common in this level of society, of saying unpleasant things about other people. Thus he does not hesitate to talk about Norpois with Madame Swann, calls him "sympathique" (p. 271) but also "une peste" according to Saint-Loup; and then Madame Swann reciprocates by telling the narrator that, at a dinner given by the Princesse de Guermantes, Norpois called the narrator "un flatteur à moitié hystérique" (p. 271). This leads to a page-long generalization on "cet écart entre notre image selon qu'elle est dessinée par nous-même ou par autrui" (p. 272). Finally the narrator tries to get Madame Swann to talk about the Duchess but she refuses to do so. That ends her appearance at the tea party. Her presence has not in any way improved the structure or heightened the action.

It is only near the end of the tea party that a definite pattern of action emerges, but it is a pattern which reaches beyond the end of *Grasset B.* In *Grasset B,* Charlus had entered, structurally speaking, at a very awkward moment since it was during the capital scene where the Duchesse de Guermantes speaks to the narrator. In the original version, the narrator sees him in the back of the room talking to Argencourt while displaying the same stereotyped smile already observed on the face of his brother, the Duc de Guermantes, and while sweeping the room with those mysterious glances which the narrator first noted at Balbec. The narrator does not dare speak to him. In the final version, while Saint-Loup is telling the narrator that he does not want to speak to Madame Swann, he suddenly exclaims: "Tiens, voici mon oncle Palamède" (p. 264). Nothing more is said about Charlus at this point; four pages later he is talking with Madame Swann; after this comes the anecdote of the money borrowed from Madame de Villeparisis and then finally a rewritten version of the original description of Charlus as seen by the narrator at a distance (269:39). This is followed by another portion of the original text of *Grasset B* which was formerly quite far from the preceding text (in the original version it came immediately after the departure of the Duchesse de Guermantes); in this portion of text, the narrator gets up his courage and does, in fact, greet the Baron de Charlus, who gives him his hand as though expecting him to kiss his "anneau épiscopal" (p. 270). Much later the Baron astonishes the narrator by pursuing him as he is about to go into the next room with Saint-Loup. Charlus wants to leave with the narrator who, however, had no intention of leaving just then. In *Grasset B,* the narrator merely says that he must speak first to Saint-Loup. Rereading himself, Proust felt a need for more action at this point since this was the beginning, at last, of a real plot sequence. Into a short space, he crammed perhaps too much action: the hat with the "G," the remark about the idiotic Duc de Guermantes, and Charlus's reproaches for the narrator's having participated in an orgy with Saint-Loup. Furthermore, the material was so badly articulated with the surrounding text that the reader does not realize immediately that the narrator is back talking to Saint-Loup (p. 278).

The original conversation between the narrator and Charlus, once they have left the tea party, is a masterpiece of style and logic and retains a certain dramatic impact because the reader understands the importance of what Charlus is saying for the future course of the action. Charlus begins by saying that he has serious doubts whether the narrator is worthy of his interest. The narrator protests that he is indeed unworthy but he adds: "quant à mon plaisir, croyez bien que tout ce qui me viendra de vous m'en causera un très grand" (p. 285). Suddenly Charlus's haughtiness changes into affection but at the same time he has the intense look which he had at Balbec. Then Charlus begins to talk of his lofty social station and about his vast knowledge of "les dessous de la politique européenne" *(p. 287)*. Next he alludes to "grands chagrins," to the death of his wife, and to the unworthiness of his son (the son vanishes in the final text and is replaced by "jeunes parents" [p. 291]). He suggests: "Peut-être . . . me mettrais-je enfin à faire des choses intéressantes où vous seriez de moitié" *(p. 291)*. Suddenly he withdraws his arm because he has noticed Argencourt coming down the street and the narrator understands that he does not want to be seen by the Belgian. When Charlus resumes the conversation, he tells the narrator that his first sacrifice must be to give up going into society. He advises him to have a mistress, if he wants, calling him a "jeune polisson qui allez avoir bientôt besoin de vous faire raser" *(p. 295)*, which is an interesting commentary on the age of the narrator. He even says that the narrator may keep Saint-Loup as a friend. The narrator makes no comment; Charlus apparently expects none and jumps into a cab.

Charlus's behavior in getting into the cab was already eccentric enough to make his madness quite obvious. However, Proust was not satisfied that he had made his point and, directly after an expanded paragraph on Charlus's lofty social station, he made the mad Baron interrupt himself "pour me poser des questions sur Bloch" (p. 287). At first Charlus is only anti-Semitic, refers to Bloch as an "étranger" and continues the same reasoning concerning Dreyfus whom he would consider guilty only "s'il avait trahi la Judée" (p. 288). Suddenly, however, he resorts to "des mots affreux et presque fous" (p. 288); he asks whether Bloch could arrange for him to witness a circumcision or could rent a hall to present a dramatic scene in which Bloch would appear as David and the father as Goliath, or in which Bloch would simply beat on "sa carogne de mère." Proust makes it quite clear that he has inserted this passage to illustrate "la bonté et la méchanceté dans un même cœur" (p. 289). Bloch *père* chancing to pass (somewhat a repetition of the Argencourt episode which is yet to happen in the final text), the narrator offers to introduce him but that only makes Charlus more furious. At this point the omniscient author interrupts to explain that Bloch *père* is greeting Madame Sazerat profusely because he has heard that she is a Dreyfusard although anti-Semitic at the same time. Resuming his discussion of the Dreyfus affair, Charlus now objects to its effect on high society, and the narrator tells him that his ideas are similar to those of the Duchesse de Guermantes. When Charlus seems to imply that the narrator cannot possibly be acquainted with the Duchess, the narrator reminds him of "la soirée de l'Opéra où il avait paru vouloir se cacher de moi" (p. 290). The text has become increasingly sketchy and enigmatic; it almost seems to be breaking down, but it will be rescued, of course, by the remaining parts of *Grasset B*, plus some additions which, although disruptive, are still logical within themselves.

Some additions were grafted, without detriment, onto the original text. Up to the beginning of the Bloch interruption, the text had been significantly expanded and improved without the least sacrifice of logic. Directly after what we have just called a breakdown of the text, there occurred what we consider an excellent addition when Charlus begins to refer to a *franc-maçonnerie* to which four European sovereigns belong. He does not explain what this is but says that some people regard it as a kind of illness of which it would be folly, however, to cure anyone.[56] Charlus is no longer speaking madly but rather eva-

[56] The historical background of this allusion to sodomy in European court circles has, of course, been treated in detail by Robert Vigneron (loc. cit. note 31).

sively, and this fits well onto the *Grasset B* text in which he states that he and the narrator could do great things together in the field of international diplomacy. Another good addition occurs after Charlus says that the first sacrifice for the narrator must be society; in the new text he goes on to say that he alone has the "Sésame" (p. 293) to the Hôtel de Guermantes and that the narrator's presence at the Villeparisis tea party was an "indécence."

Nevertheless, in spite of the success of some of these additions, it would seem that Proust is no longer sensitive to, or interested in, the orderliness of his original text. After the Argencourt episode, for no apparent reason, the narrator says: "La duchesse de Guermantes semble très intelligente" (p. 293). This remark out of context, as it were, and provoking an extensive reply from Charlus on the lack of importance of the Duchess, becomes a new introduction to Charlus's admonition to the narrator to give up society. Initially it is a bad addition but ultimately it is a good one. The most disruptive addition, since it is not in accord with the tone of the surrounding text, is Charlus's allusion to the indecency of the narrator's being at the Villeparisis tea party. Instead of reacting in depth, the narrator merely asks Charlus to tell him about the Villeparisis family, which he obligingly does by explaining the Thirion matter in detail. Even the final addition to the Grasset proofs is bothersome when Proust introduces, in parentheses, a long linguistic comment on the word "truqueur" (p. 295), but at least it does not change the tone or meaning of the surrounding text.

This is, of course, the abrupt end of the *Grasset Proofs.* In the opening pages of this commentary, we said that Proust probably stopped here because he had run out of text. Later, speaking of *Grasset B,* we hypothesized, on the basis of a letter from Proust to Grasset, that there was perhaps some more nearly finished manuscript (perhaps not yet typed) going beyond that point because of the extracts published in the July 1914 number of the *Nouvelle Revue Française.* Painter is a little more categorical about this when he says: "He added [to the *N. R. F.* extracts] the episode of the grandmother's stroke in the Champs-Elysées and her illness, which he had hitherto intended to place in his third volume between the Princesse de Guermantes's soirée and the last visit to Balbec. He had now decided that it should come immediately after Madame de Villeparisis's matinée and form the conclusion of the second volume, although he had not included it in the material sent to Grasset."[57] We do not know on what authority Painter bases this statement.

In this commentary, it is obvious that we have frequently been in disagreement with Albert Feuillerat who, in his *Comment Marcel Proust a composé son roman,* was the first to study the *Grasset Proofs.*[58] Exactly one half of Feuillerat's total study was devoted to what comes after the *Grasset Proofs* and, this being outside the scope of our commentary, we shall say nothing about his ultimate conclusions but shall stop with his preliminary conclusions, based on *Grasset B,* which are found in the middle of his book. Feuillerat's most sweeping conclusion regarding *Grasset B* is that there is a striking dichotomy in Proust himself: that an enthusiastic, lyrical young man, aged thirty-four and believing fervently in the subconscious, wrote *Grasset B;* but that a disabused, cynical and prematurely old man, aged forty-four and interested only in the wisdom which he could amass before dying, made the corrections and additions (cf. Feuillerat, p. 112). In the course of our discussion, we have already rejected this theory on the ground that the *Grasset Proofs* (including *Grasset A* which Feuillerat never saw) do not distinguish between the two Prousts who are, one might say, both present and that, although the additions seem to be more readily from the hand of the "old" Proust, there is still much of the new text which, if we did not know better, we might have attributed to the "young" Proust. Furthermore, we do not agree with Feuillerat's contention that, in *Grasset B,* "tout se suit, s'enchaîne et l'on n'éprouve aucune difficulté à saisir les idées dans leur développement naturel" (F., p. 110). Such a statement is unjustified in view of

---

[57] George D. Painter, *Proust: The Later Years,* p. 215.

[58] We cannot refrain from expressing surprise when Feuillerat says, apropos of Norpois: "Il prend Bergson pour un romancier . . ." (op. cit., p. 101). The reference which he gives in the earlier edition corresponds to vol. II, p. 222 of the Pléiade text. There is no mention of Bergson in the *Grasset Proofs* and none in the Pléiade until vol. II, p. 984.

the unfinished and often confused state of the original text to which Feuillerat, himself, gives testimony in other parts of his book. All one can say is that Proust often started with a simple text which he then proceeded to make more complicated by his additions; what we perceive about his work habits in *Jean Santeuil* and in the *Grasset Proofs* would preclude any belief that there ever could have been a simple, straightforward lyrical Ur-Proust. In fact, one would expect the exact opposite to be true in the case of an author who places such emphasis on the subconscious. With another of Feuillerat's strong statements we cannot disagree, however, when he says: "Le discontinu du développement proustien — pour employer une expression à la mode — n'a nullement été voulu par l'auteur. C'est l'effet d'un pur accident, ou plutôt c'est la conséquence inévitable de la dangereuse méthode de revision adoptée" (F., p. 109-110). Now that we are able to delineate with absolute accuracy two levels of text in the *Recherche* for the part corresponding to the *Grasset Proofs,* there is no doubt that accident, at least as frequently as design, has shaped Proust's text. Even Feuillerat acknowledges that there was also design when he says: "Si, dans la façon dont il posait les pièces, Proust travaillait à la manière d'un myope, j'entends que, regardant de trop près l'endroit à raccommoder, il perdait de vue les passages voisins, il gardait au contraire une idée très précise de la direction générale suivant laquelle il guidait l'expansion de son roman" (F., p. 110).

It has not been our purpose to prove anything in this commentary but rather to furnish a preliminary guide for comparing the *Grasset Proofs* with the final text. We consider that the more important part of this work, by far, is the tabulation of variants which follows. Other readers will discover different things in the process of comparison. But it does seem obvious that any Proust scholar, seeking to interpret the meaning of the *Recherche* or to describe its structure, would be unwise not to take this evidence into account. The *Grasset Proofs* are of great help in this effort to penetrate meaning and structure, but obviously the picture will not be complete until the vast supply of Proust *inédits* is sorted out.

If it is permissible to reach a conclusion concerning the real significance of these *Grasset Proofs*, it is that Proust's greatest effort in rewriting went to the improvement of his text *as a novel.* He was less concerned with transposing his personal reality into his work, at this stage of his writing, than he was with making what he wrote interesting and readable. Someday someone will dare to say how much of the *Recherche* is fiction and how much reality. We venture to suggest that the balance will be more heavily weighted in favor of fiction.

What we have left unsaid is any mention of stylistic problems as they became apparent in the study of these texts. That will be for someone else to work out. The supreme problem might be, usurping a title already used, to describe *The Mind of Proust.*

Part II

VARIANTS

CONCERNING THE VARIANTS

Sources. The documents from which these variants are taken are all available in the Fonds Proust of the Bibliothèque Nationale. What we have called *Grasset A* corresponds to *Dossier 29, Du côté de chez Swann, Epreuves corrigées,* and to *Dossier 30, ibid., Epreuves non corrigées.* Since *Dossier 30* has a more complete text and has not been cut apart and rearranged as is the case with *Dossier 29,* we have used *Dossier 29* only when it contained some of the parts missing from *Dossier 30.* We are concerned only with reestablishing, insofar as possible, the total printed text of the *Grasset Proofs.* Subsequent corrections do not fall within our domain, except as we have confronted the final text of the Pléiade edition with the Grasset version. In cases where there were still gaps in *Grasset A,* we have referred to *Dossiers 23-25, Du côté de chez Swann, Première Dactylographie avec corrections autographes,* and to *Dossiers 26-28, ibid., Deuxième Dactylographie avec corrections autographes.* As we have previously stated, the *Première Dactylographie,* with the exception of some pages which seem to have been confused with the *Deuxième Dactylographie,* was the manuscript used for printing *Grasset A.* Except in one instance on which we comment at the appropriate place in the variants, it seems highly unlikely that there is any difference, other than an occasional printer's error, between the *dactylographie* and the Grasset version. The missing parts thus reconstituted are as follows: (25:33. Cette opposition> 27:12. <C'est bien lui) (23:14. Les soirs> 27:13. <comme un peintre) (29:34. Je pense que Françoise> 32:28. <en sommes l'âme) (31:35. <arrière-pensée, sans> 32:21. <en me prêchant) (146:25. <jamais remarqué> 157:28. <plaisir de la possession) (222:28. <l'idéal est inaccessible> 223:7. <le contraire) (240:39. <comme tout ce qui> 238:23. <voulait le manger). In identifying these missing parts taken from the *dactylographie,* it should be noted that the *beginning* and *end* references for each of these parts delineate the text in terms of the variants hereinafter and not in terms of the Pléiade edition which has changed the order of some of the passages concerned.

Grasset B corresponds to *Dossiers 35,I-35-II, Le Côté de Guermantes, Epreuves Grasset 1914.* To fill gaps in *Grasset B,* we have consulted *Dossier 34, Le Côté de Guermantes, Dactylographie avec corrections autographes,* which is the manuscript for the section of *Grasset B* corresponding to Pléiade, vol. II, pp. 9-296. Proust's handwritten instructions to the printer indicate that the portion of *Grasset B* corresponding to *A l'ombre des jeunes filles en fleurs* was printed from a corrected set of proofs for *Grasset A* which have not survived. Since there are no lacunae in this portion, the disappearance of these proofs is of no immediate consequence to us. As for the portion of *Grasset B* to which *Dossier 34* corresponds, the reconstituted texts are as follows: (17:42. Ah! Combray> 19:30. <De bien bon monde) (107:41. <ou Alfred de Vigny> p. 118. <de Bernard Palissy) (108:4. <échelle à laquelle nous voyons> 128:13. <acteurs du théâtre* Français).

Method of Presentation. The variants which follow are identified in terms of the pagination of the Pléiade edition (*A la recherche du temps perdu,* 3 vol., Paris, Gallimard, 1954). Identification is by page and line of the Pléiade (thus 314:18, for example, signifies «page 314, line 18»). By passing back and forth from the variants to the Pléiade edition one may read consecutively the original text of *Grasset A* and *Grasset B.* The texts thus delineated fall into three categories:

1. *Texts of* Grasset A *or* B *which survive in the Pléiade edition.* These texts are identified by a reference giving the *beginning* and the *end* of the delineated passage (for example:

3:1. Longtemps> 3:5. <m'éveillait>). Sometimes the beginning or the end of the delineated passage may blend into a *major variant,* but this will never create a problem of delineation. In many cases, the delineated passage will be followed by a sequence of *minor variants* (in brackets) which do not appreciably change the sense of the passage, although they must be substituted in the delineated passage in order to reconstruct exactly the original Grasset text.

2. *Major variants.* These also are situated in their proper sequence expressed in terms of the pagination of the Pléiade edition. They will be recognized immediately by the fact that only the beginning of the passage has a Pléiade reference. Some *major variants* are passages which have no equivalent text whatever in the Pléiade and, in these cases, the identifying page and line have been assigned in a manner which indicates the relative position in terms of the surrounding text. Other *major variants* are passages which have equivalents in the Pléiade but which still differ so much from the final text that it is expedient only to quote them in their entirety.

3. *Additions found only in the Pléiade.* These are identified by page and line only (for example: {136:5-142:39}). The correct beginnings and ends of such passages can easily be determined in terms of the Grasset texts, as delineated, which surround them. It has not been possible to delineate minor additions of this kind, but they can also be distinguished, if necessary, by a comparison of the *minor variants* with the final Pléiade text.

Punctuation and Orthography

We have sought to reproduce accurately the punctuation (or often the absence thereof) of the *Grasset Proofs.* However, we have been unable to devise an efficient method for calling eccentricities in punctuation to the reader's attention. The reader must therefore assume that, if the punctuation is peculiar, it is intentionally so on our part. Proust's use of paragraphing, as we have had occasion to remark in the "Commentary," appears to be altogether arbitrary most of the time. Naturally, whenever a *major variant* included an *alinéa,* we have also included it in transcribing the passage. The reader will often note that the paragraphing distinguished in this manner differs from the paragraphing of the Pléiade. However, our method of setting forth the variants precludes giving complete information about paragraphing and anyone seriously interested in this problem will have to consult the original documents in the Fonds Proust. As for orthography, we have "respected" that of the original *Grasset Proofs* but have called attention to eccentricities by the use of an asterisk.

Symbols Used Hereinafter

* The asterisk signifies *sic.*

□ Indicates a *major variant* which is of special interest because it has no equivalent in the Pléiade or differs radically from the equivalent text.

△ Indicates a passage which moved when Proust rearranged his text. Since these passages are out of order in terms of the Pléiade pagination, a cross-reference system is provided to locate them.

(B-A) This abbreviation, used in the section (after variant 434:28) where *Grasset B* overlaps *Grasset A,* signifies that the *Grasset B* text completely replaces the corresponding *Grasset A* text. Variants from *Grasset B* are given as footnotes between pages 332 and 501.

Les Intermittences du Cœur

LE TEMPS PERDU

PREMIÈRE PARTIE

CAMBRAY*

3:1. Longtemps> **3:5.** <m'éveillait;>

□**3:5.** <je voulais jeter le journal que je croyais avoir encore en mains et souffler ma lumière; et j'étais bien étonné de voir autour de moi une obscurité qui, douce et reposante pour mes yeux, l'était peut-être plus encore pour mon esprit, à qui elle apparaissait comme une chose sans cause, incompréhensible, comme une chose vraiment obscure, et qui lui faisait sentir l'obscurité intérieure où il était lui aussi plongé.

3:24. Je me demandais> **3:30.** <qu'il doit donner à des lieux nouveaux, à des actes inaccoutumés, au vent froid sous les étoiles qui désormais toute sa vie, dans ces claires soirées qui suivent les averses réveillera en lui le désir du départ, à la causerie récente et aux adieux sous la lampe étrangère qui le suivent encore en voltigeant dans la solitude et le silence de la nuit, à la douceur prochaine du retour.

4:5. J'appuyais> **4:23.** <de goûter> [4:6. <qui, toujours pleines et fraîches,> 4:9. <en voyage et qui a dû> 4:12. <domestiques de l'hôtel seront> 4:15. <entendre un pas; le pas se rapproche puis s'éloigne. 4:19. <il lui faudra>]

□**4:23.** <de goûter (comme un pot de confitures appelé momentanément à ma vague conscience qui lui permettrait de constater qu'il fait noir dans le buffet et que le bois joue) le sommeil

où était plongée la chambre, le tout dormant* dont j'étais une petite>

4:26. <petite partie... **5:17.** <se rompre. [4:30. <mon grand-père me tirait *par> 4:35. <de mon grand-père, mais> 5:12. Un jeune homme qui dort, les bras répandus, tient>]

□**5:17.** <se rompre. Qu'il se soit endormi brusquement, tourné sur un côté où ne repose pas d'ordinaire la flexion de ses membres, aussitôt les myriades des étoiles s'échappent, tombent à terre et s'éteignent, quoique la nuit commence à peine et qu'elles brillent de leur plus vif éclat dans le ciel; s'il s'éveille alors dans ce premier somme il ne saura plus l'heure, se figurera que le matin est proche.

5:17. Que vers le matin, au contraire, après> **5:33.** <milieu de la nuit je ne savais pas où je me trouvais. [5:21. <son réveil il estimera qu'il vient à peine de se coucher. 5:27. <l'espace, et quand il rouvrira les paupières, avant d'y voir clair il se croira couché quelques mois>] {5:32-6:2}

6:3. Peut-être> **6:26.** <face au mur> [6:15. <plusieurs des lieux où> 6:17. <tourbillonnaient dans l'obscurité. Et avant même qu'aucune de ces chambres qu'il évoquait eut* permis à sa pensée, qui hésitait au seuil des temps et des formes, d'identifier le logis en rapprochant les circonstances, de choisir le pays et l'année, lui, —mon corps, —se rappelait pour chacun le genre>]

□**6:26.** <face au mur dans un petit lit de fer, et aussitôt, je me disait*: «Il va falloir me lever et allumer la lampe si je veux que mon devoir soit fait avant l'heure de la classe». Puis renaissait le souvenir d'une autre attitude, le mur filait dans une autre direction, emmenait le lit avec lui et me faisant tourner d'un demi-cercle, j'étais à la campagne chez ma grand'tante morte depuis des années; et mon corps>

6:30. <et mon corps> □**6:35.** <Sienne, le crucifix à la tête du lit, l'odeur du bénitier et du rameau, l'haleine de l'alcôve, dans ma chambre à coucher de Combray, chez mes grands-parents, en ces jours lointains (qu'en ce moment je me figurais actuels sans me les représenter exactement et que je reverrais mieux tout à l'heure quand je serais tout à fait éveillé), où il y avait encore des chambres à coucher et des grands* parents, alors

que chaque sentiment avait son caractère exclusif comme chaque chose avait son temps et sa place, où l'on n'aimait pas ses parents parce qu'ils étaient intelligents ou agréables, mais parce qu'ils étaient vos parents, où l'on n'allait pas dormir parce que l'on en avait envie, mais parce que c'était l'heure d'aller dormir et où il fallait, durant la longue cérémonie du déshabiller, goûter jusqu'à la lie le renoncement aux autres qui bavardaient en bas, l'acceptation de se coucher et la volonté de trouver le sommeil dans le grand lit exhaussé où l'on montait par deux degrés s'anéantir sous le baldaquin, entre les rideaux bientôt refermés de reps rouge aux bandes de velours frappé de même couleur; —dans ces temps où, quand on était malade, la vieille médecine vous laissait expier plusieurs jours sous vos couvertures et quelques couvre-pieds ajoutés, la faute d'avoir pris froid, et livré aux soins immoraux et vulgaires de quelques tisanes antiques comme les fleurs des champs et la sagesse des bonnes femmes, bourrache, queue de cerise ou séné, qui vous faisaient vivement tremper votre flanelle et remplir votre pot; et sans le secours d'aucun de ces produits pervers de l'immoralité moderne, antypirine*, trional, aspirine, aussi puissants désorganisateurs des lois de la famille que du fond du «tempérament», puisqu'ils ne tendent à rien moins qu'à faire croire qu'on peut dans une certaine mesure mener, quand on est malade, la vie d'un homme bien portant, qu'on peut, après être resté couché toute la matinée, descendre une heure au soleil, causer le scandale d'une promenade en robe de chambre dans le jardin, et s'ôter ainsi toute excuse de ne pas s'être levé à l'heure réglementaire et d'avoir forcé la cuisinière à servir un double «petit déjeuner».

Mais non, je devais être dans un fauteuil; j'étais dans ma chambre chez Mme de Villeparisis, à la campagne; mon Dieu! il est au moins dix heures, on devait avoir fini de dîner! J'aurai trop prolongé la sieste que je fais tous les soirs en rentrant de promenade avec Mme de Villeparisis, avant d'endosser mon habit. Car bien des années ont passé depuis Combray, où on rentrait tous les soirs au coucher du soleil et où on se mettait au lit après dîner. C'est une autre vie, un autre genre de plaisir qu'on a chez Mme de Villeparisis à ne sortir qu'à la nuit, à suivre silencieusement au clair de la lune ces chemins où je jouais jadis au soleil et à ne rentrer dîner que plusieurs heures après, quand souvent la lune était haute dans le ciel; et la petite chambre où je me suis endormi au lieu de m'habiller pour ce dîner, de loin je l'apercevais, quand nous rentrions, éclairée à l'intérieur par la lampe, seule lumière dans la nuit; tandis qu'à Combray, dans nos retours les plus tardifs, c'étaient les nuances rouges du soleil couchant que je voyais sur le vitrage de ma fenêtre, reflets de la bande de pourpre qui s'étendait au-dessus du petit bois noir du Calvaire.

Peut-être me suis-je endormi après dîner dans le jardin de Combray ou au fond d'une barque à Querqueville. Pourtant je ne me sens pas en plein air et n'entends pas le bruit de l'eau. **7:14.** Ces évocations> □**7:19.** <nous montre le cinématographe. Parfois c'était un seul de ces lieux où je ne me trouvais pas, dont venait me visiter quelque réminiscence, comme une sensation de jour tombant d'en haut par une lucarne, ou bien d'être adossé au bruit et à l'humidité d'une courette; rêverie confuse du corps, heure d'art de la matière, embryon de vie esthétique de l'organisme qui lui aussi, comme l'esprit, n'est pas* en rapport qu'avec le présent et reste agité par l'inutile passé: comme ces animaux qui l'hiver, dans un pays du Nord, écartent de la tête en dormant la mouche imaginaire de la Provence natale qui ne revient plus voltiger que dans leurs rêves.

Ainsi, je revoyais parfois l'une, parfois l'autre des chambres que j'avais habitées dans ma vie; tantôt la chambre>

7:23. See after 8:33.

8:2. <la chambre Louis XVI> **8:33.** <habitable. [8.6. <lit; tantôt celle, petite> 8:8. <étages et revêtue> 8:12. <impitoyable «glace à pied» quadrangulaire> 8:16. <accoutumé à* un emplacement> 8:17. <prévu; —où ma>]

□ **8:33.** <habitable. Maintenant du moins, ma pensée montait sans effort jusqu'à ce plafond inaccessible et je pouvais le contempler sans connaître le désir du suicide et la tristesse de l'exil. Mon âme avait même fini par prendre si parfaitement la forme de la chambre, qu'il lui fallait subir un traitement inverse et aussi douloureux quand je couchai ensuite dans une autre, laquelle était basse de plafond.

Ainsi une à une, dans ces longues rêveries qui suivaient mes réveils, je finissais par les revoir toutes, ces chambres où j'avais vécu: chambres d'hiver où, quand>

△**7:23.** <quand on est couché> **8:1.** <pointe d'un rayon> [7:28. <numéro du *Petit Temps*, qu'on> 7:40. <refroidies; chambres d'été où l'on trouve le plaisir opposé, d'être uni> 7:42. <volets entrouverts* jette>]

□△**8:1.** <pointe d'un rayon; —chambres de château où, hiver comme été, on se sent presque en pleine nature encore, où les murs et les meubles dégagent une fraîcheur humide, parfumée et salubre, comme le parc et la futaie; et qui gardent si bien de la forêt où elles sont encloses, plutôt qu'elles n'en sont séparées, les vertus de la solitude et sa puissance d'exaltation, que l'on y marche les pieds nus, en humant des senteurs naturelles comme on ferait d'une allée d'arbres; —toutes celles que mon esprit avait oubliées et qui sans ce souvenir qu'avait retrouvé inopinément mon corps, fussent restées perdues pour moi jusqu'à ma mort et avec elle les êtres qui y étaient liés et dont l'image venait de m'être à jamais rendue.

8:34. Certes> **9:7.** <raconté. [8:41. <réveil m'avait présenté côte à côte en un instant sinon l'image distincte, du moins croire* la présence possible> 8:43. <donné à ma pensée, à ma mémoire> 9:4. <grand'tante, à Querqueville, à Paris, à Venise, ailleurs>]

□ **9:9.** Ma chambre de Combray, en dehors du moment où il fallait que je me couche, était supportable; j'étais habitué à elle. Elle ne se transfigurait que certains soirs quand, pour m'amuser, on coiffait la lampe d'une lanterne magique qui, à l'instar des premiers architectes et maîtres verriers de l'âge gothique, substituait à l'opacité des murs d'impalpables irisations, de surnaturelles apparitions multicolores, où des légendes étaient dépeintes comme dans un vitrail.

9:29. Au pas> **10:16.** <transvertébration. [9:42. <écouter avec une dignité parfaite et une tristesse mystérieuse le boniment lu à haute voix par ma cousine et qu'il> 10:5. <distinguais avec effroi le cheval surnaturel de Golo.] {10:17-10:20}

10:20. Je ne peux dire quelle tristesse me causait cette intrusion de la légende, du mystère et> **10:23.** <qu'à lui-même.

△**10:24.** <inconnu; l'influence anesthésiante de l'habitude ayant cessé, je me remettais à penser, à sentir, choses si tristes. Et j'avais hâte de courir>

10:25. Ce bouton de la porte de ma chambre, qui différait en elle pour moi de tous les autres boutons de porte du monde, semblait me l'ouvrir tout seul, sans que j'eusse besoin de le tourner> **10:30.** <à Golo.

□**10:30.** Et rien que le changement que la lanterne apportait à l'éclairage habituel de la pièce en empêchant la lampe de diffuser sa lumière, me «changeait de chambre», en somme, aussi complètement que si j'étais arrivé aux bains de mer dans un châlet inconnu;>

10:31. <de courir> **10:38.** <de scrupules. [10:32. <la bonne grosse> 10:33. <et qui ne connaissait que mes>]

□**10:38.** J'y trouvais bien du charme pourtant à ces tremblantes apparitions [*cf.* 10:17] d'arc-en-ciel qui coloraient ma chambre d'un reflet d'histoire, si ancien et si poétique; elles semblaient l'émanation mystérieuse, ces vues projetées par la lanterne magique, des infortunes légendaires qu'elles racontaient et d'un passé mérovingien. Hélas! leur vue me ferait bien mal aujourd'hui, car c'est dans un passé presque aussi profond que celui-là, dans mon enfance, qu'elles me feraient descendre, c'est de souvenirs de douleurs plus réelles que celles de Geneviève de Brabant, de fautes qui me touchent plus directement que celles de Golo, qu'elles m'étreindraient le cœur. Et je crois que si un jour, entré dans la chambre enfantine de quelque petit ami, je reconnaissais sur le mur ou sur la porte leurs belles taches lumineuses et bleues pareilles à celles que l'on voit sur les ailes de certains papillons, et qui bougent avant de disparaître comme si palpitait une dernière fois au moment de s'envoler l'aile invisible qu'elles décorent, je m'enfuirais en me couvrant les yeux. Aile inconnue aux yeux d'azur et de feu, retourne à ces ténèbres dont je suis déjà si loin. Ne m'en apporte pas mes tristesses d'alors: elles me feraient courir comme autrefois sous la lampe paisible qui s'est éteinte, vers les bras fermés à tout jamais qui seuls savent me guérir.

10:39. Après le dîner, hélas, comme on me faisait coucher de très bonne heure, j'étais> **11:7.** <volonté.» [11:4. <que vous

les rendrez robustes et énergiques, disait-elle> 11:6. <petit qui a pourtant bien besoin>]

11:7. <volonté.» Pour elle, par tous les temps, même quand la pluie faisait rage>

11:13. <faisait rage> **12:31.** <cette pièce> [11:22. <nature—de son petit pas enthousiaste et saccadé, réglé à vrai dire sur> 11:26. <stupidité de notre éducation> 11:29. <hauteur qui est toujours restée pour notre femme de chambre Françoise un désespoir> 12:8. <il n'y avait de l'ironie que> 12:18. <persécution; mais alors elles me causaient encore une si douloureuse, une si intolérable horreur, j'aurais* aimé battre ma grand'tante mais dès que j'entendais les paroles atroces «Bathilde> 12:27. <aussi un lilas poussé>]

□**12:31.** <cette pièce, sans doute parce qu'elle était la seule qu'il me fut* permis de fermer à clef, servit longtemps de refuge à toutes celles de mes occupations qui réclamaient une inviolable solitude: la lecture, la rêverie, les larmes et la volupté. De là, le jour, on voyait au loin le clocher de Pinsonville et de même le soir, on distinguait confusément, tout près* la maison, les rondes collines appelées, Collines du Calvaire à cause d'un calvaire qui se dressait autrefois sur l'une d'elles au dessus* d'un vaste étang et entre lesquelles on avait établi récemment un champ de courses, et mes larmes redoublaient parce que je comparais les souffrances de ma grand'mère à la Passion du Sauveur. Hélas! <je ne savais pas>

12:36. <savais pas> **13:4.** <une* pleur involontaire. [12:39. <l'incertitude qu'elle projetait sur> 12:41. <incessantes du matin, de l'après-midi et du soir>]

13:6. Cela me faisait bien de la peine de monter tous les soirs me coucher quand tout le monde restait encore en bas à causer pendant des heures. Ma consolation était que maman venait m'embrasser quand j'étais dans mon lit.

13:8. Mais ce bonsoir> **13:16.** <tard possible. [13:14. <où elle m'avait quitté, où elle était redescendue>]

13:16. <possible. Tout le temps où maman n'était pas encore venue était un temps de répit et éloignait d'autant celui où elle serait repartie, où je ne la verrais plus.

13:18. Quelquefois> **13:32.** <présence réelle. [13:19. <pour redescendre, je> 13:30. <sa figure heureuse et aimante> 13:31. <hostie où mes lèvres>]

□**13:32.** <présence réelle et la garderaient jusqu'au lendemain; hostie pour une communion de paix, qui m'assurait un sommeil plus doux et plus calme que celui que nous trouvons dans ces autres hosties où le pharmacien enferme du sommeil, et qui sont bien miraculeuses elles aussi, bien précieuses en tous cas certains soirs, pour ceux qui n'ont plus leur mère, en leur permettant d'interrompre un moment, quand il devient anxieux, le besoin qu'ils ont encore de l'embrasser.

13:33. Mais ces soirs-là> **13:37.** <bonsoir.

□**13:37.** Le «monde» se bornait habituellement à M. Vington et à M. Swann. M. Vington, que ma grand'mère appelait la crème des braves gens, était un homme d'une politesse exagérée et d'une pudibonderie démodée. Mon père s'intéressait beaucoup aux travaux d'histoire naturelle de M. Vington et il aurait été heureux, quand il allait voir M. Vington chez lui à la Courbe, ou quand il recevait sa visite à la maison, il aurait été heureux de l'entendre lui en exposer quelques-uns. Rien n'eût pu causer autant de joie à M. Vington. Mais sensible, scrupuleux, poli à l'excès, il cherchait toujours à se mettre à la place des autres, il craignait de les ennuyer, de leur paraître égoïste, s'il suivait, s'il laissait seulement deviner son désir. Un jour que j'avais accompagné mon père à la Courbe et qu'il m'avait fait attendre devant la maison qui était dans un creux si bien que la fenêtre de M. Vington était à hauteur du sol, je pus le voir avant que mon père n'entrât, mettre vivement tout près de lui quelques notes qu'il voulait sans doute lui soumettre. Mais quand mon père fut là, je vis M. Vington éloigner le manuscrit. Il avait sans doute craint que mon père supposât qu'il l'avait fait venir à la Courbe pour le lui dire, il avait fait semblant que ces feuilles fussent là par mégarde et chaque fois que mon père insistait: «Je ne sais qui les a mises là, j'ai dit cent fois que ce n'était pas leur place» [*cf.* 113:20], et quand mon père avait insisté pour que M. Vington les lui lût, celui-là par peur d'être importun, et se laissant aller à parler des sujets qui l'intéressaient, avait détourné la conversation sur d'autres qui, en réalité, intéressaient [*sic*] mon père, comme sur le caractère de nos domestiques, l'entretien de notre jardin, s'interrompant tout le temps pour savoir si mon père n'avait pas chaud, n'avait pas froid, n'était pas mal assis. M. Vington nous faisait sourire par l'indignation avec laquelle il relevait dans le langage des «jeunes gens» du jour [*cf.* 112:5], des paroles déplacées: «Vous parlez toujours de Vington comme d'une vieille bête, disait mon père avec mauvaise humeur. C'est peut-être le plus grand naturaliste de l'époque. Si toute* ses forces n'avaient pas été brisées par la mort de sa femme et s'il ne poussait pas jusqu'au gâtisme sa tendresse pour sa fille, il aurait rassemblé les milliers d'observations qu'il a faites à l'appui d'une idée de génie et vous verriez quel livre! Mais il ne paraîtra jamais, il l'a sacrifié à sa fille. Elle n'est pourtant pas belle, la pauvre fille, avec ses taches de son, et surtout son air rude, on dirait un garçon!» Mais ma grand'mère trouvait du charme [*cf.* 113:27] à cette honnête rudesse et elle faisait remarquer quelle belle expression de douceur, presque timide, de délicatesse, de sincérité passait parfois dans le regard de la petite Vington. Quand elle venait de prononcer une parole, elle l'entendait avec l'esprit de ceux à qui elle l'avait dite, et s'alarmait des malentendus possibles. Quelquefois son visage s'empourprait après qu'elle avait dit à mes parents son désir de revenir les voir, parce qu'aussitôt elle avait pensé qu'ils avaient pu voir dans sa phrase une demande de l'inviter à dîner le soir où elle irait à Combray pour le mois de Marie, ou tel autre projet indiscret dont elle avait été bien loin d'avoir l'intention, et nous d'ailleurs de la lui prêter. «Il paraît qu'elle est très nerveuse, disait ma grand'mère, il a eu grand'peine à l'élever, elle restait des jours entiers sans pouvoir desserrer les dents et manger. Regardez, malgré cette vie d'exercice en plein air qu'elle mène, comme il la couve, comme il a toujours peur qu'elle prenne froid.»

Mes parents avaient dû être plus liés autrefois avec M. Vington car c'est de lui que venait, paraît-il, une petite collection de minéraux que mon père me donna un jour à ma fête, où il y avait différents minerais, verts, orangés, brillants comme de l'argent, une petite opale où on voyait s'allumer par parcelles, interrompu comme par le froissement d'une main, l'étincellement vert qu'il y a sous le cou d'un colibri, et une pierre, peut-être une agate brute, toute grise en sa fruste et rude enveloppe, mais dont une face sectionnée était aussi brillante qu'un miroir et laissait voir, on eut* dit, sous verre, une soie bleu-pâle sur laquelle des cercles concentriques étaient tracés comme au pastel ou sur l'aile d'un papillon. M. Vington, choqué de voir que nous continuions à recevoir en garçon, notre ami de Combray, M. Swann, après qu'il eut fait un mariage scandaleux, cessa presque complètement de venir [*cf.* 112:39] et nous ne le rencontrions plus qu'au mois de Marie ou sur le chemin du cimetière où il passait des heures à pleurer devant la tombe de sa femme.

En dehors de quelques étrangers de passage, qu'on ne conviait qu'à des dîners plus cérémonieux, M. Swann était à peu près>

13:38. <à peu près> **15:10.** <ces arbres> [14:1. <sous le cèdre, autour de la petite table de fer> 14:8. <être?» (bien que cela ne put* guère être que M. Swann); ma grand'tante> 14:27. <visage en bec d'aigle> 14:29. <à la Bressat*, parce que nous ne gardions pas de lumière pour ne pas attirer> 14:32. <dire qu'on apporte les sirops; ma grand'mère y* attachait> 14:39. <suffisait parfois à suspendre les élans du cœur, à interrompre ou à changer le cours de la pensée. 14:43. <femme qu'il adorait et avait admirablement soignée. 15:2. <dans la petite propriété qu'ils possédaient aux> 15:5. <la chambre où reposait Mme Swann et d'où il n'était pas sorti depuis plusieurs jours. 15:6. <où il y avait eu* peu>]

□**15:10.** <joli, tous ces arbres, vous avez l'air comme d'un bonnet de nuit. Ce devrait pourtant vous rappeler nos bonnes promenades d'autrefois.

15:13. Sentez-vous> **15:14.** <Amédée!»

15:14. Brusquement il retrouve le souvenir de sa femme morte et trouvant> **15:20.** <son front>

□**15:20.** <son front, de lisser les deux côtés de sa chevelure en brosse. Quelques* temps après, racontant à mon grand-père qu'un facteur voulait lui remettre à toutes forces une lettre qui n'était pas pour lui avait ajouté: «Mais pourtant votre dame m'a dit tout à l'heure», j'ai eu beau lui répéter sur tous les tons que j'étais veuf! dit-il, à mon grand-père en riant aux éclats.

15:21. Il ne put> **15:29.** <si mon> [15:26. <devenu des* phrases favorites de mon grand-père qu'il disait à propos>]

□**15:29.** <si mon grand-père ne nous avait assuré* que c'était un cœur d'or. Je m'en rapportais à lui, que je considérais comme un meilleur juge, j'ai continué depuis, et souvent avant de classer quelqu'un, en particulier moi-même, dans la catégorie des monstres, je repense au père Swann et je tâche plutôt de trouver un petit coin dans celle des cœurs d'or.

Pendant tant d'années, où, surtout avant son mariage, M. Swann, le fils, vint continuellement voir ma grand'tante et mes grands-parents à Combray, ils ne soupçonnèrent pas, à ce qu'ils m'ont raconté plus tard, que ce jeune homme—il le resta longtemps à leurs yeux—ne vivait plus>

15:38. <ne vivait plus> **16:32.** <toujours eu> [16:1. <du Comte de Chambord et du Prince de Galles> 16:4. <étions de cet «éclat» mondain de Swann tenait évidemment> 16:7. <la bourgeoisie française d'alors se faisait> 16:11. <carrière exceptionnellement brillante ou d'un> 16:18. <été les relations de> 16:19. <siennes, quelles personnes il était «en situation» de fréquenter. S'il> 16:20. <c'étaient des relations> 16:26. <étaient des gens qu'il n'aurait pas osé saluer s'il les avait rencontrés, étant avec nous. Si> 16:31. <de façon et>]

16:32. <toujours eu une toquade de botanique et de peinture, (on assurait qu'il avait même publié autrefois une brochure sur un peintre vénitien peu connu), il demeurait, depuis qu'il était orphelin, quai d'Orléans, dans une «atroce baraque», disait ma grand'tante, qui se doutait de ce que cela pourrait être! (c'était un hôtel du XVIIe siècle qui faisait rêver ma grand'mère à qui il avait promis de le faire visiter, et dont il habitait le premier, ayant logé aux étages supérieurs ses collections et ses herbiers). Ma grand'tante, qui était par certains côtés la seule personne un peu>

17:19. <un peu vulgaire de la famille, avait> **17:28.** <de lui dire> [17:21. <aurait «pu»> 17:23. <près de quatre millions>]

17:28. <lui dire: «Eh! bien, M. Swann, vous habitez toujours près du Jardin des plantes, avec vos vieilles giroflées?—Toujours, Madame.»

17:31. Et elle regardait> **17:41.** <dans tel> [17:35. <bourgeoisie» et les notaires> 17:38. <différente et l'accès d'un

monde inconnu que jamais l'œil d'aucun agent [*cf.* 17:45] ou associé d'agent ne contemple; qu'en sortant>

17:41. <tel «salon» insoupçonné et prestigieux comme l'éblouissante caverne où on voyait entrer Ali-Baba sur les assiettes à déssert* de Combray [*cf.* 18:1], quand il était sûr qu'on ne le voyait pas, cela eût paru>

17:42. <cela eût paru aussi extraordinaire à ma tante que pourrait l'être pour une dame> **18:5.** <à bras ouverts. [18:2. <aurait compris, en se rappelant les *Géorgiques,* qu'il allait>]

18:11. Un jour> **18:20.** <invitations et trouvait naturel qu'il arrivât souvent avec un panier> [18:18. Aussi, comme ma grand'tante en usait cavalièrement avec lui!]

□**18:21.** <un panier de framboises ou de pêches de son jardin, et qu'il m'eut* rapporté de Padoue des photographies des «Vertus et Vices de Giotto», (qui du reste ne m'avait* pas plu, l'Envie ayant l'air de sucer son serpent, et la Charité se déhanchant pour que Dieu puisse attraper son cœur): de l'Abraham de B. Gozzoli.

On ne se gênait guère pour lui faire pousser le piano et tourner les pages [*cf.* 18:34] les soirs où la sœur de ma grand'-tante chantait, pour l'envoyer quérir dès qu'on avait besoin d'une recette de poulet de chasseur, de perdreau à la crapaudine, de salade d'ananas, de sandwich au chester pour des dîners «à cérémonie» où on>

18:27. <où on ne l'invitait pas> **18:34.** <une lettre de Pohsdorf; et elle maniait avec une brusquerie et avec des façons comiques cet être précieux, comme s'il se plût à l'amuser et de qui se prêtait aux longs soirs comme un bibelot de collection qu'il brûlerait comme un jouet de marché! [*Syntax sic*]. C'est que même au point>

19:4. <point de vue> **19:9.** <la pensée. [19:8. <comme d'un acte de l'état civil ou d'un testament>]

□**19:9.** <la pensée des autres et le Swann que connurent à la même époque tant de clubmen était bien différent de celui que créait ma grand'tante quand le soir, dans le petit jardin de Combray, après qu'avaient retenti les deux coups hésitants de la clochette, elle injectait et vivifiait de tout ce qu'elle savait sur la famille Swann, l'obscur et incertain personnage qui se détachait

suivi de ma grand'mère sur un fond de ténèbres et qu'on ne reconnaissait qu'à la voix. L'acte si simple>

19:10. <si simple> **19:23.** <parents avaient négligé de faire>

19:24. <faire entrer> **19:29.** <à leur frontière habituelle. Mais comme, par ignorance, ils n'avaient pu loger en Swann le nom d'aucun de ses amis illustres, l'écho des fêtes fastueuses dont il était le centre et l'attrait, ils avaient entassé dans son visage vacant et désaffecté de son prestige, au fond de ses yeux dépréciés le vague et doux résidu mi-mémoire, mi-oubli, des heures>

19:31. <des heures> **19:33.** <jardin, de toute notre>

19:33. <notre vie> **19:37.** <un être> [19:34. L'enveloppe vivante de>]

□**19:37.** <un être que, pas plus que l'autre, on n'aurait pu détruire. Plus bonhomme, sans doute, plus simplet, était-il moins réel que l'élégant, ce Swann rempli de loisir, parfumé par l'odeur du grand maronnier*, des paniers de framboises et d'un brin d'estragon. Pour ma part, je ne peux passer aujourd'hui de l'un à l'autre sans avoir l'impression de dégonfler un être de chair de la substance qui le fait exister, puis d'y transvaser un autre, d'opérer une sorte de désincarnation.

Les premiers doutes de mes grands-parents à l'égard de la situation de Swann eussent pu leur venir de la marquise de Villeparisis, de l'illustre maison de Bouillon, qui avait été élevée au Sacré-Cœur avec ma grand'mère. Elles s'étaient un peu perdues de vue, mais Mme de Villeparisis aimait ma grand'mère et si celle-ci, à cause de la conception des castes, avait toujours résisté à ses prières d'échanger des visites avec elle, elle savait en revanche que si elle avait un service à demander elle était toujours sûre de trouver dans sa vieille amie le plus solide appui; ma grand'mère nous la dépeignait comme une femme d'une intelligence supérieure, peu sensible, peu aimable, avare de son affection, attachant du prix à ses moindres entretiens, à ses billets qui étaient courts mais exquis; mais aussi quand elle avait promis de faire une démarche—ma grand'mère, qui la savait proche parente du maréchal de Mac-Mahon, avait été plusieurs fois la prier d'intervenir en faveur d'amis à nous—mettant à tenir sa promesse une promptitude, une intelligence, une discrétion, une efficacité admirables.

Chaque fois que ma grand'mère eut ainsi à aller la voir, Mme de Villeparisis l'avait poussée à louer un appartement dans la même maison qu'elle ou dans des maisons contiguës et semblables qui toutes donnaient sur des jardins, d'autant plus «naturels» ceux-là, qu'aucun jardinier ne s'en occupait, et dont ma grand'-mère était revenue chaque fois plus enthousiaste, ainsi que d'un fleuriste qui avait sa boutique, où sa fille faisait aussi des réparations de broderies, dans la cour de Mme de Villeparisis, et chez qui ma grand'mère était entrée>

20:19. <était entrée> **20:25.** <social. [20:21. <gens, le fleuriste et sa fille, parfaits> 20:22. <que le fleuriste était> 20:23. <pour ma grand'mère, la distinction>]

□**20:25.** Elle s'extasiait sur les lettres d'une ouvrière en journée, disant à maman: «Sevigné n'aurait pas mieux dit!» et en revanche, d'un neveu de Mme de Villeparisis qu'elle avait rencontré chez elle: «Ah! ma fille, comme il est commun!»

Or, Mme de Villeparisis, au cours d'une de ses trois ou quatre visites, qui furent les seules que ma grand'mère lui fit pendant les quarante années qui s'écoulèrent depuis leur sortie du Sacré-Cœur, lui avait dit une fois: «Je crois que vous connaissez beaucoup M. Swann qui est un grand ami de mes neveux Villebon» [*cf.* 20:13]. Ma grand'mère n'avait pas osé demander de détails, mais cette nouvelle qu'elle nous rapporta en rougissant, car elle sentait la fâcheuse impression qu'elle allait produire, eut pour effet non pas d'élever M. Swann, mais d'abaisser les neveux Villebon sur l'échelle de notre estime mondaine et surtout d'exciter chez ma grand'tante contre Mme de Villeparisis une mauvaise humeur dont ma grand'mère était éclaboussée. Il semblait que la considération que nous accordions à Mme de Villeparisis lui créât le devoir de ne rien faire qui l'en rendit* moins digne, et qu'elle avait manqué à ce devoir en apprenant l'existence de Swann et en permettant à des parents à elle de le fréquenter. Quant à ma grand'mère on eut* dit qu'elle venait de reconnaître qu'elle nous avait trompés sur la valeur de la personne que nous avions placée si haut sur la foi de ses récits; et l'idée erronée que mes grands-parents se faisaient des relations de Swann n'ayant pas été rectifiée par cet indice qu'ils ne surent pas exactement interpréter, leur parut ensuite confirmée par son mariage avec une femme de la pire société [*cf.* 20:42], presque une cocotte, et d'après laquelle ils croyaient pouvoir juger—supposant que c'était là qu'il l'avait prise—le milieu, inconnu d'eux, qu'il fréquentait habituellement. Par délicatesse, Swann ne chercha jamais à présenter sa femme à aucun de ses amis, et continuait à aller seul chez eux; à la maison on ne lui parla jamais d'elle, mais ma mère qui savait sa tendresse passionnée pour la fille qu'il avait eue de cette femme avant leur mariage et qu'il avait reconnue (elle était un peu plus jeune que moi), priait souvent mon père, les jours où Swann venait dîner, de lui dire un mot de cette petite: «Tu lui ferais tant de plaisir, j'en suis sûre. Cela doit être si cruel pour lui» [*cf.* 23:9]. «Tu es absurde, ce serait ridicule», répondit mon père. Maman, craignant de le mécontenter, n'insista plus. Mais moi qui était* toujours à l'entrée du salon à guetter le moment où je pourrais entrer dire bonsoir à ma mère, je sais bien que toutes les fois où Swann venait de bonne heure et où maman était seule pour le recevoir en attendant que mon père et mes grands-parents descendent, la première chose qu'elle lui disait, parce qu'il n'y a pas une créature à laquelle elle n'ait cherché à faire plaisir, c'était [*cf.* 24:9]: «Eh! bien. Monsieur Swann, parlez-moi de votre fille; elle doit être bien gentille maintenant. Aimera-t-elle les arts autant que son papa? Je suis sûre que vous cherchez déjà à former son goût et à la faire vivre au milieu des belles choses.» Et Swann, heureux, ému, lui racontait qu'elle connaissait déjà tous les styles d'architecture. «Mais maintenant, elle veut absolument aller voir les cathédrales. Elle connaît Reims et encore mieux Chartres parce que ma femme y a des parents et qu'elles y passent tous les ans quelques semaines. Mais il a fallu que je promette un voyage à Bourges pour l'année prochaine si elle est bien sage.» Par instants il se taisait et lissait avec la main les deux côtés de ses cheveux en brosse. Puis quand le reste de la famille descendait, maman était obligée de changer de conversation, mais elle tirait de cette contrainte une délicatesse de plus, comme ces bons poètes à qui la tyrannie de la rime fait trouver de plus grandes beautés: «Nous reparlerons d'elle quand nous serons tous les deux. Ce n'est pas que cela ne les intéresse tous, mais il n'y a tout de même qu'une maman qui soit vraiment digne de vous comprendre. Je suis sûre que la mienne serait de votre avis.»

«Remarquez-vous comme Swann vieillit, disait mon grand-père [*cf.* 34:12]. Ce doit être les soucis que lui donne sa coquine de femme [*cf.* 34:24]. Elle a une liaison de notoriété publique avec M. de Gurcy qu'on rencontre avec elle.» «M. Swann n'a pourtant plus cet air triste qu'il a eu pendant quelque temps avant son mariage, disait ma mère.» «Oui, c'est vrai, il est même gai, mais il doit être malade car sa figure a bien changé depuis quelques années.» Mais il arriva qu'un jour, mon grand-père lut* dans un journal>

21:5. <dans un journal> **21:9.** <Louis-Philippe. [21:7. <le père et le grand-père avaient>]

21:9. <Louis-Philippe. Le fait qu'il y alla (en garçon d'ailleurs, car il ne menait sa femme nulle part) parut inexplicable à ma grand'tante qui fut néanmoins obligée de l'admettre, mais dans une acception plutôt défavorable à Swann: quelqu'un qui> {21:9-21:14}

21:15. <quelqu'un qui> **21:28.** <bontés. [21:19. <qu'on renonçait> 21:22. <prévoyantes. Ma grand'tante cessa même>]

□**21:28.** <bontés. Mon grand-père fut moins surpris. «Ça ne m'étonne pas outre mesure, dit-il. Sa pauvre mère était déjà comme ça. Souvent on rencontrait en visite chez elle des gens inconnus dans notre monde. Comme alors elle cessait d'eux* et ne faisait de frais que pour nous; les naïfs se disaient que ces inconnus devaient être des gens de peu. Mais moi qui connaissais son tact et sa délicatesse, je soupçonnais que cela devait être tout le contraire.» Or, mon grand-père [*cf.* 21:9], qui était l'homme le plus simple du monde et qui n'eût jamais voulu entrer en relations avec des gens qu'il considérait comme d'une société plus brillante que la sienne, était en revanche infiniment curieux de tous les petits détails qui le faisaient entrer par la pensée dans la vie privée d'homme* dont le rôle politique, sous la monarchie ou pendant les premières années de la République, le grand talent, la haute autorité morale, avaient tout son respect. «Savoir», «se représenter», sans être obligé de les fréquenter pour cela, par les* souvenir de gens qui les avaient connus, comment

se comportait* dans l'intimité Molé, le duc de Broglie, Casermirs* Périer, l'amusait infiniment. Aussi, quand il eut fait avouer à Swann ses relations avec M. de X..., commença-t-il à l'accabler de questions. «Voyons, Swann, vous êtes un cachotier; on nous dit que vous rencontrez souvent le duc d'Aumale; qu'est-ce qu'il dit de Thiers, de Guizot. Comment est-il avec le comte de Paris; voyons, parlez, racontez, donnez-nous une idée de tout ça.»

Malheureusement pour mon grand-père, les deux sœurs de sa femme, vieilles filles qui avaient la noble nature de ma grand'-mère sans en avoir son esprit, passaient depuis peu les vacances à Combray avec mes grands-parents.

21:34. C'étaient des personnes> **22:15.** <un peu fou. [22:5. Si alors on avait> 22:6. <fallait avoir recours> 22:12. <que ces neurologues transportent>]

22:16. Aussi, à peine mon grand-père posait-il une question à Swann sur le duc de Broglie par exemple, question qui résonnait aux oreilles des deux sœurs de ma grand'mère comme un silence profond mais intempestif et qu'il s'agissait de rompre, l'une prenait la parole avant que Swann eut* le temps de répondre et disait à l'autre> {22:16-23:11}

*23:14. **See after 27:12.***

25:1. <l'autre: «Imagine> **25:11.** <de plus intéressant. [25:4. <scandinaves les détails les plus intéressants. 25:6. <soir.» Ce sera charmant, disait l'autre. Mais je n'ai pas> 25:8. <chez M. Legrandin un vieux> 25:9. <Maubant expliquait dans>]

25:11. <de plus intéressant. Peut-être pourrait-on obtenir de lui qu'il vînt dîner un soir. Quand on le met sur Maubant ou sur Mme Materne*, il parle des heures sans s'arrêter. {25:11-25:33}

25:26. «Ce doit être> **25:33.** <vie intime>

25:33. <vie intime de Tiers* ou du comte de Chambord.

Cette opposition de natures se retrouvait jusque dans les questions littéraires. «Je relisais ce matin dans Saint-Simon quelque chose qui vous aurait amusé. Saint-Simon, dans le volume de son ambassade d'Espagne, raconte que Maulévrier avait eu l'audace de tendre la main à ses fils. «Je ne sais si ce fut «ignorance» ou «panneau» écrit Saint-Simon> {25:41-26:28}

26:36. <écrit Saint-Simon. **27:12.** <c'est bien lui!»

△**23:14.** Les soirs où des étrangers, ou seulement Monsieur Swann étaient là, maman ne montait pas dans ma chambre. Je ne dinais* pas à table, je venais après diner* au jardin, et à neuf heures je disais bon soir* et je montais me coucher. Ce baiser précieux et fragile que maman me confiait d'habitude dans mon lit au moment de m'endormir et que ces soirs-là il me fallait transporter du jardin dans ma chambre et garder pendant tout le temps que je me déshabillais, sans que se brisât sa douceur et s'évaporât sa vertu d'apaisement, justement ces soirs là* où j'aurais eu besoin de le recevoir avec plus de précaution, il fallait>

△**23:25.** <il fallait que> **23:32.** <l'ont fermée. [23:26. <le dérobe* brusquement> 23:31. <leur reviendra, s'ils l'ont fait ou non, lui opposer>]

27:13. Mais, maman pour ne pas agacer mon père, qui trouvait toutes ces «manifestations de tendresse» ridicules, ne me laissait l'embrasser ainsi devant «le monde» qu'une seconde et retirait, aussitôt approché, son visage; et moi, sachant que ce baiser serait si court et furtif, je faisais d'avance tout ce que j'en pouvais faire seul, je fixais avant que neuf heures sonnent la place de la joue de maman où je l'embrasserais, je préparais ma pensée, comme un peintre pour pouvoir>

27:23. <pour pouvoir> □**27:30.** <modèle. Quelquefois, ce commencement mental de baiser, qui me permettait de consacrer toute la courte minute que m'accordait maman, à sentir sa joue contre mes lèvres, il m'était même refusé car bien avant l'heure mon grand-père, une de mes tantes avait la férocité inconsciente de dire: «Comment! le petit n'est pas encore couché? S'il veut sortir de bonne heure demain matin...». Et mon père, qui ne gardait pas aussi scrupuleusement que ma grand mère* et que ma mère la foi des traités, disait: «mais oui, allons, monte te coucher.» Et il fallait monter. Quelquefois, à peine sorti de la maison, j'y rentrais, je demandais à ma mère de venir dans l'antichambre me dire un mot, mon père se fâchait, maman ne venait pas; cette déception avait suffi pour briser le sceau fragile sous lequel ses lèvres avaient enfermé en moi le calme et le sommeil. Et je montais dans ma chambre, désespéré, sans viatique.

Mais hélas! un jour mon père dit à ma mère: «C'est ridicule que le petit vienne dire bonsoir comme cela quand il y a du monde. Fais-le donc monter avant qu'on arrive.» Et à partir de ce jour-là, ce fut une heure, deux heures avant le moment de me coucher qu'il me fallût* demander à maman ce baiser dont la douceur si volatile devait préserver mon sommeil. Peu de temps après le jour où cette règle était pour la première fois entrée en vigueur, mon grand-père en rentrant rappela que M. Swann devait venir dîner. Sauf pour moi, c'était un plaisir pour tout le monde. «Nous allons demander à M. Swann s'il croit que le temps est au beau» [*cf.* 23:43], dit mon père qui tous les matins dès qu'il avait fini sa toilette, de la fenêtre ouverte de sa chambre, jetait cette question au jardinier en train d'inonder ses corbeilles, au mépris de l'esthétique de ma grand'mère. La météorologie comme la topographie intéressaient beaucoup mon père. Et quand après le déjeuner tandis qu'on servait le café sur la table, il allait consulter le baromètre, ma mère évitait de faire du bruit pour ne pas le troubler, le regardait avec un respect attendri, mais pas trop fixement pour ne pas chercher à percer le mystère de ses supériorités. Quand je sortis ce soir-là, c'était bientôt l'heure où M. Swann allait arriver, j'entraînai maman dans le vestibule pour lui dire bonsoir; mais je n'avais pas encore commencé à l'embrasser quand la sonnette retentit; c'était M. Swann; à ce moment, mon père ouvre la porte, dit: «Voyons, on a sonné, monte!» Maman m'embrasse à peine, me repousse pour pouvoir aller au devant de Swann. Il fallut monter>

27:41. <fallut monter> **28:19.** <insidieuse et brusque. [28:2. <m'engageais si> 28:4. <absorbé, fixé, mon chagrin et le rendait peut-être plus cruel encore pour ma sensibilité> 28:12. <de Corneille que> 28:15. <déguisement vertueux ou prosodique.]

□**28:21.** Pourvu que je ne descendisse pas près des invités, j'avais le droit de rester jusqu'à neuf heures sans me coucher et je pouvais même redescendre au petit salon quand on était «passé à la salle à manger». C'est ce que je fis. Et sentant que j'avais encore une heure avant l'instant du coucher, je m'efforçais de n'y pas penser, je regardais, dans les vases, les fleurs que le jardinier, ignorant du sentiment de la nature et de l'art des bouquets, y avait facticement disposées en masses lourdes et pressées. Dans le jardin, la lune, suspendue comme un lampion sous le feuillage du maronnier* commençait à mélanger à l'obscurité cette poussière d'argent qui, dans une heure, aurait «déposé» en revêtements fantastiques sur le paysage tout entier. Et déjà la solidité, la réalité, quittant les choses pour passer dans leurs ombres, le treillage de bois qui quadrillait le mur le long de l'allée semblait s'évanouir en clarté et avait décalqué à côté de lui un reflet plus dense et plus concret. J'écoutais un air de piano, pourtant aimé, qui venait d'une maison voisine. Mais la pensée de ceux que tend une préoccupation intérieure est comme leur regard, convexe, et ne peut laisser pénétrer du dehors en elle auçun sentiment. Je mettais devant la mienne la beauté de ce jardin, les vers que j'amais le mieux, les pensées philosophiques qui, en m'élevant dans l'éternel auraient dû m'empêcher de buter sans trêve contre la minute prochaine du coucher et ma tristesse même si je ne pouvais m'endormir, qui allait si peu durer et s'évanouit avec le matin. Mais les plus beaux vers, les plus grandes pensées, avant d'entrer dans mon esprit étaient obligées* de laisser tout leur charme, toute leur joie, comme les mets exquis perdent toute saveur dans la bouche d'un fiévreux. Enfin, il fallut monter, boucher sur moi toutes les issues en fermant les volets de ma chambre, creuser>

28:22. <creuser mon propre> **28:29.** <à ma mère> [28:25. <m'ensevelir moi-même dans>]

□**28:29.** <à ma mère pour la supplier de monter une seconde pour une chose extrêmement grave que je ne pouvais lui dire par écrit. Mon effroi était que Françoise refusât de porter ma lettre. Je savais que pour elle, faire à maman quand il y avait du monde, une commission, c'était aussi impossible que de demander au portier d'un théâtre de remettre une lettre à un acteur pendant qu'il est en scène. Elle possédait sur les choses qui peuvent se faire et ne peuvent se faire tout un code subtil, abondant et barbare, aux commandements duquel elle n'aurait pas désobéi pour un empire, et qui semblait avoir prévu des complexités sociales et des raffinements mondains tels, qu'on se demandait qui, dans son ascendance paysanne et toute primitive, dans son entourage et son ambiance de domestique de village, avait pu le lui suggérer.

Si d'ailleurs ce code tranchait aussi certaines questions ressortissant davantage du cadre restreint où elle vivait, c'était toujours avec une sorte de délicatesse inflexible, de brutalité nuancée et implacable, intransigeante sur des distinctions insaisissables ou arbitraires, ce qui lui donnait sur la modernité des cas quotidiens auxquels il s'appliquait, l'apparence singulière, à la fois dure, sophistique et oiseuse de certains codes très antiques, de la vieille loi juive par exemple, qui à côté de prescriptions féroces comme de massacrer les enfants à la mamelle et les femmes enceintes, fait voir des scrupules exagérés quand elle défend, pour la préparation culinaire du chevreau, de le faire boullir dans le lait de sa mère, ou entièrement stupides quand elle recommande, pour honorer la mémoire de Jacob, de ne jamais manger dans un animal le nerf de la cuisse. Hélas! ce code, nous l'ignorions, et quand elle nous connut* depuis assez longtemps, nous considéra suffisamment comme des «maîtres» pour nous en rendre justiciables, elle prononçait à tout moment contre nous d'implacables condamnations pour des crimes que nous avions commis sans le savoir, auxquels elle s'étonnait qu'aient pu s'abaisser des «personnes de notre rang» et que nous n'aurions même pu confesser ni comprendre si elle ne nous les eût clairement reprochés. Il est vrai que si nous étions coupables sans nous en apercevoir, c'est sans nous en apercevoir non plus que nous étions châtiés. Nous n'avions pas su en lui souhaitant une bonne nuit que nous lui faisions une injure imméritée, mais quand elle nous avait alors répondu qu'elle espérait que nous dormirions bien aussi nous n'avions pas eu davantage la notion que c'était «bien insolent à elle d'avoir répondu cela, mais cela avait été plus fort qu'elle», aussi qu'elle le racontait à l'office «aux autres», et c'est à notre insu aussi que devant cette réponse, comme elle le leur disait encore, nous étions restés «tous sots» et n'avions plus «pipé». «Et qu'ils n'y reviennent pas», avait-elle ajouté, terminant sa narration de domestique par cette vague allusion à des articles plus rigoureux visant la récidive. Répondre impoliment à une amie de mes grands-parents qui arrivait à une heure où Françoise comptait faire sa lessive ou ses comptes, était chose parfaitement permise par le code; mais demander à une dame qu'ils ne pouvaient recevoir ce jour-là si elle ne reviendrait pas les voir, attendre une réponse à une lettre qu'on l'envoyait porter, était sévèrement prohibé. Et comme dans les commissions qu'on lui donnait, les clauses illicites étaient pour elle inexistantes, Françoise se contentait de les omettre sans faire d'observation préalable. Quand on lui demandait: «Eh bien, cette dame pourra-t-elle revenir?» ou bien: «Me rapportez-vous une réponse?» les multiples stigmates d'un sourire mièvre, glacial et douloureux montaient soudain à la surface du visage de Françoise, qu'elle était tout entière visitée mystiquement à ce moment par les délicatesses, et la douceur d'une politesse impérieuse, exquise, dont elle s'affligeait que des personnes ayant reçu de l'éducation comme mes grands-parents, fussent assez grossières pour ignorer les aimables commandements et pour pousser une «simple domestique» à y contrevenir, et elle répondait: «Bien sûr que je ne lui ai pas demandé. Bien sûr que je n'ai pas attendu de réponse.» Et pour montrer à ma grand'mère que tout le monde n'était pas autant qu'elle ignare ou pervers, elle ajoutait: «Cette personne aurait été certainement très froissée; je ne sais pas pour qui elle m'aurait pris.» Malheureusement la seule partie peut-être du code de Françoise dont les dispositions fussent en harmonie avec les principes de mes parents était celle qui réglait mes rapports possibles avec maman une fois qu'elle était au «salon» ou «à la salle à manger» avec un monde; elle les réglait en les prohibant, et sauf des cas comme l'incendie [*cf.* 29:16] ou la mort subite, il était presque impossible qu'on «dérangeât» maman quand il y avait des visites ou des invités, pour une personne occupant un degré aussi infime que moi dans la hiérarchie de la maison. Aussi, pour tâcher que Françoise ne refusât pas purement et simplement, je n'hésitai pas>

29:28. <je n'hésitai pas> **29:34.** <ne me crut pas; elle regarda> {29:34-29:38}

29:38. <elle regarda> **29:40.** <la nature du contenu>

29:40. <du contenu. Puis elle sortit d'un air résigné qui semblait dire: «C'est-il pas malheureux pour des parents d'avoir un enfant pareil!» Elle vint* au bout d'un moment me dire qu'on n'en était encore qu'à la glace, qu'il était impossible au valet de chambre de remettre ainsi la lettre devant tout le monde (je dois dire que ma prétention n'allait pas jusque là) mais que, quand on «serait aux rince-bouches» avant qu'on aille prendre

le café au jardin on trouverait le moyen de le faire passer à maman. Aussitôt>

30:6. Aussitôt> **30:8.** <à ma mère; puisque>

30:8. <puisque, au moment de ces bienheureux rince-bouches, mon petit mot allait — la fâchant peut-être — me faire entrer visible et ravi dans la même pièce qu'elle, allait lui parler de moi à l'oreille, puisque cette salle à manger interdite, hostile, s'ouvrait à moi et, comme un fruit devenu doux qui brise sa dure enveloppe, allait>

30:18. <allait faire jaillir> **30:23.** <venir!

□**30:24.** Je venais peut-être d'avoir mon premier contact avec cette angoisse qu'il y a à sentir l'être qu'on aime dans un lieu de plaisir où l'on n'est pas, où l'on ne peut pas le rejoindre, angoisse en quelque sorte prédestinée à l'amour, qui sera accaparée, spécialisée par lui, mais qui, quand elle est entrée en nous avant qu'il ait encore fait son apparition dans notre vie, flotte en l'attendant vague et libre, sans affectation déterminée, au service un jour d'un sentiment, le lendemain d'un autre, tantôt de la tendresse familiale ou de l'amitié pour un camarade. Et quand Françoise revint me dire que ma lettre serait remise, je fis mon premier apprentissage avec cette joie divine et trompeuse que nous donnera souvent plus tard quelque ami>

30:43. <quelque ami> **31:17.** <aimons! [31:3. <errant devant la porte, attendant> 31:8. <parente, il> 31:10. <aimons, le parent bien intentionné>]

31:17. <aimons! Il est pourtant, le parent qui nous a accosté, un des invités de la fête, au même titre que tous les autres, un des initiés des cruels mystères. Si nous en jugeons par lui, les autres ne doivent rien avoir de bien démoniaque. Ces heures suppliciantes pour nous, inaccessibles, où elle allait goûter des plaisirs inconnus, voici que par une brèche inespérée nous y pénétrons; voici qu'un des moments, dont la succession les aurait composées, les heures de cette fête, un moment aussi réel que les autres>

31:24. <que les autres> **31:28.** <en bas. Cette fête mystérieuse, un de ces épisodes, fait d'échanges de paroles, d'allées et de venues, de sa sortie à elle, c'est nous qui en sommes l'âme, l'auteur. Et sans doute>

31:29. Et sans doute> **31:34.** <là-haut.»

□**31:35.** Hélas! la bienveillance d'un tiers ne peut agir sur l'hostilité que fait naître parfois dans le cœur d'une femme, rien qu'en l'aimant passionnément, en la poursuivant jusque dans un bal, quelqu'un qu'elle n'aime pas. Et souvent l'ami redescend seul.

D'ailleurs l'aurions-nous vue, serions-nous entré dans la fête où nous n'aurions pas osé rester de peur de l'irriter en ayant l'air d'épier les plaisirs qu'elle prend avec d'autres, et qui nous semblent illimités parce que nous sommes partis* sans en avoir vu la fin, que nous souffririons peut-être plus encore, tandis que nous resterions solitaires [*cf.* 297:18]. Aussi, s'il est bien des sortes de joies, parmi celles qu'on serait tenté, si elles ne subissaient avec tant de violence le choc en retour de l'inquiétude brusquement arrêtée, d'appeler les joies calmes, parce qu'elles consistent en un apaisement, il n'en est peut-être pas d'aussi douce que celle qu'on peut connaître par de tels soirs: quand s'apprêtant à quitter un bal où on laisse celle qu'on aime, muée en brillante étrangère, au milieu d'hommes à qui ses regards et sa gaieté qui ne sont pas pour nous, semblent parler de quelque volupté qui sera consommée ici ou ailleurs et qui nous cause plus de jalousie que l'union charnelle elle-même, parce que nous l'imaginons plus difficilement; non, je n'ai pas connu de joie plus douce que, par de tels soirs, de m'entendre rappeler, quand j'étais prêt à passer la porte, par ces mots qui, en retranchant du bal cette fin qui m'épouvantait, le rendent rétrospectivement innocent, font une chose non plus inconcevable et terrible, mais douce et connue [*cf.* 297:41], qui tiendra à côté de moi dans ma voiture, pareille à un peu de ma vie de tous les jours, du retour de mon amie, et elle-même la dépouillant de cette apparence brillante et nouvelle, me montrent que ce n'était qu'un déguisement qu'elle avait revêtu un moment, pour lui-même, non en vue de mystérieux plaisirs et dont elle était déjà lasse; de m'entendre rappeler sur le seuil du salon par ces mots qu'elle me jette: «Vous ne voudriez pas m'attendre cinq minutes, je vais partir, nous reviendrions ensemble, vous me ramèneriez chez moi" [*cf.* 298:6].

L'angoisse avec laquelle je faisais connaissance, ce soir où Françoise avait pris ma lettre pour maman; un jour, —de même que l'amour, —elle se constitue définitivement à titre de maladie chronique, dont la cause vraie est en nous, qui se développe indépendamment du monde extérieur et y cherche seulement le moindre prétexte pour déclencher des crises et nous permettre de les justifier ces crises. A partir d'un certain âge nous ne sommes plus amoureux d'une femme, mais à propos d'une femme. Nos amours ne sont en réalité, malgré la diversité des amantes, qu'un même amour latent, expectant, toujours en imminence de crise que le plus petit trait d'un visage qui a pu y donner occasion fait entrer en éruption. De même cette angoisse, un peu plus rare peut-être, qui demande des circonstances de fait un peu plus particulières pour se produire, est là aussi pourtant en nous, attendant seulement que dans la suite de nos amours en vienne un pour une femme remplissant des conditions un peu plus spéciales: une femme frivole aimant le monde, même simplement y allant à une époque, à des heures où quelque contingence (un deuil, un voyage, une différence dans l'horaire de nos journées et des siennes, tenant à nos obligations professionnelles ou autres) nous empêche de l'accompagner. C'est assez pour que l'angoisse renaisse, mêlant même aux heures où elle s'assoupit, tant de tristesse et de doute à notre amour pour une femme dont le caractère et la conduite ne nous donnent aucune raison de les ressentir; lamentable accroît de notre amour, qui nous éloigne précisément de ce que nous lui demandons de nous faire atteindre (la nature du sentiment que cette femme a pour nous, le désir de ses journées, le secret de son cœur); car il interpose sans cesse entre notre esprit et cette femme cet amas réfractaire de soupçons antérieurs à elle, qui n'ont pas leur cause en elle, et ne nous permettent plus de la connaître qu'à travers le fantôme ancien, et commun à tant d'autres de la «femme qui excite notre jalousie» dans lequel nous l'avons arbitrairement incarnée.

Et peut-être était-ce à l'heure qu'il était quand cette angoisse naquit en moi à Combray, à ce baiser de maman que j'attendais pour m'endormir, à cette influence hostile des «invités» qui m'en privaient, peut-être est-ce à ces circonstances habituelles de coucher, de «bonsoir», de «dîner» où maman était et où je n'étais pas, qui entourèrent son premier développement, que cette angoisse n'a jamais perdu chez moi, tout le long de ma vie, la marque originelle d'être vespérale. Emigrée plus tard dans l'amour, quand je fus plus âgé, elle resta soumise à l'influence trouble de l'heure à laquelle elle était née au-dessus du jardin de Combray, où on était en train de préparer des fauteuils d'osier et la table de fer pour servir le café. Même dans les amours les plus mêlées de jalousie, je réussissais habituellement à ne pas penser à ce que ma maîtresse pouvait faire pendant le jour. Mais le soir, pour avoir cette paix mêlée de trouble, la seule que peut donner une maîtresse puisqu'au moment même où on croit en elle on doute d'elle encore, et qu'on ne possède jamais son cœur comme l'enfant reçoit dans un baiser le cœur de sa mère, tout entier, sans la réserve d'une arrière-pensée, sans le reliquat d'une intention qui ne soit pas pour lui, —le soir, il fallait que je l'eusse revue le dernier, qu'elle ne vit* plus personne après moi pour que la pensée qu'elle était avec d'autres ne vint* pas me disputer ce qu'elle m'avait laissé d'elle en me quittant; il fallait qu'elle m'eût dit: «Bonne nuit, je vais me coucher», pour que je pusse m'endormir.

Hélas, d'avoir connu les souffrances que je disais, nous fait peut-être quelque soir jeter un regard d'inutile pitié, —si le hasard nous fait passer en ce moment dans le hall ou palace ou le vestibule ou cercle où elle attend, —sur une de ces pauvres filles en larmes et fardées, à qui le concierge en livrée rapporte: «Il a dit qu'il n'y avait pas de réponse» ou: «Il n'a rien dit», et qui ne veulent pas renoncer: «Comment, il n'a rien dit? mais c'est impossible! Vous avez pourtant bien remis ma lettre?... C'est bien, je vais attendre encore" [*cf.* 32:4], refusant en disant: «Je suis bien ainsi, je n'ai pas besoin de plus de lumière», le bec supplémentaire que le concierge veut allumer pour elles, et n'entendant plus, au cours de leur attente interminable et vaine que les rares propos échangés sur le temps qu'il fait, sur la saison, qui s'avance, entre le concierge et un chasseur qu'il envoie tout d'un coup, en s'apercevant de l'heure, faire rafraîchir dans la glace la boisson d'un client, mais la pitié que ces malheureuses nous font éprouver du même ordre que celle que nous essayons d'inspirer à la femme que nous aimons pour qu'elle ne nous fasse pas trop souffrir, comment ne l'éprouvons-nous jamais pour la femme aussi à plaindre qui nous aime et que nous n'aimons pas et à qui nous n'avons même pas de remords de ne pas envoyer une ligne de réponse et de refuser éternellement un rendez-vous.

31:40. Maman ne vint pas, et> **31:43.** <démentie) elle me fit dire que je devrais être endormi depuis longtemps, qu'elle était très fâchée. Françoise se retira avec la politesse résignée de ces serviteurs d'un trône chancelant, qu'ils ne tarderont pas à abandonner, en murmurant quelques condoléances qui m'exaspérèrent. Je me couchai, mais au bout>

32:17. <au bout> **32:38.** <à ne pas troubler> [32:18. <en m'approchant si près d'elle, au risque de la fâcher, que j'avais> 32:21. < et les battements de mon cœur augmentant de minute en minute, je lui faisais de plus en plus mal en essayant de me calmer, en me prêchant une résignation qui> 32:28. <revu ma mère, de> 32:30. <d'être ensuite brouillé avec elle, quand elle remonterait se coucher; je me levai. Le calme> 32:35. <mon lit; je n'osais pas faire un mouvement de peur qu'on m'entendit* d'en bas. Dehors>]

32:38. <à ne pas troubler le phénomène lunaire, prodigieux, étincelant et fragile qui maintenant avait gagné jusqu'à l'horizon et dédoublant chaque chose par l'extension devant elle de son ombre qui la reculait, avait à la fois aminci et agrandi le paysage comme un plan replié jusque-là, qu'on développe. Au pied de chaque arbre, à la porte de chaque maison se tenaient des reflets éveillés qu'on n'avait pas l'habitude de voir dehors à cette heure-là, mais contre lesquels on aurait pu buter, car aucun mouvement ne décelait leur présence, on n'avait pas entendu venir leurs grandes formes qui dans l'ombre regardaient. Ce qui avait besoin de bouger, quelques feuilles d'acacia, bougeait. Mais leur frissonnement>

33:1. <frissonnement minutieux> **33:8.** <leur pianissimo> [33:7. <détaillés avec tant de netteté qu'ils>]

33:8. <leur pianissimo, comme ces motifs d'un instrument placé dans un orchestre au milieu des autres, exécute en sourdine et que le public croit entendre bien loin de la salle de concert, quoique l'auteur se soit naturellement arrangé pour que cette distance, illusoire, n'empêche pas une seule des notes, tout le con-

tour mélodique, de parvenir aux oreilles avec la plus intacte précision.

Je ne pouvais pas me dissimuler la gravité de la situation. L'éducation qu'on me donnait plaçait en effet avant toutes dans l'échelle du mal (et comme celles contre lesquelles j'avais le plus grand besoin d'être gardé) des fautes dont je comprends maintenant>

33:27. <maintenant> **34:9.** <avait «repris» de la glace. [33:40. <couloir, je serais chassé de la maison, on me mettrait> 34:7. <fenêtre. Mes grands parents* étaient rentrés. Maman>] {34:10-35:8}

35:8. «Hé bien, si tu veux, nous allons monter nous coucher», dit mon père. «Si tu veux, mon ami, bien que je n'aie pas l'ombre de sommeil. Mais puisque je vois que la pauvre Françoise m'a attendue>

35:12. <m'a attendue> **36:37.** <qu'il appelait> [35:16. Bientôt, j'entendis ma mère qui> 35:26. <pour des fautes bien moins graves on me> 35:29. <terrible encore que le silence, comme> 35.34: <envoie «s'engager» alors> 35:41. <«bonsoir», épouvanté en voyant déjà que> 36:15. <ou bien un soir, longtemps avant> 36:21. <en deux mots>]

□**36:37.** <qu'il appelait «des sensibleries», des «manifestations ridicules». Mais je ne sais pas si on peut éprouver pour un être un sentiment de reconnaissance plus profond que celui que j'éprouvai pour lui ce soir-là; je restais sans oser>

36:37. <sans oser> **37:3.** <depuis longtemps. [36:41. <d'Abraham dans sa* gravure que m'ait* donnée M. Swann, disant à Sarah, avec ce même geste, qu'elle ait à se départir> 37:8. <longtemps que lui a cessé>]

37:8. Il y a bien longtemps> **37:10.** <pour moi. Mais je suis encore secoué, aujourd'hui, quand je repense à elles, par les sanglots que j'eus alors la force de contenir devant mon père et qui n'éclatèrent que quand je me retrouvai seul avec maman. Et il ne s'est guère passé de soir depuis sans que j'envoie à mon père dans mes prières le cri de gratitude qui ne put pas, devant lui, sortir de mes lèvres. {37:14-37:20}

37:21. Maman passa> **40:42.** <très brillants. [37:23. <à être chassé de la maison> 37:26. <grâce magnifique, la> 37:39.

<diminuer pour l'avenir ma sensibilité> 38:7. <lui demandant: «Mais> 38:31. <la maladie, les malheurs ou l'âge> 39:8. <attendrissement avec nous*, être> 39:11. <jaunet, qui> 39:13. Voyons, mon loup, puisque> 39:36. <elle-même à Chartres chez> 39:37. <je ne risque pas> 40:1. <jamais à acheter quelque chose dont on ne put* tirer> 40:14. <photographies des plus beaux monuments ou paysages. Mais> 40:20. <encore, à plusieurs degrés, comme plusieurs «épaisseurs» d'art> 40:27. <du Grand-Canal par Turner> 40:33. <grand'mère essayait de> 40:39. <avant sa complète dégradation, par Morgen*).]

40:42. <très brillants. L'idée que je pris de Venise, à qui je ne cessais de penser et où nous devions aller à une des prochaines vacances, (et aussi bien des cathédrales françaises dans les gravures d'après Turner et d'après un dessin du Titien), qui est censée* avoir pour fond la lagune>

41:1. <la lagune> **41:30.** <mystérieux. [41:2. <de vulgaires photographies. 41:3. <quand on voulait dresser> 41:6. <tentative pour s'en servir> 41:8. <d'un des destinataires.» 41:15. <une métaphore qui, dans notre moderne langage, aurait été effacée par l'habitude et l'usage. 41:18. <pleins eux aussi, comme un mobilier> 41:23. <un pigeonnier ancien ou* toutes ces choses>]

□**41:30.** <mystérieux. C'était l'année où on m'avait promis de me laisser enfin lire des romans, et aux premiers qu'on me donna, mon inquiétude était de savoir si c'étaient vraiment des romans. Je demandais à mon grand-oncle, à M. Swann: «Est-ce que vous appelleriez *Quentin Durward* un «roman»? Je savais que George Sand était le type du romancier. Cela me>

41:32. Cela me> □**41:34.** <de délicieux. Les premières pages sont bien simples: Madeline Blanchet, la meunière de Cormouer trouve dans son pré un enfant qui joue devant la fontaine où elle lave son linge. Mais le fait que cette fermière, ce petit, cette fontaine, ce pré, appartinssent à un roman leur donnait à mes yeux un attrait extraordinaire. Et puis je sentais que cette rencontre de la meunière et de l'enfant était quelque chose de plus que ce qu'elle paraissait être, qu'elle aurait plus tard de l'importance dans la vie des personnages, que ce n'était pas une scène détachée, mais un commencement qui tendait vers un

avenir inconnu. Les procédés de narration destinés à exciter la curiosité ou l'attendrissement et qu'un lecteur un peu instruit reconnaît comme communs à beaucoup de romans, à moi qui n'avais presque rien lu et qui ne considérais pas un livre nouveau comme une chose ayant beaucoup de semblables, mais comme un être unique, n'ayant de raison d'être qu'en soi, car ces façons de dire qui éveillent une sorte d'inquiétude et de mélancolie me paraissaient simplement une émanation troublante de l'essence particulière à *François le Champi.*

41:43. Sous ces> **42:29.** <jeune savant. [42:3. <accentuations étranges qui me troublaient profondément. L'action> 42:15. <qui mettait une couleur vive, empourprée et charmante sur l'enfant qui la portait sans que je susse pourquoi. 42:17. <une lectrice un peu infidèle et qui expurgeait trop, c'était> 42:25. <pourquoi. Mais les passages un peu libres, les passages à sauter devenaient trop nombreux.]

42:29. D'un de ces élans passionnés, qui n'ont ni brusquerie étourdie ni maladresse parce qu'on n'y pense qu'à ceux qui en sont l'objet et jamais à soi, et qui s'allient au contraire si bien à toutes les délicatesses, à toutes les prudences, et les inspirent, elle s'unissait à l'infortune, à la tristesse, au génie; elle devenait eux-mêmes.

42:29. De même> **42:41.** <sa sensibilité> [42:33. <lui désapprendre* que> 42:37. <reçu entier, elle> 42:39. <qui tenaient tout entières pour ainsi dire dans>]

42:41. <sa sensibilité et de son cœur.

Aux phrases les plus simples est immanent, ou plutôt préexistant un accent cordial, qui les fait attaquer dans le ton qu'il faut, mais que les mots n'indiquent pas; chemin faisant, c'est lui qui choisit les épithètes et, si on ne le fait pas sentir sous elles, on ne comprend plus la raison de leur choix, elles semblent communes; il amortit en passant toute crudité dans le temps des verbes, de façon à donner à l'imparfait et au passé défini la douceur qu'il y a dans la bonté, la mélancolie qu'il y a dans la tendresse. Puis il dirige la phrase qui finit vers celle qui va commencer, tantôt pressant, tantôt ralentissant la marche des syllabes pour les faire entrer, quoique leurs quantités soient différentes, dans un rythme uniforme. C'est cet accent, ce souffle continu qui fait vivre cette prose et que le lecteur doit trouver en soi pour pouvoir le lui donner.

43:10. Mes remords> **43:17.** <que factice. [43:12. <savais que cela ne pourrait>]

□**43:17.** <que factice, exceptionnel, unique. Demain mes angoisses reprendraient mais maman ne resterait pas là. Et pourtant j'étais heureux. D'abord parce que mes angoisses une fois calmées, je ne les comprenais plus; il me semblait dépendre de moi qu'elles ne revinssent pas; demain était lointain et serait peut-être différent. Mais surtout parce que je ne voulais pas penser au lendemain; je pressentais déjà qu'on ne peut jamais goûter du bonheur que ce qui m'en était donné: un moment, un simulacre, et je pressentais déjà ce que je devais connaître plus tard dans l'amour non partagé (je peux* dire simplement dans l'amour, il y a des êtres pour qui il n'est pas d'amour partagé) c'est que là où le bonheur vrai est impossible, il peut venir une heure pendant laquelle la bonté de celle que nous aimons ou son caprice, ou le hasard, appliquent sur nos désirs, en une coïncidence aussi parfaite, les mêmes paroles, les mêmes gestes, les mêmes actions que si nous étions aimés, que si nous étions vraiment heureux. A nous alors de savoir considérer avec curiosité et posséder avec délices, cette petite parcelle de bonheur, à défaut de laquelle nous serions morts sans avoir jamais soupçonné ce que le bonheur peut être pour des cœurs moins difficiles ou plus favorisés; à nous de supposer qu'elle n'est que le fragment d'un bonheur durable et réel qui ne nous apparaît qu'à cet endroit; et pour que le lendemain n'inflige pas un démenti à cette feinte, à nous de ne pas chercher à obtenir une faveur de plus après celle que nous n'avons due qu'à l'artifice d'une minute d'exception. Enfermons-nous plutôt dans la solitude; tâchons d'y rester longtemps en harmonie avec les dernières vibrations de la voix que nous sûmes rendre un instant amoureuse et à qui nous ne demanderons plus rien que de ne plus s'adresser à nous, de peur que par une parole nouvelle, qui ne pourrait être que différente, elle vienne blesser d'une dissonance le silence sensitif où, comme grâce à quelque pédale, survit la tonalité du bonheur.

II

43:29. C'est ainsi que, pendant bien des années, quand> **44:19.** <du premier. [43.33. < feu de bengale> 43:37. <Swann (l'auteur inconscient de mes tristesses), le> 44:7. <que neuf heures du soir. 44:8. <interrogé là-dessus que> 44:15. <Combray et encore moins d'en écrire.]

□**44:19.** <du premier. Si dans un moment d'excitation intellectuelle où quelque circonstance a suspendu notre activité physique, par exemple si, allant en voiture à un rendez-vous, nous jetons un coup d'œil sur l'objet actuel de notre pensée, nous voyons qu'il eut* dépendu d'un hasard que cet objet n'y fut* pas encore entré. Et qui sait si tout à l'heure la voiture ne sera pas brisée et si notre esprit d'où la vie se retirera ne sera pas obligé de lâcher à jamais ces quelques idées qu'en ce moment il enserre et protège anxieusement de sa pulpe frémissante. Ou encore nous sommes comme un peintre montant un chemin qui surplombe un lac dont un rideau de rochers et d'arbres cache la vue. Par une brèche il l'aperçoit, il l'a tout entier devant lui. Il prend ses pinceaux. Ainsi notre esprit est-il tout entier devant nous. Nous le possédons, nous pouvons décrire chacune des hauteurs qui le dominent, les voiles qui sont arrêtés à sa surface. Mais bientôt viendra la nuit où l'on ne peut plus peindre et après laquelle le jour ne se relève pas.

·Si c'est souvent le hasard (j'entends par là des circonstances que notre volonté n'a point préparées, au moins en vue du résultat qu'elles auront) qui amène dans notre esprit un objet nouveau, c'est un hasard plus rare, un hasard sélectionné et soumis à des conditions de production difficiles, après des épreuves éliminatoires, qui ramène dans l'esprit un objet possédé autrefois par lui et qui était sorti de lui.

44:20. Je trouve> **48:22.** <comme ses rues> [44:25. <en possession de l'outil qui> 44:28. <l'enchantement est rompu. Délivrées> 44:40. <quand un de ces hivers derniers, comme> 44:41. <ma mère me trouvant glacé, me proposa> 45:2. <appelés «Petites Madeleines» qui> 45:6. <cuillerée de thé> 45:7. <de Madeleine. 45:8. <où la gorge* mêlée> 45:17. <puissante félicité? Je> 45:34. <est à la fois le pays> 46:7. <voisine. Puis

sentant> 46:10. <avec une suprême [*blanc*]. 46:11. <je le remets en face de la saveur> 46:42. <madeleine que tous les matins à Combray, quand j'allais> 47:4. <rappelé tant que je n'y eus pas goûté> 47:5. <en ayant souvent aperçues* depuis Combray, sans> 47:13. <dévot s'étaient> 47:24. <dans le thé que me donnait ma tante, aussitôt la vieille> 47:29. <pavillon qu'on avait construit pour mes parents sur ses derrières donnant sur le jardin, ce pan tronqué que seul j'avais revu jusque-là. Et avec> 47:33. <la place où> 47:33. <déjeuner, les chemins qu'on prenait si le temps était beau, la rue où on faisait quelquefois une course avant dîner. Et comme> 47:36. <Japonais se complaisent à tremper dans un bol de porcelaine coréenne rempli d'eau ou de leur infusion favorite, de petits> 48:2. <solidité, ville et jardins, est sorti de ma tasse de thé. [*Note: There is an indentation after* 48:3, *but in* Grasset A *the figure* «II» *of the Pléiade is situated before 43:29.*]

48:22. <comme ses rues aux graves noms de saint: rue Saint-Hilaire> {48:22-48:30}

48:30. <Saint-Hilaire> **48:33.** <son jardin>

□**48:33.** <son jardin (des saints dont je connaissais plusieurs pour les avoir vus à l'église dans leurs vitraux, qui se rattachaient à l'histoire des premiers seigneurs de Combray où leur nom inscrit à la croisée des rues semblait perpétuer leur résidence immémoriale et surnaturelle); et l'Eglise les dominait toutes sur la «Place» où il y avait quelques pigeons, beaucoup de vent, et cette dame en noir que dans les villes de province on voit toujours, même en dehors des heures d'office, pousser le vantail en bois pratiqué dans le porche. Les vieilles gens mouraient beaucoup, les jeunes étaient malingres, le parler de tous était traînard, mélancolique et doux, on était souvent «content de trouver du feu», on avait peur de «se faire mouiller»; et s'il faisait beau on trouvait que le temps n'était pas sain; construites en pierre noirâtre du pays, précédées de degrés extérieurs sur la rue, coiffées de pignons qui rebellaient* leur ombre devant elles, les maisons étaient obscures et dès que le jour commençait à tomber, il fallait relever les rideaux dans les «salles»; on entendait souvent sonner pour une mort; les enterrements se déroulaient en proces-

sion dans la ville avec les prêtres en surplis, les enfants de chœur et le Saint-Sacrement. {48:33-49:4}

49:5. La cousine> **53:35.** <Françoise pleurait> [49:7. <Octave, qu'elle aimait passionnément, n'avait plus quitté d'abord Combray> 49:40. <qui la traverse> 50:3. <avant d'entrer souhaiter> 50:9. <four» ou* de campagne> 50:23. <papier à ramages et de paroissien, je> 50:43. <attention s'il n'y avait personne dans la chambre à côté, et je l'entendais> 51:20. <les eût disposées, les eût «fait poser» de la> 51:24. <mais empilées> 51:32. <de la gare, modifiées> 51:41. <lueur qui reste sur les fresques effacées, de la> 52:12. <fois du maître-autel et de la pharmacie, où> 52:18. <pepsine, ni du Salut. De l'autre> 52:30. <va-t-en, va jouer, c'est de ton âge; et si> 52:36. <pendant le temps que nous passions à Combray. Il y avait eu> 52:38. <nous allassions, à Combray> 52:39. <encore quelques mois d'hiver à Paris> 53:1. <Françoise» et je te toucherai légèrement le bras.» 53:17. <confuse mais tendre. 53:23. <famille, le charme de n'être pas> 53:30. <glacial et qu'on pouvait supporter dehors un gros pardessus et un bon feu dans la maison, quand maman>53:32. <à sa grand'mère, etc.]

□**53:35.** <Françoise pleurait comme au premier jour ses parents morts depuis des années, lui parlait d'eux avec douceur, avec tendresse, lui demandait mille détails sur ce qui avait été leur vie, sachant le bien qu'on fait en parlant de leurs morts à ceux qui les ont vraiment aimés. Et Françoise, dans son langage, parfois poétique de paysanne, trouvait pour exprimer la profondeur de son chagrin, des paroles d'une vraie noblesse.

Maman, avec cette finesse qui, s'ajoutant chez elle à la bonté, lui permettait non seulement de s'intéresser à la vie des autres, mais encore de la comprendre, avait deviné tout de suite que Françoise n'aimait pas>

53:38. <n'aimait pas> **54:19.** <à la grand'messe> [54:3. Et Françoise, émue de la sympathie de ma mère et admirant sa pénétration, disait en riant> 54:7. <qui vous voient ce que> 54:15. <sachant combien nous appréciions son service, et de fait maman était émerveillée de voir «combien cette fille était intelligente et propre», aussi «belle» dès cinq heures>]

54:19. <à la grand'messe; comme elle avait bien compris tout de suite la manière dont le médecin voulait qu'on fît* un pansement, comme elle faisait tout bien>

54:19. <tout bien> **56:28.** <en pension> [54:22. <quand on demandait> 54:27. <conquête et ne lui témoignent ni prévenance, ni respect, sachant> 54:29. <cesserait de recevoir> 55:1. <pour aller à la messe; ce ne me surprendrait point qu'elle ne soit arrivée après l'élévation. 55:22. <année.

—Françoise, vous n'avez pas>]

56:28. <en pension à Chartres.

—Ah! à moins de ça, disait>

56:30. <disait ma tante. **57:14.** <quarante voleurs ou Jeanne d'Arc à Orléans et disait en souriant: Très bien, très bien> [57:3. <pourtant, à savoir qui> 57:4. <vif et qu'elle s'apercevait malheureusement avoir à attendre>]

57:17. See after 58:43.

58:36. Madame Octave> **58:43.** <aiment bien ça. [58:38. <bientôt onze heures> 58:42. <nos parisiens!]

58:43. <aiment bien ça. Et quand je leur en donne, même rien qu'en pointes, je vous assure qu'ils n'y vont pas avec le dos de la cuillère*. Je serais>

△**57:17.** Je serais bien allée chez Camus... ajoutait-elle en voyant> **58:36.** <si galante. [57:20. <Mlle Pupin. Allez surveiller votre déjeuner, ma pauvre> 58:2. <mon cousin ne> 58:3. <que ton cousin ne> 58:6. <mon cousin était> 58:7. <Pont-Vieux? un homme que tu ne connaissais point?> 58:9. <mon cousin, c'était> 58:13. <que tu ne connaissais point!"]

59:10. See after 106:31.

67:19. See after 111:43.

68:30. Mais parfois la chronique de Combray posait des problèmes que toute la sagacité de Françoise, aidée des deux sous de sel de Camus, ne suffisait pas à résoudre. Mes parents n'étaient-ils pas un jour revenus de l'église en disant qu'ils avaient vu une échelle dressée au milieu du chœur! Françoise, envoyée au plus vite chez l'épicier, était revenue bredouille; c'était justement le jour de sortie de Théodore à qui sa double profession de chantre ayant une part de l'entretien de l'église et de garçon épicier (un peu élève amateur en pharmacie également) donnait, avec des relations dans tous les mondes, un savoir universel.

—Ah! soupirait dans ces cas-là ma tante, je voudrais bien que ce soit>

68:40. <que ce soit> **69:16.** <de la balsamine> [69:3. <pris une chambre contre l'église d'où> 69:10. <que lui servaient ses anciens maîtres>]

□**69:16.** <de la balsamine, du papier de dentelle qu'on mettait à l'église sous les vases de l'autel, du reflet que le soleil couchant mettait quelquefois sur le porche ou des «biscuits roses» de chez Camus. Ces visites>

69:16. <visites étaient> **69:42.** <répondu> [69:34. <qu'elle avait après quelques hésitations et sur les officieuses instances de Françoise «laissés monter» et qui>]

69:42. <répondu: «D'un côté ce sera une délivrance pour vous avec ce que vous souffrez depuis la mort d'Octave,» ceux-là>

69:42. <ceux-là> **73:31.** <qu'elle annonçait. [70:2. <Françoise souriait avec un peu de moquerie de l'air> 70:4. <ou si elle avait entendu un coup de sonnette, Françoise riait> 70:9. <vue, et Françoise, au fond> 70:12. <qu'on l'approuve dans son régime, qu'on la plaigne pour ses souffrances et qu'on la rassure sur son avenir. 70:29. <inopiné, et quelquefois le jeudi, étaient> 70:31. <douloureux pour peu qu'Eulalie fut* en retard, et que je ne puis comparer qu'à la faim. Trop prolongée> 70:35. <le bienheureux coup> 70:37. <presque trouver mal. 70:38. <réalité, le jeudi et le dimanche> 70:40. <monter auprès de ma tante l'«occuper». Mais> 71:1. <qu'elle ceignait comme une tour armoriée, des douze fleurons> 71:3. <venu familièrement aussi au sortir de l'église, que nous étions> 71:8. <Françoise—selon> 71:14. <vie—ajoutait: une barbue> 71:17. <marché de Troussinville, des> 71:31. <qui était amateur, inspiration, attention personnelle de Françoise, une crème au chocolat, œuvre de circonstance, nous était offerte, fugitive et légère, mais où elle avait mis tout son talent. 72:2. <dehors, mais pour ne pas lire en sortant de table, va d'abord prendre l'air un instant.» C'était aller m'asseoir> 72:9. <soignée de laquelle* s'élevait> 72:14. <temple à Vénus. 72:27. <forestière et vieille France,

qui> 73:8. <qu'on lui trouvait> 73:14. <méditation que son valet de chambre, émerveillé, aurait craint de troubler d'un seul mouvement et dont il attendait le résultat, toujours identique avec une curiosité respectueuse. Enfin> 73:21. <le lui dire>]

73:31. Si les affiches fraîchement posées humides encore et boursoufflées, en apprenant à mon cœur l'agitation inséparable de l'attente d'une fête à laquelle on pourrait assister et à laquelle on n'assistera peut-être pas, ne l'avaient troublé des incertitudes du futur et à la fois d'une odeur de colle et d'actualité, rien n'eut* été plus désintéressé et plus heureux que les rêves que chaque pièce affichée offrait à mon imagination et qui, pour chacune, étaient conditionnés par la couleur du papier sur lequel le titre se détachait et aussi par les images inséparables des mots qui le composaient. Si ce n'est une œuvre comme *le Testament de César Giraudeau** ou comme *Œdipe-Roi* qui s'incrivait*>

73:39. <s'inscrivait*> **77:18.** <à ce que devait> [74:21. <journée: 1° Got, 2° Delaunay, 3° Febvre, 4° Coquelin, 5° Thiron et qui avaient fini> 75:3. <représenter leur vie. 75:4. Sarah Bernhardt, la Berma, Bartet, Réjane, mais toutes> 75:28. Aussi, sous> 75:31. <oncle un jour> 75:33. <heure, je descendis et> 75:35. <jusque chez lui> 76:6. <instant, ce petit.» 77:10. <une cocotte chique*>]

77:18. <à ce que devait être l'immoralité de sa vie, j'étais peut-être plus troublé que si elle avait été concrétisée en une apparence spéciale, qu'en la sentant invisible comme le secret de quelque roman, de quelque scandale qui avait fait sortir de chez ses parents bourgeois et vouer* à tout le monde, qui avait fait épanouir en beauté>

77:23. <en beauté> **80:38.** <forme magnifique. [77:36. <rencontré son père chez vous. N'est-ce> 77:38. Comment aurais-je pu> 77:41. <exquis, moi qui connaissais la réserve et la froideur de mon père, j'étais> 78:2. <son insuffisante amabilité. J'ai compris plus tard> 79:3. <prix dans sa classe, ajouta-t-il> 79:16. <baisers fous et de caresses passionnées les joues> 79:20. <que je ne parle pas> 79:43. <je le souhaitais, la bienveillance dont j'étais animé à l'égard de cette présentation. 80:4. <voulurent juger l'action> 80:19. <Adolphe et m'était* attardé aux abords de l'arrière* cuisine, quand> 80:21. <laisser ma fille

cuisiner, servir> 80:28. <s'incarnait: car jamais la fille de cuisine ne fut jamais* la même>]

80:38. Ces sarraus flottants rappelaient de ces houppelandes dont Giotto a revêtu certaines de ces figures symboliques, dans les fresques dont M. Swann m'avait donné des photographies. Elle-même, la pauvre fille>

81:1. <pauvre fille> **81:36.** <envieuses pensées. [81:5. <à l'Arena. Et ces Vertus et ces Vices de Padoue> 81:11. <l'esprit, —qu'elle portait comme un simple et pesant fardeau, —de même> 81:14. <«Caritas» incarne cette vertu, sans qu'aucune> 81:19. <les tisons* de la terre> 81:26. L'envie, elle> 81:29. <il remplit>]

81:37. See after 82:15.

82:15. De même l'attention de la pauvre fille de cuisine était sans cesse> **82:23.** <l'idée de la mort.

△**81:37.** Malgré toute l'admiration que M. Swann professait pour des* fresques de Giotto, je n'avais à cette époque, et je n'eus de longtemps aucun plaisir à considérer aux murs de la petite salle d'études>

△**81:39.** <salle d'études> **82:15.** <plus frappant. [82:2. <l'opérateur, cette Justice, dont le visage grisâtre et mesquinement régulier est la caractéristique de tant de jolies bourgeoises latines, pieuses et sèches dont la plupart sont enrôlées>

82:25. Il fallait> **90:41.** <de l'Olympos.» [82:29. Et je me demande d'ailleurs si cette non participation> 82:30. <lui, n'a pas* aussi> 82:42. <cuisine, faisant> 83:2. <Vérité servait> 83:13. <de la Cure par l'emballeur (averti> 83:30. <lui, et qui offrait> 83:32. <jouir que morcelé, s'accordait bien> 83:35. <l'émouvoir), pareil au repos d'une main immobile, supportait le choc> 83:40. <survenu, mais surtout s'il faisait beau, venait> 83:42. <sous le cèdre, dans> 84:19. <intime en moi*, la poignée> 84:24. <l'épicerie orange*, trop distante de la maison pour que Françoise y put* acheter comme chez Camus, mais mieux achalandée comme papeterie et librairie, retenu> 84:28. <porte qu'ils faisaient plus mystérieuse, plus semée d'inscription* qu'une porte de cathédrale; c'est parce que je l'avais> 84:36. <croyance première qui> 84:42. <survenaient par les personnages du livre> 84:42. <vrai que ces personnages n'étaient

pas> 85:14. <partie de notre potion* totale de lui que nous pourrons en être affectés, bien plus> 85:17. <de sa notion totale de soi qu'il pourra en être affecté lui-même. 85:23. <les avons faites les* nôtres> 85:27. <la rapidité et l'intensité de notre regard. 85:29. <toute l'émotion> 85:31. <ceux qu'on a en> 85:34. <possibles que* nous> 85:38. <perception. Ainsi notre cœur change, dans la vie, et c'est la pire douleur. Mais nous ne la connaissons que dans la lecture, en imagination. Dans la réalité> 85:41. <change, mais comme> 86:2. <nous est épargnée. 86:5. <exerçait sur moi une> 86:6. <l'autre, celui que> 86:9. <j'ai eu la nostalgie> 86:16. <pensée, cet été-là il fut> 86:17. <que fut* celle que> 86:20. <couleurs complémentaires qui viennent s'ajouter. 86:27. <yeux, mais analogues. 86:32. <produit sans prestige de la fantaisie d'un jardinier—une part véritable, infiniment précieuse, de la Nature, digne d'être> 87:2. <mais le retentissement> 87:4. <a projeté sur elles, à être déçu en constatant> 87:8. <habileté, en luxe, pour> 87:12. <lieux désirés, si j'eusse> 87:19. <immobile—de ce qui n'était qu'un même et infléchissable jaillissement de toutes> 87:23. <états juxtaposés en même temps dans> 87:24. <réel qui enveloppait le tout, je trouve> 87:27. <sonnait à l'église, de> 87:38. <sonné; celle-ci venait s'inscrire tout près d'elle dans le ciel> 88:4. <effacé les rayons de la cloche sur la surface> 88:5. Beaux après-midi sous le cèdre du jardin> 88:10. <eaux vives, m'évoquent encore cette vie quand je pense à eux et la contiennent en effet> 88:15. <de leurs heures> 88:20. <coupant les doigts et se cassant des dents et criant> 88:22. <spectacle. Car c'était le jour où> 88:27. <et se faisaient voir d'eux, par la fente que laissaient entre elles deux maisons éloignées de l'avenue de la gare, la fille du jardinier avait aperçu l'éclat des casques. 88:32. <toute la largeur, il n'y avait plus de trottoir, et le galop> 88:35. <torrent déchaîné et furieux. 88:37. <sera demain fauchée> 89:5. <en 1870; ils> 89:13. <avenue de la gare qu'on voyait toujours de nouveaux casques courir et briller au soleil. 89:17. <fille s'élançant comme> 89:19. <bravé mille fois la mort, et venait> 89:22. <côté de Méséglise. 90:4. <dont la tempête laisse> 90:7. Habituellement au contraire je pouvais lire tranquille. 90:12. <décoré de grappes de fleurs, mais> 90:19.

<Bloch, qui avait été accueilli par mon grand-père aux chants répétés de: *Israël romps la chaîne* [*cf.* 91:19]. En m'entendant> 90:31. <Père Lecomte*> 90:33. <qui m'a été recommandé par cet immense bonhomme. Il tient l'auteur, le sieur Bergotte> 90:39. <*Baghanat** et le *Levier* de Magnus* a dit vrai, par Apollon, tu goûteras les joies>]

91:4. Malheureusement> **91:22.** <paroles. [91:13. <l'amenais dîner à la maison c'était toujours un juif, ce qui ne lui allait pas. De plus, en principe—son ami Swann était d'origine juive—s'il n'avait trouvé> 91:18. <qu'il ne fredonne pas> 91:21. <camarade le connût et ne* rétablît>]

91:23. Avant de les avoir vus, il devinait l'origine juive de ceux de mes amis qui l'étaient en effet, rien qu'en entendant leur nom qui, bien souvent, n'avait rien de particulièrement israélite, mais avait souvent quelque chose de fâcheux dans leurs modes.

91:28. —Et comment> **92:27.** <il est fou. [91:29. —Dumont, mon oncle. 91:38. <forcé, par un interrogatoire dissimulé, à confesser à son insu sa foi et son sang, alors> 92:2. <douce veillée*. 92:9. Mais, en revanche, Bloch> 92:12. <Bloch, vous êtes mouillé, quel> 92:16. <vis résolument> 92:18. <de me notifier. 92:20. <Bloch avait été parti.]

92:28. Et à tout le monde parce que étant venu dîner une heure et demie en retard et couvert de boue, au lieu de s'excuser il avait dit:

92:31. —Je ne me laisse> **93:25.** <plus souffrant> [92:37. <pas l'ami> 93:4. <transports ardents> 93:9. <avec amitié et n'étant pas capables> 93:11. <devoirs de l'amitié et des exigences sur> 93:14. Nos torts même font difficilement départir de ce qu'elles nous doivent. Ces* natures dont> 93:23. <Minos me fatiguaient>]

93:25. <plus souffrant qui* n'aurait fait une nouvelle conversation avec lui, bien que ma mère les jugeât pernicieuses.

Et on l'aurait encore reçu à Combray, si, après ce dîner, il ne m'avait assuré avoir entendu dire de la façon la plus certaine que> {93:27-93:33.}

93:33. <certaine que> **95:23.** <quand l'auteur reprenait son récit. [93:37. <l'abordais ensuite> 94:5. <je remarquais> 94:6. <moments, les mêmes où un flot caché d'harmonie> 94:15.

<elles qui d'elles-mêmes avaient> 94:17. <donnaient, elles et les hautes pensées qu'elles figuraient, quelque> 94:19. <donna un plaisir incomparable à celui que j'avais trouvé au premier, un plaisir que> 94:26. <qui avait* déjà été, sans que je m'en rendisse compte, la cause du plaisir que je prenais à lire Bergotte, je n'eus> 94:29. <livre de lui, traçant> 94:31. <plutôt en quelque sorte du> 94:33. <analogues qui seraient* se rapporter à lui, donneraient une sorte d'épaisseur, de volume, dont mon esprit, pour le contenir, semblait agrandi. 94:38. <lettrée. Pour lire son dernier livre paru, le Dr du·Boulbon> 95:2. <village, jusque dans les champs, la fleur charmante et commune. 95:3. <le Dr du Boulbon> 95:16. <intérieures* à sa prose et n'étaient décelés que par> 95:18. <plus douces encore, peut-être plus harmonieuses> 95:21. <il se complut>]

95:23. J'aurais voulu que tous ses livres fussent une suite de morceaux et posséder son opinion, c'est-à-dire la Vérité, sur toutes les grandes questions. Malheureusement [*cf.* 95:36] sur presque toutes son opinion m'était inconnue. Je ne doutais pas qu'elle ne fut* entièrement différentes* et bien éloignée des miennes, et persuadé qu'elles semblent de pures stupidités à cet Esprit parfait; j'avais tellement fait table rase de toutes, que quand par hasard il m'arriva de rencontrer dans un de ses livres quelque idée que j'avais eue, quelque sentiment que j'avais déjà éprouvé, mon cœur se gonflait comme si un Dieu dans sa bonté me les avait rendus, les avait déclarés légitimes et beaux, et comme si mon humble vie et les royaume* du Vraie* n'étaient pas sur tous les points séparés. Un jour ayant rencontré dans un livre de lui, à propos> {95:23-96:27}

96:27. <à propos> **96:43.** <retrouvé. [96:33. <figurer dans un miroir de la vérité une remarque analogue> 96:35. <Legrandin, remarques> 96:38. <intérêt, il me sembla que soudain mon humble vie et les royaumes du Vrai n'étaient pas aussi séparés que je n'avais cru, qu'ils> 96:42. <je pleurais>]

96:43. Chaque fois qu'il parlait d'une chose dont jusque-là la beauté [*cf.* 95:23] m'était voilée, vague, presque sans charme, des sapins, de la grêle, de Notre-Dame [*blanc*] avec une image, il en faisait exploser cette beauté qui s'approchait de moi, était claire, m'enchantait. Aussi sentant combien il y avait de parties de l'univers que ma perception infime ne dénicherait jamais s'il ne me les décrivait pas, j'aurais voulu avoir sa description, son opinion de toutes choses, surtout de celles [*cf.* 95:31] que j'avais l'occasion de voir, plus que toutes de* celles dont un mot de ses livres m'avait fait penser qu'il les aimait particulièrement, donc qu'elles étaient certainement riches de beauté, la vieille architecture de France, les paysages marins. J'imaginais Bergotte comme un vieillard faible et désillusionné qui avait perdu>

97:2. <avait perdu> **97:26.** <car Bergotte> [97:4. <plus «dolce», plus lentement peut-être> 97:8. Elle me faisait rêver du temps où je serais au collège dans la classe appelée Philosophie. 97:12. <ne ressembleraient en rien à lui, j'aurais> 97:16. Un jour pendant>]

97:26. <car Bergotte est un délicieux écrivain. Je le connais beaucoup, c'est mon plus ancien camarade.

—Oh! Est-ce que vous pourriez>

97:34. <vous pourriez> **97:42.** <dans *Le Cid*> [97:41. <leur redemander.]

97:42. <dans *Le Cid,* c'est aussi génial que les plus grandes manifestations de l'art en n'importe quel genre. Je crois que vous auriez là une vision d'une noblesse qui ne se retrouvera plus. Vous devriez profiter pendant qu'elle le joue.

—Est-ce qu'il y a [*cf.* 99:18] des ouvrages de Bergotte où il ait parlé d'elle?

—Je crois dans sa petite plaquette sur Racine, mais elle doit être épuisée. Je le lui demanderai. Je peux lui demander tout ce que vous voulez, il n'y a pas de semaine dans l'année où il ne dîne à la maison. C'est le grand ami de ma fille. Ils vont ensemble visiter les vieilles villes, les belles abbayes, les châteaux qui sont dans des sites poétiques.

Mes notions sur la hiérarchie sociale n'étaient pas assez nettes pour y mettre obstacle, l'impossibilité que mon père trouvait à ce que nous fréquentions Mme et Mlle Swann avaient* eu pour effet de me les faire situer au premier rang et de les revêtir d'un grand prestige. Je souffrais que ma mère ne se teignit* pas ses cheveux et ne se mit* pas de noir aux yeux, comme j'avais entendu dire à la maison par notre voisine, Mme Lazeret, qui n'était pas bonne langue, que Mme Swann le faisait pour plaire non à son mari, mais à M. Orgueay, et je sentais que nous devions être pour elle un objet de mépris et de risée. Ce* qui me peinait> {97:42-99:37}

99:37. <me peinait. **100:38.** <indispensable à> [99:39. <je pensais souvent> 99:40. <un même arbitraire et charmant visage. Mais quand je sus que Mme Swann> 100:1. <demandait s'il> 100:4. <Bergotte, que la causerie intime à table, ce qui correspondait pour elle à la conversation de ma grand'tante, c'était des paroles> 100:7. <tous les sujets> 100:9. <j'aurais voulu connaître ses oracles> 100:10. <d'elle inaperçu et> 100:16. <que sa pensée me remplit à la fois de désir> 100:19. <qui lui disait> 100:23. <Ile de France et des plateaux de la Normandie où j'aurais pu en voir, faisait refluer ses reflets sur l'image que je faisais d'elle. C'était être> 100:27. <pénétrer, de tout ce qu'exige l'amour pour naître. C'est ce à quoi> 100:35. <un germe* souverain pour faire>]

100:38. <indispensable à un bourgeois quelconque.

Cependant, ces jours-là—tandis que je lisais—ce que ma tante n'admettait pas en dehors du dimanche, jour où il est défendu de s'occuper à rien de sérieux et où elle ne cousait pas, me disait «comment tu *t'amuses* encore à lire, ce n'est pourtant pas dimanche» en donnant au mot amusement le sens d'enfantillage et de perte de temps, —ma tante devisait avec Françoise en attendant l'heure d'Eulalie>

101:4. <l'heure d'Eulalie. **101:38.** <faire descendre. [101:13. <arrivée hier à> 101:26. <abri.

—Comment, trois heures> 101:32. <marquant la place des>]

101:41. Un petit coup> **103:4.** <au sentiment> [102:25. <avant l'Adoration perpétuelle. 102:29. < Dieu et le bon Dieu se venge. 102:41. <bas, je l'ai fait entrer>]

103:4. <au sentiment de ma tante que le curé fatiguait toujours par des explications infinies qu'il lui donnait à propos de la moindre chose. Mais arrivant ainsi juste en même temps que celle d'Eulalie, la visite du curé lui devenait franchement désagréable.

103:13. Elle eut* mieux> □**103:20.** <qu'il y a dans votre église un homme qui fait des peintures? Dans une église? Je

peux dire que je suis arrivée à mon âge sans avoir jamais entendu parler d'une chose pareille!

—Et il paraît que ce sera comme ça jusqu'à la saint Jean, Madame Octave, répondit le curé, je n'étais pas libre de refuser. Il y a un ordre écrit de la main de Monseigneur et de l'architecte du diocèse.

—Mais soupirait ma tante qu'est-ce que le monde aujourd'hui va donc chercher!

—Et quelle partie de Saint-Hilaire croyez-vous que cet artiste va reproduire sur sa toile? Le grand vitrail de Guibert* le Mauvais qui me donne ce faux jour derrière mon autel!

—Ce qu'il y a de plus vilain dans l'église!

—Mon Dieu je n'irai pas jusqu'à dire ce qu'il y a de plus vilain, car s'il y a>

103:26. <car s'il y a> **103:43.** <abbés de Combray> [103:29. <restaurée. Passe encore pour le porche qui est sale> 103:38. <laisser des vitraux qui>]

103:43. <abbés de Combray et des comtes de Brabant. (Vous savez que les seigneurs Guermantes* descendent des anciens comtes de Brabant, et la fameuse Geneviève de Brabant était une demoiselle de Guermante* d'où l'aînée de la maison est toujours baptisée Geneviève). Voyez Méséglise ce n'est plus aujourd'hui qu'une paroisse de fermiers, quoique dans l'antiquité cette localité ait eu un grand essor au commerce de chapeaux de feutre et des* pendules. Hé bien! l'église> {104:4-104:14; 104:18-104:21}

104:21. <l'église> **104:25.** <verrière de Chartres. Beaucoup de personnes même la préfèrent et la regardent comme d'un plus beau travail. Ah! cela ne ressemble pas au vitrail de Gilbert le Mauvais!

Mais comme je lui disais>

104:28. <lui disais> **104:43.** <saint Hilaire. [104:33. <qui commençait à se fatiguer, il> 104:39. <Guermantes, recevant l'absolution>]

104:43. <saint Hilaire. Son frère Charles le Bègue, prince pieux mais qui, ayant perdu son père de bonne heure, exerçait le pouvoir suprême avec toute la présomption d'une jeunesse à qui la discipline manque, dès que> {105:1-105:13}

105:18. <dès que> **106:31.** <découpés. [105:16. <habitant. Fulbert, voulant> 105:21. <celle de Childebert, en> 105:19. <ville, il y faisait> 105:23. <d'ici à Pinsonville, pour aller combattre> 105:27. <puisque Fulbert brula*> 105:33. <sur lui [*blanc*] et lui tranchèrent> 106:2. <ajoutait-il sans apercevoir l'indignation qu'il causait à ma tante en ayant l'air de supposer qu'elle était capable de monter dans le clocher, car> 106:18. < fossés de Saint-Alise, dont> 106:19. <rideau de six grands> 106:20. <canaux de Pont-le-Vidame. Chaque fois que je suis allé à Pont-le Vidame, j'ai>]

□**106:31.** <découpés. Pour voir l'eau, pour en avoir le plaisir, il faut aller à Pont-le-Vidame même, flâner au bord du canal, seulement c'est autant dire rien. Il faudrait pour bien faire être à la fois dans le clocher de Saint-Hilaire et à Pont-le-Vidame.

Avez-vous remarqué, Madame Octave qu'il en est ainsi de bien des choses? Ainsi chaque fois que je dois aller à l'Evêché voir Monseigneur, je pense avant de partir à tout ce qu'est Monseigneur, je suis encore en haut du clocher, je me dis: es-tu heureux de pouvoir te rendre auprès de ce prélat qui approche le Saint Père, de ce grand savant, de ce grand saint! Et quand après être allé voir Monseigneur je rentre à la cure, je me dis: pense à l'homme que tu as vu tantôt, mais que dis-je c'est plus qu'un homme, c'est un personnage, c'est quelqu'un! Mais entre ces deux moments-là, c'est-à-dire quand je suis auprès de Monseigneur, eh bien! vrai, je me sens plus heureux à tailler une bavette comme en ce moment dans votre chambrette, qui n'a pourtant rien du palais d'un prince de l'Eglise, —mais qu'est-ce que vous feriez de plus, puisqu'elle est à votre convenance que vous avez le confortable et la propreté. Plut* à Dieu que je puisse en dire autant de mon église!

J'avoue que j'étais bien loin d'être aussi sévère que notre curé pour l'église de Combray, et que ce qu'il y critiquait était peut-être justement ce que j'y aimais le mieux. Le vieux porche noir, grêlé comme un* écumoire, dévié et>

△**59:11.** <dévié et> **60:15.** <douce tapisserie de verre; > [59:12. <il conduisait> 59:16. <sillons plus profonds que n'en trace la roue> 59:18. <les jours; —ces pierres> 59:19. <abbés de Combray et de Saint-Rigier faisait> 59:20. <spiri-

tuel; et qui, elles-mêmes, n'étaient plus de la matière inerte et dure car> 59:31. <distendues; —ces vitraux> 59:32. <le soleil ne se montrait pas, de> 59:34. <l'un rempli dans> 59:42. <de [*blanc*] peint> 60:3. <déjeuner); un autre où une montagne> 60:12. <pierre); tous si anciens> {60:15-60:41}

△**60:42.** <—ces deux tapisseries de haute lice représentant le couronnement d'Esther par Assuérus (où la tradition> **63:3.** <joues violettes> [60:43. <qu'on ait donné> 61:3. <amoureux), et à qui leurs> 61:14. <invisible; —tout cela> 61:18. <Dagobert, le vitrail de l'abbé Suger, le tombeau des fils de Charlemagne, en> 61:19. <émaillé), qui me faisaient m'avancer dans la nef comme> 61:23. <faisait pour moi de l'église de Combray quelque chose> 61:26. <la quatrième y étant> 61:37. <sœurs, se placent en souriant pour le cacher aux étrangers, devant> 62:11. <Combray, pourrais-je vraiment> 62:13. <religieux, auprès de tant d'absides glorieuses que j'avais vues depuis. Du dehors> 62:21. <j'ai vues, en me demandant dans laquelle le sentiment religieux est exprimé avec le plus de puissance, il ne me> 62:40. <une de ces démarcations que>]

□△**63:3.** <joues violettes contre la sombre façade de l'église, les fuchsias n'en devenaient pas pour cela plus sacrés pour moi que mon grand'oncle* quand il était agenouillé sous le vitrail de Charles le Mauvais; entre les fleurs de Mme Loiseau et la pierre noircie sur laquelle elles s'appuyaient, même imperceptible aux yeux, il y avait à l'esprit un abîme.

Quand on apercevait, rue de l'Oiseau, sa porte salie d'un noir de fumée que n'y avait déposé aucun feu, et à portée de la main à l'envers du vitrail familièrement mystérieux de Gilbert le Mauvais, quelques traits de couleur effacés, comme en ces œuvres antiques et grossières qu'un goût barbare avait surchargé de pierreries et où se trouve encore dans les rainures de la pierre, quelque coudée d'émail vert, un rubis baroque et un saphir cabochon, l'église avait l'air d'être au cœur de Combray comme son passé même, comme les jours de Saint-Hilaire qui survivaient.

△**63:9.** On reconnaissait> **64:35.** <octave au-dessus. [63:11. <pas encore; ainsi par exemple du train qui nous amenait de Paris, où mon père en l'apercevant qui filait tour à tour> 63:16. <arrivé», et aussi dans une des plus grandes promenades que

nous faisions de Combray, où la route resserrée, débouchait tout à coup sur une immense plaine semée au loin de vallées, remplie de petites collines et fermée à l'horizon de forêts déchiquetées> 63:33. <pour la regarder. 63:35. <avec cette justesse et cette originalité dans les proportions qui n'ajoute pas de beauté qu'aux visages humains, il laissait tomber> 64:3. <çà et là, immobiles en apparence, mais> 64:5. <mouette posée avec> 64:25. Et en le regardant, en regardant la douce tension>]

□△**64:36.** Ma grand'mère ne se demandait pas si cette impression de beauté *artistique* (il n'est pas question en ceci de religion, car ma grand'mère était libre-penseuse), que lui donnait le clocher de Saint-Hilaire, était quelque chose de plus réel que la vie, pouvant subsister en dehors d'elle; mais je sais bien que, sans en avoir conscience sans doute, elle le croyait, et d'une de ces croyances, qui sont les seules profondes, celles qu'impliquent certains actes. Car, quand une de ses nièces qu'elle aimait beaucoup et qui lui ressemblait, fut gravement atteinte, ma grand'mère souhaitait que si on la laissait voyager, on lui fit* voir le clocher de Combray, qu'elle ne connaissait pas. Et quand cette jeune femme fut morte, souvent ma grand'mère disait: «Je regrette qu'elle n'ait pas vu le clocher, il lui aurait plu.» Sans doute la croyance que suppose le regret est en désaccord avec la conception scientifique d'une mort totale, mais ce désaccord n'est pas une objection moins forte contre la conception scientifique que contre la croyance. Peut-être le matérialisme et la doctrine de l'immortalité de l'âme sont-ils aussi différents tous deux de la réalité, que pourrait* être par exemple, vis-à-vis de ce qui se passe dans un téléphone, les opinions de deux personnes d'un pays où l'on ne saurait pas ce que c'est que l'électricité et qui croiraient, l'une qu'il s'agit d'une simple supercherie, l'autre que c'est la voix elle-même qui est transportée à des centaines de lieues par un renforcement de sa puissance d'expension* acoustique.

△**64:36.** C'était le clocher> **67:17.** <mon cœur> [64:40. <base recouverte> 64:41. <dimanche, encore couché, je> 64:43. <faut se lever vite pour aller à la grand'messe», et je savais> 65:6. <de toile écrue et d'été, faire> 65:7. <ferait sortir, en> 65:16. <nos cousins d'Evreux avaient profité du

beau temps pour venir déjeuner, on avait> 65:40. <de Normandie, deux> 66:14. <dôme Saint-Augustin> 66:17. <gravures, —et j'en possède encore beaucoup, —que ma mémoire exécuta avec goût, elle ne put> 66:21. <aucune d'elle* avec quelque goût que ma mémoire ait pu les exécuter ne tient> 66:29. <on suivait des yeux>]

106:34. Le curé> **111:12.** <deux heures?» [107:14. <Françoise n'aurait jamais> 107:20. <Combray, Pont-le-Vidame et> 107:25. <ce qui était son> 107:43: <étaient ce qu'elle méprisait le plus s'ils ne lui disaient pas> 108:5. <à trouver qu'il y avait quelque injustice à ce que les dons n'allassent pas plus souvent à elle et à trouver bien petits ceux que ma tante lui faisait en comparaison des sommes imaginaires prodiguées à Eulalie. 108:10. <lui rapporterait* ses visites. 108:17. <jamais à médire*, en oracles sybillins, ou en sentences> 108:32. <laisse reposer. Et ma tante, épuisée, ne répondait> 109:12. <pas», ce train-train> 109:18. <cherche une à la ville voisine. Ma> 109:21. <tard dans la matinée, lui> 109:25. J'allais me retirer doucement> 110:7. <personne ait jamais> 110:10. <je ne parle pas naturellement de ces variations qui> 110:15. <marché de Troussinville, le> 110:34. <plaisir, le noyau tout prêt>] {111:12-111:18}

111:18. <tout le monde> **111:43.** <son lorgnon.

△**67:19.** Le samedi était généralement marqué par une rencontre qui, elle, ne résultait en rien de l'essence de ce jour particulier. Il était rare que nous ne croisions pas en rentrant M. Legrandin qui> **67:21.** <samedi après-midi au lundi matin.

△**67:22.** <lundi matin et qui, en descendant de wagon, allait tout de suite faire un tour de promenade, pendant qu'on apportait ses affaires chez lui.

△**67:22.** C'était un de> **67:41.** <le type de l'homme> [67:26. <dont profitent exclusivement leur conversation et leurs amitiés. 67:27. <littérateurs, doués de plus de «facilité»> 67:36. <une fière tournure> 67:38. <politesse exquise, causeur> 67:39. <entendu et qu'on feuilletait comme un livre, il était>]

△**67:41.** <le type de l'homme accompli, esprit d'élite, âme élevée, prenant la vie de la façon la plus noble et la plus délicate: ce que ma grand'mère appelait quelqu'un de vraiment bien. Elle

ne trouvait à reprendre en lui que deux choses: les tirades enflammées>

△**68:4.** <tirades enflammées> **68:8.** <rémission», et la flamme étrange qui passait parfois dans ses yeux et faisait dire à ma grand'mère: «Mes enfants, Legrandin mourrait un jour fou que cela ne m'étonnerait pas.» Mais nous savions que sa tristesse venait de la mort d'une sœur qu'il avait beaucoup aimée. L'autre était mariée dans la Manche, près de Querqueville, avec un gentilhomme bas-normand.

—Salut, amis! nous disait-il le samedi quand il nous rencontrait, jetant de loin sa cigarette si ma mère était avec nous. Vous êtes heureux d'habiter beaucoup ici; après-demain il faudra que je rentre à Paris, dans ma niche.

—Mais je crois que vous n'avez pas à vous plaindre de votre maison de Paris, lui disait mon père. Il paraît que c'est le dernier mot du confortable.

△**68:20.** —Oh! répondait M. Legrandin, avec ce sourire> **68:28.** <qu'il lui faut.

△**68:29.** Et nous le quittions afin de rentrer un peu plus tôt que les autres jours voir ma tante qui était toute seule. Et puis quand Françoise était revenue, s'informant dans les plus grands détails de ce que ma tante avait fait, si elle avait reposé, si elle avait demandé de l'eau de Vichy, on la pressait pour le dîner, si on était en mai, car alors le samedi soir, nous allions au «mois de Marie.»

112:4. Comme nous y rencontrions M. Vington, qui venait en voiture avec sa fille, ma mère prenait garde que rien ne clochât dans ma tenue, puis on partait pour l'église. C'est peut-être au mois de Marie que je vis, ou remarquai, pour la première fois des aubépines.

112:9. <aubépines. N'étant pas> **112:25.** <mystique. [114:15. <fête, enjolivées encore des festons>]

□**112:25.** <mystique. Je levai les yeux un peu plus haut: alors ce n'était pas seulement des boutons comme au bas des branches, mais des corolles qui s'ouvraient çà et là avec une grâce si insouciante qu'en suivant, qu'en mimant intérieurement le geste de leur efflorescence, je l'imaginais comme si ç'avait été le mouvement de tête étourdi et rapide d'une blanche jeune fille,

distraite et vive. Leurs pétales retenaient négligemment comme une robe de bal sa ruche qui se tient droite toute seule, un bouquet d'étamines, fines comme des fils de la Vierge, ajouté, fixé à la fleur comme un dernier atout, vaporeux, et qui l'embrunit tout entière d'un nuage de mousseline. Mais cherchant à recréer en moi, pour comprendre sa beauté, l'âme de la fleur, dix fois je fus obligé d'abandonner la forme connue au mouvement de laquelle elle m'avait semblé le moment d'avant faire allusion mais dont elle différait trop, et quand ces fines étamines avec leurs pointes minuscules avaient donné à la fleur le regard vague, aux pupilles diminuées d'une jeune fille myope, coquette, ou maniérée, aussitôt leur rayonnement au milieu des pétales me paraissait appartenir au même style catholique et flamboyant qui ajourait la rampe du jubé et les meneaux du vitrail.

C'est M. Vington près de qui j'étais placé et qu'en sa qualité de naturaliste j'avais élu pour l'interroger sur les aubépines qui prononça les mots d'étamine et de calice, que je connaissais déjà—parce que maman avait revêtu pour une soirée une robe d'étamine et que je savais le rôle du calice pendant la messe—et que, sans leur donner un autre sens, j'appliquai dès lors aux aubépines dont ils fixèrent dans mon esprit le caractère de ravissante élégance et de mysticité. Quand, le service fini, je m'agenouillai en passant devant l'autel> {112:25-113:36}

113:37. <devant l'autel> □**113:41.** <cette odeur, comme les parties gratinées... le goût d'une frangipane. Mais l'odeur des aubépines ressemblait plutôt à celle des joues de Mlle Vington que je croyais résider sous leurs taches de rousseur, en ce que comme elle, elle ne conduisait à rien de mangeable, et elle prenait quelque chose de plus pur et de plus doux d'être elle-même le seul et immatériel aliment offert à la gourmandise qu'elle avait éveillée. Mais aussi, malgré la silencieuse immobilité des fleurs sur l'autel, cette odeur était comme la révélation de leur vie intense dont vibrait l'autel, comme une haie agreste>

114:3. <haie agreste visitée par tant d'antennes vivantes, auxquelles on pensait en voyant ces rousses étamines qui semblaient> **114:11.** <aux grands. [114:6. <d'insectes métamorphosés> 114:8. <avec M. Vington devant>]

□**114:11.** Puis jetant sur les épaules de sa fille le châle qu'il portait toujours sur le bras quand il sortait le soir avec elle pour la protéger contre la fraîcheur, ce qui faisait sourire à cause de l'air robuste et rude qu'elle avait, il montait à côté d'elle dans un petit buggy qu'elle conduisait elle-même et tous deux retournaient à la Combe.

S'il faisait clair de lune et que l'air fût chaud, au lieu de rentrer directement, mon père> {114:11-114:22}

114:22. <mon père> **118:24.** <et déciderait. [114:28. <me représentait l'image même de l'exil et de la détresse> 115:2. <et qui ne me semblait pas en valoir la peine. 115:3. Des grilles> 115:6. <le soir, quand je passe dans un quartier désert, et entre lesquels, quand sur son emplacement on a créé le jardin public de Combray, dut venir se réfugier> 115:13. <par la fatigue, mais fière> 115:24. <volontaire: l'habitude> 115:25. <me portait comme> 116:3. <impérieux, d'une nécessité, fût-elle cruelle, qui les contiendrait. Sans doute> 116:17. <changements qu'elle reconnaissait utiles et auxquels> 116:34. <ferme de la Roussotte, où> 117:1. <rendre un temps sa vie> 117:10. <entrant à ce moment-là> 117:16. <immatériel de la pensée, et si> 117:19. <jouer des pièces. 117:21. <intention de s'en défairr*, et> 117:30. <de même des soupçons qui concernaient> 117:33. <si elle se levait, elle osa* se lever et descendre> 117:36. <deviner ce qu'elle* pouvait à chaque moment faire, et chercher à lui cacher Françoise. 117:38. <celle-ci, quelque contradiction> 117:41. <mot qui la faisait pâlir et que> 117:43. <cruel. Et la visite suivante d'Eulalie comme ces découvertes qui ouvrent tout d'un coup> 118:4. <l'ornière, prouvait> 118:5. <bien loin de la vérité. 118:6. <maintenant que vous lui avez donné ma* voiture.» —«Que je lui ai donné ma voiture s'écriait ma tante!» 118:11. <de Troussinville. J'avais> 118:16. <qu'elle pouvait.]

118:24. <et déciderait; de sorte que si les occupations les plus insignifiantes de la journée de ma tante, concernant son lever>

118:25. See after 119:3.

118:36. <lever, son déjeuner, non repos, avaient pris par leur> **119:3.** <Versailles> [118:39. <Versailles, elle pouvait croire>]

119:3. <Versailles et qu'ils tâchait* de savoir ensuite si on avait vu sa Majesté y jeter les yeux, ou qu'elle n'en eût jamais parlé. Et si quelque artiste lisant les Mémoires du XVIIe siècle>

△**118:25.** <du XVIIe siècle, désirant> **118:34.** <l'oisiveté> [118:28. <ou en achetant* une correspondance> 118:29. <de l'Europe, il ne se rend pas compte qu'il tourne> 118:31. <mortes, et qu'il en est plus loin qu'une vieille dame de province>]

△**118:34.** <l'oisiveté et qui n'avait jamais pensé qu'elle pût rien avoir de Louis quatorzième.

119:4. Un dimanche, où en rentrant, nous avions appris que ma tante venait d'avoir la visite simultanée du curé et d'Eulalie, mais qu'elle avait fini de se reposer, nous étions>

119:5. <nous étions> **119:32.** <étonné> [119:15. <parole dit en riant> 119:16. <profiter de ce que> 119:18. <chacun; —et, plus sérieusement—J'*ai peur que nous soyions* fâchés> 119:21. <entendre le récit, car> 119:22. <avec mon père le matin quand> 119:26. <d'un programme. 119:27. <sortant de la messe, marchant> 119:31. <arrêtions; et M. Legrandin>]

119:32. <étonné, n'ayant pas l'air de nous reconnaître, et avec cette perspective du regard particulière aux saluts peu polis, où la personne qui ne veut pas être aimable, du fond subitement prolongé de ses yeux, comme une route interminable, a l'air de vous apercevoir à une si grande distance que vous ne pouvez plus être pour elle qu'une silhouette de pupazzi par laquelle il est même extraordinaire qu'on prenne la peine de rendre un salut, si embryonnaire qu'il soit, si proportionné aux dimensions d'une marionnette.

Or, la dame qu'accompagnait Legrandin était une personne vertueuse et considérée, d'une vertu insoupçonnable; il ne pouvait donc être question d'une bonne fortune et où il eût été gêné d'être surpris, et mon père se demandait ce qu'il avait pu faire qui eût pu fâcher Legrandin. {120:1-120:6}

120:6. Mais le conseil> **120:8.** <quelque pensée. Mon père n'était pas tout à fait convaincu et gardait une crainte d'être

brouillé avec un homme qu'il appréciait. Mais elle fut dissipée dès le lendemain soir.

120:10. Comme nous> **125:21.** <à nous saluer. [120:15. <Desjardins: «Les bois sont déjà noirs, le ciel est encore* bleu»? 120:21. <aujourd'hui il s'est mué en frère> 120:22. <limpide... «Les bois sont déjà morts, le ciel est encore* bleu»... Que le ciel> 120:25. <ami, alors même> 121:13. <extinction de soir bleu, cette> 121:19. <Giotto, chargée> 121:21. <corbeille, ayant l'air douloureux, comme> 121:23. <d'azur que les asperges ceignaient au-dessus de la tunique de rose> 121:27. <Françoise faisait tourner> 121:35. Mais ce jour> 122:4. <fait quelques heures plus tard par sa> 122:16. <neveux, fût montée sur le bûcher sans une> 122:17. <singulière. Mais ma tante aimait son service! et peu à peu je découvris moi-même que la douceur, la componction, les vertus de Françoise> 122:22. <que le règne des> 122:25. <parenté, les autres humains> 122:32. <cuisine, la malheureuse fut> 123:13. <lecture du journal lui> 123:31. <elle, même malade, partait la nuit au lieu> 123:39. <personne, préférait, quand> 124:3. <charançons; des araignées> 124:4. <un savoir et une adresse merveilleuses* le centre> 124:28. <prière au point que j'aurais pu croire qu'elles ne m'avaient pas vu entrer> 124:36. <présenter à une autre châtelaine des environs. 124:40. <qui ramenait> 124:42. <qu'avait dû lui apprendre les fils* de sa sœur, Mme de Chimesey. Ce redressement> 125:15. <l'air [*blanc*], il s'y> 125:16. <inerte du bonheur.]

125:21. Au moment où nous arrivions à la maison, maman s'aperçut qu'on avait oublié la tarte du soir et demanda à mon père de retourner avec moi sur nos pas et d'entrer la commander.

125:30. Nous croisâmes> **126:26.** <M. Legrandin> [126:2. <d'amitié pour nous jusqu'aux> 126:17. <de votre oncle quand>]

126:26. <M. Legrandin malgré l'attitude étrange qu'il avait eue le matin. Mais ma grand'mère, que notre récit laissait un peu sceptique, déclara qu'à tout mettre au pire il valait mieux, s'il avait été impoli, ce qu'elle ne pouvait croire, ni surtout comprendre, ne pas avoir l'air de s'en être aperçu. {126:27-126:43}

127:1. Je dînai avec lui sur> **127:12.** <me paraissaient> [127:4. <tard l'a dit, conviennent>]

127:12. <me paraissaient encore agréables et m'avaient toujours donné envie de connaître les choses dont il parlait, les vers de Paul Desjardins, les romans de Balzac et les Roses de Jérusalem; mais troublé depuis quelques jours par le souvenir d'une femme que j'avais vu passer en voiture au cours d'une de nos promenades, et pensant, maintenant que je savais que Legrandin était lié avec plusieurs châtelaines des environs, que peut-être il connaissait celle-ci et pourrait me la faire revoir, prenant mon courage, je lui dis: «Est-ce que vous connaissez, monsieur, la... les châtelaines de Guermantes», heureux aussi en prononçant ce nom de le poser dans l'air près de moi comme une chose chère et belle sur laquelle je prenais comme une sorte de délicieux pouvoir par le seul fait de le tirer de mon rêve et de lui donner maintenant une sorte d'existence sonore objective*, qu'un autre que moi, que Legrandin, allait percevoir. Et demander: «Connaissez-vous?»—et peu après (s'il me répondait oui): «Pourriez-vous me faire connaître»—c'était renoncer à la tristesse de la résignation, c'était faire entrer l'espoir dans mon cœur.

127:23. Mais à ce nom> **129:14.** <les passions> [127:23. <milieu de l'œil bleu de> 127:25. <s'il venait d'être> 127:41. <l'idée que son aveu ne lui cause aucun embarras, qu'il est facile, agréable, volontaire, que la> 128:4. <nommément de fréquenter les Guermantes> 128:21. <comprenais très bien maintenant c'est> 128:25. <devant eux de tant de timidité et de désir de plaire qu'il n'osait> 128:27. <bourgeois, les fils de notaires et d'agents, préférant> 128:30. <dans le joli langage>]

129:14. <les passions des autres, et que si nous arrivons jamais à savoir les nôtres, ce n'est que d'eux que nous avons pu les apprendre. Sur nous elles n'agissent que d'une façon seconde, par l'imagination qui leur substitue d'autres mobiles.

129:19. Jamais le snobisme> **130:39.** <péril de la mer. [129:32. <espacées. Nous goûtions toujours le joli langage, mais nous savions qu'il n'était pas vrai et maman s'amusait infiniment> 129:38. <à Querqueville avec> 129:40. <à Querqueville, pour> 130:4. <marin, suppliait au> 130:5. <Mme de Chimesey, débarquant> 130:12. <de Querqueville, de> 130:18. <plus flo-

réal* qu'aérien> 130:20. <aussi une carnation de fleur. 130:23. <cette sortie* du règne> 130:23. Là-bas près de Brilquebec, le coucher de soleil du pays d'Auge, le coucher de soleil rouge et or que je suis loin de dédaigner, d'ailleurs> 130:34. <ou roses. Il y a là une baie charmante, dite d'opale dont les plages d'or> 130:36. <pour être alléchées* comme de blondes andromèdes* à> 130:37. <voisines, de* ce> 130:38. <hivers tant de barques>]

130:39. <péril de la mer. C'est la plus antique ossature géologique de notre sol, vraiment Ar-mor, la Mer, la fin de la terre, régions maudites qu'Anatole France, —un enchanteur que devrait lire notre petit ami—a si bien comparé* à la hekuya* de l'Odysée.

De Brilquebec surtout, où déjà>

131:2. <où déjà> **133:22.** <filtrée> [131:6. —Ah! vous connaissez Brilquebec, dit mon père. 131:15. <craindre de regarder en face, il semble avoir traversé la figure de mon père comme si elle fut devenue> 131:21. <à Querqueville, il> 131:22. <de tel regard* fait dire> 131:26. <bien Querqueville. 132:10. <à tous les yeux derrière un petit bois quelque> 132:28. <de Querqueville avant> 132:35. <situation infiniment plus> 132:39. <de Querqueville habitait> 133:14. <s'associait, je ne sais pourquoi, dans mon esprit> 133:17. <repos. En plein été nous rentrions avant le coucher et pendant notre visite à ma tante, la lumière du soleil qui baissait et touchait>]

133:22. <filtrée, et illuminait obliquement la chambre avec la délicatesse qu'elle prend dans les sous-bois, incrustant de petits morceaux d'or le bois clair de la commode.

133:25. Mais certains jours> **133:29.** <sur les vitres, mais les rayons de la lampe à l'intérieur le traversant comme les feux d'un phare inconnu. L'étang au pied du calvaire>

133:30. <du calvaire> **134:5.** <une faim! [134:4. <disais, ils seront allés>

134:5. <une faim! vos gigots, de ce moment ne sont déjà pas si gros. Celui de ce soir est-il beau au moins. Je me doute qu'il doit être tout desséché>

134:6. <tout desséché> **134:15.** <ou de l'autre: le côté de Méséglise et le côté de Guermantes. De Méséglise, à vrai dire, je n'ai jamais connu que le fameux «côté» et des gens>

134:19. <et des gens> **135:28.** <qu'elle n'avait plus> [134:40. <donnais à chacun cette cohésion> 137:17. <à l'autre, dans les vases clos d'après-midi différents et sans communications entre eux.]

135:28. <qu'elle n'avait plus d'huile ni de café qu'il n'oublie pas de lui en apporter, et l'on sortait de la ville par le chemin qui passe le long de la barrière blanche du parc de M. Swann.

On sortait du village par le chemin qui passe devant «La Frapelière», la propriété de M. Swann.

135:30. Avant d'y arriver> **139:8.** <pour n'avoir> [135:34. <du parc, leurs plumes mauves et blanches que lustrait encore l'ombre du soleil où elles avaient baigné. 135:40. <qui gardent dans nos jardins les tons> 136:2. <à La Frapelière depuis> 136:9. <hier que, sa femme et sa fille partant pour Chartres, il en profitait pour> 136:24. <pour la raconter> 136:27. A droite, le parc> 136:41. <eaux, tandis que> 137:3. <qui, en> 137:5. <et méprisé d'elle, me rendant la contemplation de la «Frapelière» indifférente> 137:11. <et comme fait en pays de montagnes> 137:15. <miracle la fît apparaître avec> 137:19. <un koufin* oublié> 137:21. <détourner de l'autre> 137:27. <oiseau s'ingéniant à> 137:36. <quelque Malestroom* imaginaire> 137:40. <plonger et je> 137:42. <j'avais à la connaître> 137:43. <mordait, quand> 138:3. <champs et dans lequel ils> 138:13. <nervures du style catholique, qui s'épanouissaient> 138:17. <comparaison semblaient les églantines, qui par ce chaud après-midi de dimanche montaient à côté d'elles en plein soleil, le chemin rustique, en soie unie> 138:25. <inattendus qui causaient le même ravissement que certains intervalles musicaux, elles m'offraient, indéfiniment, en silence, le même charme avec une profusion inépuisable> 138:38. <qui triomphera sur la lice, rares> 139:2. <terre plate une>]

□**139:8.** <pour n'avoir sous les yeux qu'elles ou que le sentiment qu'elles éveillaient en moi, et qui cherchait à se dégager, à venir adhérer à leurs fleurs, ce sentiment restait obscur, je ne parvenais pas à le formuler. Elles ne m'aidaient pas à l'éclaircir,

mais je ne pouvais demander à d'autres fleurs à le satisfaire. Il en est des créations de la nature comme de celles de l'art. L'amour pour une espèce de fleur, pour l'œuvre d'un peintre, même s'il doit initier et conduire à l'amour d'autres fleurs ou d'autres peintres, est exclusif, tant qu'il est un amour. Ce n'est qu'au peintre dont on est épris qu'on peut demander la joie que ses œuvres font désirer encore, après qu'elles l'ont données*, et redonnent, mais toujours dans les mêmes limites. Mais combien cette joie se trouve étendue et renouvelée si alors nous voyons de ce peintre un de ses chefs-d'œuvre que nous ignorions et qui diffèrent des autres, quoique analogue à eux, nous la fait éprouver de nouveau pour la première fois comme une joie autre, et pourtant la même, et qu'amplifie encore l'idée de la richesse créatrice d'un génie si varié; ou bien si l'on nous mène devant un tableau de lui, dont nous ne connaissions jusque-là, qu'une reproduction et qui nous apparaît enrichi et transfiguré, comme un morceau seulement entendu au piano et qu'on voit ensuite revêtu des couleurs de l'orchestre. C'est un peu cela que fit mon grand'-père* quand, m'appelant et me désignant la haie de la «Frapelière», il me dit: >

139:21. «Toi qui> **141:10.** <yeux bleus. [139:24. <fête, de ces> 139:28. <d'essentiellement et de nécessairement férié; mais> 140:9. <festivité dans les épines roses, mais> 140:23. <d'elle qu'une femme en robe de bal au milieu de personnes en négligé qui resteraient à la maison, prêt pour> 140:29. <bordée d'héliotropes et de verveines entre> 140:33. <circuits, aux points où il était percé dressait l'eventail vertical et prismatique de ses gouttelettes multicolores au-dessus des fleurs dont il imbibait les parfums. Tout> 140:39. Une fillette blonde, qui avait l'air de rentrer de promenade nous regardait, levant son visage semé de taches de rousseur qui étaient roses, tenant une bêche de jardinage à la main. Ses yeux noir* brillaient et comme je ne savais pas, —ce que je n'ai pas d'ailleurs appris depuis, —réduire> 141:8. <noirs, ce qui> 141:9. <voyait, je>] {141:12-141:16}

141:16. J'avais si peur que d'une seconde> **141:34.** <d'outrageant mépris> [141:17. <père, l'apercevant, ne me fissent> 141:19. <un peu en avant que je tâchais, d'un regard inconsciemment supplicateur, de la forcer> 141:25. <détourna d'un>

141:27. <visuel, et tandis qu'ils me dépassaient, elle laissa ses regards> 141:31. <que je ne pus interpréter à l'aide de toutes les notions>

141:34. <mépris, d'autant plus que sa main esquissait en même temps un geste indécent, ce qui pour moi, en public, était signe de grossièreté et d'insolence.

141:39. —Allons, Gilberte> **141:43.** <sortaient de la tête. [141:42. <un Monsieur* que je ne connaissais pas>]

142:1. Cessant brusquement de sourire, elle prit sa bêche> **143:5.** <à Paris. [142:2. <se retourner vers moi, d'un> 142:6. <venait pour moi de faire> 142:8. <au-dessus des héliotropes, des verveines et des giroflées> 142:11. <traversée et qu'il isolait de la vie de celle> 142:15. <si douloureuse, avec un inconnu où je n'entrerais pas. 142:20. <son Gurcy, car> 142:24. <d'obéir, comme n'étant pas supérieure à tout et entièrement inaccessible, calma> 142:26. Mais bien vite s'éleva de nouveau en moi cet amour comme une réaction où mon cœur humilié voulait se mettre de niveau avec elle ou l'abaisser jusqu'à lui. 142:37. <bonheur inintelligible aux> 142:39. <une petite fille blonde, à la peau>]

143:5. Ce nom de Swann, quand je causais avec mes parents, je languissais du besoin de le leur entendre dire, je n'osais pas le prononcer moi-même, mais je les entraînais sur des sujets qui avoisinaient Gilberte et sa famille, qui la concernaient, où je ne me sentais pas exilé trop loin d'elle; et je contraignais> {143:6-144:15}

144:16. <je contraignais> **145:7.** <les branches> [144:18. <la haie d'épines roses se trouvait> 144:30. <car il était si> 144:33. <discrétion, par scrupule> 144:36. <semblait alors que> 144:43. <de rentrée à> 145:5. <dans le petit chemin montant, contigu à la Frepelière*, en train>]

145:7. <les branches épineuses et, comme une princesse de tragédie à qui pesaient ces vains ornements et qu'une importune main en formant tous ces nœuds eut* pris soin sur mon front d'assembler ses cheveux, foulant aux pieds mes bigoudis arrachés et mon chapeau neuf. A la vue de la coiffe défoncée et des déchirures de la douillette, ma mère jeta un cri, mais je ne l'entendis pas:>

145:14. «Oh mes pauvres> **145:31.** <à sa suite. [145:21. <visites et d'aller écouter> 145:22. <naiseries, comme j'en entendais dire au jour de maman, de partir> 145:25. <promenade du côté> 145:28. <année, le samedi saint, le jour de notre arrivée>]

□**145:31.** Si la Semaine Sainte était un peu tard cette année là*, malgré l'hiver souvent revenu, le printemps enfin avait oublié dans les champs des arbres fruitiers dépaysés et grelottants dans leur robe rose; à l'entrée du bois de Pinconville, sous la gelée blanche, çà et là l'air avait cédé la place à la goutte de parfum d'une violette, en fléchissant le bec bleu de son corps. Je rentrais avec plus d'appétit à la maison où on refaisait du feu, et la nuit je dormais mieux qu'à Paris.

145:31. On avait toujours> **146:3.** <au passage. [145:34. <terrain depuis Chartres. Je savais que Mme Swann allait souvent y passer> 145:38. <venu de là-bas, abaisser à l'horizon les blés>]

146:10. A intervalles> **146:24.** <attention à elle.

□**146:25.** J'aimais à retrouver son image dans les tableaux et dans les livres, bien différents—du moins pendant les premières années, avant que Bloch eût accoutumé mes yeux et ma pensée à des harmonies plus subtiles, —de ceux où elle me paraîtrait belle aujourd'hui et où je ne l'eusse pas reconnu alors, comme par exemple dans un roman de Saintive* ou dans un paysage de Gleyre, où elle découpe nettement sur le ciel une faucille d'argent.

Les personnes qui pensent qu'on doit mettre devant les enfants et qu'ils font preuve de goût en aimant d'abord, les œuvres que, parvenu à la maturité, on admire définitivement, s'imaginent sans doute que les mérites esthétiques sont des objets matériels qu'un œil ouvert ne peut faire autrement que de percevoir. Ils ignorent que c'est à force de transformer nos impressions, en réfléchissant sur elles, que nous arrivons à créer en nous des équivalents de ces mérites qui nous permettent de les comprendre quand nous les rencontrons dans une œuvre d'art. Jusque-là nous ne nous plaisons qu'aux œuvres assez confuses pour paraître claires à la faible vue d'un enfant, et pour qu'il y puisse reconnaître les impressions incomplètes plutôt que fausses qu'il reçoit d'une chose. Ces impressions, nous aurons plus tard à les enrichir plutôt qu'à les détruire. Et ainsi une peinture banale, une prose poncive ne sont pas forcément horribles comme nous disons trop vite; le plus souvent elles sont simplement si rudimentaires que pour qu'un lecteur puisse s'en satisfaire, il faut que chez lui l'intelligence artistique ne soit pas développée, soit restée infantile. Elles présentent au sujet de la réalité une foule d'observations que même un raffiné trouve vraies au moment où il les déclare détestables, mais qui sont tellement connues qu'il faut que l'auteur n'ait aucune faculté d'attention pour n'avoir jamais remarqué que tout le monde les sait par cœur, les tient pour sous-entendues, et pour s'imaginer qu'il invente quelque chose en les méditant.

147:1. C'est du côté de Méséglise, à la Combe, maison> **147:20.** <relations charnelles. [147:3. <demeurait M. Vington. Ainsi croisait-on> 147:8. <définitivement à la Combe. 147:12. <pareille. Il va jusqu'à dire que cette personne aurait eu des dispositions extraordinaires pour la botanique si>]

147:20. <charnelles. Tant l'amour physique, si mystérieusement* décrié force tout être à manifester toutes les parcelles qu'il possède de bonté, d'abandon de soi et elles resplendissent jusqu'aux yeux de l'entourage immédiat. D'ailleurs pour ceux qui comme nous virent à cette époque Monsieur Vington éviter> {147:24-147:41}

147:43. <éviter les personnes> **148:1.** <quand il nous apercevait, vieillir en quelques mois, il eut* été>

148:5. <été bien difficile de supposer qu'il ne se rendait pas compte> **148:12.** <sans qu'elle le reconnaisse> [148:8. <foi. Certes il> 148:10. <complexité des êtres et des circonstances ne puissent* amener>]

148:12. <reconnaisse tout-à-fait* où il entre en contact avec elle et la fait souffrir: paroles bizarres, attitude inexplicable, un soir, de tel être qu'elle a par ailleurs tant de raisons pour aimer. Et pourtant certaines situations qu'on croit à tort être l'apanage exclusif du monde de la bohème devraient peut-être ne pouvoir exister que là où elles causeraient de moins grandes douleurs; mais, produit nécessaire d'un vice que la nature, parfois rien qu'en mêlant les vertus du père et de la mère, fait épanouir chez l'enfant comme la couleur de ses yeux, construites par lui pour lui garantir de la place et de la sécurité qu'il doit disputer à tant

d'organismes sociaux en antagonisme avec lui, on peut les rencontrer au milieu des plus saintes familles. Mais de ce que M. Vington connaissait>

148:25. <connaissait peut-être> **149:37.** <contrevenu à la Combe. [148:28. <croyances, ils ne les ont pas fait naître, ils ne les détruisent pas, ils peuvent> 148:34. <quand M. Vington songeait> 148:35. <lui-même au point de vue de leur réputation, quand il cherchait à se situer avec elle, au rang qu'ils occupaient dans l'estime générale, alors il portait ce jugement d'ordre social, exactement comme l'eut* fait l'habitant de Combray qui lui eut* été> 148:41. <reçu avec humilité> 149:2. <qui est un effet presque statistique, commun à toutes les déchéances. 149:4. <M. Vington qui debouchait* d'une autre> 149:6. <éviter, Swann> 149:13. <avec M. Vington, à> 149:16. <à La Frapelière. 149:17. <indigné M. Vington. 149:18. <reconnaissants qu'il craignait de mal les temoigner* à Swann, s'il permettait à sa fille de l'accepter. L'amabilité de Swann envers elle lui semblait> 149:23. <conserver. «Quel homme exquis», nous dit-il quand Swann nous eut quittés avec la même enthousiaste vénération—d'ailleurs, ici, moins justifiée—qui tient de spirituelles et jolies bourgeoises en respect et sous le charme devant la laideur et la sottise d'une duchesse. «Quel homme> 149:29. <tout-à-fait* déplacé, et alors, tant les gens> 149:32. <expriment d'elle dès qu'elle n'est plus là, mes parents déplorèrent avec M. Vington le mariage de Swann>] {149:38-150:2}

150:3. Comme la promenade> **150:15.** <fini accablants> [150:4. <faisions de Combray> 150:8. <de Troussinville dans> 150:10. <derrière un nuage qui> 150:14. <de Troussinville sculptait>]

150:15. <accablants. La joie qui me distrayait s'était enfuie, j'étais ramené à moi-même, j'y apercevais une obligation d'avoir plus de volonté de travailler, de préférer mon avenir qui d'ordinaire m'était cachée.

150:15. Un peu de vent> **150:36.** <sur le nez. [150:20. <la pluie dont le capucin que l'opticien avait à sa devanture nous avait menacé*; les gouttes> 150:24. <ciel, elles ne se séparent> 150:26. <la suit de si près que le ciel> 150:33. <feuille et, suspendue et reposée à la pointe brillaient* au soleil, tout>]

150:37. (*Some indecipherable and visibly incomplete manuscript fragments of the passage on Saint-André-des-Champs are found in the margin of the* Ire Dactylographie, *but, because of a lacuna in the proofs, it is impossible to say whether they belong to* Grasset A.)

152:6. Devant nous> **152:17.** <dans la maison. [152:7. <maudite, Troussinville, dans>]

152:17. Çà et là> **152:22.** <au large pour jusqu'au matin. (*As this text is found exclusively in the* 2e Dactylographie, *whereas all texts normally figure in both copies, we cannot say, because of a lacuna in the proofs, whether it really belongs to* Grasset A.)

152:23. Mais qu'importait> **153:4.** <sortais pas. [152:32. <violette. Assis> 152:39. <de La Frapelière, onduleraient>]

153:4. Mais dans l'automne où nous dûmes venir à Combray pour la succession de la tante Léonie, qui était enfin morte>

153:8. <morte, faisant> **153:14.** <aurait succombé> [153: 11. <soutenu qu'elle avait une maladie>]

153:14. <succombé, ne causant par sa mort de grande douleur que chez un seul être, mais chez celui-là, sauvage. Ce fut chez Françoise. Pendant les quinze jours que dura la maladie, Françoise ne la quitta pas un instant, ne se déshabilla pas, ne se coucha pas, ne laissa personne lui donner aucun soin, et ne quitta son corps que quand les croquemorts l'avaient emporté.

153:20. Alors nous comprîmes> **153:24.** <de l'amour. [153:21. <paroles et des>]

153:24. See after 153:28.

153:28. Il était bien loin le temps où quand nous venions passer nos vacances à Combray nous avions autant de prestige à ses yeux que ma tante. Peu à peu, au fur et à mesure que le caractère de celle-ci avait changé, un abîme s'était creusé entre elle et nous aux yeux de Françoise. Nous des hommes pareils aux autres.

△**153:24.** Sa véritable> **153:27.** <n'était plus.

153:32. Cet automne-là> **153:36.** <côté de Méséglise. [153: 34. <loisir de faire des promenades, que>] {153:37-154:31}

154:31. Quand j'étais fatigué d'avoir lu dans la salle toute la matinée et depuis le déjeuner, je sortais; mon corps obligé longtemps de garder l'immobilité>

154:34. <l'immobilité, mais qui> **155:5.** <à le connaître. [154:35. <haie de la Frapelière, les arbres du bois de Pinconville, les buissons auxquels s'adosse la Combe, recevaient>]

155:6. Je me rappelle combien dans une promenade de cet automne-là, du côté de Méséglise, près du talus broussailleux qui protégeait la Combe, je fus>

155:11. <je fus frappé> **157:28.** <plaisir de la possession> [155:15. <de la Combe, devant> 155:16. <M. Vington serrait> 155:21. <poule. Et le vent> 155:25. <l'abandon des choses> 155:37. <il faillit de* recevoir> 156:7. <reprochaient durement au moment où> 156:11. <causée par le désir qu'une paysanne surgit* devant moi> 156:14. <pensées si différentes> 156:19. <village de Troussinville> 156:31. <village de Troussinville> 156:33. <reprenant encore des> 156:41. <passante que j'appelais de mon désir> 157:4. <aux hommes forts> 157:6. <ou de Troussinville, d'une pêcheuse de Brilquebec> 157:7. <Méséglise et de Bilquebec*. 157:9. <vrai si j'en avais modifié à ma guise les conditions, je n'aurais plus cru en lui. Connaître> 157:10. <pêcheuse de Brilquebec> 157:11. <ç'aurait éte> 157:12. <pas vu* sur la plage, une fougère que je n'aurais pas vu* dans les bois. Ç'*eut* été... 157:15. <au milieu desquels ma pensée l'enveloppait. Mais avoir erré ainsi dans les bois de Troussinville sans une paysanne à chasser, c'était ne pas connaître>]

157:28. <possession, en une notion générale, des femmes différentes avec lesquelles on l'a goûté, considérées dès lors comme les instruments interchangeables d'un plaisir toujours le même, et qu'il* n'existe pas isolé, séparé et formulé dans l'esprit, comme le but qu'on poursuit en s'approchant d'elles, comme la cause du trouble préalable qu'on ressent. A peine y songe-t-on comme au plaisir qu'on aurait à l'appeler son charme à elle, car on ne pense pas>

157:37. <on ne pense pas. **158:4.** <en vain> [157:40. <nous font les doux> 157:43. <bonté du cœur>]

158:4. <en vain que je demandais au clocher de Troussinville de faire venir auprès de moi quelque enfant de son village, que je lui demandais comme au seul confident que j'avais eu de mes premiers désirs, quand au haut de notre maison de Combray, dans le petit cabinet sentant l'iris, je ne voyais que sa flèche au milieu du carreau de la fenêtre entre-ouverte*, au delà* du Calvaire, pendant qu'avec les hésitations héroïques du voyageur qui entreprend une exploration ou du désespéré qui se suicide, je me frayais en moi-même une route inconnue et que je croyais mortelle, le long de laquelle défaillait ma main sous le poids délicieux des fleurs qu'elle moissonnait jusqu'au moment où, comme un colimaçon, je laissais sur les feuilles du lilas, qui se penchaient jusqu'à moi, une trace naturelle. En vain je l'implorais maintenant.

158:17. En vain, tenant> **158:19.** <ramener une femme. {158:19-158:23}

158:23. Je fixais> **159:1.** <de mon tempérament. [158:30. <du bois de Pinconville d'entre lesquels ne sortait* pas plus d'êtres vivants que> 158:38. <d'ailleurs, aurai-je* osé> 158:39. <qu'elle m'aurait fait arrêter comme un fou>]

159:2. Il* n'avaient pas plus de lien avec la nature, avec la réalité (qui dès lors perdait tout charme et toute signification et n'était plus à ma vie que cadre conventionnel) que n'en a la fiction d'un roman avec le wagon sur la banquette duquel le voyageur le lit pour tuer le temps.

C'est peut-être d'une impression ressentie aussi auprès de la Combe, quelques>

159:8. <quelques années> **159:10.** <faite du sadisme. {159:10-159:12}

159:12. C'était par> **159:19.** <qu'il était allé> [159:16. <de la Combe où>]

159:19. <était allé voir M. Vington, et le sommeil m'avait pris. Il faisait presque nuit quand je m'éveillai, je voulus me lever, mais je vis Mlle Vington, qui probablement venait de rentrer, en face de moi, à un mètre à peine de moi, dans cette ancienne chambre où son père>

159:26. <où son père> **159:36.** <plaignait profondément. [159:35. <d'une autre grande vertu>]

159:37. Se rappelant cette triste fin de vie de M. Vington, son renoncement à l'œuvre de toute sa vie, qui, inachevée, éparse en documents qui n'auraient pris de signification que reliés entre eux, resterait inconnue, son renoncement aussi à un avenir de bonheur honnête et respecté par sa fille, cette torture constante de son cœur qu'on lisait sur son visage, ma mère en ressentait une grande tristesse et pensait avec effroi à celle combien plus cruelle et mêlée de remords que Mlle Vington devait éprouver. «Pauvre M. Vington disait ma mère, il> {159:37-160:17}

160:17. <disait ma mère, il> **160:38.** Malgré la familiarité> [160:21. Au fond de la chambre de Mlle Vington sur la cheminée était posé> 160:25. <tira près de lui* une petite table et sur laquelle> 160:26. <comme M. Vington autrefois avait mis près de lui le manuscrit qu'il avait le désir de lire à mon père. Bientôt> 160:28. Mlle Vington> 160:32. <ainsi imposer à son amie une attitude> 160:33. <aimerait mieux être> 160:35. <cœur s'en offensa et reprenant>]

160:38. Malgré la familiarité qu'elle avait avec sa camarade, je reconnaissais les gestes polis et réticents les* brusques scrupules de son père. On aurait dit qu'elle continuait sa vie. Bientôt elle>

160:41. Bientôt elle> **161:13.** <des yeux vous* voient. [161:3. <Mlle Vington. 161:9. <l'expression farouche et naïve qui plaisait>] {161:14-161:19}

161:20. —Oui, c'est probable> **161:22.** <son amie.

161:22. <amie.

—Et puis quoi? ajouta-t-elle en croyant>

161:22. <croyant> **163:24.** <et peut-être> [161:25. <agréable à Mlle Vington> 161:26. <cynique, quand> 161:28. Mlle Vington frémit> 161:29. <devaient spontanément s'adapter> 161:33. <désirait être> 161:38. <d'audace et entremêlé* de> 161:39. <d'être seule et libre.» 162:1. <Mlle Vington> 162:6. <Mlle Vington> 162:8. <sur laquelle Mlle Vington avait placé le portrait de son père. Elle comprit> 162:15. <M. Vington> 162:17. <à propos du manuscrit. Mais ce portrait> 162:26. <Mlle Vington> 162:34. <cherchai* à lui causer. Et> 162:35. <à de tels blasphèmes> 162:37. <nature si franche et si bonne> 162:38. <doucereuse de scélératesse> 163:3. <M. Ving-

ton> 163:5. <docilité qui* lui> 163:7. <Mlle Vington> 163:8. <maintenant de la pauvre orpheline. 163:11. <Mlle Vington> 163:15. <dit l'amie d'une voix qu'elle réussit à rendre brutale. 163:16. <Mlle Vington> 163:19. <M. Vington> 163:22. Et pourtant si M. Vington avait pu assister à cette scène, peut-être n'eût-il pas encore>]

163:24. <et peut-être en cela n'eût-il pas eu tout à fait tort. Certes, dans le sadisme l'apparence du mal est si entière qu'on ne pourrait la rencontrer réalisée à ce degré de perfection dans la vie, si le sadisme n'existait pas, et que si l'on voyait une fille faire cracher son amie sur le portrait d'un père qui n'a vécu que pour elle, ce serait à la lumière de la rampe d'un théâtre des boulevards, mais non pas de la lampe d'une maison de campagne. Seul le sadisme donne quelque fondement dans la réalité à l'esthétique du mélodrame. Dans la vie, en dehors des cas de sadisme, une fille aurait peut-être des manquements aussi cruels envers la mémoire et les volontés de son père mort, mais>

163:38. <mais elle> **163:42.** <de l'apparence>

163:42. <de l'apparence, dans le cœur du sadique, le mal, au début du moins, est bien loin d'être sans mélange. Le sadique est l'artiste du mal, un être entièrement mauvais ne pourrait pas être sadique car le mal ne lui serait pas extérieur, il lui semblerait tout naturel, ne se distinguerait même pas de lui; et la vertu, la mémoire des morts, la tendresse familiale, comme il n'en aurait pas le culte, il ne trouverait pas un plaisir sacrilège à les profaner. Les sadiques sont des êtres si purement sentimentaux, si naturellement vertueux>

164:9. <naturellement vertueux> **164:22.** <à ces plaisirs mais qui restait> [164:16. <plaisir. Et on comprend combien ils le désireraient en voyant combien il leur est impossible d'y réussir. Au moment où Mlle Vington se voulait> 164:20. <du vieux savant. Bien>]

164:22. <qui restait interposé entre eux et elle et l'empêcher* de les goûter directement, c'était son piège, ses gestes d'amabilité qui interposait* entre sa vie et elle une phraséologie, une mentalité qui n'était pas faite pour lui et l'empêchait de le connaître fort différent de quelque devoir de politesse. Ce n'est pas le mal qui donne l'idée du plaisir aux sadiques, qui leur est

agréable; c'est le plaisir qui leur semble malin. Et comme chaque fois qu'ils s'y adonnent il s'accompagne pour eux de ces pensées mauvaises qui le reste du temps sont absents* de leur âme vertueuse, ils finissent par trouver au plaisir quelque chose de diabolique, par l'identifier au Mal. Peut-être Mlle Vington sentait-elle que son amie n'était>

164:38. <n'était pas foncièrement> **165:5.** <de son père. □**165:6.** Peut-être si elle avait mieux su lire en son cœur, dans le cours ordinaire des actions de sa vie, eût-elle discerné qu'en elle comme en tout le monde, le mal, l'indifférence aux souffrances que nous causons (cette forme la plus terrible, parce qu'elle est permanente, de la cruauté) se rencontrent à tout moment, qu'ils ne sont pas quelque chose de rare, qu'ils dictent, quelque autre nom que nous leur donnions, beaucoup de nos actions. Elle eût cessé de penser que le mal était un état extraordinaire, étranger à sa nature et n'eût plus cherché en le faisant sien, à pénétrer comme elle croyait le faire dans la vie inconcevable et voluptueuse d'êtres d'une autre race.

165:13. S'il était en somme assez simple> **166:15.** <Saint-Marc. [165:17. <Françoise qui se désespérait qu'il> 165:18. <récoltes», ne pouvait plus voir que de rares nuages blancs nageant à la surface calme et bleue du ciel et gémissait: «Ne> 165:25. <à petit peloton*, sans> 165:26. <tombe que s'il pleuvait sur la mer»> 165:39. <rêverie, semblable> 165:28. <jardinier, de Swann et du baromètre, alors mon père annonçait au dîner> 165:33. <desquelles une guêpe passait la journée> 165:40. <de Violet le Duc*, peu en faveur aujourd'hui, qui> 165:43. <siècle, ne> 166:4. <restaurateurs—quelques> 166:6. <anéantis, —de ce qu'était> 166:9. <émouvantes, si> 166:10. <effigies glorieuses comme ces gravures anciennes de la Cène> 166:13. <voit dans un>] {166:16-166:33}

166:34. Le plus grand> **166:43.** <déjà en bleu> [166:36. <la passait une> 166:38. <dite «le pont-vieux». 166:41. <font plus ressortir les objets de ménage>]

166:43. <en robe bleu ciel dans les terres nues où çà et là étaient déjà venus s'installer tout seuls, sortis* on ne sait d'où, des bandes de primevères et de coucous. Le pont-vieux débouchait>

167:6. <débouchait dans> **171:8.** <de la recevoir. [167:7. <d'un prunier sous> 167:12. <n'ai jamais> 167:19. <jusqu'au village et à la gare> 167:24. <abbés de Troussinville. 167:28. <Novepont, Clairefontaine, Martinville, toutes> 167:37. <différente, me relevant* par son visage incompréhensible> 167:42. <d'œuf d'autant plus brillants*, me> 168:7. <venus d'Asie, mais> 168:12. <éclat d'extrême-orient. 168:24. <ne pouvait en jouir. J'obtenais qu'on> 168:31. <invisibles, sont* près> 168:36. <comme certains bacs actionnés mécaniquement il> 168:37. <pour revenir à celle> 169:4. <certains neurasthéniques qui nous> 169:16. <excita la curiosité> 169:41. <la Julienne> 170:9. <s'emplit, comme> 170:10. <rêverie du soir> 170:13. <mystérieux, avec ce qu'il y a d'infini, dans> 170:17. <j'ai vu un rameur qui> 170:25. <ciel vacant flânait> 170:31. <sons de cloche qui> 170:43. <celui qu'elle ne put garder, y est inconnu, était encadrée dans la fenêtre qui ne lui laissait pas voir plus loin>]

171:9. On sentait qu'elle avait renoncé, qu'elle avait volontairement quitté des lieux où elle aurait pu du moins apercevoir celui qu'elle aimait, pour ceux-ci qui ne l'avaient jamais vu et ne le lui montreraient jamais.

171:12. Et je la regardais> **171:31.** <de Guermantes> [171:20. <se trouvaient à un certain point du département dont on savait la distance kilométrique, que le jour> 171:23. <terre où était, dans> 171:27. <Guermantes, qui étaient des>]

171:31. <de Guermantes, dans la sacristie de l'église de Combray, tantôt de nuances changeantes comme des personnages de vitrail, tantôt impalpables comme l'image du sire et de la dame de Brabant, ancêtres de la famille de Guermantes, que projetait la lanterne magique. Et toujours enveloppés du mystère du temps mérovingiens* ils baignaient comme dans un coucher de soleil dans la lumière orangée qui émane de cette syllabe: «antes». Mais si pourtant ils étaient pour moi>

171:43. <pour moi> **174:15.** <de Léon. [172:1. <bien que singuliers, en> 172:6. <après midi. Et ils ne portaient pas> 172:19. <Guermantes, dit le Mauvais, qui occupait un vitrail dont je ne voyais que* Saint-Hilaire l'envers de laque noire> 172:23. <devant des petits> 172:28. <avec sa terre traversée

de cours> 172:30. <d'aspect dans mon imagination, s'identifia, quand j'eus entendu notre curé nous parler des fleurs et des belles eaux vives qu'il y avait dans le parc du château. Mme de Guermantes m'y faisait venir, éprise pour moi d'un soudain caprice, et tout le jour y pêcherait* la truite avec moi. 172:37. <me montrerait> 172:39. <m'apprendrait> 172:41. <composer. Et ce rêve m'avertissait que> 173:1. <un sujet d'une signification> 173:2. <s'arrêtait aussitôt de> 173:5. <maladie du cerveau qui l'empêchait> 173:12. <du ministre pour son cousin qui> 173: 15. <par une lettre autre que le sien. Si> 173:22. <attendu sans inquiétude l'heure> 173:24. <guérison. Peut-être> 173:25. <comme la réalité, qui> 173:38. <semblait que> 173:40. <eux, et parmi>]

174:16. De notre place à l'église pendant la messe de mariage, nous ne pûmes la voir. Mais au moment du défilé dans la sacristie où donnait le soleil intermittent et chaud d'un jour de vent, je vis une dame blonde avec un grand nez, des yeux bleus et perçants, une cravatte* bouffante en soie>

174:20. <en soie mauve> **174:30.** <ressemble à Mme de Guermantes; or elle venait précisément de sortir de la chapelle qui lui était réservée à Saint-Hilaire, sous laquelle étaient enterrés ses ancêtres et d'où il ne pouvait vraisemblablement y avoir qu'une seule femme ressemblant à son portrait qui eût assisté à la cérémonie, c'était elle! Ma déception était grande. Elle venait de ce que>

174:41. <de ce que je n'avais> **176:7.** <qui sont ici.» [175:1. <siècle, et jamais de la même matière que les autres personnes vivantes. 175:16. <Guermantes avaient apparu> 175:27. <fée, un mouvement de> 176:3. <dire: «Puissants dès>] {176:8-176:23}

176:24. Je trouvais important> **177:12.** <Mme de Guermantes. [176:43. <Mlle Vington», comme>]

177:13. Mais elle, je revois au-dessus de sa cravate mauve, soyeuse et gonflée, le doux étonnement de ses yeux qui, comme elle ne connaissait personne dans l'église, n'émettaient pas de ces regards actifs, qu'on adresse avec une signification précise à quelqu'un, mais laissent seulement s'échapper incessamment ses pensées devant elle, en un flot de lumière bleue qu'elle ne pouvait contenir. Comme s'il eût pu gêner ceux qu'il atteignait à tout moment, elle gardait un sourire un peu timide, un air de s'excuser auprès de tous ces gens dont l'infériorité proclamait trop sa suprématie pour qu'elle ne ressentit* pas pour eux une sincère bienveillance et à qui du reste, elle espérait imposer davantage encore à force de bonne grâce et de simplicité. Ce sourire tomba sur moi qui ne la quittait* pas des yeux et s'y arrêta avec douceur.

177:39. Je crus que> **179:7.** <vérité abstraite. [178:1. <mépris et que nous pensions> 178:4. <bonté et que> 178:10. <géranium au tapis rouge qu'on y avait étendu par> 178:20. <de Guermantes, restant un peu à l'écart de mes parents, je me livrais plus amèrement à mes regrets de me sentir sans dispositions pour les lettres, et de devoir renoncer à être jamais un écrivain célèbre. Ils me faisaient tant souffrir> 178:39. <fallait poursuivre mon>]

179:7. Du moins pour le plaisir irrésonné* qu'elles me donnaient, elles me distrayaient de penser à la littérature et à mes déboires. Mais ce devoir de conscience qu'elles m'imposaient d'apercevoir ce qui se cachait derrière elles était si ardu que je ne tardais pas>

179:15. <je ne tardais pas> **184:37.** <la figure des pays> [179:21. <rentré pour ne pas> 179:26. <les poissons que j'avais pêchés et que je rapportais> 179:37. <pourtant où> 179:42. <lui; j'eus> 180:3. <à Martinville chez> 180:10. <l'air de changer> 180:12. <élevé qu'eux, dont le lointain en semblait tout voisin. 180:24. <apercevoir dans le lointain et> 180:25. <chercher à le découvrir me> 180:32. <m'avaient causés et que> 180:36. <plus tard, le soleil tout à fait couché, j'aperçus> 180:43. <caché en elle*> 181:2. <plaisir que m'avaient* fait éprouver la vue des clochers> 181:9. <dérobaient, puis je les vis encore et enfin> 181:12. <Martinville, ce devait> 181:14. <plaisir qu'elle m'était apparue> 181:21. <perdus en campagne> 182:17. <mais au moment où dans le coin du siège> 182:22. <clochers et fait chercher ce qu'ils cachaient> 183:7. <est séparée d'une verte ou d'une noire comme par une ligne. On> 183:23. <rappeler que le soir reviendrait jamais et l'heure de quitter> 183:33. C'est ainsi que le côté> 183:41. <décou-

verte. Mais> 184:6. <rêvait, comme> 184:7. <foule, ce coin de nature où* le bout> 184:10. <parfum d'aubépine qui le soir est évaporé, un bruit sans écho de gravier sous des pas, une bulle> 184:21. <temps, peut-être de quel rêve il vient.]

184:37. <des pays où j'aimerais vivre, et les bluets, les aubépines, les pommiers qu'il m'arrive de rencontrer encore dans les champs, parce qu'ils sont attachés à la même profondeur, au niveau de mon passé, sont en communication avec mon cœur.

185:3. Et pourtant comme il y a> **185:8.** <Vivonne, pas plus que je n'aurais souhaité le soir en rentrant, que vint* me dire bonsoir une mère plus belle et plus intelligente que la mienne. Non; de même ce qu'il me fallait pour que je puisse m'endormir heureux, c'est que ce fût elle, c'est qu'elle inclinât vers moi ce visage où il y avait au-dessous de l'œil ce qui était, paraît-il, un défaut, et que j'aimais à l'égal du reste, si je veux revoir le côté de Guermantes c'est celui que j'ai connu, c'est la ferme>

185:24. <la ferme qui> **186:7.** <persistants lilas. [185:26. <chênes. Ce> 185:29. <c'est ce paysage dont la nuit parfois, l'individualité m'étreint dans mes rêves avec une puissance> 185:31. <plus exprimer au> 185:32. <pour l'avoir indissolublement uni, ce qu'ils me firent éprouver à la fois, le côté de Méséglise et le côté de Guermantes m'ont exposé> 185:39. <haie, et j'ai été> 185:42. <auxquelles ils pensent* se relier, ils leur donnent de la profondeur>]

□**186:11.** C'est ainsi que je restais souvent jusqu'au matin à songer aux jours de Combray, et par association de souvenirs, à ce que j'avais appris bien des années après avoir quitté cette petite ville, d'un amour que Swann avait eu autrefois avant que je fusse né. J'en avais connu l'histoire avec une précision qui paraîtra peu vraisemblable, mais seulement parce qu'on ne s'avise pas du moyen par lequel j'ai pu l'apprendre. Combien d'inventions de la science, de résurrections de l'archéologie, ou de découvertes de la police, qui auraient pu paraître impossibles, tant qu'on ignorait le biais par lequel cette impossibilité a été tournée. D'ailleurs n'arrive-t-il pas tous les jours qu'un hasard nous permet de connaître la vie et les amours de personnes mortes il y a des siècles, de façon bien plus détaillée que ceux de nos meilleurs amis.

Certes quand approchait le matin il y avait longtemps qu'était dominée la brève illusion de m'être éveillé à Combray. Je savais que j'étais dans ma chambre à Paris, je l'avais autour de moi reconstruite dans l'obscurité et, soit en m'arrêtant* par la seule mémoire, soit en m'orientant> {186:24-186:33}

186:38. <m'orientant> **187:15.** <levé du jour. [186:40. <croisée; je> 186:43. <portes, reposé> 187:10. <couloir; ce mur régnait là où> 187:14. <ce frêle signe qu'avait tracé au-dessous des rideaux>]

FIN DE LA PREMIÈRE PARTIE

DEUXIÈME PARTIE

UN AMOUR DE SWANN

□Il en était de M. et Mme Verdurin, comme de certaines places de Venise, inconnues et spacieuses, que le voyageur découvre un soir au hasard d'une promenade, et dont aucun guide ne lui a jamais parlé [*cf.* Pléiade III, 650:40]. Il s'est engagé dans un réseau de petites ruelles qui fendillent en tous sens de leurs rainures le morceau de Venise qu'il a devant lui, comprimé entre des canaux et la lagune, quand tout d'un coup, au bout d'une des «calli», comme si la matière vénitienne au moment de se cristalliser avait subi là une distension imprévue; il se trouve devant un vaste campo à qui il n'aurait pu certes supposer cette importance, ni même trouver de la place, entouré de charmants palais sur la pâle façade desquels s'attache la méditation du clair de lune. Cet ensemble architectural vers lequel, dans une autre ville, la rue principale nous eût conduit tout d'abord, ici ce sont les plus petites qui le cachent comme un de ces palais des contes de l'Orient où on y mène pour une nuit, par un chemin qu'il ne faut pas qu'il puisse retrouver au jour, un personnage qui finit par se persuader qu'il n'y est allé qu'en rêve.

Et en effet, si le lendemain vous voulez retourner à ce campo, vous suivrez des ruelles qui se ressemblent toutes et ne vous donneront aucun renseignement. Parfois un indice vous fera croire que vous allez retrouver et voir apparaître dans la claustration de sa solitude et de son silence la belle place exilée, mais à ce moment quelque mauvais génie sous la forme d'une calle nouvelle, vous fait brusquement rebrousser chemin et vous ramène au grand canal. Le lecteur obscur d'un journal mondain s'y retrouve chaque jour et s'y est familiarisé avec les noms d'une quantité de personnes qu'il ne connaîtra jamais et qu'ont mises en relief une fortune souvent peu élevée, un titre ou un talent même douteux; et jamais il n'y a lu le nom de Verdurin. Mais un jour, cherchant une habitation au bord de la mer, il voit plusieurs villas plus vastes que les autres et s'informe. Elles ont été louées par Mme Verdurin, pour elle et ses amis. A Versailles l'hôtel est plein; seul le plus bel appartement, rempli de meubles anciens, semble inhabité; mais il n'est pas libre, il est loué à l'année par Mme Verdurin. A cause de Mme Verdurin qui les a retenues d'avance pour elle et ses amis, on ne peut avoir la loge ou la table qu'on voulait à un grand concert ou dans un restaurant des environs de Paris. Et dans ces plans du Paris social que les courriéristes dressent avec un si minutieux détail et à une si grande échelle que souvent cent mille francs de rentes suffisent à y valoir une position pour celui qui les possède, on s'aperçoit que l'espace forcément assez vaste rempli par les Verdurin, qui dépensent de sept à huit cent mille francs chaque année, n'est nulle part mentionné ni prévu.

188:9. See after 189:32.

189:4. Les Verdurin n'invitaient jamais à dîner, mais chez eux on avait toujours «son couvert mis». Pour la soirée il n'y avait pas de programme. Le jeune pianiste dont cette année-là Mme Verdurin déclarait préférer le jeu à celui de Risler, jouait, mais seulement «si ça lui chantait», car on ne forçait personne et comme disait M. Verdurin, «tout pour les amis, vive* les camarades!» S'il jouait du Chopin par exemple, Mme Verdurin lui disait: «Ça ne devrait pas être permis de savoir jouer Chopin comme ça!» Mais si alors on lui demandait la Grande Polonaise, elle protestait, non pas qu'elle l'aimât moins, mais parce que, au contraire, son jeu causait à Mme Verdurin une trop forte impression.

189:13. «Alors vous tenez> **189:32.** <aucun étranger> [189: 14. <qu'il la joue. 189:22. <qu'elle éprouve—le docteur Cottard (un jeune débutant à cette époque, dont elle trouvait le jugement plus juste que celui de toute la Faculté) dût* un jour> 189:20. <elle a l'habitude>]

189:32. <aucun étranger au petit «groupe», au petit «noyau.» Pour être admis à faire partie du petit noyau, une condition était

suffisante [*cf.* 188:3] mais elle était absolument nécessaire, il fallait adhérer tacitement à un credo relatif au jeu du pianiste, au diagnostic du docteur, au charme du salon Verdurin, à l'horreur des ennuyeux.

△**188:9.** Toute «nouvelle> **188:20.** <sexe féminin. [188:15. <par elles-mêmes sur> 188:16. <sentant que> 188:17. <frivolité pouvaient* par> 188:18. <église, avaient>]

△**188:21.** Ils consistaient presque uniquement cette année-là (bien que Mme Verdurin fût elle-même vertueuse et d'un respectable milieu bourgeois avec lequel elle avait peu à peu cessé volontairement toute relation) à une personne>

△**188:26.** <à une personne> **189:33.** <dédaigneusement refusé.

189:33. Mais au fur et à mesure> **193:9.** <morceau de pain! [190:7. <mère, lui répliqua durement> 190:12. <le vendredi> 190:17. <le vendredi> 190:26. De même si un fidèle avait un ami ou un flirt qui serait capable de la* faire lâcher quelquefois> 190:30. <pas, lui disaient> 190:34. <s'il ne* l'était on prenait> 191:3. <Crésy*> 191:12. <je ne suis pas «fishing* compliments». 191:25. <crédit sans prix par elle-même> 191:35. <et pour le «style» de leur hôtel)> 191:37. <dont il s'éprit d'une élégance> 191:40. Ce n'est pas à un homme intelligent qu'un homme intelligent> 192:32. <écrivant à sa maîtresse> 193:8. <comme un affamé>] {193:9-193:29}

193:30. Ce n'était pas seulement> **193:40.** <identiques. [193: 39. <fait des maladresses>]

193:40. Je me suis souvent fait raconter plus tard, m'étant toujours intéressé à son caractère dans lequel je trouvais des ressemblances avec certaines parties du mien, et aussi un commentaire de certaines de mes idées, que quand il écrivait à mon grand-père (qui ne l'était pas encore, car c'est vers l'époque de ma naissance que commença la liaison de Swann qui devait finir par son mariage et qui interrompit longtemps ces pratiques), celui-ci>

194:4. <celui-ci> **197:12.** <à se retrouver> [194:18. Quelquefois l'un ou l'autre des couples de leurs amis, qui se plaignaient de ne jamais voir Swann, leur annonçait, avec une satisfaction où entrait un peu d'amour-propre et de désir d'exciter l'envie>

195:9. <n'empêchait pas qu'on rendît mondaine, alors pour elle il retournait dans le monde, mais seulement dans l'orbite où elle se mouvait ou bien dans celui où il la faisait se mouvoir. «Inutile> 195:13. <son américaine*.» Il la faisait recevoir dans> 195:16. <chaque soir, un léger crépage* ajoute* à la brosse de ses cheveux roux tempérant de quelque douceur la vivacité de ses yeux verts et son profil d'aigle, il choisissait> 195:20. <de cette coterie> 195:23. <qu'il fallait* retrouver> 195:24. <devant elle, il> 195:28. <incorporé son amour. 196:3. <un type trop accusé> 196:6. <fatiguaient tout son visage> 196:8. <après, elle> 196:9. <avait sans doute écrit> 196:14. <qu'il habitait* ce> 196:17. <tant». Et en le quittant elle lui avait> 196:23. <désabusé où l'on> 196:33. <amoureux. C'est à l'âge où il semblerait que cherchant surtout dans l'amour un plaisir subjectif, la part du goût pour la beauté d'une femme devait y être la plus grande, que l'amour peut> 196:38. <préalable. Car à cette> 197:3. <début, rempli> 197:4. <beauté, pour> 197:7. <l'autre, nous> 197:8. <pour la rejoindre tout de suite au passage> 197:11. <doute elle renouvelait à chaque fois la déception>]

197:12. <à se retrouver devant cette beauté, dont il avait un peu oublié les particularités dans l'intervalle, et qu'il ne s'était pas* rappelé ni si expressive ni si fanée, il regrettait que le visage qu'elle lui montrait pendant qu'ils causaient, que le corps qu'il sentait auprès du sien ne fussent pas tout à fait du genre de ceux qu'il aurait choisis.

197:18. Il faut d'ailleurs dire que le visage paraissait> **198:1.** <inquiet, timide> [197:20. <unie et étendue était> 197:23. <quant au corps> 197:26. <quoique Odette fut*> 197:34. <consistance de leur matière, la> 197:35. <dentelle, aux fils de grain perpendiculaires> 197:37. <busc, et nullement l'être vivant, qui>]

198:1. <inquiet, timide qu'elle avait une fois sous son chapeau de paille rond à brides de velours noir sur le devant duquel était fixé un bouquet de pensées en implorant que ce ne fût pas dans trop longtemps; «et vous ne viendriez pas une fois chez moi prendre le thé?»

198:8. Il avait allégué> **199:11.** <rêveries romanesques> [198:10. <sur *Ver Meer de Delft.* 198:17. <prend toute femme> 198:21. <moi, le peintre qui vous empêche de me voir, je n'avais> 198:25. <qu'il y a dans cette grande tête qui> 198:30. <sa part* d'être>]

199:11. <rêveries romanesques, mais qu'une circonstance vînt (ou peut-être un de ces moments qui ne* sont différents des autres où un état, latent jusque-là, se déclare) qui feraient que ces rêveries Odette de Crécy les absorberait toutes, qu'elles ne seraient plus séparables de son souvenir, alors l'imperfection>

199:17. <alors l'imperfection> **199:25.** <de ces Verdurin, qui étaient cousins des Vington.

199:25. Mais il avait> **199:30.** <les Verdurin qui possédaient, d'un maître mort récemment qui avait été leur ami un tableau de fruits qu'il désirait voir:> [199:27. <comme tombé dans la bohême*>

199:31. «A la garde! à la garde! s'écria mon> **199:37.** <petits Verdurin.»

199:38. Tout ça c'est de la racaille! Et sur la réponse négative de son* grand-père> **203:12.** <au peintre). [200:10. <pas le laisser s'affirmer> 200:13. <bon?» Et comme il> 200:31. <qu'elles n'ont l'habitude*, il> 200:33. <employer, par exemple: la> 200:36. <élégances, être> 200:37. <cas précis il> 200:38. <ses propos sans être ridicule. Quant aux noms> 201:3. <affirmer, sans souhaiter d'être cru, à quelqu'un qu'on oblige que> 201:9. <une superbe avant-scène> 201:34. <au lieu d'un rubis de trois mille francs dont il lui disait que c'était bien peu de choses*, M. Verdurin envoya au docteur Cottard pour trois cents francs une pierre reconstituée en lui laissant entendre> 202:12. <aux Verdurin qu'elle croyait que Swann allait beaucoup dans le monde, Odette> 202:20. <de* considérer>]

203:12. Pensez bien, lui rappelle-t-elle, à rendre le joli regard> **204:12.** <se sentait sûre. [203:19. <invités l'aurait* entendue> 203:23. <simplicité et sa bonté> 203:25. <d'archiviste, sa richesse, et>]

204:12. —Elle n'est pas très forte, dit Swann, en souriant à M. Verdurin qui en fut piqué.

204:15. «C'est une si> **204:17.** <seul avec elle.

204:17. <seul avec elle. Tenez, je vais vous étonner, elle écrit d'une manière charmante. Vous n'avez jamais entendu son neveu? C'est admirable, n'est-ce pas, docteur! Voulez-vous que je lui demande de jouer quelque chose, M. Swann?

—Mais ce sera un bonheur..., dit Swann, quand le docteur l'interrompit d'un air moqueur.

204:27. En effet> **206:9.** <pas la sonate> [204:33. <dans ce que le docteur appelait> 204:35. <d'ailleurs, il évoquait l'idée de quelque chose de ridicule dans l'esprit du docteur, qui interrompait la phrase commencée, et la terminait> 205:20. <fidèles, mais depuis> 205:22. <peine de rire effectivement> 205:27. <ennuyeux, et, pour> 205:29. <sa femme, mais lui qui riait de bon cœur et s'essouflait vite, avait été vite distancé> 205:31. <hilarité, elle> 205:38. <s'y fût livrée, l'eût> 205:40. <et d'assentiment, comme un oiseau dont on eût trempé le colifichet dans du vin chaud, Mme Verdurin, juchée sur son perchoir, sanglotait d'amabilité.]

206:9. <la sonate de Berget, il va nous la jouer, arrangée pour le piano.

—Ah! non, non, cria Mme Verdurin, je n'ai pas envie à force de pleurer de me fiche* un rhume>

206:13. <un rhume> **206:26.** <écoutez.»

206:26. Et le lendemain on disait que la soirée avait été encore plus amusante que d'habitude à ceux qui n'avaient pas pu venir et ils le regrettaient.

—Eh bien, voyons, c'est entendu, dit M. Verdurin, il ne jouera que le scherzo.

—Que le scherzo, comme tu y vas! s'écria Mme Verdurin. C'est justement le scherzo qui me casse bras et jambes. Il est vraiment superbe, mon mari! C'est comme si dans la «Neuvième» il disait: nous n'entendrons que la finale, ou dans la «Pathétique» que l'andante.

206:37. Le docteur> **207:18.** <remettra sur pied. [206:41. <habitude de faire fléchir> 206:42. <la vivacité de leurs prescriptions> 207:2. <fois leur* dyspepsie, ou leur* grippe> 207:11. <prenait l'âme d'un malade.]

□**207:19a.** On passa au salon. En traversant un petit salon pour s'y rendre, Mme Verdurin indiqua à Swann l'aquarelle de fruits qu'il désirait voir et qui l'intéressa en effet, au moins par la merveilleuse habileté de l'exécution.

—Je ne peux pas passer devant sans que cela me fasse quelque chose, dit-elle. Pauvre ami, je crois encore le voir les peindre ce matin-là à la campagne, chez nous! Je lui disais vous allez nous mettre en retard pour déjeuner. Justement le pauvre Nittis qui est venu me voir l'autre jour et qui m'a l'air hélas bien malade lui aussi, me rappelait ce déjeuner qui avait était* si gai!

Et c'était en effet les fruits qu'ils avaient mangé* ensuite au dessert. Leur fraîcheur, le charme de cette matinée, la longue amitié de ce grand artiste de laquelle elle s'était tant enorgueillie et sa belle main si habile qu'elle admirait tant, tout cela n'existait plus que dans cette aquarelle à laquelle elle tenait comme au résidu, au témoignage de ces choses disparues, qu'elle sentait alourdie, enrichie d'un poids et d'un prix humains, et où un peu de sa vie à elle existait plus noble, comme ce panier qu'il avait peint était celui où son vieux jardinier cueillait les fruits. Elle apprécia la délicatesse du sentiment qu'elle éprouvait, et regarda Swann avec un fixe et douloureux sourire, en fronçant sa bouche d'une moue mélancolique qui la chiffonnait comme une fleur.

207:19. Odette était allée> **208:18.** <ne dis pas que> [207:21. <ma petite nièce*, dit-elle> 207:34. Chaque attribut sur les vieux bois correspond au petit sujet du dossier; vous savez> 207:40. <plutôt un peu le dessin! Mais c'est tout un traité de viticulture que cette vigne-là. Connaissez-vous une seule botanique qui vous en apprenne autant! Est-elle assez appétissante. Mon> 207:43. <lui. Hélas! non> 208:2. <j'en jouis> 208:7. <bronzes ciselés sur l'acajou des bras et des dossiers.]

208:18. <ne dis pas que tu ne l'as pas été—je lui disais que si la jalousie n'était pas aveugle c'est des petits bronzes dorés qu'il aurait dû être jaloux.

Swann les palpait par politesse>

208:21. <par politesse> **208:31.** <et au violon. [208:24. <qu'on va caresser, caresser dans l'oreille; voilà un jeune homme qui> 208:27. <plus aimables* encore>]

□**208:32.** Et à un moment, il s'était tout d'un coup senti charmé, sans distinguer pour cela une phrase, sans pouvoir trouver un contour ni donner un nom à ce qui lui plaisait. Peut-être est-ce parce qu'il ne savait pas la musique qu'il avait pu éprouver une impression aussi confuse. Et pourtant ce sont les seules qui soient purement musicales, inattendues*, entièrement originales, irréductibles>

209:8. <irréductibles> **210:14.** <comme un homme> [209:14. <sensations du large, du menu, du capricieux. 209:17. <submergées par les sensations différentes qu'éveillent> 209:23. <ineffables, si la mémoire> 209:36. <devant lui ce quelque chose qui> 210:4. <puis là encore, vers> 210:6. <suivre d'un même pas mesuré, après>]

210:14. <comme un homme à qui vient d'apparaître une beauté nouvelle qui donne à sa propre sensibilité une valeur plus grande, sans qu'il sache seulement s'il pourra revoir jamais celle qu'il a aperçue, qu'il aime et dont il ignore jusqu'au nom. {210:20-211:19}

□**211:19.** Un deuil, brusquement survenu dans la famille des gens chez qui il avait entendu cette œuvre, l'empêcha de leur écrire pour leur demander de qui elle était. Les personnes invitées à cette soirée, qu'il interrogea, étaient arrivés* après la musique ou partis* avant; plusieurs pourtant étaient là pendant qu'on l'exécutait mais avaient été causer dans un autre salon, et d'autres restés à écouter n'avaient pas entendu plus que les premiers.

Swann avait bien des amis musiciens>

211:30. <amis musiciens> **211:33.** <de la leur chanter.

211:35. Et quant à l'un d'eux qui avait dû être à cette soirée, il se promit toujours d'aller le voir pour tâcher de savoir de lui le nom de son inconnue. Mais toujours il en fut empêché; l'ayant rencontré une fois, il ne se rappela la question qu'il avait à lui poser que longtemps après qu'ils se furent dit adieu. Puis il avait cessé d'y penser.

211:35. Or, quelques> **211:37.** <une note haute tenue pendant deux mesures, il vit apparaître, il reconnut la phrase aimée, s'échappant de sous cette sonorité prolongée et tendue comme un rideau sonore pour cacher le mystère de son incubation. Et ce fut comme quand on rencontre dans un salon ami une personne qu'on a vu passer dans la rue et qu'on désespérait de retrouver jamais. A la fin, elle s'éloigna, indicatrice, diligente, portant sur

elle le reflet d'un sourire. Mais maintenant il savait son nom, il la tenait, il pourrait l'avoir chez lui aussi souvent qu'il voudrait, essayer d'apprendre son langage et son secret.

212:11. Aussi quand le petit pianiste> **212:26.** <de cette petite> [212:15. <la comprend-t-il*>]

□**212:26.** <petite phrase et lui expliquait qu'une phrase musicale est un être invisible et proche qui s'adresse à nous, mais qui ne nous déçoit pas comme les autres êtres. Car au lieu d'un corps inerte, elle est vêtue de son qui, à chaque instant nouveau change pour refléter le désir que l'instant d'avant il a éveillé. Il lui disait cela parce qu'il ignorait qu'elle n'était pas intelligente. Mais elle avait cette grâce, innée à certains êtres médiocres, dont tous les efforts de l'intelligence et de la culture ne peuvent égaler la séduction.

Aussi quand Mme Verdurin lui ayant dit d'un peu loin>

212:27. <d'un peu loin> **213:10.** <Cottard regardait> [212:31. <sur Berget, sur> 212:32. <qu'avait signifier*> 212:39. <de Berget> 213:5. <attention. Je> 213:7. <et me perdre dans les pointes d'aiguille.* On> 213:8. <chevaux*>]

213:10. <Cottard regardait avec intérêt se jouer avec aisance au milieu de ce flot d'expressions toutes faites. Et profitant lui-même de ce que beaucoup des fidèles étaient partis, comme un nageur> {213:12-213:38}

213:39. <comme un nageur> **213:43.** <brusque résolution.

214:1. Swann apprit seulement que c'était un des maîtres de la nouvelle école, dont les œuvres étaient encore entièrement inconnues du grand public. {214:5-214:20}

214:20. Le peintre savait qu'il était> **214:27.** <de mes maîtres. [214:21. <docteur Dieulafoy> 214:24. <par Dieulafoy.] {214:28-214:37}

214:38. —Laissez-moi> **215:39.** <fort utile> [214:39. <que lui, lui répondit Mme Verdurin comme une personne qui> 215:4. C'est Dieulafoy> 215:11. Mais M. Verdurin trouvant que c'était un peu fatigant de se mettre à rire pour si peu, se contenta> 215:35. <peu, car ce n'était pas encore la>]

215:39. <fort utile, Swann qui ne parlait jamais> {215:39-215:41}

215:41. <ne parlait jamais> **216:4.** <m'en occuper, je déjeune> [216:1. <relations dans le monde officiel, répondit à Mme Verdurin.] {216:4-216:5}

216:5. <je déjeune justement> **216:27.** amis communs> [216:23. <mots, à qui il a affaire, comme> 216:26. <sur l'infirmerie spéciale du dépôt.]

216:28. <du reste> **217:36.** <instances d'Odette. D'abord il se disait que s'il lui montrait qu'il y avait des plaisirs> [216:36. <adopta immédiatement cette> 217:9. <faire «lâcher». 217:14. <déjeûners*> 217:22. <appelle gentleman.»*] {217:37-217:43}

218:3. <des plaisirs> **218:18.** <la petite phrase> [218:4. <qu'elle avait pour> 218:5. Et préférant> 218:8. <rose dont>]

218:18. <la petite phrase de Berget qui était comme l'hymne national de leur amour; elle passait, rapide, à plis simples> {218:20-218:28}

218:28. <à plis simples> **221:34.** <crapaud qu'elle appelait: «Chéris». [218:36. <même, en> 218:36. <un musicien qui ne le connaissait pas quand il l'avait composée> 218:39. <siècles, que> 219:17. <petit hôtel, derrière> 219:22. <qu'elle lui recommandait* de partir ensemble et auquel il attachait plus de prix, parce que grâce à lui, il avait> 219:27. <dans sa voiture, un soir> 219:30. <chrysanthème (c'était sa fleur préférée mais elle aimait surtout les nouveaux chrysanthèmes japonais), et le lui donna> 219:38. <courtes rues presque toutes en petits hôtels contigus, dont tout à coup venait rompre la monotonie quelque sinistre échoppe, reste du temps où ces quartiers étaient mal famés, la neige qui> 220:2. <trouvé* en> 220:4. <surélevé, sa chambre à coucher qui donnait sur> 220:9. <soie mais> 220:14. <bondé*> 220:17. <éloignés encore de> 220:21. <d'oranger*> 220:28. <cachepots*> 220:29. <des photographies et des éventails. 220:32. <qu'elle avait* eu> 220:34. <derrière sa tête, sous> 220:38. <les innombrables lampes qui presque toutes allumées dans> 220:42. <d'hiver avant ramené une couche* de soleil> 221:1. <humain, faisant> 221:4. <rallumées, elle> 221:11. <avait posé* trop près des* deux> 221:15. <bibelots chinois, et aussi aux orchidées, aux altéas* surtout, qui étaient, avec les chrysanthèmes, ses fleurs préférées, des formes

«amusantes». Elle leur trouvait le grand mérite de ne ressembler à aucune des fleurs, mais d'être en soie, en satin. 221:27. <langues de feu peintes, une potiche*, ou, brodées> 221:29. <d'argent aux yeux de rubis>] {219:38-219:42; 221:35-221:40}

221:40. Elle fit à Swann> **222:11.** <du bon thé.» [221:41. <demanda: «citron> 221:42. <riant: «un> 222:3. <une justification, peut-être pour y voir une garantie de durée dans des plaisirs qui au contraire sans lui n'en seraient pas et finissait* avec lui, que quand il était rentré chez lui à sept heures pour s'habiller, dans tout le trajet qu'il fit dans son coupé depuis chez elle, ne pouvant>] {222:11-222:20}

222:21. Une seconde visite> **222:40.** <chapelle Sixtine. [222:28. <inaccessible, le bonheur médiocre, le pessimisme vrai. Il>] {222:40-223:37}

223:37. Aussitôt il n'estima plus le visage d'Odette qui était devant lui d'après la plus ou moins bonne qualité de ses joues et pour le plaisir purement carné qu'il pouvait supposer qu'il aurait à les toucher avec ses lèvres si jamais il osait l'embrasser, mais comme un écheveau de lignes subtiles et belles que ses regards dévidèrent, poursuivant la courbe de leur enroulement, et comme dans un portrait d'elle en lequel devenait claire et intelligible sa figure, rejoignait* la cadence de la nuque dans l'effusion des cheveux et la flexion des paupières.

Il la regardait; un fragment du portrait ancien apparaissait dans son visage et dans son corps que dès lors il cherchait toujours à y trouver soit qu'il la regardat*, soit qu'il pensat* à elle, et qui bien qu'il ne tînt à lui sans doute que parce qu'il était en elle la lui rendant semblait-il plus précieuse. Alors il se reprocha d'avoir méconnu le prix d'un être qui eût paru adorable au grand Sandro, et il se félicita que le plaisir qu'il avait à voir Odette trouva* une confirmation dans sa propre culture esthétique, jugea que le choix que ses rêves avaient fait d'Odette n'était pas un pis aller si imparfait puisqu'elle contenait en lui ses goûts d'art les plus raffinés. Il oubliait qu'en lui répondant, Odette n'en était pas plus pour cela une femme selon son désir, qui avait précisément toujours été le contraire. Ces mots d'œuvre florentine rendirent un grand service à Swann. Ils lui permirent, comme un titre>

224:23. <comme un titre> **225:37.** <dont l'une> [224:26. <charnelle qu'il avait d'elle jusqu'ici en renouvelant perpétuellement ses doutes sur la qualité de son* de son corps, sur sa beauté, affaiblissaient* son amour, visage*, ces doutes furent> 224:37. <ne fit* plus que voir Odette, il se disait qu'il était naturel de donner> 225:2. <fille de Sethro*. 225:7. <il la* transformait> 225:8. <réunis, des mérites* qu'il pourrait> 225:11. <fille de Sephto*> 225:14. <ce Boticelli*> 225:15. <son Boticelli*> 225:16. <photographie de la fille de Sethro*, il> 225:18. Et quelquefois cependant> 225:19. <c'était aussi> 225:34. <jailliraient de celle-ci des mots> 225:35. <dits; et>] {225:37-225:39}

225:39. <commençait par> **226:28.** <la journée> [226:3. <ce qu'elle cachait encore de son cœur. 226:5. <Verdurin quand il apercevait les grandes fenêtres dont on ne fermait jamais les volets, éclairées par des lampes, il s'attendrissait en pensant à l'être merveilleux qu'il allait> 226:23. <le petit groupe, prenait> 226:25. <plus le* voir>]

226:28. <la journée, il était toujours certain de la retrouver le soir.

Mais une fois il arriva si tard chez les Verdurin qu'Odette, croyant qu'il ne viendrait plus, était partie. En voyant qu'elle n'était plus dans le salon, il ressentit un choc, il tremblait>

226:36. <il tremblait> **226:43.** <qu'il est pincé! [226:38. <quand il voulait> 226:41. <quand il a vu qu'elle n'était pas là, dit>] {227:1-227:10}

227:11. —Vous pensez qu'il est au dernier bien avec elle, qu'elle lui a fait> **228:26.** <encore Odette. [227:31. <ce Monsieur> 227:35. <entendu ces mots insupportables qui avaient l'air> 227:40. <ce Monsieur> 227:43. <sonate de Berget. 228:8. <n'est ni une vertu ni> 228:14. <arrivé et qui avait> 228:18. <ou par des gens qui passaient d'un trottoir sur l'autre, odieux> 228:21. <que la traversée du piéton.]

228:26. Et cette rencontre dont l'attente saccageait, dénudait à ce point les moments qui la précédaient, que Swann ne trouvait plus> {228:26-229:5}

229:5. <ne trouvait plus> **229:23.** <cocher Rémi> [229:7. <esprit, il> 229:10. <changeant visage pour savoir comment il

était fait (car il ne pouvait jamais bien se le rappeler) un regard aussitôt> 229:11. <qu'elle y vit* l'avance d'un désir et ne crut*> 229:14. <pas le* quitter> 229:19. <qu'il l'approchait*>]

229:23. <cocher Rémi que, n'ayant rien trouvé lui-même, il alla attendre à l'endroit>

229:25. <à l'endroit> **230:30.** <éteindre partout. [229:25. Sa voiture> 229:27. <dirait: «cette> 229:28. <dirait, «cette> 229:29. Et il voyait la fin de sa soirée devant lui une et alternative> 229:43. <et en lieu*, qui> 230:1. <l'âme ce manque> 230:2. <corps qui au moment> 230:16. <part, et ajoutant comme avis, en> 230:18. <quand le cocher ne> 230:27. <répondit Rémi qui était très libre de propos avec Swann, puisque>] {230:30-231:9}

231:10. Swann se fit conduire dans les derniers restaurants: ce n'est que l'hypothèse du bonheur qu'il avait envisagé* avec calme, il> **231:18.** <du boulevard. [231:17. <trouvât dans>]

□**231:19.** Il poussa jusque chez Larue, entra deux fois chez Durand et, sans l'avoir vue davantage, venait de ressortir de chez Weber, marchant à grands pas, l'air hagard, pour rejoindre sa voiture qui l'attendait au coin du boulevard Malesherbes, quand>

231:23. <quand il heurta> **232:31.** <ce prétexte> [231:24. <Odette: n'ayant pas> 231:26. <souper chez Larue dans> 231:30. <qu'il trouvait possible> 231:31. Mais cette joie d'être auprès d'Odette ce soir que sa raison n'avait cessé d'estimer irréalisable> 231:33. <car, par la prévision des vraisemblances, il n'y avait pas collaboré, elle lui restait> 231:37. <c'est elle qui projetait vers lui cette vérité qui rayonnait en elle au point de dissiper> 231:40. <rêverie heureuse, comme un voyageur arrivé> 232:5. <bouquet de [*blanc*] et Swann vit sous la dentelle qu'elle> 232:9. <velours noir qui découvrait à leur triangle, le bas d'une jupe de faille blanche, par un rattrapé- oblique, et laissait voir également un empiècement de faille> 232:13. <d'autres fleurs de [*blanc*]. Mais elle> 232:14. <frayeur qu'il lui> 232:22. <par signe* pour>]

□**232:31.** <ce prétexte, et aussi par cette tendance qu'ont les mots, les actes commencés, même s'ils sont feints, d'exiger que

nous les continuions et pour cela de nous faire croire en eux, s'écria: >

232:34. —Oh! non, surtout> **234:26.** <de sa ruse> [232:40. chatouille? [*blanc*], mais> 233:9. <qu'ont les vierges florentines avec lesquelles> 233:14. <scènes [*blanc*] comme dans les tableaux religieux de ce maître. Et> 233:15. <qui s'en* doute> 233:20. Et ce fut lui qui> 233:28. <ni-même* embrassée> 233:33. <ses [*blanc*], soit> 233:34. <de paraître rétrospectif et avoir menti, soit manque> 233:36. <que celle qu'il pouvait renouveler puisqu'elle n'avait pas fâché Odette la première fois, les jours> 233:39. des [*blanc*] à> 233:40. <les [*blanc*] n'ont> 234:2. <pas de [*blanc*] ce soir, pas moyens* de> 234:4. <temps ce* ne fut pas changé l'ordre> 234:9. <des [*blanc*], fut> 234:10. <«faire [*blanc*]» devenue> 234:12. <penser. Quand* ils voulaient signifier l'acte de la possession, survécut dans> 234:15. Et peut-être le mot différent ne signifiait-il pas exactement> 234:18. <plus différents* comme> 234:22. <nous soyions* obligés> 234:24. <l'arrangement des [*blanc*].]

234:26. <sielle* était dupe de sa ruse, ne savait pas) que c'était la possession qui allait sortir de leurs larges pétales mauves; et le plaisir qu'il éprouvait déjà et qu'Odette ne supporterait peut être* que parce qu'elle ne l'avait pas reconnu, lui semblait à cause de cela, comme il put paraître au premier homme quand il s'éveilla pour lui entre les fleurs du paradis terrestre, un plaisir qui n'avait pas existé jusque-là, qu'il cherchait à créer, un plaisir inconnu, incertain, et, ainsi que le nom spécial qu'il lui donna en garda la trace, entièrement particulier et nouveau.

234:37. Maintenant> **234:41.** <les autres?»

234:41. Un soir, où il avait oublié chez elle son porte-cigarettes, elle le lui renvoya avec ces mots: «Vous avez laissé chez moi vos cigarettes, que n'y avez-vous laissé aussi votre cœur, je ne vous l'aurais pas rendu» [*cf.* 222:18].

234:41. Les soirs où> **235:9.** <où on allait. [235:4. <victoria, répondait aux amis> 235:8. <côté, il étendait une couverture sur ses jambes, et le cocher>] {235:9-235:24}

235:24. A vrai dire> **235:34.** <voluptueuse ajoute un charme intérieur. [235:33. <existence et à qui le sacrifice>] {235:35-236:8}

236:8. Parfois, en voyant de sa voiture, dans> **236:21.** <à la porte d'entrée. [236:11. <et rose comme>]

236:21. See after 240:39.

236:28. Et une fois qu'il l'avait quittée> **238:33.** <devenir jaloux> [238:30. <victoria, bénissant Odette>]

238:33. <devenir jaloux, lui permettraient d'arriver sans avoir souffert au bout de ces heures singulières de sa vie>

238:38. <de sa vie, heures> **240:38.** <au corsage. [239:6. <il se croyait, il était peut-être artiste> 239:7. <plus le même, celui-ci> 240:4. <dire qu'elle était> 240:5. <la porte, à la matière rose de son visage, changeant la forme de sa bouche, le regard de ses yeux, le modèle de ses joues, venait se mélanger un sourire. 240:12. <désagréable en lui caressant les genoux; et la vie> 240:20. <toute vide, bien que son esprit dût penser qu'elle ne l'était pas, mais parce qu'il> 240:25. <rue Abatucci* dans une «visite» garnie de skungs*>]

240:39. Mais quand c'était devant lui qu'elle le manifestait, son mauvais goût lui plaisait au contraire comme tout ce qui venait d'elle.

△**236:21.** Sans doute quand il arrivait chez elle, le soir, et qu'il la trouvait, fredonnant au piano quelques-uns des morceaux qu'elle préférait, la *Valse des Roses* ou *Pauvre fou de Tagliafico** (qu'on devait, selon sa volonté écrite, jouer à son enterrement), il l'interrompait et lui demandait à la place la petite phrase de la sonate de Berget. Bien qu'Odette jouat* fort mal—la vision la plus claire qui nous reste d'une œuvre d'art n'est-elle pas souvent celle qui se détachait des sons faux qu'un piano désaccordé rendait sous des doigts inhabiles—il commençait [*cf.* 237:37] à se rendre mieux compte de ce que la petite phrase avait de douloureux. Mais il ne pouvait pas en souffrir: qu'importait qu'elle lui dît que l'amour est fragile, le sien était si fort. {236:31-237:37}

△**237:42.** Il jouait> **238:3.** <ne cessat* pas de l'embrasser. {238:4-238:9}

△**238:9.** Alors elle faisait> **238:23.** <avec une telle force> [238:12. <fois, saches* au> 238:17. <la Vie de Moïse, il> 238:18. <à son cou l'inclinaison> 238:19. <au quinzième siècle>]

△**238:23.** <telle force qu'il avait besoin de les contrôler, de les tenir et qu'il lui pinçait la joue de toutes ses forces, l'œil égaré, en jouant des mandibules comme s'il voulait la manger.

Mais, sauf en lui faisant jouer la petite phrase de Berget au lieu de la Valse des Roses, Swann ne lui demandait pas de jouer plutôt des choses qu'il aimait et ne cherchait nullement, pas plus en musique> {238:23-238:26}

240:42. <en musique> **241:35.** <de sa délicatesse.

241:35. Car—et cela est vrai pour de plus grands que Swann qui, tout en étant à un degré éloigné de leur famille, n'était pas un créateur,—quand un savant ou un artiste n'est pas méconnu par les êtres qui l'entourent, celui de leurs sentiments>

241:38. <de leurs sentiments> **242:21.** <de grands désirs> [241:42. <respect que lui inspirait la situation de Swann dans le monde> 242:7. <monde était>]

242:21. <de grands désirs, car il était trop éloigné de celui qu'elle connaissait pour se représenter bien nettement à elle. Elle était assoiffée de chic, mais ne s'en faisait pas>

242:28. <s'en faisait pas> **242:30.** <que le projettent dans le cercle de leurs amis ou des amis de leurs amis jusqu'à un degré assez éloigné et plus ou moins affaibli dans la mesure où l'on est distant du centre de leur intimité. Les gens du monde possèdent tous les noms dans leur mémoire, ils ont sur ces matières une érudition d'où ils ont extrait une sorte de goût, de tact, de sorte que Swann par exemple, sans faire constamment appel à son savoir mondain, s'il lisait>

242:38. <s'il lisait> **246:19.** <croyait aux revenants. [243:8. L'autre ne l'est pas moins mais il y faut> 243:37. <un homme si chic, tu> 244:17. <«du temps», d'une forme «amusante». 244:18. <d'honneur et semblait> 244:19. <familiar en> 244:35. <les [*blanc*] y étaient affreuses et la mode n'en prendraient* jamais. 244:38. <salle-à-manger*> 245:14. <réellement les goûts> 245:16. <qu'il aime flâner, se salir> 245:21. <douté!»* Elle> 245:23. <avaient réellement ces goûts> 245:29. <était le langage. 245:30. Sentant qu'il ne pouvait pas toujours réaliser> 245:31. <du moins qu'elle se plût> 245:33. <en toutes choses, et qui, d'ailleurs, l'enchantaient, car c'était autant de traits particuliers grâce auxquels l'essence de la femme qu'il aimait lui

apparaissait, devenait visible. 245:38. <aller à la «Bohême» ou que> 264:4. <maîtresse qui affleurait à> 246:16. <nuance de regrets; mais il aimait>] {246:20-246:32}

246:20. Sympathiser avec Odette, tâcher de n'avoir qu'une âme avec elle, lui était si naturel, qu'il cherchait>

246:34. <cherchait à se plaire> **250:40.** <qu'il connaissait. [246:40. <à Serge Panine* s'il> 247:6. <jusqu'à elles, il ne pensait pas que les objets de nos goûts ont en eux une valeur absolue> 247:12. <comme il trouvait que l'importance qu'Odette trouvait à avoir des cartes> 247:14. <avait attaché autrefois> 247:15. <chez le roi d'Angleterre, de même> 247:20. <d'y aller, (et même à Bruges où jusqu'ici, il s'était rendu tous les ans pour le Jour des Morts), ayant> 247:33. <dans ce petit noyau et> 247:36. <pas se croire, qu'il aimerait toujours Odette, en affirmant qu'il fréquenterait toujours les Verdurin> 247:41. <soir Odette, et, si cela ne revenait pas tout à fait au même> 247:42. <moment où il l'aimait, croire> 248:4. <malgré les petites> 248:15. <c'est simplement une> 248:24. <goûtés son amour> 248:30. <ne voulait pas avoir l'air de lui demander> 248:32. <joie en prenant l'initiative de dire: «Odette> 248:38. <campagne; Swann> 249:9. <qu'on a perdu avec> 249:10. <ajoutait-t-il*> 249:14. <elle ne venait d'ailleurs que de soi-même, le sort> 250:25. <qu'Odette venait justement de leur présenter et sur lequel ils fondaient beaucoup d'espoir*, le comte> 250:38. <Swann de répondre aux imputations trop manifestement>]

250:40. <qu'il connaissait, autrement que par un silence d'ailleurs sans mauvaise humeur et plein de cette affectueuse bienveillance, seul sentiment qu'il pût éprouver dans le petit groupe.

250:41. Quant aux tirades> **252:28.** <à cet égard. [251:16. <qui unie au scepticisme à l'égard de la science, donne> 251:18. <intelligents mais de second ordre, médecins> 251:19. <professeurs qui> 251:21. Il affectionnait* chez Mme Verdurin> 251:25. <et qu'il trouvait en action dans le petit noyau de> 251:34. <le nouveau de> 252:18. <alarmer les êtres respectueuses* s'il y en a autour de cette table, sub rosa> 252:21. <athénienne pourrait> 252:25. <Verdurin, la chronique de Saint Denis* dont>]

252:28. Blanche de Castille entrait de force dans les couvents, un bâton, j'allais dire des gants blancs à la main; nulle ne pourrait>

252:28. <ne pourrait être> **254:8.** <dans les précédentes. [252:31. <comme dit Suger et autres saint Bernard [*construction retained in* la Pléiade]> 253:2. <sentent très en> 253:17. <répugnances pour tout ce qui> 253:18. <même pour celle des parties> 253:22. <dans son habitude des bonnes manières> 253:33. <répondu: «immonde»> 253:35. <mail il n'était pas> 253:36. <Brichot qui avait commencé> 254:4. <de cet artiste>]

254:10. —Y a-t-il un sentiment un peu élevé? demanda-t-il. **254:13.** —Elevé> **256:11.** <le maîtriser. [254:35. <dans «la Ronde» ou «les Régentes»> 255:6. <ajouta: et c'est si loyal! 255:8. <que la Ronde», blasphème> 255:10. <tenait «la Ronde»> 255:11. <avec «la Neuvième», l'Ouverture des «Maîtres» et «la Samothrace», et à> 255:37. <pressés, attendez donc> 255:40. <pourtant trouver de l'assurance quand> 256:4. <salade javanaise?> {256:11-256:14}

256:15. «Je vais vous paraître bien provinciale, Monsieur, dit-elle ensuite à Swann> **259:42.** <le leur répéter. [256:35. <salade javanaise. 256:42. <salade javanaise> 257:8. <pas Francillon:> 257:10. <vaille Serge Panine> 257:13. <Théâtre français! Tandis que Serge Panine> 257:15. <Georges Olivet> 257:17. <à Serge Panine. 257:18. <lui dit Swann en souriant, mais je déteste autant l'un que l'autre> 257:28. <de Francillon, Forcheville> 257:30. <le petit «speach*»> 257:32. Monsieur a une facilité de paroles, une mémoire! avait-il dit à Mme Verdurin quand le peintre eut terminé, comme j'en ai rarement rencontrées*. Il ferait un excellent> 257:36. <avec M. Brichot, vous> 257:40. Quoiqu'il ait> 258:15. <flatter en parlant de ses belles relations, mais en homme du monde, sur un ton> 258:20. <chez les la Trémoille*, chez tout ça> 258:23. <nom des personnes> 258:26. <que ce nom d'ennuyeux, surtout lancé ainsi> 258:27. <fidèles, avait du*> 258:38. <silence n'ait pas> 258:40. <de toute mobilité; son> 258:42. <ces la Trémoille*> 259:5. <buste pour le Salon devant> 259:8. <à celle des la Trémoille* qu'ils> 259:25. Mais que me* répondait-il> 259:36. <à une rétraction*, comme>]

259:42. A quoi Swann disait en riant:

—Mais ce n'est pas du tout par peur de la duchesse. Très sincèrement, je vous assure que tout le monde adore aller chez elle, que son mari est un grand lettré et qu'elle est charmante. {260:2-260:8}

260:11. Si bien que> **260:22.** <il ne veut jamais. {260:23-260:25}

260:26. Pour vous> **260:27.** <s'insinuer? {260:28-260:34}

260:35. —Il y a> **261:18.** <hasard Mme Verdurin. [260:42. <Swann ait donné la sienne. Celui-ci se contenta de sourire sans répondre et en se dérobant> 261:6. —Ces de la Trémoille* que> 261:15. <Mme de la Trémoille*>] {261:19-262:2}

262:3. Après de dîner> **263:36.** <les médecins! [262:6. <une femme intelligente, pour moi> 262:7. Evidemment celle-ci commence> 262:15. <Gottard*> 262:32. <en face, en écoutant le peintre, fermait> 262:35. <gaieté> 263:7. —Je* trouve Odette charmante, dit> 263:26. —J'ai soigné autrefois une baronne. La baronne Picpus, les Picpus étaient aux croisades, n'est-ce pas? Ils ont en Poméranie, un lac qui est grand comme dix fois la place de la Concorde. Je l'ai soignée pour de l'arthrite> 263:35. <on voit chemin faisant qu'il connaît>] {263:37-264:38}

264:39. Tout le monde> **265:41.** <valeur particulière. [265: 10. <quand nous avons parlé de la duchesse de la Trémoïlle (qu'elle prononçait moaille au lieu de mouille). {265:42-266:22}

266:23. Swann ignorait> **268:36.** <éteindre toute lumière> [266:25. <beau, dans l'ivresse de son amour. 266:26. Il continuait à ne voir Odette, au moins> 266:35. <ressenti par Odette venant> 266:36. <immédiatement chez elle, pour> 266:42. <Verdurin, qui sait?> 267:6. <sentiment qu'il ne connût pas encore> 267:12. <influence, de ses relations, de l'utilité> 267:18. <l'autre par> 267:19. <s'il s'était figuré que> 267:21. <cet état* plus> 267:24. <voir. En attendant, en la comblant> 267:26. <reposer parfois sur> 267:34. <qualité de leur sensibilité désintéressée> 267:43. <fleurs vénéreuses*> 268:5. <ses amis, qu'il éprouvait lui-même, cette Odette dont les propos qu'elle tenait avaient> 268:9. <titres, —cette dernière image du

banquier lui rappela qu'il avait à prendre de l'argent, car si ce mois-ci> 268:12. <difficultés d'argent qu'il> 268:13. <avait donné trois mille francs, et s'il ne lui offrait pas une automobile qu'elle désirait> 268:18. <faire croire, comme elle en verrait les manifestations devenir moins grandes, que son amour pour elle avait diminué. 268:20. <se demanda si ce n'était pas> 268:25. <familier, un peu déchiré au coin, que> 268:29. <avec deux autres> 268:30. <depuis qu'elle le connaissait>]

268:36. <éteindre toute lumière à son intelligence, aussi brusquement qu'on coupe l'électricité dans une maison. Il tâtonna un instant dans l'obscurité, il releva machinalement avec le plat de sa main les deux ailes de ses cheveux en brosse, et ne revit>

268:42. <ne revit la lumière> **269:34.** <heures et demie> [268:43. <d'une pensée toute> 269:1. <prochain quatre ou cinq mille> 269:2. <de trois, à cause> 269:11. <en attendant il pouvait souvent lui être agréable> 269:13. <eue du monde> 269:18. <accoutumés aux premières qu'il eût éprouvé quelque malaise à se trouver dans les seconds.*]

269:34. <heures et demie, s'habillait et montait en voiture. Mais il ne s'y sentait pas seul, car la pensée constante d'Odette donnait aux moments où il était loin d'elle le même charme particulier qu'à ceux où il était là. Il montait en voiture mais il en sortait que cette pensée y sautait en même>

269:38. <en même temps> **270:21.** <la princesse. [270:2. <ancolies qu'il portait en souvenir d'Odette. 270:5. <Verdurin, il aurait> 270:6. <n'aurait eu> 270:12. <avant d'arriver au plat d'asperges>]

270:21. <les fidèles—qu'une fois la princesse de* Laumes qui n'était pas bonne, dit:

270:25. —Vraiment> **270:32.** <clair de lune [270:29. <trouverait du moins à Saint Cloud*. Mais il ne pouvait>]

□**270:33.** Comme un petit orchestre jouait généralement toute la soirée dans ces restaurants en plein air, Odette avait voulu qu'ils pussent jouer la petite phrase de la Sonate de Berget pour que Swann à son arrivée en eut* la surprise. Elle en parlait aux Verdurin qui mettaient le plus grand zèle à faire chercher un des violinistes, à l'aboucher avec le petit pianiste qui lui faisait répéter une ou deux fois la phrase. Ce n'est pas que Swann fut* rentré en faveur auprès des Verdurin, au contraire. Mais l'idée d'organiser un plaisir ingénieux pour quelqu'un, même pour quelqu'un qu'ils n'aiment pas, développe chez les êtres les moins tendres, pendant les quelques instants nécessaires à ses préparatifs et à sa réalisation, des sentiments de sympathie cordiale et de charité. De sorte que quand Swann arrivait il était accueilli par cette longue note ténue qui était plus belle sur le violon, instrument pour lequel elle avait été écrite et d'où s'échappait la petite phrase. Par moments il se disait>

270:43. <il se disait que> **271:20.** <situation privilégiée> {271:10-271:18}

271:20. <situation privilégiée qu'elle lui faisait et la prédilection pour lui qui y était impliquée. {271:22-271:35}

271:36. Aussi, après le dîner, la prenant> **273:38.** <qu'il leur trouvait> [271:41. <des atteintes d'un mal dont il avait souffert autrefois à l'occasion d'une autre, la jalousie. 271:43. <pleuvait averse,* il> 272:10. <particulièrement désirée.* 272:19. <pas de [*blanc*] ce soir> 272:20. <bon petit [*blanc*]. 272:23. <pas de [*blanc*] ce soir> 272:25. <fait beaucoup de bien, mes* enfin> 272:28. Mais, comme il venait de rentrer chez> 272:33. <parti, elle l'avait rallumée, et fait entrer celui> 272:38. <sur laquelle donnait* les fenêtres de son hôtel et où il allait quelquefois frapper à celle de sa chambre. 272:43. <chez elle. Dans l'obscurité> 273:2. <débordait, entre> 273:3. <dorée, la> 273:6. <annonçait: «elle> 273:10. <entre les obliques des volets> 273:14. <derrière les volets le couple> 273:25. <capturer; plus simplement il allait>]

273:39. <qu'il leur trouvait autrefois, quand son imagination n'était pas encore desséchée par la vie mondaine, mais l'avaient repris seulement là où elles étaient éclairées par le souvenir d'Odette, embellies par son passage, maintenant, c'était>

273:40. <maintenant, c'était> **276:20.** <pour lui. [274:8. <attention, nullement sa pensée véritable, qui y était> 274:14. <autrefois de l'histoire. **274:16.** <sait, demain> 274:18. <lui semblaient* plus> 274:23. Au moment de frapper> 274:36. <cette fenêtre, comme> 175:25. <curiosité qu'il avait eue, eût laissé> 275:37. <pouvaient pas la diminuer; mais> 276:15. <même et qui> 276:17. <autre, de cette>] {276:20-276:25}

276:25. De sorte qu'il> **280:27.** <trouvait d'habitude> [276: 26. <inventée, chaque grâce> 276:36. <eux, ait voulu> 276:37. <tête de turc* et briller à leurs yeux à ses> 276:38. <qu'il ait été> 277:2. <délicat pour ne pas se sentir géné* à certains moments de sa seule présence, Forcheville> 277:12. <refermée sur le vieillard, faisant> 277:16. <félicitations pour son audace, d'ironie> 277:18. <victime, lui jetant un regard> 277:21. <ses yeux le rencontrèrent, dégrisé> 277:34. <crut entendre du bruit, marcher, mais> 277:38. <d'Odette, les rideaux l'empêchant de rien> 277:39. <carreaux, appella.* Personne> 277:42. <entendre du bruit; mais> 278:18. <qui était vraie, était seule> 278:22. <faux. Ça du moins> 278:25. <trahira. Elle se trompait, elle ne se rendait pas> 278:29. <qui, quelque* fussent> 278:31. <placerait, trahiraient toujours> 278:42. <sentait, justement> 278:43. <parlant, garder> 279:10. <intéressantes, ni que les relations qu'elle pouvait avoir avec d'autres hommes n'exhalaient pas naturellement et pour tout le monde une tristesse mortelle, capable de lui donner à lui la fièvre du suicide. 279:17. <pu lui donner> 279:42. <obtenir des renseignements> 280:1. <goûts desquels il> 280:17. <je ne l'ai* pas vu.» 280:23. <ensemble qui, s'il n'était pas très grand pour elle, l'était pour lui.]

□**280:27.** <trouvait d'habitude, les florentines de ce Sandro di Mariano auquel on donne plus volontiers son surnom populaire de Botticelli depuis qu'il évoque au lieu de l'œuvre véritable du peintre l'idée banale et fausse qui s'en est vulgarisée. Elle avait en ce moment le* visage>

280:28. <visage abattu> **283:38.** <venue du dehors. [281:30. <il éprouva devant le désastre du malheureux qu'il était un sentiment de découragement, presque de compassion. Mais> 281:33. <la pitié qu'il s'inspirait à lui-même ce fut sur elle qu'il la reporta, et il murmura> 281:39. <poste, tira les lettres de sa poche> 282:4. <soupçon calomnieux peut-être pour Odette, destiné> 282:28. <avait bien lu avant: «J'ai> 282:31. <déchiffrer tout d'abord> 282:32. <phrase toute* entière. 282:39. <Swann la première fois> 282:40. <ajouté: puissiez-vous> 282:41. <reprendre. Pour> 283:9. <Forcheville pouvait-il s'expliquer qu'elle

aurait pu> 283:18. <réjouissait, comme si elle eût eu> 283:32. <l'avait peut-être trompé.] {283:38-284:9}

284:10. Quelques jours après il alla à un dîner> **285:21.** Il essaya de sourire> [284:16. <Chatou, où lui, Swann, n'était pas invité. 284:19. <sonate «clair de lune» dans> 284:36. <obtenir qu'elle n'aille pas> 284:42. <jusqu'ici:

—A demain>]

285:21. Il essaya de sourire, mais il avait l'air si atterré que son cocher lui demanda s'il n'était pas arrivé un malheur [*text repeated* 285:42].

285:22. —As-tu vu> **291:18.** <manquer l'Ouverture!» [285:23. <nous, dit Mme Verdurin à son mari en rentrant. 286:7. <à d'autre* que> 286:15. <boutique, vraiment> 286:19. «Il y aurait là les Cottard, peut-être Brichot.» «Est-ce> 286:22. <*Chatou!*» «Hélas> [*The Pléiade has kept the other quotation mark,* 286:28.] 286:39. <à rire, quand toute narine> 287:8. <s'écria-t-il, relevant> 287:10. <voulu en tirer Odette, et> 287:15. <que quelques> 287:18. <de lui.» 287:19. <sonate du Clair de lune> 287:27. <entremetteuse!» Entremetteuse, c'était> 287:37. <sociale, le lieu prophétisé par l'apôtre et dont il est écrit qu'au-dessous il n'y a rien. Nul doute que le texte sacré ne se réfère> 287:43. <dans ce «Noli tangere»* du faubourg> 288:6. <lui versaient de nouveau à chaque instant l'ivresse> 288:11. <j'ai connu* comme*, était loin> 288:14. <et qui suffit* à> 288:23. <possédées, mais n'avaient pas favorisé et protégé son amour, a provoqué* chez> 288:25. <et qui, même à travers d'autres, ne pouvait lui venir que d'Odette, de même l'immortalité, fût-elle réelle, qu'il trouverait aujourd'hui aux Verdurin s'ils n'avaient pas commencé à inviter Odette avec Forcheville et sans lui, aurait été impuissante à déchaîner> 288:39. <car quand, arrivé> 289:2. <mauvais, car il ne> 289:8. <ce soir? C'est bien ce qu'on appelle un gentleman, n'est-ce pas? il est ami personnel du> [*After* 289:22 *there is no blank in* Grasset A.] 289:30. <l'emmener à l'Opéra voir Paillasse et Swann> 289:37. <d'aller à Paillasse. C'est> 289:41. <une autre pour mépriser spontanément cette horrible musique, et surtout pour ne pas être arrivée> 290:4. <pour toute* sa qualité d'âme.» 290:8. <aller à l'Opéra> 290:24. Vois-tu, Paillasse n'est rien> 290:42. <de

renoncer à Paillasse dans l'espoir> 291:9. <supplications des hommes et dont l'habitude qu'elle avait d'eux lui permettait> 291:14. Aussi l'avait-elle* écouté avec> 219:16. <pour peu que Swann parlât encore un peu de temps>] {291:19-292:10}

292:11. Quand les Verdurin> **295:29.** <et dormait. [292:35. <Maud*> 292:39. <Violet-le-Duc*> 293:1. <d'y aller, —comme> 293:3. <disait-elle, il> 293:4. <fer, qui lui donnerait le moyen de> 293:23. <Violet-le-Duc.* 293:28. <voir aujourd'hui même> 293:33. <rencontrait, lui, elle> 293:40. <Pierrefond*> 293:41. <enmener*> 294:5. <promit* du moins> 294:10. <l'endroit exact de sa présence, à tel moment, il sentirait> 294:16. <tendre, asiles> 294:26. <il changeait vingt fois de projet, inspectait> 294:30. <qu'il l'avait trouvé> 295:8. <avait pu prendre> 295:15. <concierge, ouvrait la fenêtre pour appeler> 295:19. <rentrait. Pour la première fois il remarquait le vol incessant des voitures qui passaient. Il écoutait> 295:22. <arrêté*>] {295:30-298:8}

298:9. Et pourtant, en dehors de ces absences, elle lui réservait presque toujours la fin de la soirée et jusqu'à une heure aussi avancée de la nuit qu'il le voulait, et cette situation privilégiée qu'il conservait auprès d'elle elle ne la cachait pas, elle le* proclamait volontiers. Si Forcheville se trouvait par hasard un soir chez elle, quand Swann arrivait, et s'il demandait la permission de rester encore un moment, Odette lui répondait en montrant Swann:>

298:13. «Ah! cela dépend de ce monsieur-là> **298:33.** <toute à lui. [298:14. Enfin, restez un moment> 298:20. <voir ainsi ouvertement, en présence de Forcheville, lui adresser non seulement ces paroles d'affection, de préférence, mais encore> 298:24. <répondu pour votre> 298:26. «Avez-vous apporté seulement> 298:31. <disant tout cela>] {298:34-300:15}

300:16. Alors le lendemain, dès le matin, il courait chez son joaillier, faisait envoyer à Odette les plus beaux bijoux, parce que cette bonté de la veille avait excité sa gratitude, ou le désir de la voir se renouveler, ou un>

300:20. <ou un paroxysme> **301:42.** <si elle avait pu> [300:24. <landau de Mme Verdurin> 300:26. <invité, prier

vainement Odette, avec> 300:28. <lui, et s'en> 300:30. <rage!» ce même regard, brillant, malicieux, abaissé et sournois, qu'elle lui avait adressé le jour où il avait chassé Saniette> 301:7. <qu'il lui prêtait, il> 301:19. <reçu la lettre, non pas seulement dans son esprit mais en réalité. 301:33. <Bach et Léon Cavallo. 301:34. <vivrait tout de même plus> 301:38. <fantaisie, qu'il était possible qu'elle n'eût jamais eue de tomber>]

301:42. <elle avait pu se casser la jambe avant de partir, si le chauffeur de l'automobile qui l'emmènerait avait consenti, à n'importe quel prix, de* la conduire au lieu de Beyreuth, dans quelque lieu où elle fût restée.

302:2. <où elle fût restée> **303:22.** <maîtresse de maison. [302:11. <s'élevait, brillant dans son esprit, le visage> 302:33. <marque de désir, et même plutôt d'affection que d'amour, mais dont> 302:38. <rendait son amour moins exigeant de> 302:41. <d'où sa jalousie l'avait> 302:43. <charmante, Swann se le* figurait avec une pleine tendresse> 303:1. <consentement, de joie aussi, qu'il> 303:3. <et il lui avait de ce regard enchanteur et bon autant de reconnaissance que si elle le lui avait jeté réellement et si cela n'avait pas été seulement son imagination qui venait de le peindre pour donner satisfaction à son désir.] {303:23-303:30}

303:31. Pourquoi croire> **304:21.** <aussi artistique> [303:34. <à Paris, si Forcheville avait pensé à lui ç'aurait été comme> 303:36. <comptait dans> 303:37. <obligé de laisser la place, s'ils se rencontraient chez elle. S'ils triomphaient tous deux d'être> 304:3. Et, au> 304:4. <revu, s'il>]

304:21. <aussi artistique, que chez certaines personnes le besoin d'entendre souvent de la musique. {304:21-304:31}

304:32. Ainsi, par le chimisme> **304:39.** <son sourire. [304:37. <près de lui et, auparavant, lui avoir fait plaisir pour voir>]

304:40. Aussi Odette prenait-elle l'habitude de ne plus craindre de lui déplaire et même de l'irriter, lui refusait-elle, quand cela lui était commode, les faveurs auxquelles il tenait le plus, sûre de le voir venir après quelques jours, ausis tendre et soumis qu'avant, lui demander une réconciliation.

305:3. Peut-être> **305:25.** <jours suivants. [305:17. <il écrivait à Odette qu'étant> 305:22. <dans l'état nouveau où> 305:23. <pris dans un autre, il courait>

305:39. Mais d'autres fois au contraire—si Odette> **306:29.** désirait> [306:4. Déjà il voyait Odette> 306:7. <de le* voir. 306:15. <avait passé>]

□**306:29.** <désirait acquérir, renseignement qu'à la rigueur on pourrait avoir par le carrossier ou l'agent de change, mais qu'il était peut-être plus pratique, plus rapide de lui demander à elle-même (c'était>

306:29. <(c'était très joli> **308:21.** <du désir physique. [306:36. <présent, des> 306:40. <peine à voir venir un à un> 306:43. <qu'il* allait> 307:4. <était revenue près> 307:8. <s'étant trouvé*> 307:12. <aussi qu'elle revenait parée> 307:18. <sur le terme qu'il s'est assigné), qui, de plus, de ce qui*> 307:33. <d'avance, au* nécessaire> 307:36. <peut être*—vue du point de vue> 307:38. <tuberculeux, qui, persuadés> 308:1. <contingences, car il les considère seulement comme l'aspect qu'ont pris, pour redevenir sensible* à ces maladies, le vice et l'état morbide> 308:4. <rêves différents mais inefficaces de sa sagesse. 308:14. <que lui avait inspiré, avant qu'il aimât Odette, sa beauté trop rose, trop bouffie, lui revenait à certains jours, où sa chair qui devenait d'ailleurs plus flasque lui était apparue particulièrement congestionnée. «Vraiment> 308:19. <trouvais presque laide.]

308:39. <plus qu'un avec lui> **309:27.** <plaisait le mieux. [308:43. Cet amour avait tellement détaché Swann de tous> 309:8. <par le fait qu'il les proclamait moins précieux* qu'elle)> 309:13. <oisive, de même que> 309:16. <que jadis à lire Saint-Simon, la mécanique> 309:20. <absolu, la nouveauté du plaisir lui venait de pouvoir émigrer>]

309:27. Un jour qu'il avait voulu envoyer des fruits à la princesse de Parme pour son anniversaire parce qu'elle pouvait souvent être indirectement agréable à Odette en lui faisant avoir des places pour des galas, jubilés, couronnements, ne sachant pas trop comment les commander, il en avait chargé une cousine de sa mère qui, ravie de faire une commission pour lui, lui avait écrit, en lui rendant compte qu'elle n'avait pas pris tous les fruits au même endroit, mais les fraises chez tel marchand dont c'est la spécialité, les poires ailleurs où elles sont plus belles, etc., «chaque>

309:38. <«chaque fruit> **310:18.** <dans la famille> [309: 40. <fraises et de l'énormité des poires> 310:11. <l'amabilité de ces bourgeois était moins vive> 310:14. <de la considération et de l'estime), une> 310:15. <princiers qu'elle lui proposait*, ne>]

310:18. <dans la famille de tel vieil ami de ses parents qui le connaissait personnellement à peine, et le lui demandait comme à leur digne successeur.

310:25. Mais, par les intimités> **310:43.** <se rapportaient à Odette> [310:31. Et penser que> 310:33. <naturellement le prince de Joinville, le baron de Charlus*, le prince de Reuss et le duc de Luxembourg que son vieux valet> 310:35. <lui était d'une même consolation> 310:38. <reprisés ou> 310:39. <l'ouvrière, linceul>]

310:43. <se rapportaient à Odette, c'est-à-dire dans toute sa vie, il était si constamment dominé et dirigé par le sentiment inavoué qu'il lui était sinon moins cher, du moins moins* agréable à voir que quiconque, que le* plus ennuyeux fidèles des Verdurin, que quand il se reportait à un monde>

311:5. <à un monde> **312:29.** <quand il le rencontra. [311: 12. <excuses à ces gens pour> 311:15. <payait-il, se> 311:17. <francs, et> 311:21. <d'aucune*> 311:29. <Paris, elle le voyait> 311:30. <disait «je> 311:31. <et «qu'est-ce> 311:37. <tâcher de n'être pas privé de la rencontrer nulle part, Swann> 311:39. <mon oncle Charles dont> 311:42. <Odette. Quand elle parlait de mon oncle à Swann, elle prenait toujours des airs si poétiques, disant> 312:5. <Swann ne savait pas à quel ton se hausser> 312:9. <de sa vertu indémontrable> 312:17. <que je la rencontre. Vous> 312:19. <quelques mots, lui dire qu'elle> 312:28. <aller tuer mon>] {312:29-314:31}

314:31. Même pour leur> **315:13.** <pu le renseigner. [314:36. <réponse de la dernière importance> 314:37. <venir Swann quelqu'un d'autre offrait quand la soirée était déjà commencée de le* rejoindre au théâtre ou à souper> 315:7. <comme vous

me remerciez de vous avoir gardé> 315:10. <bon à savoir.* Parfois>] {315:13-315-23}

315:24. Certes, savoir ne permet pas toujours d'empêcher. Mais les choses que nous savons> **315:28.** <sur elles. {315:28-316:34}

316:34. Et même il lui aurait suffi. Mais elle ne voulait pas qu'elle lui permît de rester chez elle pendant qu'elle ne serait pas là; de l'attendre jusqu'à cette heure du retour dans l'apaisement de laquelle venait* se confondre les heures qu'un prestige ou un maléfice nous avait fait croire différentes des autres. {316:38-317:39}

317:40. Comme elle ne lui donnait> **318:2.** <à vide> [317:41. <sur les choses> 318:1. <imaginer, car son cerveau>]

318:2. <à vide; il relevait sa chevelure en brosse des deux côtés de son front, passait son doigt sur ses paupières fatiguées comme on essuie le verre de son lorgnon, et cessait entièrement de penser. Il surnageait pourtant de* cet inconnu certaines occupations qui réapparaissaient de temps en temps et qu'elle rattachait vaguement à quelque obligation envers des parents éloignés ou des amis d'autrefois, qui parce qu'ils étaient les seuls qu'elle lui citait souvent comme l'empêchant de la voir, sans qu'il pût tirer du néant du reste la matière d'aucun doute, d'aucune objection à élever contre eux, lui paraissaient former un cadre fixe, nécessaire, de la vie d'Odette.

318:11. A cause du ton> **318:15.** <ce jour-là> [318:12. <Hippodrome», non seulement si, s'étant senti malade et ayant pensé: «peut-être>]

318:15. <ce jour-là, ce devoir qui incombait à Odette lui semblait si inéluctable qu'il s'inclinait sans murmurer devant lui et se disait: «Ah! non, ce n'est pas la peine de lui demander de venir, j'aurais dû y penser plus tôt, c'est le jour où elle va avec son amie à l'Hippodrome. Réservons-nous pour ce qui est possible; c'est inutile de s'user à proposer des choses inacceptables et refusées d'avance»; mais encore son caractère de nécessité semblait rendre plausible et légitime tout ce qui de près, ou de loin se rapportait à lui.

318:25. Si Odette dans la rue recevait d'un passant> **318:35.** <à se les figurer. [318:27. <répondait en rattachant> 318:29. <parlait, et si>] {318:25-319:11}

319:12. Il arrivait encore parfois, quand elle sortait avec Swann et qu'elle voyait s'approcher d'elle> **319:16.** <voir quand Forcheville était là. Mais c'était rare. L'air qu'elle avait le plus souvent avec Swann et qui contrastait [*syntax sic*].

319:17. Car les jours où malgré tout> **319:24.** <par ces mots:> [319:20. <dans l'attitude qu'elle avait habituellement avec lui était l'assurance, grand contraste, peut être* revanche>]

319:24. «Ma main tremble en vous écrivant.» Elle le disait du moins et pour une petite part cet émoi devait être sincère pour qu'elle désirât d'en feindre le reste.

319:28. Swann lui plaisait> **320:4.** <cette tête-là!» [319:29. <soi, on ne craint que ceux qu'on aime. 319:34. <dire mon, mien, quand> 319:35. «Vous êtes ma chose, c'est> 319:38. Alors à tout ce> 319:41. <chauve, si caractérisée dont> 320:3. <disait:

—Si je pouvais>]

320:4. Maintenant, à tout ce qu'il disait elle répondait d'un ton parfois irrité, quelquefois indulgent:

—Ah! tu ne seras donc jamais comme tout le monde.

Elle regardait cette tête qui n'était qu'un peu plus vieillie par le souci, mais dont maintenant tous pensaient, en vertu de cette sincère aptitude qui permet de découvrir les intentions d'une symphonie quand on a lu le programme, et les ressemblances d'un enfant quand on connaît sa parenté.

—Il n'est pas positivement laid si vous voulez, mais il est ridicule: «ce monocle, ce toupet, ce sourire!» réalisaient dans leur imagination suggestionnée la démarcation immatérielle qui sépare à quelques mois de distance une tête d'amant de cœur et une tête de cocu, elle disait:

—Ah! si je pouvais changer, rendre raisonnable ce qu'il y a dans cette tête-là.

320:20. Toujours prêt> **320:43.** <il fut attendri. [320:20. <si ses* manières d'être d'Odette avec lui laissaient seulement place> 320:24. <que de l'apaiser, de le diriger, de le faire travailler, serait> 320:29. <insupportable mainmise sur la liberté.

320:31. <me transporter*> 320:32. Ainsi voyait-il dans> 320:34. <peut-être. Et> 320:42. <baiser. Elle le dit comme elle était de bonne humeur; il fut>]

321:1. Le soir il dit au marquis de Guercy: >

321:6. —Je crois pourtant> **322:21.** <pas ce soir. [321:11. <disait:

—Tiens, ce n'est pas Rémi qui est sur le siège, avec quelle> 321:14. <prendre Rémi quand je vais rue Pauquet. 321:16. <prenne Rémi> 321:20. Mais si Swann souffrait des nouvelles façons d'Odette, il ne connaissait pas> 321:29. <sentait qu'avec sa pensée il approchait d'elle, il s'éloignait vivement de peur de trop souffrir> 321:32. <où elle m'aimait> 321:37. <était serré> 321:39. <lettres où dans l'une elle disait: «Si vous aviez oublié ici votre cœur je ne vous aurais pas laissé le reprendre», dans une autre: «A quelque> 321:42. <faites signe> 322:12. <à celle-ci se demandant s'il n'était pas trop tard et s'il ne ferait pas mieux d'y renoncer, la visite du baron de Charlus* qui, bien qu'il fût allé dernièrement chez Mme de Saint-Euverte, venait offrir à Swann d'y retourner avec lui, si sa compagnie> 322:17. <ne doutez pas combien j'aimerais à être> 322:19. <plus tôt*>] {322:21-322:24}

322:24. Tâchez de la distraire> **322:37.** <Swann arriva> [322:34. <faites mon petit Mémé, vous>]

□**322:37.** <Swann arriva tranquillisé de penser qu'Odette passerait cette soirée avec M. de Charlus.*

Son indifférence mélancolique pout tout ce qu'il allait y voir, en retirant les choses de la dépendance de sa volonté dont toute action sur elles était suspendue, leur donnait à ses yeux le charme de ce qui nous apparaît en soi-même. Son attention détachée de tout but égoïste se portait sur des objets qu'elle avait toujours ignorés, et dès sa descente de voiture, les grooms, héritiers des «tigres» de Balzac, qui se tenaient devant l'hôtel, le firent penser à cette extériorisation de certains des habitants de pierre des églises romanes, qui, portant leurs insignes, sont répartis tant bien que mal à côté les uns des autres au tympan de la façade ou à l'entrée des porches. Comme les maîtresses de maison dans ce tableau fictif de leur vie domestique qu'elles offrent à leurs invités les jours de cérémonie, cherchant à respecter la vérité du costume et celle du décor, ces grooms, suivants et symboles de la promenade, intermédiaires entre l'hôtel et la nature extérieure, étaient chapeautés et bottés et restaient dehors sur le sol de l'avenue comme des jardiniers auraient été rangés à l'entrée de leurs parterres. Dans le vestibule où jusque-là, il entrait enveloppé dans son pardessus pour en sortir en frac>

323:17. <mais sans savoir> **321:21.** <allait l'introduire, et qui par l'anticipation des plaisirs de l'une ou le prolongement de ceux de l'autre ne laissant entre elles aucun intervalle, pour la première fois>

323:21. <pour la première fois> **324:29.** <escalier monumental> [323:26. <rassemblés, l'entourèrent en formant le cercle. 323:38. <touchant*> 324:3. <Martegna*> 324:9. <ou le Martyre de saint Etienne. 324:10. <disparue, ou qui> 324:11. <jamais que dans les prédelles de San Zeno> 324:13. <encore, issue> 324:16. <mais cellés*> 324:26. <jacynthes* et d'une torsade de serpent.*]

324:29. <escalier monumental où Swann s'engagea avec la tristesse de penser qu'Odette ne l'avait jamais gravi, et que leur présence décorative et leur immobilité marmoréenne aurait pu faire surnommer comme celui du Palais Ducal: «l'Escalier des Géants.» {324:33-325:5}

325:6. D'un côté et de l'autre, à des hauteurs différentes, à chaque> **325:32.** <une seule œuvre d'art> [325:10. <argentier, braves> 325:15. <industriel, attentifs> 325:21. <niche; tandis qu'un énorme> 325:23. Parvenu haut*> 325:30. <qui, tel>]

325:32. <œuvre d'art, qui en reçoivent leur nom, et dans une nudité voulue, ne contiennent rien d'autre, exhibant en son milieu comme quelque précieuse effigie de Benvenuto Cellini représentant un homme de guet, un jeune valet de pied, le corps légèrement fléchi en avant, dressant sur son hausse* col rouge une figure plus rouge encore d'où s'échappaient des torrents de feu, de timidité et de zèle, perçant la tenture d'Aubusson qui retombait sur le salon où on écoutait la musique, de son regard impétueux, vigilant, éperdu, avait l'air, avec une impassibilité militaire, ou une foi surnaturelle,—allégorie de l'alarme, incarnation de l'attente, commémoration du branle-bas,—de guetter l'apparition de l'ennemi, ou d'épier l'heure du Jugement, ange ou vigie, d'une tour de donjon ou de cathédrale, sur laquelle on sentait qu'il recevrait indéfiniment les baisers successifs des clairs de lune et des aurores, dans son ardeur immortellement immobile de statue, pour l'admiration des siècles.

326:3. Il ne restait plus> **326:7.** <clefs d'une ville. {326:7-326:10}

326:11. Swann retrouva> **326:13.** <des invités.

326:14. Mais cette laideur même et pour tant de visages qu'il connaissait si bien, lui semblait neuve depuis que leurs traits au lieu d'être pour lui des signes pratiquement utilisables à l'identification de telle personne qui lui représentait un faisceau de plaisirs à poursuivre, d'ennuis à éviter, ou de politesse* à rendre, reposaient, détachées de lui, coordonnées seulement par des rapports esthétiques, dans l'autonomie de leurs lignes. Et en ces hommes, au milieu desquels Swann se trouva enserré, et dont une soirée qui se prolonge, secrète et entasse contre les parois, près des portes, les noirs bataillons qui ne permettent pas moins d'apprécier depuis combien de temps elle dure que ne fait le degré de la chaleur qu'elle a dégagé naturellement, il n'était pas jusqu'aux monocles que beaucoup portaient et qui, jusqu'ici, auraient tout au plus permis à Swann de dire qu'ils portaient un monocle, qui, déliés maintenant de signifier une habitude, la même pour tous, lui apparaissaient chacun différent, avec une sorte d'individualité.

326:28. Peut-être parce que> **327:43.** <cache son repaire. [326:40. <au «Gibus»> 326:42. <à ses revers> 327:8. <ajouta: Vous> 327:9. <savez! pendant> 327:10. <demandant> 327:11. <ici? au romancier mondain qui, venant d'installer> 327:18. <marquis de Foustelle*> 327:29. <étincellait*> 327:33. <volupté, tandis qu'enfin, derrière> 327:36. <mendibules*> 327:41. <des Vices et des Vertus des* Giotto>]

328:1. Swann s'était avancé, sur l'insistance de Mme de Saint-Euverte et s'était mis pour entendre les morceaux de Bach qu'on jouait, dans un coin où il avait malheureusement comme seule perspective deux vieilles dames assises l'une à côté de l'autre, la marquise de Cambremer* et la vicomtesse de Franquetot, qui, parce qu'elles étaient cousines>

328:7. <étaient cousines> **328:17.** <souvenirs de jeunesse.

328:17. Avec une mélancolique ironie, Swann les regardait qui, en écoutant les intermèdes de piano qui avaient succédé au quatuor, suivaient avec anxiété le jeu vertigineux du virtuose, Mme de Franquetot avec anxiété, les yeux éperdus comme si les touches sur lesquelles il courait avec agilité avaient été une suite de trapèzes d'où il pouvait tomber d'une hauteur de quatre-vingt* mètres, lançant à sa voisine>

328:25. <à sa voisine> **329:4.** <sans aucune raison> [328:32. <telles avec> 328:35. <vous!», qu'à> 329:2. <ennuyeuse, méchante, d'une branche inférieure, ou peut-être sans raison.]

329:4. Quand elle était auprès de quelqu'un qu'elle ne connaissait pas, comme en ce moment de Mme de Franquetot, elle souffrait que la conscience qu'elle avait de sa parenté princière ne pût se manifester extérieurement en caractères visibles comme ceux qui, dans les mosaïques des églises byzantines, courent sous les pas ou s'échappent des lèvres des Saints Personnages qui sont censés les prononcer.

329:13. Elle songeait> **329:21.** <en effet la raison> [329:14. <invitation, une visite> 329:19. <Mathilde, ce> 329:21. <pardonné, elle>]

329:22. <raison pour laquelle elle n'y allait pas. Aussi tout en y pensant, ses épaules se rejetaient-elles en arrière. Elle se souvenait confusément qu'elle avait demandé plusieurs fois à Mme des Laumes comment elle pourrait faire pour la trouver, mais neutralisait et au-delà cette pensée un peu abaissante en murmurant: «Ce n'est tout de même pas à moi à faire les premiers pas, j'ai vingt ans de plus qu'elle.» De sorte que ses épaules se détachaient entièrement de son buste que sa tête était posée presque horizontalement, rapportée comme dans un orgueilleux faisan qu'on sert sur une table avec toutes ses plumes. Ce n'est pas qu'elle ne fut* assez courte, homasse*, boulotte. Mais les camouflets l'avaient redressé comme les arbres qui, nés dans une mauvaise position, sont forcés de pousser en arrière pour garder leur équilibre.

329:38. Obligée> **330:3.** <hommes de cercle. {330:3-330:11}

330:11. Quand on lui parlait d'une personne illustre, elle répondait que sans la connaître> **330:30.** <qu'il est> [330:14. <elle le répondait d'un> 330:16. <ne la* connaissait> 330:17. <principes et entêtements auxquels> 330:26. <avait pas* aucune>]

330:30. <qu'il est là, et pour ne pas avoir l'air de signaler sa présence et de réclamer des égards, bornant simplement son regard à la considération d'une étoile du tapis ou de sa propre jupe, elle était allée s'asseoir à l'endroit qui lui avait paru le plus modeste, d'où elle savait bien que l'exclamation ravie de Mme de Saint-Euverte allait la tirer dès qu'elle l'aurait aperçue, à côté de Mme de Cambremer. Elle observait la mimique de sa voisine mélomane, mais ne l'imitait pas. Ce n'est pas que, pour une fois qu'elle venait passer cinq minutes chez Mme de Saint-Euverte, elle n'eût souhaité, pour que la politesse qu'elle lui faisait comptât, se montrer le plus aimable possible.

330:43. Mais par nature> **331:4.** <coterie où elle> [331:1. <appelait les exagérations et> 331:2. <qu'elle «n'avait pas» à> 331:3. <le genre de>]

331:4. <où elle vivait, sentant* naturelle, et qui pourtant d'autre part ne laissaient pas de l'impressionner, grâce à cet esprit d'imitation voisin de la timidité que produit chez les gens les plus sûrs d'eux-mêmes l'ambiance d'un milieu nouveau, fût-il inférieur.

331:8. Elle commençait> **331:16.** <tantôt elle remontait la bride de ses épaulettes en examinant avec une froide curiosité> [331:12. <entendu*> 331:13. <à l'égard de la musique et> 331:15. <«cote» mal taillée ses>]

331:21. <sa fougueuse voisine> **331:24.** <ayant terminé le morceau de Bach, et à passant* des temps plus modernes et ayant commencé une étude de Chopin,>

331:25. <Mme de Cambremer lança> **331:31.** <de leur départ, de là ou* on avait pu espérer qu'atteindrait leur attachement, et qui ne se jouent dans cet écart de fantaisie que pour revenir plus délibérément, d'un retour plus prémédité, avec plus de précision, comme sur un cristal qui résonnerait jusqu'à faire crier, revenir frapper au cœur.

331:38. Vivant dans une famille> **332:36.** <une marque de sa délicatesse. [331:39. <guère dans le monde, elle> 331:40. <de leur manoir> 332:3. <à la voix chantante et gants blancs.* 332:8. <n'y trouvent plus> 332:10. <jeune belle-fille, pleine> 332:14. <spéciales, méprisait> 332:23. <recommencé à soixante-dix ans> 332:29. <médiocres, même de celles qui avaient> 332:32. <façon dont jouait le pianiste. La fin> 332:33. <d'elle-même sous* ses lèvres> 332:34. <charmant>] {332:36-332:40}

332:40. Cependant Mme de Gallardon> **333:7.** <avec la princesse> [332:41. <était bien fâcheux qu'elle n'eût pas l'occasion de rencontrer souvent la princesse> 333:6. <relation>]

333:7. <la princesse Mathilde, et que plus vieille que la princesse des Laumes elle n'avait pas à aller au devant* d'elle, voulut pourtant compenser cet air de hauteur et de réserve par quelque propos qui justifiât sa démarche et forçât la princesse à engager la conversation, une fois près d'elle, avec un visage dur, une main tendue comme une carte forcée, elle lui dit: «Comment va ton mari» de la même voix soucieuse que si le prince avait été malade.

333:16. La princesse> **333:25.** <dit à sa cousine:

333:27. —Ariane* (ici Mme de* Laumes regarda d'un air étonné et rieur un tiers invisible) je tiendrais beaucoup à ce que tu viennes un moment demain soir chez moi entendre un concerto de Mozart.

333:33. Je voudrais> **333:34.** <pas lui adresser une invitation, mais lui demander, et paraissait avoir besoin de l'avis de la princesse sur le concerto de Mozart, comme si ç'avait été un plat de la composition de sa nouvelle cuisinière et sur laquelle elle aurait souhaité l'avis d'un gourmet.

—Mais je connais ce concerto, je peux>

333:40. <je peux te dire> **334:4.** Tous les jours elle écrivait son regret d'avoir, à cause d'une visite de sa belle-mère, par une invitation de son beau-père, par l'Opéra, par une partie de campagne, été privée d'une soirée>

334:8. <à laquelle elle n'aurait> **334:18.** <Meilhac et Halévy,> [334:10. <qu'elle irait volontiers> 334:12. <contre temps*> 334:13. <avec leur soirée, que la princesse avouait

qu'elle leur eût beaucoup préféré*. Puis> 334:15. <dépouillé des lieux communs et des sentiments>]

334:18. <Halévy, elle l'adaptait jusqu'aux rapports sociaux, les transposait dans sa politesse qui s'efforçait d'être positive, précise, de se rapprocher de l'humble vérité. Elle ne développait pas longuement l'expression du désir qu'elle aurait à aller à une soirée; elle trouvait plus aimable de lui exposer>

334:24. <exposer quelques petits faits précis d'où> **335:4.** —Je suis ses* lumières à ce sujet. [334:32. <pourrai les quitter.] {335:5-335:26}

335:27. <sujet. Mais Ariane* ne te fâche pas, reprit Mme de Gallardon qui sacrifiait ses plus grandes espérances mondaines au plaisir obscur et prisé de dire quelque chose de désagréable, il y a des gens que* ce M. Swann c'est quelqu'un qu'on ne peut pas avoir chez soi, est-ce vrai?

335:34. —Mais> tu dois> **335:36.** <jamais venu.

□**335:37.** Et elle éclata de nouveau d'un rire qui scandalisa les personnes qui écoutaient la musique et attira l'attention de Mme de Saint-Euverte, qui, restant par politesse près du piano, s'aperçut seulement de la princesse des Laumes qui, laissant sa cousine mortifiée, alla droit à la maîtresse de maison. Mme de Saint-Euverte était d'autant plus ravie de voir la princesse qu'elle la croyait encore à Guermantes en train de soigner son beau-père malade; elle crut d'abord en la voyant s'avancer vers elle qu'elle était venue à Paris exprès pour sa soirée et la remercia avec effusion en conséquence, regardant les grains de corail givrés de diamant qui ornaient les beaux cheveux blonds de la princesse comme quelques baies de merisier que celle-ci avant de monter en voiture pour aller prendre le train, aurait été cueillir dans le parc du château et qui, doublement poétique pour provenir d'un crépuscule rural et d'un domaine princier, n'auraient pas encore perdu leur broderie de rosée et de gelée blanche.

336:1. Mais comment> **336:17.** <me faire conspuer. [336:11. <tout! je suis>]

336:18. Cependant le pianiste qui avait fait succéder Listz à Chopin redoublant de vitesse sans que cela conduisît la rhapsodie à sa fin, l'émotion>

336:18. <l'émotion musicale> **337:12.** <je n'ai pas idée d'où elle sort. [336:21. <Saint-Euverte sans qu'il la vît lui faisant des signes> 336:31. <bougie tressautait* à> 336:33. <n'y tint plus et se précipita> 336:36. <allaient-elles le* toucher que le morceau sur un dernier accord finit> 336:38. Néanmoins son initiative hardie, la courte> 366:43. <princesse de* Laumes> 337:10. <des gens de la campagne.] {337:12-337:19}

337:20. —Ah! Mais Cambremer> **337:33.** <répondit Mme des Laumes, qui voyait que le général continuait à regarder> [337:24. <pas euphonique> 337:28. <trouvez? En tous cas elle est> 337:29. <ne la perdait pas de vue>]

337:36. <continuait à regarder> **340:15.** <dit le général. [337:38. <amabilité pour lui: Pas> 337:41. <présenté, dit la princesse qui probablement n'aurait pas présenté le général à Mme de Cambremer si elle l'avait connue. 338:1. <d'une amie que je dois aller souhaiter, dit-elle> 338:6. <ses amis qui ont un nom de pont et d'avenue, les Iéna. 338:11. <moi, ajoute le général en> 338:12. <l'essuyer, comme on change un pansement> 338:27. <des _Laumes_ avait> 338:30. <connu*> 338:35. <le mobilier dont ils ont hérité. 339:1. <sur laquelle a été signée* [_blanc_]. 339:5. <beau puisque> 339:7. <dans le grenier des> 339:11. <mais je> 339:16. <une personne qu'ils ne connaissaient pas? 339:27. <de le lui entendre dire: Pourquoi? 339:29. <qu'il y a de déagréable.* 339:32. <pas, _même héroïques,_ je deviendrait* folle. 339:36. <monde. Ça m'embête déjà quelquefois de donner> 340:3. <_d'autres_ qui en ont, ajouta-t-elle en lançant joyeusement une écume de rire, les traits> 340:5. <accouplés dans la réserve* de son animation> 340:7. <gaieté que seuls avait* le pouvoir de faire rayonner ainsi, les paroles> 340:10. <votre Cambremer. Demandez-lui> 340:13. <à s'en aller, il est comme moi le pauvre Swann. Mon petit Charles.*] {340:16-341:15}

341:15. —Mon petit Charles, est-ce que vous aussi, par hasard, vous êtes voisin de campagne de cette jeune Cambremer.

—Mais vous l'êtes vous-même, princesse.

341:21. —Moi, mais ils ont> **342:15.** <la coterie Guermantes. [341:23. <les Cambremer, mais elle est une demoiselle> 342:5. <pas vrai. Et d'ailleurs Swann et la princesse n'avaient

les mêmes idées sur rien. Mais ils avaient une même façon de juger> 341:29. <suis [*blanc*] de cent> 341:37. <puisque s'il*> 342:11. <par le passe* à> 342:12. <la sonorité de sa voix, les moustaches> 342:13. <lesquelles sortait*, on>] {342:15-343:5}

343:5. —Ecoutez mon petit Charles, pour une fois> **343:9.** <Mémé. Mais pensez-vous* que je ne vous vois plus jamais!

343:11. Swann ayant prévenu de lui* M. de Fleurus qu'en quittant de chez Mme de Saint-Euverte il rentrerait directement chez lui ne se souciait pas>

343:13. <en allant chez> **343:17.** <chez son concierge. {343:17-343:29}

343:29. Mais au moment où> **343:32.** <pour la chercher. {343:33-344:15}

344:16. Quand enfin il le présenta, comme c'était> **345:35.** <et volatile essence> [344:22. <amenait, croyant que c'était l'un d'eux, et pensant> 344:25. <hésitant qui prouvait la réserve> 344:29. <déclaraient-elles*> 344:30. <préféraient avec raison avoir l'air en la faisant épouser par leur fils, d'avoir> 344:37. <fin de* nouveau> 345:3. <ne lui assusait* la réalité; il souffrait surtout,—et au> 345:5. <crier,—de prolonger> 345:10. <le violon s'était porté sur une note haute où il était resté comme pour une attente, une attente qui se prolongeait, sans que la même note cessât d'être tenue, avec une intensité croissante, dans l'exaltation où elle* était> 345:18. <qu'il puisse passer> 345:20. <eût le temps de comprendre, et de se dire: «c'est la petite phrase de la sonate de Berget; n'écoutons pas», tous> 345:24. <réussi jusque-là à> 345:26. <remonté> 345:30. <aimé», il retrouva>]

□**345:35.** <il revit tout, deux pétales neigeux du chrysanthème qu'elle lui avait jeté dans sa voiture, qu'il avait gardé contre ses lèvres et qui étaient brillants et frisés comme de la soie,—l'adresse en relief d'un restaurant sur la lettre où il avait lu, «Ma main tremble en vous écrivant»,—le rapprochement de ses sourcils quand elle lui avait dit d'un air suppliant: «Ce n'est pas dans trop longtemps que vous me ferez signe»,—l'obscurité au coin des Boulevards où on éteignait les becs de gaz le soir où il avait buté contre elle rue Royale, où dans la voiture il l'avait enfin embrassée et possédée. Il se rappela d'autres choses qu'il

avait oubliées depuis; que le premier soir Mme Verdurin l'avait fait lever d'une petite chaise pour qu'il allât s'asseoir près d'elle et l'air de conviction avec lequel Odette avait dit que ce qu'il lui disait était très beau; qu'un jour en sortant de soirée par un beau clair de lune, il avait si froid dans sa victoria en allant chez elle que Rémi avait tiré de la capote des couvertures supplémentaires; l'odeur de l'air humide et chaud dans un restaurant du Bois, le soir d'un jour où il avait tant plu qu'il avait craint qu'elle ne vînt pas, la note aiguë de sa voix qu'il s'était amusé à imiter, quand dans la peur qu'il prit* prétexte de ne pas la déranger pour ne pas la voir aussi souvent qu'elle le souhaitait, elle s'était écriée: «Mais comment! je suis toujours libre!» [*cf.* 346:16]

347:6. Et Swann aperçut> **347:12.** <qu'elle avait aimé alors qu'elle ne l'aimait plus, il fut jaloux de ceux dont il s'était dit souvent sans trop souffrir, «elle les aime peut-être», maintenant qu'il avait échangé l'idée vague d'aimer, dans laquelle il n'y a pas d'amour, par le geste que* lui avait précipitemment* jeté le chrysanthème, par l'«en-tête de restaurant», par le son aigu de la voix, qui, eux, en étaient pleins. {347:17-347:24}

347:25. Il y a dans le violoncelle et le violon, si ne voyant pas les instruments, on ne peut pas rapporter ce qu'on entend à leur image qui en modifie la sonorité, des accents qui leur sont si communs> **347:42.** <de son évocation, Swann> [347:30. <les étuis de bois, mais, par moment*, son* est>]

348:3. <Swann la sentait présente> **348:23.** <elle lui parlait> [348:8. Et tandis qu'elle glissait rapide, lui disant> 348:15. Car il n'avait plus l'impression qu'ils n'étaient pas connus de la petite phrase. 348:21. <désenchantée, il y trouvait aujourd'hui plutôt>

348:23. <elle lui parlait autrefois et que, sans être atteint par eux, il la voyait en souriant entraîner à côté de lui. Dans* son cour* sinueux et rapide, qui maintenant étaient devenus siens sans qu'il eût l'espérance d'en être jamais délivré, elle semblait lui dire comme jadis de son bonheur: «Qu'est-ce cela? tout cela n'est rien». Et Swann trouvait de la douceur à cette sagesse qui proclamait la vanité des souffrances que lui causait Odette et qui tout à l'heure>

348:36. <tout à l'heure pourtant> **349:13.** <en raisonnements. [348:38. <visages de tous ces différents> 348:43. <gens, du* moins> 349:4. <essence qui est pour eux incommunicable, et de* sembler> 349:6. <rendu*> 349:12. <codifiés ne peut pas>]

349:13. Mais ces idées d'un autre monde, d'un autre ordre que sont les motifs musicaux, idées voilées de ténèbres, inconnues, impénétrables à l'intelligence, n'en sont pas moins entre elles parfaitement distinctes les unes des autres, de valeur et de significations* inégales; le souvenir matériel des instruments nous habitue à voir les choses dans un plan faux; ce n'est pas un clavier mesquin de sept notes [*cf.* 349:37], qui est le champ ouvert à l'invention du musicien, c'est un clavier incommensurable, encore inconnu, comme inexistant, dont seules çà et là à des distances quelquefois fort éloignées, et séparées par des ténèbres, quelques-unes seulement des millions de touches de tendresse, de passion, de sérénité, de courage, chacune différente des autres, comme un univers d'un autre univers, ont été découvertes>

349:43. <ont été découvertes> **350:24.** <les ayons connues> [350:5. <néant. Berget avait été, au moins un moment, l'un> 350:10. <eux, sur le même pied que les> 350:12. <dont il savait immédiatement en quoi elle était particulière, comme il le savait pour la princesse de Clèves, ou Werther, quand leur nom se présentait à son esprit. Même> 350:18. <sans équivalent, ces notions de la lumière, du son, du relief, de la volupté physique, qui sont>]

350:24. <les ayons connues que nous ne pouvons par exemple devant les objets métamorphosés de notre chambre d'où s'est échappé jusqu'au souvenir de l'obscurité, douter de la lumière de la lampe qu'on allume. Par là la phrase de Berget avait comme certain thème de Tristan par exemple, qui nous représente une certaine acquisition originale, épousé notre condition mortelle, pris quelque chose d'humain qui était assez touchant. Son sort étant* lié à l'avenir>

350:33. <à l'avenir, à la réalité> **351:21.** <de sa main. [350:42. <de moins inglorieux, et de moins probable> 350:43. <que la petite phrase existait> 351:4. <mais que pourtant nous> 351:7. C'est ce que Berget faisait pour la petite phrase,

Swann sentait que le compositeur se contentait, avec ses instruments> 351:12. <s'altérait, s'estompait> 351:16. <réelle de la petite phrase> 351:17. <se serait tout> 351:18. <si Berget, ayant>]

351:22. Elle avait disparu. Mais Swann savait que c'était pour renaître une fois encore. {351:22-352:17}

352:17. Et il s'était> **352:37.** <si près de s'évanouir. [352:22. <apprenons à un ami en qui nous nous apercevons comme un autre dont l'émotion probable l'attendrit. 352:26. Aussi ne perdait-il> 352:32. <elle ajoute comme d'autres>]

352:37. Puis la petite phrase se défit, flotta en lambeaux où elle était à peine reconnaissable et qui bientôt se fondirent dans les phrases suivantes qui déjà avaient pris place. {352:37-353:15}

353:16. A partir de cette soirée, il sut que le sentiment qu'Odette avait pour lui ne renaîtrait jamais, que ses espérances de bonheur ne se réaliseraient pas. Et quand elle avait encore été gentille et tendre avec lui la veille, si elle avait eu quelque attention, pensé à faire enlever avant son arrivée les chrysanthèmes dont le parfum la dernière fois lui avait fait mal, il notait>

353:21. <notait ces signes> **353:36.** <s'était remis à son livre sur Ver Meer il aurait eu besoin d'aller au moins quelques jours en Hollande, à Dresde, à Londres. [353:23. <qui, veillant un ami> 353:25. <précieux «hier> 353:30. Certes il savait que s'ils avaient vécu maintenant loin l'un de l'autre, Odette aurait fini>]

353:42. Mais quitter Paris> **355:9.** <il admirait> [354:7. <en lui, sans qu'il se fût muni du souvenir de son impossibilité, et elle s'y réalisait. 354:9. <pour un an et du wagon penché vers un jeune homme qui sur le quai lui disait adieu en pleurant, cherchant à> 354:14. Alors il bénit les circonstances qui le rendaient indépendant, grâce auxquelles elles faisaient qu'il pouvait rester près d'elle, et aussi qu'elle lui permettrait de la voir, et, récapitulant tous ces avantages: sa situation, sa fortune, dont> 354:22. <lui), cette amitié de M. de Fleurus qui> 354:23. <d'Odette, mais qui> 354:26. <estime, et> 354:31. <s'il avait été pauvre> 354:33. <lié à des parents, ce rêve>]

355:9. <il admirait comme l'être humain est adroit à déjouer les périls, qu'il trouvait innombrables depuis que son secret désir les avait supputés. Et il trouvait alors bien près>

355:15. <bien près de son cœur> **355:19.** <liberté d'esprit. {355:20-355:23}

355:24. Ne pouvant> **356:30.** <avait dû naître> [355:28. <jamais, du moins savait-il que la seule grande absence qu'elle faisait était tous les ans celle du mois d'août et, comme si longtemps d'avance, il avait le temps d'en dissoudre l'idée dans tout> 355:35. <causer de souffrances> 355:39. <durcissait sa fluidité comme le faisant geler tout entier> 355:41. <énorme et dure qui pesait> 355:42. <éclater. Quand Odette lui avait dit> 356:1. <Frocheville*> 356:2. <Egypte», car il avait compris que> 356:4. <Frocheville*> 356:7. <Frocheville*> 356:9. <il voulait tâcher de savoir si elle était la maîtresse de Frocheville.* Il savait> 356:12. <pas et la crainte> 356:15. <de n'en* être> 356:18. <Frocheville*> 356:22. <lettre car> 356:24. <Swann et il chercha> 356:26. <sans liens apparents avec> 356:28. <caractère de M. de Fleurus, de M. de Guermantes, de M. de Sallemand qu'il devait>]

356:30. <avait dû naître, comme aucun de ces gens ne lui avait jamais dit qu'il approuvât les lettres anonymes et que tout ce qu'ils lui avaient dit impliquait qu'ils les réprouvaient, il ne vit pas plus de raisons pour le relier plutôt à la nature de l'un que de l'autre. Celle de M. de Fleurus était un peu détracquée*, mais foncièrement bonne et tendre, celle de M. de Guermantes un peu sèche mais saine et droite. Quant à M. de Sallemand, Swann, n'avait jamais rencontré personne qui dans toutes les circonstances même les plus tristes vînt à lui avec une parole plus sentie, un geste plus discret et plus juste. C'était au point que Swann ne pouvait comprendre le rôle peu délicat qu'on prêtait à M. de Sallemand dans la liaison>

356:43. <la liaison qu'il avait> **357:4.** <de délicatesse. [357:1. <fois qu'il pensait à M. de Sallemand il était>]

357:4. <de délicatesse qu'il avait reçu* de lui. Un instant l'esprit de Swann s'obscurcissait et il changea de pensée pour retrouver un peu de lumière. Puis il eut le courage de revenir en arrière.

357:7. Mais alors, après> **358:6.** <une fois de plus. [357:9. <M. de Fleurus l'aimait> 357:11. <colère, par quelque> 357:15. <M. de Fleurus. Mais à côté* de cela> 357:17. <froide mais> 357:20. <il réfléchissait que> 357:23. <comme était celle de M.* Fleurus, que la seule pensée de lui avoir fait cette peine eût révolté, tandis qu'un homme insensible> 357:29. <et M. de Fleurus en avait. M. de Sallemand n'en> 357:34. <de M. de Fleurus, capable> 357:37. <aimé c'était par lui. Oui, mais> 358:3. <pensons. Fleurus et> 358:4. <gens. Sallemand, n'en>]

358:6. Puis Swann soupçonna Justin qu'il* est vrai n'aurait pu qu'inspirer la lettre.

Mais comment ne pas supposer que nos domestiques, vivants* dans une situation>

358:11. <situation inférieure> **358:39.** <des gens qui le valaient> [358:13. <méprisent, ne chercheront pas à agir> 358:15. <soupçonna mon> 358:18. <agir pour son bien. Il soupçonna Bugotte*, le peintre> 358:28. Bref il se dit qu'il connaissait un être capable de scélératesse, mais qu'il ne voyait> 358:31. <tuf inexploré d'autrui, du caractère> 358:38. <ses mains le long de ses cheveux, lissa sa brosse, essuya les verres>]

□**358:40.** <valaient fréquentaient M. de Fleurus, le prince des Laumes, et les autres, il se dit que si* cela signifiait sinon qu'ils fussent incapables d'infamie, du moins, alors que c'est une nécessité de la vie à laquelle chacun se soumet de fréquenter des gens qui en sont peut-être capables, de même qu'après la mort de sa mère s'accusant de pouvoir continuer à vivre, jour par jour, il s'était persuadé qu'il n'aurait peut-être pas tort bien qu'il ne pût comprendre pourquoi, en voyant son père qui était meilleur que lui faire de même, de même encore que s'étonnant quand il avait médité sur la petitesse de notre vie perdue dans l'infini ou dans le néant, de tenir encore à des plaisirs futiles, il s'était excusé à ses propres yeux, en se rappelant qu'il avait vu le plus grand philosophe qu'il connût passer des heures à préparer sa propre élection académique. Et il continua à serrer la main à tous ces amis qu'il avait soupçonnés, avec cette réserve de pur style qu'ils étaient peut-être capables d'avoir voulu le désespérer, comme l'un d'eux Bergotte sacrifiait ses forces à élever son œuvre, tout en se disant que peut-être la gloire n'est rien,

que l'âme n'est qu'une lueur passagère de la matière, le monde que l'ombre d'un rêve. Quant au fond même de la lettre, il ne s'en inquiéta*, car rien ne pouvait s'en appliquer à Odette. Nous manquons d'invention. Nous savons bien comme une vérité générale que la vie des êtres est pleine de contrastes, mais pour chaque être en particulier nous imaginons toute la partie de sa vie que nous ne connaissons pas comme identique à la partie que nous connaissons. Nous nous imaginons que ce qu'ils nous taisent ressemble à ce qu'ils nous disent. Dans les moments où elle n'était pas avec lui, s'ils parlaient>

359:15. <s'ils parlaient> **359:41.** <même ne soupçonnait. [359:21. <s'inquiétait de son travail. Donc> 359:24. <elle n'était pas avec lui. 359:25. <qu'elle était avec lui, ou plutôt> 359:27. <eut* semblé vraisemblable> 359:39. <il lui laissait supposer>] {359:41-360:12}

360:12. Elle le regardait alors d'un air méfiant, et, à toute aventure, fâchée, pour ne pas avoir l'air de s'humilier et de rougir de ses actes.

360:17. Un jour, étant> **362:7.** <ou avec une autre. [360:25. <de marbre qu'il> 360:30. <au Salon de peinture avec> 360:37. <déplia et tourna> 361:4. <le même nom de son ami> 361:10. <vérité. Dans> 361:14. <par expérience* de> 361:16. <plus éloignées que tout* autres d'éprouver> 361:21. <cadrait au contraire avec> 361:27. <dit* il y avait> 361:31. <tutoie», et que, sans y voir l'ombre d'un rapport pour lui avec la simulation ridicule du vice, il avait accueillie> 361:36. <le souvenir de ses propos de mauvais> 361:43. <ou la colère qu'il réveillerait. Il regardait> 362:4. <demandes*>]

362:8. —Mais je te l'ai dit, tu le sais bien, répondit-elle, d'un air irrité et malheureux. **362:27.** <avec aucune femme.

362:29. —Peux tu* m'en faire le serment par ta médaille.

Cette médaille se rapportait à une des croyances les plus profondes d'Odette. Aussi ne s'en séparait-elle pour rien au monde. Et elle croyait qu'on allait en enfer si on parjurait sur elle.

362:33. —Oh! que tu me rends> **363:17.** <je faisais, une fois.* [362:37. <t'exères.* Voilà> 362:43. <douceur menteuse et persuasive. 363:1. <parles*> 363:2. <long que je dis. 363:4.

<fais*> 363:5. <actions, —je te pardonnes* tout puisque je t'aime, —mais de ta fausseté>] {363:18-365:9}

365:10. Il mit la main sur son cœur et reprit sa respiration.

—Ma chérie, vite, c'est fini>

365:10. <c'est fini> **365:35.** <Odette, mon amour.

365:36. Mais sanglotant elle lui avait dit:

—Mais tu es un misérable, tu te plais à me torturer, à me faire dire des mensonges que je fais pour que tu me laisses tranquille [*cf.* 366:8], tout ça est inventé, je n'ai jamais fait ça.

Il vit qu'il n'y avait plus rien à en attendre et lui dit:

—Mon pauvre chéri, pardonnes*-moi, je vois que je te fais de la peine, c'est fini, je n'y pense plus [*cf.* 366:27].

Mais elle vit que ses yeux restaient fixés dans le vide sur les choses qu'il ne savait pas.

Souvent du reste c'était elle qui les lui révélait, car cet écart que le vice mettait entre la vie relativement innocente que Swann avait cru qu'elle menait et sa vie réelle, elle en ignorait elle-même l'étendue;> [365:36-369:5]

369:13. <un être vicieux> **370:11.** <la trouve si détestable.» [369:17. <l'entraînât*> 369:20. <d'autres finissaient par en recevoir le reflet, par être contagionnés> 369:22. <étrange dans le milieu> 369:24. <Swann, elles épouvantaient par> 369:27. <chez les entremetteuses. 369:29. <introduit le soupçon dans> 369:30. <mécanique; il> 369:31. <fait il y était resté et> 369:32. <de sa présence matérielle mais gênante souhaitait qu'Odette l'extirpât d'un mot. 370:1. <reçu, une femme> 370:3. <tue-tête: «mais puisque je vous dis que je ne veux pas! lui ai-je répété. C'est>] {370:12-373:39}

373:40. Le Dr Cottard conseilla une croisière pour rétablir la santé du peintre qui avait été malade; les Verdurin louèrent un yacht; puis ils s'en rendirent acquéreurs et Odette fit de fréquents voyages en mer. Quand elle était partie Swann sentait>

374:3. <Swann sentait> **375:14.** <je le trouve idéal. [374:10. <et n'ait averti> 374:14. Bien que les Verdurin eussent cherché à persuader au pianiste et au Dr Cottard que> 374:18. <Paris qu'ils assuraient être en révolution, ils furent obligés de> 374:21. <de ces passagers, Swann> 374:24. <assis nez à nez avec Mme Cottard> 374:27. <de ses insignes> 374:30. <correspondan-

ces. 374:31. <que sa gentillesse native eut* pu percé* l'empesé> 374:41. <a vue le portrait>] {375:15-375:22}

375:22. Tenez, justement> **377:8.** <son manchon. [375:27. <rêve! j'ai> 376:4. Quand elle est> 376:18. <demandait: «qu'est-ce> 376:28. <jures*> 376:43. <elle, non moins que pour Mme Verdurin (et presque que* pour Odette> 377:2. <dernière, n'était* plus mêlé>] {377:9-377:19}

377:21. Jadis ayant souvent> **379:41.** <coiffé d'un fez. [377:23. <amour commençait à> 377:25. Mais à un affaiblissement de son cœur correspondait> 377:34. <souffert, mais où il avait senti si voluptueusement, et que> 377:37. <beautés, elle lui procurait plutôt une sensation agréable> 377:40. <la France, et à qui un dernier moustique prouve que l'Italie et l'été ne sont pas encore bien loin. 377:42. <vie dont il sortait> 378:6. <sentiment qu'on ne possède plus que bientôt> 378:8. <à regarder, relevait avec la main la brosse de ses cheveux, retirait son lorgnon> 378:21. <où il la* quittait> 378:23. <avait recherché à imprimer> 378:26. <voulu en pensée, au moins faire ses adieux, pendant qu'elle existait encore, à cette Odette, lui inspirant de l'amour, de la jalousie, lui causant des souffrances> 378:41. Par moment* les> 379:12. <suite avec lui. 379:14. <dit: il faut que je m'en ailles*, elle> 379:20. <éprouvait une haine affreuse pour> 379:28. <elle. C'était> 379:36. Aussi Swann>]

379:42. Quant à Napoléon III, quelque association d'idées puis, une certaine modification de sa physionomie habituelle, enfin le grand cordon de la légion d'honneur en sautoir, lui avait fait donner ce nom à quelqu'un qui, en réalité, et pour tout ce qu'il lui représentait et lui rappelait, était Forcheville. Car, d'images incomplètes et changeantes il tirait des déductions fausses>

380:7. <des déductions fausses> **380:29.** <le coiffeur est là. [380:10. <paume modelait> 380:13. <qui parallèlement, par le seul enchaînement des causes matérielles amènerait à point nommé le personnage nécessaire pour recevoir son amour ou préparer son réveil. La nuit> 380:21. <ses battements de cœur> 380:23. <nausée inexplicable> 380:24. <à Fleurus où>]

380:31. Mais ces paroles> **381:2.** <Combray, ayant> [380: 34. <soleil comme un moment avant le bruit>]

381:2. <ayant lu dans le journal que la jeune Mme de Cambremer devait y passer quelques jours. Associant dans son souvenir au charme de son jeune visage celui de cette campagne où il n'était pas allé depuis si longtemps, ils lui offraient, «l'un dans l'autre», un attrait qui l'avait décidé à quitter enfin Paris pour quelques jours. {381:8-381:39}

381:40. <jours. Et tandis qu'il donnait des indications au coiffeur pour que sa brosse ne se dérangeât pas en wagon, il repensa à son rêve, il revit comme il les avait senties* tout près de lui il y a une heure le teint pâle d'Odette, les joues trop maigres, les traits tirés, les yeux battus qu'il ne remarquait plus depuis les premiers temps de leur amour où sans doute dans son sommeil sa mémoire en avait été chercher la sensation exacte et il s'écria en lui-même:

382:11. Dire que> **382:14.** <mon genre.

TROISIÈME PARTIE

NOMS DE PAYS

383:1. Rien ne ressemblait moins que les chambres de Combray, saupoudrées, des ciels de lit en peluche aux fauteuils de velours et des couvre-pieds de lampas aux rideaux de mousseline, par une atmosphère grenue, pollinisée, comestible et dévote, que la chambre du Grand-Hôtel de la Plage à Bricquebec que j'évoquais souvent dans mes nuits d'insomnie et dont les murs passés au ripolin contenaient, comme les parois polies d'une piscine où l'eau bleuit, un air pur, azuré et salin.

383:8. Le tapissier bavarois> **384:13.** <des hommes. [383:10. <des chambres et fait courir sur trois côtés le long des murs de celle-ci, des bibliothèques> 383:13. <prévu se reflétait telle ou telle partie de* tableau changeant de la mer, déroulant une frise de claires marines, interrompues seulement par les pleins de l'acajou. 383:18. <dans les expositions du mobilier tout parés d'œuvres d'art de même style moderne et tirant logiquement leurs sujets du genre de site où l'habitation doit se trouver. 383:23. <à ce Bricquebec réel> 383:28. <et disait en gémissant que les journaux parlaient de grands sinistres et de naufrages. 384:3. <vie puissante de> 384:9. <plus réel que. 384:12. <manifeste lignée* à elle-même>]

384:13. De même, quand* elle est le beau son de sa voix, isolément reproduite, par le phonographe, ne nous consolerait pas que notre mère fût morte, de même une tempête mécaniquement imitée m'aurait laissé indifférent—comme les fontaines lumineuses de l'Exposition. Je voulais, du moment que je ne l'avais pas senti soutenue par une réalité, plus puissante et plus libre que moi, que le rivage lui-même fût un rivage naturel pour que la tempête fût absolument vraie, non une digue récemment créée par une société.

384:20. D'ailleurs la nature. **384:35.** <Terre antique. [384:22. <productions des hommes que je voyais dans la vie de tous les jours. 384:25. <nom de Bricquebec que> 384:31. <lui-même, et quand> 384:33. <terre, on>]

384:35. Des légendes païennes y renaissent à chaque pas. Et c'est> **384:38.** <ombres.» Un jour qu'à Combray j'avais cité Bricquebec devant M. Swann pour voir s'il connaissait cette plage et s'il pouvait m'assurer que c'était le point le mieux choisi pour voir les plus violentes tempêtes, il avait répondu: «Je crois bien que je connais Bricquebec, du XIIIe siècle, encore>

385:1. <encore à moitié romane> **387:9.** <changements des saisons> [385:2. <singulière, on dirait de l'art Persan*.» Et ces lieux qui jusque-là n'avaient été pour moi que> 385:5. <géologiques, et aussi en dehors de l'histoire humaine que l'Océan lui-même ou la Grande> 385:9. <il n'y avait eu de moyen âge, ç'avait un grand charme de les voir> 385:11. <siècles, avoir* connu> 385:16. <manquait, mais ils lui en conféraient une en retour. Je ne me représentais pas seulement comme ces pêcheurs> 385:19. <rapports sociaux qui s'étaient groupés là vaguement aux bords des côtes d'Enfer> 385:22. <mort; le gothique, lui aussi, me> 385:23. <villes où je l'imaginais toujours> 385:26. <clocher, il avait fleuri. J'allai voir des reproductions des apôtres moutonnants et camus, la Vierge mère, du porche, et de joie> 385:31. <éternel et salé de Bolbec.* Alors> 385:32. <le vent, en soufflant le projet d'un voyage à Bricquebec dans mon cœur, qu'il ne faisait pas trembler moins fort que la cheminée de ma chambre, mêlait en moi le désir de la tempête sur la mer et de l'architecture gothique. 385:37. J'aurais pris le lendemain ce beau train généreux d'une heure vingt-deux auquel je pensais si souvent, dont je ne pouvais> 385:40. <dans des annonces de voyage circulaire, l'heure> 385:41. <départ, qui incise à un point précis de l'après-midi une savoureuse entaille, une marque mystérieuse> 386:1. <déviées conduisent bien> 386:2. <qu'on verra non plus à Paris, à l'une de ces villes par lesquelles il passe et entre lesquelles il nous permet de

choisir; car il s'arrête à Bayeux, à Coutances, à Vitré, à Questembert, à Pontorson, à Bolbec, à Lannion, à Lamballe, à Benedet*, à Pont-Aven, à Quimperlé, telle de chaque côté de sa route [*blanc*] surchargé de noms qu'il offre et entre> 386:11. <hâte si mes parents me l'avaient permis partir le soir même et arriver à Bolbec quand> 386:13. <mer déchaînée, contre les écumes de laquelle> 386:17. <le Nord de l'Italie> 386:20. <partout, haut, toujours plus haut, jamais assez haut au gré de mon cœur qui tâchait de les soulever sur la côte la plus sauvage> 386:23. <charme, se substituaient en moi les rêves opposés du printemps le plus diapré, non pas celui de Combray> 386:31. <couleurs avaient du prix pour moi; car l'alternance des images avait amené un changement de front du désir, et aussi brusque que ceux qu'il y a parfois en musique, imprégnant de même son harmonie tout entière, un changement de ton dans ma sensibilité. Puis il arriva souvent qu'un changement de temps suffisait à cela sans avoir besoin d'un changement de saison. 386:40. <en font* désirer> 387:2. <phénomènes dont> 387:3. <santé ne peuvent bénéficier qu'accidentellement jusqu'au jour où la science s'empare d'eux> 387:8. <soumis*>]

387:9. <changements des saisons et aux variations de la température. Ils n'eurent besoin pour être déterminés en soi que de ces noms: Bricquebec, Venise, Florence (ou les noms des cités avoisinantes), dans l'intérieur desquelles avait fini>

387:12. <avait fini par s'accumuler> **387:37.** <ont les personnes! [387:12. <m'avait*> 387:14. <nom de Bricquebec> 387:17. <Venise suffisait à me donner> 387:22. <propres, et eurent ainsi> 387:33. <autres que* mon âme avait soif et aurait profit à connaître. 387:26. <d'aggraver les déceptions futures de> 387:28. <terre en augmentant leur réalité, en les faisant plus particulières. Je ne>]

387:37. Les mots sont de claires et commodes petites images comme celles qui dans les écoles montrent aux enfants comment est faite une chose, à laquelle sont pareilles les choses de même espèce, un établi, un chêne, un scaphandre, un fauteuil. Mais les noms présentent des images confuses qui tirent d'eux la couleur dont elles sont peintes comme en ces affiches bleues sur lesquelles à cause des limites du procédé employé ou par un caprice du décorateur sont bleus, non seulement le ciel et la mer mais les arbres, les femmes et les roses.

388:8. Le nom de Parme> **388:26.** <de quelque droit> [388:10. <lu la Chartreuse> 388:11. <doux, en me parlant d'une maison de Parme quelconque dans laquelle je serait* reçu> 388:16. <à l'aide de syllabe* lourde où ne circule aucun air et de tout ce que je lui avais fait absorber de douceur [*blanc*] haleine et de reflet de violette. 388:22. <et son église Sainte-Marie-des-Fleurs. Quant à Bolbec> 388:24. <vieille faïence normande>]

388:26. <de quelque droit féodal, d'un état des lieux qui ne concorde plus; et à l'aubergiste même chez qui, en arrivant le matin, j'entrerais me restaurer avant d'aller voir la tempête et l'église, je donnais quelque chose de solennel, de disputeur et de médiant* comme à quelque personnage de fabliau, je le voyais pareil à un de ces paysans d'autrefois dont en entendant ce nom de Bolbec on croyait percevoir la prononciation qui les forma dans ses syllabes hétéroclites.

388:34. Si ma santé> **389:1.** <dernière syllabe> [388:35. <à Bolbec> 388:39. <j'aurais voulu aller dans les villes>]

389:1. <syllabe, plus que ne l'est par le couchant qui s'y attarde la flèche d'aucune des cathédrales de la terre; Vitré>

389:2.<Vitré dont l'accent> **389:18.** <d'argent bruni. [389:10. <Benedet, nom> 389:14. <canal; et enfin Quimperlé> 389:16. <en grisaille>]

□**389:19.** Puis ces images étaient fausses pour une autre raison encore; c'est que pour les faire entrer dans les noms, comme ils ne sont pas vaste*, j'avais été obligé d'y faire figurer seulement deux ou trois curiosités principales, qui, à elles seules, sans intermédiaires, composaient toute la ville. Dans Bricquebec l'idée de la mer et du gothique presque persan étaient* juxtaposées*, je voyais une tempête soulevée autour d'une église dont étincelait le vitrail.

Enfin comme ce que mon imagination désirait et que mes sens ne percevaient qu'incomplètement et sans plaisir dans le présent, je l'avais enfermé dans le refuge des noms, mettant dans celui de Bolbec avec le mystère de la sculpture religieuse celui des brouillards éternels qui faisaient de ce pays comme un royaume fabuleux des ombres situées à l'extrémité, peut-être au delà* de la terre, et dans celui de Florence un printemps d'un coloris aussi frais, aussi éclatant que les fresques de ses couvents; comme ces noms par* ce qu'ils étaient pour moi les asiles du rêve étaient les aimants du désir et que je ne pensais pas à eux comme à un idéal inaccessible mais à une ambiance réelle dans laquelle un jour j'irai* me plonger; n'ayant pas en eux plus de place pour m'y figurer les moments où je jouirai d'y vivre que je n'en avais eus pour y placer leurs sites ou leurs monuments, c'était toujours à une même heure que je les voyais, dans le nom de Bolbec le jour gris venant de se lever sur la mer furieuse, dans le nom de Florence, à midi, tandis qu'on vendait des iris et des anémones en plein soleil sur la Porte* Vacchio.* Et comme cette vie que je mènerais en eux était de la vie non vécue encore, intacte, et que je ne l'éprouvais encore que par l'imagination, sans fatigue, sans déception, à l'état pur, les scènes les plus simples qu'elle offrirait me semblaient empreintes d'un charme délicieux, avaient été par moi jugées dignes, comme dans une peinture de primitif français ou italien de figurer dans le paysage simplifié de ces noms. Dans le nom de Bolbec, sous un dais architectural, étroit et qui à l'extrémité du tableau n'en occupaient* qu'une mince partie, pareil à ceux sous lesquels les vieux maîtres montrent à un moment différent de l'action, encore en train de dormir par exemple, le même personnage qu'on voit dix centimètres plus loin et une heure plus tard montant à cheval, tout en écoutant les recommandations de prudence et les indications du chemin à l'aubergiste contemporain de la reine Mathilde, j'achevais de boire avec déclice* un bol de lait brûlant avant de m'aventurer sur les rivages battus par la tempête, enveloppés de brouillard, blanchis par l'aube et d'aller contempler le vitrail d'outre-mer dans l'abside de l'église persane. Le nom de Florence était divisé en trois compartiments. A l'une des extrémités j'admirais une fresque à laquelle était partiellement superposé un rideau de lumière oblique, progressif, poudreux et blond, marque du jour déterminé et de l'heure dont je n'étais pas moins avide que de l'œuvre d'art elle-même; dans la partie médiane je traversais au soleil la Porte Vacchio*, pensant à une telle chargée* de poulets froids, de vin d'asti et de cerises, laquelle m'attendait à l'autre bout du tableau.

Justement parce que les images de ces villes étaient élaborées par ma rêverie et non par les organes de mes sens comme ce que je connaissais du monde réel, elles étaient revêtues d'une couleur, elles consistaient en une substance qui n'avait rien de terrestre, qu'aucune des villes que je connaissais ne m'avait jamais présenté, et que à cause de cela même et sans me soucier de la contradiction, j'avais d'autant plus envie de voir, de toucher, ce que je ne pouvais faire qu'en partant en voyage, car je savais que le trajet qui les séparait de moi, en moi-même, n'était pas viable, qu'il fallait me résigner à faire un détour, un crochet et ne pouvait* suivre la route de l'imagination et les aborder par la voie de terre. Je feuilletais des guides avec plus de plaisir que des poèmes, trouvant plus de rêve dans les livres de noms que dans les livres de mots, je regardais quelques gravures et sentais qu'elles ne pouvaient me donner aucune idée de l'église de Bricquebec, de Saint-Marc, ni de Sainte-Marie-des-Fleurs, car elles ressemblaient plus à des monuments que j'avais vus qu'à ceux que ces noms me montraient. Mais parce que je savais qu'elles les représentaient, parce que j'avais l'espoir d'être un jour ce personnage minuscule que le dessinateur avait figuré se promenant en chapeau haut de forme, la canne à la main au pied du portail, ces photographies rapprochaient encore ces pierres magnétiques de mon rêve, attiré, je me penchais sur une carte où leurs noms se trouvaient si près de moi que je me sentais porté jusqu'à elles d'un seul battement de mon cœur.

Deux années passèrent ainsi où je vécus tour à tour à Bricquebec, à Venise et en Toscane, car à tous les moments de notre existence le paysage qui nous entoure et nous modifie, est composé pour la plus grande partie de réminiscences et de désirs. Et je n'avais jamais séjourné, en dehors de Paris et de Combray, que dans une petite ville d'eaux allemande où pendant deux mois j'avais joué sur une petite montagne [*cf.* II, 256:33] honorée des promenades de Gœthe dominant un fleuve légendaire et des vignobles dont nous buvions au Kurhof les crus illustres, aux noms composés et retentissants comme les épithètes qu'Homère donne à ses héros. Mais enfin les temps vinrent, ce fut pendant le carême de la troisième année où mon père décida qu'en réservant les grandes vacances à une plage que connaissait mon désir, on me laissa espérer pouvoir être Bricquebec. J'irais d'abord passer les vacances de Pâques à Florence et à Venise. Je me mis à relire du matin au soir des ouvrages qu'un de mes écrivains préférés d'alors a consacré à ces deux villes. Même une fois que je les avais fermés, les pensées que me suggérait mon voyage, ne cessaient pas pour cela un seul instant d'affluer en moi, et j'éprouvais une exaltation qui, bien qu'elle eut* pour motif un désir de jouissances artistiques, devenait tout d'un coup plus profonde, plus délicieuse, dans la mesure où l'idée qui venait d'arrêter mon attention s'éloignait davantage de l'esthétique et s'abaissait vers les détails les plus vulgaires de ma propre vie.

391:29. Certes, quand je me répétais> **392:7.** <coloris avec elles. [391:37. <la Semaine Sainte, avec les violettes entr'ouvertes* et les feux rallumés), voyant> 391:40. <exacts, en tenue, à arrondir> 391:42. <en leur bloc congelé> 392:1. <poussée, je pensais que déjà le* Porte Vacchio* était jonchée* à>]

392:7. <avec elles. Mais où je ne pus plus contenir ma joie c'est quand mon père, désirant voir quels étaient les meilleurs trains, tout en déclarant qu'il ne faisait guère un temps à partir en voyage, consulta l'indicateur des chemins de fer et que je compris>

392:10. <je compris qu'en> **392:30.** <passé dans> [392:22. <moi qui crus que la joie allait me faire déraisonner, quand mon père> 392:27. <mais mille autres, simultanément et sans> 392:28. <possibles, ce>]

392:30. <dans une autre. Grâce à ces mots de «20 à 29», mon père leur consacrait des jours particuliers de ma propre vie dont le sacrifice humain allait donner à ces deux divinités de Florence et de Venise toute leur force, il leur réservait de ces jours qui sont le certificat d'authenticité, des objets auxquels on les emploie, comme la forme par rapport à nous, de leur existence, car ces jours uniques, ils se consument par l'usage, ils ne reviennent pas, on ne peut plus les vivre ici quand on les a vécus là.

Et je sentis que c'était vers une de nos particulières semaines dont elles étaient exigentes, la semaine qui commençait le lundi>

392:36. <commençait le lundi> **393:2.** <fresques de Giorgione> [392:40. <géométries, à inscrire les coupoles dans le plan de ma propre vie, et les tours. Mais>]

393:2. <fresques de Giorgione, ce n'était pas, comme, malgré tant d'avertissements, j'avais continué à l'enregistrer, ce n'était pas les hommes «majestueux et terribles comme la mer qui avaient rouillé leur armure aux reflets de bronze sous les plis de leur manteau sanglant» qui glisseraient la semaine prochaine, la veille de Pâques, mais moi-même), quand j'entendis ma mère dire à Françoise: «Il doit faire encore froid sur le Grand-Canal*, vous feriez bien de mettre à tout hasard dans la malle le pardessus d'hiver et le gros pantalon.»

393:14. A ces mots> **393:35.** <du génie, m'aurait> [393:15. <d'extase; je me sentis vraiment entre ces «roches d améthyste comme dans un bras de mer des Indes», et que, ce que j'avais craint jusque-là qui fut* impossible, je pénétrais enfin dans ce nom de Venise; par une gymnastique> 393:21. <Vénitien*> 393:31. <rétabli, se contenter de m'envoyer chaque jour jouer sans fatigue aux Champs-Elysées et de m'éviter>]

□**393:35.** <du génie, m'aurait consolé de n'aller pas à Bricquebec, en me faisant connaître quelque chose qui était peut-être aussi important et aussi beau. Mais le théâtre avait été déclaré contraire à mon régime et je ne pouvais pas regarder devant les colonnes [*blanc*] les noms des pièces que jouait la Berma. Aller aux Champs-Elysées me fut insupportable. Il n'y avait pour moi qu'une manière de désirer un endroit, c'était qu'on l'eût montré d'abord à mon imagination. Quand je croyais n'avoir envie de voir au monde que des monuments du moyen âge, il suffisait de la lecture d'une page de Bergotte pour me faire désirer passer un été dans une maison de campagne, du commencement du siècle. Il n'y avait plus que cela qui m'attirât. Si dans un de ses livres Bergotte avait décrit les Champs-Elysées avec charme, sans doute j'aurait* demandé à les voir. Mais ce jardin public destiné à nos jeux ne se rattachait par rien au monde à tout ce que me peignait* mes rêves, et comme je ne

prenais pas de plaisir que par eux, ce que mes sens seuls percevaient ne m'en donnait pas. Tout au plus, à certains jours, en passant le pont de la Concorde, je m'efforçais en regardant la Seine de penser que je voyais une eau naturelle, pareille à celle de tous les fleuves, et cherchant à lui appliquer les vers d'Heredia sur le Nil, je cherchais à reconnaître le blanchissement du fleuve noir, et ses frissons de soie chaque fois que venait de passer un bateau-mouche que je cachais avec ma main pour pouvoir croire que c'était une trirème. Ce n'est pas que je ne fusse capable d'éprouver de moi-même des plaisirs d'imagination. Un jour, aux Champs-Elysées, je me sentis saisis* par une impression délicieuse qui aussitôt abolit tous mes ennuis [*cf.* 492:10]. Ce fut en entrant par une chaude après-midi dans un petit pavillon frais et treillissé de vert, où étaient placés, en contre-bas de l'allée où je jouais, les water-closets, et où je dus attendre Françoise qui avait eu besoin de s'y arrêter. Il devait être un ancien bureau d'octroi du vieux Paris. Ses murs dégageaient une odeur—c'était une odeur de renfermé dont je ne savais pas l'origine—dans la zone de laquelle je ne fus pas plutôt* entré que je me sentis enveloppé non d'un plaisir comme ils le sont tous et au milieu desquels on se sent plus instable, plus bref et plus fragile, mais d'une félicité qui semblait au contraire me rendre plus vaste, m'étendre, m'appuyer à elle, si bien que je m'aventurais dans la zone aromatique avec une ivresse inexpliquée et tranquille, comme si j'avais traversé un monde soudain plus durable et plus vrai. J'aurais voulu, comme autrefois dans mes promenades du côté de Guermantes, quand j'étais saisi par le charme d'une impression que je ne pénétrais pas, rester immobile à respirer cette odeur, non pas pour en jouir, car, comme toutes les choses précieuses elle me proposait comme but non pas le plaisir qu'elle donnait par surcroit*, mais de tâcher de descendre dans les profondeurs qu'elle n'avait pas encore dévoilées. Je la respirais en cherchant à distinguer une image insaisissable dont elle me caressait, mais la tenancière de l'établissement, vieille femme à perruque rousse et à joues plâtrées se mit à me parler, me disant de ne pas rester au froid et m'ouvrit même un cabinet en me disant: «Vous ne voulez pas entrer, en voilà un tout propre, pour vous ce sera gratis» peut-être tout simplement comme les demoiselles de chez Boissier, quand maman entrait faire une commande, me faisaient l'offre «pour rien» d'un des bonbons qu'elles avaient devant elle* dans des cloches de verre, ce qui ne me causait d'ailleurs qu'un regret éternel, car maman me défendait de les accepter; ou peut-être moins innocemment, comme certaines vieilles fleuristes voulaient me donner des roses et me faisaient les yeux doux. Si la tenancière du pavillon avait du goût pour les garçons très jeunes, elle ne devait trouver à leur offrir les cabinets gratuit*, que le plaisir qu'on éprouve à se montrer vraiment prodigue avec ce qu'on aime, car je n'ai jamais vu assis en visite auprès d'elle que le vieux garde forestier du jardin.

Elle répondit pourtant à ma question que cette odeur venait de l'humidité du bois ancien. Mais toutes nos impressions sont susceptibles d'une explication matérielle qui satisfait notre raison mais laisse entière leur cause profonde. Et quand, rentré à la maison, un peu de bière que je pris pour prévenir ma crise d'étouffement que je redoutais eut rapproché ma pensée comme un instrument d'optique grossit les nuages lointains que je n'avais pas pu apercevoir au fond de la zone embaumée et m'eut permis de reconnaître la petite pièce de mon oncle Charles à Combray qu'exhalait* en effet la même odeur d'humidité [*cf.* 494:30], cette cause particulière de mon plaisir ainsi reconnue ne me renseigna pas sur sa raison plus générale. Si un peu de poésie se trouvait parfois se produire en moi au contact de la réalité quotidienne, c'était à mon insu, comme malgré moi, et en me rendant plus heureux que je n'étais jamais, mais sans que je sache pourquoi. Mais quant à assigner d'avance à mon imagination les désirs qu'elle devait ou non éprouver en face des choses, c'est aux œuvres des artistes que j'admirais que je demandais de le faire. Peut-être cela venait-il de l'idée trop élevée, trop mystérieuse, trop divine que je me faisais de la réalité. Mais si j'avais décidé moi-même si quelque chose était beau ou non, il m'eut* semblé que la beauté cessait d'être supérieure à mon goût, qu'elle dépendait de lui, qu'elle devenait quelque chose de facultatif et d'arbitraire.

△**496:10.** C'était notre médecin qui, malgré la désapprobation de ma grand'mère qui trouvait cela détestable pour moi et me voyait déjà mourant alcoolique, m'avait conseillé de boire de la bière et du champagne quand je sentais venir une crise d'étouffement, laquelle avorterait dans le bien-être, dans «l'aphonie*» causée par l'alcool.

△**496:16.** J'étais souvent> **497:7.** <un mal et ne faisait pas obstacle au bonheur, philosophie dont il ne se souciait pas car elle n'était pas de son ressort. [496:18. <montre de mon essoufflement. 496:19. <je sentais s'approcher une crise, toujours incertain des proportions qu'elle prendrait et de sa gravité, j'en> 496:23. <pour le garder pour lui seul, soit> 496:28. <exactitude qui devait être une sorte> 496:34. <loin; et dans le visage de ma grand'mère qui n'était plus> 496:36. <une expansion* de pitié> 496:37. <cœur éclatait, torturé par la sueur de la peine; comme> 496:38. <dû l'effacer, comme> 496:39. <pu lui donner autant> 496:41. Et maintenant que les scrupules étaient apaisés> 496:42. <malaise particulier que j'éprouvais, mon corps n'empêchait pas de lui protester que le malaise n'avait rien de douloureux, que je n'étais nullement> 497:3. <heureux. Il voulait obtenir> 497:4. <pitié physiologique et pourvu qu'on dit* qu'il avait>]

394:9. Un des premiers jours d'octobre, comme je m'ennuyais> **394:24.** <près de moi. [394:11. <excursion, au> 394:12. <bastions de marchandes de sucre d'orge, dans> 394:19. <quand, s'adressant> 394:22. <lui cria de l'allée: «Adieu>]

394:24. <près de moi, ne nommant pas seulement la personne qu'il désignait, mais s'adressant à elle en action, en sa puissance décuplée par la courbe de son jet et l'approche de son but, évoquait davantage l'existence de celle qu'il désignait parce qu'il ne la nommait pas seulement comme un objet dont on parle, mais l'interpellait; il passa ainsi près de moi, en action, en sa puissance qu'accroissait* la courbe de son jet et l'approche de son but [*repetition sic*]; transportant à son bord>

394:30. <à son bord> **394:35.** <l'une chez l'autre> [394:33. <du moins, sans le revoir, possédait>]

394:35. <l'une chez l'autre, de tout cet inconnu de moi encore plus inaccessible et plus douloureux d'être si familier et si maniable pour cette fille heureuse qui m'en frôlait sans que j'y puisse pénétrer et le jetait en plein air dans un cri; laissant s'échapper de lui l'amorce seulement mais indiquant la direction d'une des

relations (celle-ci une de camaraderie) et dont le faisceau formait la vie de Mlle Swann; faisant déjà flotter dans l'air plus dense et trop spécifique pour se mélanger à lui l'émanation délicieuse qu'il avait fait se dégager en les touchant avec précision de quelques points invisibles, du soir qu'il allait venir, tel qu'il serait, après dîner, chez elle; formant, passager céleste>

395:1. <passager céleste> **395:22.** <avec amies> [395:6. <dieux; enfin, sur cette> 395:7. <était à la fois un morceau de pelouse> 395:8. <après-midi, la blonde joueuse du volant> 395:9. <rattrapper*> 395:10. <à plumet rouge l'eut appelée), jetant une petite bande> 395:15. <«Allons, boutonnez votre> 395:18. <plumet rouge à>]

395:22. <avec ses amies, si bien qu'elle me fit demander par l'une d'elles si je voulais compléter leur camp, la première fois qu'elles ne se trouvèrent pas en nombre pour leur partie de barres; et je jouai>

395:25. <je jouai> **397:21.** <que Gilberte sortît> [395:28. <mienne que j'avais par deux fois sentie passer si douloureusement près de moi condensée dans le nom de Gilberte, dans le raidillon> 395:37. <matinée, et si ne le sachant pas je lui demandais si elle viendrait jouer, elle me répondait: «j'espère> 395:41. <verrait*> 396:1. <sorti> 396:9. Si je voyais la dame d'en face qui mettait son chapeau près de la fenêtre, je me disais: cette dame> 396:11. <sortir. Pourquoi> 396:13. <dame? Mais> 396:16. <pleuvrait. Et s'il> 396:17. Aussi après le déjeuner> 396:27. <de nouveau ternie, mais> 396:35. <découpé*> 396:36. <une témérité* dans la déclination* des moindres>]

□**397:21.** <que Gilberte sortît, et que maman disant*: «Ce n'est pas la peine que tu ailles aux Champs-Elysées, il ne fait même pas de soleil, tu ne trouveras personne», alors tout d'un coup, faisant dire à ma mère: «Tiens>

397:22. <«Tiens voilà> **398:10.** <chevaux de bois immobiles> [397:23. <même», sur le manteau> 397:26. <noirs. Ces jours-là> 397:35. <tous les grands avantages et bonheurs de la vie. 397:40. <relations de sa mère. 398:5. <nous allions jusqu'au>]

398:10. <chevaux de bois immobiles, les chaises en bordure le long du massif de lauriers, désertées par l'assemblée frileuse des institutrices et dans le réseau noir des allées dont on avait enlevé la neige, la pelouse blanche sur laquelle la statue [*syntax sic*].

398:14. La vieille dame> **399:2.** <jour de départ> [398:16. <disant: «comme> 398:20. <l'air se déchirait> 398:22. <le plumet jaune de> 398:31. <«Bravo! Bravo!> 398:32. <c'est chic, si je n'étais pas> 398:35. <pour la remercier d'être venue> 398:38. <à mes Champs-Elysées, une vieille intrépide. 398:41. Et elle rit avec satisfaction. 398:42. Ce jour auquel la neige, image>]

399:2. <jour de départ en nous retirant l'aspect et presque l'usage du lieu habituel de nos seules entrevues, maintenant changé, tout enveloppé de housses, ce jour faisait pourtant faire un progrès à mon amour, car il était comme un premier chagrin qu'elle eût partagé avec moi.

399:7. Il n'y avait que> **399:9.** <un commencement d'intimité, d'être là un jour pareil. Mais aussi de sa part, comme si elle fût venue rien que pour moi, par un jour pareil, cela me semblait aussi touchant>

399:12. <touchant que si> **403:34.** <était devenu> [399:14. <Champs-Elysées; et je> 399:15. <et à* l'avenir> 399:32. <que je vienne sur> 399:34. <l'usure argenté* des> 399:35. <faisait un noir* camp du drap d'or. 399:41. <dire de suite que> 399:43. <aux Champs-Elysées; ces moments où> 400:23. <elle, «ce> [*punctuation sic*]. 400:26. <Gilberte». 400:35. <mon désir> 400:41. <impatient de voir Gilberte auraient> 400:43. Plus tard, en effet, il> 401:1. <nous nous contentons> 401:3. <être ni* inquiets> 401:6. <renoncions à celui de lui> 401:9. <fleur, lui en sacrifient> 401:11. <dehors de moi, que, en permettant seulement que nous écartions les obstacles, il nous offrait> 401:14. <changer, et que si j'avais> 401:18. <fabriquée*> 401:22. <Champs-Elysées et que j'allais pouvoir enfin confronter> 401:25. <indépendantes* de moi, dès que> 401:31. <pied avant l'autre> 401:36. <joies* pleines> 401:42. <de celle à> 402:6. <comme une œuvre qu'on compose, la jeune fille me passait> 402:12. <tendait, comme> 402:14. <rejoindre, me> 402:20. <décisifs auxquels* j'étais> 402:26. <pain

d'épices, et> 402:29. <garçons que je me rappelle comme le petit coloriste> 402:30. Car l'un refusait un sucre> 402:34. <mieux cette prune-là, parce qu'elle> 402:35. <billes d'un coup.* 403:18. <demandé, me> 403:19. <envoyé.» Mais>]

403:24. <était devenu un des petits bleus qu'Elle* avait reçus ce jour-là, pouvant figurer au milieu des mêmes incidents de sa vie, —j'eus peine>

403:25. <peine à reconnaître> **404:37.** <j'éprouvais une allégresse> [403:27. <qu'y avait ajoutés au crayon un des facteurs, signes de réalisation effective> 403:30. <ceintures symboliques, hygiéniques, de la vie, qui> 403:43. <dans ma* bouche> 404:4. <qu'elle faisait pour articuler les mot* qu'elle> 404:7. <un fruit qu'on veut avaler nu, tandis que> 404:9. <m'atteignant ainsi plus> 404:23. <m'expliquant pourquoi elle> 405:25. <restai*> 404:26. <devant moi, à ne pas regarder les petits avantages qu'elle m'avait donnés non pas>]

404:37. <une allégresse qui me semblait seulement l'anticipation d'un grand bonheur qu'elle me laisserait quand, entrant dès le matin au salon pour embrasser maman, déjà toute prête, la tour de ses cheveux noirs entièrement construite avec ses étages d'arceaux superposés, et ses belles mains blanches et potelées sentant encore le savon, j'avais reconnu, en voyant la colonne de poussière qui se tenait toute seule en l'air au-dessus du piano en entendant «en revenant de la revue», qu'un orgue de barbarie* jouait sous les fenêtres, que l'hiver en fête avait pour jusqu'au soir, la visite inopinée et radieuse d'une journée de printemps.

405:4. Pendant que nous déjeunions> **405:13.** <avant trois heures, je regardais le désert de notre cour de récréation où un mirage me faisait apercevoir la pelouse des Champs-Elysées et quand Françoise étant venue me chercher à la sortie, nous prenions ces mêmes rues que nous suivions tous les jours pour aller aux Champs-Elysées et qui justement, étant plus larges, étaient celles que le soleil avait choisies pour son passage au devant duquel tout le monde se pressait, et sans m'arrêter à ces colonnes polychromes des théâtres dont souvent, attentif et fiévreux stylite, je restais méditer longuement les mystérieuses inscriptions, cherchant à en dégager ce que pouvait être le génie de la Berma, je quittais à tout instant le trottoir pour être en plein soleil sur la

chaussée, faisant entrer mon corps dans l'armure de lumière aux fines mailles qui me faisait valeureux et confiant comme un saint Georges, en levant les yeux en l'air vers les balcons qui, descellés par le soleil et vaporeux, flottaient devant les maisons comme des nuages d'or.

405:19. Hélas aux> **405:29.** <bénédiction du soleil.

405:30. La dame qui lisait les *Débats* était assise> **407:11.** <battements de cœur> [406:2. J'entraînai Françoise au-devant d'elle jusqu'à l'Arc-de-Triomphe, nous ne la rencontrâmes pas> 406:12. <et son père allait venir la chercher. Aussi> 406:22. <sentais sans la connaître la raison> 406:26. <les Ambassadeurs et> 406:27. <je devinais toutes les occupations où> 406:30. <troublait encore quand> 406:34. <Débats qui> 406:35. <feu», lui> 406:37. <que Gilberte était chez> 407:2. <moi, —comme Gilberte> 407:3. <Gilberte, comme des dieux tout puissants sur elle en qui il aurait eu> 407:4. <source—un inconnu>]

407:11. <de cœur qu'avait excité* l'apparition de son chapeau gris, de son manteau à pèlerine et de sa cravate à pois, son aspect>

407:13. <aspect impressionnait> **407:33.** <surtout son père> [407:16. <le comte de Chambord qui> 407:17. <quand j'entendais*> 407:20. <jamais connu de Bourbon; elles> 407:29. <connaître. Cela> 407:30. <bien souvent à Combray depuis que j'étais tout petit; souvenir>]

407:33. <son père, un personnage nouveau; comme les idées sur lesquelles j'embranchais maintenant son nom étaient différentes des idées au réseau desquelles il était autrefois rattaché et que je n'utilisais plus jamais quand j'avais à penser à lui, il était devenu un personnage nouveau; je le rattachais pourtant par une ligne artificielle à notre invité d'autrefois>

407:40. <d'autrefois; et comme> **408:25.** <un prénom différent> [407:43. <je retrouvais les> 408:11. <que Henri V avait> 408:12. <nous commençâmes à jouer> 408:16. <en lieu* d'asile (cependant qu'ils en complétaient la signification), tel> 408:21. <émail dont la>]

408:25. <un prénom différent, une nouvelle divinité, trois de ces jours-là je n'eus pas le courage de cacher ma déception à Gilberte.

408:29. —J'avais justement> **411:12.** <à mon bonheur> [408:37. <j'ai un arbre de Noël; après-demain> 408:41. <après cela c'est le jour de Noël> 408:42. <midi.* Ce que ce serait chic! en tout cas, j'irai faire des visites avec maman. Je ne viendrai pas ici. Adieu> 409:10. <mes sanglots ces mots que m'avait dit* Gilberte, où elle laissait éclater> 409:11. <venir aux Champs-Elysées. 409:14. <songeait à Gilberte, à la position particulière, unique, fut-elle* déplorable, où me plaçait inévitablement par rapport à elle, une contrainte> 409:22. <autres: je> 409:23. <et va m'expliquer la> 409:25. <de faire semblant d'être heureuse, de* ce qui l'empêche de me voir, de prendre l'apparence de la Gilberte simple camarade. 409:35. <que j'aurais aimé lire, de peur qu'en les énonçant j'exclue justement ceux-là, les plus chers, les plus désirés, du champ des réalisations possibles. 409:40. <que de sont* côté m'eût adressé* Gilberte> 410:4. <mais que* du moins, m'avait été donnée par elle, cette> 410:6. <fille* d'agate> 410:14. <raisons nouvelles d'aimer, les* qualités fussent-elles les plus opposées à celles que le sien recherchait tant qu'il était spontané, moi, qui l'avais d'abord aimée dès Combray> 410:21. <m'étais*> 410:22. <cette vie> 410:24. <collaboratrice de mes travaux, qui le soir collectionnerait* pour moi des brochures. 410:27. <devin*> 410:30. <plaisir que la page sur Racine> 410:33. <me l'avait apporté*. 410:38. <cette pierre, même la beauté de cette page de Bergotte que> 410:40. <amour comme si> 410:42. <néant, elle* lui donnait une> 410:43. <antérieures à mon amour pour Gilberte, qu'elles> 411:5. <pas aimé et rien ne me permettait par conséquent de lire en eux un message de bonheur.]

411:12. <à mon bonheur, mais aucun intérêt particulier pour mon amour dans un ordre différent qu'elle donnait à tous ses ouvrages, ne portant aucun intérêt particulier à mon amour, et ne pensant pas d'abord que j'étais aimé, elle recueillait les actions>

411:15. <les actions de Gilberte> **411:22.** <du jour de l'an> [411:19. <Gilberte, au lieu de venir aux Champs-Elysées, aller>]

411:22. <du jour de l'an, je pouvais me dire, elle est frivole ou docile; j'aurais dû comprendre qu'elle eut* cessé d'être l'un et l'autre si elle m'avait aimé, et que si elle avait été forcée d'obéir ç*'eût été avec le même désespoir que j'avais les jours où je ne devais pas la voir. Il disais* encore que je devais pourtant>

411:27. <je devais pourtant savoir> **413:1.** <d'une nouvelle amitié. [411:28. <Gilberte; il me faisait remarquer que le souci perpétuel de me faire valoir à ses yeux, et à ceux* duquel* j'essayais> 411:32. <avec un épi jaune, ou> 411:36. <dévouée), ce besoin> 411:42. <montrer que sous les actions de Gilberte je ne trouverais ni l'un ni l'autre. 412:3. <Champs Elysées* pour aller faire des emplettes avec elle, agréable> 412:7. <endroit s'occupait-elle du désir> 412:16. <qu'elle me dise que> 412:22. Il disait que si> 412:32. <jours; que dans les sentiments de Gilberte pour moi, trop anciens pour pouvoir changer, c'était l'indifférence> 412:35. <aimais. C'est vrai répondait>]

413:4. See after 417:11.

416:30. Ces jours où Gilberte m'avait annoncé qu'elle ne devait pas venir aux Champs-Elysées, j'entraînais Françoise en pèlerinage devant la maison qu'habitaient les Swann. {416:34-416:41}

416:41. J'aimais Gilberte: si sur le chemin j'apercevais leur vieux maître d'hôtel promenant un chien, l'émotion m'obligeait à m'arrêter, j'attachais sur ses favoris blancs des regards pleins d'amour. Françoise me disait:

417:3. —Qu'est-ce que> **417:11.** <sur laquelle les fenêtres> [417:4. <jusque devant la porte où un concierge>]

417:11. <les fenêtres de l'entre-sol* semblaient conscientes d'être refermées entre la noble retombée de leurs rideaux de mousseline ressemblaient* beaucoup moins à n'importe quelle autre fenêtre qu'aux regards de Gilberte. D'autres fois j'emmenais Françoise jusqu'au Bois où se promenait presque chaque jour Mme Swann, et parfois dans la rue Duphot qui, parce qu'on assurait qu'il arrivait à M. Swann d'y passer pour se rendre chez son dentiste, et qui à cause de cela (car mon imagination différenciant* tellement M. Swann du reste de l'humanité que sa présence au milieu du monde réel y introduisait du merveilleux) me

donnait autant d'émoi qu'à un paysan un chemin hanté par les fées. J'avais toujours à portée>

417:28. See after 637:40.

△**413:4.** J'avais toujours à portée> **413:20.** <ne me suffisait pas. [413:9. <père qui n'était pas comme ma mère et ma grand'mère au courant de mon amour [*syntax sic*]. 413:17. <le nom de Swann, car si je me le répétais mentalement sans cesse, j'avais besoin aussi>] {413:20-413:43}

△**414:1.** Je ne tarissais plus non plus sur la beauté, la magnificence, la noblesse de la vieille dame qui lisait les *Débats* (et j'avais insinué à mes parents que ce devait être une ambassadrice ou peut-être une altesse) jusqu'au jour>

△**414:5.** <jusqu'au jour où> **414:25.** <mon temps à table> [414:7. <je vois que* c'est, s'écria ma mère. A la garde! > 412:12. <enfant des* manèges> 414:18. <vraiment M. Swann. 414:20. <il a toujours fallu qu'elle> 414:21. <est la* horrible>]

△**414:25.** <mon temps à table à rentrer ma tête dans mes épaules. Mon père disait: cet enfant est idiot, il deviendra bossu».

△**414:27.** J'aurais surtout> **415:39.** <des Trois Quartiers> [414:28. <semblait quelqu'un de si> 414:29. <des personnes que je connaissais aussi le connussent et que> 414:31. <amener* à la* rencontrer. 414:38. Quelle volupté, quelle souffrance d'apprendre> 415:1. <disais*> 414:4. <et, disait-on, son> 415:6. Mais combien j'avais envie de savoir si Swann avait sa cravate à pois. 415:11. <plus qu'elle n'eût souhaité, à> 415:16. <j'avais voulu attenter à la> 415:30. <plus, que j'y existasse d'une façon assez complète> 415:33. <ma personnalité de camarade> 415:35. <grands parents*>]

△**415:39.** <des Trois Quartiers où, Swann l'ayant eue devant les yeux, elle avait représenté pour lui une personne définie avec qui il avait des souvenirs communs qui avaient motivé chez lui le mouvement de s'approcher d'elle, le geste de la saluer, quelques paroles, elle ne semblait pas mettre à part ce moment de sa journée sur lequel l'attention de Swann avait passé et pour moi resterait à jamais peinte*, comme sur la terre qu'il a rasée un moment, l'ombre des ailes d'un oiseau merveilleux.

Et mes parents ne semblaient pas trouver non plus à parler des grands parents* de Swann>

△**416:2.** <de Swann, du titre> **416:16.** <rien d'unique. [416:7. <sculpté le porche et>]

△**416:16.** <rien d'unique, parce que mes parents étaient dépourvus de ce sens supplémentaire et momentané qui me permettait de percevoir dans tout ce qui entourait Gilberte une qualité inconnue, analogue dans le monde des émotions à ce que peut être dans celui des couleurs l'infra* rouge [*cf.* 416:27].

△**416:16.** Ce qu'au contraire ils y appréciaient, ils le trouvaient à> **416:19.** <d'une autre, qui n'avait rien à voir avec Gilberte et qui l'était mieux, ou à* des financiers d'un cran supérieur à son grand-père; et s'ils avaient>

△**416:22.** <s'ils avaient eu> **416:24.** <à se dissiper.

□ △**416:24.** Je ne me rendis peut-être jamais compte plus douloureusement de ce désaccord qui existait entre moi et les autres personnages au sujet de Swann, qu'un jour où vint dîner à la maison un ancien diplomate que mon père avait connu depuis peu dans une commission dont ils faisaient tous deux partie au ministère, et pour qui il avait une grande considération, le Marquis de Norpois*, jour qui m'est resté mémorable parce que dans l'après-midi duquel* j'avais entendu pour la première fois la Berma.

434:28. M. de Montfort avait été ministre plénipotentiaire avant la guerre et ambassadeur au moment du Seize Mai. Ses

---

434:28. ([1]*It is curious that Proust made so many corrections but failed to eliminate this repetition in* Grasset A *which was therefore reproduced in* Grasset B. *Later, to be sure, he crossed out the first three sentences, but we shall not take account of handwritten corrections in* Grasset B.) ([2]appeler des hommes) ([3]recueillir sans compensations des risques d'un manque de). 435:11. ([1]sait) ([2]peut se dispenser car ils ne lui* ajouteraient rien, de ces) ([3]la haute aristocratie de* celle au-dessous de laquelle elle est immédiatement située, elle sait). 435:23. ([1]pas pour l'inutile) ([2]politiques, fussent-ils francs-maçons, qui) ([3]priment, à tous ceux qui peuvent conférer une illustration) ([4]Norpois). 436:11. ([1]préféreront même des). 436:19. ([1]se traduissent, —dans un discours, dans un document—, par). 436:21. ([1]Norpois). 436:22. ([1]que sans qu'à vrai dire personne et surtout mon père eût jamais su pourquoi, lui témoignait l'ancien ambassadeur). 436:35. ([1]Norpois). 436:38. ([1]personne. Je suis sûr qu'il va). 436:39. ([1]Norpois) ([2]peut-être, il). 437:8. ([1]Norpois). 437:9. ([1]vers). 437:37. ([1]Norpois). 438:11. ([1]Norpois). 439:9. ([1]avait toujours fait). 439:40. ([1]Norpois). 440:6. ([1]Norpois). 440:19 (Norpois) ([2]que le vide). 440:32. ([1]désir de recevoir). 440:41. ([1]de San Giorgio) ([2]les Carpaccio). 441:9. ([1]davantage, si). 441:36. ([1]était l'étoile). 441:41. ([1]deux actes) ([2]étaient, comme celui de Phèdre, transparents) ([3]m'était connue, illuminés). 442:19. ([1]*Phèdre,* dont le titre n'était pas). 442:21. ([1]caractères

attaches, ses opinions auraient dû le rendre suspect à la République qui au contraire lui offrait et lui faisait accepter les missions les plus importantes, sous des ministres où un simple bourgeois réactionnaire se serait récusé. Mais une certaine aristocratie a une conscience si évidente et perpétuelle de sa supériorité originelle

---

différents). 442:25. ([1]l'autre leurs points successifs et traçant sur la scène, avec leurs points successifs* une mince ligne invisible mais qui pour Phèdre ne serait qu'un côté d'une figure qui s'étendait). 442:34. ([1]peut compenser.). 442:36 ([1]ce que je demandais à cette représentation). 444:6. ([1]elle et mon père). 444:17 ([1]ne me disaient). 444:21 ([1]c'eût été pour abréger). 444:30. ([1]*Phédre*). 444:31. ([1]ma). 444:34. ([1]l'affiche). 445:7. ([1]deux). 445:9. ([1]Norpois). 446:24. ([1]plateau: et en effet dans un moment sa calèche) ([2]elle en descendrait). 446:32. ([1]que contrairement) ([2]enfantines, il) ([3]et où au contraire, par une) ([4]s'adressèrent) ([5]voir—, mon plaisir). 448:11. ([1]encore dans ce commencement du second acte) ([2]rideau fut). 448:17. ([1]femme de Thésie*) ([2]actrice lui donna). 448:23. ([1]nobles). 448:33. ([1]celle qu'en pouvait la). 449:2. ([1]esprit vers). 449:24. ([1]Berma quittant la scène reste immobile un instant, le bras levé à la hauteur de l'épaule, devant) ([2]éclata). 449:37. ([1]d'une mélopée) ([2]débita) ([3]temps d'apprécier. 450:14. ([1]disait à côté de moi une femme assez commune, elle). 451:4. ([1]Persée). 451:18. ([1]Norpois). 452:26. ([1]Norpois). 453:32. ([1]façon qui n'avait rien de défavorable, à). 453:40. ([1]Norpois). 455:23. ([1]Norpois). 456:36. ([1]Norpois). 456:40. ([1]Berma. Je n'avais) ([2]Norpois). 457:8. ([1]Norpois). 457:18. ([1]Hé). 457:20. ([1]Norpois). 457:22. ([1]de politesse envers la maîtresse de maison, c'est). 457:33. ([1]exagérés. Et puis) ([2]Berma n'avait cessé de grandir depuis que la représentation était finie parce qu'il) ([3]extérieure: mais j'éprouvais le besoin de lui trouver des explications; de plus il s'était porté avec une intensité égale, pendant que la Berma jouait, sur tout) ([4]distingué; aussi fut-il heureux de se découvrir une justification dans ces éloges que M. de Norpois donnait à la) ([5]artiste, il les attirait à lui par) ([6]s'emparait) ([7]*Phèdre*) ([8]Norpois). 459:34. ([1]pas au trône (car vous saviez* qu'il y a été appelé par un congrès européen et il a même fort hésité à l'accepter, jugeant cette royauté un peu inégale à sa race, la plus noble). 460:33. ([1]Vaugoubert). 460:36. ([1]Cette surprise). 463:2. ([1]Vaugoubert) ([2]assistants m'ont) ([3]prononcé à merveille) ([4]intentions, toutes les finesses. Je me suis laissé raconter ce fait assez piquant, que précisément à ce mot d'«affinités» qui était en somme la grosse innovation) ([5]gagne si bien les cœurs) ([6]Vaugoubert) ([7]Oettingen) ([8]d'«affinités»). 463:25. ([1]Vaugoubert). 464:8. ([1]Norpois). 464:22. ([1]Balbec). 464:23. ([1]Balbec). 464:26. ([1]Balbec). 464:28. ([1]Balbec). 464:29. ([1]Balbec). 464:35. ([1]Balbec). 464:37. ([1]Balbec). 465:4. ([1]Balbec). 465:21. ([1]Norpois). 466:2. ([1]m'amusais hier à). 467:7. ([1]même quand il ne les lui avouait pas) ([2]pas, de lui manifester implacablement, quand il la ressentirait enfin) ([3]Alors commence une période pendant laquelle il voulait) ([4]la) ([5]brûlé la partie) ([6]il aurait pu y songer et qui ne s'éclairait plus.) ([7]passer sa main sur ses yeux et) ([8]semblait peut-être aussi). 468:35. ([1]Swann) ([2]ces). 468:38. ([1]aimée; et certes) ([2]encore, pendant cette période qui dura quelque temps, de la) ([3]sorte; nous) ([4]traits particuliers de) ([5]même à ceux) ([6]l'habitude) ([7]traits particuliers) ([8]avaient malgré tout en) ([9]ces traits là*) ([10]faisait métier d'écrivain, quand il publiait des

et ineffaçable! M. de Norpois* avait été ministre plénipotentiaire avant la guerre et ambassadeur au moment du Seize Mai [*repetition sic*].[1] Au grand étonnement de beaucoup il avait été depuis prié plusieurs fois—et avait accepté—de représenter la France dans des missions extraordinaires sous des ministres radicaux qu'un simple bourgeois réactionnaire se fut* refusé à servir, et auxquels le passé de M. de Norpois*, ses attaches, ses opinions auraient dû le rendre suspect. Mais ces ministres avancés semblaient se rendre compte au contraire qu'ils pouvaient à bon compte par de telles désignations montrer la largeur d'esprit qu'ils avaient dès qu'il s'agissait des intérêts supérieurs de la France, se mettre hors de pair des hommes politiques, en se faisant appeler[2] patriotes et hommes d'état, bénéficier enfin du prestige qui s'attache à un nom aristocratique et de l'intérêt qu'éveille comme un coup de théâtre un choix inattendu. Et ils savaient aussi que ces avantages ils pouvaient, en faisant appel à M. de Norpois*, les recueillir.[3] Les compensations de risques, de man-

---

études.) ([11]conversation où ils abondaient.) ([12]ce qu'il écrivait.) ([13]Mais ce temps, heureux, d'affection) ([14]pas été bien long.) ([15]eue, elle) ([16]mauvais et factice) ([17]mais être reçue chez) ([18]Norpois venant* de) ([19]des personnes qui allaient) ([20]Laumes devenue bientôt duchesse des* Guermantes à la mort de son beau-père.) ([21]revêtit jamais dans son imagination son ambition) ([22]inventait) ([23]son) ([24]indestructible) ([25]déterminent, on verra plus tard qu'elle) ([26]réalisa d'une façon bien autre qu'il) ([27]faisait mais bien différente de celle dont il avait souffert si longtemps et qu'à* vrai dire était son amour même. Cette nouvelle curiosité était haineuse et ressemblait à celle qu'on éprouve) ([28]qu'on répétât à Odette) ([29]«idiots», (maxime qui se) ([30]semblant dire) ([31]Cette seconde maxime c'était) ([32]peut) ([33]Swann était) ([34]changeant) ([35]d'avis, se) ([36]qu'elle lui avait souvent témoignée) ([37]que c'était son devoir de) ([38]songeant) ([39]humaine comme toute autre,) ([40]ne peuvent jamais être) ([41]judiciaires, qui se servent) ([42]fortune qui sait si ce n'était pas d'une de ces criminelles (qu'il avait crues à tort enfermées dans une caste spéciale), qu'il voulait) ([43]attarder) ([44]l'autre, à celle de la femme entretenue, il essuyait ses paupières avec sa main, et ne pensait plus) ([45]pliait depuis longtemps sans) ([46]qu'Odette était maintenant avec) ([47]lequel) ([48]formé des soupçons atroces) ([49]nouveau elle ne le laissait plus) ([50]coïncidence? il) ([51]Swann) ([52]devenir une méchante femme) ([53]Pourtant depuis et, même) ([54]appliquant) ([55]travaillait) ([56]en commun avec) ([57]se mesurait pour Swann, non pas en fonction des gens plus brillants qu'il avait commis* avant son mariage et continuait à fréquenter, mais en fonctions* des relations) ([58]du) ([59]Au «fils Swann» et au Swann élégant, s'était ajouté le Swann mari d'Odette. A vrai) ([60]femmes tarées, parure) ([61]de) ([62]étroitement il semble) ([63]Wickenham) ([64]Norfrois*) ([65]Norpois).

que de loyalisme politique contre lesquels ils pensaient que la naissance du marquis devait non pas les mettre en garde, mais au contraire les garantir.

435:7. Et en cela la République> **435:11.** <peut lui enlever, dont ses pairs ou ceux qui sont plus haut* encore connaissent assez exactement la valeur pour qu'elle n'ait pas besoin de le montrer, soit*[1] qu'elle peut[2] s'en dispenser car ils n'ajouteraient rien de ces efforts de ne professer que des opinions bien portées et de ne fréquenter que des gens bien pensants dans lesquels on voit se consumer tant de bourgeois sans qu'ils arrivent à obtenir ce qu'elle a eu au berceau. En revanche, soucieuse de se grandir aux yeux de la[3] plus haute aristocratie, elle sait qu'elle ne le peut qu'en ajoutant à son nom ce qu'il ne contenait pas et ce qui fait>

435:2. <fait qu'à nom égal> **435:23.** <grande fortune.

435:23. Et les frais qu'elle ne fait pas*[1] l'inutile hobereau auprès duquel les bourgeois se dépensent et de la stérile amitié duquel un prince ne lui saurait aucun gré, elle les prodiguera aux hommes politiques[2] qui peuvent faire arriver dans les ambassades ou patronner aux élections, aux artistes et aux savants qui peuvent aider à se faire connaître dans la branche où ils peinent*,[3] de tous ceux qui sont peuvent* espérer une illustration nouvelle ou faire un riche mariage. Puis surtout dans une longue pratique de la diplomatie, M. de Montfort[4] s'était imbu>

435:35. <imbu de[1] cet esprit. **436:22.** <à la Commission> [435:37. <et surtout sous> 435:38. <l'esprit de la chancellerie. Il y avait puisé l'aversion> 436:3. <du genre de M. Le Gouvé*> 436:5. <Mézières, qu'il n'applaudirait à celui de Boileau par Claudel. 436:8. <entre lui et Georges Berry> 436:10. <politiques mais non son genre> 436:11. <lui préféreront[1] des adversaires> 436:12. <de fidèles royalistes se> 436:15. <par habitude professionnelle de> 436:19. <se traduisent,[1] ou dans un discours, ou dans un document, par> 436:21. <M. de Montfort[1] passait>]

436:22. <Commission, où chacun félicitait mon père de la sympathie que[1] lui témoignait l'ancien ambassadeur sans qu'à vrai dire personne et surtout mon père eût jamais su pourquoi. Car étant généralement peu aimable, mon père avait l'habitude

de n'être pas recherché en dehors du cercle de ses intimes et l'avouait volontiers, car il était extrêmement modeste.

436:27. Il avait conscience> **436:39.** <sur la guerre de 1870.» [436:30. <sympathies, et duquel toutes> 436:32. <qu'elles ennuient et agacent une> 436:35. «De Montfort[1] m'a invité à dîner> 436:38. <personne.[1] Et il va encore>

436:39. <la guerre de 1870.» Mon père trouvait un vif plaisir à la conversation pleine de souvenirs de M. de Montfort.[1] Il savait que seul peut-être[2] dès 1866, il avait inutilement averti>

436:40. <averti l'empereur> **437:9.** <le genre d'intelligence> [437:3. <avait eu avec M. de Montfort. Il faudra> 437:4. <a beaucoup d'importance, nous> 437:8. <peut-être M. de Monfort*[1] n'avait pas>]

437:9. <le genre d'intelligence par[1] lequel elle se sentait le plus attirée. Mais c'était une délicate flatterie qu'elle aimait réserver à mon père que de lui parler avec admiration de cet homme qui lui marquait une prédilection si rare. Elle sentait qu'en fortifiant dans l'esprit de mon père la bonne opinion qu'il avait de M. de Norpois, et par là en le conduisant à en prendre une bonne de lui-même, elle remplissait un de ses devoirs d'épouse qui était de rendre la vie agréable à son mari, comme elle faisait> {437:10-437:27}

437:33. <comme elle faisait> **438:11.** <sans songer que> [437:34. <la cuisine fut* bonne et> 437:37. <admirer M. de Monfort*[1] pour> 437:38. <elle aimait naturellement> 438:3. <ponctualité si surprenante> 438:5. <reconnaissait son écriture sur> 438:7. <croisée, et qu'il semblait exister pour lui à la poste des levées supplémentaires et de luxe.]

438:11. <les quoiques* sont toujours des parce que, et que c'était les mêmes habitudes qui permettaient à M. de Montfort[1] de satisfaire>

438:16. <satisfaire à tant> **438:33.** <chez nous. [438:20. <mettait tout ce qui la concernait au-dessous, et par conséquent en dehors, des autres choses, et ainsi la réponse> 438:23. <adresser exactement parce qu'il> 438:27. <M. de Monfort* un> {438:34-438:43}

439.1: Ce fut sans doute en voyant l'abattement> **439:8.** <t'y emmener> [439:4. <qu'un jour ma mère me dit:

—Si tu as encore>]

439:9. Mais ce fut parce que M. de Norpois lui avait dit: «Oh! elle est superbe, la Berma, vous devriez bien laisser votre fils aller l'entendre, c'est un beau souvenir à garder pour un jeune homme», que mon père qui jusque-là avait[1] fait une violente opposition à ce que j'allasse perdre mon temps et risquer de prendre mal pour ce qu'il appelait au grand scandale de ma grand'mère, des inutilités, n'était plus loin de considérer cette soirée préconisée par ce «vieux malin de père Norpois» comme faisant vaguement partie d'un ensemble indivisible de recettes précieuses pour faire une brillante carrière. Ma grand'mère qui avait fait un gros sacrifice en renonçant pour moi au profit que, selon ce qu'elle croyait, j'aurais trouvé à entendre la Berma, mais qui l'avait fait à l'intérêt de ma santé, s'étonnait que cet intérêt devînt négligeable>

439:21. <devînt négligeable> **439:39.** <du côté de Guermantes. [439:22. Mettant une espérance invincible de> 439:31. <avait changé les intentions de mon père sur un point bien plus important pour moi. Mon père avait toujours> 439:34. <même si je pouvais pendant de longues années être attaché au ministère, ce serait ensuite être envoyé dans des capitales que Gilberte n'habitait[*] pas.]

439:40. Mais mon père s'était montré entièrement hostile à la carrière des lettres qu'il estimait fort inférieure à celle des ambassades et à laquelle il refusait même le nom de carrière, jusqu'au jour où M. de Montfort[1] qui n'aimait pas beaucoup les agents des nouvelles couches lui avait assuré>

440:2. <assuré qu'on pouvait> **440:18.** <de Gilberte> [440:6. <le père Montfort[1] n'est> 440:7. <tout hostile à> 440:10. <ne se réglât dans la conversation> 440:13. Ecris aussi quelque> 440:15. <entrer, il arrangera cela>]

440:18. <Gilberte me donnait le désir mais non le moyen d'écrire quelque chose qui pût être montré à M. de Montfort.[1] J'avais beau m'installer devant un bureau me répéter combien il était souhaitable que j'écrivisse un ouvrage merveilleux, mon

esprit ne montrait que[2] du vide. Et après quelques pages préliminaires>

440:21. <pages préliminaires> **440:41.** <Titien des Frari> [440:23. <doué pour la littérature et ne pourrais> 440:26. <profiter de cette chance de rester auprès de Gilberte. Seule> 440:27. <Berma venait me distraire de cette tristesse. Mais> 440:29. <où elles étaient les plus fortes, de même je n'aurais voulu voir la Berma que> 440:32. <c'est l'espoir d'une découverte précieuse que recèle pour nous le désir[1] d'avoir, de recevoir de telles impressions de la nature ou de l'art, nous avons une sorte de scrupule> 440:39. <c'était une de ces choses fameuses que mon imagination avait le plus désirée.]

440:41. <Titien des Frari ou des Carpaccio de[1] Giorgio, si jamais j'entendais dire à la Berma les vers: «Oui Prince, je languis, je brûle pour Thésée,» que j'admirais d'après la simple reproduction qu'en donnent les éditions imprimées, mais qui faisaient battre mon cœur quand je pensais, comme à la réalisation d'un voyage, que je les verrais enfin baigner effectivement dans l'atmosphère et l'ensoleillement doré de sa voix les[2] Carpaccios* de Venise, la Berma dans Phèdre*, chefs-d'œuvre>

441:9. <chefs-d'œuvre d'art pictural> **441:15.** <les yeux ouverts après une si longue attente devant l'objet inconcevable et unique de tant de milliers de mes rêves. Puis si j'attachais depuis tant d'années une telle importance à pouvoir entendre la Berma, c'est que d'après ce qu'on m'avait dit de la beauté de son jeu si douloureux et si noble, j'en attendais des révélations sur certains aspects de la noblesse, de la douleur, que je ne pourrais connaître si je ne l'entendais pas. Or ce qu'il y avait de beau, de réel dans ce jeu, me semblait devoir l'être davantage,[1] et si elle le superposait à une œuvre d'une beauté véritable que si elle brodait en quelque sorte du vrai et du beau sur du faux et du vulgaire. Enfin, si j'allais, pour entendre la Berma, à une pièce nouvelle, il ne serait pas difficile de juger son jeu, sa diction dans un rôle où je ne pourrais pas faire le départ entre un texte que je ne connaissais pas d'avance et ce que lui ajoutaient des intonations et des gestes qui me sembleraient faire corps avec lui; tandis que les œuvres anciennes, où je n'aurais plus à m'occuper du texte que je savais par cœur, m'apparaissaient>

441:30. <m'apparaissaient comme> **441:41.** <jour de l'an> [441:32. <en toute liberté> 441:36. <elle était[1] la vedette et l'étoile> 441:37. <consulter l'annonce des représentations, je ne voyais que des pièces du jour, fabriquées>]

441:41. <j'y vis pour la première fois, comme lever de rideau, une de ces nouveautés probablement insignifiantes dont le titre sur l'affiche me semblait opaque parce qu'il contenait tout le particulier d'une action que j'ignorais, en fin de spectacle les[1] derniers actes de *Phèdre* avec Mme Berma, et aux matinées suivantes *Le Demi-Monde*, les *Caprices de Marianne*, dont les noms au contraire étaient[2] transparents, remplis seulement de clarté, tant l'œuvre était[3] connue de moi et de tous, illuminés jusqu'au fond d'un bénévole sourire d'art qui ennoblissait jusqu'à Mme Berma elle-même. Car une note indiquait au bas du programme qu'elle avait résolu de se montrer de nouveau au public dans quelques-unes de ses anciennes créations. Cette décision donnait au passé de l'actrice quelque chose de plus artistique encore, en prouvant que celle-ci savait que certains rôles ont un intérêt qui survit à la nouveauté de leur apparition ou au succès de leur reprise, et qu'elle les considérait, interprétés par elle, comme des pièces de musée qu'il pouvait être instructif de mettre sous les yeux de la génération qui l'y avait admirée ou de celle qui ne l'y avait pas vue.

442:17. En faisant afficher> **442:25.** <a cité les autres:> [442:19. <soirée, ce[1] titre: *Phèdre,* qui n'était pas plus long> 442:21. <en[1] d'autres caractères, elle>]

□**442:25.** <les autres: M. Bergotte ou M. Anatole France. Certes, Phèdre[*] allait être pour un jour une pièce comme ces autres nouveautés, une pièce qui se développerait face au public de trois heures à six, chaque mot des rôles, chaque moment de la pièce, s'anéantissant l'un après l'autre;[1] aussitôt prononcés, aussitôt révolus, leurs points successifs traceraient sur la scène une mince ligne parallèle à la rampe, évanouie comme dans les autres pièces, à mesure qu'elle se prolonge, mais qui pour *Phèdre* ne serait qu'un côté d'une figure qui s'étendait, immense et permanente, en largeur dans les esprits de tous ceux qui relisaient sans cesse le chef-d'œuvre, en profondeur sur deux siècles de gloire.

442:27. Le médecin> **443:6.** <récitais sans cesse> [442:31. <crainte m'eût peut-être arrêté si> 442:32. <attendu de cette soirée avait été seulement> 442:34. <peut[1] compenser, étant de même ordre. Mais> 442:35. <voyage à Bricquebec, au> 442:36. <désirés), ce[1] que je lui demandais, c'était> 442:38. <réel, plus précieux que celui où je vivais, et dont l'acquisition une fois faite ne pourrait pas m'être enleveée par des modalités insignifiantes, fussent-elles douloureuses, de mon> 442:42. <pendant cette soirée m'apparaissait-il>]

443:6. <récitais sans cesse les vers: «Oui, Prince, je languis, je brûle pour Thésé*,» cherchant]

443:10. <cherchant toutes> **443:27.** <quand ma mère> [443:10. <pouvait leur donner, afin> 443:13. <trouverait pour eux. Cachée> 443:15. <Bergotte (dans la page retrouvée par Gilberte) que> 443:20. <jour, comme sur un autel allumé sans cesse, trônait>]

443:28. <mère (bien que cette représentation eût lieu précisément le jour de la séance de la Commission après laquelle mon père devait ramener dîner M. de Montfort. Mais comme c'était en matinée cela ne m'empêcherait pas de causer avec lui) m'eût dit: «Hé bien nous ne voulons pas te chagriner, si tu crois que tu auras tant de plaisir», quand>

443:32. <quand cette journée> **444:34.** <la première fois> [443:35. <impossible, pour la première fois aussi je me demandai si, même possible, elle était de plus souhaitable> 443:38. <après que j'avais détesté> 443:40. <peine me causait une tristesse à travers> 444:1. <parents étaient heureux> 444:2. <doit vous ennuyer», dis-je en pleurant à> 444:4. <pût être triste> 444:6. <duquel ils[1] étaient> 444:14. <mettais d'un côté «sentir> 444:15. <Champs-Elysées», de l'autre> 444:17. <esprit, ils[1] ne disaient plus rien; peu> 444:21. <pour toutes, et c'eut*[1] été abréger> 444:23. <l'espoir d'une connaissance intellectuelle et> 444:30. <joie la soirée de Phèdre,[1] parce qu'étant> 444:31. <théâtres une[1] station quotidienne de stylite, depuis peu si cruelle, j'avais vu l'affiche>]

444:34. <la première fois. A vrai dire, le reste de la distribution ne m'intéressant pas, cette affiche n'apportait aucun attrait nouveau pour me décider. Mais elle donnait à un des buts entre

lesquels oscillait mon indécision—aller à la matinée de *Phèdre*—une forme plus consistante, plus concrète, et (comme elle[1] était datée non du jour où j'étais mais de celui de la représentation et de l'heure même du lever du rideau) presque imminente>

444:41. <presque imminente> **445:9.** <grande déception. [444:43. <jour-là, à cette heure-là, je serais assis à ma place, prêt à entendre la Berma, et de peur> 445:7. <fermée à huit[1] heures.»]

445:9. <grande déception. Nous avions été déposés devant le square du théâtre ma grand'mère et moi, par mon père qui se rendait à la Commission et qui en quittant la maison avait dit à ma mère sur l'escalier: «Je ramènerai sans doute de Montfort,[1] tâche d'avoir un bon dîner.» {445:14-446:7}

446:7. Tant que je n'eus pas> **446:9.** <le théâtre et dont les marronniers dénudés luisaient avec des reflets métalliques dès que les becs de gaz était* allumés sous la lumière qui éclairait le détail de leurs ramures; devant le contrôle où les employés dont le choix, l'avancement, le sort dépendaient de la grande artiste qui seule avait le pouvoir dans le théâtre où des directeurs éphémères et purement nominaux se succédaient obscurément prirent nos billets>

446:17. <prirent nos billets> **446:24.** <poussière du plateau,[1] car bientôt sa calèche à deux chevaux à longue crinière allait s'arrêter devant le théâtre, elle[2] allait en descendre enveloppée dans les* fourrures>

446:27. <fourrures, et, répondant> **446:32.** <n'étant pour elle que le milieu plus ou moins bon conducteur que son talent avait à traverser, qu'un second vêtement plus extérieur dans lequel elle entrerait et qu'elle se préoccupait de trouver à la fois assez lâche pour ne pas y être gênée et assez épais pour n'y pas* avoir froid. J'eus aussi du plaisir dans la salle même, où depuis que je savais que[1] contrairement à ce que m'avait* si longtemps représenté mes imaginations enfantines,[2] il n'y avait qu'une scène pour tout le monde, je pensais qu'on devait être gêné par les autres spectateurs comme dans une foule, et[3] au contraire, comme par une disposition d'optique qui semble un symbole de toute perception chacun se sent le centre du théâtre, si bien que tout adolescent qui y va pour la première fois, tout domestique qu'on

envoie au paradis assure que sa place était la meilleure qu'il pût avoir, et au lieu de se trouver trop loin, s'est senti intimidé par la mystérieuse proximité du rideau. J'en eus davantage encore quand je commençai à distinguer derrière ce rideau baissé de la vie, des bruits confus comme on en entend sous la coquille d'un œuf, quand le poussin va sortir, qui bientôt grandirent, et tout-à-coup, de ce monde impénétrable à nos regards, mais qui nous voyait des siens, s'adressa*[4] indubitablement à nous sous la forme impérieuse de trois coups qui me firent battre le cœur, comme des signaux qu'on nous aurait faits de la planète Mars. Et, au lever du rideau, quand sur la scène une table à écrire et une cheminée assez ordinaires d'ailleurs signifièrent que les personnages qui allaient entrer seraient—non pas des acteurs venus réciter comme j'en avais vus* une fois en soirée—mais des hommes en train de vivre chez eux un jour de leur vie dans laquelle j'entrerais par effraction sans qu'ils pussent me voir,[5] à ce moment-là mon plaisir durait encore; il fut interrompu par une courte inquiétude quand, juste comme je dressais l'oreille avant que commençât la pièce, deux hommes entrèrent par la scène, bien en colère sans doute parce qu'ils parlaient assez fort>

447:24. <assez fort pour que> **447:34.** <entr'acte si long> [447:25. <avait mille> 447:28. <se sont colletés; mais> 447:31. <clapoter ici un rire, puis là un autre, je> 447:32. <et que le petit lever de rideau venait de commencer. Il fut suivi>]

447:34. <si long que le public revenu à ses places s'impatientait, tapait des pieds. J'étais effrayé; car de même que dans un procès je lisais que quelque noble cœur allait venir>

447:38. <venir, au mépris> **448:29.** <à ce qu'il voulait dire. [447:41. <pas généreusement, et> 448:1. <dépitée par la mauvaise éducation de ce public (dans lequel> 448:5. <importance), ne lui> 448:6. <mal, et je regardais> 448:8. <fureur stupide l'impression> 448:11. <n'y paraît pas encore.[1] Pourtant quand le rideau[2] se fut levé> 448:14. <écarté, qui protégeait la scène dans toutes les pièces où jouait la Berma, une actrice> 448:17. <rôle de la veuve[1] d'Hector devenait inutile. Mais une actrice[2] vint lui donner la réplique. J'avais> 448:20. <prenant la première pour la Berma, car celle-ci lui> 448:23. <de beaux[1] gestes> 448:24. <comprenais le rapport avec le texte, tandis

qu'elles soulevaient les beaux péplums—et aussi à tout moment des intonations> 448:27. <qui souvent me faisaient> 448:33. <celle[1] qu'avait la Berma>]

448:30. Mais tout d'un coup, de derrière le rideau rouge pareil à celui du sanctuaire, une femme sortit et à la peur que j'eus aussitôt—plus que celle qu'avait la Berma elle-même—qu'on la gênât en ouvrant une fenêtre>

448:32. <une fenêtre, qu'on> **449:23.** <par un autre. [448:36. <ne l'applaudissant pas assez, à ma façon—plus absolue encore que ne devait être celle de la Berma—de ne considérer> 448:41. <inflexions de la voix qui parlait, je compris> 448:43. <ressemblance avec la Berma. Mais> 449:2. <tendre mes yeux, mes oreilles, mon esprit,[1] tout ouverts vers la Berma, pour ne pas laisser> 449:9. <*Phèdre,* comme j'aurais vu vivre Phèdre, sans que son talent semblât y avoir rien ajouté. 449:12. <pouvoir les approfondir, pour tâcher d'y découvrir ce qu'elles avaient de beau—arrêter> 449:14. <moi chaque intonation de voix, chaque expression de la physionomie de la Berma; du> 449:19. <geste, et, à force d'intensité, d'arriver> 449:22. <était-il recueilli par mon>]

449:24. A un moment où la Berma[1] reste immobile, au fond de la scène, dans une attitude d'offrande, devant le décor qui représente la mer, la salle éclate*[2] en applaudissements, mais déjà elle avait changé>

449:28. <changé de place> **449:29.** Je ne pus m'empêcher de dire à ma grand'mère que je ne voyais pas bien, elle me passa sa lorgnette. Mais quand on croit à la réalité des choses, de les faire montrer au moyen d'un expédient artificiel n'est pas tout à fait la même chose que se sentir près d'elles.

449:34. Je pensais> **449:37.** <l'éloignement, était-elle plus inexacte encore. Laquelle des deux Berma était la vraie, celle que je voyais avec mes yeux ou celle que je voyais dans la lorgnette. Comment n'avais-je pas essayé avant la représentation de savoir de quel point exact et de quelle façon elle estimait qu'elle devait être vue? Cependant le moment de la déclaration à Hippolyte arriva; je l'attendais à ce morceau où à en juger par les ingénieuses significations que ses camarades me découvraient dans des parties moins belles, elle trouverait sans doute des intonations

plus surprenantes que celles que j'avais tâché d'imaginer à la maison; mais elle n'atteignit même pas celles que certes ses camarades eussent trouvées, elle passa tout le morceau au rabot d'un[1] ton uniforme, mettant ensemble dans le même sac des oppositions pourtant si tranchées, qu'une actrice à peine intelligente, qu'un élève de lycée n'en eût pas négligé l'effet; d'ailleurs elle le dit[2] tellement vite que ce fut seulement quand elle fut arrivée au dernier vers que ma pensée eut le temps[3] de dépouiller la façon dont elle avait dit les précédents.

450:11. Enfin éclata> **450:14.** <les prolonger pour que par reconnaissance, elle jouât de son mieux.

D'ailleurs au fur et à mesure que j'applaudissais, il me semblait qu'elle avait mieux joué. «Au moins, disait[1] une femme assez commune à côté de moi, elle> {450:19-450:41}

451:1. <elle se dépense> **451:18.** <auquel je devais> [451:3. <de ça, ça c'est jouer.» 451:4. <me doutant qu'elles n'en rendaient pas plus compte que de celle de la Joconde, ou de Pensée*[1] de Benvenuto> 451:9. <de l'enthousiasme> 451:10. <tombé, la déception que> 451:12. <prolonger, de l'approfondir, de ne pas quitter pour jamais, en sortant du théâtre, cette vie qui> 451:15. <espéré y apprendre>]

451:18. <auquel je devais qu'on m'est* permis d'aller l'entendre, M. de Montfort.[1] Je lui fus présenté avant le dîner par mon père qui m'appela pour cela dans son cabinet. M. de Norpois* à mon entrée se leva aussitôt, me tendit>

451:22. <me tendit la main> **452:18.** <il[1] ne me détourna pas> [451:24. <présentés, quand il était Ambassadeur, étaient> 451:27. <marque dont il pourrait dire> 451:32. <connaître, mais encore, persuadé que dans la vie des grandes capitales, en* contact> 451:35. <approfondie de l'histoire> 451:38. <sur le nouveau> 452:4. Ainsi, tout en> 452:5. <qui sait qu'il a acquis une immense expérience> 452:6. <avec sagacité, comme si j'avais été> 452:8. <tournée, et de la sorte, témoignait à la fois à mon endroit de la majestueuse> 452:14. <avaient été jusqu'ici ma vie>] {452:19-452:26}

452:26. <il ne me détourna pas de m'y adonner, mais aussitôt me parla d'elle d'une façon qui me la montra si différente de l'idée que je m'en étais faite à Combray, que je compris que

j'avais eu doublement raison de me résoudre à y renoncer, car, si je m'étais rendu compte alors que je n'avais pas de dons pour y réussir, maintenant que je voyais plus exactement ce que c'était, je n'avais même plus le désir de m'y livrer.

—J'ai justement le fils d'un de mes amis qui est comme vous, me dit M. de Montfort,[1] prenant pour parler de nos dispositions communes le même ton rassurant que si elles avaient été des dispositions non pas à la littérature mais au rhumatisme et voulant me montrer qu'on ne mourait pas. Aussi il a préféré ne pas suivre la carrière des Ambassades qui était celle de son père et il s'est mis à écrire. {452:32-453:10}

453:21. Il n'a certes pas> **453:32.** <d'úne façon[1] favorable à l'Académie des Sciences morales. [453:24. <un ouvrage sur le sentiment religieux au bord du lac Victoria-Nyanza> 453:27. <alerte, sur la réforme du recrutement dans l'armée bulgare, qui l'ont> 453:29. <joli chemin et je sais que>] {453:34-453:38}

453:39. Mon père, me voyant académicien> **454:4.** <d'un voilier. [453:40. <M. de Montfort[1] porta>] {454:5-455:19}

455:19. Mon père m'envoya chercher un petit poème en prose que j'avais fait à Combray autrefois en revenant> **455:23.** <à tous ceux qui le liraient. Mais il ne dut pas la produire sur M. de Montfort,[1] car ce fut sans nous la communiquer, sans dire une seule parole qu'il me le rendit. {455:26-455:29; 455:38-456:14}

456:15. —Eh bien, as-tu été content> **456:18.** <la Berma tantôt> [456:18. <M. de Montfort. «Il>]

456:19. <tantôt, vous vous rappelez nous en avions parlé ensemble, lui dit mon père, de même qu'à tout moment il lui rappelait [*cf.* 445:30] quelque mesure utile qu'ils avaient décidé de soutenir à la prochaine séance de la Commission, et sur le ton particulier qu'ont ensemble dans un milieu différent deux collègues à qui leurs habitudes professionnelles créent des souvenirs communs où n'ont pas accès les autres et auxquels ils s'excusent de se reporter devant eux.

456:23. —Vous avez dû> **456:40.** <j'avais eu de voir> [456:24. M. votre père> 456:25. <cette journée pouvait> 456:27. <délicat, je crois, mais je l'ai rassuré. 456:32. <l'Angleterre, qui ont encore une formidable> 456:36. M. de Montfort,[1] mille> 456:39. <question; je le prierai de>]

456:40. <j'avais eu de voir la Berma,[1] l'intérêt qu'elle excitait en moi, et qui avait encore grandi quand la représentation avait pris fin. Je n'avais qu'un moment pour lui demander cela, il fallait en profiter et faire porter mon interrogatoire sur ce qui était le plus précieux à apprendre de lui, mais qu'était-ce? Fixant mon attention tout entière sur mes impressions si confuses, je ne pouvais arriver à les exprimer, et ne songeant nullement à me faire admirer de M. de Montfort,[2] mais à obtenir de lui la vérité souhaitée, je ne cherchais pas à remplacer les mots qui me manquaient par des expressions toutes faites, de sorte que je restais d'abord balbutiant, et que finalement pour tâcher>

457:5. <tâcher de le provoquer> **457:22.** <afin de remplir> [457:8. <ennuyé de voir la mauvaise impression que l'aveu de mon incompréhension produisait sur M. de Montfort,[1] comment> 457:16. <avait de si bien. Evidemment elle est> 457:18. Et*[1] bien, si elle est> 457:20. <dit M. de Montfort[1] en>]

457:22. <remplir consciencieusement le devoir professionnel de[1] la politesse, c'est le goût parfait qu'elle apporte dans le choix de ses rôles. Elle joue> **457:28.** <dans son jeu. {457:28-457:33}

457:33. Jamais de couleurs trop voyantes, de cris exagérés,[1] la simplicité des grands artistes. Et puis cette voix admirable qui la sert si bien et dont elle joue à ravir, je dirais presque en virtuose, en musicienne!

Mon intérêt pour le jeu de la Berma[2] qui grandissait depuis que j'avais cessé de l'entendre parce qu'il était plus comprimé et limité par une nécessité extérieure[3] mais qui avait besoin de s'expliquer à moi-même et qui pendant qu'elle jouait, porté avec une intensité égale sur tout ce qu'elle offrait, dans l'indivisibilité de la vie, à mes yeux, à mes oreilles, n'avait rien séparé et distingué,[4] fut heureux de se trouver des mobiles dans ces éloges que M. de Montfort douait* à la simplicité de l'artiste,[5] les attirant par son pouvoir d'absorption, s'empara[6] d'eux comme l'optimisme d'un homme ivre enveloppe les actions de ses voisins et y trouve des raisons d'attendrissement. «C'est vrai, me disais-je, quelle belle voix, quelle absence de cris, quels costumes simples, quel goût d'avoir été choisir Phèdre*,[7] quelle grande artiste!»

—Vous avez un chef de tout premier ordre, madame [*cf.* 458:14], dit M. de Montfort[8] en reprenant d'un poulet pour lequel

Françoise, surexcitée par l'ambition de réussir pour un invité de marque un dîner semé de difficultés dignes d'elle, s'était donnée* une peine qu'elle ne prenait plus quand nous étions seuls et avait retrouvé sa manière incomparable de Combray. Ma mère attendait M. de Montfort[8] à la salade de truffes [*cf.* 459:19]. Mais l'Ambassadeur, après avoir exercé un instant sur ce mets la pénétration de son regard d'observateur, le mangea en restant enveloppé de mystère diplomatique et ne nous livra pas sa pensée. {458:11-458:13; 458:25-459:17; 459:22-459:26}

459:27. —Nous avons lu dans les journaux que vous> **460:24.** <singulièrement heureuse. [459:34. <pas[1] encore à ce trône (non sans qu'il y a* été appelé par un congrès européen, et il a même fort hésité à l'accepter, jugeant une royauté étrangère indigne de la race la plus noble> 460:2. <se tirerait de ces conjonctures assez délicates> 460:5. <renseignements tout à fait autorisés, avait> 460:7. <était tout à fait digne>] {460:26-460:28}

460:27. La chose était> **460:31.** <il a porté.

460:33. —Votre ami, M. de Norpois*,[1] qui en somme préparait> **460:43.** <dans l'événement. [460:36. <surprise. Elle[1] a été> 460:39. <ne l'aurait pas trouvée>] {461:1-463:27}

463:2. Quant à Norpois*,[1] il s'attendait à un toast correct et rien de plus. Plusieurs personnes qui étaient au nombre des assistants[2] et qui m'ont assuré qu'on ne peut pas en lisant ce toast se rendre compte de l'effet qu'il a produit, prononcé[3] et détaillé à merveille par le roi qui est un maître diseur et qui en soulignait au passage toutes les intentions,[4] m'ont raconté ce fait assez piquant, c'est que précisément à ce mot d'affinité»* qui était en somme la grande innovation du discours, et qui défraiera encore longtemps, vous verrez, les commentaires des chancelleries, Sa Majesté, avec cette bonne grâce juvénile qui lui gagne[5] tous les cœurs, sachant toute la joie qu'elle allait causer à notre ambassadeur, qui allait trouver là le juste couronnement de ses efforts, de ses rêves, pourrait-on dire et, somme toute, le bâton de maréchal de sa vieillesse, se tourna à demi vers Norpois*[6] et fixant sur lui ce regard si prenant des Gettingen*,[7] il détacha ce mot si bien trouvé «d'affinités»[8] sur un ton qui faisait savoir à tous qu'il était employé>

463:24. <employé à bon escient> **463:31.** <cher marquis?» [463:25. <que Norpois*[1] avait> 463:27. <comprends. On m'a même affirmé que le roi s'était approché de lui après le dîner quand il a tenu cercle et lui aurait dit>]

463:31. Il est certain qu'un pareil toast a plus fait que vingt ans de conversations diplomatiques pour resserrer encore les «affinités» des deux pays, selon> **463:37.** <il a rendu. [463:35. <mais vous voyez comme toute la presse européenne>] {463:38-464:1}

464:1. Je suis d'autant moins suspect en la matière> **464:9.** —«Ah! celui-là!» [464:3. <innovation de ce> 464:5. <télégramme du jeune empereur d'Allemagne> 464:8. <Norpois*[1] leva>] {464:9-464:14}

464:15. —Et mon mari> **464:28.** <surtout celle de Bricquebec.[1] [464:16. <peut-être cet été en Espagne> 464:18. <projet dont je me réjouis beaucoup. J'aimerais> 464:21. <l'emploi de votre été? 464:22. <à Bricquebec,[1] je> 464:23. —Ah! Bricquebec[1] est> 464:24. <construire de coquettes villas> 464:26. <choisir Bricquebec?[1]]

464:29. J'ai appris qu'on vient de construire à Bricquebec[1] un excellent hôtel qui lui permettra de vivre dans des conditions de confort qui lui sont nécessaires. {464:33-464:34}

464:35. —L'église de Bricquebec[1] est> **465:10.** <dit mon père. [464:37. <attraits de Bricquebec[1] pût être ses coquettes villas. 464:43. —Mais elle est> 465:4. L'église de Bricquebec[1] mérite> 465:6. <pluie vous ne pouvez aller sur la plage, vous>]

465:11. —Non, répondit M. de Monfort* avec un sourire, hier je dînais chez une femme dont vous avez peut-être entendu parler, la belle Mme Swann. {465:15-465:21}

465:21. Ma mère, curieuse de savoir quel genre de personnes les Swann pouvaient recevoir, s'enquit auprès de M. de Montfort*[1] de celles qu'il y avait rencontrées.

465:23. —Mon Dieu> **465:29.** <discrétion tempéraient la malice.

—Je dois dire, ajouta-t-il, qu'il ne faudrait pas exagérer, il y va cependant des femmes, mais... appartenant plutôt... au monde républicain qu'à la société>

465:35. <société de Swann> **465:37.** Du reste il faut dire que c'est, je crois, ce qu'ils préfèrent. {465:38-466:2}

466:2. Car Swann avait beaucoup d'amis, et sans trop s'avancer*, ni vouloir commettre d'indiscrétion, je crois pouvoir dire que non pas toutes, ni même le plus grand nombre, mais quelques-unes des amies de Swann et qui sont de fort grandes dames, ne se seraient peut-être pas montrées entièrement réfractaires depuis son mariage à l'idée d'entrer en relations avec sa femme, et vraisemblablement tous les moutons de Panurge auraient suivi. Mais il ne semble pas qu'il y ait eu du côté de Swann aucune démarche esquissée en ce sens auprès d'elles. Il est d'ailleurs curieux de voir combien Swann, qui connaît tant de monde et du plus choisi, montre d'empressement auprès de personnes qui, évidemment, sont fort loin de celles qu'il fréquentait. Moi qui ai toujours connu Swann si réservé dans le monde et portant avec tant de modestie et de tact une situation véritablement privilégiée, je m'amusais[1] à observer la satisfaction qu'il laissait éclater, sa fierté d'avoir chez lui des fonctionnaires en somme obscurs et même pour un homme aussi bien élevé que lui, j'ai été surpris de le voir remercier avec effusion le Directeur du Cabinet du ministre* des Postes, d'être venu et lui demander si Mme Swann pourrait *se permettre* d'aller voir sa femme. {466:12-466:27}

466:37. Il doit pourtant> **466:39.** <soit malheureux. {466:38-467:7}

□**467:7.** On plaisante beaucoup la façon dont il parle de sa femme comme d'une excellente épouse. Ce n'est pas aussi faux qu'on le croit. A sa manière qui n'est évidemment pas celle que tous les maris préféreraient, mais enfin, entre nous, il me semble difficile que Swann qui la connaissait depuis longtemps et qui est très fin, ne sût pas à quoi s'en tenir, il est indéniable qu'elle semble avoir de l'affection pour lui. Je ne dis pas qu'elle ne soit pas volage, et Swann lui-même ne se fait pas faute de son côté de l'être, à en croire les bonnes langues. Mais elle lui est reconnaissant de ce qu'il a fait pour elle, et ils sont tellement habitués l'un à l'autre que je crois qu'il lui aurait manqué à elle, autant qu'elle à lui. C'est, à mon avis, ce qui explique en partie ce mariage qui, il faut bien le dire, a paru au premier abord si singulier qu'on a été jusqu'à prétendre que Swann l'avait fait par intérêt et pour jouir d'une fortune assez peu honorablement acquise, version qui d'ailleurs ne tient pas debout. Je crois tout simplement qu'ils se sont mariés parce qu'ils ne pouvaient se quitter.

J'ai su depuis que ce que M. de Norpois* disait là était vrai. Du jour où Swann avait cessé d'être amoureux de Mme de Crécy, d'exiger d'elle de l'amour (auprès de quoi toute affection semble nulle), il s'était aperçu de celle qu'elle avait pour lui et que d'ailleurs elle lui manifestait moins au temps où il la persécutait de ses soupçons jaloux, même[1] inavoués. Autrefois, quand il souffrait par elle, il s'était juré que si jamais il cessait de l'aimer il vengerait son orgueil humilié, qu'il n'oublierait pas,[2] quand il la ressentirait enfin, de lui manifester implacablement, cette indifférence qu'il avait souvent jouée quand il l'aimait, mais jamais jusqu'au bout par crainte d'être pris au mot et d'être privé, par représailles, de ces rendez-vous dont il ne pouvait alors se passer. Mais une fois qu'il eut cessé d'être épris d'Odette, avec son amour même disparut le désir de lui montrer qu'il ne l'aimait pas. Il[3] voulait au contraire lui témoigner l'affection qui en lui avait survécu à l'amour, et le lui exprimait même plus tendrement qu'autrefois parce qu'il ne cherchait plus à le[4] dissimuler pour piquer au vif chez Odette un sentiment amoureux que maintenant il ne souhaitait même pas lui inspirer puisqu'il ne le ressentait plus. Il la trompait, ses amis, mon grand père* même, recommençaient à recevoir de lui des lettres où il leur demandait de le mettre en rapport avec telle ou telle personne. Elle-même menait toujours sa vie scandaleuse. Mais le chagrin trop vif qu'il en avait ressenti avait entièrement consumé,[5] comme une lampe électrique, la partie de son cerveau où il[6] avait pu y songer. S'il se disait qu'il aurait peut-être dû lui donner des conseils, au même instant il éprouvait la lassitude, l'incapacité de penser de quelqu'un qui n'a pas mangé depuis plusieurs jours, et après un ou deux efforts sans résultat, trouvait plus sage d'épargner une fatigue inutile à ses circonvolutions inanitiées*. Même comme son corps s'était usé, que son cerveau avait vieilli, il ne se contentait pas comme il eût fait autrefois de limer[7] la brosse de ses cheveux et d'essuyer son monocle, il répétait deux ou trois fois: «après tout je m'en fiche» en penchant la tête et haussant les épaules. D'ailleurs quelque plaisir qu'ils cherchassent séparément, aucun ne leur semblait[8] aussi profond que celui qu'ils avaient chacun à retrouver dans l'autre toute sa vie passée, que, sans s'en apercevoir, il y avait jour par jour enclose. Si même Odette n'avait jamais compris l'intelligence de Swann, du moins> {467:25-468:32}

468:32. <du moins savait-elle> **468:38.** <ressemblante et aimée;> [468:35. <couturier; de lui,[1] elle connaissait à fond les[2] traits particuliers du caractère que>]

□**468:38.** <et aimée.[1] Certes Swann ne connaissait plus le trouble mystérieux qu'il ressentait autrefois quand il voyait Odette dépositaire de cette sorte de portrait tout intime de lui-même. Car il n'avait plus d'amour pour elle. Mais l'amour de soi suffisait à ce qu'il trouvât encore[2] de la douceur quoique d'une autre sorte[3] nous tenons tellement aux moindres particularités[4] de notre nature, même[5] celles que nous voudrions le plus corriger, que c'est parce qu'elles ont fini par en prendre une habitude indulgente et doucement railleuse, pareille à celle[6] que nous en avons nous-mêmes, que les vieilles liaisons ont quelque chose de la douceur et de la force des affections de famille. Le lien qui nous unit à un être se trouve sanctifié quand cet être se place au même point de vue que nous pour juger une de nos tares. Et parmi ces particularités,[7] il y en avait aussi qui appartenaient autant à l'intelligence de Swann qu'à son caractère, et que pourtant en raison de la racine qu'ils avaient[8] en celui-ci, Odette avait plus facilement discernées. Elle se plaignait que ce ne fussent pas ceux-là[9] qu'on reconnût quand il écrivait,[10] autant que dans ses lettres ou dans sa conversation.[11] Elle lui conseillait de leur faire la part plus grande. Elle l'aurait voulu parce que c'était ceux qu'elle préférait en lui, mais comme elle les préférait parce qu'ils étaient plus à lui, elle n'avait peut-être pas tort de souhaiter qu'on les retrouvât dans ses[12] études. Cette[13] période heureuse d'affection et de calme qui avait suivit* la fin de l'amour de Swann, n'avait pas[14] duré. A cause de la fille qu'ils avaient eue[15] et qu'il adorait, elle trouvait qu'il aurait dû l'épouser comme d'autres hommes du monde avaient épousé des amies à elle, vis-à-vis desquelles elle souffrait de sa situation restée irrégulière, mais elle était persuadée que Swann ne le voudrait pas, et il s'était déve-

loppé chez elle un caractère mauvais[16] qu'elle tenait des circonstances, une aigreur qui ne lui était pas naturelle et qui lui inspirait à l'égard de Swann de méchants propos. Et certes, quand elle avait rêvé d'être sa femme, elle n'avait pas plus souhaité qu'autrefois se lier avec les amies de Swann, qu'elle ne connaissait pas, et que déjà au temps où il était le plus épris d'elle, elle avait elle-même déclaré qu'elle ne voulait pas connaître, mais[17] chez* des personnes placées plus immédiatement au-dessus d'elle —celles probablement que M. de Montfort[18] vient de nous dire qu'elle les recevait maintenant—; qui[19] allaient aux bals de l'Elysée où on lui avait refusé une invitation, qu'elle rencontrait en visite chez ses anciennes amies mariées et à qui on évitait de la présenter [*cf.* 470:27]. C'était Swann au contraire qui dans les heures où il s'imaginait Odette devenue sa femme se représentait invariablement le moment où il l'amènerait et surtout amènerait sa fille chez la princesse des Laumes.[20] C'était la seule image que revêtit[21] son ambition mondaine pour elles deux. Il ne désirait pas les présenter ailleurs, mais il s'attendrissait quand il imaginait[22] ce que la princesse dirait de lui à sa femme, ce que sa femme dirait de lui à la princesse, comme la princesse aimerait sa fille, la gâterait, l'en rendrait fier.

Les Laumes n'étaient pas pour lui des gens du monde comme les autres. Il les aimait, ils avaient gardé dans leur*[23] esprit un indéluctable*[24] prestige; il se savait apprécié d'eux; il caressait l'idée de leur montrer son bonheur. L'image de cette première entrevue de sa fille avec la princesse l'aurait décidé au mariage. Comme toutes les images antérieures qui nous déterminent,[25] elle ne se réalisa pas, ou se réalisa[26] bien autrement qu'il l'avait esquissée.

Cependant quand Odette était devenue aussi violente et disputeuse, lui-même alors avait été atteint d'une sorte de jalousie sans désir et sans amour, d'une curiosité de ce qu'elle faisait[27] comme on en éprouve à l'égard d'une domestique par qui l'on se croit bafoué. Il se vengeait en disant à ses amis, en s'arrangeant à ce qu'on[28] lui répétât, non pas même qu'il ne l'épouserait jamais, mais qu'il romprait prochainement tout à fait avec elle. Et elle n'était pas sûre que ce ne fut* pas vrai, car si elle était conduite dans une moitié de son existence, (qui en tant qu'il s'agissait de Swann était terminée), par le* seule maxime qu'elle eût longtemps été capable de concevoir et qui était qu'on peut tout faire aux hommes qui vous aiment, car ils sont si «idiots»,[29] se traduisait dans son visage par un petit clignement d'yeux méchants qui[30] semblait dire: «Ayez pas peur, il ne cassera rien» [*cf.* 468:6],—en revanche une femme sculpteur dont elle avait fait la connaissance quelques années auparavant et pour qui elle avait une grande admiration, lui avait appris une autre maxime qui se présentait maintenant souvent à l'esprit d'Odette quand on lui parlait de Swann, et lui faisait alors lever les sourcils et les épaules d'un air découragé comme si elle avait voulu dire: «Après tout, il n'y aurait rien d'impossible. Ce serait bien ma chance!» C'était:[31] «qu'on pût*[32] s'attendre à tout des hommes quand ils n'aiment plus, parce qu'ils sont si mufles» [cf. 467:38]. Mais Swann[33] au contraire était persuadé qu'elle n'ajoutait pas foi à ses menaces et qu'elle en riait. Pour ce* qu'elle s'effrayât, il la laissait sans argent, décidait de rester des semaines sans la voir, mais aussitôt, changement[34] d'avis,[35] en se rappelant de nouveau la bonté qu'elle[36] avait eue pour lui, des* choses charmantes qu'elle avait faites, il allait revenir près d'elle, trouvant qu'il[37] devait l'épouser, quand elle, irritée et de plus en plus amère, refusait de lui envoyer sa fille, disant qu'elle allait l'emmener avec elle en voyage. Comme c'était toujours après quelque plaisir dont Swann l'avait privée, qu'elle mettait ainsi un obstacle à ce qu'il vit* leur enfant, tout d'un coup se désagrégeaient dans son esprit, tant de doux souvenirs qui adhéraient à Odette pour lui faire une sorte de personnalité de tout repos, pareille à celle de tel ou tel des membres de sa propre famille que Swann avait le plus aimés.

Et réfléchissant[38] qu'elle était seulement de la matière humaine[39] sur laquelle aucune garantie sociale, aucun nom respecté, ne[40] sont jamais imprimés que superficiellement, et dans laquelle le crime peut toujours apparaître comme le cancer ou la mort dans un organisme sain ou une vie jeune, de même qu'autrefois il s'était demandé si Odette n'était pas une femme entretenue, maintenant il se disait qu'elle était peut-être une de ces aventurières dont parlent souvent les chroniques judiciaires[41] et qu'il avait crues enfermées dans une certaine caste, qui se servent de l'enfant qu'elles ont eu d'un homme riche pour le faire chanter, se faire épouser par lui et l'assassiner après avoir capté sa fortune,[42] que c'était d'une de ces criminelles qu'il voulait faire sa femme. Mais cette supposition il ne pouvait pas plus s'y attendre[43] qu'autrefois à l'autre,[44] il relevait avec sa main la brosse de ses cheveux, et ne pensait plus à cela, car ses idées s'étaient brouillées. Ce n'était pas ses amis qui auraient pu sur ce sujet les rendre plus claires et lui faire adopter un avis. Sans doute, ils ne se faisaient pas faute de lui en donner, blâmaient à qui mieux mieux ce qu'ils appelaient la honteuse faiblesse de Swann à l'égard d'Odette. Mais lui savait bien que cette faiblesse c'était lui-même qui, soit pour se faire plaindre, soit par adresse de narrateur ou malice de taquin, et pour grossir ses effets, la leur avait ainsi dépeinte, qui les en avait habilement persuadés comme malgré lui, si bien qu'ils croyaient l'avoir constatée. Mais il savait lui-même que ce qu'il leur avait raconté était incomplet ou tendancieux, qu'il leur avait tu bien de ses exigences auxquelles Odette se pliait[45] sans un murmure, ce que n'auraient jamais fait les femmes ou les maîtresses de ces amis que ceux-ci croyaient de bonne foi plus douces avec eux qu'Odette[46] avec Swann. S'ils avaient tout su, s'ils avaient pu voir la fréquente docilité, la résignation d'Odette, ils eussent été étonnés et auraient sans doute échangé leur opinion contre une opposée qui n'eût peut-être pas été plus vraie car ils n'étaient pas plus intelligents, ni plus sages que Swann, qui[47] n'avait pas réussi à s'en faire une définitive sur Odette.

Quand il la revoyait, la gentillesse qu'elle lui montrait, les bons sentiments qu'elle lui exprimait, le rendaient honteux d'avoir formé[48] de tels soupçons, de ne pas l'avoir encore épousée. Et pourtant s'il lui refusait encore quelque chose, de nouveau[49] il ne pouvait plus voir sa fille. Etait-ce une coïncidence, [50] il aurait voulu le savoir, mais une fatigue cérébrale l'empêchait d'y songer longtemps. Après tout puisque c'est en tout être et sans acception d'origine que le mal peut se former, puisque le père de l'un des plus honnêtes gens avec qui il[51] fut lié, avait, illustre grand seigneur français, étranglé sa femme, si Odette était en train de devenir[52] méchante, peut-être n'y était-elle pas fatalement prédisposée et était-ce lui qui était en partie responsable des mauvais sentiments qu'il faisait naître en elle. Pourtant,[53] même une fois marié, il se demandait encore parfois si ce mariage n'avait pas été le résultat d'un chantage, s'il n'était pas une victime, si Odette ne l'empoisonnerait pas un jour. Mais il trouvait impossible de découvrir l'origine cachée d'actions pareilles sous les propos qu'elle lui tenait et qui depuis que contre tout espoir il l'avait épousée, n'étaient plus que de tendresse et de bonté, le bonheur n'ayant pas rendu sa nature meilleure, mais entièrement effacé cette acrimonie du langage, cette violence du caractère qui n'étaient pas foncières chez elle, ne venaient que des souffrances de son amour-propre, comme ces états morbides dont la cause accidentelle est due à une mauvaise hygiène et qui cèdent entièrement à un changement de régime. Elle était heureuse de pouvoir recevoir chez elle des personnes avec qui elle n'aurait jamais cru qu'elle put* entrer en relations. Et Swann appliquait[54] peut-être un peu en cela ces mêmes dispositions qui, si souvent, dans des pays ou des milieux différents, l'avaient poussé à se rebâtir une position nouvelle et appropriée, travaillant[55] de tout son cœur à servir les ambitions de sa femme. Il avait épousé avec Odette ses goûts, sa situation. Tout en continuant à fréquenter seul ses relations d'autrefois à qui sa délicatesse lui interdisait d'imposer Odette quand elles ne lui demandaient pas spontanément à la connaître, avec[56] sa femme c'était une nouvelle vie qu'il recommençait à pied d'œuvre, au milieu d'êtres nouveaux, dont le rang (et par conséquent le plaisir d'amour-propre qu'il pouvait avoir à les recevoir) ne[57] lui apparaissait pas relativement aux gens plus brillants qu'il connaissait, mais relativement aux relations antérieures d'Odette et au[58] but qu'elle se proposait.[59] A vrai dire, si maintenant c'était avec ces inélégants fonctionnaires, avec ces femmes,[60] parure équivoque des bals du[61] ministère, qu'il ambitionnait de se lier plus étroitement[62] en relations, il semble qu'il aurait dû ne parler de ces amis nouveaux qu'avec discrétion, cette modestie qu'il montrait autrefois chez une* grand'tante quand il dissimulait de son mieux ses invitations à Frohsdorf[63] ou à Buckingham-Palace, et dont, au dire de M. de Montfort,[64] il se départissait maintenant. Mais c'est que nos vertus ne restent pas quelque chose de libre, de flottant, dont nous gardons la disponibilité perpétuelle; elles finissent par s'associer si étroitement dans notre esprit avec les actions à l'occasion desquelles nous nous sommes faits* un devoir de les exercer, que si surgit pour nous une activité d'un autre ordre, elle nous prend au dépourvu et sans que nous ayons même l'idée qu'elle pourrait comporter ces vertus. Swann, empressé avec ces nouvelles relations et les citant avec fierté, était comme ces grands artistes modestes ou généreux qui, s'ils se mettent à la fin de leur vie à se mêler de cuisine ou de jardinage, étalent une satisfaction naïve des louanges qu'on donne à leurs plats ou à leurs plates-bandes et n'admettent pas pour eux la critique comme ils font pour leurs chefs-d'œuvre; ou qui donnant une de leurs toiles pour rien, ne peuvent sans mauvaise humeur perdre quarante sous aux dominos.

—M. Swann est ami du Comte de Chambord, je crois, dis-je à M. de Montfort, dans la peur que la conversation ne changeât de sujet.

—Oui, en effet répondit M. de Montfort[65] en se tournant vers moi et en appliquant visiblement à ma modeste personne ses grandes facultés> {468:38-471:35}

471:35. <facultés de travail> **473:15.** <n'est pas grand'chose. [471:38. <du profond respect que j'éprouve pour> 471:39. <le Prince sans cependant avoir de relations personnelles avec lui, ce que rendrait difficile ma situation, si peu officielle qu'elle soit, en vous citant> 472:2. <permis de lui demander comment il avait trouvé Mme Swann. Cela> 472:10. <de Chambord[1] demanda> 472:12. <M. de Montfort;[1] les> 472:12. <de Chambord[2] a> 472:19. <esprit, bien loin d'être un sot. 472:22. <été, monsieur, demanda> 472:24. Alors avec une> 472:25. <la mesure habituelle> 472:26. <répondit M. de Montfort.[1] 472:28. <rentre dans une forme particulièrement appréciée de l'esprit de conversation à condition qu'on l'accompagne d'enjouement, il éclata> 472:31. <instants, humecta les> 472:32. <et fit vibrer> 472:34. —Elle est *charmante.* 472:37. <le sujet enivrant

---

471:37. <je ne crois pas que ce soit franchir les bornes du respect que je professe, à l'égard du Prince sans cependant>

472:10. ([1]Paris). 472:12. ([1]Norpois) ([2]Paris). 472:26. ([1]Norpois). 472:38. ([1]Norpois). 472:41. ([1]importance et même aux) 473:2. ([1]avait dit). 473:6. ([1]Norpois). 473:36. ([1]tout cela). 473:42. ([1]dit à M. de Norpois, mais). 474:1. ([1]vous n'êtes pas).

des> 472:38. <de Montfort,[1] inclinant> 472:39. <avec politesse, comme> 472:41. <importance[1] aux* questions> 473:2. <dont mon père nous disait[1] que Bismarck> 473:6. <de Montfort[1] (qui> 473:7. <doutes encore plus affreux que> 473:9. <moi-même, que ce que> 473:10. <plus divin au> 473:11. <partage pas complètement cette> 473:13. <il faut avouer qu'il en joue>] {437:16-473:20}

473:20. Dans un temps> **473:30.** <ceux du dedans. [473:25. <partout, on a le droit de demander à un écrivain autre chose que d'être un bel esprit à la façon de Voiture et que de nous faire oublier> 473:28. <sur les mérites de pure forme>]

473:30. On a le droit, à une époque comme la nôtre de demander à un auteur de faire plus que d'agencer des mots d'une façon plus ou moins harmonieuse. {473:30-473:34}

473:35. Celle de Bergotte est agréable, je n'en> **474:1.** <péchés de jeunesse. [473:36. <total elle[1] est bien mièvre, bien mince et bien peu viril*. 473:42. <(je l'avais dit[1] mais je ne le pensais pas)>]

474:1. Après tout, pour*[1] n'être* pas le seul qui se croit* un poète à son heure et qui n'en ait pas de pareils sur la conscience. Mais on y voit la mauvaise>

474:5. <mauvaise influence> **474:12.** <avant les bœufs, [474:6. <qu'il n'y a là aucune des qualités de Bergotte> 474:7. <dans l'art du style dont à votre âge> 474:10. <déjà ce défaut ce contresens>] {474:12-474:22}

474:12. Et j'avoue que toutes les chinoiseries de forme me semblent bien vaines, même dans l'œuvre de Bergotte. Il n'empêche que chez Bergotte cette œuvre est infiniment>

474:22. <infiniment supérieure au personnage. Ah!> **474:32.** <de Phœbus et qui rend plus déplaisantes encore les choses qu'il dit tant et les dit mal. [474:27. <compagnie que ce Bergotte.]

□**474:39.** Le[1] hasard voulut qu'à un moment je me souvins de cette pièce de mon oncle Charles*[2] à Combray [*cf.* 494:28]

474:34. Je ne sais si c'est Vaulabelle ou Sainte-Beuve qui dit que Vigny était de même. Mais Bergotte n'a jamais écrit Cinq-Mars ni le Cachet rouge.

474:39. ([1]Ce nom de Vaulabelle me fit souvenir de cette petite pièce) ([2]Adolphe) ([3]pavillon des Champs-Elysées). 475:2. ([1]impressions). 475:5.

devant laquelle je passais après le déjeuner avant de monter lire du Bergotte, et d'où s'échappait, comme elle était plus basse que le jardin, cette odeur humide et renfermée, qui m'avait enveloppé d'une telle atmosphère de joie quand je l'avais retrouvée, sans la reconnaître d'abord, dans le petit pavillon[3] aux water-closets des Champs-Elysées. Et rapprochant ce plaisir si humble et si vif de ceux que j'avais trouvés dans les livres d'un simple «joueur de flûte» tandis que j'avais tant de difficultés à écrire un essai>] {474:39-474:42}

474:42. <un essai ou seulement> **475:4.** <une grande valeur> [474:43. <ma médiocrité intellectuelle> 475:2. <certaines confessions,[1] ou une lecture>]

475:5. <valeur et me faisait juger par moi-même à ces moments-là comme un être sublime. Mais cet état, mon poème en prose le reflétait: nul doute que M. de Montfort[1] n'en eût saisi de suite ce que j'y trouvais beau et ce que je n'avais[2] vu ainsi qu'à travers une illusion aussi factice que celle que produit l'ivresse. Il[3] vient de m'apprendre que jugé au contraire du dehors, objectivement, par le connaisseur le mieux disposé et le plus intelligent, quelle place infime j'occupais parmi les plus *[blanc]* je me sentais>

475:12. <me sentais> **475:39.** <qu'analyses perpétuelles> [475:16. <génie,[1] maintenant c'est tout entier dans l'étroite médiocrité où l'opinion de M. de Montfort l'avait soudain enfermé et restreint. 475:25. <s'inscrire à l'Ambassade et> 475:27. <honneur dans une certaine mesure par ses écrits, j'aurais passé> 475:30. <seul et il prétendait ne pas être invité seul> 475:32. <étant en somme célibataire> 475:34. <si j'avais été> 475:37. <moral que prend Bergotte>]

([1]Norpois) ([2]n'avais cru tel qu'à travers) ([3]Il venait de m'apprendre au contraire quelle place infime était la mienne (quand j'étais jugé du dehors, objectivement, par le connaisseur le mieux disposé et le plus intelligent [*parenthesis not closed*] 476:16. ([1]génie, tenait maintenant contracté tout entier dans l'étroite médiocrité où M. de Norpois l'avait soudain enfermé et restreint.) (475:39. ([1]remords maladifs). 476:2. ([1]doive). 476:10. ([1]Norpois). 476:15. ([1]Monfort*). 476:19. ([1]dirai). 476:25. ([1]Norpois). 476:42. ([1]jolie; c'est le moment). 477:1. ([1]fou. M. de Norpois savait qu'il n'y a rien que de naturel dans le plaisir de regarder). 477:7. ([1]disant qu'il parlerait de moi).

475:39. <perpétuelles de scrupules douloureux, de remords[1] angoissés et maladifs, pour des peccadilles, et même pour rien du tout, quand il montre tant d'inconscience et de cynisme dans sa vie.

476:1. Bref, j'éludai> **476:19.** <notre amphitryon. [476:2. De sorte que je ne suppose pas que je ne dois*[1] pas* être> 476:3. <auprès de Bergotte, et> 476:5. <l'inviter avec moi. 476:7. <car c'est au fond un malade. 476:10. <de Montfort,[1] profitant> 476:15. <Montfort[1] parut> 476:17. —Oui, en effet, une>]

476:19. Je vous dirais*[1] que je l'ai peu vue, elle est partie après le dîner.

476:22. Mais je vois> **477:6.** <seconder ses desseins. [476:25. <de Montfort[1] était pour un instant encore dans> 476:39. <d'une jolie maison> 476:42. <maison aussi jolie,[1] le moment où> 477:1. <aperçu que son interlocuteur est fou.[1] Ainsi M. de Montfort savait qu'il est naturel d'avoir du plaisir à regarder> 477:4. <quelqu'un vous* parle avec chaleur d'une femme, de faire> 477:5. <amoureux, et de l'en>]

477:7. Mais en offrant[1] de parler de moi, ce qui me permettrait, comme une divinité de l'Olympe qui a pris la légèreté d'un souffle ou plutôt l'aspect du sage Mentor, de pénétrer, invisible>

477:11. <invisible, dans le salon> **477:21.** <dans l'eau. [477:16. <de sa famille, ce potentat qui allait user pour moi du grand>] {477:21-477:23}

477:23. Il est difficile à chacun> **477:34.** <qu'ils ont dit> [477: 25. <ses gestes apparaissent> 477:26. <grandissant jusqu'à l'infini le champ sur lequel est obligée de s'étendre la mémoire des autres> 477:29. <accessoires de notre gesticulation,[1]

477:20. <blanches et si fripées, qu'elles avaient l'air> [*Here, on the other hand,* Grasset A *conforms with the Pléiade.*]

477:29. ([1]discours). 477:34. ([1]même en ce qui concerne la) ([2]du feuilletoniste selon qui) ([3]événement ou d'un) ([4]«Qui s'en souviendra dans dix ans?» à la troisième) ([5]ne parle-t-il pas souvent d'un fait) ([6]d'un) ([7]valeur, qui date de l'époque des Pharaons et qu'on connaît encore intégralement. Peut-être) ([8]dans laquelle) ([9]cela, si vous parlez de moi à Mme Swann, ma) ([10]vanté, au cas où M. de Norpois m'aurait mal) ([11]vrai.) ([12]Mais en le disant je sentais bien que c'était devenu) ([13]j'avais essayé) ([14]Norpois)

de> 477:30. <dans la conscience de ceux avec qui nous causons et que>]

477:34. <ont dit et dont il ne pensent pas qu'on pourra confronter cette variante à aucun souvenir subsistant. Mais il est au fond bien possible que, même[1] pour la vie millénaire de l'hu-

---

([15]regard vertical, étroit et oblique) ([16]solide, la ligne fuyante d'une de ses faces) ([17]circonstance et pour M. de Norpois, c'était moi) ([18]Norpois) ([19]diaboliquement des personnes) ([20]fou insoupçonné avec) ([21]sur des passants que nous nous accordions à trouver vulgaires, nous montre) ([22]Norpois) ([23]Norpois) ([24]prix (par conséquent, sans doute d'une grande difficulté), pensa) ([25]essentielle—à cause) ([26]de ma part) ([27]donc, et que je connaissais) ([28]elle, et ce fut peut-être un malheur moins grand que je ne croyais.) ([29]en l'esprit de qui) ([30]demeure) ([31]aurais) ([32]Norpois) ([33]de la maîtresse de la maison que) ([34]la) ([35]maison) ([36]Norpois) ([37]soir; je songeais de nouveau) ([38]entendre avait d'autant plus besoin d'être complété qu'il était bien loin d'égaler) ([39]promis; aussi s'assimilait-il) ([40]le nourrir, par exemple ces mérites que M. de Norpois avait) ([41]et que mon esprit avait bu) ([42]Or mon) 480:42. ([1]esprit). 481:1. ([1]d'art, etc.», celle-ci). 481:8. ([1]Chateaubriand) ([2]étaient apparues mais la leur ajoutant, et risquant un acte de foi dans la valeur de leur œuvre, se disent: «Après tout!»; et qu'on pense à ceux qui croient) ([3]future des écrits de laquelle ils pourront jouir ainsi et) ([4]intelligence) ([5]future; qu'on pense encore à ceux). 481:33. ([1]n'ait). 481:37. ([1]«hautes et pures» impressions). 483:11. ([1]Norpois). 483:13. ([1]Paris). 483:15. ([4]mère, j'aime). 483:21. ([1]Norpois). 483:25. ([1]a-t-il donc dit... «avec les princes on ne sait jamais>»). 483:39. ([1]Mais de tous) ([2]qu'il) ([3]celui qui) ([4]plusieurs) ([5]Norpois). 486:38. ([1]air, au coin de la Rue Royale, et j'en achetai une de la Berma. Les admirations). 487:2. ([1]répondre, comme) ([2]rechange, et). 487:23. ([1]que le jour de l'an n'était pas un jour différent des autres, qu'il n'était pas le premier). 487:33. ([1]univers). 487:37. ([1]était la même, comme sont les années nouvelles que notre désir, sans pouvoir les atteindre elles-mêmes et les changer, recouvre) ([2]jour de l'an) ([3]en vain; je sentais qu'il ne savait pas qu'on l'appelait le jour de l'an, qu'il finissait dans le crépuscule d'une façon que je me rappelais: dans le vent). 488:31. ([1]comme doués d'une). 488:41. ([1]grande que) 490:35. ([1]dire: «Vous savez ils ne vous gobent pas!»). 490:42. ([1]d'un œil favorable). 491:20. ([1]douté: en effet la lettre). 491:21. ([1]Norpois) 491:22. ([1]que celles-là). 491:28. ([1]Mais moi). 491:29. ([1]Car que ce fut* une erreur, je) ([2]Et) ([3]décrit avec tant d'exactitude, dans ma lettre, certaines) ([4]des sentiments généreux que, pour que d'après elles Swann ne les eût pas aussitôt reconstitués et ne) ([5]ces nobles sentiments, il ne les eût jamais ressentis lui-même, il fut*). 492:7. ([1]prévoir) ([2]j'avais pu). 493:37. ([1]résistait; ses pommettes enflammées par l'effort étaient rouges et rondes comme des cerises; par moment elles* les secouaient*, riant sans fin comme si je l'eusse chatouillée; je la tenais serrée entre mes jambes comme un cerisier après lequel j'aurais voulu gripper*; et au milieu) ([2]goûter; aussitôt je pris la lettre). 494:15. ([1]Peut-être c'est du moins une supposition que j'ai faite beaucoup plus tard en me rappelant ces paroles avait-elle obscurément senti que) ([2]su remarquer que) ([3]s'en fut*) ([4]quoi) ([5]que de rester tranquille auprès d'elle. 495:9. ([1]moins;

manité, la philosophie des[2] feuilletonistes pour qui tout est promis à l'oubli soit moins vraie qu'une philosophie contraire qui prédirait la conservation de toutes choses. Dans le même journal où le moraliste de la première colonne nous dit d'un événement,[3] d'un chef-dœuvre: qui[4] s'en souviendra dans dix ans; à la troisième page, le compte rendu de l'Académie des Inscriptions rappelle[5] un fait par lui-même moins important, un[6] poème de bien moindre valeur[7] et qui datait de l'époque des Pharaons. Peut-être n'est-ce pas aussi vrai pour la courte vie humaine. Toujours est-il que dix ans plus tard dans une maison d'où M. de Norpois* venait de partir, on me raconta qu'il avait parlé d'une soirée d'autrefois où[8] il avait «vu le moment où j'allais lui baiser les mains», je fus aussi étonné que quand je lus pour la première fois qu'on savait [*cf.* 478:25] exactement la liste des chasseurs qu'Assourbanipal invitait à ses battues, dix siècles avant Jésus-Christ.

—Oh! monsieur, lui dis-je, si vous faisiez cela,[9] ma vie vous appartiendrait. Mais je tiens à vous faire remarquer que je ne connais pas Mme Swann et que je ne lui ai jamais été présenté.

J'avais voulu ajouter cela par scrupule et pour ne pas avoir l'air de m'être vanté,[10] si M. de Montfort m'avait mal compris, de quelque chose qui n'était pas rien.[11] Et[12] je le dis pour achever ce que je voulais dire mais en sentant bien que c'était devenu inutile, car dès les premiers mots par lesquels j'essayais[13] de remercier M. de Monfort*,[14] j'avais vu passer sur son visage une expression d'hésitation et de mécontentement et dans ses yeux, de regard[15] étroit vertical et oblique, (comme dans le dessin en perspective d'un solide,[16] une de ses faces opposées au spectateur), qui s'adresse à cet interlocuteur invisible qu'on a en soi-

---

ils). 495:17. ([1]lequel) ([2]ne les entend). 495:23. ([1]celle de). 495:28. ([1]manger, je me mettais à table, quand). 496:8. ([1]«insidieuses» et plus «larvées».) 497:22. ([1]de mouillé). 499:33. ([1]de ces) ([2]*rectam*, et beaucoup de mots, de cette lettre, d'une grande écriture, semblaient soulignés, parce que la barre des *t* étaient* tracée non au travers d'eux, mais au-dessus, et traçaient un trait sous le mot correspondant de la ligne supérieure: «Mon). 500:18. ([1]vais guère non plus). 502:33. ([1]Norpois). 502:39. ([1]pu dire, en effet, c'était). 502:41. ([1]Mais d'ailleurs ce) ([2]n'influa probablement que). 503:11. ([1]qu'embaumait). 503:42. ([1]perpétuellement, plus formidable et plus désirée qu'à Versailles jadis l'apparition du Roi, la possibilité de les rencontrer, et où habituellement). 504:7. ([1]Swann, si au moment où je passais, l'un) ([2]ils me serraient) ([3]disaient).

même, au moment où on lui dit quelque chose que l'interlocuteur vivant avec qui on parlait jusqu'ici—dans la circonstance,[17] moi—ne doit pas entendre. Je compris aussitôt que ces mots que je venais de dire et qui, à peine en rapport avec l'effusion reconnaissante qui m'avait envahi, m'avaient paru devoir toucher M. de Monfort*[18] et achever de le décider à une intervention qui lui eût donné si peu de peine, et m'eut* causé tant de joie [*cf.* 479: 10], étaient peut-être entre tous ceux qu'auraient pu chercher diaboliquement[19] et inutilement des personnes qui m'auraient voulu du mal, les seuls mots qui pussent avoir pour résultat de l'y faire renoncer. En les entendant en effet, de même qu'au moment où un homme[20] avec qui nous causions agréablement, et venions d'échanger des impressions que nous avions pu croire semblables, sur[21] la vulgarité d'un cortège d'invités, nous montre tout à coup l'abîme qui le sépare de nous en ajoutant négligemment en tâtant sa poche: «c'est malheureux que je n'ai* pas mon revolver, il n'en serait pas resté un seul» [*cf.* 479:21], M. de Monfort*[22] qui jusque-là avait cru que je pensais volontiers à Mme Swann et à sa fille parce que c'étaient de jolies femmes et comme j'aurais pensé à d'autres folies femmes, que je m'intéressais aux relations de Swann comme à celles de tout autre homme à la mode, M. de Monfort*[23] qui savait que rien n'était moins précieux et plus facile pour l'ordinaire des gens que d'être recommandé et présenté à Mme Swann, en voyant que cela était pour moi d'un tel prix[24] ce qui signifiait probablement que c'était d'une grande difficulté, pensa que le désir, normal en apparence, que j'avais exprimé devait cacher quelque pensée différente, quelque visée suspecte, quelque faute antérieure, peut-être une indignité essentielle[25] à cause desquelle* étant sûr de déplaire à Mme Swann en lui faisant une commission de[26] moi, personne n'avait jusqu'ici voulu s'en charger. Et je compris aussitôt que cette commission, il ne le* ferait jamais, qu'il pourrait voir Mme Swann tous les jours sans pour cela parler une seule fois de moi. Il lui demanda [*cf.* 479:35] cependant un renseignement que je désirais avoir, et chargea mon père de me le transmettre. Mais il n'avait pas cru devoir dire pour qui il le demandait. Elle ignorerait donc,[27] et ce fut peut-être un malheur moins grand que je ne croyais, et que je connaissais M. de Norpois* et que je désirais tant aller chez elle.[28] Car la seconde de ces nouvelles eut* probablement ôté à la première beaucoup d'une efficacité qui n'était du reste peut-être pas si grande. Car pour Mme Swann en[29] qui l'idée de sa propre vie et de sa propre maison[30] n'éveillaient* aucun trouble mystérieux, une personne qui la connaissait, qui allait chez elle, ne lui semblait pas un être fabuleux comme à moi aurait*[31] jeté dans ses fenêtres une pierre si j'avais pu y écrire que je connaissais M. de Monfort*,[32] persuadé que la connaissance d'une telle nouvelle m'eut* donné beaucoup plus de prestige aux yeux de[33] Mme Swann que ne l'eût indisposée contre moi cette grossièreté. Mais même si j'avais pu me rendre compte que la commission de M. de Monfort* fut* restée sans grande utilité pour moi ou même n'eût pu que me nuire, je n'aurais pas eu, s'il avait consenti à le*[34] faire, le courage de l'en décharger et de renoncer à la volupté, si funestes qu'en pussent être les suites, que mon nom et ma personne pénétrassent un moment auprès de Gilberte dans sa demeure,[35] dans sa pensée, dans sa vie inconnues.*

Quand M. de Montfort[36] fut parti [*cf.* 480:19], mon père jeta un coup d'œil sur le journal du soir,[37] tandis que ma mère qui avait remarqué pendant la soirée qu'il venait un peu de froid par une porte, essayait une combinaison de tenture qui put l'intercepter dorénavant. Je songeais de nouveau à la Berma. Le plaisir que j'avais eu à l'entendre[38] avait été bien loin d'égaler celui que je m'étais promis.[39] Mais d'autant plus mon impression avait-elle besoin d'être complétée et s'assimilait-elle immédiatement tout ce qui était susceptible de la[40] nourrir, comme ces mérites que M. de Monfort* avait reconnus à la Berma et[41] qui y avait bu d'un seul trait comme un pré trop sec sur qui on verse de l'eau. Mon[42] père me passa le journal en me désignant cet entrefilet: «La représentation>

480:29. «La représentation de *Phèdre*> **481:4.** <je m'écriai:> [480:34. <éclatant. Nous reviendrons. 480:42. <assister.» Aussitôt que mon intelligence[1] eût* formé cette idée> 481:1. <«d'art»,[1] elle se> 481:2. <théâtre, elle lui ajouta>]

481:4. <je m'écriai:

—Quelle grande artiste!

481:5. Sans doute> **481:8.** <du génie> [481:6. Mais plutôt, qu'on pense à tant>]

481:8. <génie de Châteaubriant*,[1] se remplissent tellement de cette idée de génie que, repensant alors à leurs propres pages ils ne les voient plus telles qu'elles leur avaient[2] apparues* d'abord mais en les leur ajoutant, et se disent: «après tout», risquent un acte de foi dans la valeur de leur œuvre à ceux qui croient en l'amour qu'a pour eux une maîtresse dont ils ne connaissent que les trahisons, à ceux qui espèrent alternativement une survie incompréhensible dès qu'ils pensent à la gloire future[3] de leur œuvre dont ils pourront aussi jouir et un néant rassurant quand leur pensée[4] se reporte au contraire aux fautes que sans lui ils auraient à expier dans une vie future,[5] à ceux qu'arrête la beauté totale d'un voyage>

481:30. <d'un voyage dont> **481:36.** <qui lui manquait. [481:33. <une seule de celle qui nous rendait le plus heureux qui n'aient*[1] été>]

481:37. Je me persuadai que je n'avais pas de regret à avoir. J'avais en somme assisté à une interprétation qui était capitale au regard des plus grands critiques et qui me permettrait s'ils écrivaient des études sur le* Berma dans le rôle de Phèdre de savoir exactement de quoi ils voulaient parler, de pouvoir me reporter à une des plus curieuses[1] impressions d'art de ce temps que je savais posséder dans ma mémoire. {481:37-483:7}

483:8. Cependant, mon père> **483:23.** <à ce qu'elle croyait. [483:11. <père Montfort[1] a été un peu vieux jeu. Quand> 483:13. <de Chambord,[1] j'ai> 483:15. <tout, dit ma mère[1] cessant d'arranger la portière, j'aime> 483:20. <intelligent, moi qui le vois> 483:21. <mon père qui, heureux de voir que ma mère appréciait M. de Montfort,[1] voulait lui persuader>] {483:24-483:25}

483:25. Comment a-t-il[1] dit... avec des princes on ne sait jamais?> **483:39.** <*de M. Poirier.* [483:30. <gens bien, des> 483:32. <pêcher tous ces gens là?* 483:33. <remarqué, dit ma mère, avec quelle finesse il a dit: «C'est> 483:38. <quelque intonation remarquable de>]

483:39. Mais[1] celui de tous les mots que M. de Montfort[2] avait dits ce soir-là, celui[3] de tous qui fut le plus goûté, le fut par

Françoise qui riait encore quelques[4] années après, d'avoir été traitée par l'Ambassadeur de «chef de premier ordre», ce que ma mère était allée lui raconter à la cuisine en la complimentant pour son poulet. Le titre d'ambassadeur n'en imposait pas d'ailleurs beaucoup à Françoise qui disait de M. de Montfort[5] avec la cordialité due à quelqu'un qui l'avait prise pour un chef: «c'est un bon vieux comme moi.» {484:1-486:7}

486:8. Quand vint le premier janvier, après avoir fait avec maman nos visites de famille, je courus> {486:8-486:25}

486:25. <je courus aux Champs-Elysées> **486:38.** <péril qui pourrait> 486:27. [<Swann lui acheter du> 486:28. <lettre que j'avais, dès le jour où Gilberte m'avait fait tant de peine, décidé> 486:32. <déceptions et qu'avec l'année nouvelle c'était>]

□**486:38.** <pourrait l'endommager, le moindre signe de refroidissement entre nous. En rentrant, Françoise, qui désirait acheter pour ses étrennes une photographie de Pie IX et une de Raspail, me fit arrêter devant un marchand en plein air[1] qui vendait au coin de la rue Royale, à côté de ces hôtels que j'aurais dû par la pensée rattacher à Versailles, mettre à côté de tant de façades qui continuent ça et là en France, à faire mousser et gonfler leur plâtre ancien, au milieu d'un espace nu et réservé comme celui d'un vase, sous les joies[*] d'une Renommée qui souffle dans une trompette ou d'un amour qui touche les cordes d'une petite lyre, mais qui me semblaient laides parce que je ne les séparais pas de ce que je voyais tous les jours que je les croyais frères du marchand de photographies de la rue Royale et contemporains du mastroquet du coin de la rue Boissy-d'Anglas.

Pendant que Françoise demandait ses photographies, j'en achetai une de la Berma. Les admirations innombrables qu'elle excitait donnaient>

487:1. <donnaient quelque chose> **487:37.** <nouvelle amitié> [487:2. <y répondre,[1]—comme ce vêtement immuable des personnes qui n'en ont pas de rechange,[2]—et où elle> 487:5. <le relèvement des sourcils au-dessus de l'œil, quelques> 487:9. <pas semblé beau> 487:11. <supporter, et de ceux que du fond de la photographie, il semblait> 487:14. Car elle devait> 487:22. <j'eus à la fois la> 487:23. <que[1] ce jour qu'on appelait le nouvel an n'en savait rien, était un jour comme beaucoup d'au-

tres, qui finissait dans le crépuscule d'une manière que je me rappelais, et qu'il n'était pas le premier d'un> 487:26. <comme au premier jour du monde, comme> 487:28. <comme si étaient anéanties> 487:32. <qu'elle m'aimât. Je sentis que> 487:33. <lui d'un monde[1] qui ne l'avait pas contenté, c'est> 487:35. <et qu'il n'y avait pas>]

487:37. <nouvelle amitié était,[1] comme la nouvelle année, la même sous un nom différent, comme les années que notre désir, sans pouvoir l'atteindre elle-même et la changer, recouvre à leur insu d'un nom différent. J'avais beau dédier celle qui commençait à Gilberte, comme on superpose une religion aux lois aveugles de la nature, j'avais beau essayer d'imprimer au nouvel[2] an l'idée particulière que je m'étais faite de lui, c'était en vain:[3] dans le vent doux qui soufflait autour de la colonne d'affiches, j'avais reconnu, j'avais senti reparaître la matière irréparable et commune, l'humidité familière, l'ignorante fluidité des jours. {488:7-488:19}

488:20. Quand je fus> **488:31.** <savait d'ailleurs> [488:25. <vue affichée pour le soir même. Je n'avais même pas, pour calmer l'agitation que cette pensée faisait naître en moi dans ce soir d'insomnie, l'idée que>]

□**488:31.** <d'ailleurs si bien elle-même, qu'elle en faisait apparaître les troubles connus, comme[1] d'une violence et d'une douceur insoupçonnées à des spectateurs dont chacun pourtant l'avait ressenti par soi-même, et qui, enflammés, émerveillés, éclataient en applaudissements. Et combien la passion qu'elle montrait devait être irrésistible, quand elle la déclarait non plus à un Hippolyte de théâtre mais quand elle avait devant elle les objets vivants de ses flammes réelles.

488:35. Je rallumai> **488:41.** <une nostalgie à laquelle ajoutait encore le son d'un cor de chasse qui venait d'un mastroquet voisin, comme ceux qu'on entend la nuit de la Mi-Carême et dont la tristese est plus grande[1] encore que dans les bois parce qu'elle est sans poésie. {489:2-490:27}

490:27. Quelques jours plus tard, Gilberte revint aux Champs-Elysées, mais Swann avait-il surpris la lettre que je lui avais écrite, ou ne faisait-elle> **490:35.** <dire[1] que ses parents étaient loin de me rendre la sympathie que j'avais pour eux. {480:35-490:39}

490:39. Ils ne demandaient pas> **491:29.** <de mon âme! [490:41. <aimé, croyait-elle, que> 490:42. <voyaient pas favorablement[1] ses relations avec moi, ne me croyaient pas d'une grande moralité et ne pensaient pas que j'exercerais une bonne influence sur elle. Ce> 491:2. <scrupuleux dont Swann voulait sans doute parler et auquel il croyait que je ressemblais, je> 491:8. <traits avec quelle> 491:11. <animé pour Swann> 491:12. <que je ne doutais pas s'il les eût soupçonnés qu'il> 491:15. <dans une lettre> 491:17. <il me croyait donc un plus> 491:19. <peindre avec> 491:20. <douté,[1] car la lettre que je lui avais écrite, aussi ardente> 491:21. <de Montfort,[1] n'eut> 491:22. <succès de* lui que[1] les autres auprès du vieil ambassadeur. 491:23. <derrière le massif> 491:28. Moi[1] je savais>]

491:29. <mon âme! Ma lettre n'avait même pas effleuré l'absurde erreur de Swann. Etait-ce[1] une erreur, je n'en doutais pas alors?* Or[2] je sentais que j'avais décrit[3] dans ma lettre avec tant d'exactitude certaines caractéristiques irrécusables du[4] sentiment généreux que j'éprouvais que, pour que d'après eux Swann ne l'eût pas aussitôt reconstitué et ne fût pas venu demander pardon de son erreur, il fallait que ce[5] noble sentiment, il ne l'eût jamais ressenti, il fut* incapable de le comprendre.

491:40. Or, peut-être> **492:7.** <généralité des autres> [492:4. <fatalement dirigés>]

492:7. <généralité des autres et à en deviner[1] expérimentalement les conséquences. Si du moins je[2] pouvais avoir avec lui une explication?* Gilberte me dit qu'elle la lui avait proposée, mais qu'il la jugeait inutile et ajouta:

—Tenez, ne me laissez pas votre lettre, il faut rejoindre les autres. {492:8-493:26}

493:30. Peut-être* si Swann était> **493:37.** <empêchez-moi de la prendre, nous allons voir qu'est-ce qui* sera le plus fort.

Elle la mit derrière son dos, les bras passés derrière le cou l'un de l'autre, nous luttions, arc-boutés. Je tâchais de l'attirer, elle résistait,[1] mes jambes glissèrent contre celles de Gilberte, et au milieu de la gymnastique que je faisais pour attraper la lettre, sans que l'essoufflement que me donnait* l'exercice musculaire et l'ardeur du jeu en fut* à peine augmenté, je jetai comme quelques gouttes de sueur arrachées par l'effort, mon plaisir auquel je ne pus m'attarder même le temps de le goûter,[2] et aussitôt j'attrapai la lettre.

494:11. Alors, Gilberte> **494:15.** Peut-être[1] avait-elle senti que mon jeu avait un autre objet, mais n'avait-elle pas remarqué[2] que je l'avais atteint. Et moi qui croyais qu'elle s'en était[3] aperçue, j'acceptai de lutter encore de peur qu'elle pût croire que je ne m'étais pas proposé d'autre but que celui après lequel[4] je n'avais plus envie que[5] de souffler.

494:25. See 474:39.

494:39. Depuis quelque temps> **495:41.** <languissant et perméable> [494:42. <réputé dont elles connaissent trop d'erreurs de diagnostics pour avoir confiance en lui; on prétendait qu'ils ne réussissaient pas aux enfants> 495:4. <dont leur atmosphère était responsable> 495:5. <la tendresse de ma mère> 495:8. Les êtres nerveux sont> 495:9. <moins,[1] précisément parce qu'ils entendent> 495:14. <quand il allait seulement tomber de la neige ou qu'on allait partir en voyage, qu'ils> 495:17. <avertissements qu'un homme de guerre qui,[1] dans le feu de l'action, n'entend[2] même pas et peut, étant très malade, continuer encore> 495:23. <que de la[1] circulation de> 495:26. <froid signifie non> 495:27. <mais qu'on a> 495:28. <pas manger[1] quand> 495:32. <dont mon indifférence de glace avait> 495:39. <j'avais 41° de fièvre>]

495:41. <et perméable dont j'étais enveloppé, d'une pensée souriante je rejoignais, j'exigeais le plaisir> 496:2. <goûter encore. {496:3-496:5}

496:5. Le médecin déclara le soir «préférer»> **496:8.** <plus «insidieuses.»[1]

496:9. Pourtant ma convalescence fut longue. J'avais presque chaque jour de longues crises d'étouffement pendant lesquelles ma grand'mère restait auprès de moi. Et soit que l'intransigeance de sa raison diminuât avec l'âge, ou qu'il ne lui permit* plus de supporter la vue de la souffrance de ceux qu'elle aimait, d'elle-même elle m'offrait de me donner de la bière ou du cognac.

496:10. See after 393:35.

497:11. Un soir qu'elle m'avait> **497:22.** <que tu profites> [497:12. <chambre presque au milieu de la nuit, et> 497:14. <Dieu, tu souffres> 497:20. <yeux avaient une expression>]

497:22. <que tu profites un peu pour te reposer puisque tu es mieux, me dit-elle.

Et quand je l'embrassai je sentis sur ses joues fraîches quelque chose d'humide[1] dont je ne sus pas si c'était l'humidité de l'air nocturne qu'elle venait de traverser ou bien une larme qui était en train d'y sécher. Mais elle me quitta brusquement avant que je commence à boire. Puis j'allai mieux mais on parlait> {497:27-499:14}

499:14. <on parlait de ne plus m'envoyer> **499:24.** <chagrins qu'ils ont? [499:17. <ne puisse plus>] {499:25-499:32}

499:33. Un jour, à l'heure du courrier, ma mère posa sur mon lit une lettre et s'éloigna aussitôt. Je l'ouvris distraitement puisqu'elle ne pouvait pas être de la seule personne à qui je tenais, Gilberte avec qui je n'avais pas de relations en dehors des[1] Champs-Elysées où je n'irais plus. Sur le papier était timbré un casque d'argent bruni sous lequel cette devise était gravée: *Per viam rectam*,[2] une grande écriture avait écrit cette lettre dont presque tous les mots saillaient, soulignés par la barre des t d'en dessous*, laquelle était tracée au-dessus de la lettre au lieu de la couper: «Mon cher ami> {500:1-500:16}

500:16. «Mon cher ami> **500:27.** <amitiés, Gilberte.» [500:18. <vais[1] plus très souvent non plus>] {500:28-502:21}

502:21. Cette lettre avait peut-être été indirectement provoquée par un incident que j'avais cru au contraire de nature à me perdre à jamais dans l'esprit des Swann. Peu de temps auparavant Bloch et le Dr Cottard, nouveau médecin de mon père, étant venus dîner à la maison, on les avait fait entrer un moment pour me distraire dans ma chambre où j'étais encore alité. Bloch ayant dit qu'il avait entendu dire que Mlle* Swann m'aimait beaucoup>

502:29. <m'aimait beaucoup> **502:41.** <dîné à côté> [502:31. <Mme Swann, j'allais lui dire> 502:33. <de Montfort[1] et de> 502:34. <Mme Swann l'apprenant me prit* pour> 502:36. Mais au moment de rectifier l'erreur de Bloch, je n'eus pas le courage, en devinant qu'elle était volontaire> 502:39. <pu[1] en

effet lui dire, c'était tout simplement pour faire savoir ce qu'il jugeait flatteur, qu'il avait>]

502:41. <dîné à côté d'une amie de Mme Swann. Or si M. de Montfort apprenant que je ne connaissais pas Mme Swann et aurait* aimé la connaître, s'était gardé de lui parler de moi, le Dr Cottard, médecin de Mme Swann, ayant induit de ce qu'il avait entendu dire à Bloch que Mme Swann me connaissait beaucoup et m'appréciait, pensa que dire à Mme Swann que j'étais un charmant garçon avec qui il était lié ne pourrait en rien être utile pour moi et serait flatteur pour lui, deux raisons qui le décidèrent à parler de moi dès qu'il la vit. Et elle pensa qu'il était regrettable qu'elle ne me connût pas. Mais[1] ce mensonge de Bloch ne[2] dut avoir influencé que d'une façon accessoire sur la lettre de Gilberte, qu'aujourd'hui encore je crois plutôt avoir été due à une démarche, d'ailleurs créée par elle, de ma mère qui savait depuis longtemps que j'avais du chagrin [*cf.* 501:1].

503:9. Alors je connus> **503:26.** <neveu de la maîtresse de la* maison. [503:11. <mais qui*[1] embaumait> 503:12. <douloureux de la vie> 503:14. <demandais à monter voir Mlle Swann, de> 503:15. <casquette d'un geste propice> 503:16. <prière. Ces fenêtres> 503:19. <semblait celui même de Mme Swann, il> 503:23. <réception de Mme Swan*, pour> 503:25. <faisaient un bonjour>] {503:27-503:40}

503:41. Les parents de Gilberte> **504:7** <pour Mme Swann)> [503:42. <maintenant quand j'entrais dans la sombre antichambre où planait perpétuellement[1] la possibilité de les rencontrer plus formidable et plus désirée qu'à Versailles jadis l'apparition du Roi (et où habituellement, après avoir buté contre l'énorme>]

504:7. <pour Mme Swann,[1] si l'un d'eux, M. ou Mme Swann, la traversait en même temps que moi, loin d'avoir l'air irrité, il[2] me serrait la main en souriant et me disait:[3] {504:11-504:15}

504:15. —Gilberte sait-elle> **504:34.** <d'en distinguer> [504:18. <la plus inéluctable des séparations que le destin avait

---

504:11. —«Comment allez-vous (qu'ils prononçaient comman* allez-vous sans faire la liaison du *t*. Gilberte sait-elle>

504:18. ([1]devenaient maintenant au contraire). 504:24. ([1]humoristique écrite en anglais). 504:25. ([1]quelquefois timbré d'une) 504:43. ([1]qu'elle cherchait à se rappeler ceux dont). 505:2. ([1]entière. Comme). 505:11. ([1]brus-

accumulées entre elle et moi, maintenant[1] ils devinrent au contraire une occasion de nous réunir dont elle m'avertissait par un mot écrit sur un papier à lettre orné parfois d'un caniche> 504:24. <humoristique[1] en anglais> 504:25. <d'exclamation, quelquefois[1] d'une ancre marine, ou encore du chiffre> 504:28. <feuille, ou d'une branche de myosotis, ou du nom «Gilberte»> 504:30. <imitaient sa signature et finissaient> 504:33. <en majuscule* sans>]

504:34. <d'en distinguer une seule, ou encore portant, comme la première fois> {504:35-504:38}

504:38. <comme la première fois> **505:2.** <envoyer le même> [504:40. <*rectam,* au-dessus du> 504:41. <bruni, chacun choisi> 504:43. <plutôt, comme je le crois maintenant, parce qu'elle[1] se reportait à celui dont elle s'était servie>]

505:2. <envoyer le même à un de ses correspondants qu'aux intervalles les plus éloignés possibles*, et après avoir épuisé la série entière[1] de ceux qu'elle possédait.

505:5. Comme à cause> **506:27.** <l'intérieur d'un Temple> [505:11. <brusquement[1] les liens> 505:13. <à ma vie antérieure et m'ôtaient> 505:14. <une fois au chaud> 505:17. <rapport qui étaient de style Henri II, et pourvu> 505:20. <équivalent dans le nôtre sur laquelle> 505:22. <de si prestigieux> 505:25. <hésité à donner[1] à mes parents ce renseignement faux qui seul pouvait> 505:28. <le même respect que moi, de même que devant un ignorant> 505:34. <choses que j'avais sous les yeux, et seulement que> 505:36. <certain qu'en faisant cette description à mes parents je commettais[1] un mensonge. Mais*[2] cela ne me parut pas certain, mais cela me[3] parut probable, car quand mon père m'interrompit en disant: «je connais> 505:42. <pareilles; c'est Berlier> 506:1. <construites», je piquai un fard. Il> 506:3. <et l'allée*[1] pas assez claire, je sentis alors indistinc-

---

quement bien avant que j'atteigne le palier, les liens). 505:25. ([1]donner sciemment à). 505:36. ([1]commisse) ([2]Cela ne) ([3]dut me paraître). 506:3. ([1]l'entrée). 506:6. ([1]moi). 506:11. ([1]ces). 506:13. ([1]mémoire, n'étant plus que le jouet). 506:27. ([1]semblait, aussi débonnaire et familier qu'il était). 507:29. ([1]mère, si Mme Swann, —dont) ([2] «le jour»—, après) ([3]visite entrait) ([4]habillée de velours bleu, souvent dans* robe de satin noir couverte de dentelles). 508:7 ([1]tableau de Jérôme*).

tement que mon esprit> 506:6. <intérieure, j'écartai à tout jamais de lui*[1] la pensée> 506:9. <que l'appartement des Swann> 506:11. Cependant, les[1] jours> 506:13. <mémoire,[1] jouet mécanique, maladroit et rougissant des plus vils réflexes, j'arrivais> 506:15. <gâteau de Savoie, entouré> 506:19. <semblait suspendu, comme l'univers nécessaire de Kant, à un> 506:21. Car nous étions tous dans le petit salon de Gilberte, quand, tout d'un coup, regardant l'heure, elle disait: >]

506:27. <d'un Temple peint par Rambrandt*, et où le gâteau de Savoie semblait[1] aussi accoutumé qu'il était magnifique, trôner là à tout hasard pour le cas où il aurait pris fantaisie à Gilberte de manger. Bien mieux, elle ne consultait pas seulement sa faim à elle, mais, tandis qu'elle m'offrait un gâteau, s'informait de la mienne, et même de l'heure à laquelle mes parents dînaient. Comme* si je l'avais su encore, comme si le trouble> {506:31-506:34}

506:41. <trouble qui me dominait> **506:43.** <dans mon estomac et mon souvenir également paralysés! Si plusieurs de ses amies refusaient une tasse de thé, elle disait: > {507:1-507:21}

507:21. «Décidément> **507:29.** <permission à sa mère> [507:22. <effacer encore l'idée de cérémonie, dérangeait l'ordre des chaises autour de la table en disant: «Nous avons l'air d'un dîner de noces; mon> 507:26. <côté sur sa chaise, placée en travers. 507:27. <si Gilberte eût> 507:28. <avoir à sa disposition tant de petits fours, sans>]

507:29. <mère,[1] Mme Swann, dont c'était habituellement le jour,[2] si après avoir reconduit une visite[3] elle entrait un moment en courant, quelquefois en[4] velours bleu, souvent en robe de satin noir couverte de dentelles blanches, disait d'un air étonné: >

507:36. —Tiens, ça> **507:41.** <j'ai encore> [507:37. <de vous voir manger.]

507:41. <j'ai encore Mme Trombert et Mme Cottard; s'il ne vient plus personne> {507:41-508:2}

508:2. <personne, je reviendrai> **508:8.** <jours prendre> [508:3. <vous, ce qui m'amusera beaucoup plus quand elles seront parties. 508:6. <j'ai eu quarante-cinq visites et il y en a eu> 508:7. <parlé du portrait[1] de Machard.]

508:8. <fera prendre *votre* thé avec Gilberte; Gilberte vous le fera comme vous l'aimez, ajoutait-elle, en s'adressant à moi tout en s'enfuyant vers ses visites et comme si c'était quelque chose d'aussi connu de moi que mes habitudes que j'étais venu chercher dans ce monde mystérieux. Alors M. Swann> {508:16-508:29; 509:1-511:12}

□**511:14.** Alors M. Swann entrait à son tour. Que sa femme fût sortie ou non, il rentrait d'habitude fort tard et à ce moment de cinq heures où il se sentait jadis si malheureux, il ne se demandait pas comme autrefois ce qu'elle pouvait faire. Il se rappelait bien quelquefois qu'il avait un jour essayé de lire une lettre adressée par Odette à Forcheville. Même il ne lui était pas désagréable de se rappeler qu'il l'avait fait, et plutôt que d'approfondir la honte qu'il en ressentait, préférait se livrer à une petite grimace du coin gauche de sa bouche [*cf.* 523:20]. Mais ce problème qui lui avait paru si passionnant et qu'il se promettait alors d'éclaircir quand il ne serait plus jaloux, par amour de la vérité, savoir si Odette avait ce jour-là ou tout autre jour été possédée par Forcheville, ce problème depuis que Swann n'était plus galant avait entièrement perdu de son intérêt à ses yeux. Il lui eût été désagréable d'en vouloir à Odette et d'ailleurs il n'éprouvait aucun besoin d'être renseigné. Vers sept heures, le jour de Mme Swann, nous le voyions, Gilberte et moi, entrer dans la salle à manger.

Alors M. Swann entrait à son tour.

511:15. —Sais-tu si ta mère> **511:18.** <être brisée. {511:18-511:21}

508:29. Et moi qui aux Champs-Elysées, avait* eu si peur, de la fâcheuse impression qu'avait dû produire Françoise, j'entendais Mme Swann me dire que c'était tout ce que Gilberte avait raconté de notre vieille servante qui leur avait donné, à elle et à son mari tant de sympathie pour moi. «On sent qu'elle vous est si dévouée, qu'elle est si bien.» Je changeai entièrement d'avis sur Françoise. Par contre* coup avoir une institutrice pourvue d'un caoutchouc et d'un plumet ne me semble* plus une chose si nécessaire.

508:37. Enfin je> **508:43.** <chez les Swann.

511:13. Quand Mme Swann était retournée près de ses visites, M. Swann entrait à son tour.

511:18. <brisée. C'est> **511:21.** <l'*o* bref, ce qui m'étonna beaucoup la première fois. Pensez> [*Parenthesis not closed*].

511:21. Pensez, depuis> **512:15.** <d'honneur. [511:21. <après-midi! disait-il en> 511:24. <douze, je suis bête, je crois> 511:26. <jour, quand j'ai vu> 511:28. Et depuis que je suis> 511:36. <juste le grade, disait> 511:38. <comme un enfant de deux> 512:4. <parents et[1] pensait d'ailleurs qu'on ne pouvait qu'ajouter à une relation> 512:7. <d'importance.] {512:22-512:41}

512:42. —Hé bien! sa femme ne me plaît pas.

512:43. —Mais tu as le plus grand tort> **513:5.** <des Dieux. {513:6-515:15}

515:15. Je crois que Swann n'était pas fâché de penser qu'ainsi mes parents apprendraient que Mme Bontemps venait voir sa femme. A vrai dire, chez eux, le nom des personnes avec[1] qui* Mme Swann arrivait successivement à connaître, piquait>

515:20. <piquait plus la curiosité> **515:40.** <les un tel. [515:21. <Mme Bontemps, ma> 515:27. <les Bontemps sont> 515:32. <quelque Expédition[1] fructueuse chez les Masséchutos, les Cynglalais* et les Bontemps. 515:34. Mais[1] toutes> 515:36. <avaient souvent été assez difficilement amenées>]

515:41. Quand*[1] à Mme Cottard dont mon père s'étonnait que Mme Swann put* trouver quelque avantage à attire*[2] cette petite bourgeoise si peu élégante, il répétait:

—Pour Mme Cottard j'avoue que je ne comprends pas.

Ma mère, elle, comprenait très bien, car elle savait>

516:2. <elle savait> **516:7.** <il faut. [516:5. <pouvait faire informer>]

516:7. <il faut un témoin, quelqu'un qui vienne dans ce monde nouveau et délicieux, comme un insecte dans une fleur,

---

512:4. ([1]et pouvait d'ailleurs penser qu'elle ne faisait qu'ajouter).

512:15. <d'honneur.» «C'est un homme délicieux même fort joli garçon.» Sa femme d'ailleurs l'avait épousé envers et contre tous. C'était un être de charme. Et en effet il avait, ce qui constitue un ensemble délicat et rare, une barbe blonde et soyeuse, de jolis traits, une voix nasale et un œil de verre.

515:15. ([1]que Mme Swann). 515:32. ([1]expédition). 515:34. ([1]Et). 515:41. ([1]Quant) ([2]attirer).

516:7. (*B-A*) <il faut un témoin, quelqu'un qui vienne dans ce monde nouveau et délicieux comme dans une fleur, un insecte bourdonnant et volage et qui ensuite, au hasard de ses visites répandra, on l'espère du moins, la nouvelle>

et qui répandra ensuite, on l'espère du moins, au hasard de ses visites, la nouvelle qu'elle aura emportée avec elle, tel des germes d'envie et d'admiration. Mme Cottard rentrait dans ce que ma mère appelait les «Etrangers* va dire à Sparte» et était en effet bien choisie pour ce rôle car, bienveillante, résumée et modeste,

---

516:11. <la nouvelle, le germe> **516:14.** <d'invités que ma mère appelait des: «Etranger va dire à Sparte!" D'ailleurs—en dehors d'une autre raison qu'on ne sut que bien des années après—bienveillance réservée et modeste*. Mme Swann n'avait pas à craindre en confia* à ses jours brillants d'introduire chez soi un traître ou une concurrente. Elle savait le nombre énorme de calices bourgeois que pouvait visiter en un seul après-midi cette active ouvrière quand elle était armée de l'aigrette et du porte* cartes. Elle connaissait son pouvoir de dissémination et en se basant sur le calcul des probabilités, Mme Swann pouvait s'imaginer sans invraisemblance tel habitué des Verdurin. Apprenant* dès le surlendemain que le gouvernement* de Paris avait mis des cartes chez elle, ou tel autre entendait raconter que M. de Fressagny les avait emmenés, elle et Swann, au gala du roi Théodose; ou enfin telle autre de ces matérialisations particulières et assez peu nombreuses sous lesquelles nous nous représentons, et nous poursuivons la gloire, faute de pouvoir l'imaginer sous toutes les autres formes que nous espérons bien d'ailleurs—en gros—qu'elle rêvait* également.

523:10. Les jours où sa femme ne donnait pas de thé, Swann rentrait généralement plus tard. Il ne s'inquiétait pas qu'elle fut* sortie à ce moment de six heures du soir où jadis il se sentait si malheureux éprouvait* une telle angoisse, il ne se demandait plus ce qu'elle pouvait être en train de faire. Il se rappelait bien [*cf.* 511:14 *in Grasset A*] parfois qu'il avait bien des années auparavant essayé un jour de lire à travers l'enveloppe une lettre adressée par Odette à Forcheville. Mais le souvenir ne lui était pas agréable et plus tôt* que d'approfondir la honte qu'il ressentait d'avoir fait cela, il préférait se livrer à une petite grimace du coin de la bouche. Certes il se rendait bien compte maintenant oue l'hypothèse à laquelle il s'était souvent arrêté jadis et d'après quoi, c'était les imaginations de la jalousie qui seules noircissaient la vie, en réalité innocente d'Odette, il se rendait bien compte que cette hypothèse (en somme bienfaisante puisque tant qu'avait duré sa maladie amoureuse elle avait diminué ses souffrances en lui faisant croire qu'elles étaient imaginaires)>

523:29. <imaginaires) n'était> **523:31.** < davantage.

523:31. Mais il ne pouvait penser longtemps à cela. Autrefois> **523:43.** <d'être jaloux.

□**523:43.** <jaloux. Il lui eût été maintenant désagréable de poser des questions à ce sujet à Odette et sa réponse d'ailleurs l'aurait laissé indifférent. A peine pouvait-il se représenter l'angoisse qu'il avait éprouvée autrefois. Elle avait cependant été si forte qu'il ne pouvait se figurer alors qu'il ne s'en délivrerait jamais et que la mort d'Odette lui semblât seule capable de lui faire le chemin libre pour qu'il pût continuer à vivre; c'est ainsi que souvent un effet de perspective nous fait croire qu'une hauteur qui est devant nous barre entièrement la route; mais Swann avait continué

Mme Svann* n'avait pas à craindre en l'invitant à ses jours brillants d'introduire chez elle un traître ou une concurrente, et, en revanche en se basant sur le calcul des probabilités, elle pouvait

---

d'exister et s'était aperçu que le chemin contournait l'obstacle mais n'en était pas obstrué. Et pourtant cette angoisse qu'Odette avait fait éprouver à Swann (pareille à celle avec laquelle j'avais connaissance à Combray le soir où il venait à la maison) il lui était réservé—et, d'après ce que me raconta M. de Charlus ne dut pas être longtemps après que j'eus commencé à aller chez eux—de la ressentir encore, non à propos d'Odette, mais d'une autre femme. C'est que cette angoisse, Swann était arrivé à l'âge, où elle se constitue en nous à titre de maladie chronique dont le principe est en nous, et qui cherche seulement dans le monde extérieur, indépendamment duquel elle se développe, des occasions pour déclancher et justifier ses crises. A partir d'un certain âge nous ne sommes plus amoureux d'une femme mais à propos d'une femme. Nos amours ne sont, malgré la diversité des amantes, qu'un même amour latent, expectant, toujours en imminence de crise et que le plus petit trait d'un visage qui a pu y donner prétexte fait entrer en éruption. De même cette angoisse, un peu plus rare pourtant, qui demande pour se produire des circonstances un peu plus particulières est là aussi en nous, attendant seulement dans la suite de nos amours, qu'en survienne un pour une femme remplissant des conditions un peu spéciales, par exemple une femme frivole aimant le monde, y allant à une époque ou à des heures où quelque contingence nous empêche de l'y accompagner. Celle qui était sur le point d'aimer Swann quand Gilberte m'écrivit pour me demander de venir désormais goûter avec elle, celle qui devait réveiller en lui cette angoisse dont selon M. de Charlus, Swann est mort, ne lui donna cependant à ce qu'on m'a dit aucune raison d'être jaloux, elle lui fut toujours fidèle. Mais il ne le croyait pas. Obligé de rester beaucoup avec sa femme, de partir avec elle quand elle voulait voyager, il lui arrivait souvent de ne pouvoir suivre dans le monde cette jeune femme dont il était épris, qui s'y plaisait, qui s'y montrait gaie disait-on. C'était assez pour que renaquit* en lui l'ancienne angoisse, lamentable accroît de son amour, qui éloignait Swann précisément de ce qu'elle était comme un désir d'atteindre (la nature, la sincérité du sentiment que cette jeune femme avait pour lui, le désir caché de ses journées, le secret de son cœur); car elle interposait,—cette angoisse,—entre Swann et celle qu'il aimait, cet amas réfractaire de soupçons antérieurs, ayant leur cause en Odette ou en telle autre qui avait précédé Odette, et qui ne lui permettaient plus de connaître sa maîtresse actuelle qu'à travers le fantôme ancien, et commun à d'autres, de la «femme* excitait sa jalousie» dans lequel il l'avait arbitrairement incarnée. Souvent Swann l'accusait, cette jalousie, de le faire croire à des trahisons imaginaires; mais alors il se rappelait qu'il avait fait bénéficier Odette du même raisonnement et à tort. Et tout ce que faisait la jeune femme qu'il aimait aux heures où il n'était pas avec elle cessait de lui paraître innocent. Comme il aurait souhaité quand il souffrait par Odette de pouvoir un jour lui laisser voir qu'il en aimait une autre. Maintenant il l'aurait pu et au contraire il prenait mille précautions pour qu'Odette ne soupçonnât pas ce nouvel amour.

s'imaginer que tel belâtre de Verdurin apprendrait probablement le surlendemain que le Gouverneur de Paris avait mis des cartes chez l'ancienne Odette ou telle autre de ces réalisations particulières et assez peu nombreuses sur lesquelles nous nous représentons et nous poursuivons la gloire, faute de pouvoir l'imaginer sous toutes les autres formes que nous espérons d'elles—en gros—qu'elle revêt. {516:39-523:9; 523:22-525:35}

525:37. Ce ne fut pas seulement à ces thés, d'ailleurs à cause desquels> **525:42.** <m'avaient privé> [525:39. <que maintenant je pris part, mais ces sorties> 525:41. <promenade, ou au théâtre, ou à des réceptions, et qui>]

525:42. <privé de la voir, ces jours où je restais près de la pelouse, l'imaginant qui participait avec ses parents à une sorte d'existence supérieure comme celle que mènent les Dieux, ces sorties maintenant M. et Mme Swann m'y admettaient, j'avais une place dans leur landau à côté de Gilberte, même c'était moi à qui l'on demandait si je[1] voulais plutôt aller au Jardin d'Acclimatation ou à l'Eden, à une leçon de danse chez une amie de Gilberte ou visiter les Tombeaux de Saint-Denis. Souvent pendant que Gilberte [*cf.* 536:15] allait se préparer, je restais seul avec M. et Mme Swann qui me découvraient les vertus vraiment rares de Gilberte. Et tout ce que j'observais me montrait qu'ils disaient vrai> {526:8-536:14}

536:18. <disaient vrai> **536:35.** <pour une raison> [536:21. <domestiques, des attentions> 536:23. <par des riens qui> 536:25. <pour la[1] marchande des Champs-Elysées et alla par la neige le lui porter, pour le lui remettre elle-même et sans> 536:28. <cache,[1] c'est une grande âme, disait> 536:31. <mais elle ne prenait pas un air de blâme, car elle avait un culte pour son père. 536:34. <de Mlle Vington,[1] elle>]

536:35. <pour une raison, c'est qu'il paraît qu'elle n'est[1] pas gentille pour son père, qu'elle lui fait[2] de la peine. Vous ne pouvez pas plus comprendre cela que moi qu'on fasse de la peine à son père, n'est-ce pas, vous qui ne pourriez sans doute pas plus

---

525:42. ([1]j'aimais mieux aller). 536:25. ([1]notre). 536:28. ([1]cache, disait). 536:34. ([1]Venteuil*). 536:35. ([1]n'était) ([2]faisait). 537:23. ([1]si parfaites). 537:34. ([1]connaissance que) ([2]les)

survivre au vôtre que moi au mien. D'ailleurs je trouve cela tout naturel. Comment oublier jamais quelqu'un qu'on aime depuis toujours.

Et un jour qu'elle était plus particulièrement câline avec son père, comme je le lui fis remarquer quand il se fut éloigné:

537:1. —Oui, pauvre> **537:7.** <trop bon. [537:6. <méchante que d'habitude, il vous trouve une perfection.] {537:8-537:14}

537:15. Dès le premier jour où je restai un moment seul avec les parents de Gilberte, ayant demandé à Mme Swann> **537:21.** <le grand favori. [537:19. <Mme Svann* m'avais* répondu:]

537:23. Sans doute dans ces coïncidences parfaites,[1] au moment où nos actes se replient et s'appliquent exactement sur ce que nous avons si longtemps rêvé, ils nous le cachent entièrement, se confondent avec lui, comme deux figures égales superposées qui>

537:27. <n'en font plus> **538:7.** <rayons infrangibles> [537:29. <de notre rêve, dans le moment même où par la réalisation nous les touchons> 537:34. <connaissance[1] nouvelle que nous avons faite, le souvenir de ces heures inespérées que nous venons de passer, ces[2] propos> 537:39. <imagination, rétroagissant* davantage> 537:40. <plus libres de> 538:1. <passé dix minutes chez> 538:4. <a exclu. Comment aurais-je pu encore rêver> 538:5. <comme à un lieu> 538:6. <un pas dans ma pensée sans>]

538:7. <infrangibles qu'émettaient à l'infini derrière eux, jusque dans mon passé le plus ancien, les œufs sur le plat que je venais d'y manger. Et quand> {538:10-538:28}

□**538:9.** <d'y manger. Et il devait se passer quelque chose d'analogue pour Swann: car cette salle à manger et cet appartement où il me recevait étaient le lieu où étaient venus s'appliquer et se confondre, coïncider non pas seulement l'appartement idéal que mon imagination avait engendré, mais un autre encore, celui que la jalousie de Swann, aussi inventive que mes rêves, avait si souvent décrit devant lui et lui avait fait apparaître, à lui aussi, comme inaccessible et délicieux, cet appartement commun à Odette et à lui dont il avait rêvé, tel soir où Odette l'avait ramené avec Forcheville prendre de l'orangrade* chez elle; et ce qui était venu s'absorber, pour lui, dans la salle à manger où nous dépensions*, c'était ce paradis inespéré où jadis il ne pouvait pas défaillir* imaginer qu'il aurait dit à «leur» maître d'hôtel ces mots: «Madame est-elle prête? que je lui entendais prononcer presque chaque fois mais seulement avec une légère

538:28. Et quand Gilberte elle-même me disait: «Qu'est-ce qui vous aurait dit il y a six mois que la petite fille que vous regardiez jouer aux barres sans lui parler serait votre grande amie chez qui vous iriez tous les jours où cela vous plairait», elle parlait d'un changement que j'étais bien obligé de constater du dehors, mais que je ne possédais pas intérieurement car il se composait de deux parties que j'arrivais difficilement à penser à la fois.

C'était ainsi; et pourtant malgré tout ce charme mystérieux de la vie de Swann, je ne l'avais pas chassé entièrement de leur maison parce que j'y avais pénétré; je l'avais fait seulement reculer>

539:1. <reculer, dompté> **540:4.** <nous allions> [539:7. <Gilberte, pendant que j'attendais seul au salon,[1] sur le tapis, sur les bergères, sur les consoles, sur les paravents, sur les tableaux, j'imprimais avec mon regard comme avec un cachet l'idée gravée en lui que Mme Swann> 539:13. <prendre leur parfum. Est-ce parce que, sachant> 539:20. <fois je* pense> 539:20. <ce salon qui n'existe plus et que Swann,[1] sans prétendre en rien à contrarier les goûts de sa femme, trouvait si disparate parce

---

impatience mêlée toutefois à une certaine satisfaction d'amour* propre qu'il* avait adopté à la longue cette opinion d'Odette qu'être toujours en retard est une habitude particulière aux femmes élegantes. Pas plus que lui, je ne pouvais arriver à connaître mon bonheur et quand Gilberte elle-même me disait>

□**538:37.** *(B-A)* C'était ainsi; et pourtant cet appartement parce qu'il avait été si passionnément désiré par la volonté de Swann, devait conserver pour lui quelque douceur, car pour moi dont l'imagination en avait tant rêvé, il n'avait pas perdu tout mystère. Ce charme étranger que pendant si longtemps j'avais supposé à ce charme* la vie des Swann, je ne l'avais pas chassé entièrement de leur maison parce que j'y avais pénétré; je l'avais fait seulement reculer>

539:7. ([1]salon, j'imprimais avec mon regard comme avec un cachet, sur le tapis, sur les bergères, sur les consoles, sur les paravents, sur les tableaux, l'idée gravée en moi que Mme Swann). 539:20. ([1]Swann (sans que cette critique impliquât de sa part l'intention de contrarier en rien les goûts de sa femme) trouvait). 539:30 ([1]au contraire) ([2]souvenir ce salon composite une). 539:36. ([1]chose que nous voyons une). 539:37. ([1]dans). 539:41. ([1]était pour> [*Grasset B conforms here with the Pléiade*]... amalgamées, indéfinissables,—partout également troublantes—dans la place). 540:4. ([1]yacht) ([2]j'avais autrefois*) ([3]qu'il semblait). 540:24. ([1]et son manteau à pélerine*, ce manteau à pélerine* dont) ([2]le pareil) ([3]remplacer).

que conçu encore dans le goût moitié serre> 539:24. <appartement, où il l'avait connue, elle avait commencé> 539:27. <maintenant «tocards», par de nombreux petits meubles en soie Louis XVI> 539:29. <compter des chefs-d'œuvre de peinture apportés> 539:30. <du Quai d'Orléans, il a[1] dans mon souvenir[2] une cohésion> 539:36. <à elles et rien qu'à elles, donner> 539:36. <choses[1] une âme> 539:37. <développement de[1] notre souvenir. Toutes> 539:41. <qui était[1] comme le corps du temps de leur vie et devait en exprimer la singularité, toutes ces idées en étaient réparties, amalgamées, indéfinissables, dans la place> 540:3. <dans les allées et venues des domestiques>]

540:4. <allions prendre le café comme des touristes sur le pont d'un yascht*[1] dans la grande baie du salon, dont les vitres étaient fermées, mais que le soleil caressait comme une brise, à mes pieds ce n'était pas seulement le tabouret de soie que me passait Mme Swann (tout en me demandant combien je voulais de morceaux de sucre dans mon café) qui continuait à dégager avec le charme douloureux que j'avais[2] entendu autrefois sous l'épine rose puis à côté du massif de lauriers, dans le nom de Gilberte, le sentiment hostile qu'avaient eu ses parents pour moi et qui[3] lui semblait avoir si bien su et partagé que je ne me sentais pas digne, et que je me trouvais un peu lâche de lui imposer mes pieds à son capitonnage sans défense>

540:15. <défense; une âme> **540:24.** <M. Swann>{540:17. <dans ce golfe ensoleillé où>}

540:24. <M. Swann et[1] que sa cravate à pois, cette cravate à pois dont j'avais tant désiré porter la[2] pareille et que maintenant Mme Swann lui demandait de changer,[3] pour être plus élégant, quand je leur faisais l'honneur de sortir avec eux, tandis qu'elle-même allait ôter la robe de chambre de crêpe de Chine ou de soie vieux rose, cerise, rose vénitien, blanche, mauve, verte, rouge, jaune, unie ou à dessins, dans laquelle elle avait déjeuné, pour mettre une de ces toilettes souveraines qui s'imposaient à tous, et entre lesquelles pourtant c'était moi qui avais eu à choisir celle que je préférais qu'elle revêtit*. {540:33-540:41; 541:11-543:21; 543:31-544:40}

540:42. Au bois de Boulogne, au Jardin d'Acclimatation dans tous les lieux de promenade où nous allions, que j'étais fier quand nous étions des-

544:41. Une fois seulement à une de ces sorties Gilberte me causa un profond étonnement.

544:42. C'était justement> **545:1.** <son grand-père.

545:1. Nous devions[1] aller, Gilberte et moi, avec son institutrice, à un concert et Gilberte s'était préparée avec l'indifférence qu'elle avait[2] pour l'endroit où nous allions, pourvu que>

545:7. <pourvu que cela me plût> **545:25.** <elle n'en avait> [545:9. <pour dire à Gilberte que cela ennuyait son père que nous allions au concert ce jour-là. Je répondis que> 545:11. <devint d'une pâleur[1] qu'elle ne put cacher, et elle ne dit> 545:15. <Gilberte, et l'emmena dans la pièce à côté. On entendait> 545:17. <sage, lui résistât un jour pareil> 545:18. Enfin son père sortit> 545:23. <déjeuner. Après le déjeuner nous allâmes dans sa chambre>]

545:25. <n'en[1] avait jamais eu:

—Deux heures! mais vous savez>

545:26. <vous savez que> **546:2.** <dure, en dégageant vivement son bras. [545:35. <trouve cela grotesque> 545:38. <vais pas l'empêcher[1] pour faire>]

□**546:4.** Plus précieuses encore que les après-midis* au Jardin d'Acclimatation, dans tous ces lieux de promenade où j'étais

---

cendus de voiture de marcher à côté du beau manteau de Mme Swann! Tandis que dans sa démarche nonchalante elle le laissait flotter, je jetais>

541:2. <je jetais sur> **541:5.** <rencontrions l'une* ou l'autre des camarades de Gilberte>

541:6. <Gilberte, qui> **541:9.** <et était* mêlé à cette autre partie de sa vie qui ne se passait pas aux Champs-Elysées.

543:21. Nous fûmes ainsi salués dans une allée du Jardin d'Acclimatation, Mme Swann et moi par quelqu'un qui lui dit bonjour sans s'arrêter et que je ne savais pas qu'elle connut* Bloch. Elle me dit qu'il lui avait été présenté par Mme Bontemps, qu'il était attaché au cabinet du ministre. Elle ne devait pas d'ailleurs le connaître beaucoup car elle croyait qu'il s'appelait M. d'Echebrune. Je lui dis qu'elle confondait et qu'il s'appelait Bloch. Souvent, au lieu de nous promener, nous allions au théâtre, au concert. Une fois, à propos d'une sortie de genre* Gilberte me causa un profond étonnement. C'était justement>

545:1. ([1]devions elle et moi, assister, avec) ([2]montrait toujours pour la chose que nous devions faire pourvu que). 545:11. ([1]pâleur de colère qu'elle). 545:25. ([1]n'en ait eue* à aucun moment). 545:38. ([1]l'en priver pour).

546:4. *(B-A)* Faveur plus> **546:11.** <devais lui inspirer> [546:7. <Bergotte, qui avait>]

si fier de marcher à côté du beau manteau de Mme Swann sur lequel, tandis que d'une démarche nonchalante elle le laissait flotter [*cf.* 541:2], je sentais des regards d'admiration auxquels elle répondait coquettement par un long sourire, et à mon tour, si nous rencontions* quelques camarades de Gilberte qui nous saluaient de loin, me sentant régardé par elles comme un de ces êtres que j'avais tant envié*, un ami qui connaissait ses parents, qui était mêlé à cette autre partie de sa vie qui ne se passait pas aux Champs-Elysées, les Swann ne m'excluaient même pas de leur amitié avec Bergotte qui avait été à l'origine du charme que je leur avais trouvé quant* avant même de connaître Gilberte, je pensais que son intimité avec le divin vieillard eût fait d'elle pour moi la plus passionnante des amies si le dédain qu'elle avait pour moi ne m'avait pas interdit d'espérer qu'elle m'emmènerait avec lui visiter les villes qu'il aimait. Or un jour que Gilberte m'avait invité à déjeuner pour aller après nous promener ensemble, ses parents avaient pour convives quelques personnes à qui Mme Swann me présenta, quand tout d'un coup, de la même façon [*cf.* 547:12] qu'elle venait de dire mon nom comme si nous étions seulement deux invités du déjeuner qui devaient être chacun également content de connaître l'autre, elle prononça le nom du doux chantre aux cheveux blancs. {546:14-547:12}

547:17. Ce nom de Bergotte> **547:13.** <devant moi. [547:22. <par un petit homme rude, jeune[1] et trapu, à nez camard et à barbiche noire. Et cependant j'étais mortellement> 547:25. <réduit en poussière, la bourre de revolver qui n'était plus qu'un peu de cendre, c'était le langoureux>] {548:14-548:33}

546:11. <lui inspirer l'espoir* ne m'avait pas interdit qu'elle m'enmènerait* avec lui visiter les villes qu'elle aimait. Or un jour que Gilberte m'avait invité à déjeuner pour aller après nous promener ensemble, ses parents avaient pour convives quelques personnes à qui M. Swann me présenta, quand tout d'un coup, de la même façon>

547:22. ([1]jeune, trapu et myope, à nez rouge en forme de coquille de colimaçon, et à barbiche noire).

547:33. <devant moi. Tout le Bergotte que j'avais lentement et délicatement élaboré moi-même avec la transparente beauté de son œuvre, comme une stalactite est faite avec des gouttes d'eau, tout ce Bergotte là* se trouvait tout d'un coup ne plus pouvoir servir qu'il* fallait conserver le nez en colimaçon et utiliser la barbiche noire comme* n'est plus bonne

548:34. Il semblait bien> **549:6.** <d'homme à barbiche. [548: 36. <montra pas d'étonnement> 548:38. <autre, et ne sembla> 548:40. <d'un corps qui pensait au déjeuner prochain et à d'autres réalités> 549:1. <costume de* duc de Guise qu'il aurait mis>] {549:18-549:35}

549:36. Puis je l'entendis parler. Je compris l'impression de M. de Monfort*. Il avait en effet un organe bizarre mais rien n'altère>

549:39. <n'altère autant les qualités matérielles de* voix> **551:5.** <permettaient nullement à ceux qui n'avaient pas de génie d'augurer ce qu'il découvrirait dans une chose donnée et autre*. [549:41. <labiales en sont tout influencées. 549:42. <semblait pourtant entièrement différente de son style> 550:1. <celles qu'il écrivait. Mais la parole humaine sort> 550:5. <Bergotte se mettait à parler> 550:7. <qu'à M. de Norpois*> 550:8. <avec ces* parties de ces* livres où son style devenait si poétique et si musical. 550:13. <style, il avait> 550:14. <poursuivait sous eux> 550:18. <esthétique des choses qu'il

---

à rien, du moins la solution que nous avions trouvée pour un problème dont nous avions incomplètement la donnée et sans tenir compte que le total devait faire quarante-cinq. Le nez rouge en colimaçon et la barbiche noire étaient des éléments aussi inéluctables et d'autant plus gênants qu'ils ne me forçaient pas seulement à recouvrer entièrement mon personnage physique de Bergotte, mais encore semblaient impliquée*, produire, secréter incessamment un certaine genre d'esprit actif, satisfait de soi, ce qui n'était pas du* jeu, car cet esprit-là n'avait rien à voir avec la sorte d'intelligence répandue dans les livres de Bergotte, je ne serais jamais arrivé au nez rouge en colimaçon; mais en partant de ce nez qui n'avait pas l'air d'ailleurs de s'en inquiéter faisait* cavalier seul>

548:10. <seul et «fantaisie»> **548:15.** <et si on leur déclare: «X... a pour vous beaucoup d'amitié, finissent-ils plutôt eux-mêmes en ajoutant: Vous êtes bien aimable de vous faire ainsi l'écho.» Il semblait bien>

549:7. Il* me disais qu'il avait dû s'y appliquer mais qu'il avait vécu dans une île où il y avait des huîtres perlières, il aurait pu se livrer avec succès au commerce des perles. Son œuvre ne me semblait plus aussi inévitable. Et alors je me demandais si l'originalité des œuvres d'art prouvent* vraiment que nous soyions* des Dieux régnant>

549:13. <régnant chacun> **549:17.** <diverses personnalités.

550:18. ([1]dans sa conversation). 550:24. ([1]du). 550:41. ([1]sorte la petite quantité de Bergotte enfouie dans). 551:36. ([1]positif, de particulier). 552:29. ([1]qui «m'intriguait»). 553:5. ([1]façon à ce qu'ils). 553:27. ([1]cela qui portera). 554:5. ([1]comprendre (et même jamais dans les Maîtres-Chanteurs), comment). 554:7. ([1]pourtant Bergotte). 554:11. (dans* ouverture). 554:17. ([1]lui à partir

disait et l'effet, dans[1] la causerie, de ce> 550:20. <apercevoir tout de suite que les choses qu'il disait> 550:23. <parce qu'elles étaient vraiment> 550:24. <d'être de[1] Bergotte. 550:25. <dans ce qu'on appelait le genre Bergotte et que> 550:35. <vrai, qui était caché> 550:36. <chose, que Bergotte grâce à son génie parvenait à en extraire, ce qui était son but et non de faire du Bergotte. 550:41. <était en quelque sorte[1] Bergotte enfoui dans une chose que Bergotte en avait tiré*.] {551:6-551:28}

551:29. Aussi—de même que la diction de Bergotte eût été sans doute fort agréable si lui n'avait été que quelque amateur récitant plus ou moins du Bergotte, au lieu qu'elle était liée avec la pensée> **552:4.** <siennes propres. [551:35. <appliquait sa pensée à la chose qui lui> [551:36. <de positif,[1] particulier, de trop> 551:42. <question, négligeant ses aspects> 552:1. <faux, dans le paradoxe, et> 552:2. <confuses, car chacun appelle idées>] {552:4-552:27}

552:27. En réalité des paroles méconnaissables> **554:22.** <pour toujours. [552:29. <yeux et qui[1] m'intriguait* c'était bien au Bergotte que> 552:30. <elles ne s'inséraient pas dans> 552:34. <que je lui avais entendu dire> 552:37. <m'en avait paru> 552:42. <emphase, en faisant> 553:2. <nombre de v, d's, de g, semblant tous exploser de sa main qu'il ouvrait à ce moment-là) correspondait> 553:5. <aimés de façon[1] qu'ils y fussent en pleine lumière, précédées> 553:9. <dans son langage certain éclairage qui chez Bergotte comme chez quelques autres modifie> 553:12. <l'aspect des mots> 553:20. <séparable de son moi le plus intime. 553:21. <qui, dans les moments où il était entièrement naturel> 553:22. <les mots souvent fort insignifiants qu'il écrivait alors. Il n'est pas noté> 553:24. <ne l'indique> 553:25. <aux mots, on> 553:27. <chez l'auteur et c'est cela[1] qui n'est [*blanc*] en rien qui portera témoignage sur

---

du moment où il les transporta dans ses livres, il cessa d'en). 554:20. ([1]et bien plus quand je le connus, sa). 555:21. ([1]la). 555:23. ([1]qu'il répétait). 555:35. ([1]n'étant pas doué comme). 555:39. ([1]alors) ([2]original) ([3]Par réaction encore sans doute contre) ([4]Bergotte) ([5]rationnelle qu'il tappelait*, qui semblait). 556:13. ([1]*Rancé*). 556:15. ([1]un malade assure) ([2]lui). 556:17. ([1]harmonie pareille à) ([2]laquelle) ([3]donnaient à certains de leurs orateurs).

la plus intime essence de sa nature. 553:32. <traces chez Bergotte> 553:34. <frères et sœur, je> 553:38. <qui l'avait connu enfant> 553:39. <lui, comme chez> 553:35. <eux mais bien> 553:41. <tour à tour ces cris de violente gaieté et ces abandons de lente tristesse> 554:2. Si spécial qu'il> 554:3. <êtres est éphémère et> 554:5. <comprendre[1] dans les Maîtres-Chanteurs* et en général n'importe où de comprendre comment un artiste> 554:7. <écoutant chanter les oiseaux, en[1] revanche Bergotte> 554:9. <mots qui se prolongent en> 554:11. <telles fins de phrase, où l'accumulation des sons se prolonge comme d'une[1] ouverture d'Opéra> 554:14. <finir et répète dix fois sa dernière phrase avant que le chef d'orchestre ne pose son bâton, en laquelle je retrouvai> 554:17. Mais pour lui,[1] quand il les transpose dans ses livres, il cesse d'en user> 554:20. <il commença d'écrire et[1] quand je l'ai connu, sa> {554:23-555:16}

555:17. C'était, non plus> **555:39.** <seconde main> [555:21. <lui, le[1] manifestaient> 555:23. <prépositions que[1] lui répétait> 555:27. <gens n'avaient-ils> 555:29. <syntaxe et de l'accentuation qui est en> 555:35. <qu'il avait imité sans le vouloir, mais qui, lui, n'était[1] pas doué de génie comme Bergotte, n'avait>

555:39. <main, tandis[1] que, influencé dans le domaine de la conversation par son ami, il avait été originel*[2] et créateur quand il écrivait. Par[3] une autre réaction, ses doutes contre la précédente génération trop éloquente, trop amie des abstractions, des grands lieux communs, quand il[4] voulait dire du bien d'un livre, c'était toujours quelque scène faisant image, quelque tableau sans signification rationnelle[5] qui semblait lui être resté dans l'esprit.

556:4. «Ah! si, disait-il> **556:21.** <modernes d'où nous ne cherchons pas tirer* ce genre d'effets. [556:8. <son temps, car le mot qui> 556:13. <celui de *René*,[1] il> 556:15. <qui on[1] assure que le lait vous[2] fait> 556:16. <doux, il me semble que c'est ce qu'il y a de plus doux.» 556:17. <harmonie[1] douce à l'oreille et pareille à celle pour lesquels*[2] les anciens donnaient[3] à certains de leurs poètes, à certains de leurs orateurs des louanges>] {556:23-557:15}

557:16. Pourtant, malgré tant de correspondances que je perçus dans la suite, je n'avais pas cru au premier abord que c'était Bergotte que j'avais sous les yeux mais un tout autre homme à barbiche. Et peut-être d'ailleurs j'aurais eu en quelque manière raison de ne pas croire que cet homme qui se tenait là devant moi, fut* l'auteur des livres divins car lui-même, au sens vrai du mot croire, ne le croyait pas non plus. Il ne le croyait pas non plus puisqu'il avait si longtemps traité avec déférence des gens du monde, sans être d'ailleurs le moins du monde snob, des gens de lettres, des journalistes, qui étaient si inférieurs à ce grand écrivain. Maintenant par le suffrage de tous, il avait appris qu'il avait du génie, à côté de quoi le monde et les positions officielles ne sont rien. Il l'avait appris mais il ne le croyait pas puisqu'il continuait>

557:30. <continuait à simuler> **557:39.** <fauteuil académique[1] de telle duchesse utile[2] sans qu'aucune personne qui eut* estimé que c'était un vice, eut* pu le voir faire. [557:33. <éternel qui est> 557:36. <sait qu'il> 557:37. <barbiche[1] avait

---

557:16. *(B-A).* Si, pourtant, malgré> **557:18.** <au premier* que ce fut* Bergotte, que ce fut* l'auteur de tant de livres divins qui se trouvât devant moi, chez Mme Swann, peut-être n'avais* pas absolument tort, car lui-même (au vrai sens du mot) ne le «croyait» pas non plus. Il ne le croyait pas non plus puisqu'il montrait un grand empressement envers des gens du monde (sans être d'ailleurs le moins du monde snob), des gens de lettres, des journalistes, qui lui étaient si inférieurs. Maintenant par le suffrage des autres, il avait appris qu'il avait du génie, à côté de quoi le monde et les positions officielles ne sont rien. Il l'avait appris mais il ne le croyait pas puisqu'il continuait>

557:37. ([1]barbiche et à nez en colimaçon avait). 557:39. ([1]académique espéré de) ([2]utile, mais de s'en rapprocher sans entâchant* qu'aucune personne qui eut* estimé que c'était un vice, put* voir son manège.). 558:8. ([1]amour à demi incestueux). 558:16. ([1]prouvaient pas cependant, à supposer qu'on les lui imputât justement, que cette). 558:20. ([1]semblable, sont dus, certains à un excès d'autres à une insuffisance). 558:29. ([1]connaître les péchés de tous). 558:39. ([1]ou). 558:40. ([1]frappait) ([2]s'épurait la notion de moralité, d'autre) ([3]qu'il avait encore fait jusque là* de la vie privée des écrivains; et certains soirs, au théâtre on se montrait parfois Bergotte dans une loge dont la seule composition) ([4]sa dernière œuvre). 559:11. ([1]caché de sa profonde sensibilité). 559:18. ([1]eut*). 559:27. ([1]quand l'occasion). 559:29. ([1]langage de ceux qui continuent). 559:35. ([1]peindre) ([2]comme). 560:1. ([1]les) ([2]en vue) ([3]n'apercevrait certainement pas). 560:5. ([1]reste le bras levé à la).

des ruses d'homme du monde kleptomane, pour>] {557:43-558:6}

558:7. Quant à ces vices auxquels avait fait allusion M. de Norpois* > **558:39.** <ménage que*[1] le mauvais ton de leur foyer. [558:8. <amour[1] incestueux> 558:9. <d'indélicatesse d'argent> 558:13. <leurs personnages en> 558:16. <supporter, ils ne trouvaient*[1], pas cependant que cette littérature fût absolument mensongère, et tant de sensibilité une pure comédie. 558:20. <semblable[1] peuvent être tout différents selon qu'ils sont dus à un excès ou à une insuffisance de tension, de sécrétion, etc., de même qu'il peut> 558:25. <force anxieuse. Et l'artiste lui donne> 558:29. <l'Eglise commencent tout en étant bons par sentir[1] le mal de tous les hommes et en tirent la sainteté de leur vie personnelle, souvent> 558:33. <tous. C'est toujours plus spécialement les vices> 558:35. <les propos inconséquents de leur fille, l'adultère de> 558:37. <les écrivains ont flétri* dans>]

558:40. Mais ce contraste frappant[1] moins autrefois qu'à l'époque de Bergotte, parce qu'au fur et à mesure que se corrompait la société et que s'épuisait[2] le sentiment moral, d'autre part le public se mettait au courant plus qu'il[3] ne l'était autrefois de la vie privée des écrivains et se montrait parfois dans une salle de théâtre la loge du romancier dont la seule composition semblait un commentaire singulièrement risible ou poignant de la thèse qu'il venait de soutenir dans ses[4] dernières œuvres. Ce n'est pas ce que chacun put* me dire qui>

559:8. <me dire qui> **560:13.** <dans les musées. [559:11. <trait touchant car il avait été évidemment destiné à rester caché[1] de la sensibilité profonde. 559:13. < avait traité sa femme avec cruauté. Mais> 559:15. <veiller une pauvre malade dont le fils avait été tué, et quand> 559:18. <malheureuse et ait[1] des attentions pour elle. 559:20. <se développa en lui aux> 559:27. <quand[1] par hasard l'occasion> 559:27. <s'adresser à eux, au moins> 559:29. <point de vue mais au point de vue même de celui qui souffrait et d'où lui aurait fait horreur le langage[1] de devoir compassion à ceux qui continuent à penser à leurs petits intérêts personnels devant la douleur d'autrui. 559:33. <de lui à côté de rancunes justifiées des gratitudes ineffaçables.

559:35. <homme qui n'aimait que certaines images; que les composer et les prendre[1] sous les mots, couper[2] une miniature au fond d'une boîte. Pour> 559:40. <se montrait souvent insatiable dans> 559:42. <devant une Cour d'assises, malgré> 560:1> produire sur des[1] juges, mais d'après[2] des images que le juge ne[3] verrait pas. 560:4. <je lui racontai que> 560:5. <où elle revoit[1] Thésée, la main levée à la hauteur> 560:6. <précisément la scène où> 560:7. <elle avait eu le génie d'évoquer exactement avec un art très noble, et jusque dans la couleur même, les vierges de l'ancien Eréchtchéion* qu'elle n'a peut être* d'ailleurs jamais vues.] {560:13-560:17}

560:18. —Ce[1] sont des cariatides? demanda Swann. **560:22.** <bien plus ancien> [560:29. <sa passion à [*blanc*][1] et> 560:21. <mouvement d'Hégeso* dans le* stèle de Céramique>

560:22. <ancien qu'elle évoque. Le portrait des Koraï de l'ancien Eréchtchéion*. {560:23-560:31}

560:32. Je savais ce qu'il voulait dire, car je connaissais ces statues archaïques par un livre de lui où il leur adresse une invocation qui est une de ses plus belles pages.

560:7. *(B-A).* <elle avait su> **560:11.** <de l'ancien Erechtchéion*.

560:18. ([1]—Vous parlez des). 560:29 ([1]Œnone).

560:22. *(B-A).* <ancien qu'elle évoque. Je parlais des Koraï> **560:25.** <une de plus. Oh! et puis si elle est bien jolie la petite Phèdre du VIe siècle reste* son bras levé. C'est très fort d'avoir trouvé ça. Il y a beaucoup plus d'antiquité dans ce geste là* que dans bien des livres qu'on appelle en ce moment «antiques».

560:32. *(In the text of* Grasset B *this sentence was eliminated.)* 561:1. ([1]existait effectivement). 564:3. ([1]années, pendant). 564:9. ([1]eut* fait poser à demi déguisée, prête pour un dîner de «têtes», en vénitienne.) ([2]bruns) ([3]intérieur le grimage) ([4]seulement) ([5]incarné; figurant quelque animal). 564:32. ([1]soulexait* pour garder intacts les deux grains). 564:35. ([1]démarcation entre les deux ressemblances). 564:41. ([1]cet ovale se). 565:5. ([1]maintenant lui saient* brusquement changer) ([2]en). 565:24. ([1]Mélusine). 566:36. ([1]quand* en pensant à) ([2]remarquer, mais d'un ton détaché, ennuyé, comme s'il voulait rester en quelque sorte en dehors de ce qu'il disait, avec quelle intelligence, quelle ingéniosité elle disait à Œnone: «Tu). 567:22. ([1]Bergotte me demanda comment j'avais trouvé la Berma.) ([2]que je n'avais pas eu de plaisir, et) ([3]pas lui dire les raisons de ma déception. Il parla) ([4]produire sur lui). 568:17. ([1]et que cet) ([2]j'avais aimé) ([3]étranger). 568:30. ([1]en me les entendant). 568:34. ([1]passé dans ses). 568:36. ([1]saints, ayant). 568:38. ([1]ayant la plus grande) ([2]J'aurais dû me dire tout cela, mais je ne le disais pas, j'étais persuadé que j'avais paru stupide à Bergotte, et j'étais entrain* de me désoler, quand) ([3]accompagnée).

—C'est[1] à ce moment-là une véritable statue du VIe siècle, c'est d'un art très noble.

Voilà qui me donnait une nouvelle raison de m'intéresser au jeu de la Berma. Je tâchais de revoir la Berma celle* qu'elle était dans cette scène où je me souvenais qu'elle avait élevé les mains à hauteur d'épaule. Et je me disais: «Voilà une de ces admirables orantes de l'Acropole, voilà ce que c'est qu'un art noble.» Mais pour que cette idée pût embellir pour moi les gestes de la Berma, il aurait fallu que Bergotte me l'eût fournit* avant la représentation.

561:1. Alors pendant que cette attitude de la Berma aurait[1] existé effectivement> **561:12.** <sanction objective. [561:3. <lieu est encore pleine des profondeurs de la réalité, j'aurais pu essayer d'en extraire ou d'y mêler l'idée de la sculpture archaïque et de l'en embellir. Mais> 561:7. <comme une simple image, sans ces dessous du présent d'où l'on peut tirer> 561:9. <nouveau et à laquelle je ne pouvais imposer> 561:11. <qui n'aurait plus été>] {561:12-564:2}

564:3. Pendant que nous causions avec Bergotte (et de ma part peut être* plus librement que je n'aurais cru car depuis des années[1] que pendant tant d'heures de lecture et de solitude où il n'était pour moi que la meilleure partie de moi-même, j'avais pris avec lui l'habitude de la sincérité, de la franchise, de la confiance et j'étais moins intimidé devant lui que devant un autre, parce que c'était bien loin d'être la première fois que je causais avec lui) [*cf.* 568:1], Gilberte à qui on avait déjà dit deux fois d'aller se préparer>

564:4. <préparer pour sortir> **564:9.** <en Gilberte les traits, l'expression, les mouvements de sa mère; elle avait l'air d'un portrait de Mme Swann que le peintre par un caprice de coloriste, eut*[1] fait poser en vénitienne. Et comme elle n'avait pas seulement une perruque blonde, mais que tout atome sombre avait été expulsé de sa chair qui, dévêtue de ses voiles blancs,[2] semblait plus nue, en le seul duvet des rayons dégagés par un soleil incorporé,[3] le grimage ne semblait pas sûrement[4] superficiel, mais incarné;[5] animal fabuleux, elle avait l'air d'un travesti mythologique. Cette peau rousse de Gilberte c'était celle de son père

au point que la nature semblait avoir eu à résoudre le problème quand elle avait créé Gilberte de refaire Mme Swann, en n'ayant>

564:28. <en n'ayant> **565:5.** <alors on voyait> [564:32. <nez de Mme Swann parfaitement reproduit, la peau se reflait*[1] sur les grains> 564:35. <blanc à côté d'un lilas violet. Mais la ligne de démarcation[1] n'était pas nette. Par> 564:29. <on voyait l'ovale> 564:41. <mélange; il[1] se précisait>]

565:5. <on voyait dans ses yeux ce regard incertain, dissimulé et triste qu'avait sa mère quand elle mentait, quand Swann lui demandait où elle était allée, et qu'elle lui faisait une de ces réponses qui jadis désespérait l'amant et maintenant[1] laissait [*blanc*] changer la conversation au[2] mari prudent et sans curiosité. Mais si souvent aux Champs-Elysées ce regard-là m'avait inquiété, c'était à tort. Car chez elle, survivance toute physique de sa mère, il ne correspondait plus à rien.

565:16. C'est quand> **565:24.** <de cette mélusine*.[1] [565:18. <que des pupilles exécutaient> 565:19. <d'Odette étaient* causés par la peur de trahir qu'elle> 565:21. <pressée d'aller à>] {565:25-566:32}

566:33. —Allons, va> **566:36.** <en cachant sa tête entre les genoux de son père qui, passant tendrement les doigts dans la chevelure blonde, dit: «tu es bonne* fille» en prenant soudain l'air tout proche des larmes que nous avons quand[1] nous pensons à la trop grande tendresse d'un être qui est destiné à nous survivre. Mais pour ne pas laisser voir cette impression, il se mêla à notre conversation sur la Berma. Il me fit remarquer[2] avec quelle intelligence, quelle ingéniosité dans le vrai elle disait à Osmone*: «Tu le savais!» Il avait raison: cette intonation était clairement intelligible. Et comme on pouvait expliquer nettement ce que signifiait cette intonation, il semblait qu'elle eût dû satisfaire à mon désir> {566:39-567:6}

567:16. <désir de trouver> **567:22.** <quiconque la concevrait> [567:19. <si intelligente, d'une>]

□**567:22.** <la concevrait aussi clairement la possèderait aussi pleinement. Sans doute la Berma l'avait trouvée mais est-ce vraiment trouver que de trouver quelque chose qui ne serait pas différent si on l'avait reçu, quelque chose qui ne tient pas es-

sentiellement à votre être puisqu'un autre maintenant peut le reproduire sans le concours de cet être.

«Avez-vous[1] été content, me dit Bergotte.» Mais comme devant un médecin de qui on attendrait un diagnostic d'où la santé dépend, on s'attache à décrire exactement ce qu'on éprouva et non à faire des phrases, je lui avouai que[2] non, et ne pus pas[3] plus lui dire les raisons de ma déception qu'on ne peut souvent définir au médecin ce qu'on éprouve. Il parla ensuite à d'autres personnes, à Gilberte; je pensais à la mauvaise impression que j'avais dû lui[4] produire, d'autant plus qu'il devait être plus sévère encore que M. de Norpois*, ayant dit de ce diplomate quand on avait prononcé son nom: «qu'il l'avait trouvé assommant.» D'ailleurs ce n'était pas d'aujourd'hui mais dès les premières lectures que j'avais faites de ses livres dans le jardin de Combray qu'imaginant son intelligence comme une inaccessible perfection, j'avais pensé au mépris qu'il aurait sans doute pour mes idées. Pourtant j'aurais dû me dire que puisque> {567:29-568:5}

568:11. <puisque c'était sincèrement> **568:25.** <ses regards> [568:14. <théâtre une déception dont> 568:17. <l'autre, devaient obéir aux mêmes lois et[1] cet esprit de Bergotte que j'aimais[2] dans ses livres ne devait pas être quelque chose de si étrange,[3] de si hostile> 568:22. <peut-être n'existe-t-il même qu'une seul* intelligence dont tout le monde est colocataire*, une intelligence>]

568:25. <ses regards, comme au théâtre, contrairement à ce que j'avais cru quand j'étais enfant, si chacun a sa place, en revanche il n'y a qu'une seule scène, commune pour tous.

568:26. Sans doute les idées que j'avais l'habitude d'expliquer n'étaient pas celles que considérait d'ordinaire Bergotte dans ses livres. Mais> **568:38.** <qu'ils ne commettent pas> [568:30. <avions à notre disposition, il devait, comme[1] les entendant exprimer> 568:31. <aimer, me sourire ayant sans doute, à mon grand étonnement, devant son œil intérieur, toute une autre partie> 568:34. <découpure avait fait*[1] ses livres> 568:36. <que les saints[1] sont ceux qui ayant>]

568:38. <pas, de même les génies étant[1] ceux qui ont la plus grande expérience de l'intelligence, peuvent le mieux comprendre

les idées qui sont les plus opposées à celles qui sont le fond de leurs œuvres. Et[2] de même de* Bergotte j'aurais dû me dire [*blanc*], mais je ne le disais pas, j'étais désolé, j'étais persuadé que je lui avais paru stupide, quand Gilberte que j'avais accompagné*[3] dans sa chambre pendant qu'elle mettait son chapeau me dit: {568:43-569:5}

569:9. —Je nage> **569:11.** <extrêment intelligent.

□**569:23.** Ce fut avec Bergotte, pendant que les Swann étaient dans une autre voiture que je fis route en allant au[1] Jardin d'Acclimatation. Il me parla de ma santé, et me dit:

569:25. —Nos amis> **569:30.** <les connaissent.

569:31. Hélas il disait cela mais combien je sentais que c'était peu vrai pour moi, comme tout raisonnement me laissait froid, comme je n'étais heureux que dans les moments de pure flânerie, quand j'éprouvais du bien-être; combien ce que je désirais dans la vie était purement matériel, et avec quelle facilité je me passerais de l'intelligence. Comme je ne distinguais pas entre les plaisirs ceux qui venaient en moi de différentes sources et plus ou moins profonds* et durables, je pensai que j'avais une vie où j'aurais été lié avec la duchesse de Guermantes, et où j'aurais souvent senti comme dans les water-closets des Champs-Elysées une odeur qui m'eût rappelé Combray. Dans cet idéal>

570:1. <idéal de vie> **570:17.** <dégoût de moi-même. [570:4. <monsieur,[1] lui dis-je, les> 570:7. Vous croyez vraiment,[1] me dit-il. Eh bien> 570:11. <étroit. Au[1] lieu de ce que m'avait dit M. de Monfort*,[2] j'avais>]

569:12. C'est à Saint-Cloud que nous allons avec lui n'est-ce pas? demandai-je à Gilberte. —«Oh! où on voudra, moi vous savez aller ici ou là.»

569:14. Mais depuis l'incident du concert je me demandais si le caractère de Gilberte n'était pas le contraire de ce que j'avais cru> **569:22.** <par hasard contrariés.

569:23. ([1]à Saint-Cloud).

569:31. *(B-A)* Hélas! ce qu'il> **570:1.** <cet idéal de vie> [569:34. <moments de pure flânerie>]

570:4. ([1]monsieur, les). 570:7. ([1]vraiment, lui dis-je* avec le scrupule du malade qui a peur de mentir au médecin. Eh bien) 570:11. ([1]A cause de ce) ([2]Norpois). 570:17. ([1]Norpois) ([2]le jugement sans appel, il ôtait à ce jugement beaucoup) ([3]comprimée.) 573:33. ([1]en). 573:34. ([1]cette personne). 573:40. ([1]semblait prophétiser). 573:42. ([1]raconté). 574:1. ([1]qu'elle fut* encore un peu plus mauvaise, n'avait). 575:3. ([1]ce verdict de Bergotte pour). 575:9. ([1]cela commun).

570:17. Surtout par ce qu'il avait dit de M. de Monfort*,[1] dont j'avais cru l'opinion[2] irrésistible, il ôtait à cette opinion beaucoup de son poids. Et ma propre opinion de moi-même, moins confirmée,[3] recommençait à occuper plus de volume. {570:20-573:22}

573:7. Mes parents furent désolés d'apprendre que j'avais passé la journée avec Bergotte. «Mauvaise relation», dit ma mère. Hélas quand j'eus ajouté qu'il ne goûtait pas du tout M. de Norpois*:

—Naturellement! s'écria mon père. Cela prouve bien que c'est un esprit faux et malveillant.

Mes parents n'étaient pas déjà enchantés que j'allasse tant chez les Swann. {573:19-573:22}

573:24. La présentation> **575:25.** <inviter Gilberte. [573:25. <leur apparaissait comme> 573:26. <avaient eue de me laisser aller dans ce milieu, de ce que mon grand-père eut* appelé un «manque le circonspection». Je sentis> 573:30. <M. de Norpois*> 573:33. <moi à[1] ce> 573:34. <si elle[1] avait> 573:35. <quelqu'un qu'il n'estimait pas> 573:37. <lui en paraissait que plus étendu. 573:40. <réformes dont il fallait[1] proclamer l'imminence. 573:42. <comme, ne l'eussé-je pas dit[1]> 574:1. <parents, qu'elle[1] le fit* un peu plus ou un peu moins, n'avait pas grande importance. 574:8. <les gens intelligents bêtes, qui était> 574:9. <gens et dont la louange me paraîtrait enviable et m'encourageait* au mal> 574:11. <d'un air désespéré que> 574:18. <préjugé contre Bergotte, contre lequel> 574:20. <faire toutes les louanges que je lui aurais données, seraient demeurées vaines. 574:26. —Ah! il a dit cela reprit> 574:27. <rien son talent devant lequel tout> 574:30. <père Monfort*> 574:35. <interrompit ma mère> 574:37. <Montfort est> 575:1. <doigts les mêches de mes cheveux> 575:3. <attendu cela[1] pour> 575:5. <quand j'avais> 575:5. <n'osais pas pour> 575:7. <contraire, dans nos goûters, maman> 575:9. <cela[1]

575:34. Ce fut vers cette époque que Bloch changea ma conception du monde, ouvrit pour moi des possibilités nouvelles du* bonheur qui se changeaient plus tard en possibilités de souffrance, en m'assurant que, contrairement à ce que je croyais à Combray les désirs que j'avais ressentis si souvent du côté de Méséglise n'avaient rien d'irréalisable et que les femmes ne demandaient pas mieux que de faire l'amour.

bien commun> 575:11. <jamais arriver à> 575:16. <quand arriverait Gilberte> 575:19. Mais puisque je ne la connais pas. 575:23. <Mme Swann n'a pas>] {575:27-575:33; 577:31-579:8}

575:40. Il compléta> □**576:2.** <figure vague, sorte de moyenne entre les différentes beautés je* connaissais déjà. Les maisons de passe devaient un jour me permettre on le verra plus tard de substituer des visages particuliers à ce type abstrait. De sorte que si j'avais à Bloch, par sa bonne nouvelle, le bonheur, la possession de la beauté ne sont pas choses inaccessibles et qu'il est inutile d'y avoir à jamais renoncé, une obligation de même genre qu'à tel psychothérapeute ou tel philosophe optimiste qui nous fait espérer la longévité dans ce monde et de ne pas en être entièrement séparé quand on aura passé dans l'autre, les maisons de passe que je fréquentais quelques années plus tard, elles, en me fournissant des échantillons du bonheur, en me permettant d'ajouter à cette beauté des femmes cet élément>

576:15. <cet élément que> **576:32.** <d'anciennes curiosités> [576:18. <nous-même, dans lequel> 576:21. <individuel, méritèrent> 576:24. <séduction de Martagnan*, de> 576:27. <symphoniques et les voyages d'art. Mais celle où>]

□**576:32.** <curiosités ou en contracter de nouvelles.

La maquerelle ne connaissait aucune des femmes qu'on aurait voulu lui demander et elle nous en proposait toujours dont on n'aurait pas voulu. En éteignant la lumière dans la chambre où j'étais, et en laissant la porte ouverte, elle me les faisait voir sans que je fusse vu d'elles. La maquerelle m'en voulait* toujours une qui avait le sourire plein de promesses (comme si ç'avait été une rareté et un régal) elle* prétendait juive et qu'à cause de cela sans doute elle appelait Rachel. Elle était brune pas belle, mais avait l'air intelligent semblait* bonne fille et non sans passer un bout de langue sur ses lèvres, souriait d'un air plein d'impertinence aux michés qu'on lui présentait et que j'entendais du fond de mon obscurité entamer la conversation avec elle. Elle avait autour de son mince et étroit visage de beaux cheveux noirs frisés qui l'exprimaient comme dans un dessin à l'encre de Chine. Chaque fois je promettais à la maquerelle qui la proposait avec une insistance particulière en vantant sa grande intelligence et son instruction que ce serait mon tour de faire la connaissance de Rachel, surnommée par moi «Rachel quand du Seigneur». Mais le premier soir je l'avais attendue* au moment où j'arrivais et où elle partait dire à la maquerelle:

577:15. —Alors> □**577:19.** <générale de personnes, dont l'habitude commune et quelle que put* être la profession de chacune dans la journée était de venir là le soir voir s'il n'y avait pas quelqu'un et un louis ou deux à gagner. Elle variait seulement la forme de la phrase en disant:

—Si vous avez besoin de moi «si vous avez besoin de quelqu'un.

La maquerelle qui ne connaissait pas l'opéra d'Halévy ne savait pas pourquoi j'avais pris l'habitude de dire «Rachel quand du Seigneur» (aussi invariablement que Rachel: Vous me ferez chercher si vous avez quelqu'un). Mais pour ne pas comprendre cette plaisanterie elle ne la trouvait pas moins drôle et c'est chaque fois en riant de tout son cœur qu'elle me disait:

—Alors, ce n'est pas encore ce soir que je vous unis à «Rachel quand du Seigneur.»

579:9. Mes parents cependant auraient voulu que> **579:24.** <posais à moi-même> [579:14. <quand la demeure des Swann me> 579:15. <assis à ma table que> 579:17. <rentré chez moi, mon> 579:19. <paroles auquel je m'étais machinalement laissé entraîner> 579:21. Seul à ma table, je> 579:23. <je tenais moi-même la place>]

579:24. <à moi-même une question fictive obéissant au principe de finalité et dont mes traits brillants n'étaient[1] que l'heureuse répartie. Bien qu'il fût silencieux, cet exercice était une conversation>

579:27. <conversation et non une méditation> **579:33.** <plaisir tout passif> [579:28. <non moi-même, mais> 579:30. <former, non les pensées que je croyais vraies mais celles> 579:32. <dehors au[1] dedans>]

579:33. <passif que trouve à faire le moins de mouvements possibles* quelqu'un qui est alourdi par un[1] mal d'estomac. Si j'avais été moins>

579:36. <moins résolu à me mettre> **580:5.** <quelques pages> [579:42. <ne pas faire* un soir où j'étais si mal disposé un début> 580:1. <hélas! ne[1] se montraient pas plus favorables. Mais j'étais raisonnable. Ce[2] qui avait attendu> 580:4. <jours. J'étais si certain que>]

580:5. <pages, que de ma résolution je ne disais pas un seul mot à mes parents; ils avaient pu le prendre pour une bonne parole; j'aimais mieux>

579:24. ([1]ne seraient). 579:32. ([1]vers le). 579:33. ([1]une mauvaise digestion.). 580:1. ([1]ne devaient pas se montrer plus) ([2]De la part de qui). 580:15. ([1]partant, plus autant de courage). 580:22. ([1]*In* Grasset A *and* Grasset B *there is an indentation here.*) 580:25. ([1]peut-être) ([2]par l'énervement). 580:28. ([1]son scepticisme venait). 580:36. ([1]le) ([2]talent. Et pourtant croire que quelqu'un) ([3]peut le recevoir). 581:21. ([1]venir le lendemain prendre). 592:5. ([1]*choufleuri*). 592:9. ([1]toujours un peu tard). 592:25. ([1]attelés. Non*. Le passant croyait, et non sans un certain émoi, à une modification survenue dans cette cause mystérieuse, quand il voyait l'un de ces coupés). 592:38. ([1]P.-S.* Stahl). 592:41. ([1]ne pourrait pas contenir pas* deux fleurs—il semble, à cause). 593:1. ([1]dû). 593:19. ([1]A travers). 593:29. ([1]Odette). 594:36. ([1]y manquait le moins souvent possible, ayant) ([2]elle à la même heure. Les jours où Mme Swann n'était pas sortie de chez elle, on la trouvait dans une robe). 595:20. ([1]portières et desquels ce que).

580:6. <mieux patienter> **580:22.** Hé bien> [580:9. <vaste que j'attendais dans> 580:10. <fini, simplement ma> 580:11. <internes avait* duré> 580:15. <immédiatement, n'ayant[1] plus le même courage> 580:17. <pour me décider à me coucher. 580:19. <fallait pour reprendre> 580:20. <détente, et le seul jour où>]

580:22. Hé bien, ce travail, on n'en parle même plus.

Je lui en voulus, persuadé[1]>

580:23. <persuadé> **580:36.** <en étant paresseux> [580:24. <voir que ma résolution de travailler était définitivement prise, elle> 580:25. <venait d'ajourner encore une fois et pour longtemps [*blanc*][1] l'exécution, l'énervement[2]> 580:28. <que sa[1] parole sceptique venait de heurter sans l'avoir vue une volonté silencieuse et ferme. Elle> 580:31. Et pour que je ne décourageasse* pas> 580:34. D'ailleurs en passant> 580:35. <ne faisais-je pas comme Bergotte? Il semblait presque à mes parents que>]

580:36. <paresseux, si je vivais dans un[1] même salon qu'un grand écrivain, je menais la vie la plus favorable au talent,[2] comme si croire que quelqu'un peut être dispensé de faire son talent soi-même, par le dedans, et le[3] recevoir d'autrui, n'était pas aussi absurde que croire qu'un homme peut se faire une bonne santé tout en manquant à toutes les règles de l'hygiène et en commettant tous les excès, rien qu'en dînant souvent en ville avec un médecin. Même, quand je disais à Mme Swann que je ne pouvais pas venir goûter, elle avait l'air de trouver>

581:5. <trouver que je faisais> **581:8.** <n'est pas bien. [581:6. <paroles elle dit:] {581:8-581:13}

581:14. Et elle ajoutait> **581:21.** <venir[1] prendre une tasse de thé chez elle avec Bergotte vers six heures. [581:17. <un volontaire avec> 581:18. <son colonel, dans>] {581:22-592:3}

592:4. Car ce n'était pas seulement à Gilberte que je faisais des visites. Mme Swann m'avait tout de suite dit:

592:5. —C'est très bien de venir chez Gilberte, mais je veux aussi que vous veniez me voir, moi, pas à mon *choupfleury*[1] où vous vous ennuyeriez* parce que> 592:9. <trouverez toujours[1] tard. {592:10-592:16}

592:16. Dans ce quartier> **593:4.** <morte décoration. [592:17. <aujourd'hui qui, même au centre> 592:19. <salon presque au

rez-de-chaussée tel qu'était celui de Mme Swann, suffisaient> 592:25. <attelés.[1] Non sans un certain émoi le passant croyait à quelque modification survenue dans la cause mystérieuse, en voyant l'un de ces coupés> 592:29. <craignant que ses chevaux ne prissent froid> 592:30. <faire ainsi de temps> 592:35. <rue, si l'hôtel ou l'appartement n'étaient pas> 592:38. <P.-S. Stehl*> 592:41. <col qui ne[1] contiendrait pas deux fleurs—il semble bien, à cause> 593:1. <avoir du*[1] répondre chez les maîtresses de maison plutôt>] {593:4-593:19}

593:19. Et[1] à travers les arborescences des espèces variées qui faisaient ressembler la fenêtre éclairée au vitrage de la serre d'enfant qu'on donne à Mlle Lili pour ses étrennes, le passant>

593:21. <passant, se hissant> **593:37.** <singulier qui commandait* la déférence et exigeait* de l'attention. [593:25. <deux entailles* dans une topaze> 593:26. <salon ambré par le samovar—invention nouvelle alors—> 593:29. Mme Swann continuait à tenir à ce thé autant que quand elle était Mme[1] de Crécy; elle> 593:36. <note avec un air grave>] {593:38-594:36}

594:36. Dès la fin d'octobre elle n'y[1] manquait pas un seul jour, ayant entendu dire que si Mme Verdurin s'était fait un salon c'était parce qu'on était toujours sûr de le* trouver chez elle,[2] on la trouvait dans une robe de chambre de crêpe, blanche comme une première neige, souvent aussi> {594:42-595:11}

595:14. <aussi dans un> **595:29.** <ce qui ajoutait> [595:17. <peu approprié* à l'hiver> 595:20. <fermés de portière[1] et dans ce que> 595:22. <capitonnés»—l'air frileux des roses qui pouvaient> 595:24. <l'hiver, roses et nues comme au printemps. 595:27. <maison n'était pas avertie>]

595:29. <ajoutait encore à l'impression de romanesque, d'une sorte de secret surpris que nous donne aujourd'hui le souvenir de ces robes que Mme Swann était peut-être la seule à porter encore et qui nous donnent l'expression* que la femme qui le* portait devait être une héroïne de roman parce que nous ne les avons pour la plupart vues que dans les illustrations de certains romans d'Henry Gréville comme [*blanc*]. Elle avait maintenant, au commencement de l'hiver, des chrysanthèmes énormes et d'une variété

595:29. *(B-A)* <ajoutait encore> **595:37.** <d'Henry Gréville.

de couleurs comme Swann jadis n'en eût pas pu voir chez elle. Mon admiration pour eux, quand j'allais faire une visite à Mme Swann, venait sans doute>

596:2. <sans doute de ce que, rose pâle comme> **596:13.** <les avoir aperçus> [596:4. <chambre de crêpe,[1] ou d'un> 596:5. <samovar[1] de vieux cuivre anglais, ils superposaient une seconde décoration à celle du salon, d'un coloris> 596:8. <j'étais moins touché> 596:9. <avaient d'éphémère, que par ce qu'ils avaient de relativement> 596:10. <tons, eux aussi roses ou cuivrés>]

596:13. <aperçus s'éteignait au ciel, avant d'entrer chez Mme Swann, je retrouvait* prolongés, transposés dans cette palette enflammés* des fleurs, comme dans la toile d'un grand coloriste qui eut* orné l'intérieur d'une demeure humaine par [*blanc*] des feux du dehors arrachés à l'instabilité de l'atmosphère et du soleil. Ils m'invitaient, ces chrysanthèmes, à goûter avidement>

596:20. <avidement pendant> **596:24.** <l'atteindre; elle leur ressemblait si[1] peu. [596:23. <dans la conversation que>]

596:24. Même avec Mme Cottard, et quoique l'heure fût avancée, Mme Swann se faisait [*blanc*][1] pour dire: «mais non il n'est pas tard» et[2] en faire accepter une tasse de plus à la femme du docteur[3] toujours son porte-cartes à la main.

—On ne peut pas s'en aller de chez vous, disait Mme Bontemps à Mme Swann>

596:4. ([1]grèbe*). 596:5. ([1]samovar, ils).

596:13. *(B-A)* <aperçus avant que> **596:19.** <goûter avidement>

596:24. ([1]bien). 596:24. ([1]caressante) ([2]et faire) ([3]docteur qui gardait son). 596:39. ([1]—«Et Mme Bontemps se plaignait de l'ennui que lui causaient [*the punctuation of direct discourse is retained*]). 599:18. ([1]Rauthnitz). 606:42. ([1]demandait). 607:1. ([1]s'écriant*) 607:28. ([1]plaisirs de l'hiver dont) ([2]Ils n'étaient pas venus et cependant) ([3]«on ferme!») ([4]j'aurais) ([5]plaisirs inconnus.) ([6]trouvaient-ils donc pas situés). 615:11. ([1]la rue Lapérouse) ([2]de matières précieuses). 615:34. ([1]Mme Swann entassait et pétrissait derrière mon dos les coussins, ils). 616:7. ([1]élevée. Car) ([2]tendresse; celle-ci) ([3]charmantes) ([4]pouvait pourtant pas) ([5]imposer) ([6]possédait, lui, qu'ils* semblaient si naturellement incorporés à ses mains ou à sa voix.) 616:18. ([1]avec des) ([2]indispensables, de la même). 616:30. ([1]de sorte que) ([2]si l'on avait appris qu'ailleurs, chez les Verdurin par exemple, elle passaît pour bête, tout le monde eut* été bien étonné. Je). 616:42. ([1]finement et disait: «On). 618:28. ([1]lui avaient ajouté si longtemps à Odette un ventre postiche dont). 619:10. ([1]en). 620:2. ([1]«choufleuri»). 620:12. ([1]sa taille et à). 620:37. ([1]cela).

596:32. <Swann, tandis que> **596:39** <peu aimable> [596:33. <sa surprise naïve d'entendre> 596:34. C'est ce que je dis toujours», approuvée>]

596:39. <aimable, et restant devant les brillants amis d'Odette, sur la réserve, sinon sur la défensive.

—Voilà[1] j'adore causer avec une petite femme intelligente comme vous, reprenait Mme Bontemps s'adressant à Odette et en profitant pour exprimer par contraste l'ennui que lui causaient> {596:41-597:43}

598:1. <causaient les femmes> **598:18.** <puisque votre père> [598:8. <obligations. Ah bien vous avez> 598:12. <langue, c'est tel que je vous le dis! Et ma fille est comme moi. 598:17. <répondu ma fille avec>]

598:19. <père était marmiton.» Comme ça, dans la figure, vlan, tel que je vous le dis. Vous avez de la chance de pouvoir vous retenir, j'envie les gens qui savent déguiser leur pensée.» —«Mais je n'en ai pas besoin, madame; je ne suis> {598:20-598:24}

598:30. <suis pas si difficile> **599:18.** <je suis une fervente> [598:31. Mme Cottard, d'abord> 598:36. <l'admiration de son mari> 598:38. <utile à la carrière du docteur> 598:42. <mets à faire comme elle. C'est> 599:1. <dire qu'elle faisait des grimaces; mon> 599:10. <lettres, tel que je vous le dis. Je> 599:12. <comme les méchancetés.]

599:18. <une fervente de Rothnitz*.[1]

—Oh! bien> **599:22.** <chiffre. {599:23-599:26}

599:26. Et montrant à Mme Swann un tour de cou que celle-ci lui avait donné.

—Vous reconnaissez? {599:29-603:40}

603:40. —Oh! Madame Bontemps, je vois que vous vous levez, disait Mme Swann, c'est très mal de donner le signal de la fuite, vous me devez une compensation de n'être pas venue jeudi dernier... Mais non, ne regardez pas la pendule, ce n'est pas l'heure, elle ne va pas.

—Allons je me rassieds un instant, vous savez, moi, j'adore causer avec une petite femme intelligente comme vous [*cf.* 604:18 and 596:39]. {603:43-605:1}

605:1. Parlez-moi de ça; mais le monde officiel, toutes ces femmes d'Excellences qui ne savent que parler de chiffons! Tenez, madame, pas>

605:4. <pas plus tard> **605:12.** <je n'ai pas raison? [605:5. <*Lohengrin* la femme du ministre de>] {605:13-606:40}

606:40. Mais elle avait entendu Mme Cottard qui venait de dire à Mme Swann:

—«Le docteur a une passion.»

606:40. Et l'œil brillant> **607:4.** <pour sa vue. [606:42. <madame?» avait demandé[1] Mme> 607:1. <s'écria[1] Mme Bontemps.] {607:5-607:6}

607:6. A propos de vue, Odette, savez-vous que> **607:8.** <à l'électricité? {607:8-607:13}

607:13. C'est évidemment> **607:23.** <un vrai casse-tête. [607:15. <du nouveau. Il y a la belle-sœur> 607:19. <j'ai intrigué> 607:20. <pas l'avoir à>]

607:26. Allons, Odette, je me sauve, vous me faites> **607:27.** <après mon mari!»

607:28. Et moi aussi, il fallait que je rentre, désolé de partir avant d'avoir goûté à ces plaisirs[1] dont les chrysanthèmes m'avaient semblé être l'enveloppe éclatante. Cependant[2] on n'avait pas l'air d'attendre autre chose, Mme Swann laissait les domestiques emporter le thé comme elle aurait dit «enferme»*[3] et je sentais que j'aurai*[4] pu rester encore sans rencontrer ces plaisirs.[5] Ne se trouvait-il*[6] donc pas situé sur cette pente insensible, sur cette route battue, des heures qui m'avaient mené, si vite, à l'instant du départ, mais sur quelque chemin de traverse où je n'avais pas su bifurquer. {607:42-615:11}

615:11. Avant cet instant du départ Mme Cottard n'avait pas manqué de féliciter Mme Swann sur les meubles nouveaux, les récentes acquisitions qu'elle avait remarquées dans le salon de celle-ci. Elle pouvait d'ailleurs y reconnaître mais en petit nombre quelques objets qu'Odette avait autrefois dans son petit hôtel de l'Arc-de-Triomphe,[1] notamment tous ses animaux en[2] substances précieuses, tous ses fétiches.

Mais Mme Swann, ayant appris d'un ami qu'elle vénérait un mot nouveau—le mot «tocard»—qui avait ouvert des* nouveaux horizons à sa vie, parce qu'il désignait précisément pour elle toutes les choses qu'elle avait trouvé* «chic» quelques années auparavant; successivement le treillage doré qui servait d'appui aux chrysanthèmes, les louis en carton semés sur la cheminée, avaient suivi dans leur retraite mainte bonbonnière de chez Giroux et le papier à lettres à couronne. D'ailleurs dans le désordre artistique et un pêle-mêle d'atelier, des pièces> {615:26-615:29}

615:30. <pièces aux murs> **615:34.** <du XVIIIe siècle> [615:32. <blancs d'aujourd'hui, l'Extrême-Orient>]

615:34. <siècle, et quand, pour que je fusse plus «confortable», elle[1] entassait derrière mon dos et pétrissait les coussins, ils étaient semés de bouquets Louis XV, et non plus comme autrefois de dragons chinois. {615:38-616:2}

616:2. Elle était entourée> **616:7.** <auxquels elle faisait> [616:5. <Saxe) pour lesquels elle redoutait plus encore qu'autrefois pour ses>]

616:7. <faisait expier par ses emportements les transes qu'ils lui avaient données. Et Swann si poli et doux avec eux n'était pas choqué de la voir si mal élevée,[1] car sans doute la vie lucide de certaines infériorités n'ôte rien à la tendresse,[2] qui les fait au contraire trouver charmants*,[3] car Swann mettait sa femme au-dessus de presque tous les autres êtres, et ne pouvait[4] pas ignorer qu'elle disait: «vas-tu chez les «de un tel», et «eccetera». Mais il ne cherchait pas à lui apprendre[5] certains raffinements qu'il possédait[6] pourtant si naturellement qui s'étaient incorporés à ses doigts ou à sa langue. Ce n'était plus dans des chambres japonaises qu'elle recevait>

616:14. <recevait ses intimes> **616:30.** <ministre de Belgique> [616:15. <Watteau dont> 616:18. <peau, de[1] respirations si profondes, qu'elle avait l'air de les considérer non pas comme décoratives et comme flatteuses à la façon d'un cadre, mais comme indispensables[2] et de la même manière> 616:23. <hygiène. D'ailleurs elle> 616:26. <que bien des personnes qu'elle connaissait, que des «*foultitudes* de personnes» disait-elle. 616:29. <valaient presque une fois>]

616:30. <Belgique, si[1] bien que dans le groupe dont elle était le soleil, chacun[2] eut* été bien étonné d'apprendre qu'ailleurs, chez les Verdurin par exemple, elle passait pour bête. Je l'aurais été tout le premier mais pour une autre raison. C'est que

je ne pouvais séparer ses paroles de son visage, de sa bouche, de ses yeux dont elles me semblaient couler.

616:33. A cause de> **617:4.** <avaient vu Mme de Crécy auraient pu avoir peine à reconnaître. [616:38. <orthographe, de faux sourcils. Pour certaines au contraire qui lui avaient montré de l'indulgence> 616:42. <si elles étaient malheureuses. Elle les défendait finement[1] et gentiment et disait: «on est> 617:3. <c'était elle-même> 617:4. <avaient vu Mme>] {617:6-617:7}

617:7. Sans doute> **617:23.** <jeunesse immortelle. [617:7. <tenait un peu à> 617:8. <portante, plus calme, plus reposée, plus fraîche et d'autre> 617:10. <nouvelles avec les cheveux> 617:12. <semblaient résorbés. Mais cela tenait aussi à ce que arrivée au milieu de la vie elle s'était enfin découvert> 617:19. <fatigue des années pour un instant, une>] {617:25-618:16}.

618:16. Son corps lui aussi était maintenant découpé> **619:5.** <volants d'autrefois. [618:25. <parcours aussi bien aux défaillances de la chair qu'à celles de l'étoffe. Les coussins> 618:28. <baleines lui[1] avaient fait si longtemps une partie postiche dont Swann il est vrai connaissait la fausseté et lui avaient donné> 618:41. <travailler, j'allais à l'improviste chez les Swann, je la trouvais souvent dans>]

619:6. Quand par un jour encore froid de printemps elle nous enmenait* Gilberte et moi au Jardin d'Acclimatation, souvent sous sa veste> 619:21. <ne se portaient plus. [619:10. <«dépassant» de[1] dents> 619:13. <années plutôt> 619:20. <qu'on pensât* invinciblement>] {619:21-619:24}

619:24. Ainsi comme dans un> **620:1.** <d'une civilisation. [619:31. <inachevée, d'autres formes qu'on aurait pu> 619:38. <ou encore à cause d'une sorte>]

620:2. Quand, quittant ses visites pour venir assister un instant à notre goûter, elle entrait dans la salle à manger vêtue de quelqu'une de ces merveilleuses robes qu'elle portait à son «choufleury»[1] quelquefois en taffetas, d'autrefois* en faille, ou en velours>

620:7. <velours, ou en crêpe> **620:42.** <Henri II>. [620:10. <sortie dehors, donnaient ce jour-là à> 620:12. <d'agissant; sans doute la simplicité hardie de leur coupe, était bien appropriée à la[1] taille de Mme Swann et à ses mouvements dont elles* avaient

l'air d'être la couleur, changeante selon les jours; et on aurait dit> 620:26. <dans le cerne de ses yeux> 620:30. <il y avait sur le corsage même tel dessin> 620:35. <la discrétion d'une «allusion» délicate qui, tout> 620:37. <n'ayant sans elle[1] aucune> 620:40. <superstition, d'engendrer le souvenir> 620:41. <philippine. Ou bien, dans>]

620:42. <Henri II, aux manches de la robe de satin noir un léger ronflement près de l'épaule qui faisait penser aux «gigots dix-huit cent*» ou, d'autres fois dans la jupe aux paniers Louis XV, donnaient à la robe un air imperceptible d'être un costume et insinuant sous la vie présente comme une réminiscence du passé et* mêlait à la personne de Mme Swann le charme de certaines héroïnes historiques romanesques.*

□**621:7.** Cherchant à m'expliquer le plaisir que me donnait sa toilette, je lui demandais quel était le nom de ces soutaches, de ces boutons, de cette cravate, comme j'aurais demandé à un musicien comment s'appelait cette sorte de finale, de trait, d'arpège, par cette tendance que nous avons à croire faussement qu'une classification générique nous élucidera le secret d'un charme. Et Mme Swann me répondait: «Mais cela s'appelle des boutons, des soutaches, une cravate» comme le musicien eut* dit: «Mais cela s'appelle une finale, un trait, un arpège», peut-être aussi pour dissimuler toute trace d'effort, avoir l'air de n'avoir imité personne, et être sûre* de ne pouvoir être imitée par personne, avec un sourire qui exprimait sa satisfaction qu'une question qui était un hommage,[1] et qui allait quelquefois jusqu'au rire afin de souligner cet hommage aux personnes présentes en

---

620:42. *(B-A)* <Henri IV> **621:7.** <historiques ou romanesques. [620:43. <qui aux manches de satin noir près de l'épaule> 612:2. <«gigots» dix-huit cent trente ou, d'autres fois, dans la jupe>]

621:7. ([1]hommage, (et qui) ([2]excessif), mais) ([3]qu'éprouve l'artiste) ([4]Mme Swann) ([5]la voyant si) ([6]cru garder fermée) ([7]devaient rester) ([8]entendre; on* quand) ([9]gothiques dissimulées) ([10]bas reliefs extérieurs). 636:12. ([1]l'environnait; Swann). 636:25. ([1]ne gênait). 636:27. ([1]élegante, elle* la portant). 636:36. ([1]même sur son ombrelle mauve que souvent elle tenait encore fermée dans ses mains quand elle arrivait, elle laissant* tomber par moments comme sur un bouquet de violettes de Parme, son regard heureux). 636:41. ([1]encore. Elle). 637:2. ([1]profane, un). 637:18. ([1]liturgie et des rites dans lesquels Mme Swann était profondément versée, sa). 637:26. ([1]un autre ciel). 637:37. ([1]s'étant).

ayant l'air de trouver ma question risible, mon hommage excessif,[2] mais où il y avait aussi du bonheur de[3] l'artiste quand il s'est soumis par conscience à des règles que la foule ne connaît pas mais dont l'observance entre à son insu pour une grande part dans le plaisir qu'elle éprouve. Ces canons selon lesquels elle s'habillait en tenant compte de la saison, de l'heure, de la circonstance, il m'était impossible de n'avoir pas l'impression que c'était pour elle-même que madame[4] y obéissait, comme à une Sagesse supérieure dont elle eut* été la grande prêtresse, quand, me promenant avec elle, je[5] le* voyais si elle avait trop chaud ouvrir sa jaquette qu'elle avait entière[6] fermée j'y découvrais mille détails d'exécution [*cf.* 638:4] qui auraient[7] restés* inaperçus comme ces parties d'orchestre auxquels* le compositeur a donné tous ses soins quoique le public ne doive jamais les entendre,[8] et quand, portant sur mon bras son manteau, j'y apercevais dans la doublure de la manche un détail exquis, une bande d'une teinte merveilleuse, une satinette mauve cachée aux yeux de tous mais aussi délicatement travaillées* que les parties qui leur étaient montrées, comme des sculptures gothiques[9] invisibles dissimulées au revers d'une tour inaccessible et aussi parfaites que les sculptures[10] extérieures du porche principal. Quand furent venus les beaux jours qui ne commencèrent que très tard dans cette première année où je la connus, comme je savais qu'avant le dîner elle sortait un peu de chez elle et allait faire quelques pas avenue du Bois, j'obtins> {621:7-635:28}

635:34. <j'obtins de mes parents> **635:38.** <pendant tout ce mois de mai.

635:40. J'arrivais à l'arc-de-triomphe* vers midi.

Je guettais de l'entrée de l'avenue le coin de la petite rue>

635:42. <rue par où Mme Swann> **636:27.** <ne se soucie plus> [636:2. <étaient moins nombreux et presque tous des gens élégants> 636:10. <ombrelle de même nuance> 636:12. <l'environnait;[1] Gilberte, Swann> 636:13. <matin ou qu'elle venait de rencontrer: et leur agglomération obéissante, sombre, exécutant> 636:16. <autour d'elle, donnait à cette femme qui seule avait de l'intensité dans les yeux, l'air de regarder> 636:25. <qui ne[1] la gênait pas>]

636:27. <plus du reste, certaine qu'elle portait—dussent des passants vulgaires qui ne comptaient pas ne pas l'apprécier—la toilette la plus élégante,[1] la portant naturellement, pour elle-même et ses amis, sans y prendre garde, mais cependant sans avoir l'air non plus de ne pas tenir compte d'elle, n'empêchant pas>

636:31. <n'empêchant pas> **637:40.** <toilette champêtre. [636:35. <jeux, à leur rythme personnel, pourvu> 636:36. <même[1] laissant tomber par moment* sur son ombrelle—qu'elle tenait encore fermée à la main quand elle arrivait—un bouquet* de violettes de Parme, son regard heureux> 636:41. <l'air de leur sourire encore,[1] elle réservait> 636:42. <elle faisait ainsi occuper> 636:43. <les hommes avec qui elle causait le plus> 637:2. <déférence du profane[1]; un> 637:3. <et sur laquelle* ils reconnaissaient à Mme Swann comme> 637:9. <Swann, par l'heure tardive> 637:10. <passé une si longue matinée> 637:12. <semblait indiquer la proximité par la lenteur de sa promena-de> 637:14. <jardin et on aurait> 637:15. <qu'elle en portait> 637:18. <liturgie[1] de ces rites dans lesquels cette tendance était profondément pensée, sa toilette était liée à la saison> 637:23. <naître plus naturellement au mois de mai que les fleurs des jardins et des bois> 637:26. <tendue comme un[1] ciel rond, clément> 637:35. <poignets et fît pour eux enfin tous> 637:37. <qui s'était[1] gaiement abaissée> 637:39. <connaît, qui n'en a pas>]

□**637:40.** Dès son arrivée, je la saluais, elle m'arrêtait en souriant. Elle ouvrait son ombrelle, sous laquelle nous causions comme sous un berceau de glycines et qui versait sur son visage et sa toilette l'onde d'une lumière dans la transparence liquide et le vernis de laquelle Mme Swann, reconnue par des cavaliers attardés qui passaient au galop en mouvements décomposés sur l'ensoleillement blanc de l'avenue comme sur la toile d'un cinématographe, leur répondait d'un bonjour de la main amical, conscient de leurs noms, notoires pour le public mais familiers pour elle, souverain, printanier, matinal, irisé, d'un reflet bleu. Et de tous

---

637:40. ([1]mois de mai [*the* Grasset B *text stops here and then, only with an indentation, resumes at 642:18*]).

les cadrans solaires et fleuris que ma mémoire se rappelle c'est peut-être en celui-là que je peux distinguer le plus exactement aujourd'hui les minutes entre midi et quart et une heure au mois de mai.[1]

Mais la beauté, l'infaillible appropriation des toilettes de Mme Swann n'eut* pas suffi à me les faire considérer avec ces dispositions d'esprit, faites de curiosité esthétique et de respect, si spécial qu'on m'eût bien étonné en me disant que telles des personnes que mes parents connaissaient et auxquelles je ne faisais aucune attention s'habillaient presque aussi bien qu'elle, si je n'avais pas préalablement introduit en elle ma croyance en son élégance. Et cette croyance avait dû naître en moi un peu plus tôt, quand mon amour pour Gilberte—conspirant quoique dans un cercle restreint avec l'ignorance de cet âge où ne sachant rien de la vie et ne la connaissant que par l'imagination nous lui prêtons encore la réalité que seules les idées possèdent—me faisait tout ce qui entourait la fille de Mme Swann comme doué d'une existence extraordinaire, comme incomparable au reste.

Alors, rien ne me causait plus d'émoi que de me trouver sur le passage de M. ou de Mme Swann et peut-être celle-ci, quand enfin j'allai ensuite chez elle, avait-elle reconnu en moi—mais je n'osai pas le lui demander,—l'adolescent qui un ou deux ans plus tôt ne perdait pas une occasion de l'apercevoir, et même quoiqu'elle ne sût pas à cette époque qui j'étais, de la saluer, se croyant autorisé à le faire parce qu'il avait connu son mari et jouait aux barres avec sa fille. Ayant appris cette année-là où je n'étais encore point allé chez Mme Swann et ne pensais pas y aller jamais, qu'elle se promenait autour du grand lac, allée de la Reine Marguerite ou allée des Acacias, presque tous les jours, ceux où je savais que Gilberte ne viendrait pas aux Champs-Elysées, je dirigeais> {638:22-641:11}

△**417:28.** <je dirigeais Françoise> **418:39.** <interdite), et enfin> [417:29. <où on voit> 417:32. <rivière, une ferme, une colline> 417:42. <quelque promeneur rapide—, il était le Jardin des femmes; et comme l'allée des Myrtes de l'Enéide, plantée> 418:10. <légère et même*, d'une élégance> 418:13. <comme des colonnes ailées et vibratiles, parasites> 418:19. <que j'y verrais certaines> 418:28. <le pouvoir de réaliser, j'attendais,

j'acceptais> 418:33. <c'est surtout Mme Swann>] {418:39-418:41}

△**418:41.** <ce sentiment de vénération> **421:17.** <aucune attention> [419:6. <Acacias comme le chemin> 419:11. <mettais au premier rang. Si, après> 419:14. <pendant des heures, je voyais> 419:22. <siège comme un cocher de grande maison anglaise, un énorme> 419:25. <je sentais, imprimant sa forme> 419:28. <cri» une allusion aux> 419:35. <d'une majesté> 419:43. <oisif, tourné> 420:3. <et qui voulait dire: «Oui> 420:5. <vous taire* de parler> 420:15. <l'allée, marchant> 420:19. <femmes ne portent pas> 420:22. <but avait* été> 420:33. <quelque personne commune.* 421:15. <que n'étant pas un banquier]>

△**421:18.** <saluer sans la connaître, à vrai dire, cette femme> **426:28.** <parties d'un souvenir> [421:25. Quant à elle, elle ne savait pas mon nom, ne se rappelait plus qu'elle m'avait vu à la cascade, mais j'étais> 421:36. <souvent en «tube»> 422:2. <où dans les maisons, à Paris, la> 422:4. <assiste, donne* une nostalgie> 422:7. Dans une chambre> 422:9. <auquel s'appliquait*, les faisant bouillonner comme ces taches jaunes qui parfois quoique* nous regardions, dansent> 422:14. <fermés comme d'une bouche> **422:16.** <les voir traversées> 422:18. <ne pouvant pas plus me> 422:36. <trapu, entété* et têtu> 422:41. <fleur. Ainsi le bois> 423:1. <arbres d'espèce commune> 423:2. <trois essences précieuses> 423:5. <clarté. Aussi c'était> 423:7. <parties différentes en> 423:8. Dans les parties où les arbres gardent la lumière avec leurs feuilles> 423:9. <altération dans leur> 423:17. <incendié. Elle épaississait> 423:20. <feuilles de ces maronniers*> 423:24. <bouquet de fleurs> 423:26. <parties du Bois de Boulogne mieux> 423:29. <toutes ou un feuillage> 423:38. <arbres, la joie que> 424:11. <délimitant, ensoleillant l'alentour, soit> 424:15. <elles semblaient seules, trempées> 424:16. <émerger de l'atmosphère> 424:17. <futaie toute* entière> 424:22. <faîte des chênes, rondes> 424:23. <dans la création de Michel-Ange> 424:28. <saison, le temps> 424:31. <féminine dont je rêvais et que je brûlais de contempler, se réaliseraient> 424:33. <que faisait* désirer les sapins et les acacias du bois de Boulogne> 424:37. <temple à l'amour>

424:39. <du lac, j'allais> 424:41. <je l'avais fait tenir dans la hauteur d'une victoire*, dans la maigreur> 425:13. <chapeaux si bas> 425:18. <gréco-saxonne relevant* avec> 425:19. <des Tanagras, et> 425:22. <Swann allée> 425:23. <ni même d'autres. Ils> 425:34. <avons pensé donner> 425:36. <c'était en elle* et non> 425:39. <trouver élégantes comme étaient les anciens attelages, les automobiles; je suis> 426:4. Ma consolation les femmes vraiment élégantes que j'ai connues> 426:6. <gens qui voient ces horribles créatures sous des chapeaux>]

△**426:31.** <j'aurais voulu> **426:33.** <couleurs sombres, comme>

△**426:34.** <comme était jadis celui de Mme Swann où luiraient les feux> **427:34.** <perçus par les sens. [426:39. <ceux où je n'avais pas> 472:2. <ne rentrait plus> 427:12. <toilette m'intéressaient*> 427:20. <les chemins vides. Le> 427:21. La nature reprenait sur le Bois> 427:24. <le vent ridait de petites vaguelettes le Grand-Lac, comme>] {427:34-427:43}

□**642:18.** Quand nous partîmes cette année-là pour Balbec, mon corps qui n'avait opposé aucune résistance à ce voyage tant

---

642:18. ([1]appelerait*) ([2]qu'on m'habituat*) ([3]Balbec) ([4]exquis (il). 646:13. ([1]trouver). 646:14. ([1]Balbec) ([2]mal: Celui-ci qui) ([3]comme un obstacle) ([4]situation, car) ([5]jamais, du) ([6]préférant, louer) ([7]mes). 646:30. ([1]Mais elle avait été obligée). 647:12. ([1]départ et du plus grand bonheur possible. Et comme la détermination). 647:25. ([1]j'enveloppais). 647:27. ([1]traverse). 647:27. ([1]autres trains; et). 647:36. ([1]Bolbec*). 647:39. ([1]Bolbec*). 647:40. ([1]Bolbec-Plage). 648:3. ([1]l'ancienne; maman devait nous conduire au train. Comme) ([2]d'avoir) ([3]jusqu'à ce départ). 648:19. ([1]dans la suite de ce récit que) ([2]en tout vent*) ([3]masque) ([4]nue) ([5]dépouillée) ([6]si elle veut). 644:42. ([1]Bolbec*). 648:20. ([1]moi, autrement que pour moi, d'une autre vie que moi.) ([2]j'éprouvais) ([3]de) ([4]de) ([5]qu'elle était peut-être le premier essai) ([6]ma mère commençait à se résigner) ([7]demandant au concierge s'il). 648:43. ([1]Bolbec*). 649:26. ([1]les avait placés). 649:29. ([1]peignaient par* un). 650:26. ([1]Ma mère). 651:6. ([1]appelait «euphorie»). 651:8. ([1]eu de mon côté le droit). 651:21. ([1]bière, si). 651:30. ([1]Bolbec*). 651:31. ([1]vite). 652:11. ([1]pourtant ma propre voix articulant les moindres mots me donnait). 652:14. ([1]s'attardât). 652:17. ([1]moins belle) ([2]linéaments) ([3]exécuté) ([4]après l'avoir conduite et resté* quelques heures chez). 654:18. ([1]puis). 654:21. ([1]maintenaient). 655:19. ([1]dont un changement interne de densité rompt l'équilibre, il) ([2]frémir, n'attendant) ([3]à s'y) ([4]enmanchant*). 655:26. ([1]Roussainville). 655:29. ([1]jarre). 655:37. ([1]qu'ils sont individuels et) ([2]dans). 656:8. ([1]baille*). 656:11 ([1]Que ce soit) ([2]de Bugotte*, et aussitôt) ([3]blasé) ([4]sent) ([5]dépeinte). 656:34. ([1]sédentaire et) ([2]et toutes mes) ([3]avaient*) ([4]accourus*) ([5]remplacer, rivalisant entre elles de zèle, de la plus basse à la plus noble, de la respira-

que je m'étais contenté en y pensant, d'apercevoir du fond de mon lit de Paris, l'église persane à côté de la tempête, mon corps se révoltât* aussitôt qu'il eut compris qu'il était de la partie [*cf.* 645:37], et qu'à mon arrivée on me conduirait à une chambre qu'on appelait[1] ma chambre et que je n'aurais jamais vue. A partir de ce jour-là j'eus l'air si malheureux que le nouveau médecin qui me soignait et qui avait conseillé de[2] m'habituer à tout ce dont le précédent m'avait prescrit de m'abstenir, me dit:

—«Ça n'a pas l'air de vous amuser de partir. Ça ne vous dit rien Bricquebec.[3] C'est drôle de ne pas aimer les voyages. Moi je trouve ça exquis[4] (qu'il prononçait esquis). {642:1-644:19}

644:26. See after 648:19.

646:13. Je vous réponds que si je pouvais prendre[1] seulement huit jours pour aller prender le frais au bord de la mer, je ne me ferais pas prier. Et puis il y aura des courses, des régates, vous vous amuserez beaucoup.»

□**646:14.** Il est probable pourtant que le désir que j'avais de voir Balbec* était beaucoup plus fort que celui du docteur, et que j'aimais tout autant que lui les voyages. Mais j'avais soupçonné, quand j'avais été entendre la Berma, et toutes les fois où j'allais jouer aux Champs-Elysées avec Gilberte, que ceux qui aiment et ceux qui ont du plaisir, ne sont peut-être pas les mêmes. La contemplation de Bricquebec[1] ne me semblait pas moins désirable parce qu'il fallait l'acheter au prix d'un mal,[2] qui était au contraire comme le symbole de la réalité de l'impression que j'allais chercher, et qu'aucun spectacle équivalent, aucune vue stéréoscopique qui ne m'eut* pas empêché de rentrer coucher chez moi, n'aurait pu remplacer. Et comme je sentais déjà que

---

tion, de l'appétit et de la circulation sanguine à la sensibilité et à l'imagination. Je ne sais) ([6]que cette fille) ([7]leur) ([8]vertus) ([9]rivales) ([10]sculpté) ([11]ciseau qui) ([12]donc introduit dans sa pensée). 657:8. ([1]l'appelai.). 657:11. ([1]Elle) ([2]avec rapidité et adresse le café) ([3]J'essayai) ([4]à me trouver près d'elle). 658:15. ([1]ciel moins rose que son visage). 658:16. ([1]villes, Vezelay* ou Jumièges, Bourges ou Beauvais, servent à désigner leur église principale. Cette acception). 658:24. ([1]nom de Bolbec*). 658:31. ([1]Bolbec-le-Vieux, Bolbec-en-Terre). 658:40. ([1]Bolbec-Plage). 659:8. ([1]j'allais devoir retourner). 659:14. ([1]moulées au musée) ([2]baie profonde du porche). 659:24. ([1]Bolbec). 659:26. ([1]Bolbec). 659:34. ([1]statue de la Vierge). 660:1. ([1]ma canne). 660:10. ([1]ma). 660:12. ([1]beauté, la Vierge de Bolbec, l'unique). 660:23. ([1]Bolbec-Plage). 660:24. ([1]Bolbec*). 660:34. ([1]Bolbec*). 660:41. ([1]pression).

quelle que fut*, plus tard, la chose que j'aimerais, elle ne serait jamais placée qu'au bout d'une poursuite douloureuse où j'aurais d'abord à sacrifier mon plaisir à ce bien suprême au lieu de l'y chercher, et à traverser comme[3] obstacle*, à vaincre, ma propre santé, je n'aurais pas voulu demander à ne pas faire ce voyage—tout en souhaitant secrètement que quelque incident imprévu vint* l'empêcher—ce qui m'eût semblé renoncer dès la première expérience, sinon à connaître la sensation[4]—car je ne l'éprouverais jamais[5]—du moins à posséder l'objet du bonheur. Mais les résistances de mon corps furent cette fois-là d'autant plus difficiles à dominer que mon père, n'étant pas encore revenu du voyage en Espagne qu'il était allé faire avec M. de Norpois, et préférant,[6] paraît-il, louer une maison pour l'été dans les environs de Paris [*cf.* 646:1], ma mère décida, ce qu'elle ne m'annonça que la veille de mon départ pour abréger nos*[7] angoisses, qu'elle ne nous accompagnerait pas et que ma grand'mère irait seule avec moi à Bricquebec.

Celle-ci, toujours désireuse de donner aux présents qu'on me faisait un caractère artistique, avait d'abord voulu m'offrir de ce voyage une «épreuve» ancienne, et que nous reprissions moitié>

646:28. <moitié en voiture> **646:30.** <par «le» Pont-Audemer. Mais[1] tout en trouvant que «c'était une pitié» de me laisser passer près de belles choses sans les voir, elle fut obligée d'y renoncer, sur la défense de mon père, que maman tenait au courant par lettres, et qui savait, quand ma grand'mère organisait>

646:33. <organisait un déplacement> **646:37.** <et de contraventions. [646:35. <pronostiquer d'avance de trains>] {646: 37-647:11}

647:12. Bref nous partirions simplement de Paris par ce train de une heure ving-deux que pendant des années j'avais souvent cherché dans l'indicateur où son heure de départ me donnait l'émotion, presque l'illusion du départ.[1] Le prendre, descendre à Bayeux ou à Coutances me représentait depuis longtemps l'un des plus grands bonheurs possibles; et comme la détermination des traits d'un bonheur dans notre imagination vient beaucoup plus de ce que nous avons de lui des désirs toujours identiques que des notions précises, je croyais>

647:20. <croyais connaître> **648:2.** <accepterais d'y vivre. [647:24. <train réveillait toujours> 647:25. <villes que je[1] coulais dans la lumière> 647:27. <qu'il traversait,[1] me> 647:27. <de tous les autres;[1] et> 647:29. <vu mais auquel on rêve sans cesse, par> 647:33. <au pied d'une cathédrale, avant> 647:36. <à Bricquebec,[1] elle> 647:27. <amies, d'où je> 647:39. <de Bricquebec,[1] qui> 647:40. <de Bricquebec-Plage[1]>]

648:3. Mais il fallait d'abord quitter l'ancienne[1] et maman nous accompagnerait. Elle nous conduirait à la gare. Comme elle devait passer l'été avec mon père à Saint-Cloud, elle avait arrangé d'y aménager ce jour-là même et avait pris, ou feint de prendre, toutes ses dispositions pour y aller directement en quittant la gare, sans repasser par la maison où elle craignais[*] que je ne voulusse, au lieu de partir, rentrer avec elle. Et même elle avait pris le prétexte d'avoir beaucoup à faire dans la maison nouvelle et à[2] avoir peu de temps, afin de ne pas rester avec nous (pensant que je serais moins malheureux de la quitter), jusqu'au[3] départ du train>

648:13. <du train où> **648:18.** <impuissante et suprême. [648:14. <qu'elle ne l'est déjà plus à éviter>]

□**648:19.** Elle entra avec nous dans la gare, dans ce lieu tragique [*cf.* 645:16] et merveilleux où il fallait abandonner toute espérance de rentrer tout à l'heure dans les lieux familiers où j'avais vécu, mais aussi où le miracle devait s'accomplir grâce auquel ceux où je vivrais bientôt seraient ceux-là mêmes qui n'avaient encore d'existence que dans ma pensée.

Sans doute, aujourd'hui, ce serait en automobile qu'on ferait ce voyage et on penserait le faire ainsi plus agréable et plus vrai, suivant de près aussi les diverses gradations par lesquelles change la face de la terre [*cf.* 644:25]. J'ai dit ailleurs, et à d'autres points de vue, je montrerai plus tard ici[1] que je ne méconnais pas l'automobile. Mais je n'apprécie pas cet esprit nouveau qui, à[2] tort veut nous montrer à côté des choses ce qui les entoure dans la réalité, supprime l'essentiel, l'acte intellectuel qui les en isolait, et presque[3] sous une satisfaction médiocre qu'il vient nous accorder par surcroît, le plaisir original qu'elles devaient nous donner. On prétend qu'il faut voir un tableau du XVIIIe siècle au milieu de meubles, de bibelots, de tentures de l'époque [*cf.* 645:4], et on ne reconstitue que le fade décor que nous montrent tous les hôtels d'aujourd'hui où Rembrandt humilié finit par refléter le pauvre goût d'une maîtresse de maison qui a d'ailleurs passé des années aux archives comme toutes ses pareilles font maintenant, et où rien que le temps d'un dîner on s'ennuie au milieu de chefs-d'œuvre qui ne nous redonneront l'enivrante joie qu'on doit leur demander que* sur les murs d'une salle de musée, jamais assez nus,[4] assez dépouillés[5] de toutes particularités s'ils[6] veulent symboliser les espaces intérieures* où l'artiste s'abstrayait de son milieu pour créer. Le plaisir spécifique>

△**644:26.** <spécifique du voyage> **644:42.** <de même que sur son écriteau elles portent son nom> [644:27. <fatigué, la vraie vérité du voyage c'est de rendre> 644:29. <peut, de la conserver totale, intacte telle qu'elle était dans notre pensée quand> 644:36. <que schématisait (mieux qu'une promenade toute réelle où> 644:37. <veut qu'il n'y a pas pour ainsi dire plus d'arrivée)> 644:39. <gares, qui ne font pas partie pour ainsi dire de la ville>]

△□**644:42.** <son nom, laboratoires fumeux, antres empestés mais où on accédait au mystère, grands ateliers vitrés, comme celui où j'entrai ce jour-là cherchant le train de Bricquebec[1], et qui déployait au-dessus de la ville éventrée un de ces immenses ciels crus et tragiques comme certains ciels> {644:43-645:13}

△**645:29.** <ciels d'une modernité> **645:32.** <Croix. [645:29. <Mantégna*> 645:31. <comme le départ>]

648:20. Pour la première fois je sentais que ma mère pouvait vivre sans moi.[1] Je sentais qu'elle pouvait vivre de son côté avec mon père, à qui peut-être elle trouvait que ma mauvaise santé, ma nervosité faisaient la vie un peu difficile et triste. Si bien que je ressentais[2] de cette séparation un plus sombre désespoir, en me disant qu'elle était peut-être pour ma mère le terme des[3] déceptions successives que je lui avais causées et qu'elle m'avait tues et après lesquelles elle avait compris les difficultés des[4] vacances communes;' et aussi comme[5] le premier essais* d'une existence à laquelle elle[6] finissait par se résigner pour l'avenir, au fur et à mesure que les années viendraient pour elle et pour mon père, d'une existence où je la verrais moins, où ce que même dans mes cauchemards* je n'avais jamais entrevu, elle serait déjà pour moi un peu étrangère, une dame qu'on verrait rentrer seule dans une maison où je ne serais pas, demandant[7] s'il n'y a pas de lettres de moi.

648:38. Je ne pus répondre> **649:5.** <de ta maman. [648:39. <valise, les sanglots étouffaient ma voix. Ma> 648:43. <de Bricquebec[1] si>] {649:6-649:8}

649:9. Puis elle cherchait à me distraire, elle me demandait ce que je commanderais pour le dîner, admirait la tenue de Françoise et lui en faisait compliment.

—Mais Françoise vous êtes magnifique! Où avez-vous déniché ce chapeau, ce manteau?

Françoise répondait que nous les connaissions bien et forçait ma mère à se rappeler un ancien chapeau, un ancien manteau de ma grand'tante, lesquels avaient excité l'horreur de ma mère quand ils étaient neufs, l'un>

649:14. <l'un avec l'immense> **649:28.** <devenu charmant. [649:17. <un envers de drap rouge, uni et> 649:18. <longtemps qu'il était cassé. Et, comme il est quelquefois troublant de trouver les raffinements> 649:21. <dans quelque chanson> 649:23. <blanche ou soufre[*] juste à la place qu'il fallait,—le nœud> 649:26. <Françoise l'avait[1] placé avec>]

649:29. Mais surtout les sentiments qui lui étaient habituels, sa tendresse pour les siens, son respect pour ses maîtres, l'orgueil de son honnêteté qui lui permettait de «porter le front haut», la modestie pour sa condition dont elle trouvait que c'était «à la bêtise» de vouloir sortir, tout cela n'avait pas seulement donné une noblesse singulière à son visage régulier qui avait dû être charmant au temps de sa jeunesse, mais avait gagné son maintien et son port de tête; et même, les vêtements inattendus qu'elle avait revêtus pour le voyage afin d'être digne d'être vue avec nous sans avoir l'air de chercher à se faire voir,—depuis le drap cerise mais ancien de son manteau, jusqu'aux poils comme il faut et sans raideur de son collier de fourrure, pareils à ceux qui ombrageaient sa bouche,—avaient contracté cette expression réservée et sans bassesse d'une femme qui sait à la fois «tenir son rang et garder sa place» et faisaient penser à ces portraits où les vieux maîtres peignaient[1] un vitrail d'église ou pour un livre d'heures quelque Anne de Bretagne en prière, et où tout est bien en place, où le sentiment de l'ensemble s'est si bien résorbé dans toutes les parties que la riche et désuète singularité du costume n'exprime plus que la même piété, la même gravité douce que les lèvres et que les yeux. {650:1-650:25}

650:26. Mais ma mère,[1] voyant> **650:28.** <circonstances...» puis se rappelant que l'affection pour autrui vous détourne des douleurs égoïstes, elle tâchait> {650:28-650:32}

650:32. <tâchait de me> **651:7.** <moins vulnérable. [650:34. <trajet à Saint-Cloud> 650:39. <vérité son départ pour Saint-Cloud et c'est> 650:42. <dans cette robe> 651:1. <faisaient autre, qui la faisaient déjà appartenir à cette demeure où je ne la verrais pas. 651:5. <un peu trop de bière afin> 651:6. <appelait[1] l'euphorie où>]

651:8. Je n'étais pas décidé à le faire, mais je voulais au moins que ma grand'mère reconnût que si je l'avais fait, que* j'aurais eu pour [*blanc*][1] le droit et même la sagesse pour moi si je le faisais.

651:10. Aussi j'en parlais> **651:20.** <tu me donnes!» [651:12. <l'endroit où je prendrais de la bière, buffet> 651:15. <me révoltant* soudain avec une violence indignée, à cet acte d'aller boire>]

□**651:21.** Et m'apercevant seulement alors, tant le chagrin de quitter maman avait absorbé jusque-là mon attention, que la crise que je redoutais était déjà amorcée, le remords physiologique d'avoir trompé ma grand'mère par un air de bonne santé apparent me poussa à me plaindre, à confesser par des signes extérieurs le mal que j'éprouvais et que j'avais omis de manifester.

Ma grand'mère eut un air si désolé, si bon, en me disant: «Mais alors vas* vite chercher de la bière[1] ou une liqueur, si cela doit te faire du bien» que je me jetai sur elle et la couvris de baisers par lesquels ma tendresse s'imaginait effacer le chagrin que je n'avais pas hésité à lui causer pour satisfaire au désir que mon corps avait d'être plaint. Et si j'allai cependant boire de la bière, boire trop de bière, ce fut parce que je sentais que sans cela j'aurais un accès trop violent et que c'est encore ce qui peinerait le plus ma grand'mère. Mais il fallut en prendre bien davantage que si je n'avais eu qu'à prévenir une crise possible; c'était une crise commençante qu'il fallait bien faire rétrocéder.

651:28. Quand, à la première> **651:35.** <ne paraissait pas> [651:29. <dans le wagon> 651:30. <à Bricquebec,[1] comme je sentais> 651:31. <m'habituerais bien[1] à>]

651:35. <ne paraissait pas éprouver de toutes ces bonnes nouvelles que je lui donnais la même joie que moi. La tête tournée vers la fenêtre elle me répondait en évitant de me regarder:

—Tu devrais peut-être essayer de dormir un peu. {651:38-652:4}

652:5. Mais quand elle croyait> **652:17.** <temps habituel. [652:7. <puis lancer sur moi un regard puis le retirer> 652:11. <pourtant[1] le défi de ma propre voix> 652:14. <durer, j'attendais que chacune de mes inflexions s'attardait[*1] longtemps aux mots>]

□**652:17.** Pour compenser, le sacrifice de bien-être que je faisais à mon amour de l'architecture en me faisant voir un beau monument de plus, vers le milieu de la journée, comme nous approchions de la ville où nous devions nous arrêter chez son amie, ma grand'mère me dit:

—Tu sais que la station après celle-là est Bayeux, ne préfères-tu pas ne descendre que là pour voir la cathédrale, au lieu de venir avec moi. Il fait beau, le soleil n'est pas couché, tu auras encore le temps de bien voir.»

Je me rappelais tout ce que j'avais lu sur la cathédrale de Bayeux, sur la tapisserie de la reine Mathilde, mais ma grand'mère était là, je n'avais pas la force de me séparer d'elle; elle me redevenait brusquement plus chère que tout au monde; la haute dentelle artistique et dorée du nom de Bayeux me parut [*blanc*];[1] pourtant par raison pendant un instant j'hésitai et comme la seule idée d'une résolution (à moins qu'on n'ait rendu cette idée inerte en décidant qu'on ne prendrait pas la résolution) développe en un moment comme une graine vivace les [*blanc*][2] tout le détail des émotions qui naîtraient de l'acte agréable[3] je me fis dans mon hésitation effleurer et déchirer le cœur tout autant que si j'eusse quitté ma grand'mère, d'un chagrin que j'aurais pu m'épargner puisque quand le train repartit j'étais descendu avec elle.

Quand le soir, après[4] être resté quelques heures avec ma grand'mère chez son amie, j'eus repris seul le train, du moins je trouvai courte cette nuit-là; c'est que> {652:17-654:6}

654:10. <c'est que je n'avais pas à la passer encore dans> **654:32.** <les jeux de cartes> [654:11. <l'ensommeillement même me> 654:12. <entouré au contraire par l'activité calmante de tous> 654:13. <compagnie, me veillaient, s'offraient à causer avec moi si je ne pouvais pas dormir, me berçaient> 654:18. <égales, tantôt[1] une double> 654:19. <noire, neutralisant la force> 654:21. <sur moi des> 654:21. <me soutenaient[1] en> 654:24. <rafraîchissante que j'aurais eue de repos, dû à la vigilance des forces plus puissantes>]

654:32. <les jeux de cartes, les barques qui s'évertuent sans avancer sur une rivière au soleil couchant, sous un store bleu à-demi* baissé. A un moment, où je dénombrais les pensées que j'avais eues dans le temps qui avait précédé pour me rendre compte si je venais ou non de dormir et où l'incertitude même qui me faisait me poser la question, me permit de me répondre à moi-même, par une affirmation certaine, dans le carreau>

654:36.<carreau de la fenêtre> **655:18.** <versatile afin d'en avoir une vue> [654:43. <je sentais bien que cette> 655:1. <n'était ni caprice, ni inertie, mais> 655:2. Bientôt je sentis s'amonceler derrière> 655:4. <yeux au carreau, de> 655:11. <me désolais de l'avoir perdue quand je l'aperçus, mais rouge> 655:13. <abandonna à un nouveau coude>]

□**655:19.** Mais j'en fus empêché par le soleil lui-même, car tout à coup, mécaniquement propulsé comme un œuf qui[1] jaillit en vertu du seul changement de densité [*blanc*] sa coagulation, il bondit de derrière le rideau à travers la translucidité duquel je le sentais depuis un moment frémissant[2] et n'attendant que l'instant d'entrer en scène et dont il effaça sous un flot de lumière la pourpre mystérieuse. Déjà il illuminait des paysages matinaux dans lesquels il donnait à mon imagination une joyeuse envie d'aller vivre que ne neutralisait aucune appréhension de mon corps assuré de ne pas avoir à y*[3] transporter et à y arriver sans habitudes. Celui d'entre eux que le train longeait était sillonné par une rivière où les arbres exposaient sous le vernis de l'eau le tableau doré de leurs feuillages, comme à l'heure où le promeneur qui a fait sa sieste à l'ombre pendant la chaleur du jour, se lève pour se remettre en marche, en voyant le soleil baisser; des bateaux dans le désordre des brouillards bleus de la nuit qui traînaient encore sur les eaux encombrées des débris de nacre et de rose de l'aurore, passaient en souriant dans la lumière oblique qui, comme quand ils rentrent le soir, mouillait et jaunissait le bas de leur voile, en marchant*[4] à leur beaupré une pointe d'or: scène imaginaire, grelottante et déserte, pure évocation du couchant, ne reposant pas sur la suite des heures du jour qui doivent la précèder*, interpolée, inconsistante comme une image du souvenir ou du songe. Puis la rivière disparut, le paysage devint accidenté>

655:19. <accidenté, abrupt> **655:37.** <et du bonheur. [655: 23. <être la fleur d'un> 655:26. <de Troussinville,[1] ce> 655:29. <vers le train en portant une jate*[1] de lait. 655:35. <rose que le ciel rose. 655:35. <ce délicieux désir>]

655:37. Nous oublions toujours que[1] comme elle, soit individuelles* et leur substituant dès*[2] notre esprit un type de convention> **655:42.** <nous portons en nous des images abstraites auxquelles manquent précisément le caractère individuel dans lequel consistent beauté et bonheur, qui sont languissantes et fades.

656:3. Et nous portons> **656:7.** <où il ne reste pas un atome de beauté et de bonheur. [656:5. <cru faire> 656:6. <avons mis* et replace* par>]

656:8. C'est ainsi que brille*[1] d'avance d'ennui un lettré> **656:11.** <livres qu'il connaît, tandis qu'un beau livre est particulier, c'est-à-dire imprévisible. Ce sera[1] la *Chartreuse de Parme,* un roman d'Emilie Bronté*, une nouvelle de[2] François* James et aussitôt le lettré, tout à l'heure blessé*,[3] se sert*[4] de l'intérêt pour la réalité que lui aura parut*[5] le nouveau grand écrivain. Telle, étrangère aux modèles de beauté qu'imaginait ma pensée quand j'étais seul, apparurent à mes yeux, les traits énergiques et doux, la souple démarche de la belle fille. Et leur vie me donna aussitôt le goût d'un certain bonheur (seule forme sous laquelle nous puissions connaître le goût du bonheur), d'un bonheur qui se réaliserait en vivant auprès d'elle.

Peut-être la faisais-je un peu bénéficier de ce que c'était mon être au complet, un être nouveau, goûtant de vives jouissances, qui était en face d'elle. [656:23-656:25]

656:27. C'est d'ordinaire> **656:33.** <présence indispensable. [656:32. <voyage dans ce wagon, l'interruption>]

656:34. Mon habitude était si[1] active et n'était pas matinale, et elle faisait défaut, et[2] [*blanc*] toutes mes facultés étaient[3] accourues[4] pour le remplacer;[5] mes simples fonctions organiques, d'appétit ou de respiration, rivalisaient de zèle avec leurs sons plus nobles. Je ne sais si, en me faisant croire qu'elle[6] n'était pas pareille aux autres femmes, le charme sauvage de ces lieux ajoutait au sien, mais en tous cas elle le lui[7] rendait bien. L'assurance singulière et gracieuse de ses mouvements, la farouche franchise de son regard vif et borné, et toutes ces qualités[8] naïves et vivantes[9] qui avaient arrêté[10] la forme de son nez, la rondeur de son menton, le dégagement de ses épaules, avec la décision d'un ciseau[11] de sculpteur qui avait fait d'elle la statue de toutes les qualilités* qui m'étaient étrangères et comme une personnification d'une vie à laquelle je ne participais pas, tout cela donna tout à coup quelque chose de si doux à l'endroit qu'elle habitait, aux occupations insignifiantes qui remplissaient son temps, que la vie m'aurait paru délicieuse si seulement j'avais pu, heure par heure, la passer avec elle, l'accompagner jusqu'au torrent, jusqu'à la vache, jusqu'au train, me sentant à côté d'elle, et connu d'elle, donc[12] aussi en elle.

657:5. Elle m'aurait initié aux charmes de la vie rustique et des heures matinales. Je lui> **657:8.** <je l'appelai,[1]> {657:9-657:11}

□**657:11.** <l'appelai, elle[1] revint sur ses pas, me fixant de son regard droit et perçant, et comme les employés commençaient à fermer les portières, me versa avec[2] une rapidité et une adresse merveilleuses le café au lait bouillant. Je la regardais, elle ne détournait pas les yeux. J'essayais[3] de l'attirer dans le wagon, elle se dégaga* en riant: «Allons, voyons, on part», le train se mit en marche; je la vis s'éloigner de la gare et reprendre le sentier. Que l'état d'exaltation dans lequel je me trouvais eût été produit par elle, ou au contraire eût causé la plus grande partie du plaisir que j'avais eu à[4] la voir, en tout cas elle était si mêlée

à lui, que mon désir de la revoir, comme la prédilection qui attache les fumeurs d'opium à leurs compagnons de fumeries, était avant tout le désir moral de ne pas laisser cet état d'excitation périr entièrement, de ne pas être séparé à jamais de l'être qui y avait participé.

657:27. Ce n'est pas seulement que cet état fut* agréable. C'est surtout que, (comme> **657:37.** <plus les mêmes> [657:29. <nerf comme une note ou> 657:31. <voyais, il me mettait comme> 657:33. <fille que je voyais encore> 657:34. <sa marche, reprendre le sentier par où elle était venue; c'était comme> 657:36. <liséré, parmi lequel les sensations>]

657:37. <mêmes; il semblait que ce liséré fut* impossible à retraverser et maintenant que j'étais dans cette vie nouvelle, en sortir eût été comme mourir à moi-même. Pour avoir la douceur de m'y sentir du moins rattaché, il eut* suffi>

657:39. <suffi que> **658:15.** <du dehors. [657:40. <de cette petite> 658:3. <page. Projet>]

□**658:15.** Tel mon esprit combinait les itinéraires qui me permettraient de retrouver la belle fille tandis que je l'apercevais encore qui regagnait la maison du garde d'une marche assurée et vive, sous le ciel[1] qui moins que son visage était rose.

658:16. Certains noms de villes[1] servent par abréviation à désigner leur église principale. Quand on dit aimez-vous mieux Vezelay* ou Jumièges, Bourges ou Beauvais, tout le monde comprend que c'est de l'abbaye ou de la cathédrale qu'on veut parler. Cette acception—s'il s'agit de lieux que nous ne connaissons pas encore,—sculpte le nom>

658:20. <nom tout entier> **658:24.** <en fera comme une grande cathédrale. Ce fut pourtant au-dessus d'un buffet, en lettres blanches sur un avertisseur bleu que je lus le nom[1] Bricquebec, à l'ornementation presque persane. Je traversai vivement la gare et la Place, je demandai la plage pour>

658:28. <pour ne voir que> **659:14.** <éternelle des sculptures> [658:31. <dire! Bricquebec-le-vieux*,[1] Bricquebec-ville*, Bricquebec-en-Terre, où> 658:33. <les pêcheurs, selon la légende, avaient trouvé> 658:36. <découverte; c'est bien dans les falaises battues> 658:40. <à Bricquebec-Plage[1]> 659:2. <où s'embranchaient deux lignes de tramway en face d'un café>

659:4. <«Billard» et sur un fond de maisons aux cheminées desquelles> 659:6. Et l'église, entrant dans mon attention avec le café, le passant> 659:8. <chemin, la gare où il[1] allait falloir retourner> 659:10. <d'après-midi, où sa coupole>]

659:14. <sculptures, en reconnaissant les Apôtres dont j'avais vu les statues moulées[1] si facilement au musée du Trocadéro et qui m'attendaient des deux côtés de la Vierge, devant la baie[2] du porche profond comme pour me faire honneur.

659:18. La figure bienveillante et douce> **660:12.** <d'une intangible beauté> [659:20. <l'alleluia d'un beau jour> 659:22. <était immuable et ne se modifiait que si on se déplaçait autour d'eux comme il arrive quand on a tourné autour d'un chien mort. Et je me disais> 659:24. <de Bricquebec.[1] Cette> 659:26. <de Bricquebec.[1] Ce> 659:28. <célèbres, un moulage au musée du Trocadéro. 659:29. <elle-même, ce sont elles, elles, les uniques> 659:32. <le fait qu'on lui a demandé, la balle> 659:34. <courage qu'il possède et qu'il* aurait voulu faire entrer dans sa réponse ou dans son action, de même dans mon esprit qui avait dressé la statue[1] hors des reproductions que j'en avais eu* sous les yeux> 660:1. <de mon[1] parapluie, enchaînée> 660:4. <couchant et dans une heure de clarté du même reverbère* dont le bureau> 660:7. <en même temps que lui par le relent> 660:9. <particulier> 660:10. <tracer une[1] signature>]

660:12. <beauté,[1] que j'avais cru la dégageant des images qu'on me montrait, intacte si on les déchirait, si on les brisait, sensible aux vicissitudes qui pouvaient les frapper, c'est elle la Vierge de Bricquebec, l'unique (ce qui hélas voulait dire la seule), qui>

660:13. <qui, sur son> **661:2.** <plus désormais de les contenir. [660:17. <trace de ma craie> 660:22. <immortelle que j'étais venu chercher, que> 660:23. <ensemble Bricquebec-Plage.[1] 660:24. <sur Bricquebec,[1] les mots de> 660:26. <que des circonstances particulières, la mauvaise> 660:30. <pour moi, et que ma grand'mère me permettrait d'aller visiter, que je pourrais> 660:34. <pour Bricquebec,[1] dès> 660:41. <poussés par une passion*[1] extérieure, par une force> 660:43. <syllabes qui s'étaient refermées sur eux, les laissaient encadrer le porche de l'église>]

661:3. Ma grand'mère, seule—car pour que tout fut* préparé d'avance elle avait imaginé de faire partir Françoise avant elle, mais lui ayant donné un faux renseignement n'avait réussi qu'à faire partir dans de mauvaises directions Françoise qui en ce moment sans s'en douter filait à toute vitesse sur Nantes et [*blanc*] peut* être à Bordeaux—m'attendait dans le petit chemin de fer d'intérêt local qui devait nous conduire à Bricquebec-Plage. A peine dans le wagon>

661:11. <wagon rempli> **661:21.** <auquel mon corps> [661:13. <de tout l'après-midi, la première> 661:15. <fatiguée, elle> 661:16. «Hé bien Bricquebec?» avec un sourire si ardent de l'espoir de la grande joie qu'elle pensait que j'avais éprouvée, que je n'osai pas lui avouer tout d'un coup que cette joie ne s'était pas produite. D'ailleurs>

661:21. <corps aurait à s'accoutumer. Au bout de ma pensée je cherchais **à inaugurer*** le directeur de l'hôtel de Bricquebec[1]

661:3. *(B-A)* Ma grand'mère m'attendait dans le petit chemin de fer d'intérêt local qui devait nous conduire à Bolbec-Plage, mais elle m'attendait seule—car pour que tout fut* préparé d'avance elle avait imaginé de faire partir avant elle, —mais lui ayant donné un faux renseignement n'avait réussi qu'à faire envoyer dans une mauvaise direction, —Françoise qui en ce moment sans s'en douter filait à toute vitesse sur Nantes et se réveillerait peut être* à Bordeaux—m'attendait* dans le petit chemin de fer d'intérêt local qui devait nous conduire à Bolbec-Plage. A peine dans le wagon>

661:21. ([1]Bolbec) ([2]certainement) ([3]d'une morgue certaine, mais très) ([4]Bolbec-Plage) ([5]précédaient et dont). 661:40. ([1]au-dessus) ([2]ces) ([3]qui parce que je les avais entendu prononcer). 662:12. ([1]ont à traverser). 662:16. ([1]que prolongeait). 662:19. ([1]vent fraîchissant, évidé et anxieux). 662:21. ([1]habituel). 662:32. ([1]Bolbec*). 662:36. ([1]sorte de poussah à la figure et à la voix pleines de cicatrices qu'avaient laissées l' xtirpation). 662:41. ([1]de l'«omnibus»). 664:12. ([1]faire les cent pas dans les rues). 664:21. ([1]devant). 665:1. ([1]s'interrompre) ([2]seconde, je). 665:4. ([1]«lift», et qui à ce point). 665:36. ([1]extérieur—de l'objectivité de la vie, —que le changement de position). 665:41. ([1]où, à six heures, il y avait une impossibilité d'imaginer) ([2]personnel, et une attente vague et craintive) ([3]cette même place il y avait maintenant les boutons) ([4]directeur, son geste pour sonner le lift) ([5]posais à leur sujet dans le petit chemin de fer ne me semblaient) ([6]poussah) ([7]toujours connu et que si j'avais voulu reprendre) ([8]imaginer ce que serait mon arrivée à l'hôtel, je) ([9]Mais du moins ce changement) ([10]d'objectif, —si insignifiant que cela fut* d'ailleurs en soi—et j'étais comme brisé) ([11]qui, ayant eu le soleil). 666:32. ([1]Bolbec). 667:2. ([1]présence de petites bibliothèques à vitrines qui couraient le long des murs, mais surtout par une grande glace à pieds, arrêtée en travers de la pièce et avant le départ de laquelle je sentais). 667:17. ([1]hôtel et qu'avait tenté* pour moi ma grand'mère; et jusque).

pour qui j'étais encore inexistant, et j'aurais voulu me présenter à lui d'une façon plus prestigieuse que devancé par ma grand'-mère qui allait silencieusement*[2] lui demander des rabais. Je l'imaginais d'un[3] dédain certain très vague de contours. Ce n'était pas encore Bricquebec-Plage,[4] à tout moment le petit chemin de fer nous arrêtait à l'une des stations qui précédaient[5] Bricquebec-Plage et dont les noms même* (Bergeville, Criqueville, Equemanville, Couliville) me semblaient>

661:34. <semblaient étranges> **661:40.** <de l'orchestration. [661:36. <étaient près de Combray.]

661:40. De même, rien ne me faisait moins penser que ces tristes noms de sable, d'espace trop aéré et vide et de sel, au dessus*[1] desquels le mot ville s'échappait comme vole dans Pigeonvole, que Troussainville, que Roussainville, que ce*[2] noms

---

667:42. ([1]une pitié plus vaste encore, que). 668:27. ([1]caressée) ([2]un tel plaisir dans). 668:34. ([1]en touchant). 668:43. ([1]que, une semaine plus tard, quand je fus souffrant, je renouvellai* pendant quelques jours tous les matins parce que ma grand'mère voulait me donner du lait de bonne heure. Alors). 669:34. ([1]de laquelle). 670:13. ([1]Bolbec*). 670:30. ([1]ne résignaient pas). 671:15. ([1]Ce n'est pas que notre cœur ne doive les éprouver aussi quand). 672:3. ([1]les nerfs). 672:35. ([1]le nom de l'Hôtel et avec laquelle). 672:41. ([1]laissaient). 673:13. ([1]l'émeraude (dans ces montagnes où le soleil s'étale ça et là comme un géant qui en descendrait capricieusement les pentes), moins). 673:43. ([1]que, de la gourde de cuir d'un citron, nous répandions quelques). 674:10. ([1]me demandais si le) ([2]ce n'était pas). 674:20. ([1]projetait Geneviève de Brabant aussi). 675:9. ([1]casquettes de toutes les personnes qui étaient en train de déjeuner; elle-même). 675:17. ([1]Bolbec*). 675:18. ([1]banalement). 676:9. ([1]Car—comme) ([2]Bolbec*). 676:12. ([1]Rivelelle*). 676:15. ([1]Bolbec*) ([2]Bolbec*). 676:18. ([1]Bolbec*). 676:19. ([1]longtemps, faisaient charger leurs malles sur une barque, quand les pluies et les brumes arrivaient et traversaient). 676:22. ([1]Rivelelle*). 677:18. ([1]de laquelle). 680:18. ([1]Bolbec*). 681:39. ([1]jousjous*) ([2]glace, et tous les quatre s'engouffrant) ([3]les quatre gourmands discuter) ([4]longuement) ([5]un* autre aile de l'hôtel) ([6]de notre étage nous). 677:41. ([1]avec). 678:1. ([1]sert). 678:2. ([1]avec un geste distant, un air renseigné et une moue) ([2]l'espèce de certaines) ([3]d'être* relations) ([4]convaincre). 678:19. ([1]séduire, en se renouvelant soi-même, à s'attacher la sympathie) ([2]où) ([3]ricaner) ([4]aurait, en l'apercevant dans le hall, murmuré) ([5]braqué la lentille). 679:14. ([1]entre elle d'une part, les domestiques de l'hôtel et les fournisseurs de l'autre, ses). 679:28. ([1]garantissent pour elle, au milieu d'un sol étranger, le privilège de son extraterritorialité*. Elle). 679:37. ([1]vîmes, en revanche, au bout d'un instant en revanche* un hobéreau*). 680:8. ([1]de). 680:17. ([1]malveillant de ce genre à). 680:38. ([1]«Renaissance» authentiques). 681:10. ([1]d'un). 681:14. ([1]attendait. Et le soir quand). 681:14. ([1]Balbec).

qui[3] pour les avoir entendu prononcer si souvent par ma grand'tante>

662:5. <grand'tante à table> **662:43.** <des grands seigneurs. [662:8. <remontent du fond de ma mémoire comme une bulle gazeuse> 662:10. <spécifique au milieu des couches> 662:12. <qu'ils ont traversés avant[1] d'arriver jusqu'à> 662:13. C'étaient—dominant> 662:14. <au pied des collines> 662:16. <comme sur le canapé d'une chambre d'hôtel l'on* vient d'arriver—composées de quelques villas que[1] où* prolongeait> 662:19. <au vent,[1] évidé, rafraîchissant et anxieux, de petites> 662:21. <fois mais par leur dehors quotidien,[1] des joueurs de tennis en casquettes blanches, le> 662:24. <une dame qui, décrivant> 662:27. <allumée, et blessaient> 662:32. <grand-hôtel de Bricquebec[1] en> 662:36. <directeur, homme[1] à la figure et à la voix pleines des cicatrices qu'avait laissé* l'extirpation> 662:40. <cosmopolite, au smoking> 662:41. <psychologue qui s'exerçait* à l'arrivée de l'omnibus[1] et prenait infailliblement les grands>] {663:1-663:22}

663:23. Tandis que j'entendais ma grand'mère demander sur une intonation artificielle: «et> **663:40.** <gravir le faux marbre du grand escalier. [663:30. <à la surface insensibilisée de mon corps, (comme l'est celle des animaux qui par inhibition font les morts quand on les blesse), afin de ne pas> 663:35. <moment, la dame> 663:37. <familiarités avec son petit chien, le jeune gandin qui, la plume au chapeau, rentrait en sifflotant et demandait «est-ce que j'ai des lettres»>]

664:12. Mon impression de solitude s'accrut quand un moment après ma grand'mère étant partie en courses (je lui avais avoué que je n'étais pas bien, que je croyais que nous allions être obligés de revenir à Paris, et sans protester elle avait dit qu'elle était obligée d'aller faire quelques emplettes utiles aussi bien si nous partions que si nous restions ici et que je sus ensuite m'être toutes destinées, Françoise ayant avec elle des affaires qui m'auraient manqué, comme des tricots, des chaussons, une boule d'eau chaude), j'allai en l'attendant par[1] les rues encombrées d'une foule>

664:20. <foule qui> **664:42.** <causé une désillusion profonde> [664:21. <où était* encore ouverte la boutique du coif-

feur, et le salon d'un pâtissier où des habitués prenaient des glaces jusqu'à*[1] la statue> 664:25. <plaisir qu'une image d'elle sur la couverture d'un journal en procure au malade> 664:33. <exagérer, mais qui pourtant s'adressait> 664:34. <clientèle et dont il connaissait bien les goûts> 664:35. <pour les faire venir au Grand Hôtel de Bricquebec, non>]

□**664:42.** <désillusion profonde en lui disant, que j'étais malade et qu'il valait mieux ne pas persévérer dans ce voyage sur lequel elle avait fondé tant d'espérance pour ma santé.

664:42. Elle devait> □**665:1.** <désespérer que rien put* me faire du bien. Je voulais lui parler, j'étais retourné deux fois à l'hôtel et elle n'était pas encore rentrée. En songeant que peut-être je ne la verrais pas, ne pourrais pas essayer de la consoler avant une heure encore, me représentant sa tristesse qui durerait jusque-là, mon angoisse était si aiguë qu'elle obligeait ma pensée à cesser[1] aussitôt comme il arrive quand on essaye d'imaginer qu'on tombe d'un ballon dans le vide, en une chute qu'on ne peut pas continuer à se figurer plus de l'espace d'une seconde;[2] je touchais le néant, j'étais obligé de m'arrêter même de marcher pour reprendre mon souffle et recommencer à vivre.

665:1. Je me décidai> **665:11.** <nef commerciale. [665:4. <appelait lift,[1] et à ce point le plus haut de l'hôtel où serait le lanternon d'une église normande, était installé comme un photographe derrière son vitrage ou plutôt comme un organiste dans sa chambre, se mit>] {665:12-665:18}

665:18. Pour dissiper l'angoisse mortelle que> **665:41.** <la même âme. [665:22. <water closet*> 665:24. <captivité, qui continuait> 665:27. <donner autant de peine> 665:36. <extérieur[1] et de l'avis par le changement de la position, par rapport à nous, d'une personne même insignifiante, avant et après que nous l'ayons connue. 665:40. <de Bricquebec, je>]

665:41. Mais dans cette âme, à l'endroit où[1] tandis que le petit chemin de fer m'emportait vers Bricquebec il y avait une impossibilité à imaginer le directeur, l'hôtel, son personnel,[2] une [*blanc*] et craintive du moment où le directeur m'apercevrait, à cette[3] peur même il y avait les boutons extirpés dans la figure du directeur[4] et son geste pour [*blanc*] le lift, le lift lui-même, toute une frise de personnages semblables à des personnages de guignol sortis de cette boîte de Pandore, indéniables, inamovibles, qui me connaissaient, si bien que les questions que je me posais[5] ne me semblaient plus avoir de sens puisque je possédais dans mon souvenir la figure du personnel*[6] boutonneux comme si je l'avais toujours[7] connu et qui me prouvait qu'il s'était passé quelque chose si [*blanc*] que ce fut* d'extérieur à moi, d'objectif et par conséquent d'essentiel, comme [*blanc*] le voyageur qui, ayant vu le soleil devant lui pendant la première partie de la route, le voit derrière lui pendant la dernière. Il y avait là quelque chose à quoi je ne pouvais rien. Toutes ces pensées que j'avais dans le train cherchait* à me renseigner sur l'hôtel, le personnel, n'avaient plus aucun sens. Si j'avais voulu reprendre mon effort pour imaginer,[8] je serais retombé immédiatement sur la figure boutonneuse, sur la présence stérilisante pour l'inspiration du fait accompli qui nous donne d'une façon insignifiante et inéluctable la réponse que nous aurions dû trouver nous-même et sublime*. Et[9] ce changement dans lequel je n'étais pas intervenu me prouvait qu'il s'était passé quelque chose d'extérieur à moi d'objectif,*[10] comme le voyageur qui[11] avait le soleil devant lui en commençant une course constate que le temps a passé en le trouvant derrière lui. J'étais brisé de fatigue, j'avais la fièvre, je me serais couché, mais je n'avais rien de ce qu'il fallait pour cela. {663:3-666:7}

666:19. J'aurais voulu> **667:2.** <tiers les irrite. [666:21. <repos à ce système de sensations> 666:28. <cardinal La Ballue* dans> 666:32. <chambre de Bricquebec[1] qui n'était mienne que de nom, car elle était pleine>] {667:2-667:6}

667:2. J'étais tourmenté par la présence[1] d'une glace arrêtée en travers de la pièce et par de petites bibliothèques vitrines, en glace aussi qui couraient le long des murs avant le départ desquelles je sentais>

667:10. <sentais qu'il> **668:19.** <enfant qui téte*. [667:12. <mes regards,—dont les objets de ma chambre de Paris ne gênaient plus l'expansion que> 667:17. <hôtel;[1] et jusque dans cette région plus proche que celle> 667:35. <sa robe de servante, son habit de religieuse ou de garde. 667:42. <dans une[1] plus vaste pitié, que tout> 668:1. <vouloir, y serait étayé>

668:6. Et comme> 668:11. <insecte, trompé> 668:13. <dans ses bras, et je suspendis> 668:15. <m'ouvrait et qui était plus à moi que le mien. Et quand>]

668:20. Sur sa prière et comme elle me sentait fatigué, je me rassis, je regardais sans me lasser son visage découpé>

668:21. <découpé comme> **668:34.** <déshabiller moi-même> [668:27. <que si c'était sa bonté que j'y avais caressé*.[1] Elle trouvait une[2] telle douceur dans>]

668:34. <moi-même, elle m'arrêta d'un regard suppliant comme si mes mains en[1] les* touchant aux premiers boutons de ma veste et de mes bottines, allaient briser sans pitié son fragile bonheur.

668:37. —Oh, je t'en prie> **669:29.** <tous ses manèges. [668:38. <grand'mère de t'être bonne à quelque chose. 668:43. <coups—que[1] je renouvellai* une semaine plus tard quand je fus souffrant pendant quelques jours et que ma grand'mère voulu* me donner du lait le matin. Alors> 669:9. <elle aurait dormi> 669:16. <et bientôt ma grand'mère> 669:23. <entre la peur de>]

669:30. Elle me donnait mon lait, entr'ouvrait* les volets; à l'annexe de l'hôtel qui faisait saillie, le soleil> **669:40.** <personne n'assiste> [669:34. <et dont[1] l'immobilité> 669:36. <que j'aille jusqu'à>]

669:40. <n'assiste, et ou* des habitants de l'hôtel nous étions seuls présents; petit morceau de vie qui n'était qu'à nous deux, que j'évoquerais volontiers dans la journée devant Françoise ou des étrangers en disant: «Il y avait pourtant un fameux brouillard ce matin à six heures», avec l'ostentation non d'un savoir que j'aurais été seul à posséder, mais d'une marque de tendresse que ma grand'mère n'avait donné* qu'à moi; doux instant>

670:3. <instant matinal> **672:20.** <plafond inaccessible. [670:13. <à Paris quand j'avais compris qu'en partant pour Bricquebec[1] je disais adieu à ma chambre. Peut-être> 670:22. <horreur que me faisait éprouver> 670:26. <je ne verrai plus> 670:28. <survie comme Bergotte le* promettait dans> 670:30. <caractère qui ne[1] pouvaient se résigner à l'idée> 670:38. <ne verrais plus> 671:1. <c'est que tu seras heureux là-bas. 671:15. <désespoir. Certes[1] notre cœur aussi les éprouvera quand la sépa-

ration> 671:20. <aimons et dont nous tirons> 671:23. <pensons s'ajoutera pour ce qui nous* semble> 671:27. <amis qui ne seraient plus autour de nous, mais notre affection pour eux; elle aurait été> 671:35. <moi condamné à> 671:38. <rébellions qui ne sont que la forme secrète, partielle, tangibles* et vraie> 671:43. <à tout moment> 672:3. <mienne, c'est-à-dire chez qui les intermédiaires nerveux[1] ne remplissent pas leurs fonctions> 672:8. <disparaître, l'anxieuse>]

□**672:22.** Mais le lendemain matin!—comme à Combray, après une nuit de tristesse, à l'heure où le soleil qui, les effaçant toutes à la fois, entrait par la fenêtre et semblait me dire: descends au jardin; où, voyant flamboyer les ardoises du clocher de Saint-Hilaire, je m'apprêtais pour aller sur la place, à l'église, au bord de la Vivonne, —le lendemain matin, après qu'un domestique>

672:22. <domestique fut venu> **673:16.** <mobilité de la lumière> [672:23. <chaude, tout en faisant ma toilette et en essayant vainement> 672:35. <écrit le[1] mot: Grand-Hôtel, avec laquelle> 672:37. <sécher et que je dépliais avec peine, je retournais> 672:40. <d'émeraude, çà et là polis et translucides qui avec> 672:41. <léonin laissèrent[1] s'accomplir> 673:4. <désirée, ici> 673:13. <alpestes*, translucides comme l'émeraude,[1] moins l'humidité>]

□**673:16.** <lumière dans ces montagnes où le soleil s'éveille çà et là comme le géant qui en descendait capricieusement les pentes.

673:16. Au reste> **674:18.** <bleues, comme si quelque géant s'était amusé à les déplacer en bougeant un miroir dans le ciel. [673:25. <le matin, la lumière venait> 673:29. <poursuivre sur sa route tournante un voyage> 673:32. <soleil me montrait au> 673:40. <l'impression de désordre. Hélas, ce vent> 673:43. <que[1] nous répandions de la gourde de cuir d'un citron quelques gouttes> 674:5. <clos qui nous séparait de la plage comme une vitrine, tout en nous la laissant entièrement voir et dans lequel le ciel entrait> 674:10. <«boudoir» je sentais[1] que le «soleil rayonnant sur la mer» de Baudelaire, c'était[2]—bien différent>]

□**674:20.** Et cette instabilité de la lumière, qu'on ne rencontre que sur la mer et dans la montagne, faisait penser aux incertitudes, à la perpétuelle mise au point de quelque sublime lanterne magique, tant les accidents sur lesquels elle se jouait semblaient avoir peu d'importance; une grande clarté joignait le rivage aux flots, puis le désertait, s'isolait au milieu de la mer, réunissait deux bateaux, coupait un vapeur en deux moitiés dont l'une restait à l'ombre, avec autant d'indifférence que ma lanterne magique de Combray projetait[1] la guerrière de [*blanc*] aussi bien sur les rideaux de la fenêtre que sur le bouton de la porte ou l'encoignure de la cheminée. {674:20-675:5}

675:6. Mais ma grand'mère ne pouvant supporter l'idée que je perdais* le bénéfice d'une heure de mer, ouvrit> **675:39.** <cinq cent mille. [675:9. <coup, menus, journaux, voiles et casquettes;[1] elle-même> 675:15. <méprisants, décoiffées et furieux. 675:17. <à Bricquebec,[1] donnait> 675:18. <d'ordinaire franchement[1] riche> 675:22. <président du Mans, d'un> 675:23. <notaire de Nantes qui> 675:27. Ils y avaient toujours> 675:28. <chambres, et leurs femmes> 675:36. <la grande ville> 675:37. <deux mille même au>]

675:42. Ils le disaient> **677:35.** <chagrin ses parents. [676:2. <président de Rennes de venir à la Cour> 676:9. Car[1] comme la baie de Bricquebec[2] était> 676:12. <seulement par les jours où on apercevait Riuelelle*, ce> 676:15. <à Bricquebec[1] mais encore que quand l'automne et les froids avaient gagné Bricquebec,[2] on était certain de trouver encore sur cette> 676:17. <mois de chaleur> 676:18. <habitués de l'hôtel de Bricquebec[1] dont> 676:19. <longtemps,[1] quand les pluies et les brumes arrivaient, faisaient charger leurs malles sur une barque> 676:22. <l'été à Costedor ou à Riuelelle.*[1] Tout ce petit> 676:24. <et, tout en ayant l'air de ne pas s'intéresser à lui, interrogeaient> 676:30. <pièce du trousseau tout en> 676:33. <société de Nantes ni d'Alençon. 676:36. <proclamé roi d'un petit îlot de l'Océanie habité par quelques sauvages. 676:40. <parce qu'elle leur jetait des pièces de cinquante centimes. 677:14. <leur or, que> 677:18. <courant desquelles[1] était> 677:27. <fêtard d'un coulissier millionnaire et qui> 677:33. <femme déclarait tenir de bonne source que ce jeune>]

677:39. See after 681:39.

□**680:18.** Ce sentiment, peut-être la colonie avait-elle moins l'occasion de l'éprouver à l'égard d'une actrice, mais connue comme telle, car elle avait joué peu de rôles à l'Odéon, qu'à cause de sa grâce, de son esprit, de son élégance, de son goût, de ses précieuses collections de porcelaine allemande, et qui était au grand hôtel de Bricquebec[1] avec son amant, jeune homme très riche pour qui surtout elle s'était cultivée, et avec deux hommes en vue de l'aristocratie, quatre personnes formant par le plaisir qu'elles avaient à causer ensemble, à jouer aux cartes ensemble, à manger ensemble (car les quatre étaient atteints au même degré de gourmandise), une petite société que les déplacements d'été ne désunissaient pas et qui se transportait, intacte et au complet, tantôt ici, tantôt là. Mais la femme du premier président, la femme du notaire se voyaient refuser la joie qu'elles auraient eue à souffrir d'une promiscuité avec cette demi-mondaine. Car la petite société qui avait toujours des menus spéciaux pour l'élaboration desquels chaque fois un ou deux de ses membres avait* de longues conférences avec le cuisinier, ne venait déjeuner qu'extrêmement tard, quand tout le monde était sur le point de sortir de table. Ils prenaient leurs repas à l'écart, entrant par une petite porte, ne gênant personne; la femme toujours admirablement mise, avait des robes toujours renouvelées mais peu voyantes, avec un goût, particulier à elle, d'écharpes qui plaisaient à son amant. On ne voyait aucun d'eux dans la journée qu'ils passaient tout entière à jouer aux cartes.

680:34. See after 681:39.

□**681:39.** Le soir quand on sortait de table, on apercevait tout au plus les trois hommes en smoking attendant la femme en retard qui bientôt, après avoir de l'étage sonné le lift, sortait de la cage de l'ascenseur comme d'une boîte de joujou*[1] [*cf.* 682:1], toute parée avec une écharpe nouvelle, se regardant un instant dans la glace,[2] remettant un peu de rouge, et toute la société s'engouffrant dans une voiture fermée attelée de deux chevaux, qui attendait, allaient dîner à une demi lieue* de là dans un petit restaurant réputé pour sa table et où comme il y avait peu de monde, le chef pouvait soigner davantage la cuisine, et euxmêmes[3] discuter plus largement[4] avec lui de l'opportunité d'ajouter ou non tel ou tel ingrédient. De telle sorte ils passaient presque inaperçus des habitants de l'hôtel. Il n'en allait pas de même à l'égard d'une vieille dame riche [*cf.* 677:37] et titrée dont, quoiqu'elle fut* à un[5] autre étage, le valet de chambre du nôtre[6] nous avait parlé, impressionné comme tous ses camarades parce qu'elle avait amené avec elle, femme de chambre, cocher, chevaux, voitures, et avait été précédée par un maître d'hôtel chargé de choisir les chambres et de les rendre, grâce à des bibelots, à de précieuses vieilleries qu'il avait apportées, aussi peu différentes que possible de celles que sa maîtresse habitait à Paris. Le bâtonnier et ses amis ne tarissaient pas de sarcasmes au sujet de ce respect du personnel pour une dame à particule qui ne se déplaçait qu'avec tout son train de maison.

△**677:39.** Chaque fois> **678:2.** <observation méthodique> [677:41. <insolemment de[1] leur> 678:1. <suspecte comme on en voit[1] souvent dans les grands hôtels, qu'après>]

△**678:2.** <méthodique ou* peut éloigner, par[1] le signe d'un geste distant, d'un air renseigné et d'une moue de dégoût.

Sans doute par là la femme du notaire et du premier président voulaient montrer, comme fait tout le monde, que s'il y avait certaines choses dont elles manquaient—dans l'espèce[2], certaines prérogatives de la vielle dame, et des[3] relations avec elle—, c'était non pas parce qu'elles ne pouvaient pas les avoir, mais parce qu'elles ne le voulaient pas. Mais le malheur était que cherchant seulement à en persuader les autres, elles avaient fini par s'en persuader[4] elles-mêmes. Et c'est la suppression>

△**678:10.** <suppression de tout désir> **678:19.** <à l'amour-propre> [678:12. <êtres, de l'effort pour plaire, remplacés chez ces dames par>]

△**678:19.** <amour-propre comme elles faisaient, du moins à un certain principe d'éducation, ou à certaines habitudes intellectuelles, le trouble délicieux qu'il y a à se mêler à une vie inconnue, à poursuivre l'objet de ses désirs, à séduire,[1] à s'attacher, en se renouvelant soi-même la sympathie mystérieuse des êtres nouveaux. Sans doute le microcosme dans lequel s'isolait la vieille dame noble n'était pas empoisonné de virulentes aigreurs comme celui que[2] le clan du premier président laissait exulter, ricanant[3] de rage. Mais il était embaumé d'un parfum vieillot et fin, de bon ton, qui n'était pas moins factice. Je me plaisais à penser qu'elle

avait peut-être au fond d'elle de la sensibilité et de l'imagination, et que le charme que dégage un être inconnu aurait agi plus profondément sur elle que par le plaisir sans mystère qu'il y a à ne fréquenter que des gens de son monde et à se rappeler que ce monde est le meilleur qui soit; qui sait si ce n'était pas en pensant que si elle arrivait inconnue à l'hôtel, faisant peu d'effet ou faisant rire avec sa robe de laine noire et son bonnet démodé, en l'apercevant dans le hall un jeune fétard* qu'elle eût trouvé joli garçon—comme celui qui cette année se ruinait au jeu—aurait[4] même murmuré de son rocking chair «quelle purée» et où* quelque homme de valeur, ayant gardé, comme le premier président entre ses favoris poivre et sel, un visage sain et des yeux spirituels, comme elle les aimait, aurait désigné à sa femme en souriant l'apparition de ce phénomène insolite sur lequel celle-ci eût braqué,[5] et non par mauvaise humeur, la lentille de son face à main comme un instrument de précision, qui sait si ce n'était pas par effroi de cette première minute qu'on sait courte mais qui n'est pas moins redoutée—comme la première tête qu'on pique dans l'eau—que cette dame envoyait d'avance un domestique mettre l'hôtel au courant de sa venue, de sa personnalité et de ses habitudes, et qu'en descendant de voiture elle s'avançait rapidement entre sa femme de chambre et son valet de pied, coupant court aux salutations du directeur avec une brièveté où il voyait de l'orgueil et où il n'y avait que de la timidité. Rapidement elle gagnait sa chambre où des rideaux personnels ayant pris la place de ceux qui pendaient aux fenêtres, des paravents, des photographies, des bibelots apportés, mettaient>

△**679:9.** <mettaient si bien> **679:28.** <portes d'une ambassade> [679:14. <entre[1] elle et les domestiques de l'hôtel, les fournisseurs*, ses domestiques qui> 679:16. <le contact douloureux ou charmant de cette> 679:18. <entre elle et les autres touristes étrangers et baigneurs> 679:21. <la correspondance échangée et reçue, par le>

△**679:28.** <ambassade ayant les couleurs du pays dont elle dépend, garantissait*[1] par un lien d'un sol étranger, le privilège de son internationalité. Elle ne descendit pas de sa chambre et nous ne l'aperçûmes pas>

△**679:33.** <pas dans la salle> **680:17.** <pas» se fussent mis à sa place. [679:37. <vîmes au bout d'un instant en revanche un hobéreau* et sa fille> 679:40. <M. et Mlle de Silaria, dont le directeur nous avait> 679:41. <soir. Ceux-là venus seulement à Bricquebec pour retrouver des châtelains qu'ils connaissaient dans le voisinage, ne passaient entre les invitations acceptées et les visites rendues que le temps strictement nécessaire dans la salle à manger de l'hôtel. C'était> 680:4. <pour tous les inconnus assis aux tables voisines, et au milieu desquelles M. de Silaria gardait> 680:8. <milieu des[1] voyageurs> 680:10. <froid et sa place dans> 680:12. <M. de Silaria, lequel>]

△**680:17.** Et certes dans le désir d'isolement qui poussait le jeune homme riche, sa maîtresse et ses deux amis à ne voyager qu'ensemble, à ne prendre leurs repas qu'après tout le monde, il n'y avait aucun sentiment malveillant[1] à l'endroit des autres et par conséquent désagréable et d'un goût aigre pour eux-mêmes mais seulement les exigences du goût qu'ils avaient pour certaines formes spirituelles de conversation, pour certains raffinements d'élégance et qui leur eût rendu insupportable la vie en commun avec des gens qui n'y avaient pas été initiés.

△**680:34.** Même devant une table servie ou devant une table à jeu, où ces connaisseurs ne trouvaient par* leur emploi, chacun d'eux> **680:38.** <tant d'hôtels parisiens se parent comme d'un «moyen âge» ou d'une «Renaissance[1] authentiques», la finesse d'esprit qui empêche de se plaire à un calembour bête, une expérience de la bonne société qui fait dépister tout de suite des façons prétentieuses ou communes, en somme des critériums communs à eux tous pour distinguer en toutes choses le bon et le mauvais.

△**680:42.** Sans doute> **681:14.** <le goûter attendait.[1] [681:3. <un poker avec ces trois hommes, toujours les mêmes, que se manifestait la vie spéciale> 681:7. <ambiante. Pendant les longs après-midi où ils restaient à jouer aux cartes, la mer> 681:10. <d'une[1]>]

△**681:14.** Il en était de la campagne comme de la mer et des hommes. Et le soir quand ils allaient dîner au dehors, la route bordée [*cf.* 682:8] de pommiers qui part de Bricquebec,[2] n'était pour eux que la distance qu'il fallait franchir, —peu distincte à la nuit noire, de celle qui séparait leurs domiciles parisiens du café anglais ou de Joseph—avant d'arriver au restaurant élegant et champêtre où ils faisaient leur fin dîner, et où tandis que> {681:14-682:10}

682:12. <tandis que les amis> □**682:18.** <tous ces gens, dont beaucoup d'entre eux je me souciais; je n'aurais pas voulu être méprisé par eux. Je n'avais pas encore eu à cette époque le réconfort d'apprendre les traits de caractère de Swann qui aurait cru en faisant venir de Paris sa maîtresse pour passer sur elle le désir qu'une inconnue lui avait inspirée*, ne pas croire à ce désir, substituer une réalité particulière à laquelle on ne pouvait pas souhaiter être inconnue* d'un homme au front déprimé, au regard fuyant entre les œillières de ses préjugés et de son éducation. Le grand seigneur de l'arrondissement était beau-frère* de Legrandin, qui venait quelquefois en visite à Bricquebec et qui dépeuplait l'hôtel d'une partie de ses habitués, chaque dimanche, par sa garden-party hebdomadaire, parce qu'un ou deux d'entre eux y étaient invités et parce que les autres pour ne pas avoir l'air de ne pas l'être, choisissaient ce jour-là pour faire une excursion qui les éloignaient* de Bricquebec. {682:29-683:2}

683:21. J'aurais aimé> **683:26.** <trésors d'affections; je me souciais> [683:22. <roi en Océanie> 683:23. <tuberculeux[1] auquel je pensais sans cesse, supposant qu'il cachait> 683:24. <sous des dehors>] {683:26-683:33}

683:33. <je me souciais> **684:36.** <joyeuse surprise. [683:34. <ces personnalités momentanées> 683:38. <été plus[1] bas>

682:18. *(B-A)* <tous ces gens. De beaucoup d'entre eux> **682:29.** <pour faire une excursion qui les éloignait de Balbec. [682:23. <Legrandin, venait> 682:24. <et chaque dimanche, par sa garden-party> 682:27. <eux y étaient invités et parce que>]

683:23. ([1]tuberculeux, supposant).

683:36. <recréer en moi leur>

683:38. ([1]fort). 683:39. ([1]Balbec) ([2]commune mesuré*). 684:7. ([1]peignent). 684:9. ([1]la bonne voie). 685:40. ([1]Balbec). 686:1. ([1]que Mme de Villeparisis jouissait) ([2]Silaria. Non d'ailleurs que l'amie de ma grand'mère, me représentât une personne). 686:14. ([1]penser à une personne d'un monde spécial, que son cousin) ([2]lui ancien Président de) ([3]maréchal. Ma grand'mère avait pour). 686:39. ([1]Cambrimer*). 687:14. ([1]Cambremer). 687:15. ([1]ai). 687:24. ([1]coin.»—«Mais vous). 687:43. ([1]Bolbec*). 688:7. ([1]Cambremer). 688:17. ([1]Cambremer). 688:40a. ([1]faute.) [*In* Grasset B *the remainder*

683:39. <à Bricquebec[1] où l'absence de commerce[2] mesuré* leur> 683:41. Mais d'aucun le mépris ne m'était aussi pénible que de M. de Silaria. 684:4. <raison l'hérédité et l'éducation aristocratique de cette jeune fille mais d'autant plus clairement que je savais son nom et qu'il était noble, —comme> 684:7. <qui peignait*[1] splendidement> 684:9. <auditeurs qui ont d'abord aiguillé leur imagination dans la[1] voie en lisant le programme. Cette hérédité et cette éducation en ajoutant aux charmes de Mlle de Silaria l'idée> .684:16. <à ce teint qu'elle avait composé> 684:20. <le moyen de nous donner aux yeux de tous ces gens un prestige immédiat. 684:23. <chez elle, coiffée d'un bonnet à brides et peu imposante par son corps, mais, grâce au valet de pied qui la précédait, au valet de chambre qui portait ses affaires, à la femme de chambre qui courait derrière avec un livre et une couverture oubliées*, exerçant une action> 684:28. <personne, peut-être parce qu'il avait plus de données sur elle et sur sa famille, M. de Silaria, le directeur se pencha> 684:30. <Perse à un spectateur> 684:32. <peut être intéressé à l'avoir vu à quelques pas de lui, il lui coula> 684:35. <moment la Marquise apercevant>] {684:37-685:33}

685:34. Malheureusement s'il y avait quelqu'un qui vivait encore plus enfermé dans son univers particulier que ne faisaient toutes les autres personnes de l'hôtel, c'était ma grand'mère. Je ne peux pas dire qu'elle m'aurait méprisé, mais plutôt qu'elle ne m'aurait même pas compris, si elle avait su>

685:38. <su que j'attachais> **685:43.** <parce que je sentais> [685:39. <remarquait même pas> 685:40. <quitter Bricquebec[1] sans>]

686:1. <sentais qu'à[1] cause de sa nombreuse domesticité Mme de Villeparisis jouissait dans l'hôtel d'un grand prestige et que son amitié nous eut* posés aux yeux de M. de Silaria,[2] étant d'ailleurs l'amie de ma grand'mère, me représentant une personne de l'aristocratie: j'étais trop habitué>

686:5. <habitué à son nom> **686:14.** <ne me faisait pas plus penser> [686:11. <Lord-Byron ou dans la rue de Grammont*>]

---

of this passage is eliminated] 689:32. ([1]davantage. Et dans). 689:33. ([1]romanesque et légendaire peut-être aurions-nous). 689:35. ([1]luiraient).

686:14. <penser[1] à quelqu'un d'une vie particulière, que son cousin Mac Mahon que je ne différenciais pas de M. Grévy, qui avait été comme lui[2] Président de la République et de Raspail dont Françoise avait acheté la photographie avec celle du maréchal[3] chez le marchand en plein vent qui faisait le coin de la rue Royale. D'autre part ma grand'mère avait pour principe qu'on n'a plus de relations en voyage, qu'on ne va pas>

686:20. <va pas au bord> **686:32.** <dans le vague. [686:29. <contenta de répondre: «Ah», détourna les yeux et eut l'air>] {686:32-686:35}

686:36. Elle prenait aussi> **688:1.** <grand regret du bâtonnier> [686:39. <même M. de Soulangy;[1] en effet> 687:9. <étonnement simulé avec exagération; à cause> 687:14. <*de* Soulangy,[1] n'est-ce pas? 687:15. Je les avais[1] bien reconnus. C'est une comtesse. Et> 687:24. <restons dans notre petit coin.»[1] Mais vous> 687:28. <pas mangé ces gens. 687:31. <traitez des comtesses! 687:38. Mais vous allez aussi chez eux, dit le président au notaire. 687:43. M. de Silaria n'avait pas déjeuné ce matin-là à Bricquebec,[1] au>]

□**688:1a.** <bâtonnier, qui depuis le jour où un garçon lui avait appris le nom de cet inconnu avait trouvé qu'on voyait tout de suite que c'était un homme parfaitement bien élevé.

688:1. Mais insidieusement> **688:18.** <justement nous réunir> [688:3. <de Silaria qu'il> 688:7. <c'est le comte de Soulangy.[1] 688:14. <M. de Silaria, qui ne savait pas* que> 688:17. <de Soulangy,[1] voulaient>]

688:18. <réunir, dit effrontément le bâtonnier, nos jours n'ont pas coïncidé, enfin je ne sais plus. {688:19-688:24}

□**688:25a.** Comme toujours, mais plus facilement pendant que son père s'était éloigné pour causer avec le bâtonnier, je regardais Mlle de Silaria. Je savais dans quel milieu presque féodal encore, elle avait vécu en Bretagne, et (autant que la singularité>

688:25. <singularité hardie> **688:40.** <moment faisait faute> [688:30. <avant-bras pareils aux deux branches d'un vase), la sécheresse> 688:37. <vers la race qui>]

□**688:40a.** <faute,[1] et vers cette éducation qui avait borné le monde pour elle à son oncle l'évêque, à sa tante l'abbesse. De jeunes cousins nobles devaient avoir pris la douce habitude, le

contact familier de son corps au cours de chasses, de jeux loin desquels hélas! j'avais vécu au fond de cette baie grise, semée de mille petits rochers qui, les soirs calmes comme celui où la [*blanc*] de Tristan y était apparue [*blanc*], à l'infini des nuances du coucher de soleil, dans cette île où les chênes reflétaient des clartés vertes au dessus* des fontaines des fées et des bruyères roses et qui me semblait* avoir tant de charme parce qu'elle enfermait la vie de Mlle de Silaria et reposait dans la mémoire de ses yeux.

688:40. Mais à certains regards> **689:37.** <clapotement des vagues que par les gros temps le vent pousse sur l'île. [689:8. <vinsse goûter sur elle à cette vie si éloignée, si poétique, si ancienne, à laquelle, soit> 689:19. <repas me la faisait paraître plus douce> 689:27. <mais les attraits du sexe et de l'âge. Si un jour M. de Silaria> 689:29. <une bonne opinion> 689:32. <davantage[1] et dans un mois d'hiver où elle serait restée> 689:33. <romanesque,[1] légendaire aurions-nous> 689:35. <où luisaient[1] plus>] {689:38-689:41}

689:41. Car il me semblait> **690:37.** <les gens avec qui l'on[1] se trouve. [689:43. <lieux qui enveloppaient Mlle de Silaria de tant de souvenirs et me séparaient d'elle, —voile que> 690:11. <détourner nos* regards de Mlle de Silaria, car> 690:12. <connaissance d'une notabilité était> 690:15. <n'exigeait en dehors d'une poignée de mains et d'un coup d'œil pénétrant aucune conversation immédiate et nulles relations ultérieures, son père> 690:18. <et revenait s'asseoir> 690:22. <autres jours, on entendait par moments sa* voix du bâtonnier s'adressant au maître d'hôtel> 690:34. <disposition, où il attire*[1] à la fois de la timidité, de la vulgarité et de la sottise,[2] à croire qu'il est>]

690:37. Il le répétait sans cesse, mais comme il tenait à étaler à la fois ses bonnes relations avec le maître d'hôtel,[1] sa supériorité sur lui, il accompagnait cette interpellation d'un sourire comme celui qu'on garde quand on fait la conversation avec un enfant.

689:38. Ensemble nous avions* parcouru> **689:41.** <de ses yeux. [689:40. <de Mlle de Silaria et>]

690:34. ([1]entre) ([2]sottise, qu'ont certaines personnes à croire). 690:37. ([1]elles se trouvent). 690:37. ([1]d'hôtel et sa). 694:5. ([1]tard, ma grand'mère). 694:14. ([1]s'aperçoivent n'en* peuvent). 694:19. ([1]la retenir jusqu'au).

690:40. Et le maître d'hôtel> **690:42.** <la plaisanterie. {691:1-694:5}

694:5. Mais quelques jours plus tard,[1] le lendemain de celui où étaient partis M. et Mlle de Silaria, ma grand'mère et Mme de Villeparisis tombèrent le matin l'une sur l'autre> **694:21.** <elle faisait pour avoir> [694:11. <joie en vertu d'une convention analogue à celle qui règle certaines scènes du théâtre de Molière où deux acteurs> 694:14. <s'être encore vus> 694:14. <s'aperçoivent[1] l'un l'autre, n'en peuvent croire les yeux, s'assurent, et finalement tombent dans les bras l'un de l'autre> 694:19. <préfèra* rester[1] avec elle jusqu'au déjeuner, désirant apprendre d'elle comment>]

694:21. <pour avoir des grillades à son repas et son courrier plutôt* que nous. Et Mme de Villeparisis prit l'habitude> {694:22-694:26}

694:26. <l'habitude de venir> **694:29.** <nous nous dérangions en rien pour elle. {694:33-696:31}

696:37. —Je dirai à ma femme de chambre> **696:41.** <à vous dire! [696:39. Comment, vous vous écrivez *tous les jours* avec votre fille? Mais>]

696:41. Cette parole valut à Mme de Villeparisis un tel dédain de la part de ma grand'mère, que celle-ci ne daigna même pas protester quand sa vieille amie lui dit: {696:42-697:17}

697:12. —Qu'est-ce que vous avez là! Ah! oui, je vous voyais toujours avec les lettres de Mme de Sévigné (elle oubliait> **697:26.** <posant son sac>

□**697:26.** <sac dessus, les mémoires de Mme de Charlus.[1] En revanche si ma grand'mère avait remarqué un livre que Mme de Villeparisis lisait ou admiré*[2] des fruits qu'elle avait à son des-

---

694:30. Tout au plus> **694:33.** <serviettes défaites> <694:31. <moment quotidien et sordide où>]

696:32. <défaites. «Mais il me semble> **696:37.** <côte. Ah! je dirais> [696:37. <Bolbec>]

697:26. ([1]Beausergent) ([2]trouve* beaux des) ([3]dessert, une heure) ([4]montait nous remettre livre ou fruits. Et quand) ([5]de la mer.» [Grasset B *stops here and resumes at 698:6*]). 698:8. ([1]grand'mère sans se rendre compte que ses paroles excitaient mon indignation.). 698:19. ([1]des fruits superbes et d'autant plus rares qu'ils unissaient en cette corbeille diverses saisons avec une).

sert[3] ou trouvé beaux*, une heure après un valet de chambre montait[4] chez nous et priait Françoise—flattée de la provenance—de nous remettre livre ou fruits «de la part de Madame la Marquise» [*cf.* 696:24]. Et quand nous la voyions ensuite, pour répondre à nos remerciements, elle se contentait de dire, ayant l'air de chercher une excuse de son présent, dans quelque utilité spéciale: «C'est toujours plus prudent d'avoir du fruit dont on est sûr au bord de la mer»[5] ou «c'est toujours assez difficile d'avoir de bons fruits au bord de la mer quoique* ils aient ici des petites poires assez agréables, mais pour mon goût pas assez juteuses. Mais vous les aimez, ajouta-t-elle d'un air entendu comme si le goût que nous avions était une chose importante», ou «ce sont des mémoires assez amusants à lire pour tout ce qui touche aux Orléans que l'auteur a bien connus, mais la partie sur les Bourbons* est faite de chic et ne vaut rien. On sentait une femme qui déteste les phrases qui s'attachait* aux détails précis, particuliers, aux goûts matériels, avec une sorte de parti pris, en vertu d'une sorte d'esthétique comme celle d'un [*blanc*] social. {697:28-698:5}

698:6. —Il faudra> □**698:8.** <grand'mère[1] qui excite* mon indignation en ayant l'air de ne pas comprendre qu'elle* vie à part de tous les autres humains menaient les descendants de Geneviève de Brabant, lesquels n'eussent jamais voulu prendre connaissance de Mme de Villeparisis.

698:9. Comment aurais-je pu> **698:12.** <d'or de l'imagination. Mais nous vîmes à l'hôtel un jour des fruits plus beaux que ceux que Mme de Villeparisis avait sur sa table.

698:13. On voyait souvent> **698:24.** <être destinés ces fruits. [698:13. <en grand équipage> 698:15. <fort, une dame d'honneur à côté d'elle, la princesse> 698:19. <rapporté les[1] superbes fruits avec une carte: «La princesse> 698:23. <quel hôte princier demeurant incognito dans l'hôtel pouvaient être destinés ces fruits>]

□**698:28.** Car ce ne pouvait être à Mme de Villeparisis que la princesse avait voulu faire visite. Comment[1] l'aurait-elle connue?

698:24. <ces fruits, ces prunes> **698:28.** <d'un outremer célestes*.

698:28. *(B-A)* Car ce ne pouvait être à Mme de Villeparisis que la princesse avait voulu faire visite. Pourtant le lendemain soir> **698:37.** <se

Pourtant une heure après Mme de Villeparisis nous envoya des poires et des raisins que nous reconnûmes. Le lendemain matin nous rencontrâmes Mme de Villeparisis en sortant du concert symphonique qui se donnait sur la plage. J'y avais la veille rencontré Bloch qui n'en manquait pas un, m'avait-il dit, parce que le chef d'orchestre, un grand musicien selon lui, jouait de nombreuses scènes de Wagner et des transcriptions de Schumann. Et il m'avait cité de belles phrases de Baudelaire sur Wagner et de Schopenhauer sur la musique. C'est ainsi que j'entendis des fragments de *Lohengrin,* de l'*Or du Rhin,* qu'après ma nuit en chemin de fer j'avais reconnus pour les avoir si souvent vus au [*blanc*], le *Réveil de Brunhilde*—où les mêmes phrases que j'avais entendues dès la fin de la *Walkyrie* prirent, retrouvées à une autre place préparant non plus le sommeil de la vierge mais sa résurrection la même acception nouvelle et mystérieuse que certaines lueurs roses, certains rayons obliques du soleil, pareils à ceux que j'avais vus si souvent au couchant mais qui cette fois signifiaient le levier*—et enfin le *Carnaval* de Schumann. Sachant que la musique reflétait la «Volonté du roi et tous les spectacles de l'univers» je ne m'arrêtais pas un instant à l'idée que Schumann avait pu chercher à peindre quelque chose d'aussi limité, d'une importance spirituelle aussi médiocre, et, si je m'en apportais à mes propres goûts, d'aussi ennuyeux et d'aussi vulgaire qu'un soir de carnaval. C'était les alternatives d'irrésistible allégresse et d'ineffable mélancolie auxquelles l'âme se donne tour à tour que je cherchais à saisir dans cette musique.

698:38. Et persuadé que les œuvres que j'entendais exprimaient les vérités les plus hautes, je tâchais de m'élever aussi haut que je pouvais pour atteindre jusqu'à elles, je tirais de moi pour tâcher de les comprendre, je leur remettais tout ce que je recelais alors de meilleur, de plus profond.

699:1. Or, en sortant> **699:14.** <l'armature d'invisibles tiges inflexibles et obliques qui l'auraient traversé. [699:1. <chemin de promenade qui monte à l'hôtel> 699:5. <des «croque Monsieur» et> 699:7. <venir vers nous la>] {699:16-699:21}

---

donnait sur la plage. [698:31. <dorée comme un beau jour d'automne et des prunes> 698:33. <les prunes comme la mer à l'heure de notre dîner eussent passé au mauve>]

699:21. Mme de Villeparisis présenta> **699:25.** <avait marié sa fille. [699:22. <mais ne savait pas mon nom. 699:23. <l'avait probablement jamais>]

□**699:25.** Mon nom parut lui faire une grande impression. Cependant la princesse de Luxembourg nous avait tendu la main, en riant, comme pour une plaisanterie. Un marchand de plaisirs ayant passé, elle lui acheta tout ce qu'il avait et nous en tendit à moi et à ma grand'mère comme à un bébé et à sa nourrice, et m'en mit de plus un paquet tout ficelé dans ma poche en me disant: «Vous les ferez manger à votre grand'mère.» Elle appelait Mme de Villeparisis par son prénom et l'invita à dîner pour le lendemain. De temps en temps elle posait ses yeux sur nous en souriant avec mille signes d'intelligence comme sur des muets avec qui on ne peut pas causer mais à qui on veut montrer qu'on les aime. Et ce sourire était si doux que je croyais qu'elle allait tendre la main pour nous caresser, ma grand'mère et moi, comme des animaux étranges et sympathiques qu'on a devant soi au Jardin d'acclimatation*. Un autre marchand passa avec des babas, elle les acheta encore et les mit dans mon autre poche. Puis elle dit adieu à Mme de Villeparisis, et se tournant vers nous nous prit la main en riant comme à des petits enfants à qui on s'amuse de dire bonjour comme si c'était des grandes personnes, et reprit sa promenade sur la digue ensoleillée en incurvant sa taille magnifique qui se tordait comme un serpent autour de son ombrelle blanche imprimée de bleu. {699:28-701:4}

701:5. —Est-ce que vous êtes le fils du Directeur au> **702:23.** <son ouvrage et> [701:6. <me demanda Mme de Villeparisis> 701:11. <M. de Monfort*[1] avaient> 701:14. <nous sachions comment> 701:28. <relief et dans tant de détails l'agrément de sa conversation, les contingences> 701:31. <pour le Grec* et changeant pour Mme de Villeparisis l'échelle de sa vision, lui faisait voir ce seul homme plus grand que les autres au milieu des petits humains, comme ce Jupiter> 701:37. <nous puissions rester> 702:9. <mari de lui dire que> 702:19. <d'égards, auxquels toutes> 702:20. <qu'elle n'avait aucun droit>]

701:11. ([1]Monfort [*sic*]).

□**702:23.** <regardait avec son face à main d'un air d'examiner un plat dans lequel on n'a pas confiance et auquel on ne touchera pas, qui faisait mourir de rire ses amies.

702:25. —Oh! moi, vous savez> **703:10.** <de me méfier. [702:28. <actes de mariage. Du reste> 702:31. <riant au devant* la femme du Premier.] {703:10-704:10}

704:11. Comme le médecin de Bricquebec que ma grand'mère avait fait venir pour moi trouvait que je n'aurais pas dû passer toute la journée au bord de la mer surtout avec la grande chaleur qu'il faisait sur le sable, sans ombre (il avait aussi écrit pour moi de nombreuses ordonnances de médicaments que ma grand'mère avait prises avec un respect apparent où j'avais reconnu tout de suite sa ferme décision de n'en faire exécuter aucune), ma grand'mère accepta l'offre de Mme de Villeparisis de nous faire faire quelques promenades en voiture.

704:21. Ces jours-là pour ne pas me fatiguer, je devais rester couché jusqu'au déjeuner, et à cause de la trop grande lumière garder fermés le plus longtemps possible les grands rideaux rouges qui m'avaient témoigné tant d'hostilité le premier soir. Mais comme malgré les épingles avec lesquelles pour que le jour ne passât pas Françoise les attachait chaque soir et qu'elle seule savait défaire comme [*blanc*][1] les couvertures, les étoffes prises ici ou là qu'elle y ajustait,[2] placées*, elle n'arrivait pas à les faire joindre exactement, ils laissaient se répandre sur le tapis comme un écarlate effeuillement d'anémones parmi lesquelles je ne pouvais m'empêcher de venir un instant poser mes pieds nus. Et sur le mur qui leur faisait face un cylindre d'or que rien ne soutenait était verticalement posé et se déplacait* lentement comme la colonne lumineuse qui précédait les Hébreux dans le désert. Je me recouchais, obligé de goûter, sans bouger, par l'imagination, et tous à la fois, les plaisirs de jeux, du bain, de

---

704:11. *(B-A)* Le médecin de Balbec> **704:20.** <promenades en voiture.

704:20. <en voiture. D'ailleurs je ne regrettais pas trop d'être empêché de rester au bord de la mer; d'abord parce que les jours chauds, le manteau ensoleillé me semblaient jetés comme un déguisement morne, momentané et hideux sur la sauvage beauté du «pays des Cimériens», dissipant ces brouillards éternels dans lesquels j'avais rêvé de venir m'ensevelir. Ces jours-là>

704:21. ([1]malgré) ([2]ajustait, elle n'arrivait).

promenade, auxquels la matinée invitait, la joie faisait battre bruyamment mon cœur comme une machine en pleine vitesse mais immobile et qui est obligée de la décharger sur place en tournant sur elle-même. Parfois c'était l'heure de la pleine mer. J'entendais du haut de mon belvédère le bruit du flot qui déferlait doucement, ponctué par les appels des enfants qui jouaient, des marchands de journaux, des baigneurs comme par des cris d'oiseaux de mer. Soudain à dix heures le concert symphonique éclatait sous mes fenêtres. Entre les intervalles des instruments reprenait, coulé et continu, le glissement de l'eau d'une vague qui semblait envelopper les traits du violon dans ses volutes de cristal et faire jaillir son écume au-dessus des échos intermittents d'une musique sous-marine. Pour voir si Françoise ne venait pas défaire les rideaux et m'apporter mes affaires,—car l'heure du déjeuner approchait,—je courais jusqu'à la chambre de ma grand'mère.

704:22. Elle ne donnait pas> **705:2.** <pétales de rose. [704:25. <était autrement meublée> 704:29. <brisaient les côtés dans les angles du mur, changeaient la forme de la chambre, à côté d'un reflet de la plage, mettaient> 704:35. <fenêtre, regardant une courette latérale au fond de laquelle un mur blanchi à la chaux portait l'enseigne [*blanc*] de midi, ajoutaient>]

705:2. Je rentrais dans ma chambre: Françoise entrait pour me donner du jour et je me soulevais dans l'impatience de savoir quelle était la mer qui jouait ce matin-là au bord du rivage comme une nymphe.

705:5. Car chacune ne restait> **705:24.** <la fraîcheur très lucide et verte de sa molle palpitation. [705:6. Le lendemain j'en voyais une autre> 705:10. <la fenêtre en s'ouvrant découvrit-elle> 705:19. <surprise, comme devant un miracle. 705:12. <la nymphe Alecto, dont> 705:17. <autour d'elle et censé* dans des couleurs uniques, plus abrégée et plus saisissante, comme ces déesses> 705:20. <dégrossir, elle nous invitait> 705:22. <d'où dans la calèche>]

□**705:25.** Mais d'autres fois il n'y avait pas cette opposition si grande entre une promenade agreste et ce but inaccessible, ce voisinage fluide et mythologique. Car la mer semblait alors rurale elle-même et la chaleur y avait tracé comme à travers champs une route poussièreuse* et blanche derrière laquelle la fine pointe d'un bateau de pêche dépassait comme un clocher villageois. Un remorqueur dont on ne voyait que la cheminée fumait au loin comme une usine écartée, tandis que seul à l'horizon un carré blanc et bombé, peint sans doute par une voile mais qui semblait compact et comme calcaire, faisait penser à l'angle ensoleillé de quelque bâtiment isolé, hôpital ou école. Et les nuages et le vent les jours où il s'en ajoutait au soleil, parachevaient sinon l'erreur de jugement, du moins l'illusion du premier regard, la suggestion qu'il éveille dans l'imagination. Car l'alternance d'espaces de couleurs nettement tranchées comme celles qui résultent dans la campagne, de la contiguïté de cultures différentes, les inégalités âpres, jaunes, et comme boueuse* de la surface marine, les levées, talus qui dérobaient à la vue la barque où une équipe d'agiles matelots semblait moissonner tout cela par les jours orageux faisait de l'océan quelque chose d'aussi varié, d'aussi consistant, d'aussi accidenté, d'aussi populeux, d'aussi civilisé que la terre carrossable d'où, en voiture avec Mme de Villeparisis nous le regarderions.

Mais parfois aussi, et pendant des semaines de suite, le beau temps fut si éclatant et si fixe que quand Françoise venait ouvrir la fenêtre j'étais sûr de trouver le même pan de soleil plié à l'angle du mur extérieur, et d'une couleur immuable qui n'était plus émouvante comme une révélation de l'été, mais morne comme celle d'un émail inerte et factice. Et tandis que François ôtait les épingles des impostes, détachait les étoffes, tirait les rideaux, le jour d'été qu'elle découvrait semblait aussi mort, aussi immémorial qu'une somptueuse et millénaire nomie que notre vieille servante n'eût fait que précautionneusement désemmailloter de tous ses linges, avant de la faire apparaître, embaumée dans sa robe d'or.

705:26. Mme de Villeparisis> **705:36.** <non seulement les personnes> [705:27. <d'aller jusqu'à Couliville, jusqu'aux rochers d'Erméez, ou quelque* autre but> 705:31. <journée; dans la joie> 705:32. <entreprendre, je faisais les cent pas devant l'hôtel et fredonnais quelque air récemment appris, en attendant> 705:34. <prête. Quand c'était>]

705:36. <les personnes qui allaient chez Mme de Chemusey*,[1] mais celles qui n'y étaient pas invitées et trouvaient désagréable qu'on s'aperçut qu'elle* ne l'était pas, plutôt que de rester là comme des enfants punis déclaraient que le dimanche était un jour assommant à Bricquebec et partaient dès après déjeuner se cacher dans une plage voisine ou visiter quelque site. Et même souvent si on demandait en vain à la femme du notaire si elle avait été chez Mme de Chimesey elle répondait péremptoirement: «non, nous étions aux cascades d'Allaire», comme si c'était là la seule raison pour laquelle elle n'était pas chez Mme de Chimesey.

706:3. Et le bâtonnier> **706:6.** <intéressant.

706:7. Mme de Villeparisis ne tardait pas à descendre suivi de son vieux maître d'hôtel qui portait ses affaires et nous regardait partir en accompagnant d'un sourire approbatif, attendri et complice, comme celui qu'on a pour deux fiancés, les relations nouvelles que d'un œil favorable, il voyait se nouer entre sa maîtresse et nous, cependant que parfois, levant les yeux en entendant une fenêtre qui s'ouvrait je voyais apparaître et disparaître aussitôt l'œil avide et indifférent de Françoise qui, incapable de se priver de ce spectacle, ne voulait pas avoir l'air de manquer à la défense établie à Paris par maman, de jamais* se mettre aux croisées. Peu après avoir tourné* la station> {706:7-707:6}

707:8. <la station du chemin de fer> **707:19.** <fleurs rougissantes. [707:10. <s'amorçait jusqu'au> 707:12. <labourées. Le long de la route j'avais la joie de voir ça et là> 707:15. <suffisait à me faire battre le cœur parce que> 707:17. <tapis d'une fête>]

707:20. Combien de fois à Paris dans le mois de mai suivant —gardant de cette route et aussi de certains clos qu'il y avait quelque* distance, le même souvenir présent, fixe, immuable que jadis de certaines scènes classiques que je me récitais, et que j'aurais voulu entendre dire par la Berma,—combien de fois j'ai acheté une branche de pommiers chez le fleuriste et j'ai ensuite

705:36. ([1]*From this point on, except for additions, Proust made almost no corrections in* Grasset A, *so that proper nouns remained unchanged.*)
707:43. ([1]de yachts, de plaisance (n'avait-on pas eu l'idée abominable d'organiser des régates). Mais).

passé la soirée devant elle, devant les fleurs où s'épanouissaient* la même essence crémeuse>

707:24. <crémeuse qui poudrait> **708:4.** <détails contemporains> [707:29. <lampe,—quelquefois si longtemps que l'aurore souvent leur apportait la même rougeur qu'elle faisait en même temps sur les hauteurs de Bricquebec—et je cherchais> 707:36. <voulu revoir au moment où avec> 707:41. <à Bricquebec je> 707:43. <cabines, de paquebots.[1]]

708:4. <contemporains qui m'empêchaient de me rendre compte que j'avais devant moi l'océan de Baudelaire, la mer antique de Leconte de Lisle, déferlant encore le même flot sonore que «tel qu'un vol d'oiseaux carnassiers dans l'aurore» battaient les cent mille avirons «des nefs erronées», mais, en revanche>

708:11. <en revanche, je n'étais plus> **708:15.** <foncée que lui. [708:15. <aussi consistante* que>]

708:16. Parfois sachant faire plaisir à ma grand'mère, elle demandait au cocher de couper par les bois de l'Arbonne. L'invisibilité des innombrables oiseaux qui s'y répondaient tout à côté de nous dans les arbres, donnaient cette impression de repos qu'on a quand on reste les yeux fermés; enchaîné sur mon strapontin>

△**720:12.** <strapontin comme Prométhée> **720:18.** <sans regard. [720:13. <j'écoutais comme lui des Océanides.]

□**708:17.** Le cocher qui ne connaissait pas encore bien le pays demandait un renseignement à quelque paysan et souvent j'entendais qu'on lui citait comme point de repère, ce village dont je voulais tant voir l'église, Blenpertuis. Comme il n'était pas directement sur notre chemin, je ne pouvais, à cause de Mme de Villeparisis, demander qu'on s'y arrêtât, mais je donnais à son nom une place à part, un tour de faveur, dans ma mémoire, me promettant que si cette année ma santé ne s'améliorait pas assez pour qu'on me laissât faire des promenades seul et visiter cette église, du moins l'année suivante, je viendrais, fût-ce de Paris exprès pour cela. Et en me persuadant, en prenant vis-à-vis de moi-

---

708:4. *(B-A)* <contemporains qui la relieraient en quelque sorte de* la nature et de l'histoire, et je pouvais> **708:11.** Mais, en revanche>

708:17. ([1]que je désirais tant voir).

même l'engagement que mon pèlerinage n'était qu'ajourné, je pouvais sans trop de regret voir notre voiture continuer sa route et laisser loin derrière elle, sur les côtés, l'église de Blenpertuis. Je savais pourtant bien que si entre toutes les autres églises aussi intéressantes que signalait mon Précis d'archéologie monumentale de l'ouest, c'était elle que[1] j'avais désiré voir, elle n'avait pas de supériorité intrinsèque qui justifiât cette préférence exclusive. Mais à partir du moment où je l'eus arbitrairement choisie, c'est sur elle uniquement que s'était dirigé, chaque fois qu'il renaissait, mon désir d'églises de village. Elle lui avait donné un objet à aimer, à nommer, à se représenter. Dans l'étendue informe et vide de la France entière je ne voyais que le clocher bleu de Blenpertuis. Renoncer à Blenpertuis c'eut* été le premier pas que je ne voulais pas faire vers cette déchéance où je tomberais peut-être un jour de ne plus considérer la vie comme la connaissance et la possession de ce que j'avais désiré, c'eut* été de demander à la réalité ce dont mon imagination et mon intelligence avaient d'abord fixé le prix.

Mme de Villeparisis voyant que j'aimais les églises avait voulu que nous puissions passer devant celle de Brissinville «toute cachée>

708:19. <cachée sous> **708:26.** <dont elle parlait. [708:20. <un geste de la main qui enveloppait avec goût la façade absente sous un feuillage> 708:23. <avait d'ailleurs souvent> 708:24. <particularité d'une église, évitant>]

708:25. Elle semblait chercher à s'en excuser sur ce qu'un des châteaux de son père, et où elle avait été élevée, était situé dans une région où il y avait des églises du même style et comme si l'architecture —dont il eût été honteux, disait-elle, ce château étant le plus bel exemple de celle de la Renaissance, qu'elle ne prit* pas le goût de la peinture... dont il était un vrai musée, la musique même et la littérature*. Chopin venant de jouer du piano et Lamartine réciter des vers pour sa mère eussent été une sorte d'annexe de sa large enfance aristocratique et cultivée. Peut-être même à force d'attribuer, soit par grâce* d'une bonne éducation, ou manque de vanité, ou manque d'esprit philosophique, cette origine purement matérielle à ses goûts artistiques, avait-elle fini par les en faire dépendre trop exclusivement. Elle ne se serait pas dérangée pour aller voir un chef-d'œuvre dans une de ces collections faite à coup* d'argent où «on n'est pas sûr si tout n'est pas faux, où on ne sait pas ce qu'on voit. Ma grand'mère ayant admiré deux grains d'un collier rouge qui passait sous son manteau, elle lui répondait:

—C'est gentil, n'est-ce pas? Cela m'amuse de le porter parce qu'il est dans le portrait du Titien de la bisaïeule de laquelle* il me vient, comme le portrait d'ailleurs. Il était dans ma chambre d'enfant. C'est un des plus beaux Titien* qu'il y ait et il n'est jamais sorti de la famille. Comme cela on est sûr de l'authenticité. Mais ne me parlez pas de ces tableaux, achetés on ne sait pas comment, je suis sûre que ce sont des faux, ça ne m'intéresse pas. Ma grand'mère n'était pas du reste étonnée de la voir si au fait de la peinture sachant qu'elle faisait des aquarelles de fleurs, et elle luit dit qu'elle les avait même entendu vanter.

709:12. Mme de Villeparisis changea> **709:17.** <si les fleurs> [709:14. <ni de satisfaction qu'une artiste assez connue>]

□**709:17.** <si les fleurs sorties du pinceau n'étaient pas fameuses, les fleurs vivantes dans la société desquelles cela faisait vivre avaient une beauté dont on ne se lassait pas. Elle ne travaillait pas à Bricquebec où elle avait donné vacances complètes à ses yeux qui baissaient, mais à Paris elle serait contente de nous donner quelques fleurs à* sa façon.

Mais si la nature, quelques églises, quelques tableaux, avaient leur part dans les petites vignettes perlées dont Mme de Villeparisis ornait sa conversation, celle-ci autant que j'en pus juger au cours de nos promenades, était surtout humaine et décrivait* beaucoup plus souvent des anecdotes mondaines auxquelles le caractère public des personnes que la vieille dame avait connues dans sa jeunesse donnait presque un petit intérêt historique ou littéraire. Et avec le même petit geste de la main, la même épithète modérée que pour un clocher ou une meule, elle nous montrait la reine des Belges en visite, Louis-Philippe entrant chez son père quand elle était enfant, Mérimée faisant des caricatures, l'atelier de Delacroix. Mais il semblait que ce fût malgré elle, et parce qu'elle les revoyait tels dans son souvenir, si le nom des personnages qui figuraient dans ces historiettes, la familiarité de leur attitude et de leurs propos, montraient dans l'intimité de combien de gens brillants elle avait vécu. Car elle ne cherchait jamais à parler d'elle; dans les plus petites circonstances, dans les plus futiles incidents de nos promenades, elle nous disait toujours la chose qui la mettait, elle, au second plan, mais pouvait nous faire valoir, se montrait toujours pleine de tact, d'à-propos, d'agrément, de cœur (le contraire vivant de mon ami Bloch); bien plus tandis que dans les préoccupations d'une société moins brillante les privilèges du grand monde, soit dénigrés, soit loués, toujours enviés et respectés, tiennent une place importante, Mme de Villeparisis parlait de la naissance et du rang, comme venant bien après le talent et l'intelligence.

Elle poussait cette modestie jusqu'à rejeter les idées qui sans être inévitablement aristocratiques ou mondaines, nous semblaient cependant devoir être professées par l'aristocratie et dans le grand monde.

709:26. Elle s'étonnait> □**709:29.** <Espagne. Elle disait: «Un homme qui ne travaille pas, pour moi ce n'est rien», défendant contre nous la République qu'elle acceptait et à laquelle elle ne reprochait son anticléricalisme que dans cette mesure: «Je trouverais tout aussi mauvais qu'on m'empêche d'aller à la messe si j'en ai envie que d'être forcée d'y aller si je ne le veux pas», lançant même certains mots comme: «Oh! la noblesse d'aujourd'hui! Qu'est-ce que c'est», qu'elle ne disait peut-être que parce qu'elle sentait ce qu'ils prenaient de piquant, de savoureux, de mémorable dans sa bouche. En un mot elle professait en toutes choses ces opinions d'une bourgeoise conservatrice mais libérale en la justesse desquelles nous n'avions pas osé croire complètement jusque-là, que grand'mère et moi, parce qu'elles répondaient trop à nos désirs, et que nous nous efforcions quand nous cherchions la vérité de faire, par effort d'impartialité, la part de ceux qui devaient penser autrement que nous et peut-être après tout mieux que nous, d'une Mme de Villeparisis par exemple. Mais quelle détente, ces opinions, de les recevoir cette fois sans scrupules d'un esprit si différent, dans lequel elles étaient chez nous instinctives et si naturelles, prenaient l'autorité d'idées vraies et devenaient méritoires. En entendant Mme de Villeparisis les exprimer, notre sympathie pour elle s'élevait jusqu'à l'admiration et nous faisait prendre un plaisir extrême dans cette conversation

où deux instincts qui semblent contradictoires, mais qui coexistent pourtant chez beaucoup de gens, pouvaient trouver à se satisfaire: l'horreur du snobisme dans ces éloges de la médiocrité, ces railleries de la noblesse, ces vues élevées, et le goût du snobisme, parce qu'en écoutant ce langage élevé on entrait plus avant dans l'aristocratique fréquentation de Mme de Villeparisis et ses interlocuteurs princiers. A ces moments-là je n'étais pas loin de croire qu'en Mme de Villeparisis trônaient la mesure et le modèle de la vérité en toutes choses.

710:7. Mais—comme> **710:30.** <conseil des ministres> [710:12. <puisque n'y éclate pas> 710:13. <aussi bien que dans leurs fragments sur Marcel et sur Baudelaire,—Mme de> 710:16. <Hugo riait> 710:18. <piquants et agréables comme sur les grands seigneurs et les hommes politiques, et les jugeait sévèrement, précisément parce> 710:24. <qualités de mesure de jugement> 710:26. <qu'atteint l'homme de valeur> 710:28. <hommes qui peut-être en effet étaient pourvus de ces qualités-là et avaient sans doute l'avantage sur>]

710:30. <des ministres, Molé, Barat, Fontanes, Vitroles*, Pasquier, Lebrun ou Daru. Eux aussi pourtant, Chateaubriand quand elle était petite, Balzac chez Mme de Castries, Stendhal, elle les avait connus, elle avait d'eux des autographes, des souvenirs.

Elle semblait se prévaloir de ces relations particulières pour penser que son jugement sur eux était plus juste que celui des jeunes gens qui comme moi n'avait* pas pu les fréquenter. «Je crois que je peux>

710:32. See after 721:20.

711:5. <peux en parler> **711:10.** <telles labourées> [711:6. <M. Sainte-Beuve, qui lui au moins avait beaucoup d'esprit> 711:8. <ont pu juger ce qu'ils>]

□**711:10.** <labourées; tout d'un coup les champs qui étaient des deux côtés de moi me semblaient des champs miraculeusement vrais, des champs beaux comme ceux de la Bible, et un souffle me parcourait. C'est que je venais de voir quelques bleuets hésitants qui sur le talus suivaient notre voiture. Or depuis Combray, certaines choses très communes que je regrettais, avaient fini par prendre ce caractère précieux, inaccessible, de tout ce qui est dans notre pensée, c'est-à-dire si près de nous sans que nous

puissions le toucher. Un bleuet exposant au bas d'un champ sa signature pour en certifier l'authenticité me semblait quelque chose de plus estimable que ces fleurettes par lesquelles certains maîtres anciens signaient leurs toiles.

711:14. Bientôt nos chevaux> **712:19.** <plus intéressant. [711:17. <bleue; d'autres s'enhardissaient> 711:24. <champs, car il reste à chacune quelque chose qui n'est pas ailleurs et qui n'empêchera pas que nous puissions contenter avec une pareille le désir qu'elle a fait naître en nous—quelque paysanne poussant> 711:32. <Bloch, autant qu'un grand savant ou un fondateur de religion, m'avait> 711:33. <de la vie et du bonheur, le jour> 711:39. <ne songeaient qu'à faire l'amour. 711:41. <seul, jamais pouvoir le faire avec elles, j'étais comme un enfant né dans une prison ou dans un hôpital et qui croirait que l'organisme humain ne peut digérer que du pain sec et des médicaments, et qui apprend tout d'un coup> 712:5. Même si les ordres de son geôlier et de son garde-malade ne lui> 712:7. <lui paraîtrait meilleur, et la vie plus clémente. Car un désir nous paraît plus beau> 712:11. <réalité lui obéit, même> 712:12. <à une vie qui sait l'assouvir, à une vie où, à condition que nous écartions pour un instant de notre pensée le petit obstacle accidentel et particulier qui nous empêche de le faire, nous pouvons nous imaginer nous-même l'assouvissement.]

712:20. La voiture de Mme de Villeparisis passait vite. A peine avais-je le temps de voir la fillette qui venait dans notre direction; et pourtant—comme les beautés des êtres ne sont pas comme celles des choses, et que nous sentons que ce sont celles d'une créature unique, consciente et volontaire—à peine l'individualité de la fille qui s'approchait—conscience vague, volonté inconnue de moi—se peignait-elle, en une petite image prodigieusement réduite, embryonnaire mais complète au fond de son regard distrait, aussitôt—ô mystérieuse réplique des pollens tout préparés pour les pistils—je sentais saillir en moi l'embryon aussi vague, aussi minuscule, et aussi entier du désir de ne pas laisser passer cette fille, sans que sa pensée eût conscience de ma personne, sans empêcher ses désirs d'aller à quelqu'un d'autre, mais de venir me fixer, dans sa rêverie et de saisir son cœur.

712:34. Cependant notre voiture> **712:38.** <m'avaient déjà oublié> [712:36. <constituent une preuve, ses>]

□**712:38.** <oublié, si même elle ne s'était pas moquée de moi. Etait-ce à cause du passage si rapide que je l'avais trouvée si belle? Si j'avais pu descendre lui parler, aurais-je été déconcerté par quelque défaut de sa peau que de la voiture je n'avais pas distingué? peut-être* un seul mot qu'elle eût dit, un sourire m'eût fourni une clef, un chiffre maltendus*, pour lire l'expression de son visage et de sa démarche, de son individualité, qui seraient aussitôt devenues banales? C'est possible, car je n'ai jamais rencontré dans ma vie de filles aussi désirables que les jours où j'étais avec quelque grave personne que je ne pouvais quitter, malgré les mille prétextes que j'inventais [*cf.* 713:33]. Celui d'être pris d'un brusque mal de tête, qui ne céderait que si je quittais la voiture et rentrais à Bricquebec à pied, ne convainquaient* ni Mme de Villeparisis, ni ma grand'mère qui refusaient de me laisser descendre. Et mon grand regret de ne pas m'être arrêté auprès de la belle fille, de ne pas l'avoir connue, était plus amer que celui que m'avait laissé l'église du village ou le clocher, et mon désir de la trouver elle et non une autre plus exclusif. Car je savais que sous la grâce de la belle fille, il y avait autre chose que sous la grâce des vieilles pierres: ma pensée si vaste dans laquelle je ne serais pas, pour qui je continuais à ne pas exister quand même je serais connu, aimé de toutes les autres filles du monde, mais je n'avais pas comme pour l'église le point de repère d'un nom, ou pour le champ d'une borne kilométrique. Elles étaient bien vagues les particularités que je tâchais de me rappeler. Elle avait passé à telle heure sur une charrette, ou dans une victoria, à tel endroit allant vers tel village; mais cela me permettrait-il de la retrouver? en* attendant je me disais que le monde est beau qui fait> {712:39-714:40}

714:41. <fait ainsi croître> **715:11.** <l'illusion. [714:43. <à la fois uniques et communes> 715:6. <pourrais faire sur d'autres routes de semblables rencontres, je commandais* déjà à sentir ce qu'a>]

715:12. Mme de Villeparisis nous mena une fois à Briseville où était cette église couverte de lierre dont elle avait parlé. Bâtie sur un tertre, elle dominait le village, la rivière qui le traversait et gardant son petit pont du moyen âge! Ma grand'mère, pensant que je serais content d'être seul pour regarder l'église, proposa à Mme de Villeparisis d'aller>

715:18. <d'aller goûter> **715:27.** <ils sont accoutumés> [715:22. Dès* le bloc de verdure> 715:26. <on les force par>]

715:28. <accoutumés, j'étais obligé de faire perpétuellement appel à cette église, cette idée d'église dont je n'avais guère besoin d'habitude devant des clochers qui se faisaient reconnaître d'eux-mêmes, j'étais obligé de faire perpétuellement appel pour ne pas oublier qu'ici l'arcade, cette corbeille de lierre était celle d'une verrière ogivale, là que le ronflement vertical des feuilles était le relief d'un pilier.

715:34. Mais alors un peu> **716:13.** <vivait en lui> [715:40. <pont les filles du village qui comme c'était un dimanche se tenaient> 716:1. <les dominer les autres par> 716:2. <disaient, l'une*, plus grosse et plus volontaire, il y en avait> 716:5. <poissons qu'elle avait peut-être péchés> 716:8. <forme petite, fine et charmante>]

716:13. <en lui, cette pensée qui est en chacun et avec laquelle il n'est qu'une sorte d'attouchement qui est de frapper son attention, qu'une sorte de pénétration, y éveiller une idée.

716:16. Et cette personne intérieure de la belle pêcheuse, semblait m'être close encore> **717:2.** <idée de moi. [716:17. <doutais que* si> 716:19. <dans la mémoire* de son regard> 716:22. <ne m'aurait pas> 716:24. <moi qui était en elle, qui s'y> 716:26. <désir, et me gardât son souvenir>]

□**717:2.** <de moi, et j'avais eu si peur qu'elle ne m'écoutât pas jusqu'au bout, que j'avais tenu la pièce de cinq francs devant ses yeux (pour avoir plus de chance qu'elle acceptât la commission) avant de commencer ma phrase et que je n'osai pas lever les yeux avant de l'avoir finie, de peur d'apercevoir un geste de refus qui l'eût interrompue et m'eût ôté tout prétexte d'apprendre à cette villageoise que j'étais attendu par la voiture à deux chevaux d'une marquise. Mais quand j'eus prononcé les mots marquise et deux chevaux, soudain un grand apaisement se fit en moi. Je sentis qu'elle se souviendrait de moi; je sentais se dissiper mon effroi de ne pouvoir le* retrouver, et avec lui une partie de mon désir de la retrouver.

717:7. Il me semblait> **717:11.** <physique.

974 (page 717, note 2). <physique. Je levai... regarder>

□**974:27.** <à nous regarder partir avec des yeux écarquillés. Mais l'être que j'avais composé avec quelques traits aperçus de son visage et que d'autres avaient contredit, avec mon imagination qui m'avait fait supposer en elle une hautëur que je pensais [*blanc*] qu'elle imaginait en moi, cet être n'existait plus. Il ne restait qu'une fille assez laide avec un grand corps et un joli nez, et par laquelle il me fut indifférent d'être contemplé au moment glorieux où aussitôt que je fus monté dans la voiture, celle-ci démarra, nous faisant faire un départ retentissant et solennel aux yeux de tous les habitants de Briseville attirés sur le pas de leur porte.

□**717:12.** Une fois, comme nous prenions une route de traverse qui descendait sur Couliville, je fus rempli de ce bonheur profond que je n'avais pas* ressenti qu'une fois en respirant l'odeur humide du petit pavillon des Champs-Elysées, depuis ces promenades autour de Combray où il me saisissait si souvent. Du strapontin où j'étais assis en face de ma grand'mère et de Mme de Villeparisis, je venais d'apercevoir en retrait de la route en dos d'âne que nous suivions trois arbres qui devaient être l'entrée d'une allée couverte et formaient un dessin que je sentis en même temps qu'il passait devant mes yeux, palpiter mon cœur.

Dans ces lieux que je voyais pour la première fois ils intercalaient un fragment du site que je n'avais pas reconnu mais que je sentais si bien m'avoir été familier autrefois que mon esprit ayant trébuché entre quelque année lointaine et le moment présent, les environs de Bricquebec vacillèrent, et je me demandai si toute cette promenade n'était pas une fiction, Bricquebec un endroit où je n'étais jamais allé que par l'imagination, Mme de Villeparisis un personnage de roman et les trois vieux arbres la réalité qu'on retrouve en levant les yeux de dessus le livre qu'on était en train de lire et qui vous retraçait si bien le milieu dans lequel il se passe qu'on avait fini par s'y croire effectivement transporté.

Cette illusion ne dura qu'une seconde, je sentis que les trois arbres n'étaient pas pareils à trois autres arbres qui ailleurs devaient s'ouvrir de la même manière sur un paysage qui m'était familier. Mais lequel? Je les regardai, je les voyais bien> {717:12-717:33}

717:33. <voyais bien, mais non> **718:1.** <mes parents! {718:1-718:11}

718:11. Je mis un instant> **718:30.** <qu'on croyait n'avoir jamais lu, ils surmégeaient* seuls du livre oublié de ma première enfance. [718:18. <eux la même réalité connue mais> 718:20. <voiture s'avançait, je les voyais approcher. 718:21. <déjà vus? 718:22. <Combray ni du côté de Guermantes, ni du côté de Méséglise, où>]

718:31. Appartenaient-ils seulement au contraire à ces paysages de rêve toujours les mêmes, à cause de cela assez commun* quoique plus surnaturels que ceux de la terre, devant lesquels je revivais en dormant, l'effort que pendant la veille j'avais fait vers le mystère et dont leur aspect étrange n'était que l'objectivation pendant le sommeil soit pour l'atteindre dans un lieu derrière l'apparence duquel je le pressentais, comme cela m'était arrivé si souvent du côté de Guermantes, soit pour essayer de le réintroduire dans un lieu que j'avais désiré connaître et que du jour où je l'avais connu m'avait paru tout superficiel, comme Bricquebec?

718:41. N'étaient-ils> **719:21.** <les abandonna. [718:42. <déjà devenu* si flottant et si vague qu'il me semblait> 719:2. <arbres, tel clocher, telle touffe de plus* que j'avais vu du côté> 719:3. <obscur, aussi disciplinaire qu'un passé lointain si bien que> 719:6. Ou ne cachaient-ils> 719:11. <normes*, qui me proposaient leurs oracles> 719:13. <compagnons de ma jeunesse, des> 719:15. Comme les ombres autour d'Enée ils semblaient> 719:19. <parole, sait qu'il> 719:21. <de routes, la>] {719:21-719:25}

719:24. Je les vis s'éloigner> **719:29.** <jamais au néant.

719:30. Enfin je ne sus jamais plus tard ce qu'ils voulaient dire, ni où je les avais vus.

719:35. Et quand la voiture bifurquat*, je leur tournai le dos et cessai de les voir, tandis que je répondais en souriant à Mme de Villeparisis, me demandant pourquoi j'avais l'air rêveur, mon cœur battait d'angoisse comme si à ce moment-là et pour toujours je venais de perdre un ami, de mourir à moi-même, de renier un mort ou de méconnaître un dieu.

719:41. See after 722:40.

720:12. See after 708:16.

721:20. Le jour tombait souvent avant que nous fussions de retour. Timidement> **721:32.** <premiers à plaisanter. [721:27. <me disait-elle. Je vous dirai>]

△ □**710:32.** C'est comme les romans de Stendhal. Vous l'auriez beaucoup surpris en lui en parlant sur le ton que vous preniez tout à l'heure. C'était un homme de bonne compagnie et aux éloges [*blanc*] de M. de Balzac (sous lesquels il y avait d'ailleurs une vilaine histoire d'argent) avance* qu'il n'avait pu se retenir d'un éclat de rire.

721:32. On ne prodiguait> **722:2.** <les plus insensés. [721:36. <lune. Je vous dirais que j'ai> 721:40. <à poser et était ridicule>] {722:2-722:4}

722:4. Quant à ses phrases sur le clair de lune je vous dirais qu'elles étaient devenues> **722:28.** <pour le lecteur. [722:22. <d'importance, il n'y a rien à dire.] {722:29-722:39}

722:40. De même elle reprochait à Balzac> 723:8. <divagations des socialistes. [722:43. Quant à M. Victor Hugo, elle nous disait que M. de Villeparisis son père>]

△ □**719:41.** Il fallait songer au retour, Mme de Villeparisis qui avait un certain sentiment de la nature—plus froid que celui de ma grand'mère mais se retrouvant avec lui pour admirer les mêmes beautés—et qui sur les routes comme sans doute dans les musées montrait ce goût élevé et clairvoyant, qui distingue, qui sait reconnaître les choses plus belle* d'autrefois, dit un jour au cocher de revenir sur la vieille route de Bricquebec qu'on ne prenait presque jamais et qui est bien plus belle que l'autre, plantée de vieux ormes qui transportèrent ma grand'mère.

Mme de Villeparisis à cause du genre d'éducation et même de culture littéraire qu'elle avait reçu, aurait trouvé ridicule de faire des phrases admiratives sur ces ormes séculaires. Pourtant elle les appréciait puisqu'elle choisissait de rentrer par la vieille route pour passer devant eux et elle pouvait sourire de l'enthousiasme de ma grand'mère qui sans elle ne les eût sans doute jamais vus. Mais la familiarité de certaines personnes de goût avec les objets plus récents pour nous, de notre admiration, ne procure pas que, chez elles, cette admiration ait été la même. Mme de Villeparisis n'éprouvait pas un sentiment d'admiration pour lui-même, ne cherchait pas à le comprendre, à l'analyser. Elle le laissait toucher immédiatement dans le domaine obscur de la vie pratique et se composait ainsi des habitudes noble* qui pour les autres faisaient un beau cadre à sa vie, sans que son esprit à elle s'y arrêta* beaucoup.

Une fois que nous connûmes la vieille route, pour changer, si nous n'avions pas passé par là à l'aller, nous prenions au retour une route qui traversait la forêt, route pareille à tant d'autres de ce genre qu'on rencontre souvent en France, montant en pente assez raide, puis redescendant sur une assez grande longueur.

△**720:21.** Au moment> **720:23.** <rentrer.

△□**720:23.** Il faisait frais, les feuilles sentaient bon. Mme de Villeparisis jetait une couverture sur mes jambes. Je commençais à avoir faim. Parfois, d'une voiture qui passait à toute vitesse, une dame envoyait des bonjours à Mme de Villeparisis. C'était la princesse de Luxembourg qui allait venir* chez une de ses cousines: on apercevait un village, et au delà dans les arbres, comme un site plus éloigné, comme la localité suivante, distante et forestière et qu'on ne pourrait pas atteindre ce soir-là, le coucher du soleil. Mais cette route devint pour moi dans la suite une cause de joies en restant dans ma mémoire comme une amorce où toutes les routes semblables sur lesquelles je passerais plus tard au cours d'une promenade ou d'un voyage s'embrancheraient aussitôt sans [*blanc*] de continuité et pourrait grâce à elle, communiquer immédiatement avec moi-même. {720:23-720:29}

△**720:30.** Car dès que la voiture ou l'automobile s'engageraient* dans une de ces routes qui auraient l'air d'être la continuation de celle que je suivais avec Mme de Villeparisis, à qui ma conscience [*blanc*] se trouvait immédiatement appuyée comme à mon passé le plus récent, ce serait (toutes les années intermédiaires se trouvant abolies, aux impressions que j'avais de ces fins d'après-midi-là en promenade près de Bricquebec), raccordées>

△**720:42.** <raccordées à celles> **721:9.** <grande de réalité> [721:3. <autres, elles se renforceraient>]

△☐**721:9.** <réalité évoquée, songée, (et par conséquent non seulement belle mais irretrouvable) pour me faire éprouver plus qu'un sentiment esthétique, cette sorte de désir exalté, impossible à assouvir qu'éveillent en nous certains lieux au milieu desquels nous passons, auxquels nous voudrions nous attacher, nous jurant de vivre désormais parmi eux pour toujours.

Bien des années après, sur de belles routes, quelquefois à la fin de la journée, quand les feuilles sentent bon, que la brume s'élève, et qu'au delà du prochain village, on aperçoit entre les arbres le coucher de soleil comme un site plus éloigné, comme la localité suivante, distante et [*blanc*] mais qu'on n'atteindra pas ce soir>

△**721:12.** <soir, que de fois tandis que je me souvenais de cet été à Bricquebec, que de fois être assis sur un strapontin en face de Mme de Villeparisis, croiser dans la forêt qui lui envoyait des bonjours de sa voiture la Princesse de Luxembourg, rentrer dîner au grand hôtel où les lumières seraient déjà allumées, ne m'est-il pas apparu comme un de ces bonheurs ineffables que ni le présent ni l'avenir ne peuvent pas* nous rendre et qu'on ne goûte qu'une fois dans la vie.

☐**723:9.** Nous apercevions déjà l'hôtel. Et les globes lumineux du hall, ces ennemis fascinants du premier soir, maintenant c'était pour moi la lumière amie du foyer, douce et protectrice comme une lampe [*blanc*]. C'était rentrer chez moi, retrouver dans la chambre qui avait fini par devenir réellement ma chambre, que revoir les grands rideaux et les bibliothèques basses c'était me retrouver seul avec moi-même. Et quand la voiture arrivait près des degrés de la porte>

723:12. <porte, le concierge> **723:21.** <car ils contiennent plus de notre actuel nous-même. [723:13. <naïfs, vraiment inquiets> 723:14. <attendre, c'était, hostiles, [*blanc*] comme les choses, ces êtres> 723:18. <trouvons tant de douceur.] {723:22-723:28}

723:28. Nous descendions> **723:31.** <obligé* d'y jouer un rôle. J'étais harassé, affamé. Souvent pour ne pas trop retarder le moment de dîner, nous ne remontions pas dans nos chambres avant de nous mettre à table et nous attendions tous ensemble dans le hall le maître d'hôtel qui viendrait nous dire>

723:38. <dire que nous> **724:9.** <l'excès de ses politesses. [723:29. <d'«écouter» Mme de Villeparisis. 723:41. —Mais nous vous dérangeons: nous abusons> 723:42. <m'enchante, disait Mme de Villeparisis avec> 724:2. <coutumière de vieille dame un peu bougonne. 724:6. <heureuse d'être avec>]

□**724:9.** En ce qui nous concernait personnellement, Mme de Villeparisis avait certainement le désir de continuer avec nous dans son salon de Paris des relations auxquelles sa crainte était au contraire que ma grand'mère mît fin en quittant Bricquebec. Mais elle avait pris une fois pour toutes ce pli professionnel dans la personne du faubourg Saint-Germain voyant>

724:11. <voyant toujours> **724:17.** <ne les invitera pas. [724:13. <occasions où elle peut, dans le livre de compte* de son>]

724:17. Ainsi le génie de sa caste, agissant une fois pour toutes et ignorant que les circonstances étaient autres, les personnes différentes et qu'à Paris Mme de Villeparisis nous inviterait sans cesse, la poussait cependant avec une ardeur fiévreuse et comme si le temps qui lui était concédé pour être aimable était court, à multiplier dans ses relations de bain de mer avec nous, les envois de roses, de melons, les prêts de livres, les promenades en voiture et les effusions verbales. {724:26-724:35}

724:36. —Mais non, au contraire je suis charmée, restez, finissons ensemble cette bonne journée. Donnez vos manteaux pour qu'on les remonte.

Ma grand'mère les passait au directeur qui murmurait en les emportant qu'il n'était pas un domestique.

724:41. —Je crois que ce Monsieur est> **726:32.** <duc qui avec un des jugements les plus faux que j'aie jamais connus ne manquait pas d'un certain esprit. [724:43. <prendre votre manteau. Je vois encore le Duc de Nemours> 725:9. <disait le Prince à mon père> 725:13. <ficelle. J'espère que je n'ai rien abimé*, disait le Prince en riant.» Maintenant> 725:33. <de plus grande maison, ils> 725:35. <en Basigny*. J'admets que trop [*blanc*] par les alliances et les illustrations, l'ancienneté> 725:40. <dames à se résigner au premier pas. Elles> 726:1. <entend une calèche dans> 726:7. <escalier, et souffle> 726:11. <qu'on a de braves> 726:13. <difficilement, était énor-

me> 726:19. <malgré cette, comment dire, cette... importance.]

□**726:35.** Après le dîner, dans la chambre de ma grand'mère, en causant avec elle, je contrôlais d'après les siennes la justesse de mes impressions si favorables à Mme de Villeparisis. Et ma grand'mère m'approuvait pleinement. Mais aussitôt je lui soumettais mes doutes, mes scrupules. Mme de Villeparisis était-elle si intelligente que cela, et étions-nous bien sincères au moment où nous l'admirions: Je lui rappelais ce qu'elle avait dit sur les grands écrivains et j'avouais que cela me faisait me demander non seulement si avoir connu un artiste, avoir sur lui dans des archives des documents inédits, aide à le mieux comprendre, mais même si des qualités de mesure, de tact, de finesse, de modestie comme Mme de Villeparisis avait, conduisaient à rien de bien précieux puisque ceux qui les possédaient au plus haut degré ne furent que des Molé et des Vitrolles, et si leur absence qui peut rendre les relations quotidiennes désagréables, est bien grave, puisqu'elle n'a pas>

726:42. <n'a pas empêché> **727:2.** <se récriait. Elle profitait du contraste désagréable qu'il faisait avec Mme de Villeparisis pour reprendre l'éloge de celle-ci, d'abord parce qu'elle avait une sincère admiration pour elle. Ensuite parce que comme on dit>

727:3. <on dit que c'est> **727:13.** <trouver une distraction> [727:11. <jugement, particulières à une société>]

727:13. <une distraction, un apaisement, où l'on vit fleurir l'esprit d'un Doudan, d'un M. de Rémusat, d'un M.* de Charlus, voire d'une Mme de Sévigné, et qui mettent plus de bonheur, plus de dignité dans la vie que les raffinements opposés qui ont conduit un Beaudelaire*, un Poë à des souffrances, à une déconsidération dont elle ne voulait pas pour son petit-fils. Elle redisait les jolis mots, elle rappelait les gentilles attentions qu'avaient eu* Mme de Villeparisis dans la journée.

727:21. Je l'interrompais> **727:26.** <le degré d'estime> [727:25. <l'avouait. Aussi soumettai-je[1]>]

727:25. ([1]soumettais-je). 730:39. ([1]tâcher et* d'effacer). 781:40. ([1]Montargis—qu'elle fut* intelligente ou non, je n'en savais rien—lui). 782:35. ([1]parmi les jeunes auteurs et acteurs lui avaient).

727:26. <d'estime et de goût que je devrais avoir pour quelqu'un que quand elle me l'avait indiqué.

Le plaisir d'un trait spirituel, ou d'un geste gentil, je ne le* goûtais que longtemps après les avoir remarqués quand je pouvais, entre deux baisers, les apprendre ou les rappeler à ma grand'mère. Je ne me plaisais avec les gens quand* pensant que je pourrais les lui peindre dans ces causeries du soir où pour permettre à ma pensée d'entrer en contact avec la sienne et d'en connaître de nouveaux aspects, je venais lui apporter et lui soumettre les croquis que j'avais pris dans la journée d'après tous ces êtres inexistants qui n'étaient pas elle. Car ma grand'mère était pour moi plus qu'une cour suprême qui fixait une jurisprudence, plus que le milieu de culture favorable où des observations purement intellectuelles que j'avais faites, devenaient un bonheur. Elle était l'être suprême, l'être réel auquel toutes les personnes que nous fréquentions s'opposaient comme de falotes silhouettes dont je n'avais qu'une connaissance seconde à travers elle, qui n'existaient pour moi que par ce qu'elle m'en dirait. Souvent je lui disais:

—Sans toi je ne pourrai pas vivre.

727:32. —Mais il ne faut pas> **727:41.** <nous regarder. [727:33. <dur que cela. Sans>]

727:41. Pourtant le sentiment de son angoisse fut plus fort que le mien. Je m'approchai de la fenêtre et distinctement je lui dis.

728:1. —Tu sais> **728:9.** <parler de philosophie. [728:4. <autant je m'habitue, ma vie> 728:7. Je ne pus pas en dire plus, je regardais par la fenêtre. Grand'mère sortit>]

728:9. <philosophie, sujet sur lequel [*blanc*] que la plus récente, et après les questions essentielles, tout ce qu'on pouvait savoir de vérité; alors je lui dis que ce philosophe et avec lui les plus grands savants, —matière sur laquelle ma grand'mère s'en rapportait beaucoup à moi. Et je dis sur le ton le plus indifférent que je pus, et en m'arrangeant pour que ma grand'mère fit* attention à mes paroles, que c'était>

728:12. <c'était curieux> **728:14.** <et leur réunion.

728:15. Bientôt Mme de Villeparisis cessa de nous voir aussi souvent. Un jeune neveu récemment entré à Saint-Cyr dont elle attendait la visite pour quelques semaines était arrivé et elle passait beaucoup de son temps avec lui. Elle nous avait parlé de lui au cours de nos promenades, ventant* son intelligence, surtout son cœur, et déjà je me figurais qu'il allait se prendre de sympathie pour moi, que je serais son meilleur amie*, et quand>

728:24. <quand, avant son arrivée, sa tante lui avait laissé entendre> **728:38.** <interstices laissaient> [728:28. <fatalement par la folie, le crime> 728:32. <dont un médecin vient> 728:35. Un jour de grande chaleur>]

728:38. <laissaient passer le clignotement bleu de la mer, quand je vis passer dans le hall qui, allant de la plage à la route, traversait toute le* largeur de l'hôtel, un jeune homme, habillé d'une étoffe grise, presque blanche, comme je n'en avais jamais vue* sur personne, comme je n'aurais jamais cru qu'aucun homme osât en porter, dont la fraîcheur évidente évoquait autant que celle de la salle à manger la chaleur et le beau temps dehors. Son visage et ses cheveux étaient d'une blondeur qui semblait dû* à l'absorption, —comme dans le raisin ou le miel, —à l'absorption des rayons du soleil, et ses paupières dans leur mince écartement laissaient passer un œil vert et bougeant de la couleur de la mer. C'était le neveu de Mme de Villeparisis, le comte de Beauvais, qui était arrivé le matin. Devant lui voltigeait son monocle qu'il semblait poursuivre comme un papillon. {729:9-729:31}

729:34. Il venait> **730:1.** <et tandis que> [729:36. <portraits d'aujourd'hui des peintres intelligents prétendent sans tricher en rien sur l'observation le* plus exacte de la vie actuelle, mais en choisissent* pour leur> 729:40. <course, entreport* de yacht>]

730:1. <et tandis que son monocle, un moment posé et captif, reprenait sur la route ensoleillée ses ébats lumineux et ailés, avec l'élégance et la maîtrise qu'un grand pianiste trouve le moyen de montrer dans le trait le plus simple, où on n'aurait pas pu croire qu'il saurait se montrer supérieur à un exécutant de deuxième ordre, le neveu de Mme de Villeparisis décacheta une lettre que le directeur d'hôtel lui donna, et prenant les guides que lui passa le cocher, s'assit à côté de lui et fit partir les bêtes.

730:10. Quelle déception> **730:24.** <à la morgue que devaient au contraire pratiquer impitoyablement les jeunes contes*. [730:11. <hôtel—équilibrant> 730:14. <gravité—en voyant qu'il ne cherchait pas à se rappeler* de nous et ne nous saluant* pas quoiqu'il ne put* ignorer> 730:19. <elle, M. de Monfort*, je> 730:21. <l'aristocratie y permettait peut-être aux femmes et aux marquis de manquer>] {730:26-730:38}

730:39. Cette morgue que je devinais chez M. de Beauvais, son mépris pour nous et tout ce qu'il supposait de dureté naturelle, se trouva vérifié chaque jour par son attitude; chaque fois que nous passions à côté de lui dans l'hôtel ou dehors, il posait sur nous un regard impassible, implacable, dépouillé de ce vague respect pour les droits d'une autre existence qu'on a en face d'une créature humaine, ne le* connaît-on pas, et comme s'il ne nous distinguait pas des meubles du hall ou des pierres du chemin. Et cette preuve que ces regards, cette attitude venaient apporter ainsi à mon hypothèse sur sa nature insensible, orgueilleuse et méchante, en avaient fait une certitude [*blanc*] si absolue que quand Mme de Villeparisis, sans doute pour tâcher[1] d'effacer la mauvaise impression que devait nous causer cette attitude dont elle était sans doute elle-même gênée, nous parla de l'inépuisable bonté de son neveu, j'admirai comme dans le monde, au mépris de toute vérité et sans doute pour donner une apparence honorable et légitime de* goût qu'on a pour eux, on attribue des qualités de cœur à des êtres qui sont peut-être aimables avec des gens brillants comme eux mais qui font preuve à l'égard du reste de l'humanité d'une sécheresse affreuse. D'ailleurs devant Mme de Villeparis* même il ajouta une confirmation nouvelle à la loi d'ailleurs déjà bien établie pour moi, de sa nature. Car un jour où je le rencontrai avec sa tante dans un chemin étroit où elle ne put faire autrement que de me présenter, tandis que mécaniquement il jetait en avant sa main que je pris, son visage dont aucun muscle ne bougea resta le même que s'il n'avait pas entendu que sa tante me nommait et ses yeux où ne se forma aucun regard, d'où était absente la virtualité de toute sympathie possible, ne se contentèrent pas de garder l'insensibilité qu'ils avaient eue d'un miroir sans vie; ils [*blanc*] à un degré où la créature vivante se révélait derrière la prunelle morte par une exagération dans l'inanimé de l'apparence qui ne connaissait pas les objets inanimés, par la trace d'un effort pour expulser des yeux la notion qu'il pouvait y avoir devant eux une personne pensante non loin de qui sa main avait été projetée par l'avant-bras, et non tendue par sa volonté.

Or il se trouva que cette attitude qui contenait si bien les sentiments que je lui avais prêtés était* tout simplement le résultat d'une habitude mondaine—particulière d'ailleurs à sa famille sous cette forme extrême et à laquelle on avait plié son corps dès son enfance; comme celle qu'il avait prise aussi de se faire présenter> {731:5-731:13; 731:39-732:4}

732:13. <présenter immédiatement> **732:21.** <bouillante et sans le préservatif duquel il y eût un* péril à demeurer une seconde de plus. [732:19. <eût été quelque réflexe défensif>] {732:23-732:34}

732:35. Mais, ces formalités remplies, je vis que ce jeune homme qui> **732:42.** <et passent* des heures à étudier Proudhon. [732:39. <tante, imbu d'autre part>] {732:43-734:14}

734:15. Dès le premier jour il fit la conquête> **734:32.** <raideur et sans empois. [734:22. <Combray, des plates-bandes> 734:30. <vêtements de Montargis, d'une>]

734:32. Elle le prisait davantage encore dans la façon négligente et libre que le jeune homme riche avait d'user du luxe, sans «sentir l'argent», sans en être gonflé, sans airs importants; elle en retrouvait même le charme dans l'incapacité qu'il avait gardée et qui généralement>

734:37. <généralement disparaît> **735:1.** <une grimace de plaisir s'emparait aussi irrésistiblement de son visage que font certains éternuments* ou certains fou-rires*; la peau>

735:2. <la peau trop> **735:5.** <gracieuse apparence> [735:3. <laissait transparente une vive>]

735:5. <gracieuse apparence, à cet incarnat passager de la franchise et de l'innocence et qui d'ailleurs chez lui ne trompent pas. Mais chez bien d'autres, sa sincérité physiologique n'exclut nullement la duplicité morale; bien souvent il* prouve simplement la vivacité avec laquelle ressentant* le plaisir jusqu'à être désarmées devant lui et à être forcées de le confesser aux autres,

des natures capables d'ailleurs des fourberies les plus viles pour l'obtenir.

735:14. Mais où ma grand'mère> **736:24.** <que pour soi-même> [735:15. <de Beauvais c'était> 735:18. <comme ma grand'mère n'eut* pas pu en trouver, disait-elle> 735:19. <aimants, et qu'eussent contresignés «Sévigné ou Charlus»; il> 735:22. <amusée, mais les plaisantait comme elle-même> 735:30. <rester plus tard, le soir avec moi s'il> 735:36. <convenu tacitement entre nous que> 736:2. <rien de cette joie qu'il> 736:3. <quand j'étais seul. Alors quelquefois, je> 736:6. <j'étais avec Montargis, que je parlais à quelqu'un, mon esprit> 736:10. <me donnaient aucun> 736:11. <que je l'avais quitté, je> 736:12. <mots comme de l'ordre dans les minutes> 736:14. <rare et je goûtais ce plaisir de me sentir entouré de biens> 736:16. <acquérir qui> 736:17. <naturel, le plaisir d'avoir> 736:20. <avec Montargis et> 736:22. <seul et de m'être enfin mis à travailler.]

736:24. <soi-même, que les plus grands désirent être appréciés, que je ne pouvais pas considérer comme perdues des heures où j'avais bâti une grave idée de moi dans l'esprit de moi aussi* et si je n'éprouvais rien de la joie que j'avais eu* à éclaircir la plus petite pensée de moi, des mois* je me persuadais facilement que je devais être heureux et je souhaitais d'autant plus vivement que ce bonheur ne me fût jamais enlevé que je ne l'avais pas ressenti. On craint plus que tous les autres la disparition des biens qui n'existent en dehors de nous que parce que notre cœur ne s'en est pas aperçu.

736:33. Je me sentais> **736:36.** <pas pour moi. [736:34. <beaucoup parce que>]

736:37. Mais je me sentais incapable de connaître la joie pour tout sentiment qui au lieu d'accroître les différences qu'il y avait entre mon âme et celles des autres—comme il y en a entre les âmes de chacun de nous—les aplanirait, et notamment la joie de l'amitié.

736:40. En revanche> **737:4.** <approfondir. [736:41. <en Beauvais un> 736:42. <le «noble», qui>]

737:4. J'éprouvais à retrouver toujours en lui le noble—antérieur à la propre naissance de Beauvais et quoiqu'il aspirait* lui-même à être tout autre chose, —mais c'était une joie intime et non pas une joie d'amitié.

737:7. Dans l'agilité morale> **737:37.** <prétentieux et mal mis> [737:9. <il offrait à ma grand'mère sa voiture et> 737:11. <adresse et sa simplicité à> 737:17. <d'elle, bien* que pour pouvoir mieux faire fête à ses amis> 737:22. <à Beauvais ce> 737:22. <est «autant qu'eux*, cette peur> 737:32. <qualités personnelle, intellectuelle et morale à laquelle* il attachait>]

737:38. <mal mis, et notamment Bloch à qui il me demanda de rappeler qu'il l'avait rencontré dans une université populaire, avaient chez lui> **737:40.** <il cherchait sincèrement à se faire pardonner par eux, cette origine aristocratique qu'il exerçait sur eux était au contraire une séduction qu'ils dissimulaient sous de la froideur et de l'insolence, et à cause de laquelle ils le recherchaient. Et les opinions qu'il professait n'étaient pas dictées chez lui comme elles l'étaient chez eux sans qu'ils se l'avouassent, par le désir de faire une brillante carrière. Tout au plus> {738:1-738:18}

738:19. <plus souriai-je parfois de retrouver chez lui les leçons> **738:32.** <prévenir de suite. [738:23. <lui, Montargis, n'attachait> 738:26. <c'était Montargis qui> 738:31. <dites au lift* de>] {738:32-740:3}

740:3. Montargis quant à lui trouvait d'autant moins grave que Bloch ne sut* pas prononcer le mot lift, qu'il y voyait surtout dans cette faute un manque de savoir vivre que lui, Montargis, pratiquait à merveille mais méprisait absolument. Mais la peur qu'on ne la révélât un jour à Bloch qui croirait avoir été trouvé par lui ridicule fit qu'il se trouva coupable comme s'il avait trouvé son ami ridicule en effet et que la rougeur qui colorerait sans doute les joues de Bloch à la découverte de son erreur, il la sentait par anticipation et réversibilité monter aux siennes propres. Car il pensait que Bloch attachait bien plus d'importance que lui à cette faute. Ce que Bloch prouva quelques temps après un jour qu'il m'entendait dire lift, en disant:

—Ah! on dit lift.

Et d'un ton sec et hautain:

—Cela n'a d'ailleurs aucune espèce d'importance. Phrase peu réflexe [*cf.* 740:20], qui, identique chez tous les hommes, dans les grandes circonstances comme dans les petites dénonce l'importance qu'il attachait à une chose qui manque et s'échappe, la première de toutes si lamentables et si navrantes, des lèvres de tout homme un peu fier dont on vient de tirer la dernière espérance en lui refusant un service:

—Cela n'a aucune espèce d'importance, je m'arrangerai autrement.

L'autre arrangement est* sans aucune espèce d'importance était quelquefois le suicide...* Mais si Beauvais rougit de l'erreur de Bloch, il n'en rit pas comme Bloch n'aurait pas manqué de rire de lui. Et si, de cette bienveillance, je sentais l'aristocrate devenir exempt de la timidité et de l'envie qui se cachent souvent sous l'ironie méchante des petits bourgeois, là encore en lui l'aristocratie, en maintenant la grande pureté de son atmosphère morale, avait favorisé l'éclosion de certaines vertus. Et c'est cette grande pureté qui, ne pouvant [*cf.* 779:37] se satisfaire entièrement dans un sentiment égoïste comme l'amour, se rencontrait d'autre part en lui comme elle s'est rencontrée en moi l'impossibilité de trouver sa nourriture spirituelle autre part qu'en soi-même, le rendait vraiment capable d'amitié. Personne moins que lui n'avait le préjugé des classes. Un jour qu'il s'était emporté contre son cocher et que je lui en avais fait reproche.

—Pourquoi affecterais-je de lui parler poliment? {740:33-748:38}

△**780:10.** <poliment? N'est-il pas mon égal? n'est-il> **780:22.** <ma cousine. [780:11. <cousins. Tu as l'air> 780:13. <inférieur. Tu parles comme> 780:21. —Oh! une carpe>]

□ △**780:23.** —Comment est-elle votre cousine?

Il me répondit distraitement et avec ennui.

—Oh! je n'en sais rien, je vous dirai que ces questions de généalogie me laissent froid. La vie est courte et il me semble qu'il y a vraiment des choses plus intéressantes dont nous pouvons parler dans le monde le plus récent* possible.

L'habitude qui avait été pour lui la conséquence de cette sorte de préjugé contre les gens du monde et ces jours où il y allait, l'attitude méprisante ou hostile qu'il y gardait le plus souvent, augmentait encore chez tous ses proches parents leur chagrin de sa liaison avec une actrice, liaison>

△**780:27.** <liaison qu'ils accusaient de ne lui avoir fait que du mal, que de lui être fatale> **780:30.** <complètement. {780:31-780:36}

△**780:36.** Car il n'était pas> **781:12.** <d'un jeune clubman> [780:39. <monde. Mais lui, sa> 780:41. <pour les jeunes gens du monde—qui sans> 781:7. <délicatesses, elle respecte>].

△**781:12.** <clubman comme Montargis ou d'un jeune ouvrier, son amant l'admire trop pour ne pas respecter ce qu'elle respecte et pour lui l'échelle>

△**781:17.** <l'échelle des valeurs> **781:31.** <croire, qu'il respecte maintenant sans avoir besoin pour cela de le connaître, qu'il respectera même quand ce serait d'autres qui lui en parleront. [781:20. <une autre femme, chez une de ses parentes aurait fait rire ce jeune homme robuste. 781:23. <comme Montargis a>]

△**781:34.** La maîtresse> **781:40.** <les bêtes. Une actrice comme celle avec qui vivait Montargis[1]—et une cocotte y eût suffi—lui avait procuré aussi cet avantage de lui faire trouver ennuyeuse la société des femmes du monde, considérer comme une corvée l'obligation d'aller dans une soirée, elle l'avait guéri du snobisme et de la frivolité. Mais si grâce à>

△**782:3.** <grâce à elle> **782:35.** <bien qu'elle pouvait> [782:5. <vie du jeune amant> 782:8. <lui avait enseigné à> 782:14. <de Montargis qui> 782:15. <préférer. Elle apprenait à son amant à éprouver> 782:18. <bientôt Montargis, sans> 782:20. <à Bricquebec où> 782:21. <moi qu'elle n'avait pas connu, de lui-même il fermait> 782:25. <à dire adieu à la fois à plusieurs personnes, s'arrangea à les quitter un peu avant moi afin de me garder le dernier et seul, de me traiter> 782:31. <vie, elle avait ennobli son cœur, mais tout>]

△**782:35.** <pouvait pour lui, et maintenant elle ne faisait plus que le faire souffrir, car elle l'avait pris en horreur. Elle avait commencé par le trouver bête et ridicule, parce que les amis qu'elle avait dans[1] la jeunesse littéraire lui avaient appris qu'il l'était, et elle le répétait à son tour avec cette passion, cette absence de réserves avec lesquelles on adopte les opinions ou les usages qu'on ignorait entièrement et qu'on a reçu* tout faits du

dehors. Elle professait volontiers comme eux qu'entre elle et Montargis le fossé était infranchissable>

△**783:3.** <infranchissable, parce qu'ils> **783:8.** <son amant. [783:4. <intellectuelle et lui, quoiqu'il* prétendit*, était>]

△**783:8.** Mais ce mépris pour lui était devenu de l'horreur quand les mêmes amis l'avaient convaincue qu'elle détruisait dans une compagnie aussi peu faite pour elle les grandes espérances qu'elle avait données, que son amant finirait par déteindre sur elle, qu'elle gâchait son avenir d'artiste. Alors elle ressentait pour Montargis la même haine que s'il s'était obstiné à vouloir lui inoculer une maladie mortelle. Elle le voyait le moins possible tout en hésitant encore à rompre définitivement avec lui. {783:18-784:7}

△**784:8.** Cette période orageuse de leur liaison—et qui était arrivée maintenant à son point le plus aigu, le plus cruel pour Montargis, car elle lui avait défendu de rester à Paris où elle était exaspérée par sa présence et l'avait envoyé seul à Bricquebec, —avait commencé à une soirée où Montargis avait obtenu d'une de ses tantes chez qui cette soirée avait lieu que son amie viendrait y réciter des fragments d'un drame symboliste qu'elle

---

□**783:16.** <tout en hésitant encore à rompre définitivement avec lui, si même elle en avait vraiment l'intention, ce qui me semblait bien peu vraisemblable. Car Saint-Loup faisait pour elle de tels sacrifices que* à moins qu'elle ne fut* ravissante—il n'avait jamais voulu me montrer sa photographie, me disait, «d'abord ce n'est pas une beauté et puis elle vient mal en photographie. Ce sont des instantanés que j'ai fait* moi-même avec mon kodecq* et ils te donneraient une fausse idée d'elle», il me semblait difficile qu'elle trouvait* un second homme qui fut* d'une pareille bonté pour elle. Mais Saint-Loup qui, sans bien comprendre ce qui se passait dans la pensée de sa maîtresse, ne la croyait qu'à demi sincère, ni dans les reproches injustes ni dans les promesses d'amour éternel, qu'elle lui faisait souvent, avait pourtant à certains moments le sentiment qu'elle romprait quand elle le pourrait, avait, par une sorte d'intérêt pratique qui se conciliait chez lui, avec les plus grands égarements du cœur, refusé de lui constituer un capital. Il avait emprunté des sommes énormes pour qu'elle ne manquât de rien, mais ne lui remettait d'argent qu'au le jour le jour, non sans doute par un instinct de conservation de son amour, plus clairvoyant que Saint-Loup n'était lui-même. Et sans doute, au cas où elle eut* vraiment songeait* à le quitter—si* elle était belle et avait de l'avenir, au théâtre, attendait-elle froidement d'avoir «fait sa pelotte*». Avec tout ce que Saint-Loup lui donnait elle ne pouvait pas donner un temps bien long mais enfin qui lui était tout de même concédé pour prolonger son bonheur—ou son malheur.

avait joué une fois sur une scène d'avant-garde et pour lequel elle>

△**784:17.** <elle lui avait> **785:3.** <à se venger. [784:20. <«Ancille*> 784:21. <à Montargis être> 784:22. <assemblée de clubmen et de> 784:24. <de sa psalmodie> 784:28. <de Montargis avait> 784:29. <grotesque. Le Duc d'Albon, un des hommes le plus en vue de la société, ne lui> 784:33. <encore elle avait> 784:40. <à Montargis:> 784:41. quelles p.... sans éducation> 784:43. <dire, dans les hommes qui étaient là il n'y avait pas un de ces hommes qui ne m'éût fait de l'œil>]

△□**785:4.** Et ce qu'elle lui avait dit alors avait changé l'antipathie qu'il avait pour les gens du monde en une horreur autrement profonde et qui lui faisait endurer d'incessantes souffrances. Tous ceux de ses cousins, de ses camarades qu'il lui avait présentés, elle lui avait assuré, —soit pour couper les ponts entre lui et des jeunes gens qui peut-être avaient pris le parti de ses parents et avaient dit à la jeune femme la peine que cette liaison leur faisait et tâché de lui faire accepter l'idée d'une rupture, soit pour exciter sa jalousie, soit pour expliquer l'insuccès qu'elle avait eu quand elle était allée réciter chez sa tante, soit tout simplement parce que c'était vrai, —elle lui avait avoué qu'ils avaient tous essayé de coucher avec elle et même de la prendre de force. Et Montargis quoiqu'il se fut* et elle aussi brouillé* avec eux pensant que peut-être quand il était loin d'elle comme en ce moment à Bricquebec, ceux-là ou d'autres en profitaient pour revenir à la charge. C'est bien souvent [*cf.* 785:37] les mains vides et le front soucieux que je le voyais rentrer de la poste où seul de tout l'hôtel avec Françoise, lui par impatience d'amant comme elle par méfiance de domestique, il allait chercher et porter les lettres lui-même.

△**785:15.** Et quand il parlait d'un de ces viveurs> **785:23.** <misère et la cruauté des riches. [785:18. <respirait la douleur et la haine.]

□**785:23.** Le nombre des lettres et des dépêches qu'il envoyait à sa maîtresse était incalculable. Tout en l'empêchant de venir à Paris, chaque fois qu'à distance elle trouvait le moyen de se brouiller avec lui, on le voyait à sa figure décomposée. Le chagrin qu'il éprouvait avait pour singulier effet de le persuader qu'il avait eu tort. Comme sa maîtresse ne lui disait

△ □785:35.. Comme ma grand'mère approuvait que je fusse le plus possible avec Montargis elle permit même que nous sortissions ensemble le soir. Nous avions commencé par ne pas revenir dîner un jour que nous étions allés ensemble à un ancien moulin, situé à quelques kilomètres de Bricquebec, et qui était devenu le restaurant des sous-officiers de la garnison voisine, et où des employés venaient se reposer de la sécheresse de leurs occupations quotidiennes, de la chaleur et de la poussière de la ville, en louant une barque et en dînant au bord de l'eau. Montargis m'avait dit: «ta grand'mère est si bonne, elle ne te grondera pas si nous ne rentrons qu'à neuf heures», nous avions commandé des truites, et Montargis m'avait promené sur l'eau que frappait le soleil oblique jusqu'à ce que la servante nous eût fait signe que le dîner était prêt. Je lui demandais* s'il croyait qu'on pourrait facilement faire monter la servante dans la petite chambre qu'on louait en haut. Il ne le croyait pas; d'ailleurs je trouvais plus simple de rester avec lui et je me contentais de la regarder en mangeant la truite, au gazouillement de l'eau, sous les feuillages pleins d'oiseaux. Et je lui posai des questions sur la vertu de telle ou telle femme; personnellement il s'en désintéressait, car il gardait loin de sa maîtresse une chasteté qui lui coûtait peu, les autres femmes lui étant devenues indifférentes et qui l'apaisait beaucoup parce que par sa propre fidélité il cherchait à se prouver qu'elle n'est pas

---

jamais ce qu'elle avait à lui reprocher, tout en soupçonnant que si elle ne lui disait pas c'est qu'elle ne servait* pas et qu'elle avait simplement assez de lui, il avait voulu avoir des explications, il lui écrivait: «Dis-moi ce que j'ai fait de mal. Je suis prêt à reconnaître mes torts». L'espèce de douleur au cœur qu'il gardait pendant ces jours-là était quelque chose de constant, d'atroce, qui lui donnait envie de se tuer; mais l'accablante fixité physique de cette souffrance avait pour correspondant moral des états bien plus mobiles. Car quand il voulait, soit en lui-même, soit en causant avec moi, soit en écrivant à sa maîtresse, «parler sa souffrance, en donner une traduction rationnelle, tantôt le mal, pourtant toujours le même, né de leur brouille et qui durait autant qu'elle, était une terrible colère contre sa maîtresse pour qui il avait tout fait, tantôt une crainte anxieuse de n'avoir pas bien agi avec elle. Et quand elle se conciliait, ses scrupules comme son indignation s'épanouissaient avec sa souffrance. Seulement il gardait une crainte pour l'avenir et se félicitait de ne pas lui avoir constitué un capital. Vous comprenez me dit-il d'un ton à la fois triste et content. De cette façon j'ai barré sur elle.»

Ce mot excite* en moi moins d'agacement que ce qu'il exprimait d'heureuse sécurité que de pitié parce qu'il impliquait des doutes douloureux.

une vertu impossible et à se persuader que peut-être sa maîtresse la mettait en pratique comme lui. Mais je ne lui causais pas en l'interrogeant sur la légèreté certaine ou possible d'une femme ou d'une autre, le même malaise insupportable que si je lui avais parlé d'hommes débauchés; parce que eux sans s'en rendre compte c'était toujours sa maîtresse qu'il les imaginait en train à* désirer. Il m'assura que les jeunes filles étaient souvent moins farouches que je ne croyais.

—Pour Mlle de Silaria que je connais un peu, me dit-il, je n'ai presque aucun doute. Je regrette de ne pas avoir été là, je vous aurais abouchés.

J'en profitai pour lui parler d'une grande jeune fille à qui il m'avait présenté devant l'hôtel, une de ses cousines, en villégiature chez la princesse de Parme. Il me semblait impossible de confondre avec aucune autre cette majestueuse et souple nymphe de Jean Goujon ou du Primatrice avec son haut diadème de cheveux blonds, son front prolongé par un nez pur, cette beauté radieuse, grecque dans la mesure où le sont des déesses de cour, affinées et hautaines que croyait emprunter à l'antiquité l'école de Fontainebleau. Et pourtant si Montargis ne m'eut* pas dit qu'elle était une de ses parentes j'aurais cru la reconnaître, l'avoir rencontrée plusieurs fois dehors dans mon quartier de Paris. Elle m'y avait frappé par quelque chose—que je ne voyais jamais aux bourgeoises comme il faut—de trop élégant et de trop négligé à la fois dans la mise—d'oisif, d'inconscient d'une foule* ambiante et affinée dans la démarche—qui donnait rétrospectivement dans mon souvenir à la promeneuse de Paris l'air de s'y trouver comme sur une de ces promenades sortant de la ville* d'une amie, en toilette de plage. Or, à Paris, cette belle-fille* en m'apercevant s'était arrêtée net, m'avait regardé dans les yeux, souriante, les lèvres tendues, avec une impudeur que n'aurait pas eue une cocotte. Et je l'avais vue faire de même devant un autre jeune homme. J'interrogeai donc Montargis sur sa cousine. Elle était au contraire d'une vertu revêche.

—Elle est odieuse, me dit-il, si elle n'est pas encore mariée c'est qu'elle ne veut qu'une altesse ou au moins le chef d'une grande maison ducale. Mais je t'assure que c'est à peine si elle dit bonjour à ma tante Villeparisis. C'est ignoble! Elle n'a pour elle que d'être belle comme un antique et d'être austère. On ne peut pas lui refuser cela, à Claremonde. Mais elle croit que cela lui donne le droit d'être le dédain même.

En effet elle ne m'avait même pas fait un signe de tête quand Montargis m'avait présenté.

J'appris qu'il ne pouvait y avoir rien de commun entre cette jeune fille et mon inconnue de Paris. Je fus effrayé de penser aux risques qu'il y a d'identifier une image présente à une autre qui n'est plus que dans notre mémoire toujours incertaine et où nous ne pouvons ne pas apercevoir la petite différence qui eut* suffi à nous détromper. Et par une bizarre coïncidence que ne pu* me rejeter dans des perplexités parce que les renseignements fournis par Montargis m'avaient démontré mon erreur et donné une certitude, étant allé quelques jours après me promener seul sur la digue jusqu'à son extrémité, là où il n'y a presque plus de maisons, là où commencent les dunes du pays avoisinant, je croisai Mlle Claremonde qui se retourna trois ou quatre fois et s'arrêta même, et fit même un signe sans que j'eusse pu apercevoir les amis qu'elle avait sans doute aperçus et qui arrêtaient son attention. Montargis ne put m'accompagner dans une visite que je fis à quelque distance de Bricquebec chez le peintre Elstir dont nous avions fait tous deux connaissance. Attendant ce jour-là un de ses oncles qui devait venir passer deux ou trois jours auprès de Mme de Villeparisis, Montargis avait préféré, puisque je ne serais pas là, lui consacrer cette première après-midi pour être plus facilement excusé de passer les autres avec moi.

748:38. Mais ce n'était pas d'une façon tout à fait certaine que son oncle s'était annoncé ce jour-là, car très adonné aux exercices physiques, surtout à la marche, c'étaient* en partie à pied, en couchant dans les fermes, qu'il devait faire la plus grande partie de la route, depuis le château où il était en villégiature ce qui laissait assez incertain le moment où il serait à Bricquebec. Cet oncle s'appelait Palamède, d'un prénom qu'il avait hérité des princes de Sicile dont il descendait. Et plus tard quand je retrouvais dans mes lectures historiques, appartenant à tel podestat ou tel pape, non pas un prénom semblable, mais celui-là même, belle médaille de la Renaissance, —d'aucuns disaient véritable, antique, —toujours restée dans la famille, ayant glissé de descendant en descendant depuis le cabinet du Vatican jusqu'à l'oncle de mon ami, j'éprouvais le plaisir réservé à ceux qui ne pouvant pas faire de collections de statues ou de camées font, s'ils ont de l'imagination, faire des collections de vieux noms, noms de localité dans lesquels survit l'état ancien d'un usage ou d'une région—documentaires et pittoresques avec une carte ancienne, même cavalière, une enseigne ou un couturier, —vieux prénoms dans les belles finales françaises desquels résonne et [*blanc*] comme un défaut de langue, l'intonation d'une vulgarité ethnique, la faute de prononciation législatrice et grammairienne, avec laquelle nos ancêtres villageois faisaient subir aux mots latins ou saxons des mutilations augustes et durables, —font en un mot des collections dans ces sonorités anciennes avec lesquelles je me donnais à moi-même des concerts, comme certains qui recherchent les violes de Gambe et les violes d'amour jouant de la musique d'autrefois sur des instruments anciens. Montargis me dit que>

749:27. <dit que, même dans> **749:43.** <de sa fierté. [749:33. <arrivé que des personnes qui désiraient le connaître avait* essuyé un refus de la part de son frère même. «Non> 749:40. Au jockey*, lui et quelques amis il* avait désigné 200 membres> 749:42. <il est connu>]

□**749:43.** Cet orgueil aristocratique, bien atténué paraît-il par la dévotion et les années, aurait dû particulièrement déplaire à Montargis. Mais il m'assurait que, malgré ce qu'il appelait «des idées de l'autre monde», personne n'était aussi intelligent, ni doué pour les arts que son oncle Palamède lequel vivait dans ce milieu isolé, lointain, ravissant comme un rocher de corail dans les mers australes, apparaissait à mon esprit, non avec les disparates et l'opacité d'un homme réel, mais avec la translucide homogénéité d'un personnage légendaire. Il me donnait l'idée d'une puissance, non pas seulement plus grande que celle des autres hommes comme est celle des rois, mais d'une puissance autre, particulière au noble Palamède et qui ajoutait quelque chose de si flatteur par la vanité aux images que son nom éveillait, mais en même temps restait tellement sous leur dépendance, que sous le plaisir d'imaginer ce grand seigneur, se cachait inaperçue à mes yeux, l'ambition de le connaître, laquelle par contre ne se trouvait nullement satisfaite s'il ne ressemblait pas au personnage que je m'étais figuré.

Montargis me parla de la jeunesse de son oncle [*cf.* 750:1]. Il amenait tous les jours des femmes dans une garçonnière qu'il avait avec deux de ses amis, tous deux beaux comme lui, ce qui faisait qu'on les appelait «les trois Grâces.»

—Un jour, un des hommes qui est aujourd'hui des plus en vue dans le faubourg Saint-Germain, mais qui dans sa jeunesse avait des goûts bizarres avait demandé à mon oncle de venir dans cette garçonnière. Mais voilà qu'il ne fut pas aux femmes mais à mon oncle qu'il se mit à faire une déclaration.

750:12. Mon oncle fit> **750:19.** <à le* faire renoncer. [750:15. <jusqu'au sang, et le jetèrent>]

750:19. Naturellement il ne ferait plus cela aujourd'hui quoiqu'il déteste ce genre d'homme. Mais il est au contraire très bon et tu n'imagines pas le nombre de gens du peuple qu'il prend en affection, qu'il protège, quitte à être payé d'ingratitude.

750:24. Ce sera> **750:26.** <métier.

750:26. Il n'est pas si méchant qu'il n'en a l'air il* paraît qu'on ne peut s'imaginer comme>

750:36. <comme il faisait> □**750:41.** <se remplissaient de rafraîchissements. Si pour une pièce pour laquelle il était utile de voire* toute la scène, il quittait sa loge et descendait à l'orchestre, c'était les fauteuils qui devenaient les places recherchées.

750:42. Un été> **751:27.** <pendant des années. [751:1. <dans une vigogne> 751:3. <respecté les jolies rayures bleues et oranges.* 751:5. <bleus et orangés, à longs> 751:6. Si par exemple pour une raison quelconque> 751:11. <veston. Si pour manger un gâteau il demandait une fourchette au lieu de sa cuiller, on commandait à un orfèvre un couvert de son invention, on se servait de ses doigts, il n'était plus> 751:17. <de Beethoven et avait fait> 751:20. <chambre. Ah! je crois qu'il> 751:22. <femmes, je ne sais d'ailleurs pas exactement>]

□**751:27.** Ainsi Montargis, tout en m'accompagnant à la gare où j'allais prendre le train pour aller chez Elstir me parlait de cet oncle dont il escomptait l'arrivée. Mais il attendit en vain. Le soir quand je revins de chez Elstir, l'oncle Palamède n'était toujours pas arrivé.

Le lendemain matin comme je passai* devant le casino en rentrant de* l'hôtel>

751:32. <l'hôtel, j'eus> **753:41.** <celle-ci, voilà que je t'appelle le baron de Guermantes. [751:36. <nerveusement avec une badine son pantalon de toile blanche, fixait> 751:37. Par moment* des regards d'une extrême activité les perçaient en tous sens comme en ont seuls> 751:41. <pour une raison quelconque, elle inspire des pensées que n'auraient pas les autres, par exemple un fou ou un espion. Il lança sur moi un dernier regard à la fois hardi, prudent, rapide et profond, comme> 752:3. <avoir jeté un coup d'œil tout> 752:8. Il tira de sa poche> 752:9. <annoncé car c'était dimanche et il y avait grande matinée, tira deux> 752:13. <n'arrivait pas, et fit avec la main le geste mécontent par lequel> 752:25. <change il cherchait seulement> 752:26. <exprimer l'indifférence et le détachement> 752:30. <je lui aurait* infligé> 752:33. <taille d'un air de fronde, pinçait des* lèvres> 752:38. <pour un fou. 752:40. <à Bricquebec, il> 753:2. <où elle était allée chercher quelque chose, quand> 753:3. <avec Montargis et> 753:5. <traversa comme un moment où> 753:8. <neutre qui paraît ne rien> 753:10. <qui n'exprime que la satisfaction de sentir autour de lui les [*blanc*] qu'il écoute* de sa> 753:15. <élégance intimide moins, est moins loin de la simplicité que la fausse; mais ce n'était pas que cela; d'un> 753:24. <sombre au pantalon s'harmonisait à la rayure> 753:26. <d'un goût [*blanc*] ailleurs et à qui> 753:34. <de: heue, heue, heue, pour> 753:36. <doigt, l'annulaire et le pouce> 753:37. <l'annulaire que je m'empressai de serrer sous mon* gant de suède*; puis>]

753:43. Après tout, l'erreur> **754:13.** <professionnelle. [754:6. <de Montargis ne> 754:6. <dévisageait les gens qu'il ne connaissait pas (et> 754:11. <qu'il connaissait ou qui se trouvaient avec d'autres qu'il connaissait, comme>]

754:13. Les laissant, ma grand'mère, Mme de Villeparisis et lui causer, je retins Montargis en arrière:

—Dis-moi> **754:17.** <un Guermantes.

754:18. Mais ou, naturellement, il est> **754:29.** <actuel du château. [754:21. <Combray, qui descendent de> 754:23. —Mais absolument: mon oncle qui est plus héraldique que moi te répondrait que notre *cri*, notre cri de guerre, était même Combraysis>]

□**754:30.** Comment connaissez-vous donc ce château? Vous l'avez visité, ou vous connaissez peut-être les Gilbert de Guermantes, ma tante de Guermantes-La Trémoille* qui l'habitait avant, me dit-il, soit que, trouvant tout naturel qu'on connut* les mêmes gens que lui, il ne se rendait pas compte que j'étais d'un autre milieu ou par politesse, faisait semblant de ne pas s'en rendre compte [*cf.* Pléiade I, p. 977, ligne 47].

—Non... mais... j'ai entendu parler de ce château. Il y a là tous les bustes des anciens seigneurs de Guermantes, n'est-ce pas?

—Oui, c'est un beau spectacle, dit ironiquement Montargis, moitié par modestie, puisqu'il était à mon grand étonnement parent des Guermantes, moitié à cause de son indifférence sincère, voire de son préjugé hostile à tout ce qui concernait la noblesse. Il y a, ce qui est plus intéressant! un superbe portrait de ma tante par Carolus Duran et de magnifiques dessins de Delacroix. {754:30-754:43}

△**755:10.** Ma tante est> **755:30.** <voudrais voyager incognito.» [755:14. <le Duc de Guermantes> 755:16. <baron de Fleurus. Régulièrement> 755:17. <Pélaméde*> 755:18. <de Prince des> 755:21. <a sur la noblesse des idées> 755:22. <un peu dans la famille des> 755:23. <espagnoles et jusqu'à des titres du pape> 755:25. <de Fleurus, par>]

755:30. Il vous prouvera du reste qu'il n'y a pas du* titre plus ancien, bien qu'il est* antérieur à celui des Montmorency qui se disaient faussement les premiers barons de France. Mais, ajouta Montargis, vous n'allez pas me faire parler généalogie. Il n'y a rien qui m'assomme autant.

755:42. Je reconnaissais> **756:2.** <appelé Gilberte. [755:42. <regard qui> 756:1. <à la Frapelière au>]

756:3. —Mais est-ce que votre oncle ne passe pas pour avoir été l'amant de Mme Swann.

756:6. Oh! pas du tout!> **756:22.** <ne se servait> [756:8. Vous laisseriez* beaucoup> 756:11. <répondre que j'aurais causé bien plus d'étonnement à Combray si j'avais eu> 756:13. <de Fleurus. Sans doute elle avait remarqué l'importance qu'avaient pour lui les questions de naissance et de situation mondaine, mais

précisément parce qu'elle n'y en attachait elle-même aucune, elle l'avait remarqué sans rien de cette sévérité où il y avait souvent une secrète envie> 756:20. <grand'mère qui était contente de son sort et ne regrettait nullement>]

756:22. <ne se servait pour observer les travers de M. de Fleurus que de son intelligence, que dans le jugement qu'elle portait sur eux, son caractère ne l'intéressait pas, qu'il en restait extrêmement détaché, elle parlait de l'oncle de Montargis avec cette absence de mauvaise humeur, cette bienveillance souriante, presque sympathique, avec laquelle nous récompensons l'objet de notre observation désintéressée du plaisir que celle-ci nous procure, et d'autant plus que cette fois l'objet était un personnage dont elle trouvait les prétentions légitimes, du moins pittoresques, qui était amusant pour elle par la façon dont il tranchait sur les personnes qu'elle avait habituellement l'occasion de voir.

756:31. Mais c'était surtout en faveur de l'intelligence et de la sensibilité qu'on sentait en lui, qu'elle avait aisément pardonné à M. de Fleurus un préjugé aristocratique qui d'ailleurs chez lui ne s'opposait pas à elle* comme chez ces nobles que raillait Montargis que pourtant il ne leur avait pas non plus sacrifiées mais qu'il avait plutôt conciliées avec elles.

756:39. Possédant comme> **757:1.** <souvenirs de famille> [756:41. <Némours*, des princes de Lamballe, des La Trémoille* et des Choiseuil, des archives> 756:42. <Boucher, pouvait dire>]

757:2. <famille, il avait à cause de tout ce qu'elles ont de précieux pour l'imagination replacé au rang où son neveu l'avait déchu l'héritage de l'aristocratie française.

757:3. Peut-être aussi> **757:8.** <être souvent pour> [757:4. <idéologue que son neveu, se> 757:6. <prestige sur eux et qui>]

757:9. <pour son action utilitaire un mobile puissant. Le débat reste éternellement ouvert entre les hommes de cette sorte et ceux qui obéissent à l'idéal intérieur qui les pousser* à renoncer à leurs propres avantages pour chercher à le réaliser, artistes qui renoncent leur virtuosité, peuples artistes qui se modernisent en peuples guerriers qui rêvent de désarmements et gouvernements, qui se font démocratiques ou législateurs humains, de

même que la réalité employée à leur rêve en faisait perdre aux uns leur talent, aux autres leur prestige séculaire, en multipliait les guerres, les crimes, les tyrannies, même un peut* d'une estétique.* Si le goût de M. de Fleurus était [*blanc*], il semblait fermé à l'art moderne que depuis le romantisme il considérait comme en décadence, il était permis de nommer cette étroitesse plus avisée que l'effort de l'émancipation qu'avait fait Montargis si l'on en jugeait sur les résultats extérieurs, sur l'hôtel où M. de Fleurus avait transporté une grande partie des admirables boiseries de l'hôtel Guermantes*, au lieu de les échanger comme avait fait son neveu pour celles qu'il avait possédées contre un mobilier moderne style et des statues polychromes de Gêrome*.

757:32. A quelques femmes> **758:28.** <spirituelle, à part* qu'elle trouvait enviables, par-dessus tous les hommes, les pinces*, parce qu'ils peuvent avoir un Labruyère*, un Fénelon comme précepteurs. [757:42. <qui le laisseraient indifférent> 758:1. <lui ce qu'est> 758:8. <par conséquent nous rappelle des connaissances> 758:11. <de Fleurus se> 758:14. <sang moins noble, les offrait intactes à son admiration, dans leur noblesse> 758:18. Enfin M. de Fleurus célébrait> 758:23. <des êtres à qui> 758:26. <reste, eussent* semblé trop ridicule et particulièrement pour ma grand'mère toujours sans défense>]

758:32. Mme de Villeparisis emmena son neveu faire une petite promenade. {758:32-758:41}

758:42. Quoique ce fût dimanche> **759:10.** <faire que du bien. [759:3. <pour aller chez les [*blanc*], et elle> 759:5. <que Mme Bruland est> 759:9. <ai persuadé de descendre>]

759:11. Quand Mme de Villeparisis en rentrant de sa promenade nous fit demander à la fin de la journée de venir prendre le thé avec M. de Fleurus, je pensai que s'étant peut-être aperçue de l'impolitesse qu'il avait marquée à mon égard elle avait voulu lui donner l'occasion de la réparer. Mais quand dans le petit salon de son appartement où elle nous reçut je voulus saluer M. de Fleurus, j'eus beau tourner autour de lui qui faisait un récit d'une voix aiguë à Mme de Villeparisis, je ne pus pas>

759:18. <je ne pus pas attraper> **759:32.** <venir la police. [759:26. <ses yeux en effet qui> 759:30. <et montrent leur

marchandise illicite, scrutent sans cependant tourner>] {759:32-760:43}

□**761:1.** Sans doute s'il n'y avait pas eu ces yeux, le visage et le corps de M. de Fleurus étaient semblables au visage et au corps de beaucoup de beaux hommes et même je m'imaginais un «grand seigneur» comme un être si différent des autres que j'avais été déçu de voir M. de Fleurus avoir une taille élancée, un profil régulier et de fines moustaches de la même façon que beaucoup d'autres gens que j'avais vus ou que je connaissais. Je pensais que seul ce grand seigneur faisait exception parmi les autres en revêtant le corps d'un homme quelconque. Et quand Montargis en me parlant d'autres Guermantes me dit:

761:4. «Dame> **762:12.** <portât de bagues. [761:10. <je sentis s'envoler une de mes illusions. Mais ce visage semblable à d'autres, auquel> 761:13. M. de Fleurus avait> 761:14. <l'expression, ces yeux> 761:16. <laquelle, selon les mouvements qu'il faisait, ou le point où on se plaçait, on se sentait brusquement croisé du reflet de quelque engin qui semblait en équilibre instable et n'avait rien de rassurant> 761:22. <circonspecte, incessante et inquiète de ces yeux> 761:23. <cerne très bas descendu, en> 761:26. <d'un homme puissant ou seulement dangereux, mais> 761:30. <rendu son regard si énigmatique quand> 761:33. <ni, avec ce que j'entendais de sa conversation> 761:35. <était si aimable avec ma grand'mère> 761:37. <personnelle contre moi, car> 761:39. <départir d'une grande> 761:43. De deux ou trois qui étaient de la famille ou de l'intimité de Montargis et dont Montargis cita par hasard le nom, il dit avec> 762:7. <mépris. Mais qui n'eût pas semblé efféminé, jugé d'après la vie qu'il voulait> 762:10. <virile? (lui-même racontait que dans ses voyages à pied, après des heures de marche, il se jetait>]

762:13. Et je remarquai que même autour de cet annulaire qu'il savait tendre il n'y en avait aucune.

762:14. Mais ce parti pris sa* virilité> **762:28.** <avec sa fille. [762:21. <vrai, c'est par là que les lettres de Mme de Sévigné sont vraiment profondes, humaines. C'était du reste> 762:23. <de Lafontaine*.] {762:28-763:1}

763:2. —Mais une fois seule avec elle, elle n'avait rien à lui dire.

763:4. <Certainement> **763:26.** <ignorance de la vie. [763:5. <qui les remarquons»*. Et même si elle n'avait rien à lui dire, elle était du moins près d'elle. Et Labruyère* nous dit> 763:9. <de Fleurus d'une> 763:13. <que d'autre*. Elle a en somme passé> 763:18. <d'un ton plus péremptoire et presque tranchant> 763:24. <Dieu. Ses démarcations>] {763:27-763:37}

763:38. Ces* réflexions sur la tristesse> **764:16.** <fines mouches. [763:39. <devaient le même soir amener ma grand'mère à me dire que M. de Fleurus comprenait> 763:41. <œuvres que Mme de Villeparisis, et surtout> 763:43. <club, souvent grossiers, et lui donnait des intuitions presque féminines), il n'y laissait pas seulement paraître une délicatesse de pensée que montrent> 764:6. <où il parlait de ces sentiments si fiers, sur> 764:8. <chœurs de sœurs, de mères, de fiancés, qui> 764:10. <de Fleurus, avec>]

□**764:16.** —Mon Dieu, j'aurais pu vous faire aller dans ce château qui vous intéresse, dit-il à ma grand'mère, quand il y avait encore des Montmorency, mais leur famille est éteinte.

—Tu es aimable pour ton cousin le duc de Montmorency, dit Montargis.

—Ah! permets, je parlais des Montmorency, des membres de la famille de Montmorency. Le charmant homme auquel tu fais allusion ne sachant probablement pas quel nom prendre et refléchissant qu'il n'y avait plus de Montmorency, a trouvé sans inconvénient d'arborer le nom de cette station de la ligne du Nord. Il avait peut-être une maison de ce côté-là, on ne sait jamais! ajouta-t-il en rentrant pudiquement dans sa poche un mouchoir brodé dont il venait d'apercevoir que le liséré de couleur dépassait, avec la mine effarouchée d'une femme pudibonde, mais point innocente, cachant des appâts que par excès de scrupules elle jugerait indécents [*cf.* 765:2]. Toujours est-il, ajouta-t-il en se tournant vers ma grand'mère, que les propriétaires de ce château dont vous me parliez montrent en ce moment combien ils étaient peu dignes de le posséder, car ils vont le vendre, et malheureusement il est à craindre que ce soit des gens plus indignes encore qui vont l'acheter. En tout cas, je ne peux* plus rien savoir [*cf.* 764:30] d'une demeure sotte et infidèle qui s'est laissée vendre à de tels gens et défigurer par eux. Je ne veux plus avoir rien de commun avec elle qu'avec une belle cousine Avaray qui a mal tourné et qui n'est plus belle. Mais je garde le portrait de la maison comme celui de la cousine, et je regarde souvent ces beaux traits qui ignoraient encore la trahison. Je ne vais pas jusqu'à le porter sur moi mais je pourrai vous en faire donner communication. La photographie acquiert un peu de la dignité qui lui manque quand elle nous montre des choses qui n'existent plus.

764:17. Il raconta> **764:30.** <que je mets mes balais.» [764:18. <où Marie-Antoinette avait passé, dont le jardin était> 764:19. <riches financiers Gebzeltern qui l'avaient achetée.

—Avoir été la demeure des Guermantes et appartenir aux Gebzeltern!! s'écria-t-il.]

765:3. Ces gens ont commencé par détruire le jardin et le remplacer par un jardin anglais. Une personne qui détruit un jardin de Lenôtre est aussi coupable que celle qui lacère un tableau de Poussin. Pour cela, les Gebzelter* devraient être en prison.

765:6. Il est vrai> **765:22.** <avait fait allusion> [**765:11.** <est du style du Trianon, dit> **765:14.** <dépare entièrement la façade de Gabriel, dit M. de Fleurus. Evidemment> 765:18. <Mme Gebzeltern ait> 765:21. <malgré les prières de Montargis qui>]

765:22. <allusion devant M. de Fleurus—qui avait dû trouver cela bien peu viril—à la tristesse que j'éprouvais souvent le soir avant de m'endormir. Je tardai encore un peu, puis m'en allait*, et je fus>

765:26. <je fus bien étonné> **766:21.** <en quels termes le faire. [765:27. <frapper à ma porte et ayant> 765:28. <de Fleurus qui> 765:30. C'est Fleurus. Puis-je> 765:30. <monsieur? Monsieur me dit-il, du même ton, mon neveu disait tout à l'heure> 765:34. <j'en ai un dans ma malle que vous> 765:37. <pas content. 765:38. <de Fleurus avec> 765:39. <que Montargis lui> 765:43. <répondit-il d'un ton plus doux. 766:1. <personnel, si peu> 766:12. <pas cruelles, je>] {766:22-766:39}

766:39. Quelques minutes se passèrent ainsi, puis, de sa voix redevenue cinglante, il me jeta: «bonjour, monsieur» et partit.

767:1. Aussi après tous les sentiments élevés que je lui avais entendu exprimer fus-je bien étonné le lendemain matin qui était le jour de son départ, sur la plage, au moment où j'allais prendre mon bain, comme M. de Fleurus s'était approché de moi pour m'avertir que ma grand'mère m'attendait aussitôt que je serais sorti de l'eau, de l'entendre me dire>

767:7. <me dire, en me pinçant> **767:23.** <costume de bain. [767:11. <je l'adore, je n'aime rien autant qu'elle au monde> 767:19. <précaution, à l'instant vous vous seriez>] {767:23-767:26}

767:26. Vous me faites> **767:35.** <je reçus dans une reliure sur laquelle mes initiales étaient entourées d'une branche de myosotis, le livre de Bergotte qu'il m'avait prêté et que je lui avais fait rapporter au moment de son départ. {767:42-779:34}

780:10. See after 740:3.

786:1. Quand quelques jours après le départ de M. de Fleurus ma grand'mère> **786:11.** <de ce qui la concernait personnellement. [786:2. <que Montargis venait> 786:3. <quittât Bricquebec elle> 786:7. <enfantillage, de cette coquetterie qui>]

786:11. Cette semaine-là, je ne pus pas plus l'avoir à moi le jour que le soir. Si je rentrais pour être un peu seul avec elle, on me disait qu'elle n'était pas là; ou bien elle s'enfermait avec Françoise pour de longs conciliabules qu'il ne m'était pas permis de troubler.

786:14. Malheureusement je laissai apercevoir le mécontentement que me causa le projet de photographie et surtout la satisfaction puérile que ma grand'mère paraissait en ressentir, pour que Françoise> **787:13.** <lui dire bonsoir> [786:19. <l'accroître par la façon sentimentale et attendrie dont elle me parla et à laquelle je ne voulus pas> 786:23. <Françoise lui a> 786:28. <tour, en souriaient elles-mêmes aussi. Mais ma grand'mère s'aperçut aussi que j'avais l'air ennuyé, si bien qu'elle me dit que si cela pouvait me contrarier elle renoncerait à ce projet. 786:33. <preuve de finesse et de puissance en ajoutant quelques paroles désagréables destinées> 786:36. <voir son magnifique chapeau, je réussis> 786:42. <manifestation de travers mesquins que nous détestons et cherchons à détruire plutôt que comme

la forme> 787:1. <procurer. Le point de départ de ma mauvaise humeur venait surtout de ce que cette semaine-là ma grand'mère avait paru une fois et que je n'avais pas pu l'avoir un instant à moi. 787:9. <avec Montargis je> 787:10. <j'allais avoir à retrouver et à embrasser ma>]

787:13. <bonsoir, je n'entendais rien et finissais par me coucher, en larmes et lui en voulant un peu de cette indifférence nouvelle avec laquelle elle me privait ainsi d'une joie dont j'avais tant besoin, sur laquelle j'avais tant compté et je m'endormais dans les larmes. {787:22-798:33}

□**798:34.** Si je rentrais ainsi assez tard à Bricquebec, c'est que depuis quelque temps ma grand'mère qui ne désapprouvait guère pour moi des projets, s'il* devaient être réalisés de concert avec Montargis dont elle estimait que l'influence sur moi était salutaire, avait permis que j'allasse une fois ou deux par semaine dîner avec lui. Et à l'heure où les autres jours j'étais déjà à table, Montargis qui avait fait atteler m'emmenait dîner fort loin de Bricquebec au grand restaurant de Rivebelle où se réunissaient à certains jours toutes les élégances de cette côte beaucoup plus à la mode alors qu'aujourd'hui et où des spéculateurs audacieux avaient ouvert des lieux d'attractions et de plaisirs qui sont aujourd'hui désertés. Ces jours-là ma grand'mère exigeait que contre mon habitude je rentrasse me reposer une heure sur mon lit avant de partir avec Montargis, et dès six heures et demie je rentrais à l'hôtel>

799:22. <hôtel, sonnant maintenant sans timidité et sans tristesse le lift qui ne restait pas silencieux comme autrefois pen-

---

□**799:22.** *(B-A)* <je rentrais à l'hôtel; j'adressais un sourire au directeur et en recueillais un, sans l'ombre de dégoût, dans sa figure que depuis que j'étais à Bolbec mon intelligence injectée et peu à peu transformée comme une préparation d'histoire naturelle. Ses traits étaient* devenus courants, changés* d'un sens médiocre mais intelligible comme une écriture qu'on lit et dès* ne ressemblent* plus en rien à ces caractères bizarres, affreux, intolérables que son visage m'avait présentés ce premier jour où j'avais devant moi un personnage maintenant oublié, et si je pouvais* à l'évoquer méconnaissable, difficile avec la personnalité insignifiante et polie dont il n'était que la caricature, hideux* et sommaire. Sans timidité ni tristesse maintenant, je sonnais le lift qui ne restait pas silencieux comme autrefois pendant que je m'élevais à côté de lui dans l'ascenseur, dans une sorte de cage>

dant que je m'élevais à côté de lui dans l'ascenseur, comme dans une cage>

799:25. <cage thoracique mobile, qui se fût déplacée le long de la colonne montante et qui cherchant parce qu'il avait un engagement dans une plage plus méridionale pour la fin de la saison à faire fermer l'hôtel le plus tôt possible, me répétait:

—Cela commence à devenir vide, on s'en va, les jours baissent.

800:26. Et c'était lui qui restait sans recevoir de réponse* au cours de la courte traversée> **800:37.** <fenêtre des cabinets. [800:29. <ramifications de couloir dans>]

802:15. Arrivé au dernier étage, je quittai l'ascenseur. Mais au lieu d'entrer chez moi je m'engageai plus avant> **802:25.** <était adossé l'hôtel> [802:19. <bout qui regardait le côté de la colline et de la vallée>]

□**802:25.** <l'hôtel et d'où, sous une brume précoce qui la gazait déjà, s'échappait par saccades un bruit secret d'infiltration ou de source, ne contenait>

802:25. <ne contenait qu'une> **803:9.** <verreries de Gellé*. [802:29. <ces petites architectures> 802:40. J'entrais dans> 803:4. <de la baie des triangles [*blanc*] d'une immobile écume [*blanc*] avec la délicatesse>]

□**803:9.** Mais le plus souvent il faisait beau. Et parfois sur la mer calme des mouettes éparpillées flottaient comme des nymphéas que selon l'heure je voyais blancs, jaunes, ou quand le soleil était couché, roses. Elles semblaient offrir un but si inerte aux petits flots qui les ballotaient que ceux-ci par contraste semblaient dans leur poursuite avoir une intention, prendre de la vie. Puis tout d'un coup, s'échappant comme d'un déguisement de leur incognito de fleurs, les mouettes montaient toutes ensemble vers le soleil, tandis que de l'extrémité la plus éloignée de la côte, ne daignant pas voir leurs yeux, un grand oiseau solitaire et hâtif, fouettant l'air du mouvement régulier de ses ailes, passait à toute vitesse au-dessus de la plage tachée çà et là de reflets pareils sur le sable à de petits morceaux de papier rouge déchirés, et la traversait dans toute sa longueur, sans ralentir son allure, sans détourner son attention, sans dévier de son chemin comme un émissaire, qui va porter bien loin de là un ordre urgent et capital.

803:10. Bientôt les jours diminuèrent et au moment où je poussais ma porte, en entrant, celle-ci faisait refluer une lumière rose qui remplissait la chambre et changeait les rideaux de mousseline blanche en lampas* aurore; elle émanait du ciel violet qui [*blanc*] par la figure raide, géométrique, passagère et fulgurante du soleil, pareille à la représentation de quelque* signes miraculeux, de quelque apparition mystique s'inclinait>

803:14. <s'inclinait vers la mer> **804:14.** <des images de la mer. [803:31. <bande du ciel> 803:42. <élevées penchent* au-dessus>]

804:31. Mais bien souvent ce n'était, en effet, que des images, tant ma pensée, habitant à ces moments-là la surface de mon corps que j'allais habiller pour tâcher de paraître le plus plaisant possible aux regards féminins qui me dévisageraient dans le restaurant illuminé de Rivabella*, était incapable de mettre de la profondeur derrière la couleur des choses, et si, sous ma fenêtre>

804:31. <ma fenêtre, le vol> **805:18.** <vaporeux du ciel. [804:43. <rouge comme la lune>] 805:4. <deux côtés duquel> 805:6. <tirer jusqu'à son lit. Et> 805:8. <femme entrée, entre deux visites, dans une galerie> 805:13. <l'horizon tellement de la même couleur que lui, ainsi que dans une toile apparaissait impressionniste*, qu'il semblait>]

805:18. Parfois la mer emplissait presque toute ma fenêtre, surélevée qu'elle était par une bande de ciel> **806:27.** <entre les spécimen* de tous les genres de l'histoire naturelle et les provenances de tous les pays, les plats inusités, aussitôt commandés par Montargis, qui tenteraient ma gourmandise ou mon imagination. [805:22. <croyais être entre les deux de la mer encore> 805:26. <horizontales, qu'elle avait l'air par une préméditation> 805:29. <bibliothèque montraient* des nuages> 805: 31. <lumière, semblaient comme> 805:42. <maître. Le rose> 805:43. <rien à voir. Je> 806:5. <m'attrister que je laissais ainsi mourir au haut des rideaux et sans lui donner de regrets l'heure où d'habitude> 806:13. Je me disais: il est temps, je m'étirais> 806:24. <joie que je me rendais plus complets* par

tous ces appâts> 806:25. <dipos à toute une> 806:27. <de Montargis et>] {806:32-808:4}

808:5. Les premiers temps> **809:6.** <j'étais à Bricquebec, un contrôle minutieux et constant> [808:12. <l'air d'une arborisation qu'on> 808:13. <d'onyx ou d'agate> 808:14. <de voiture de Rivebelle, souvent même que nous y montions à Bricquebec si> 808:19. <ne signifiait pas abandon de mes projets, réclusion dans une chambre, dans la grande salle> 808:22. <musique des Tziganes> 808:23. <lampes triomphèrent* aisément> 808:25. <montais gaiement à côté de Montargis dans le coupé qui nous attendait tout attelé sous l'averse. 808:38. Peut-être des chefs-d'œuvre ont-ils été écrits en bâillant.» 808:41. Et,—comme* un médecin ayant trouvé> 808:43. <santé, m'avait tracé> 809:2. <accident—subordonnant tous les plaisirs>]

□**809:7.** <constant, faisant toujours attention à l'état de chaleur, d'appétit, de fatigue où je me trouvais pour savoir si je pouvais ôter mon manteau, manger d'un plat, faire un tour, me rappelant exactement avant de boire, combien j'avais déjà pris de bière pour rester un peu au-dessous de l'unique verre qu'en dehors des périodes de crises je ne devais pas dépasser.

809:7. On ne m'aurait pas fait toucher à la tasse> **809:9.** <lendemain. Mais nous arrivions à Rivebelle, et aussitôt, comme s'il ne devait plus jamais avoir de lendemain, ni de fins élevées à réaliser, disparaissait ce mécanisme précis de prudente hygiène qui fonctionnait pour les sauvegarder.

809:17. Tandis qu'un valet> **809:37.** <général vainqueur. [809:18. <paletot, Montargis me disait:

—Tu n'auras pas froid? tu ferais peut-être> 809:23. <mais en tout cas j'avais oublié la peur de tomber malade> 809:27. <Tziganes> 809:35. <venant de* chanter> {809:38-809:41}

809:42. La dose de bière qu'à Bricquebec je> **810:8.** <ne me rappelais même plus. [810:2. <lucide sa saveur représentait> 810:3. <appéciable et pourtant aisément> 810:4. <en une heure sans même la goûter et je donnais au violoniste qui avait bien joué les deux>] {810:8-811:26}

811:27. J'entendais le grondement> **811:33.** <de la couleur. [811:28. <il y avait du plaisir indépendant>] {811:33-811:37}

811:33. Tout ce que je demandais c'était à* ne pas sortir de cette passivité, je laissais la musique> **812:23.** <je répétais à mi-voix> [811:38. <note où elle devait se poser> 811:39. <chimiques qui débitent en quantité des corps qui ne se rencontrent accidentellement dans la nature que dans ces cas fort rares—ce restaurant> 812:17. <inconnu; il* sont l'enfer le plus impitoyable, le plus privé d'issue*, pour le malheureux jaloux; pour eux le plaisir physique existe seul. Et ils sont l'enfer le plus impitoyable [*repetition sic*], le plus dépourvu> 812:22. <celle qui la remplit tout entière>]

□**812:23.** <à mi-voix les mots de cet air, je lui ai rendu son baiser. Cette volupté particulière à lui, il me la faisait éprouver; inconnue de moi il y a un instant et maintenant si chère, que j'aurais quitté mes parents pour suivre le motif dans le monde singulier qu'il construisait en lignes tour à tour pleines de langueur et de vivacité. Quoiqu'un tel plaisir ne soit pas d'une sorte qui donne plus de valeur à l'être auquel il s'ajoute car il n'est perçu que de lui seul, et quoique chaque fois dans notre vie nous avons déplu à une femme qui nous a aperçu elle ne peut* pas savoir si à ce moment-là nous ne possédions cette félicité intérieure et subjective qui par conséquent ne changeait rien au jugement qu'elle a porté, les données sur lesquelles elle l'a fondé restent les mêmes malgré la joie nouvelle que nous ressentons, je me sentais plus puissant, presque irrésistible. Et quand un musicien se détachant et se plaçant devant l'orchestre chanta la belle mélodie de Reynaldo Hahn: «Je sais un coin perdu de la grève Bretonne* où j'aurais tant aimé pendant les soirs d'automne, chère à vous emmener; il me semble que mon amour pour Mlle de Silariat* (à qui j'adressais mentalement cette proposition) n'était plus quelque chose de déplaisant et dont elle pourrait sourire, mais avait précisément la beauté touchante, la séduction de cette musique. La mélodie comme un milieu sympathique où nous nous serions rencontré* avait établi entre Mlle de Silariat* et moi tant d'intimité que le mot chère adressé à elle me semblait aussi naturel dans ma bouche que l'était l'accent que la phrase musicale lui donnait. Et ne doutant pas que mon projet ne lui parut* aussi voluptueux que me semblait cette phrase, mon amour timide et malheureux se sentit soudain consolé par toute la poésie que je sentais se dégager pour Mlle de Silariat* et par cette nouvelle qu'en ce moment «par ce soir d'automne» elle était occupée à la tristesse que je ne l'eusse pas «emmenée dans un coin perdu de la terre bretonne.» {812:43-814:26}

814:22. Si par hasard pour finir la soirée avec telle bande d'amis de Montargis que nous avions rencontrée, nous allions au Casino d'une autre plage, si Montargis allait avec eux et me mettait seul dans une voiture, je recommandais>

814:31. <je recommandais au cocher> **814:43.** <nécessaire pour l'amener jusqu'à ma raison. {815:1-815:28}

815:28. Ne faisant en somme que concentrer dans une soirée la paresse qui pour les autres hommes est diluée> **816:6.** <l'espoir de sa ruche. [815:35. <cerveau, l'œuvre dont> 815:36. <raison d'être de leur vie. 815:38. <venu pour me tuer> 816:2. <ne pas être séparé d'elle, je me serais laissé> 816:4. <fumée des cigarettes, qui>] {816:7-817:20}

817:21. Montargis, avant qu'il eût fait la connaissance de sa maîtresse actuelle, avait tellement vécu> **818:1.** <peut lui trouver. [817:23. <qui se tenaient ces soirs-là> 817:26. <retrouver leurs amants, d'autres tâcher* d'en trouver> 817:29. <une nuit annuelle. Il> 817:32. <savait pour toutes les autres femmes que son actrice> 817:35. Et l'une chuchotaient*: «C'est le petit Montargis. 817:36. <toujours son actrice. C'est> 817:42. Mais ce n'est pas ça; il ne lui faut pas de gueuses*.] {818:1-818:2}

818:2. Elle a des pieds comme des bateaux, des faux sourcils, et des dessous sales! **818:40.** <au lieu d'être ces médailles sous lesquelles se cachaient des souvenirs d'amour. [818:5. Regarde-moi> 818:8. <il me reconnaissait bien> 818:8. <moi.» Mais pourtant entre elles> 818:12. <pas pu m'y rendre. 818:13. <éternellement incomplet, dans> 818:18. <dans le regard une fois qu'il nous connaît et s'adresse à nous dans le sourire qui acquiesce> 818:20. Et pourtant même aussi réduit que je le voyais leur visage, était> 818:25. <pour Montargis qui> 818:36. <qu'elles suivraient pendant>] {818:42-825:18; 825:34-826:6; 827:7-827:16; 828:11-828:21; 828:33-840:24; 842:30-866:2}

□**825:20.** Ce fut dans ce restaurant de Rivebelle que nous fîmes connaissance du peintre Elstir dont on verra plus tard que l'influence sur ma vie devait être grande. Sans savoir son nom nous l'avions remarqué qui venait quand tout le monde commençait à partir, dîner seul à une table mise à l'écart. C'était un homme grand, d'un visage régulier et d'un corps athlétique, mais de qui le regard songeur restait fixé avec application dans le vague.

—Comment vous ne connaissez pas le célèbre peintre Elstir, avait répondu le restaurateur quand nous lui avions demandé qui était ce dîneur tardif et solitaire.

J'avais entendu prononcer son nom par Swann, je ne me rappelais pas ce qu'il avait dit de lui ni s'il le connaissait personnellement, mais j'ignorais que je ne me le rappelais pas car je ne me le demandai pas un instant. Swann avait certainement voulu parler de lui comme d'un de ses amis et d'un grand artiste.

—C'est un grand ami de Swann, dis-je de la meilleure foi à Saint-Loup. Il a un immense talent.

□**826:7.** Elstir n'était peut-être pas encore à cette époque aussi célèbre que prétendait le patron de l'établissement. Mais il avait été un des premiers à habiter ce restaurant alors que ce n'était encore qu'une sorte de ferme et à y amener une colonie d'artistes. (Ils avaient du reste tous émigré ailleurs dès que la ferme où l'on mangeait en plein air sous un ample auvent était devenu* un centre élegant et Elstir ne revenait en ce moment à Rivebelle qu'à cause d'une absence de sa femme avec laquelle il était fixé non loin de là).

826:18. Mais un grand talent> **826:37.** <pas une fortune. [826:21. <questions de quelque anglaise*> 826:24. <recevait, même de l'étranger> 826:29. <admiration des étrangers injustifiée> 826:33. Il y a bien les> 826:35. <petit lever de soleil sur la mer qu'Elstie*>]

□**826:38.** Nous étions encore à certains points de vue si près de l'enfance, Saint-Loup et moi que la vue d'Elstir de qui nous supposions qu'il était un grand artiste nous causa autant d'émotion que si nous eussions connu et admiré ses œuvres. Puis nous supportions impatiemment qu'il ignorât, et aussi que les gens qui étaient encore dans le restaurant et se montraient Elstir ignorassent comme lui, que nous étions Saint-Loup et moi liés avec son brillant ami M. Swann. Notre enthousiasme, notre incognito nous étouffant, nous fîmes remettre à Elstir une lettre signée de nous deux [*cf.* 826:1] où nous lui disions que son grand ami M. Swann nous avait cent fois parlé de lui, et que nous demandions à lui présenter l'hommage de notre admiration.

826:38. Nous le vîmes> **826:43.** <remarqués par lui. [826:39. <dîner, se mettre à fumer, demander ses affaires> 826:42. <nous aurions autant souhaité maintenant—autant qu'avant nous l'aurions craint—de partir>]

□**827:17.** Mais au moment où il arrivait près de la porte, il avait fait un crochet et était venu à nous. J'avais pensé que le nom de Saint-Loup l'impressionnerait particulièrement mais ce fut avec moi qu'il causa davantage ce soir-là, et un jour suivant, où j'allai le voir comme il m'y avait invité et où Saint-Loup n'avait pu m'accompagner, il prodigua pour moi seul une amabilité—me donnant même une étude qu'il venait de finir—qui était>

827:36. <qui était aussi supérieure> **828:11.** <ou froissé.>

828:21. Mais ayant voulu produire pour les autres, en produisant> **828:32.** <être pour nous dès que nous l'avons connue. [828:32. <société dont il était devenu indifférent à elle; la pratique>]

828:32. Le plus grand charme qu'eut pour moi cette visite que je fis à l'atelier d'Elstir, ce fut d'ouvrir un champ nouveau aux désirs que j'avais apportés à Balbec et auxquels la réalité si différente n'avait guère répondu. Sans doute pour ce qui était par exemple, de l'église de Balbec la conversation d'Elstir, les paroles qu'il me dit furent aussi efficaces que ses tableaux pour me faire oublier ma déception et à* me faire souhaiter de revenir devant la vieille façade.

840:25. —Comment vous avez été déçu par ce porche, mais c'est la plus belle Bible historiée que le peuple ait jamais pu contempler, je vous assure en aucun temps, on n'a jamais rien fait d'aussi chouette.

840:27. Cette Vierge> **842:20.** <tout orientales. [840:41. <était tout autre> 841:2. <le geste d'Elisabeth qui> 841:14. <aidant sa jeune femme> 841:15. <cœur pour qu'elle voie qu'il bat vraiment; et l'ange qui> 841:27. <et des joies des élus> 841:30. <c'est autrement chouette que tout ce que> 842:3. <ce n'est pas lui que j'avais vu. 842:5. <échasses et* forment>]

842:20. <tout orientales; et tenez j'ai là la photographie d'un chapiteau qui reproduit> **842:23.** <par des navigateurs.

842:23. <par des navigateurs.

Je vis en effet des dragons presque chinois qui se dévoraient> **842:.28.** <presque persane.

□**842:29.** N'importe ces autres mots, «délicieuse poésie, profondes pensées, poème d'amour en l'honneur de la Vierge», mon esprit les avait maintenant accueillies*, ils l'avaient enflammé; ils lui avaient rendu un désir nouveau d'aller devant le porche où je pourrais voir «la plus belle Bible historiée que le peuple ait jamais eu* devant lui et les balustrades de la Jérusalem céleste». Un homme de grand goût venait de jeter en moi les fondements de nouveaux désirs. Et plus tard cet homme de goût je n'ai pas eu besoin d'aller le consulter dans un atelier, à Balbec; car peu à peu il s'en est développé un en moi-même qui, devant les monuments, séance tenante, et même plus tard encore au fur et à mesure que les déceptions de la vie, l'affaiblissement de ma pensée ou le desséchement* de mon cœur eurent diminué ma faculté d'admirer, j'eus soin d'ajouter en moi à l'homme de goût qui vieillissait un peu, un historien, un érudit qui à Balbec par exemple devant les statues des porches ou les vitraux des chapelles, au lieu d'écouter en lui ce qu'y éveillait leur vue cherchait à leur trouver un autre intérêt que leur beauté artistique, en les rattachant à l'histoire d'un saint dont le culte avait Balbec pour principal centre au moyen âge, parce que l'église possédait les reliques de ce saint, en compulsant les vieux lectionnaires*, en cherchant dans les chansons de geste où il est question des miracles de ce saint, pour voir si Balbec ou quelque lieu approprié n'y était pas nommé, et quand j'abaissais mes yeux sur le pavage de la nef et du chœur, en cherchant à y lire les relations de la vieille église avec l'histoire de France, les raisons qui firent que tel grand écrivain y avait sa sépulture, que tel prince, dont je savais que par son testament il avait demandé que son cœur fut* déposé dans un couvent de Paris, avait été enterré ici—me consolant de ne pas recevoir la même impression poétique que j'avais eue jadis à Combray devant les pierres tombales pareilles aux alvéoles d'un miel durci, doré et doux.

Mais bien plus que ces conversations, ces tableaux avaient changé la forme de mes rêves, avaient dirigé constamment mes désirs sur ce qu'ils avaient dédaigné jusque-là. Par exemple, à Balbec, je m'étais toujours devant la mer, efforcé d'expulser du champ de ma vision les baigneuses du premier plan, les yachts de plaisance aux voiles trop blanches comme un costume de plage en coutil blanc, tout qui ce m'empêchait de me persuader que je contemplais le flot immémorial qui déroulait déjà cette même vie mystérieuse avant l'apparition de l'espèce humaine jusqu'à ce que j'eusse vu dans l'atelier d'Elstir une marine de lui ou une jeune femme en robe de barège dans un yacht échenillant le long de ses drisses au soleil et au vent, ses flammes multicolores, mit dans mon imagination le «double» spirituel d'une robe de barège et du grand pavoi d'un yacht, qui réchauffa, y couva un désir insatiable d'en voir le plus tôt possible comme si cela ne m'était jamais arrivé. Malheureusement il était trop tard dans la saison et je ne rêvais que de revenir à Balbec en plein été, pendant ces jours dont jusque-là l'ensoleillement d'un temps radieux me semblait simplement cacher sous la parure banale de l'universel été, cette côte de brumes et de tempêtes, et ces beaux jours n'être qu'une simple interruption au lieu de la réalité véritable, l'équivalent de ce qu'on appelle en musique une mesure pour rien. Maintenant vivait en moi le désir qu'ils revinssent, éveillé non seulement par l'aquarelle qui représentait les yachts mais aussi par une autre où au bord de la mer, pâlie, vaporisée par le soleil, et où les ailes blanches de quelques bateaux semblaient engourdies de chaleur comme des papillons pâmés, j'avais vu en contraste, dans l'eau encore mais tout au pied de la falaise, rose, gigantesque, friable et dentelée comme les arc-boutants d'une cathédrale, les ombres qui étaient mises à l'abri et au frais, j'avais attendu avec impatience, la prochaine journée brûlante où je pourrais aller guetter dans l'eau entre les rochers, ces déesses cachées qui évoquaient la luminosité et la chaleur d'un temps radieux, mieux peut-être que ne faisait l'horizon ensoleillé et blanc par leur beauté d'un vert glissant et verni, par leurs prunelles d'un blanc intense et sombre.

Quand j'avais vu, en descendant du train, l'église de Balbec j'aurais voulu pouvoir la séparer des gens qui prenaient du café où était écrit le mot: «Billard». Mais Elstir, me rendit moins exclusif, d'abord en me montrant de petites études de lui. Le charme qu'il faisait ressortir comme caractéristique d'une ville de province française—certes on ne voit pas cela en Amérique—c'était celui qui est fait de la juxtaposition des scènes pittoresques de la vie populaire famillèrement dominées, au-dessus du «marché», du magasin de bonneterie ou du grand café, par deux vieilles tours de la vieille église abbatiale, image d'une aïeule authentique qui n'était pas mise là pour orner mais qui faisait vraiment partie de l'histoire et du passé de la ville, née à ses pieds.

Mais le même goût d'harmoniser la vieille église avec ce qui l'entourait, certains tableaux d'Elstir me l'avaient doué* plus que ces petites études et d'une manière plus profonde. Dans ces petits dessins, presque tous à la plume, il n'était qu'un homme de goût, qui se souvient habilement de ce qu'il sait. Mais quand il faisait vraiment œuvre de créateur, dans ses grandes toiles, c'était merveille de voir comme tout ce qu'Elstir pouvait savoir—et Dieu sait si dans sa curiosité d'historien, d'amateur d'art et de savant, il s'était instruit—il avait le courage de les oublier quand il faisait un tableau afin de prendre les choses comme elles apparaissent, à ce moment premier le seul vrai, où notre intelligence n'étant pas encore intervenue pour nous expliquer ce qu'elles sont, nous ne substituons pas à l'impression qu'elles nous ont donnée les notions que nous avons d'elles, où devant une impression de bleu aérien comme en donne si souvent la mer, ou du bleu compact et liquide comme on* donne si souvent le ciel, nous n'avons pas encore reconnu notre erreur et conclu à la suite d'un raisonnement que nous ne pouvons pas être en présence de celui de ces deux éléments que nous avions cru d'abord. Quand il peignait il n'avait plus de connaissances en archéologie; les monuments anciens et les bâtisses modernes étaient alors pour lui sur un tel pied d'égalité, l'église avec ce qui l'entourait, deux tableaux d'Elstir que non seulement son «Ecole communale» à Nemours valait, si elle ne lui était supérieure, son Abbaye de Verclay, mais que dans une même toile, représentant un coucher de soleil, la contemplation du peintre, placée comme au cœur des rayons roses du soir enveloppait d'un même amour et fondait dans une seule lumière la cathédrale et la poste. On lui reprochait dans ces tableaux-là où il se rapprochait un peu des impressionnistes de ne faire que des «effets» et de se contenter d'un air matériel, sans se rendre compte qu'an contraire aucun art n'était aussi purement spirituel. C'est parce qu'Elstir arrivait à composer entièrement sa toile, rien qu'avec des parcelles de réalité qui toutes avaient été personnellement senties, sans l'adjonction d'une seule qu'il se fut* contenté matériellement de transcrire, qu'elle avait cette même unité profonde qu'ont nos impressions, et que les objets les plus différents pour l'érudit ou l'homme pratique—le chef-d'œuvre d'architecture et la bâtisse moderne médiocre mais utile—y semblaient des accidents homogènes produits par un même regard. Et cette unité correspondait à celle de la nature; car tous ces monuments qui chez de très grands peintres, ayant traité les mêmes sujets, continuaient à rester isolés, comme dans une description exacte et composite, manifestent tous dans la nature à cette heure-là la loi d'optique. Ces tableaux d'Elstir rendaient pour moi semblables à eux, c'est-à-dire me permettaient d'admirer des choses naturelles auxquelles je n'avais jamais fait attention et par là me permettaient de les aimer. En me montrant une petite étude qu'il venait de terminer et qui représentait une huître entrouverte en son bénitier calcaire doublé d'émail, sur les beaux plis d'une nappe damassée à côté d'un couteau brillant des reflets d'un jour terne, il avait fait autant que s'il m'eut* donné ce chef-d'œuvre, ou plutôt il m'en avait donné mille, (le chef-d'œuvre quotidien que me présenterait indéfiniment, après chaque déjeuner, cette chose que jusque-là j'avais regardée avec ennui, une table desservie. De beaucoup des endroits dont j'avais entendu la première fois le nom quand avec ma grand'mère j'étais arrivé à Balbec par le petit chemin de fer d'intérêt local, Briseville, Fourgeville, Marville en me montrant une étude, en me disant un mot, il m'avait désigné le charme, auquel parfois il ajoutait le charme plus général, —et entièrement renouvelé—de la saison ou de l'heure.

C'est ainsi que jadis aux Champs-Elysées capable d'aimer la neige unie et pure, j'avais tant cru que Gilberte de* viendrait pas, de voir la Seine déjà à demi libre, avec la glace attaquée partout par les pics des terrassiers; mais un «Effet de dégel à Briseville» que je vis dans l'atelier d'Elstir et où la dissimulation de toutes limites sous la glace cassée en mille morceaux et du milieu de laquelle s'élevaient des arbres presque entièrement défeuillés, empêchait de savoir si on avait devant soi le lit d'un fleuve ou une clairière dans les bois, m'avait appris la beauté qu'il y avait dans cette immense équivoque de reflets où l'œil ébloui est incertain s'il voit briller

866:2. Le séjour de Montargis à Bricquebec toucha à sa fin, et ma grand'mère était désireuse [*cf.* 825:7]> **866:24.** <l'en excuser, le lendemain> [866:6. <venir pour lui de nombreuses>

---

un morceau de glace azurée, ou une lueur de soleil sur l'eau, tandis que les feuilles mortes mêlées à la neige et aussi à la rousseur des cimes des arbres réverbèrent dans le ciel et son miroir glacé des lueurs roses comme un coucher de soleil qui dure du matin au soir. Aussi ce tableau me donna-t-il l'envie d'aller à Equenonville et j'avouai à Elstir qu'avec la Pointe du Raz, c'était maintenant ce que j'avais le plus envie de voir.

—La Pointe du Raz, d'ici, me dit-il, ce serait tout un voyage [*cf.* 854:32]. Et puis même si Equenonville n'était pas si près, je vous le conseillerais malgré cela davantage. La pointe* du Raz c'est épatant, mais enfin c'est toujours la grande falaise normande ou bretonne que vous connaissez, poussée seulement au gigantesque. Equenonville (je vous parle de la côte) c'est tout autre chose, avec les rochers sur une plage basse; je ne connais rien en France d'analogue. Cela rappelle plutôt certains aspects de la Floride. C'est très curieux.

Et il m'avait aussitôt donné le goût que je n'avais eu* jusque-là de regarder les plages pour elles-mêmes en ajoutant:

—Et puis la plage même, la ligne de la plage y est ravissante tandis qu'à Balbec la plage est quelconque.

C'est ainsi qu'il introduisait en tout ces différences, des qualités esthétiques qui m'enflammaient, comme quand, à propos d'une porte de l'église de Balbec lui ayant dit avec dédain, mais avec ennui, ce que je ne faisais que répéter un lieu commun:

—Ce n'est pas intéressant, c'est restauré.

—Oh! il y a restauration et restauration. C'est une très belle restauration qui a été admirablement faite au XVIIe siècle par un grand architecte; c'est loin d'être sans beauté.

Le matin où j'étais allé le voir, il m'avait retenu à déjeuner heureux d'avoir auprès de lui quelqu'un par qui il se sentait admiré, il avait su mettre un sens riche dans son invitation, dans l'acte de m'accompagner à la gare, dans tous les gestes et démarches de l'amabilité devenus nécessaires pour exprimer ce qu'il ressentait, et que les autres hommes qui n'en usent que par habitude ont laissé s'évider et devenir si secs. Au moment de me quitter il m'avait fait don de deux «Variations en opale» qu'il venait de finir et qui représentaient l'une, un curieux effet produit par des globes de gaz allumés sur la plage dans la nuit et en* feu d'artifice qu'on tirait, l'autre la plage de Balbec irisée comme un arc-en-ciel par le prisme qu'y émiettaient d'innombrables méduses, transparentes comme de grandes girandoles mauves, bleuâtres et rosées. En le quittant j'aurais peut être* dû chercher à approfondir et à rendre féconde l'exaltation que cette visite m'avait donnée; mais cette joie était restée stérile car je l'avais usée en courant de droite et de gauche dans un wagon noir où j'étais, me suspendant aux embrasses des portières, répétant tout haut: «Quel être adorable! quel homme de génie», tandis que les employés criaient successivement: Appolloville*, Briseville, Transville, tous les noms de stations que j'avais entendus une première fois dans des dispositions bien différentes, quand j'avais fais* avec ma grand'mère, le jour de l'arrivée à Bolbec* le même petit chemin de fer d'intérêt local.

866:8. <Montargis vint en prendre connaissance à l'hôtel> 866:17. <état organique qui> 866:19. <grand'mère avait été beaucoup> 866:20. <qu'il avait fait* sans y réussir d'ailleurs pour>]

866:25. <le lendemain, du wagon, de l'en excuser auprès d'elle, puis le surlendemain> {866:25-868:5}

868:8. <le surlendemain, dans une lettre> **868:13.** Le papier était armorié d'un lion que surmontait une couronne formée par un bonnet de pair de France.

«Après un voyage qui s'est assez bien effectué, me disait-il, en lisant>

868:17. <en lisant> **868:21.** <me voici revenu, disait-il, au milieu de cette vie grossière que vous méprisez sans doute et qui n'est pourtant pas sans charme. Tout m'y semble changé>

868:27. <changé depuis que> **868:31.** Je n'ai parlé de notre amitié, de vous, qu'à une seule personne, qu'à mon amie que j'ai vue à mon passage à Paris.

868:32. Elle aimerait beaucoup> **868:39.** <incapables de comprendre. J'aurais presque aimé mieux pour le premier jour évoquer leur souvenir pour moi seul>

868:41. <moi seul et sans> **869:3.** <subtil et plus digne de vous.»

Et à partir de ce moment-là quand on apportait le courrier je reconnaissais tout de suite si c'était de lui que venait une lettre, cet autre visage que nous montrons quand nous sommes absents et dans les traits duquel, à savoir les caractères de l'écriture, il n'y a aucune raison pour que nous ne croyions pas aussi bien saisir une âme individuelle que dans la ligne du nez ou les inflexions de la voix. {869:18-951:45}

951:2. Mais nous restâmes peu de temps à Bricquebec après le départ de Montargis dans l'hôtel qui n'allait pas tarder à fermer et n'avait jamais été si agréable, où parfois la pluie nous retenait, le casino étant fermé, dans les pièces presque complètement vides>

952:3. <vides, comme à> **952:10.** <inventaient> [952:9. <entamait la conversation.]

952:10. <conversation (ce qui me donnait le plaisir de rester longtemps à table, au moment admirable et quotidien où sur la table desservie les coûteaux traînent au milieu des serviettes défaites), inventaient>

952:20. Je fis> **952:38.** <dîner avec nous? [952:24. <rentré plus tôt à Paris. Ils m'invitèrent à venir> 952:26. <que je n'accepte pas. 952:28. <et bien que ce fût en réalité le jeune homme riche qui m'eût invité puisque les autres personnes n'étaient pas ses hôtes> 952:37. <s'effaçant pour laisser plus de prix à l'invitation qui me dit>]

□**952:41.** J'étais désolé de partir. Certes, surtout depuis que Montargis m'avait fait connaître des plaisirs mondains, Bricquebec m'avait donné bien peu d'impressions, mais enfin je savais que j'y demeurais effectivement et que c'était le nom qu'on était obligé de mettre comme adresse sur une lettre pour qu'elle me parvînt, et je sentais que la possibilité restait du moins près de moi des impressions que je n'avais pas eues. D'ailleurs comme dans ces lettres on me demandait si je ne reviendrais jamais, comment je pouvais rester à Bricquebec quand tout le monde était parti depuis longtemps [*cf.* 953:1], je me persuadais par raisonnement, si je ne l'éprouvais pas directement, que par la prolongation de mon séjour j'acquérais une connaissance plus approfondie de cette côte, et que je prouvais mon amour pour elle. Contre le témoignage opposé de mon ennui, de mon manque d'impressions, j'appelais à mon secours cette opinion que j'avais souvent entendu émettre et qui pouvait être vraie que nous som-

---

952:19. La brièveté des journées me donnaient d'ailleurs le plaisir de pouvoir allumer l'électricité de bonne heure dans ma chambre et m'enchanter de ces effets qu'Elstée* avait rendus avec subtilité. Malheureusement il n'y avait plus de feux d'artifice. J'aurais tant aimé en voir.

—On n'en tirera plus, demandais-je au directeur.

—Oh! non, nous sommes tout à fait à la fin de la saison.

C'était aussi l'avis du lift qui voyant l'amabilité* de ses efforts pour nous décider à rentrer à Paris avait fini par partir.

—Et des régates il n'y en aura plus.

—Encore moins.

—J'aurais si envie d'en voir.

—Mais vous en avez vu de magnifiques il y a deux mois.

—Oui... mais... .

—Il faudra revenir l'année prochaine; je pourrai vous donner de meilleures chambres [cf. 953:12].

—Oh! j'aime mieux celle que j'ai, elle est très bien.

□**952:39.** Au fond j'en avais été ravi parce que je pensais qu'à leur restaurant on devait servir des huîtres. Il n'y avait plus moyen d'en avoir à l'hôtel et j'en étais extrêmement curieux, j'aurais été bien loin pour en avoir et pour en manger.

mes souvent mal renseignés par notre sensation intime et mauvais juges pour nous même*, nous trouvant moins bien portants après un traitement qui nous a réussi étant mécontents de notre œuvre la meilleure, nous croyant plus méchants que nous ne sommes. Et comme ma fenêtre donnât*, au lieu que ce fût sur une campagne ou sur une rue, sur les champs de la mer, que j'entendais pendant la nuit sa rumeur montagneuse, étendue comme un paysage dans les ténèbres qu'elle accidentait et à la résistance de laquelle j'avais avant de m'endormir, confié comme une barque mon sommeil [*blanc*], il me semblait que cette [*blanc*] avec la mer devait matériellement, à mon insu, faire pénétrer en moi la notion de son charme à la façon de ces leçons qu'on apprend en dormant. Et je profitais des derniers jours du soleil pour m'exposer à ses rayons marins, comme s'il y avait eu en moi, ignorées de moi, des impressions qu'ils muriraient* nécessairement, comme les raisins d'une vigne.

□**952:40.** Et le peu de joie que j'avais en somme reçues* de la mer, de la campagne et des églises normandes ne me faisait pas>

□**952:41.** <faisait pas souhaiter moins, mais au contraire davantage, non seulement de rester plus tard cette année, mais de revenir l'année suivante. Car c'est bien moins le plaisir que la déception, qui donne ce désir de la répétition et du recommencement, véritable aveu de l'inachevement.* Et puis mon besoin de savoir que je reviendrais naissait aussi de cet attachement aux choses qui avaient quelques mois plus tôt causé ma souffrance quand j'avais dû quitter ma chambre de Paris pour celle à laquelle je m'étais maintenant habitué, où j'entrais sans plus jamais sentir l'odeur du vetiver et dont ma pensée, qui s'y élevait jadis si

---

□**952:40.** *(B-A).* J'eus un vrai plaisir un jour avoir* qu'un gros temps avait déposé sur le sable d'innombrables méduses. Je m'enchantais à voir le soleil briller dans les lustres d'opâles, même je touchai leur délicate ceinture lilas avec autant de joie que si ç'avait été l'écharpe d'Iris. De dégoût je n'en avais aucun car le sentiment esthétique nous fait franchir les limites qu'impose* à nos goûts les préférences du corps. C'est ainsi qu'un grand artiste pourra comparer à de belles Muses, pourra s'enchanter à regarder de jeunes hommes que trouverait écœurant un homme de club, livré aux étroites répulsions de l'instinct sexuel. Malgré cela j'avais en somme reçu bien peu de joie de la mer, de la campagne et des églises normandes; mais cela ne me faisait pas souhaiter>

difficilement, avait fini par prendre si exactement les dimensions que je fus obligé de lui faire subir un traitement inverse quand je dus coucher dans une chambre nouvelle, laquelle était basse de plafond [*cf.* 953:19].

Et quand j'eus quitté Bricquebec sans jamais y avoir connu ce dont le désir m'avait fait surmonter maladie et tristesse—des flots soulevés par la tempête qui battaient une église persanne*, au milieu d'éternels brouillards, tandis qu'au petit jour je buvais du café au lait dans l'auberge—il se trouva qu'ensuite, chaque fois qu'à ces image* le souvenir, pour me donner envie de retourner à Bricquebec, substitua les siennes, il ne les choisit pas moins arbitraires que celles de l'imagination, elles furent aussi étroites, aussi délimitées dans leur cadre, aussi instantanées dans leur durée, aussi exclusives de toute autre, aussi privilégiées, aussi excitantes pour mon désir, aussi impérieuses pour ma volonté. Ce qui maintenant me faisait rêver, de revenir un jour à Bricquebec, c'était le désir, par un temps de soleil et de vent, remontant de la place avec Mme de Villeparisis qui en passant envoyait un bonjour de la main à la princesse de Luxembourg et m'annonçait que nous allions avoir des œufs à la crême et des soles frites, d'entrer à midi dans la salle à manger à travers le grand vitrage azuré de laquelle je verrais des ombres promenées du ciel sur la mer comme par un miroir; ou bien d'être dans une barque arrêtée au fil de l'eau devant l'ancien moulin, sous la lumière abaissée de la fin du jour, pendant que la servante—la même—se pencherait pour annoncer que les truites sont prêtes. Ce n'était pas une promenade en barque ailleurs qu'il me fallait, ni sur une autre rivière les mêmes rayons; je voulais que ce fût devant l'ancien moulin; transportées dans un autre lieu, la même servante, les mêmes truites n'étaient rien; mais pourtant sans la servante et les truites, la promenade en barque et la lumière ne suffisaient pas. Sans doute certains de ces plaisirs étaient eux-mêmes insignifiants. Mais le souvenir les maintenait dans un assemblage, dans un équilibre où il n'était pas permis de rien distraire et de rien refuser sans altérer son authenticité. Or je sentais bien que toutes ces circonstances je ne pourrais pas les retrouver semblables. La servante aurait peut-être changée* et peut-être même, une fois à Bricquebec, pris dans l'engrenage d'une vie que je ne pouvais prévoir, je n'irais peut-être jamais jusqu'au moulin. L'hôtel pourrait rester le même. Mais Mme de Villeparisis n'y viendrait pas, ou serait alors trop âgée pour se promener, la princesse de Luxembourg ne serait plus là cette année-là. Et dès lors le petit chemin qui nous ramenait de la plage, ne serait plus de même. Car les lieux n'appartiennent pas qu'au monde fixe de l'espace où nous les situons pour plus de commodité.

Ils n'étaient quand nous les avons connus qu'une mince tranche au milieu d'impressions contiguës qui étaient notre vie d'alors, le souvenir d'une certaine image n'est au fond le* regret d'un certain instant, et les maisons, les routes, les plages, sont aussi fugitives que les années. Mais même si à peu de temps de distance j'avais pu artificiellement réunir les éléments de ce souvenir, je me serais aperçu qu'il était pourtant impossible de l'atteindre. Car il était d'essence spirituelle, perçu par la pensée et le désir de déjeuner à Bricquebec un jour de vent n'était au fond comme jadis le désir de voir Bricquebec dans le brouillard, qu'une forme de ce besoin contradictoire que nous avons de tâcher de connaître par l'expérience de nos sens ce que nous apercevons en nous-mêmes. D'ailleurs, à l'église de Bricquebec, sa solidarité avec les différentes parties de la ville qui lui donnait dans mon souvenir non seulement cette même lumière qui la baignait comme le Comptoir d'escompte et le café-billard, mais la même qualité d'état d'esprit dans lequel je les avais vus—état d'esprit fait de mes dispositions et de mes rêveries d'une journée de voyage, auxquelles la ville s'était opposée comme une réalité qui n'avait rien de subjectif et à laquelle je ne pouvais rien modifier, —cette solidarité qui m'avait gêné ce jour-là assurait au contraire au monument cette vive saveur d'être d'une certaine ville, d'être unique, que je lui imaginais quand je donnais une existence individuelle au nom de Bricquebec. J'aurais voulu revoir ces bons apôtres qui m'avaient reçu sur le seuil de leur église, j'aurais voulu les revoir comme des hôtes chez qui on a passé de bons moments sans qu'on sache au juste si le charme qu'on leur a trouvé ne venait pas un peu de la nouveauté de l'endroit où on était allé les voir, de l'amusement, du changement de vie et de l'excitation du grand air. Comme en les contemplant devant l'église j'avais tâché de me pénétrer uniquement de la signification de la sculpture, la sensation du beau temps, l'odeur du train que je gardais sur moi, n'avaient pas été affaiblies par ma réflexion qui s'était détournée d'elles, me revenaient particulièrement intenses, si bien que quand je revoyais ces bienveillants seigneurs de pierre, c'était toujours dépliant autour d'eux la lumière qui s'enfonçait dans le porche comme sur un berceau de vignes—comme il arrive pour certains passages d'une beauté intellectuelle et d'une si noble signification que dès qu'on pense à eux on se rappelle le goût du vin qu'on a bu et du cigare qu'on a fumé devant eux. Quant aux images d'une église persane dans le brouillard et la tempête, l'expérience les avait détruites. Détruites, mais non sans les laisser renaître quelquefois. Quand le temps était doux, que j'entendais le vent souffler dans la cheminée, le désir d'aller voir une tempête au bord de l'église persane de Bricquebec, de prendre le beau train d'une heure cinquante, renaissait en moi pareil à ce qu'il était autrefois. Et j'oubliais un instant ce* que cette église de Bricquebec je la connaissais, qu'elle n'était pas au bord de la mer, dans des brumes éternelles, mais éclairée par le même bec de gaz que la succursale du Comptoir d'Escompte dans une ville traversée par un tranway.

De la même façon renaquit aussi en moi le désir de Florence. Et ce fut le souvenir du désir de Florence (et non comme c'était autrefois le souvenir de ces vacances de Pâques passées à Combray) qui donna pour moi cette année-là et les suivantes, sa tonalité et ses images aux temps du Carême. La semaine sainte comme j'avais dû l'année précédente y voir Florence, continuait pour moi à s'entourer comme si elle avait été son atmosphère naturelle. Comme cette ville, elle semblait avoir une physionomie spéciale, en harmonie avec la sienne. La semaine sainte, la semaine de Pâques, avait quelque chose de toscan, Florence quelque chose de pascal, chacune des deux m'aidait à pénétrer le secret de l'autre. Je savais cependant bien que les raisons pour lesquelles je n'avais trouvé à l'église de Bricquebec le charme qu'elle avait dans mon imagination ne lui étaient pas plus particulières que ne le sont à l'eau qu'en se penchant d'une barque on puise dans le creux de sa main, les raisons qui la dépouillaient des reflets dont de loin elle semblait revêtue. A

Florence quand j'y arriverais, pas plus qu'à Bricquebec, mon imagination ne pourrait se substituer à mes yeux pour regarder. Je le savais. Mais j'avais mis autrefois dans le nom de Florence, dans le nom de Parme, dans le nom de Venise, un monde particulier, sans lien avec un autre et j'avais beau me dire que les villes ne peuvent pas être si différentes des villes voisines, malgré cela leur nom continuait à me montrer l'âme individuelle que j'y avais mise et qui s'en laissait difficilement déloger. D'autre part je savais tout aussi bien que l'individualité que nous prêtons aux jours, ils ne la possèdent pas, je me rappelais encore la bouffée d'air qui m'en avait averti, un soir du jour de l'an, devant une affiche de théâtre. Je savais que ces jours de la semaine sainte qui approchait seraient des jours comme les autres, mais je ne pouvais empêcher que mes souvenirs les fissent différents. Dans la rangée des jours qui s'étendait devant moi, quelques-uns se détachaient plus clairs, entre les jours contigus, comme s'ils avaient été d'une autre matière, ou touchés d'un rayon ainsi que sont quelques-unes seulement des maisons d'un village qu'on aperçoit au loin dans un effet d'ombre et de lumière. Comme elles ils retenaient sur eux tout le soleil, c'étaient les jours saints. Il gelait, l'hiver semblait recommencer et Françoise, dernière sectatrice en qui survivait obscurément la doctrine de ma tante Léonie, voyait dans ce temps hors de saison une preuve de la colère du bon Dieu. Mais je ne répondais à ces plaintes que par un sourire plein de langueur, car un état de faiblesse analogue à celui de convalescence, quand il n'est pas la cause du goût que nous reprenons aux choses, du réveil de nos désirs de vivre et de voyager, en est l'effet. Comme pour la ville bretonne qui ne remonte du fond de la mer qu'à une certaine époque de l'année, les jours étaient venus où Florence renaissait pour moi.

La semaine sainte toucha à sa fin. Ce fut la veille de Pâques, Françoise mettait une bûche dans le feu, allumait la lampe, annonçait de la pluie pour le lendemain. Pour moi, il ferait certainement beau car je me chauffais au soleil de Fiesole et la violence de ces rayons me forçait à fermer à demi les yeus et à sourire. Ce n'était seulement les cloches qui revenaient d'Italie, c'était l'Italie même [*cf.* II, 148:32]. Et mes mains fidèles ne manqueraient pas de fleurs pour honorer l'anniversaire du voyage que j'avais dû faire l'an passé, car, depuis qu'à Paris le temps était redevenu froid et sombre, comme cela avait eu lieu déjà cette autre année à la fin du Carême, dans l'air liquide et glacial qui baignait les maronniers* de l'avenue et les platanes des boulevards, s'entrouvraient pour comme* dans une coupe d'eau pure, les narcisses, les jonquilles, les anémones de la Porte* Vecchio.

Recherche du temps perdu pl. 1

LE CÔTÉ DES* GUERMANTES

{9:1-10:36} **10:37.** A l'âge où les Noms> **13:19.** <lumière orangée> [11:12. <d'église, s'éteignait peu à peu, quand de nouveaux rêves l'imprégnirent* de l'écumeuse humidité des torrents. 11:16. <à laquelle correspond le nom de la fée car cette> 11:22. Alors le Nom, —le nom—sous> 12:6. <ayant repris par instant ou après tant d'années> 12:16. <Combray ou un autre gaz de cette> 12:17. <d'une odeur des aubépines agitées par le vent> 12:24. <rares instants comme ceux-là, où> 12:38. <quand ma nourrice qui sans doute ne savait pas—ni moi-même aujourd'hui—en honneur* de qui> 13:2. <chocolat, je ne le sais pas> 13:15. <rêveries, ne contenant pas un seul élément qui ne dérivât de ses syllabes, les reflétait>]

13:19. <orangée et du haut duquel la duchesse décidait de la vie et de la mort de ses vassaux, avait fait place à cette terre torrentueuse où elle m'apprenait>

13:24. <m'apprenait à pêcher> **15:36.** <privilèges féodaux. [13:25. <violettes et jaunes qui> 13:28. <une tour jaunissante fleuronnée qui doit traverser les âges> 13:30. <encore vide devait surgir plus tard Notre-Dame de Paris et Notre-Dame de Chartres aux endroits où alors* au sommet de la colline de Laon ne s'était pas posée comme l'Arche du Déluge au sommet du mont Ararat debordante* de Patriarches et de justes qui se penchait* anxieusement aux fenêtres> 13:38. <terre, emplie d'animaux, qui en débordent comme ces bœufs qui s'échappent par l'embouchure des tours et se promenant* paisiblement sur les toits regardant de haut les plaines de Champagne. 14:1. C'était,

comme le cadre d'un roman, un paysage de roman que j'avais peine à me représenter enclavé, et d'autant plus que le désir d'y découvrir au milieu de terres et de routes réelles, qui tout d'un coup> 14:32. <connu Montargis, il> 14:36. <et son titre venait du midi. 14:38. <perspectives anciennes [*blanc*] en vigueur> 14:40. Quant aux tapisseries, c'était des tapisseries de Boucher. 15:1. <un fort vilain salon d'andrinople et de peluche. Par là Montargis avait> 15:4. <permirent plus de continuer à faire réciter uniquement de la sonorité des syllabes la maçonnerie des constructions> 15:13. <comprenait toutes les personnes qui partageaient la vie de la duchesse mais ces personnes que je n'avais jamais vues n'étant pour moi que des noms célèbres et poétiques, et ne connaissant eux-mêmes que des personnes qui n'étaient elles aussi que des noms, ne faisaient qu'agrandir et protéger le mystère de la duchesse de Guermantes en étendant autour d'elle un vaste halo dégradé. 15:29. <quand Montargis m'eut> 15:34. <ses terres possédé héréditairement>]

15:36. Mais cette dernière demeure s'était elle-même évanouie quand ma grand'mère cédant aux conseils de Mme de Villeparisis était venue occuper avec nous un des appartements voisins à* celui de Mme de Guermantes dans une aile de son hôtel.

15:40. C'était de ces vieilles demeures comme il y en a peut-être encore> **17:14.** <de son mécontentement. [16:11. <jardinet de la loge à côté du cocher, un valet de pied qui descendait corner des cartes à chaque hôtel aristocratique du quartier, envoyait indistinctement des sourires et des petits bonjours de la main dans son affabilité dédaigneuse et sa morgue égalitaire aux enfants et aux locataires bourgeois de l'ensemble qui passaient à ce moment-là et qu'elle confond dans sa dédaigneuse* amabilité et sa morgue* égalitaire. 16:18. <habiter, la comtesse au fond de la cour était une duchesse> 16:22. Car les Guermantes qu'elle désignait souvent, par les mots de «en dessous», en bas* étant sa constante préoccupation depuis le matin où jetant> 16:29. <le duc aura été à la chasse», jusqu'au soir où si, en me donnant mes affaires de nuit, elle entendait un bruit de piano, un écho de chansonnette, elle disait: «Ils ont> 16:42. <battants, Mme de Guermantes montait>] {17:15-17:19}

17:20. Les derniers rites> **17:41.** <à Combray.

□**17:42.** —Ah! Combray, Combray s'écriait-elle en une invocation. Ce ton chantant révélait chez Françoise non moins que la pureté arlésienne de son visage une origine méridionale et que la patrie qu'elle regrettait n'était qu'une patrie d'adoption. Oh! Combray, quand est-ce que je te reverrai>

18:10. <reverrai, pauvre terre> **18:41.** <causer par la fenêtre> [18:24. <coups de la sonnette qui m'auront déjà damnée* d'avance dans ma vie> 18:26. <appels du fleuriste de> 18:30. <de Françoise, et qui ayant levé la tête en entendant ouvrir notre fenêtre cherchait> 18:34. <pour M. Borniche le visage> 18:38. <au fleuriste un>

18:43. Elle lui montrait la calèche attelée en ayant l'air de dire: «Des beaux chevaux, hein», mais en réalité parce qu'elle savait qu'il allait lui répondre, en mettant la main devant la bouche pour parler à mi-voix:

—Vous aussi vous pourriez en avoir si vous vouliez, et même peut-être plus qu'eux, mais vous n'aimez pas tout cela.

19:8. Et Françoise après> **19:12.** <Guermantes, c'était nous> [19:8. <ravi qui pourrait signifier: «Chacun>]

19:12. <nous, mais Borniche avait raison de dire «vous» car, comme ces plantes qu'un animal à qui elles sont entièrement unies> {19:14-19:17}

19:19. <unies nourrit> **19:30.** <indispensable à sa vie. [19:21. <vivait en symbiose avec nous> 19:26. <coutume ancienne, la petite gorgée>]

□**19:30.** <sa vie. Aussi notre départ d'un immeuble que nous avions longtemps habité, «où on était si bien estimé de partout» [*cf.* 9:16], l'installation dans une nouvelle maison où les premiers jours, où le concierge ne nous connaissait pas, Françoise avait cesse* momentanément de recevoir les marques considération* nécessaire* à sa bonne nutrition morale l'avait jetée dans un état de dépérissement pendant la durée duquel elle faisait continuellement entendre des lamentations mais elle se releva rapidement car les Borniche—«De bien bon monde ces Borniche, de braves gens»— lui procurèrent un plaisir, aussi vif et plus raffiné que celui qu'elle aurait eu si nous avions pris une voiture, en sachant tout de suite confondre et répéter dans toute

la maison que si nous n'avions pas d'équipage, c'est que nous ne voulions pas. {19:31-19:41; 20:4-21:20}

21:21. Et quand un fournisseur ou un domestique> **21:30.** Si elle tenait tant d'ailleurs à ce que l'on nous sait* riches, ce n'est pas que la richesse> {21:31-21:33}

21:34. <richesse sans plus> **21:43.** <refermée elle commençait en soupirant à ranger la table de la cuisine.

22:4. —Il y a des Guermantes> **22:8.** <piqueur du Baron* de Guermantes. {22:9-22:36}

22:37. —La duchesse doit être alliancée avec tout ça, c'est de la même parenthèse, disait Françoise. {22:38-22:42}

22:42. C'est une grande famille> **23:6.** <certaines pierres, ayant ainsi par endroit* un défaut et qui projetait de l'obscurité jusque dans la pensée de Françoise.

—Je voulais demander à leur maître d'hôtel si c'est eux qui ont leur château à dix lieues de Combray, mais c'est un vrai seigneur un grand pédant qui ne cause pas, on dirait qu'on lui a coupé la langue. {23:11-24:19}

24:19. Ah! si c'était à moi le château> **24:37.** <gondole à Venise. [24:23. <misérable ville, quand ils seraient libres d'aller à Combray. Qu'est-ce qu'ils>] {24:38-25:2}

25:3. —Au moins> **25:35.** <en riant finement> [25:5. <à Pâques qu'à la Noël, et que je n'ai pas seulement un petit angelus* quand> 25:14. <madame, interrompit le>]

25:35. <finement; mais comment que tu as entendu parler, toi de Meséglise*?

—Comment j'ai entendu parler de Meséglise*? mais c'est bien connu; on m'en a causé et même souvent, répondait-il>

25:39. <répondait-il avec> **26:2.** <près du fourneau. [26:1. <vous promets qu'il>]

26:3. See after 26:32.

26:13. —Mais c'est à Combray> **26:14.** <vous étiez, alors?

26:16. —Oui chez Mme Octave> **26:22.** <tout ce qu'il fallait. [26:18. <du bon, que vous pouviez arriver>]

26:29. Comme nous disait M. le Curé, s'il y a une femme qui est sûre d'aller près du bon Dieu, c'est celle-là.

26:32. Pauvre Madame> **26:35.** <si je mangeais.

△**26:3.** Elle leur parlait aussi d'Eulalie comme d'une bien bonne personne; depuis qu'Eulalie était morte, elle avait en effet complètement oublié qu'elle l'avait peu aimée durant sa vie.

Mais déjà depuis un quart d'heure maman disait: {26:6-26:12; 26:35-27:29}

27:30. —Mais qu'est-ce> **27:31.** <à table.

27:31. Et elle sonnait> **34:33.** <au duc de Bavière. [27:38. <les coups commençant à se répéter et à devenir plus insolents nos domestiques> 28:1. Françoise montait ranger> 28:6. <dans une chambre> 28:7. Malgré la morgue de> 28:16. <que péages*, ni aiguilles> 28:18. <de Criquebec, ayant perdu son mystère, étant* devenue> 28:26. <parlant de Mme de Guermantes: «Elle> 29:39. <un bouton d'or ou> 30:4. <enfermant bien réellement enfin, objectivement> 30:11. <soirées de Mme de Guermantes la> 30:43. <Faubourg, dans certaines> 31:11. <dîners de douze, assemblés> 31:23. <Afrique? Et il n'y a> 32:4. <de Supien* lequel> 32:8. <de la part de cet homme de> 32:15. <plus de mécontentements. 33:9. <bientôt ce quidam vous> 34:2. <nommer beaucoup des salons> 34:11. <duc de Chartres, mais> 34:22. <duchesse de Vermandois, mais> 34:24. <y allez quelquefois. 34:38. <voit il y a tragédie, opéra tout.] {34:34-35:23}

35:24. Cette villa> **35:26.** Les noms de Vermandois, de Parme, de Guermantes-Bavière, différenciaient les villégiatures où se rendait Mme de Guermantes, les fêtes quotidiennes que le sillage de sa voiture reliaient* à son hôtel, non pas seulement entre elles, mais de toutes autres.

35:30. S'ils me disaient> **35:35.** <évaporer du sien, qui lui permettait de se déplacer, protégée par une cloison, enfermée dans un vase, lui-même aussi mystérieux, au milieu des flots de la vie de tous. Mme de Guermantes pouvait déjeuner>

35:38. <déjeuner devant> **36:17.** <glacées de nacre rose. [35:39. <de Vermandois, où> 35:40. <robe de drap blanc> 36:13. <de satin rose>]

36:19. Mon père reçut d'un ami un fauteuil pour l'un de ces soirs de gala de l'Opéra-Comique et comme la Berma> {36:19-36:25}

36:25. <Berma que je n'avais> □**36:41.** <la Berma que je portais dans mon cœur. C'est pour voir ces tapisseries, ces tableaux, que je serais parti comme jadis, quand je partais pour Balbec, heureux de sacrifier pour eux ma santé et mon repos que ma foi, mon désir ne venant plus lui rendre un culte incessant, peu à peu, ce «double» de l'art de la Berma qui était en moi, y avait dépéri comme ces «doubles» des trépassés, de l'ancienne Egypte qu'il fallait constamment nourrir et maintenir en vie. Cet art était devenu mince et minable. Aucune âme profonde ne l'habitait plus et il ne consistait plus qu'en une mince croûte de sang et d'attitude. Maintenant, c'est pour aller voir tel tableau d'Elstie*, telle tapisserie gothique que j'aurais fait litière de ma santé, peut-être bon marché de ma vie. Mais je me disais que dans quelques années sans doute, ces œuvres-là je me trouverais peut-être à quelques pas d'elles sans même désirer les regarder et à sentir la vanité des efforts que j'aurais fait montre pour les contempler, les nuits sans sommeil, les crises d'étouffement en wagon je sentais pour la première fois l'énormité de cet effort comme les nerveux qui ne sont fatigués que quand on présente à eux la notion de leur fatigue. Au moment où je montai le grand escalier du théâtre j'aperçus devant moi un homme que je pris d'abord pour M. de Charlus duquel>

37:9. <duquel il avait le maintien> **38:29.** <vers de douze pieds. [37:14. <aux ouvreuses. Car> 37:37. <c'est sa cousine> 37:43. <disait: «sa cousine> 38:12. <n'avais en somme devant> 38:23. <*Phèdre* que je ne me rappelais pas> 38:25. <je n'essayai pas>]

38:30. Mais tout à coup je me le rappelai exactement; il entre* aussitôt dans la mesure d'un alexandrin, ce qu'il avait de trop>

38:33. <de trop se dégagea> **39:40.** <le profil incliné du duc d'Aumale. [38:36. <n'était qu'une seule syllabe. 38:38. <achetés par une foule de snobs> 39:20. <des spectateurs qu'il fit lever. Au contraire> 39:35. <l'esprit. D'abord que* des ténèbres on rencontrait tout d'un coup comme le rayon d'une pierre précieuse>] {39:41-40:3}

40:4. Mais presque partout, les blanches déités qui> **45:6.** <dont disait la Berma. [40:17. <après commençait l'orchestre> 40:20. <liquide, et pleine, les yeux> 40:22. <l'orchestre, s'y

peignaient suivant> 41:13. <corolle, comme sont certaines> 41:23. <mosaïque marine et vague qui> 41:29. <n'était pas toute* entière> 41:34. <prolonger, merveilleuses uniques, engendrées autour de la Princesse comme> 42:1. Et cependant tous ceux qui cherchaient à savoir qui était dans la salle, reconnaissant la Princesse sentaient se relever> 42:25. <sorte d'évocation, de scène> 42:31. <de Guermantes Condé*> 42:32. <en moi, me donnant des plaisirs dont je ne reconnaissais pas l'origine que je rapportais à la princesse. Il me fallait> 42:40. <de moi, qu'ils feignaient en ce moment d'offrir> 42:42. <d'avance comme celui d'une danseuse> 43:9. <où ils se remettaient* à vivre la vraie vie> 43:15. <que Maillac* eût> 43:22. <oblique, se déplaçant lentement dans l'ombre transparente, son gros œil rond collé contre le verre du monocle ne paraissait pas plus voir> 44:3. <de ces parures> 44:10. <rose de ces joues> 44:17. <d'autrefois quand> 45:4. <delà existait* d'une>] {45:7-45:14}

45:14. Mais maintenant> **45:17.** <plus que des choses pareilles aux autres, dont je prenais connaissance parce que j'étais là; les artistes des gens de même essence que ceux que je connaissais tâchaient de dire le mieux possible ces vers de Phèdre qui eux ne formaient plus un être sublime et individuel, séparé de tous les autres, mais étaient des vers plus ou moins réussis, près* à rendre l'immense matière des vers français où ils étaient mêlés comme des choses entre d'autres. Je n'eus plus> {45:25-46:9}

46:10. <plus la même indulgence> **46:42.** <dans ses yeux. [46:19. <contraire: «sois furieuse»> 46:21. <frénésie. Mais leur voix inextingible* et rebelle restait, extérieure à leur diction, leur voix naturelle, avec ses> 46:36. <la petite femme qui>] {46:42-47:11}

47:12. C'était une actrice qui> **47:32.** <qu'un avec lui. {47:32-47:43}

47:43. Les intentions entourant> **49:40.** <impression individuelle. [48:7. <résorbés. Sa voix, en laquelle> 48:12. <d'Aricie où elles n'avaient pu s'imbiber, mais avait> 48:21. <froide. Ses bras que> 48:28. <mais de raisonnements ayant pris vie, ayant perdu> 48:40. <n'est pas devant l'âme comme un obsta-

cle opaque qui empêche de l'apercevoir mais comme un vêtement purifié, vivifié où elle s'est diffusée et où on la retrouve, que des enveloppes> 49:8. <le génie. Par le génie de Racine? 49:33. <c'est un ton bizarrement interrogatif, c'est l'impression despotique d'un être qu'on>]

49:41. Maintenant je me rendais compte que les mérites [*blanc*] d'interprétations* puissance* et c'était cela. Ou plutôt que c'était cela qu'on est convenu de décerner>

50:2. <décerner ces titres> **51:27.** <de terreur, de tendresse> [50:8. C'est bien peu cet intervalle, cette faille, que j'avais à franchir> 50:13. <qu'après une certaine impression de vide> 50:34. <lesquels la vieille actrice rageuse> 51:1. Mais je n'avais pas comme pour une pièce classique cette déception> 51:7. <fameuse, j'ajoutais à défaut de la célébrité qu'elle aurait dans l'avenir> 51:11. <être mis un jour, confondu> 51:13. Et ce rôle serait mis> 51:18. <indifférente en elle-même, pour>]

51:27. <de tendresse, sur les mots fondus tous aplanis ou relevés, et qu'une artiste médiocre eût détachés. Sans doute chacun avait une inflexion propre. Mais elle les faisait obéir à des systèmes plus vastes qu'eux-mêmes à la frontière desquels>

51:40. <desquels c'était un charme> **52:31.** <je mets en premier»> [51:43. <musicien à faire entrer ensemble les mots divers du livret> 52:14. <mon désir d'alors était>]

52:31. <en premier», tout en sentant confusément quelque calme que cette affirmation de ma prédilection m'apportât, que le génie de la Berma pouvait ne l'être* traduit plus exactement que dès l'affirmation quelque calme d'ailleurs qu'elle m'apportât de ma prédilection.*

Au moment où cette seconde pièce commença, je regardai du côté de la baignoire de Mme de Guermantes. Cette princesse venait par un mouvement générateur d'une ligne délicieuse que mon esprit poursuivait dans le vide, de tourner la tête vers le fond de la baignoire, les invités étaient debout, tournés vers le fond, et entre la double haie qu'ils faisaient, dans son assurance et sa grandeur de déesse, mais avec une douceur inconnue que lui donnait* les mousselines blanches dans lesquelles elle était enveloppée et l'air habilement naïf, timide et confus que son arrivée tardive et tout le monde qu'elle faisait lever au milieu de la représentation, mêlait à son sourire victorieux, la Duchesse de Guermantes qui venait d'entrer alla vers sa cousine>

53:5. <cousine, fit une profonde> **53:12.** <avec eux depuis quinze ans. [53:9. <—qui à ce moment là* furent les hommes et particulièrement M. de Palancy, que j'aurais le plus aimé être>

53:12. Mme de Guermantes laissait sentir le mystère dès que je pusse sans vue* distinguer dans l'énigme de ce regard souriant>

53:14. <souriant qu'elle adressait> **54:24.** <de poésie personnelle> [53:20. <les reflets de son monocle> 53:25. <aux monstres inférieurs> 53:30. <spirituellement froncées* et> 53:40. <un flot de blanche mousseline> 54:7. Peut-être la Duchesse aurait un sourire quand elle parlerait de la coiffure un peu trop compliquée de sa cousine, mais> 54:13. <dont s'habillait la Duchesse, trouvait peut-être dans cette>]

54:24. <personnelle, on n'avait qu'à donner le rôle qu'elle jouait et qu'elle seule pouvait jouer, à n'importe quelle autre actrice, lever les yeux vers les premières, on y aurait vu un «arrangement» qu'elle croyait rappeler ceux de la Princesse de Guermantes donner* simplement à la Baronne de Morienval l'air excentrique>

54:30. <excentrique, prétentieux> **55:7.** <flamme d'un incendie. [54:34. <montée sur fil de fer et piquée droit, sèche et pointue> 55:1. <bientôt, mais en ce moment immobilisé par l'attention>]

55:8. Mais la Princesse de Parme avait cédé çà et là quelques loges à des femmes comme Mme de Cambremer qui ne faisaient pas partie>

55:14. <partie de la haute> **56:25.** <aigrette, son collier> [55:18. <Guermantes et le pouvait d'autant plus facilement que ne les connaissant pas elle ne pouvait avoir l'air de quêter un salut. Certes, entrer en relations avec elles était pourtant le but> 55:25. <elle savait le caractère> 56:1. Il acceptait souvent d'aller au théâtre avec Mme de Cambremer, au théâtre et à la sortie, dans le vestibule, il restait>]

56:25. <collier, son corsage diamanté qui devaient faire honneur à son hôtesse et aussi vers celle de la princesse elle-même dont son invitée semblait se proclamer la sujette>

56:27. <sujette, l'esclave> **56:37.** <y était encore. [56:28. <pris fantaisie à celle-ci de s'en aller> 56:30. <comme composée* d'étrangers curieux à considérer le reste de la salle>]

56:37. Mais elle savait que quelquefois quand il y avait à Paris un spectacle qu'elle jugeait intéressant, de faire atteler* une de ses voitures aussitôt qu'elle avait pris le thé avec les chasseurs et au soleil couchant d'aller au grand trot à travers la forêt crépusculaire, puis par la route, prendre le train à Combray pour être à Paris le soir.

57:1. «Peut-être vient-elle> **58:6.** <piliers du Ciel. [57:8. <du nom de Guermantes et du nom de Condé la vie> 57:10. <visages puisque je les connaissais)>]

58:7. Tandis que je contemplais cette apothéose momentanée avec un trouble que mélangeait de paix le sentiment d'être ignoré des Immortels, la Duchesse, qui m'avait vue* une fois avec son mari, mais avait dû oublier mon visage et mon nom, se trouvait par la place qu'elle occupait dans la baignoire, regarder les Madrépores* anonymes et collectifs du public de l'orchestre, dans lequel je sentais heureusement mon être dissous>

58:15. <au milieu d'eux> **58:37.** <attendu à la voir. [58:36. <et levait* les yeux>] {58:38-59:17}

59:18. Souvent avant cette soirée> **60:8.** <et d'un catéchisme. [59:19. <quand il faisait beau; et s'il> 59:24. <le soleil, d'apercevoir une pensionnaire> 59:27. <mon cœur, s'élancait* déjà vers une vie étrangère le désir nouveau qu'une image serait* s'y faire affluer, refluait ou s'échappait déjà, s'élançait vers cette vie étrangère; je tâchais> 59:30. Heureusement la frugalité* de ces rencontres empêchait l'image caressée et que je me promettais de chercher à revoir, de se fixer fortement dans mon souvenir. 59:42 <de l'Opéra-Comique, j'avais> 60:4. <de la baignoire. Je>] {60:8-61:10}

61:10. Or chaque jour maintenant sans doute au moment> **61:25.** <pas lui plaire. [61:16. <l'air de ne pas m'attendre à rencontrer Mme de Guermantes que>]

61:25. Et pourtant au bout de quelques jours, je ne m'occupais plus que de Mme de Guermantes, je ne songeais plus aux fillettes, ni de* la laitière, quoique je n'espérasse plus de ce que j'étais venu chercher ni la tendresse promise au théâtre dans le sourire, ni même de retrouver de près la silhouette, ni le visage clair>

61:38. <clair sous la chevelure blonde> **62:11.** <divinité égyptienne? {62:11-62:20}

62:21. Tel jour> **62:42.** <même lui répondre. [62:39. <rond au bas]> {62:42-63:8}

63:9. Et à cause de ces apparitions successives de visages différents, occupant une étendue> **63:24.** <pour moi de leur importance.

□**63:24.** <leur importance. Même le visage que avant de m'endormir je revois clair et brillant étant le plus souvent, quand je le voyais le matin de près, rouge, bientôt le désir qui chaque soir me décidait de ne pas manquer de sortir le lendemain, ce ne fut plus celui de retrouver une tête blonde et dorée, mais de revoir une peau couperosée. Je n'aurais pas senti>

63:25. <pas senti moi-même> **64:4.** <ces propos à Françoise. [63:33. <sentais que je n'arriverais à rien.] {64:5-65:25}

64:5. Mais plus probablement la crainte, l'attention et la ruse avaient fini par donner de nous à notre servante, cette sorte de connaissance intuitive et presque devinatoire que le matelot a de la mer, le gibier du chasseur et le malade de la maladie. Je n'ai jamais>

65:26. <jamais dans ma vie éprouvé> **66:4.** <ou un moyen de centupler ses* revenus. [65:29. <et si, quand dans ma colère>] 66:1. <lu dans un journal> 66:2. <quelconque put*, contre>] {66:5-66:9}

□**66:10.** Mais la première, Françoise me donna l'exemple (que je ne devais comprendre que plus tard quand il me fut donné de nouveau et plus douloureusement, comme on le verra dans le dernier volume de cet ouvrage, par une personne qui m'était plus chère), que la vérité n'a pas besoin d'être dite pour être manifestée>

66:15. <manifestée, et qu'on peut> **66:34.** <pour les apercevoir. [66:24. <de mon corps et de mes actions, furent* bien interprétées par Françoise. Mais pour cela>]

□**66:34.** <apercevoir. Quoiqu'il en soit ce fut Françoise la première qui me donna l'idée qu'une autre personne, avec ses qualités, ses défauts, ses intentions à notre égard n'est pas un tableau visible comme celui que fait un jardin avec ses plates-bandes et qu'on aperçoit à travers une grille. Mais une ombre où nous ne pouvons pas pénétrer. Quand Françoise>

66:35. Quand Françoise> **66:42.** <tout le mal possible. [66:38. Mais Jupien révéla depuis>] {66:42-67:22}

67:22. Le pensait-elle vraiment.* L'avait-elle dit seulement> **67:28.** Et ainsi ce fut elle la première qui m'enleva l'idée qu'une autre personne que nous est devant nous immobile et visible, avec ses qualités, ses défauts, ses projets, ses intentions à notre égard, comme un jardin qu'on regarde, avec toutes ses plates-bandes à travers une grille, mais qu'une autre personne est une ombre où nous ne pouvons jamais pénétrer par laquelle il n'existe pas de connaissance directe, mais seulement par des convictions nombreuses et par lesquelles les paroles et même les actions donnent des renseignements insuffisants et d'ailleurs contradictoires, une ombre>

67:39. <ombre où nous pouvons> **68:8.** <des impressions d'autrefois. [68:3. <ni gens qui> 68:5. J'imaginais qu'elle le faisait.]

68:8. Au lieu de profiter des forces de renouvellement ou* une perspective vient de former marbre* en moi, au lieu de les employer à déchiffrer en moi-même des pensées qui d'habitude m'échappent au lieu de me mettre enfin au travail, je préférais parler tout haut, penser d'une manière mouvementée, extérieure, qui n'était qu'un discours et une gesticulation inutiles et me dispensaient de me retirer et comme j'aurais fait pour devenir un enfant, tout un roman purement d'aventures, stérile et sans vérité, comme à un enfant que la Duchesse, tombée dans la misère venait demander asile, à moi qui était* devenu par suite de circonstances inverse* riche et puissant, et je me raconte à moi-même ce roman purement d'aventures, stérile et sans vérité. Et quand j'avais>

68:22. <j'avais choisi précisément> **68:41.** <je n'en avais pas le courage. [68:29. <en allant ainsi au-devant> 68:35. <sur sa route, il faudrait qu'en m'arrangeant>]

68:41. Mais dans une direction qui me rapproche d'elle. Ce n'était pas impossible. Car ne serait-ce pas être plus près de Mme de Guermantes que je n'étais d'elle, le matin dans la rue, solitaire>

69:11. <solitaire, humilié> **69:20.** <le lui faire savoir qui, en tous cas bien qu'on envisageât avec lui, s'il pourrait ou non se charger de tel ou tel message auprès de Mme de Guermantes, je donnerais à mes songeries solitaires, muettes et* une forme nouvelle parlée, active, qui me semblerait un progrès presque une réalisation. Ce qu'elle faisait durant sa vie mystérieuse de la «Guermantes» qu'elle était, cela qui était l'objet de ma rêverie constante y intervient* même indirectement comme on pénètre dans une machine non avec sa main mais avec une* un levier, en gouvernant quelqu'un à qui n'était pas interdit son hôtel, ses soirées, la conversation prolongée avec elle, n'était-ce pas un contact plus distant mais plus effectif que ma contemplation dans la rue tous les matins.

69:34. L'amitié> **70:7.** <possibilité d'avantages> 69:36. <j'y attachais du> 70:1. <qu'on possède et qu'on ne porte pas écrits sur soi, on voudrait> 70:5. <justement parce qu'ils ne sont jamais écrits sur quelqu'un, peut-être>]

□**70:7.** <d'avantages qu'on ne sait pas. L'ivrogne, rempli de son bonheur et de la facilité qu'il voit* à dénoncer les choses, ne songe pas que la personne qu'il rencontre ne lui tiendra aucun compte d'un état qu'elle ne partage pas et ne comblera pas plus aisément ses vœux qu'il y a une heure avant boire quand tous les obstacles lui apparaissent clairement. Mais il y a des avantages plus réels d'un optimisme subjectif et momentané et sur lesquels le passant n'est pas mieux renseigné qu'ils influenceraient peut-être. Qui sait si le monsieur que nous rencontrons ne vient pas de quitter la plus flatteuse maîtresse, peut-être la nôtre?

70:8. Saint-Loup ne pouvait pas> **70:35.** <rester dans la ville> [70:14. <où Saint-Loup avait quitté> 70:16. <reçue de lui. C'était dans le nord, une de ces petites cités> 70:21. <buée

intermittente et solitaire qui> 70:30. Elle était située assez près de Paris pour qu'en descendant du train il me fut* possible, si j'étais monté dans le prochain, de rentrer, de retrouver ma mère et ma grand'mère et de coucher dans mon lit.]

70:35. <ville; mais j'en eus assez pour laisser un employé porter ma valise jusqu'à un fiacre, pour prendre en marchant derrière lui l'âme dépourvue sans arrière-pensées d'un voyageur qui surveille ses affaires et qu'aucune grand'mère n'attend pour monter dans une voiture avec la désinvolture de quelqu'un qui ayant cessé de penser à ce qu'il veut, a l'air de savoir ce qu'il veut, et pour donner au cocher l'adresse du quartier de cavalerie.

70:43. Je pensais que> **71:34.** <de vieilles tapisseries> [71:6. <et d'où, à tout moment, deux à deux, car c'était six heures du soir, des hommes sortaient dans la rue> 71:23. <directement de son œil nu, les autres traversant son monocle.]

71:34. <tapisseries, c'est ravissant. Moins artiste que lui, —ou davantage—le plaisir que donne une jolie demeure était pour moi superficiel et ne pouvait pas calmer mon angoisse commençante, dis-je, aussi profonde que celle que> {71:34-72:15}

72:15. <celle que j'avais jadis> **72:36.** <par la bride, le calma et le rendit alors à son camarade.

—Oui, me dit-il en revenant à moi, je vous assure>

72:37. <vous assure que> **74:6.** <se préparer à y monter> [73:31. <force, redressant son corps en arrière d'un mouvement> 73:37. <qui venaient de faire* et ceux> 73:42. <capitaine me dit Saint-Loup à mi-voix, soyez> 74:4. <le majestueux et lent>]

74:6. <monter, avec une noblesse de gestes étudiée comme dans quelque tableau historique et s'il allait partir pour une bataille. {74:9-74:13}

74:13. Je m'engageai> **74:21.** <feu allumé. Il ne pouvait pas se tenir tranquille et à tous moments il remuait les buches* et fort maladroitement. Il en laissa rouler une, en fit fumer une autre. Et même quand il ne changeait rien de place, comme les gens vulgaires il faisait tout le temps entendre les bruits qui du moment que je voyais monter la flamme me paraissaient des bruits de feu, mais que si j'avais été de l'autre côté>

74:28. <côté du mur> **74:35.** <et avec calme. [74:30. <de Liberty et>]

74:35. <calme, dans un repos sûr. Saint-Loup y semblait amusé* par les livres de travail qui étaient sur la table à côté de photographies parmi lesquelles je reconnus la mienne et celle de Mme de Guermantes, par le feu qui avait fini par s'habituer à la cheminée et comme une bête couchée en une attente ardente, silencieuse et fidèle, laissant seulement de temps à autre tomber une braise qui se brisait ou léchait>

74:42. <léchait d'une flamme> **75:9.** <n'ont pas de lieu. [75:7. <plus. Du moins je croyais>] {75:9-78:5}

78:5. La porte s'ouvrit> **78:37.** <pour cacher mes larmes> [78:17. <fanfare des sonneries dont> 78:33. <difficulté. Maintenant laissez-moi>]

□**78:38.** <mes larmes; mon angoisse venait de se détacher de moi, elle ne m'étreignait plus, elle n'était plus mienne, j'avais assez de détachement, d'insincérité, de loisir, pour pouvoir pleurer.

78:39. Plusieurs fois> **79:3.** <j'ai tant désirés. {79:4-79:34}

79:35. Je regardais la photographie de sa tante et tout d'un coup la pensée que Saint-Loup, possédant cette photographie, il pourrait> **80:11.** <valeur pour moi. [79:41. <Mme de Guermantes. Mais c'était une rencontre prolongée> 80:1. <chapeau de campagne, et> 80:3. <de sourcils, jusqu'ici voilés pour moi par la rapidité de son passage, l'étourdissement de mes impressions, l'inconsistance du souvenir et desquels la contemplation>]

80:11. <pour moi. Telle fut mon impression à ce moment-là. Mais plus tard, ce qui m'avait d'abord paru être le plus précieux dans cette photographie—l'immobilité de Mme de Guermantes, la durée, la permanence de son apparition—devait m'en paraître le défaut. Je sentis que cette femme qui n'avait qu'un seul profil, qui ne pouvait s'empêcher de regarder mon attendrissement s'augmentait d'un bien-être> {80:17-80-31}

80:31. <bien-être causé par la chaleur> **80:38.** <dans un presbytère). {80:38-82:2}

82:3. Mais, dès le second jour> **82:33.** <je les rencontrais se montaient* pour moi d'une prévenance silencieuse. [82:18. Hé bien, je m'étais trompé.] {82:34-83:6}

83:7. Si je voulais sortir> **83:11.** <gradation, de ces propositions parfaites qui dans certains genres de couleurs, de saveurs viennent émouvoir en nous une sensualité particulière.

Mais si les sensations de la vue et de l'odorat la réveillent souvent en nous, il n'en est pas de même de celles du toucher il m'avait fallu venir dans cette demeure pour connaître la volupté qu'il peut y avoir à monter et à descendre. De même qu'il faut aller dans certaines stations clématériques*, pour apprendre que respirer est quelquefois un acte délicieux. D'ailleurs cette dispense d'effort que nous accordent seules les choses dont nous avons un long usage, quand je posai mes pieds pour la première fois sur ces marches, familières avant d'être connues, comme si elles possédaient, incorporé*, peut-être déposé* en elles par les maîtres d'autrefois qu'elles accueillaient chaque jour, la douleur anticipée d'habitudes que je n'avais pas contractées encore et qui même ne pourraient que s'affaiblir quand j'y serais moi-même accoutumé.

83:27. J'entrai dans une chambre, la double> **84:5.** <concentration, mais encore également au plaisir de ma solitude qui restait inviolable et cessait d'être enclose sentiment* de ma liberté à sa manière presque aussi exaltant que celui que j'éprouvais à Combray en regardant le donjon de Roussainville sous les toits dans un cabinet semblable de Roussainville.* Celui dont je jouissais maintenant dans ce vieil hôtel ne donnant que sur une cour>

84:8. <cour, belle solitaire> **84:34.** <clair de lune. {84:34-85:19}

85:19. <lune. Le lendemain je fus réveillé par la fanfare d'un régiment qui tous les matins passait sous mes fenêtres. Mais deux ou trois fois mon sommeil interposé fut assez résistant> {85:21-85:24}

85:25. <résistant pour> **86:9.** <l'illusion d'assister. [85:29. <par qui seule la fin d'une cautérisation, restée d'abord insensible, est perçue comme une légère brûlure> 86:4. Car souvent quand je dormais ou* j'avais cru être réveillé, je crois* l'être encore pendant une heure et je me jouais>] {86:11-86:35}

88:36. Quand j'avais fini de dormir> **89:12.** <une pure vision. [88:41. <l'air, mêlées par une trame> 89:2. <pas la même chose; à> 89:9. <pipe et me donnant comme elle un plaisir>] {89:13-89:23}

89:24. Certains jours agité* par l'envie> **90:10.** <fait semblable> [89:38. Je savais qu'elles* étaient>]

90:11. <semblable à lui, je [*blanc*] occupations importantes qui le faisaient si pressé, si alerte, si content et à côté desquelles les ennuis qui m'empêchaient tout à l'heure de rester un instant sans souffrir, étaient négligeables, comme pour lui; j'étais>

90:14. <j'étais comme> **90:23.** <maintenant? [90:20. <se chargeait de mettre. La>]

90:24. —Je vais> **90:43.** <ce soir à dîner. [90:33. <beaucoup de vous voir manœuvrer, et> 90:35. <pas: vous n'avez pas dormi, vous vous êtes mis> 90:39. <et dormez; pas trop vite parce que notre garce>] {91:1-92:17}

92:18. Les jours où il y avait repos et où il ne> **92:23.** <et emplissait tous les bâtiments du quartier qui grondaient sans cesse (et même plus que le Grand Hôtel de Balbec à la fin de la saison) comme un grand antre des vents. Tandis que j'attendais Saint-Loup (pendant qu'il était occupait* à quelque service) avec tels de ses amis auxquels il m'avait présenté et que je venais quelquefois voir même quand Saint-Loup ne devait pas être là, devant sa chambre ou au réfectoire, voyant par la fenêtre>

92:30. <fenêtre, à cent> **93:40.** <espèces de palmes> [93:3. <de saluer, de lancer son monocle, dans «la fantaisie»> 93:8. <lundi, au retour des* permission, pour l'un d'eux qui était de la compagnie de Robert>]

93:40. <de palmes, épatant*;*

—Pour les anciens, hommes du peuple qui ignoraient le Jockey, qui mettaient>

93:42. <mettaient seulement Saint-Loup> **96:16.** <d'être bien reçu. [94:12. <soldat. Le café du matin semblait meilleur dans la chambrée, ou le repos sur les lits dans la journée quand quelque ancien servait> 94:20. <un jeune licencié-ès-lettres* qui cherchait par ce langage à ne pas avoir> 94:25. <le lieutenant colon* ne le quittait pas des yeux, je craignais de le voir mis au bloc. Et> 94:29. <ce que le capiston va dire. Ah* il se peut> 94:33. —Comment que tu le sais vieux, demanda le jeune licencié> 94:42. —Je comprends. Et encore> 95:2. <amené et la cantinère en a entendu> 95:9. <où j'allais chaque soir dîner> 95:23. <cris, décrivant des cercles> 95:35. <de l'hôtel,

luttait> 96:4. <riches d'un contenu divin, de toute une sorte d'existence à laquelle leur souvenir m'invite à goûter et qu'il me semble> 96:10. <comme un être relié>]

□**96:16.** <reçu. Cette vie était-elle différente en elle-même et les charmes que je lui trouvais était-ce seulement ce temps exultant d'extrême automne qui me les versait dans son breuvage frais, vif et doré? Ou bien est-ce un repos pour nous de concentrer sur quelques êtres comme étaient Montargis* et ses amis, sur un point fixe tout l'intérêt de notre vie, de faire porter par quelques êtres comme étaient Saint-Loup* et ses amis tout l'effort de notre intelligence, de notre art de plaire, de notre bonté* de ne chercher à recueillir que là des satisfactions, fût-ce d'amour-propre? Ou bien mon amour pour Mme de Guermantes qui savait quelle bonne situation je m'étais faite dans la garnison de son neveu, cet amour était il* l'armature cachée qui soutenait pour moi cette vie, et sans quoi elle s'effondrerait. L'amour sait si bien infuser dans les habitudes organisées autour de lui un agrément que nous nous figurons leur appartenir en propre. Swann, on l'a vu, moi, on le verra plus tard, ne crûmes-nous pas aimer pour elle-même la vie qu'on menait dans le salon de* Verdurin et dans le casino de Balbec?

En attendant l'heure de partir dîner avec Saint-Loup, j'écrivais à ma grand'mère que je me sentais bien, que j'allais enfin commencer à me bien porter et à travailler. Le nombre de fois que cette espérance avait déjà été trompée, ne l'avait pas affaiblie en moi. Chaque jour j'étais convaincu que le lendemain j'arrangerais ma journée à merveille et travaillerais plusieurs heures comme les personnes qui s'imaginent que si elles se trouvaient dans une bataille ou dans un procès en trois ou quatre mouvements elles mettraient l'ennemi en fuite ou rétorqueraient toutes les accusations. Non pas que la cause qui me rendait malade et m'otât* le courage de travailler ne fut* permanente, mais je ne la connaissais que par ses effets passés; je ne le sentais pas en moi où chaque soir, se trouvaient seulement en présence dans un espace imaginé et vide d'obstacles, que j'appelais le lendemain d'une part quelque projet à réaliser, quelque travail à faire, et d'autre part une volonté pure, intacte, qui viendrait aisément à bout d'eux. Malheureusement dès que ce lendemain devenait aujourd'hui, il laissait aussitôt entrer sous sa cloche pneumatique une atmosphère dans laquelle je me remuais, avec infiniment moins de facilité que dans l'«avenir». Mais le résultat était que je prolongeais ainsi indéfiniment une paresse que je croyais passagère.

Il est du reste probable que non, l'idée de la date de leur échéance que nous ajoutons aux choses au moment où nous les pensons les modifie extrêmement pour nous. De même que nous rendons l'idée de la mort à peu près nulle en écartant du présent immédiat l'attente de sa réalisation de même que les gens les plus sages, les plus vertueux, deviennent capables de mener jusqu'à la fin l'existence la plus coupable ou la plus folle en comptant sur les hasards du lendemain pour amener la résiliation d'une habitude dégradante ou ruineuse et qu'ils n'acquièrent pas* toujours que parce qu'ils ne s'engagent jamais que pour un jour ou deux.

A sept heures je m'habillais et ma lettre pour ma grand'mère à la main, je ressortais pour aller dîner avec Saint-Loup à son hôtel.

96:19. J'aimais m'y rendre> **96:31.** <d'aller d'un endroit> [96:25. <dans la garnison de Saint-Loup. Mais un souvenir, un chagrin, sont choses mobiles.]

96:31. <endroit à un autre; elles me semblaient nouvelles, douées d'une existence propre, contenant des femmes qui leur étaient particulières. La vie que menaient> **97:19.** <onctueux et dorés. [97:14. <élément qu'ils n'avaient fait le jour, nageaient lentement dans la grasse liqueur des lampes qui chaque soir à la tombée de la nuit sourd>

97:19. Je reprenais mon chemin, et parfois dans la ruelle noire qui passe devant la cathédrale, comme jadis dans le chemin de Méséglise, je m'arrêtais, et la force de mon désir était telle qu'il me semblait qu'une femme allait surgir pour le satisfaire; si dans l'obscurité je sentais tout d'un coup passer une robe, son contact me causait un tel plaisir qu'il me semblait impossible que son frôlement fortuit ne fut* pas une caresse volontaire et que j'essayais de refermer les bras sur la passante effrayée. Cette ruelle-là avait pour moi>

97:28. <pour moi quelque chose> **97:36.** <facile peut-être. {97:37-98:7}

98:8. Le vent> **99:25.** <pas encore soupçonnée. {99:26-99:39}

99:40. A la table de Saint-Loup, dans notre petite salle je trouvais quelques-uns de ses amis> **100:20.** <pas autrement. {100:21-100:32}

100:33. <autrement. Je ne peux pas vous dire> **103:1.** —On fera les deux. [101:15. <d'amour-propre vous le savez. Aussi> 101:36. <en disant à Robert que j'avais oublié sa [*blanc*] et pour ne pas laisser à Saint-Loup le temps de me poser sur mes motifs des questions qui> 102:27. <l'égard de la seule chose qui me semblait importante>]

103:2. —Comme je vous aime! Ecoutez dis-je encore> **103:22.** <je le détestai. {103:23-104:22}

104:23. Le troisième jour, un> **104:42.** <de cette petite pièce. [104:30. <qui n'ayant pas d'attrait physique à leur base sont les seules> 104:38. <de gaz, dont il parlait en souriant.] {104:42-105:16}

□**105:17.** Saint-Loup m'avait parlé de ce jeune homme; je savais que seul d'eux tous il était partisan de la révision du procès Dreyfus.

—Il n'est pas de bonne foi me dit Saint-Loup; au début il disait: il n'y a qu'à attendre>

105:23. <attendre, il y a là> **105:42.** <ces idées-là. [105:29. <sincèrement (quoique personne ne soit, ou du moins n'était, aussi clérical, avant son Dreyfus, que mon ami, ajoutait Saint-Loup). Alors> 105:33. <républicain, (mon ami était d'une famille ultra-monarchiste) était> 105:39. <Saussier (et remarque que>]

105:43. —Vois-tu, dis-je à Saint-Loup, c'est que> **106:9.** <modifient en rien; et comme une idée est quelque chose qui ne peut participer aux intérêts humains et ne pourrait jouir de leurs avantages, les hommes d'une idée ne sont pas influencés par leur intérêt.

—Vous êtes épatant. {106:10-107:16}

107:17. De même qu'un frère de cet ami.* Saint-Loup soit* élève de la Schola Cantorum> **107:41.** <du genre de Victor Hugo ou Alfred de Vigny. [107:40. <Schéerazade*>]

108:4. See after 128:1.

117:35. Je me sentais séparé> **118:28.** <pour lui?» [118:1. <d'épaisseur, par la chaleur de cette petite> 118:14. <dans son cadre naturel> 118:19. <un cercle d'animalcules, de coquillages satellites, crabes> 118:25. <conversations a parte que j'avais avec le sous-officier dreyfusard. Est-ce>]

□**118:28.** <pour lui?» Me* disait* Saint-Loup et ses camarades. Dès que la conversation devint générale, comme lui était pour l'état-major on évitait de parler de Dreyfus de peur de froisser mon nouvel ami. Celui-ci n'étant pas là le lendemain un autre ami de Saint-Loup me dit combien il était curieux que leur camarade, vivant dans un milieu si militaire, fut* tellement Dreyfusard*, presque antimilitariste.

C'est dis-je ne voulant pas entrer dans les détails que l'influence du milieu n'a pas grande importance, bien que je comptasse m'en tenir là de ce que j'avais développé quelques jours plus tôt à Saint-Loup, comme ces mots-là je les lui avait* dits presque textuellement, j'allais m'en excuser auprès de son ami en disant: C'est justement ce qu'avait* hier etc.», quand non sans en être un peu agacé je vis Saint-Loup, absolument comme si cette idée avait toujours habité son cerveau et si je ne faisais en ce moment que chasser sur ses terres, me souhaiter la bienvenue avec chaleur et m'approuver.

119:12. —Mais oui!> **119:19.** <regard comme une vrille sur l'œil de son ami:

—Tous les hommes d'une même idée sont pareils, lui dit-il, d'un air de défi. Il n'avait sans doute aucun souvenir de ce que je lui avais dit deux jours avant. Un souvenir, un chagrin, sont choses mobiles [*cf.* 96:25 and 119:26]. Un moment on ne les apercevait plus, aussitôt ils reviennent, de longtemps ils ne vous quittent plus. Il y avait des soirs où en traversant la ville pour aller vers le restaurant j'avais peine à marcher on aurait dit>

119:32. <on aurait dit qu'une partie> **120:8.** <blés de Méséglise> [119:38. <viscères, il semble qu'il tienne plus de>]

120:8. <Méséglise: parce qu'on ne change pas, parce qu'on fait entrer dans le sentiment qu'on rapporte à un être bien des éléments qui lui sont étrangers. Et puis ces sentiments particuliers toujours quelque chose en nous s'efforce de l'amener* à plus de vérité, c'est-à-dire de le* rejoindre au sentiment général, commun

à toute l'humanité, avec lequel les individus et les peines qu'ils nous causent sont seulement une occasion de communier. C'est peut-être ce qui mêlait à ma tristesse un certain plaisir. Car je savais qu'elle est une partie de l'amour. Et ainsi en étant triste à cause de Mme de Guermantes c'était—comme quand on replie en géométrie deux plans l'un sur l'autre—certains points de plus où mon état particulier coïncidait avec la passion appelée amour. Et sans doute>

120:18. <doute, de ce que je croyais> □**120:36.** <Mme de Guermantes». Et aussitôt ce n'était plus seulement les étoiles et la brise mais jusqu'aux divisions arithmétiques du temps qui prenait quelque chose de douloureux et de poétique. Je me disais: «elle n'attendra peut-être pas plus longtemps pour venir à récipiscence. Quatorze jours, quatorze jours d'attente, c'est une bien longue attente.» Et je ne songeais pas qu'elle n'attendait pas, et que ces quatorze jours de séparation, immenses à travers le microscope de mon regret qui m'avait permis d'en compter chaque dixième de seconde, étant infimes peut-être pur néant, et resteraient tels même quand à eux se seraient ajoutés cent fois quatorze jours pour Mme de Guermantes qui pendant tout ce temps n'avait pas pensé, ne pensait pas une seule fois à moi.

120:42. Chaque jour était> **121:17.** <entre deux trains et sans que je l'aie su. [121:1. <l'oubli, de l'autre était* emporté> 121:15. J'appris peu à peu qu'une>]

□**121:17.** En tous cas la querelle se poursuivit par lettres; elle lui déclarait qu'elle allait le quitter. Il lui écrivait à toutes minutes. Il avait beau savoir qu'elle ne lui avait jamais rien livré de sa pensée, qu'il ne la connaissait pas, que c'était seulement de ce qu'elle faisait et jamais de ce qu'elle disait—qui n'était même pas assez uniformément mensonger pour qu'il suffit* d'en prendre le contrepied—qu'il pouvait induire ce qu'elle désirait, ce qu'elle voulait, malgré cela il attachait à ce qu'elle disait une importance extraordinaire. Aussi quoique persuadé d'avoir fait pour elle tout ce qui était possible, dans un moment comme celui-ci où elle était méchante avec lui, il éprouvait le besoin de lui demander, de la supplier de lui dire ce qu'elle pouvait avoir à lui reprocher et si en effet elle finissait par formuler un reproche, immédiatement il se mettait devant de longues pages à y répondre, à le réfuter. Pourtant bientôt, ce ne fut plus avec sa maîtresse qu'il correspondait directement, car il ne voulut pas transiger sur certaines choses et crut devoir accepter sincèrement ou par feinte une rupture. Peut-être sincèrement le tourment de quitter sa maîtresse pouvait lui sembler moins cruel encore que celui de rester avec elle dans certaines conditions. {121:17-122:34}

122:35. See after 124:4.

123:16. Tout en lui donnant plus* signe de vie, il passait tout son temps au télégraphe et au téléphone qu'on venait d'installer dans cette ville pour pouvoir demander des nouvelles, ou donner des instructions à la femme de chambre qu'il avait placée auprès de son aime*. Ces communications étaient du reste d'autant plus compliquées et lui prenaient d'autant plus de temps que son amie n'habitait plus Paris même. Mais peut-être après les opinions de ses amis littéraires relativement à la laideur de la capitale et à l'influence de la «nature» qu'en considération de ses bêtes, de ses chiens, de son singe, de ses serins et de son perroquet que son propriétaire de Paris avait cessé de tolérer à cause de leurs cris incessants qui incommodaient les voisins, elle venait de louer une petite propriété aux environs de Versailles. Il ne dormait plus un instant la nuit.

123:29. <la nuit. Une fois> **124:3.** <tout essoufflé; [123:34. <chef. Il avait remarqué que celui-ci avait tâché de l'écarter d'une certaine partie de la maison. Il avait deviné> 123:39. <les cris que poussaient sa maîtresse à certains moments voluptueux. Il avait voulu>]

124:4. Mais je vis bien que pendant une heure il fut sur le point de télégraphier à sa maîtresse que la réconciliation était faite. Puis son rêve s'effaça un peu de son esprit. Pour moi, sans rien savoir il me semblait impossible qu'elle eut* réellement l'intention de quitter Saint-Loup. Lui-même ne savait que trop qu'en penser.

△122:35. Il souffrait> **122:41.** <malade et qui> [122:37. <qui préparent toutes> 122:38. <vue d'un départ qui> 122:41. <à ces cœurs qu'on>]

△122:41. <et qui continue à battre, détaché de tout corps. En tout cas c'est cette espérance que sa maîtresse reviendrait à lui, lui donnait* le courage>

△**123:1.** <courage de persévérer> **123:6.** <plus désolé>

□△**123:6.** <désolé, il aurait peut-être en pratiquant d'abord la rupture par feinte fini par s'y accoutumer sincèrement. Tous les matins il venait chez moi l'œil distrait et fixe et ces jours où il souffrit tant l'un après l'autre dessinèrent dans mon esprit comme la courbe magnifique et dure de quelque rampe d'escalier en fer forgé d'où Robert restait à sonder ce mystère qui l'occupait toujours, —ce que pensait réellement sa maîtresse, ce qu'elle faisait ce qu'elle était, —mais était maintenant devenu autre* urgent et douloureux puisce* qu'il fallut déchiffrer ce n'était pas seulement ce qu'elle pensait, mais ce qu'elle voulait, se* qu'elle avait résolu, puisque ce qu'elle était en réalité, et en particulier et par rapport à lui, son amie pour toujours ou son esclave haineuse, n'était pas seulement une essence intime sur laquelle on pouvait discuter, mais allait devenir, effectivement, une réalité, se traduire en actes.

124:19. Enfin, elle lui demanda> **124:29.** <au Ier janvier. [124:21. <il vit tous les inconvénients d'une réconciliation lui apparurent*. D'ailleurs> 124:24. <la morsure, s'il recommençait sa liaison. Il>]

124:29. <janvier. Lui-même aimait mieux lui montrer qu'il pouvait se passer d'elle, mais n'avait pas le courage d'aller à Paris sans la voir. De sorte que la visite qu'il devait me faire faire à ce moment là* à sa tante Guermantes se trouva supprimée.

Cela m'ennuie à cause de notre visite chez ma tante.

—Je retournerai sans doute à Paris à Pâques. Nous ne pourrons pas aller chez Mme de Guermantes à ce moment-là car je serai déjà à Balbec. Mais çà* ne fait absolument rien. {124:30-124:33}

124:40. —A Balbec?> **124:43.** <m'y envoyer à Pâques.

125:13. Je cherchai pendant tout le dîner> □**125:18.** <à Balbec. Sans doute là-bas dans cette visite à son atelier qui m'avait laissé une si forte impression, le désir que la peinture qu'il m'avait montrée avait exécuté* en moi, était moins de voir d'autres œuvres de lui, que les choses mêmes qu'il représentait et dont son art me proposait la beauté.

Ses tableaux avaient été pour moi, surtout, des clefs ouvrant de nouveaux domaines de beauté que je ne connaissais pas. Aussi, à Balbec, si j'avais été riche, ce que j'aurais souhaité ce n'eut* pas été d'acheter des tableaux d'Elstir mais de pouvoir lui en commander représentant tous les lieux de la terre, tous les moments du jour dont je ne suis pas arrivé à découvrir tout seul la beauté. J'aurais voulu qu'il peignit* de ces aubépines et de ces épines roses desquelles à Combray le charme m'était resté en partie obscur et que ses doutes, descendaient* plus avant que moi au cœur des choses, il aurait mieux su dégager. Et si j'avais pu lui faire faire le portrait des êtres, des choses, des lieux que j'aimais ce n'eut* pas été pour moi conserver leur beauté mais me* pour la découvrir. Mais depuis que j'avais quitté Balbec ces tableaux auxquels j'avais demandé seulement de mettre au jour pour moi des parties nouvelles de la réalité, comme j'aurais fait un livre de Bergotte ou une interprétation de la Berma, maintenant, c'est le souvenir de leur originalité, de leur séduction particulière qui ne cessait d'occuper ma pensée; et le désir qu'il développait en moi ce n'était plus tant de voir dans la nature les choses qu'Elstir avait peintes, que de nouveaux tableaux de lui. Peut-être l'amour que j'avais pour sa peinture était-il, en cela, devenu moins noble que quand je croyais qu'il devait seulement me conduire à l'amour des choses meilleures et plus vraies qu'elle-même et dont elle n'était qu'un reflet, quand le désir qu'éveillait en moi «la glace à Briseville», le «jour de marché», la «Solate», les «Femmes sur la Plage», le «Grand Pavois», j'en attendais impatiemment la satisfaction d'un temps de dégèle* du retour de la saison ou des bains d'un voyage à Venise, d'une journée de régates. Peut-être au contraire, en reportant mon désir de l'objet représenté sur la représentation elle-même, me rendais-je mieux compte de la nature du plaisir que j'avais ressenti et que ce dont mes yeux se repaissaient dans ces toiles c'était la vision d'Elstir qui l'y avait projeté mais que cela ne se rencontrait ni en Italie, ni par les temps de dégel, ni les jours de marché ou de régates. Peut-être aussi voulais-je maintenant retrouver les sensations mêmes que me donnait la vue de ces tableaux—de leur facture dont le caractère particulier m'avait d'abord été caché par leur signification générale—tout simplement parce que tout souvenir cherche à renaître; tandis qu'au moment où je les voyais, j'aurais voulu devant moi les pavillons rouges et jaunes amenés le long des drisses sous un ciel bleu, et la glace cassée à petits morceaux entre les peupliers, et le reflet rose sur le grand Canal—parce que le charme de ces tableaux était lui-même analogue à celui d'un souvenir, désireux de se prolonger revenir* à la vie, spirituel tyranique indivisible. De même que quand pénétrat* en moi le désir de Florence, il y effaçait le désir de Balbec, de même cet amour des œuvres d'Elstir, toujours présent à ma pensée l'occupant tout entière, y refusait aux œuvres des autres peintres même de ceux que je savais plus grands que lui le souvenir effectif, immédiat qui seul eût pu me donner le désir d'aller les revoir.

125:30. Il me semblait d'ailleurs que ses moindres pages* à lui était* encore quelque chose d'autre que leurs plus grands chefs d'œuvre*.

125:32. Son œuvre était> **127:1.** <vous l'aviez promis. [125:37. <mais qu'il avait peint d'abord des tableaux> 126:3. <pierre marbrière* duquel> 126:11. <importantes d'Elstir étaient> 126:15. <annoncé son voyage à Bruges> 126:27. <dame vous savez toujours bien laquelle.]

127:3. *J'espère que> **127:8.** <oublier son absence. [127:5. <Saint-Loup s'absente, cela ne doit rien changer pour nous. Ce>] {127:9-127:43}

128:1. Et tous me dirent qu'aussi longtemps que je resterais ici, ou à quelque époque que je revinsse, si Robert n'était pas là, leurs voitures, leurs chevaux, leurs maisons, leur temps seraient à moi et je sentais que c'était de grand cœur que ces jeunes gens comme je n'en avais encore jamais rencontré d'aussi aimables mettaient leur luxe, leur jeunesse, leur vigueur au service de ma faiblesse.

—Pourquoi ne reviendriez-vous pas tous les ans, vous voyez bien que cette petite vie vous plaît! Et encore vous vous intéressez à tout ce qui se passe au régiment comme un ancien.

C'était vrai. Grâce à cet agrandissement d'échelle à laquelle>

△**108:4.** <à laquelle nous voyons> **108:13.** <sous mes fenêtres. [108:9. <prend, à côté, l'inconsistance>] {108:13-117:34}

□**128:13.** <fenêtres. Aussi avec Robert et ses amis ce dont j'aimais surtout à causer, c'était du quartier des officiers de la garnison, de l'armée en général. C'est surtout sur la valeur militaire de ces différents officiers que j'interrogeais mes nouveaux amis, sur ce qu'ils entendaient par valeur militaire, par intelli-

gence militaire, par génie stratégique. Peut-être craignant que ces officiers dont j'entendais parler pendant que je buvais du sauterne, et qui recevaient sur eux son reflet charmant, ne passassent dans mes souvenirs à un plan aussi effacé que maintenant tant de personnages qui à Balbec m'avaient paru énormes, le premier président, le souverain d'Océanie, la petite société des trois gourmets, le beau frère de Legrandin, ce qui voudrait dire que ce qui me plaisait aujourd'hui me serait indifférent, que l'être que j'étais encore n'existerait plus, je tâchais de trouver à l'intérêt que je trouvais, ardent et fugitif comme une ivresse, que je trouvais pour quelques soirs, à cette vie militaire un fondement intellectuel, permanent, qui me permit* de croire qu'une fois parti je continuerais à m'intéresser aux faits et gestes de la garnison, et ne tarderais pas à revenir. Et pour bien comprendre ce que c'était que la valeur militaire, je faisais comparer à mes nouveaux amis les différents officiers dont je savais les noms, je leur demandais lequel avait le plus une nature de chef, des dons de tacticien, comme jadis je faisais faire par mes camarades des classements entre les différents acteurs du théatre* Français.

128:17. Si à la place> **130:36.** Mais au contraire> [128:19. <Négrier un des camarades de Saint-Loup disait: «Mais Négrier est un officier des plus médiocres»> 128:25. <épanouissement arrivant et* soudain> 128:33. <souvent, et que dès mon arrivée, comme il avait été obligé d'avoir Saint-Loup à dîner dans un repas de corps il m'avait invité avec lui, c'était son capitaine, le Prince de Borodino. 128:40. <farouche et risible d'adjudant, les amis de Saint-Loup ne semblaient pas classer M. Borodino*> 128:43. <beaucoup d'attitude> 129:21. <—on l'appelait à cause de cela au faubourg Saint-Germain comte refait—> 129:25. <qui était cousin de l'Empereur. 129:26. <que cousin peut-être. 129:34. <Napoléon III d'une façon> 130:2. <beaucoup un chef d'escadrons* roturier qui était un homme agréable), c'est que, les considérant les uns les autres du haut> 130:16. <inviter, et lui demanda> 130:21. <aristocraties: entre l'ancienne>]

130:37. <contraire d'une noblesse dont les titres gardaient encore leurs significations de riches majorats récompensait* de glorieux services, de hauts postes occupés dans lesquels on commande à beaucoup d'hommes et où l'on doit connaître les hom-

mes, le Prince de Borodino, —considérant son rang comme une prérogative effective et à ces mêmes bourgeois que Saint-Loup eut* touchés à l'épaule>

131:4. <l'épaule et pris> **132:17.** <du regard. [131:8. <voulue, sans doute parce qu'il était moins> 131:10. <avait eu de grandes charges> 131:12. <mais surtout parce que cette> 131:16. <un Ronher*, un Fould. <131:24. <s'étaient en lui matérialisées> 131:26. <reproche à un caporal> 131:29. <rues de la ville, un> 131:32. <bureau du sergent-major, suivi> 131:35. <pour sa compagnie, il fixait sur le caporal tailleur> 131:40. <une Italie comme Napoléon III. Mais aussitôt, devenant Napoléon Ier, il faisait>] {132:18-132:37}

132:38. Un matin> **132:40.** <l'idée, comme un service téléphonique avec Paris venait d'être installé de causer avec moi. Bref le même jour elle devait me demander au téléphone, il me conseilla d'être vers quatre heures moins un quart à la poste. Ma grand'mère m'avait déjà demandé: j'entrai> {132:41-134:26}

134:26. <j'entrai dans la cabine> **134:38.** <j'entendis cette voix [134:32. <dès que je ramenai* près de moi, il se remettait à parler>]

134:38. <voix que je connaissais si bien, car jusque là, quand ma grand'mère me parlait je savais ce qu'elle me disait je l'avais toujours suivi sur son visage comme sur une partition ouverte, et en somme parlait avec les yeux, mais sa voix>

134:43. <voix elle-même> **135:4.** <combien elle était douce; peut-être d'ailleurs ne l'avait-elle jamais été autant, car ma grand'mère me sentait loin et triste, croyait pouvoir s'abandonner à l'effusion d'une tendresse que, par «principes» d'éducatrice, elle contenait et cachait d'habitude. Et aussi combien elle était triste, d'abord à cause de sa douceur même presque décantée, combien peu de voix humaines ont jamais dû l'être, de toute dureté, de tout élément de résistance aux autres, de tout égoïsme, fragile à force de délicatesse, elle semblait>

135:14. <semblait à tout moment> **135:43.** <après sa mort> [135:22. <un symbole, plus une évocation, plus encore un effet direct> 135:25. <que m'adressait à tout moment ma grand'mère dans l'ordinaire> 135:31. <tout à fait ici, on> 135:33. <pos-

sible puisque ma santé et mon travail pouvaient s'en bien trouver); >]

135:43. <sa mort quand je l'aimerais encore et qu'elle aurait à jamais renoncé à moi, alors seulement parce que je ne faisais que l'entendre, je la *vis* seule; cette voix avec le pouvoir d'un magicien m'évoqua la solitude de ma grand'mère en me permettant comme dans une apparition soudaine, dans une féerie, de voir, malgré la distance, de tant de lieues qui nous séparaient, ma grand'mère et la vie qu'elle menait en ce moment sans moi, loin de moi, et alors je criai:

—Grand'mère, grand'mère et j'aurais voulu l'embasser [*cf.* 136:2] mais je n'avais plus devant moi que cette voix que je ne pouvais étreindre, vrai fantôme aussi impalpable que celui qui reviendrait peut-être me visiter quand ma grand'mère serait morte. Grand'mère parle moi*; mais ne m'entendais* plus; alors il arriva que me laissant plus seul encore, je cessai tout d'un coup d'entendre cette voix, la communication avait dû être coupée et que grand'mère non plus ne m'entendait plus, dans l'immensité de la distance nous nous étions perdus, je restai là longtemps, puis je dus quitter la poste avec la même angoisse que j'avais eu* un jour tout petit enfant quand j'avais perdu ma grand'mère dans une foule, angoisse moins de ne pas la retrouver que de sentir qu'elle me cherchait, surtout de sentir qu'elle se disait que je la cherchais. J'allai retrouver Robert à son restaurant et en arrivant je lui dis que allant peut-être recevoir une dépêche qui m'obligerait à revenir, voudrais* savoir à tout hasard l'horaire des trains.

Je ne lui dis pas que mon cœur n'était plus avec eux mais auprès de ma grand'mère, que mon départ était irrévocablement décidé; il parut me croire, mais j'ai su> {136:29-136:40}

137:1. <j'ai su depuis> **137:30.** <à deux heures. [137:13. <quand je sentis s'y employer l'activité> 137:17. <soir de la ville de garnison où nous étions, à Paris> 137:24. <sans cela j'aurais risqué de>] {137:31-138:5}

138:6. Le matin quand je vins il était trop tard, Saint-Loup était parti à son déjeuner dans un château voisin. Vers une heure>

138:8. <une heure et demie> **139:22.** <sais, je pense. [138:11. <je vis se dirigeant vers le quartier un tilbury> 138:14.

<déjeuné, un qui avait son château dans le voisinage et que j'avais déjà vu une fois à l'hôtel où Robert dînait. Je n'osais pas> 138:22. <il vit bien qu'on le saluait et répondit au salut, mais> 138:32. <malades, recrues dispensées de marche, jeune bachelier*, un ancien qui> 138:43. <des bonnes> 139:9. <qui s'appelle [*blanc*], ayant> 139:12. <émotion il se donnait le temps de retrouver ses mots en disant deux ou trois fois «monsieur», puis après>]

139:25. —Ah! alors> **139:37.** <le régiment sortir> [139:30. <partout dirent-ils en riant. 139:35. <cheval, ayant conscience d'être à Austerlitz. Quelques passants tôt réveillés, étaient assemblés>]

□**139:38.** Droit sur son cheval, le visage plein, l'œil lucide et résolu le capitaine de Borodino leva le bras et d'un beau geste tira son sabre, et avec la voix calme des suprêmes résolutions lança: «Face en arrière». «Demi-tour, ette» cria à sa section. Saint-Loup qui pirouettait* sur lui-même faisait adhérer à son épaule remontée son oreille crispée par un mouvement nerveux, et rendit brusquement la liberté à son monocle qui s'envola. Mais il fallut que je quittasse le quartier, le régiment était déjà si loin, que je ne pus pas distinguer si c'était ces fanfares qu'entendait encore mon oreille ou si elle était le jouet de quelque hallucination quand après le passage du tramway le silence qui suivit* son roulement, me sembla parcouru et strié par une vague palpitation musicale, j'étais désolé de ne pas avoir dit adieu à Saint-Loup, mais je partis tout de même car je ne pensais qu'à rejoindre ma grand'mère, moi qui jusqu'à ce jour, dans cette petite ville, quand je pensais à ce que ma grand'mère faisait sans moi, je me la représentais telle qu'avec moi, sans tenir compte des effets sur elle de cette suppression, ce qui n'était pas du tout la même chose, maintenant, j'avais>

140:7. <j'avais à me délivrer> **140:39.** <permanent dans son esprit> [140:11. <et qui* était arrivée une lettre> 140:36. <puisque les joues, les épaules de ma grand'mère>]

140:39. <esprit, comment n'en eussé-je pas omis ce qui en elle avait pu épaissir et changer>

140:42. <changer, alors que> **141:11.** <de même quand quelque maudite ruse du hasard empêche notre intelligence et

pieuse tendresse d'accourir comme elle fait d'habitude pour cacher à nos regards ce qu'ils ne doivent jamais contempler quand elle est devancée par nos regards, qui, arrivés les premiers sur place et laissés à eux-mêmes, fonctionnent mécaniquement à la façon d'un appareil photographique, et nous montrent à la place de l'être chéri qui>

141:18. <qui n'existe plus> **142:23.** <d'Elstir. [141:21. Et, comme un malade qui ne s'était pas regardé> 141:31. <contigus, tout> 142:19. <l'aime, car pendant>]

□**142:23.** <d'Elstir. S'il n'eût pas dû m'éloigner de Mme de Guermantes, c'est avec joie que j'eusse vu approcher notre départ pour Balbec. Certes j'avais quitté Criquebec* sans y avoir connu ce dont le désir m'avait fait, la première fois surmonter, pour partir, maladie et tristesse: des flots soulevés par la tempête autour d'une église persane, parmi l'immense brouillard, au petit jour, tandis que je buvais du café au lait dans une auberge.

Mais mon désir d'aller à Balbec n'était pas moins fort parce qu'à ces images, la mémoire en avait substitué d'autres, choisies par elle, et aussi arbitraires, aussi étroites, aussi fugitives dans leur durée, aussi fixes dans leur aspect, aussi délimitées dans leur cadre, aussi exclusives de toutes autres, aussi excitantes pour mon désir aussi dominatrices de ma volonté et que le lecteur pourait* sans doute énumérer aussi bien que moi, si en les lui décrivant, tandis que je racontais mon premier séjour à Balbec, j'ai su les lui rendre chers. Ce que je voulais maintenant c'était par un jour de soleil et de vent remonter de la place avec Mme de Villeparisis qui en passant envoyait un bonjour de la main à la Princesse de Luxembourg et m'annonçait que nous allions avoir à déjeuner des œufs à la crème et des soles frites [*text from the end of* Grasset A]; c'était d'entrer à midi dans la salle à manger à travers le grand vitrage azuré dans laquelle je verrais des ombres promenées ciel* sur la mer comme par le jeu d'un miroir mobile; ou bien être dans une barque arrêtée au fil de l'eau devant l'ancien moulin, pendant que la même servante se pencherait pour annoncer que les truites étaient prêtes. Je sentais bien que tous ces tableaux-là étaient les uns et les autres d'essence spirituelle que je ne les atteindrais jamais, pas plus ceux qui étaient maintenant formés par ma mémoire que ceux qui l'avaient été autrefois par mon imagination et que la réalité avaient détruits. Détruits? pas pour toujours; quand le temps était doux que j'entendais le vent souffler dans la cheminée, que je me rappelais certaines phrases de Bergotte sur les églises du moyen âge ou sur les mers brumeuses de Bretagne, alors, tout d'un coup ce désir qui m'avait tant de fois agité, de prendre le beau train d'une heure cinquante renaissait en moi pareil à ce qu'il était autrefois. J'oubliais que cette église de Balbec je la connaissais, qu'elle n'était pas au bord de la mer, dans des brumes éternelles, mais sur une place traversée par un tramway, qu'elle était éclairée le soir par le même réverbère que la succursale du Comptoir d'Escompte. Comme autrefois, je me voyais arrivant à l'aube, pendant que des flocons d'écume volaient autour de la façade persane.

Puis tout à coup je me rappelais; ce tableau c'était avec des phrases, avec des noms, avec des désirs qu'il s'était composé en moi, il n'existait pas dans la réalité. Je ne pourrais pas plus le voir qu'étreindre une héroïne de roman et je maudissais la médiocrité d'un monde où les plus beaux rêves de notre jeunesse sont dus à notre ignorance de la réalité, à notre foi excessive en certaines paroles et ne peuvent jamais être caressés que de loin sans que nous soyons jamais transportés parmi eux.

Nous le trouvons pourtant dans notre sommeil. Là le rêve, l'inaccessible est à côté de nous. Nous avons pu enfin atteindre le but du voyage et il n'a pas cassé d'être conforme à ce que nous avions imaginé. Nous entendons le clapotis, nous sentons la fraîcheur des eaux mystérieuses, les fleurs inconnues sont à la portée de notre main. Cela m'était souvent arrivé pour Balbec, et ma nostalgie la plus profonde, la plus insensée, avait pour but, ce Balbec non pas même de mon imagination mais de mes songes, longtemps, découvrant dans la journée parmi les souvenirs oubliés de la nuit qu'on retrouve tout à coup comme un objet perdu, le lieu étrange que j'appelais Balbec en dormant, je crus que c'était la première fois que je faisais ce rêve et que c'était seulement une des illusions dont il était composé, qui me faisait l'avoir rêvé souvent. Mais si c'est souvent, un des effets de songe de nous faire paraître une nouveauté familière et reconnaître ce que nous n'avons jamais vu, il est facile de se référer dans les «souvenirs de rêves» qui eux appartiennent au jour, à des jours qu'on ne peut se rappeler. Aussi je me rendis compte que je faisais souvent un même rêve à propos de Balbec. Et je le fis en effet si souvent que le lieu que je voyais alors finit par prendre dans ma mémoire une place fixe et je me demandais si je ne l'avais pas vu réellement autrefois, s'il ne me serait pas donné de le voir réellement un jour. Objectivant sans doute dans une réalisation synthétique ce que mon imagination avait souvent cherché pendant la veille à se représenter du paysage marin de Balbec et à la fois son passé médiéval, je voyais en dormant une cité du moyen âge [*cf.* 146:7] au milieu des flots immobiles comme sur un vitrail. Un bras de mer divisait en deux la ville de la baie de Balbec de son passé immémorial.* Je voyais l'eau verte à mes pieds; sur la rive opposée elle baignait une église orientale (sans doute l'église persane) puis des maisons gothiques qui existaient encore dans le passé, si bien qu'aller vers elles, comme j'allais avoir l'ivresse de pouvoir le faire, c'était comme remonter le fleuve des âges. Mais je songeais que le désir de cette synthèse où la nature avait appris l'art, où l'océan était devenu gothique, où le présent pouvait approcher le passé révolu depuis des siècles, ce n'était que dans un rêve qu'il était donné de l'atteindre car c'était le désir de l'impossible.

142:32. Cependant l'hiver finissait. Un matin, après quelques semaines de giboulées et de tempêtes, ce que j'entendis dans ma cheminée, au lieu du vent informe élastique et sombre qui me secouait, de l'envie d'aller au bord de la mer, ce fut le roucoulement>

142:36. <roucoulement des pigeons> **142:42.** <beau jour. Et comme était semé dans la tempête le désir que j'avais eu de Balbec avant d'y être allé, ce qui renaquit en moi, avec les premiers soleils à l'approche du carnaval, ce fut le souvenir de projets inexécutés de voyage à Venise et à Florence. {142:42-143:7}

143:8. Je sentais bien> **143:13.** Je le sentais> [143:10. <avait dans mon imagination, qu'à Florence>]

1142:1. <sentais, mais j'avais> **1142:4.** <déloger.

143:14. De même, un soir> **143:37.** <n'eût-elle pas existé> [143:18. <le souvenir des jours pendant lesquels j'avais cru

l'année précédente, passer à Florence la Semaine Sainte, ne continuât à faire d'elle comme l'atmosphère de Florence, à donner> 143:25. <des jours contigus. 143:33. Mais parce que j'y rencontrais Mme de Guermantes, je pensais>]

□**143:37.** <existé, je n'en eusse pas moins manqué à* faire mes sorties tout de même. Cependant sachant que je sortais le matin bien des amis, et surtout depuis qu'on avait appris notre projet de passer une partie de l'année loin de Paris, m'avaient dit que chaque jour avant déjeuner ils m'attendraient l'un chez lui, l'autre avenue du Bois, l'autre au Louvre où il faisait une copie. Et sans doute supputaient-ils si j'avais plus ou moins de chances de venir, si tel empêchement ne serait pas plus fort que mon intention de les retrouver. Or ces empêchements qu'ils imaginaient eussent été tout à fait inutiles.

Car pendant des semaines pas une seule fois ne se présentait à moi le matin le souvenir que l'un était au bois, l'autre au Louvre et qui m'attendaient et si je les avais aperçus, j'aurais eu le brusque mouvement de quelqu'un qui se rappelle une obligation oubliée. Tandis que le passage de Mme de Guermantes dans ces rues, ce n'est pas seulement que je ne l'anéantissais pas par l'oubli, je le multipliais des centaines de fois par l'imagination et l'attente, son apparition était un dessin que ma pensée avait indéfiniment esquissé, avant que mes regards lui donnassent sa forme définitive.

143:39. Hélas! si pour moi> **145:22.** <chefs-d'œuvre. [144:7. <elle sentait avec exaspération que c'était elle qu'elle eut* retrouvés*. Aussi même si j'avais> 145:5. <mettait autour d'elle et>] {145:22-146:37}

146:38. Saint-Loup vint à Paris pour quelques heures seulement me dit-il, tout en m'assurant qu'il n'avait pas eu l'occasion de parler de moi à sa cousine.

—Elle n'est pas gentille>

146:40. <gentille du tout> **147:8.** <et plus jeune. {147:8-148:16}

148:17. Le temps était redevenu froid et Françoise, dernière sectatrice en qui survivait obscurément la doctrine de ma tante Léonie, touchant le* physique, disait de ce temps hors de saison: «C'est le restant de la colère de Dieu!» Mais je ne répondais à ses plaintes que par un sourire plein de langueur plus indifférent aux prédictions de Françoise, que de toutes manières il ferait beau pour moi>

148:27. <moi; déjà je voyais> **149:23.** <ta vocation. [148:29. <rayons; leurs forces me forçait* à> 148:43. <maintenant où allait> 149:16. <intéressants. Il m'a dit un grand bien de toi>] [*From 148:28 to 148:42* Grasset B *picks up a fragment from the end of* Grasset A.]

□**149:23.** Mais je ne pouvais trouver belle qu'une carrière qui contrariée par mes parents me laissait du moins la douceur de faire leur volonté, et je ne pus que répondre à mon père, en couvrant de larmes et de baisers ses joues colorées et sa barbe.

—Non je ne serai pas bientôt un homme, je ne serai jamais que ton petit garçon. D'ailleurs je n'ai aucune vocation pour écrire. Permets-moi d'avoir la même profession que toi. Quand* à Mme de Villeparisis, puisque Saint-Loup vient à Paris avant notre départ c'est lui qui m'y mènera.

Si au moins j'avais pu commencer une œuvre qui parut* assez belle à mon père pour qu'en me demandant d'écrire il ne fit* que m'exprimer connaître* son désir au lieu de se résigner au mien.

Mais quelques* fussent les conditions dans lesquelles j'abordasse le projet de travailler, (de même>

149:26. <même, hélas!> **150:27.** <idée plus avantageuse. [149:29. <promenade, en me la réservant pour après comme une récompense> 150:2. <si je prétendais me coucher de bonne heure, ne boire que de l'eau, travailler, vraiment elles s'irritaient> 150:8. <d'être moins sage c'est-à-dire plus raisonnable> 150:21. Ma mère avait un immense respect pour mon père le voyant>] {150:27-150:35}

150:36. Quant à moi> **150:39.** <du reste, arriva. {150:40-152:40}

152:42. Saint-Loup devant venir à Paris quelques jours avant notre départ pour Balbec m'avait promis> **153:5.** <où elle habitait. [153:3. <que nous devions conduire à ses répétitions. Nous>]

□**153:6.** Bien qu'il fit* du vent, que «le fond de l'air» selon Françoise fut* assez froid, il y avait tant de soleil que j'avais mis une redingote grise; et cette journée-là—comme je ne me servais jamais de l'air et des sales temps ambiants que comme une matière à incorporer dans un rêve incessant que je faisais jusqu'à ce que je l'eusse remplacé par un autre—cette journée-là fut d'abord pour moi une journée de Balbec. Car j'avais demandé à Saint-Loup que le déjeuner eut* lieu de préférence dans certain restaurant où Aimé m'avait dit qu'il devait entrer comme maître d'hôtel en attendant la saison de Balbec. C'était un grand charme pour moi qui rêvai* à tant et accomplissais si peu de voyages, de revoir quelqu'un comme moi qui faisait partie>

153:14. <partie plus que> **153:28.** <charme du voyage. [153:24. <vitrine. Aimanté lui-même>]

153:28. <voyage. J'avais envie de causer avec lui de Balbec comme j'avais eu envie de causer avec Saint-Loup de Mme de Guermantes. {153:29-153:34}

153:35. Saint-Loup devait m'attendre devant sa porte; de là nous irions ensemble chercher sa maîtresse. Avant d'arriver chez lui, je rencontrai Legrandin>

153:36. <Legrandin, que nous> **154:12.** <le cou à tous. {154:12-154:14}

154:14. Pendant que vous irez> **154:17.** <lune rose. {154:17-154:21}

154:21. Adieu, ne prenez pas> **154:35.** Adieu, ami. [154:28. <pour les palais>] {154:36-154:41}

154:42. Ayant vu à Paris malgré le printemps commençant les arbres des boulevards à peine pourvus> **155:26.** <que j'avais vus. [155:5. <une des fêtes> 155:12. <froid, que c'était de la neige fondue ailleurs qui était encore restée après les arbustes. 155:16. <unie, plus certaine, plus éclatante et comme si>

1142 (P. 155, note 5). <formaient... fleurs>

155:28. <fleurs blanches> **155:39.** <ensoleillée et mousseuse. [155:32. <retrouver dans quelque Crête*; et> 155:35. <on voyait des branches, selon>]

□**155:39.** <mousseuse. Mais il fallait gagner le village où habitait la maîtresse de Robert. C'était sur une route en dos d'âne, très ancien régime, un village ancien avec sa route droite, sa vieille église cuite et dorée, sa vieille mairie devant laquelle en guise de mats* de cocagne et d'oriflames*, trois grands poiriers

étaient comme pour une fête civique et locale galamment pavoisés de satin blanc. Jamais Robert ne me parla plus tendrement [*cf.* 156:1] de son amie que pendant ce petit voyage. Je sentis ce qu'elle était pour lui, je sentis que tout le reste, sa fortune, son avenir, sa situation mondaine ne comptaient pas pour lui, que seule elle avait des racines dans son cœur. Lui si délicat il envisageait la perspective d'un brillant mariage rien que pour avoir des sommes d'argent assez énormes, pour que vaincue par une richesse pareille, elle renonçât à l'idée de le quitter.

Seule elle avait des racines dans son cœur [*cf.* 156:3]; l'avenir qu'il avait dans l'armée, sa situation mondaine, sa fortune personnelle, sa famille, tout cela ne lui était pas indifférent certes. Mais cela ne comptait en rien auprès des moindres choses qui concernaient sa maîtresse. C'était à elle qu'il pensait sans cesse. C'était de là que lui venaient toutes ses inquiétudes, c'était de là que lui venait par moments une ineffable douceur. C'était la seule chose qui ait du prestige pour lui infiniment plus que les Guermantes et tous les rois de la terre. Je ne sais pas s'il se formulait à lui-même qu'elle était d'un* essence supérieure à tout, mais je sais qu'il n'avait de considération, de souci, qu'il ne pouvait éprouver de fièvre, d'audace que pour ce qui la touchait. Par elle, il était capable de souffrir, d'être heureux, peut-être de tuer. Il n'y avait vraiment d'intéressant de passionne* pour lui que le présent, ce que voulait ce que ferait sa maîtresse, que ce qui se passait, discernable tout au plus par des expressions fugitives, dans l'espace étroit de son visage et sous son front privilégié. Si on s'était demandé à quel prix il l'estimait, je crois qu'on eût jamais* pu imaginer un prix assez élevé. Car pour la garder il eut* certainement donné toute sa fortune, et il eut* sacrifié avec joie les choses que souvent le titre sert seulement et peut ne pas suffire à procurer, une grande situation mondaine. Car s'il ne l'épousait pas c'est parce qu'un instinct pratique lui faisait sentir que dès qu'elle n'aurait plus rien à attendre de lui elle le quitterait ou du moins vivrait à sa guise et qu'il lui fallait la tenir par l'attente du lendemain. Car il sentait bien qu'elle ne l'aimait pas ou du moins l'affection générale appelée amour, et malgré ses diversités habituelles chez tous les hommes, la forçait bien puisque cela fait partie de ses syndromes (autre mot) à croire par moments qu'elle l'aimait.

156:29. Mais pratiquement> **157:1.** <me le réserve. [156:33. <s'empresserait (victime des théories de ses amis de la littérature) et tout en l'aimant de le quitter. 156:37. <Boucheron. Cela me gêne bien parce qu'il coûte vingt-cinq mille francs. Mais>] {157:1-157:9}

157:10. Pour gagner la maison qu'elle habitait, nous passions devant de petits jardins> **157:29.** <entresol de verdure. [157:12. <car ils étaient en floraison des cerisiers et des poiriers, et qui sans doute vide et inhabitée encore comme une propriété qu'on n'a pas louée, était subitement peuplée et embellie par ces nouvelles venues> 157:20. <Robert, attends-moi là>]

□**157:29.** <verdure. Mais j'ai tort de dire les yeux seulement. Car j'avais reconnu en elles les pelotons violets disposés à l'entrée du parc de M. Swann, passé la petite barrière blanche, pour* les chauds après-midi de printemps, tandis que pêchait le pêcheur à la ligne; et cette ravissante tapisserie provinciale que je connaissais si bien n'appartenait pas seulement au monde que nous observons froidement avec nos regards. Elle en faisait commencer devant moi un autre dont nous sentons que la vision, —seul véritable enrichissement, seul sentiment de réelle plénitude, seule source de pure joie—s'étend aussi dans notre cœur. Je pris un sentier qui aboutissait à une prairie, une de ces parcelles de vraie nature qu'on rejoint, qu'on identifie presque, en faisant tomber les esclaves hétérogènes de la ville voisine à des lieux semblables qu'on a aimés. Un air froid>

157:33. <froid y soufflait> **157:41.** <par les rayons.

□**157:41.** <rayons. J'étais transporté par cette fantaisie, la plus enchanteresse, celle qu'on sent jaillir de la vie la plus simple, de la plus solide nature. Et je le quittai à regret pour retourner au jardin devant lequel m'avait quitté Saint-Loup. Car ainsi que quand nous nous émerveillons de ce qu'est le baiser, nous cherchons à penser jusqu'à quelle douceur il pourrait atteindre s'il était appliqué sur des lèvres chères et que nous n'avons jamais effleurées, j'aurais voulu pour sentir encore avec plus de force ce qu'avait de naturel et d'émouvant l'efflorescence du beau poirier, réussir à l'ajouter par la pensée à une certaine prairie,

au coin de la route que j'avais si souvent prise dans mes promenades avec Mme de Villeparisis et par laquelle on sortait de Balbec. Saint-Loup n'était pas encore revenu devant le petit jardin quand j'y arrivai. J'avais passé à Combray et en effet c'était bien les fleurs de Combray, les fleurs qui avaient fait rêver mon enfance, ces tels* enchantements que je ne croyais plus que, dans le monde médiocre, elles existaient réellement, c'était bien ces fleurs-là de poiriers, de cerisiers, que je voyais attachées aux arbres au-dessus de l'ombre propice de la sieste, à la lecture, à la pêche.

157:42. Tout à coup> **158:2.** <personnalité plus mystérieusement enfermée dans un corps que le Saint des Saints dans le Tabernacle était l'objet encore sur lequel travaillait sans cesse l'imagination de mon ami, qu'il sentait qu'il ne connaîtrait jamais, dont il se demandait perpétuellement ce qu'il était en lui-même, derrière le voile des regards et de la chair, dans cette femme je reconnus à l'instant «Rachel quand du seigneur» celle qui disait à la maquerelle: >

158:10. «Alors> **158:12.** <chercher.»

158:13. La pitié que j'aurais dû éprouver pour Robert ne fut pas le sentiment qui m'envahit alors. Non si ces larmes me vinrent aux yeux, ce fut plutôt par l'excès de la joie que me donna l'apparition au fond de moi d'une sorte de vérité confuse encore, mais générale et qui dépassait Robert et son amie. Je me rendais> {158:13-158:43}

159:1. <rendais compte> **159:31.** <de soupçons, de rêves. [159:4. <d'abord; et inversement je me rendais compte en quels misérables matériels* et sans prix pouvait> 159:6. <rêveries, si au contraire elle avait été comme d'une manière opposée par la connaissance la plus triviale.* 159:12. < qu'un million, que la famille, que le [*blanc*] s'il avait commencé par imaginer en elle un être inconnu, curieux de* connaître, difficile à saisir, à garder. Sans doute> 159:19. <communiqueront jamais> 159:22. <d'une forme* quelconque> 159:25. <m'avait* paru> 159:26. <et sans eux>]

□**159:31.** <rêves. Ce qui m'avait été offert pour vingt francs, il donnait plus d'un million pour l'avoir pour que ce ne fut* pas offert à d'autres. Il avait* su maintenant que cela avait été

offert à tout le monde pour vingt francs, qu'il eut* sans doute terriblement souffert mais n'eût pas moins donné un million pour le conserver, car tout ce qu'il eût appris n'est pas de faire sortir tout ce qui est au-dessus des forces de l'homme et ne peut arriver que malgré lui par l'action de quelque grande loi naturelle—de la route dans laquelle il était et d'où ce visage ne pouvait lui apparaître qu'à travers les rêves qu'il avait formés d'où ces regards, ces sourires, ce mouvement de bouche étaient pour lui la seule révélation d'une personne dont il aurait voulu connaître la vraie nature et posséder à lui seul les désirs. L'immobilité de ce mince visage comme celle d'une feuille de papier soumise aux colossales pressions de deux atmosphères, me semblait équilibré par deux infinis qui venaient aboutir à elle sans se rencontrer car elle les séparait. Et en effet la regardant tous les deux Robert et moi nous ne la voyions pas du même côté du mystère. Et en même temps ces jours où il avait tant souffert ne sachant pas si elle allait le quitter et où sans doute elle ne songeait qu'à rire de lui, ou à l'allécher davantage, à moins que la fortune tellement inspirée et folle qu'elle avait lui ait tourné la tête, ces jours qui avait* dessiné en moi comme le* courbe dure et magnifique en fer forgé de laquelle Saint-Loup se penchait vers le mystère, je croyais en voir se profiler ironiquement l'ombre inconsistante et exactement inverse.

Je revoyais ([*blanc*] avec le reste) de Rachel, le petit air impertinent qu'elle prenait quand le [*blanc*] et je comprenais que pour Robert c'était cela les signes comme tracés de l'intérieur par la personnalité de cette femme et pour lesquels il eut* tout donné.

Il aurait su maintenant qui elle était qu'il eut* souffert davantage bien qu'il ne l'aurait* pas moins aimée. Je la regardais, je me disais c'est elle, elle qui ne vaut pas vingt francs pour tout le monde, qu'on peut payer un million, préférer à la vie, pour quoi* on commettrait peut-être un crime. Et ce n'était pas>

160:27. <n'était pas> **161:23.** <contente de tout. [160:30. <l'amour qui me semblaient grandes> 160:31. Je détournais> 161:5. J'échangeais> 161:8. <avaient un air> 161:12. <ses ailes d'innocence en fleurs. 161:14. <quelques pas devant avec> 161:15. <puissions nous attendre j'aurais même été plus content

de déjeuner seul avec toi, et à ce que* nous restions>] {161:24-164:38}

164:39. Mais en réalité ces déjeuners «chose si gentille», se passaient> **165:1.** <s'amusait à attiser> [164:42. <hommes qui étaient là il>]

165:1. <attiser; elle faisait semblant> {165:1-165:3}

165:4. <semblant de ne pas détacher ses yeux d'un homme d'ailleurs*, et d'ailleurs> **165:27.** <d'un nez grec. [165:17. <tranquillisât, consentait* à aller faire une course et lui laissât le temps> 165:22. <soucieux. C'est qu'il avait> 165:24. <vulgaires, Clodion* avec>] {165:27-165:42}

□**165:40.** Clodion vint prendre notre commande. Il s'informa de la santé de ma grand'mère, je lui demandai des nouvelles de sa femme et de ses enfants. Il m'en donna avec émotion car il était homme de famille. Je voulais lui poser quelques questions sur Balbec, mais je vis bien vite que ses réponses ne me feraient pas entrer plus avant dans le charme de Balbec que la lecture d'un ouvrage sur les modèles qui ont servi à Stendhal pour *Lilin Sorel** ou la suzeraine dans le charme du *Rouge et le Noir* ou de la Chartreuse.* Je ne savais même pas que lui dire.

166:2. Il avait un air> **166:9.** <le joli dessin> [166:5. <enfoncés de Clodion, auxquels>]

166:9. <dessin qu'était sa figure, un peu jauni et fatigué maintenant, et que pendant tant d'années, comme telle gravure représentant le prince Eugène ou l'incendie de Chateaudun? Voir*, toujours à la même place, au fond de la salle à manger, n'avait pas dû attirer de regards bien curieux.

166:14. Il était donc resté> **167:8.** <et des ateliers. [166:25. Pourtant Clodion dut> 166:32. <renvoyé Clodion assez>] {167:8-167:27}

167:28. Mais quand on toucha au théâtre je cessai de prendre part à la conversation. Car, sauf peut-être de la Berma dont elle prit la défense contre Saint-Loup en disant: «Oh! non c'est>

167:33. <c'est une femme> **167:38.** <un si grand cœur,»> [167:34. <ne nous intéresse plus>]

167:38. <cœur,» la maîtresse de Saint-Loup—lequel enchérissait sur elle—parlait des artistes les plus connus sur un ton d'ironie et de supériorité, qui m'irritait parce que je savais que

c'était elle qui leur était inférieure. Elle s'aperçut> {167:38-168:4}

168:8. Elle s'aperçut très bien> **168:23.** <que la mienne. {168:23-168:39}

168:39. Mais bientôt> **169:7.** <t'attendre au théâtre. [168:41. <avec Clodion, elle>] {169:8-169:33}

169:34. —Allons bon!> **169:36.** <ces conditions. {169:36-169:39}

169:40. Et elle se mit> **170:22.** Mais pas plus que ça. [170:9. —Non, c'est là que j'ai besoin> 170:11. <tout fâché contre moi; sa colère> 170:14. <mais sous lesquelles elle étend comme un même sentiment. 170:16. <appela Clodion et>]

170:22. <que ça. Robert a tort de se faire des idées.» Tout ça se forme dans ma tête. Tenez, regardez>

170:27. <regardez les yeux> **170:35.** <buvaient du champagne. {170:35-170:38}

170:38. J'avais mal déjeuné, j'étais mal> **171:18.** <leurs façons de maintenant. [171:5. <perdues pour moi puisque par elle j'ai, chose gracieuse et qu'on ne peut payer trop cher, une rose> 171:8. <c'était assigner un caractère esthétique> 171:11. <j'éprouvais de trouver une raison>] {171:18-172:19}

□**172:20.** <maintenant. Ce fut pour moi, d'aller dans les coulisses, et avant cela, dans la salle où Saint-Loup m'avait pût* donner un fauteuil pour la première pièce, pourtant insignifiante, un plaisir d'autant plus vif que je n'avais plus la passion du théâtre. Dans ce temps-là les acteurs ne me semblaient exister que dans leurs relations avec la vérité d'art que je pourrais extraire de leur diction, de leur jeu. Car de même que du jour où je cessai de chercher une grande impression d'art dans les pierres des cathédrales, elles m'intéressèrent en elles-mêmes comme se rattachant à de petits problèmes d'hagographie* et d'histoire, de même depuis que les acteurs>

172:21. <acteurs n'étaient plus> **173:8.** <réalité du moi et méditer le mystère de la mort. [172:30. <dame dont les magnifiques perles l'avaient frappé dans une loge voisine> 172:34. <artistes (comme il l'avait à Rivebelle fait sur celle des femmes qui dînaient près de nous) je> 173:6. <d'elles, ce à cause de

quoi leur dissolution, le spectacle fini, fait comme celle>] {173:10-176:2}

176:3. Quand le rideau tombé nous passâmes sur la scène, intimidé de me promener sur le plateau, je voulus> **176:43.** <le salut militaire! [176:13. <sujet de conversation. 176:23. <dénonçant qu'il me connaissait sans> 176:27. <rôles il était véritablement mon frère; il l'avait été, il l'était redevenu> 176:41. <qui, levant les guides, le>]

177:1. Cependant j'étais content de cheminer parmi les décors, tout ce cadre qu'autrefois mon amour de la nature m'eut* fait trouver ennuyeux et factice mais auquel sa peinture par Goethe dans Wilhelm Meister*, avait donné pour moi une certaine beauté; et j'étais déjà charmé d'apercevoir au milieu de journalistes ou de gens du monde amis des actrices, qui saluaient, fumaient comme à la ville, un jeune homme en toque de velours noir> {177:1-177:18}

177:19. <noir, en jupe> **179:1.** <Marsantes, Meter Semila*, ça sent la race. [177:23. <mains, bondissant> 177:41. <aller après se> 178:20. <s'écria-t-elle en> 178:26. <mal, me dit Saint-Loup avec cette<] {179:1-179:9}

179:9. Mais tout n'est pas fini> **179:35.** <ce qu'il fait là. [179:16. <a mille fois> 179:17. Et si je ne puis m'empêcher>] {179:36-179:40}

108:1. —Ecoute, pour> **180:20.** <innocente d'ingénue. [180:9. —Mais mon petit me dit Saint-Loup ne reste pas là je te dis tu vas te mettre à tousser.] {180:20-180:22}

180:23. —Il n'est pas défendu> **182:9.** <tu t'emballes.» [180:27. <folle lui cria-t-elle. 181:6. <quand ils ne parlent que d'une rectification de frontière, ou la mort d'un malade, alors qu'il n'était question que> 181:14. <le journaliste qui avait pâli et hésité un instant ne riposta pas. 181:22. <souffrance, et le troisième s'était> 181:33. <répondre. Quant aux amis du journaliste, voyant que tout était terminé, ils revinrent>] {182:11-182:12}

182:12. Pauvre Robert, j'avais beau avoir senti le matin devant les poiriers en fleurs l'illusion sur laquelle reposait son amour pour> **182:18.** <dans ses yeux: je lui demandai ce que nous allions faire; il me demanda d'aller de mon côté chez Mme de Villeparisis, il m'y retrouverait> {182:18-183:30}

183:32. <retrouverait, mais aimait mieux> **183:36.** <l'après-midi.

□**183:38.** Comme je l'avais supposé avant de faire connaissance à Balbec, il y avait une grande difficulté* entre le milieu où vivait Mme de Villeparisis et celui de Mme de Guermantes. Mais cette différence dont je ne me rendis peut-être compte que plus tard, tenait à des raisons de fait et n'avait pas ce caractère absolu, uni, poétique, des différences que l'imagination met entre les choses rien qu'en répandant sur elles ses tonalités diverses.

183:41. Mme de Villeparisis était> **184:9.** <trop ancienne. La liaison que Mme de Villeparisis avait depuis vingt ans avec M. de Norpois n'était certainement pas la raison de son déclassement dans un monde> {184:9-184:13}

184:17. <monde où les femmes> **185:26.** <résister quelques années. [184:31. <avait-elle, à ce moment-là fait> 185:5. <scandales qu'ont* probablement effacés l'éclat de son nom. 185:14. <qui supposent quelque exaltation. Sans doute j'avais remarqué>]

185:27. Ce que les artistes appellent intelligence semble-t-il* prétention pure à la société élégante qui incapable de se placer au seul point de vue d'où ils jugent tout, ne comprennent* jamais l'attrait particulier auquel ils cèdent en choisissant une expression ou en faisant un rapprochement, éprouvent* auprès d'eux une fatigue, une irritation d'où naît très vite l'antipathie.

185:33. Pourtant dans sa conversation> **187:13.** <qu'elle reçoit. [185:39. <vécu et ne dépeignait, d'ailleurs avec beaucoup de justesse et de charme, que ce qu'elles> 186:3. <frivole eut été* incapable> 186:13. <Villeparisis, rien que de telle épithète juste, de telles métaphores qui se suivent, le lecteur pourra induire le salut profond> 187:10. <qui les dépréciait>]

187:13. Certes le désir mondain, l'ambition de Mme de Villeparisis avait été bientôt de conserver, puis de reconstituer cette situation mondaine qu'elle tenait de sa grande naissance que son genre d'esprit son caractère particulier, s'étaient exercés à défaire avec une industrie persévérante et naturelle. {187:19-188:2}

188:2. De même l'isolement> **188:13.** <à son désir. {188:14-188:40}

188:41. <désir. D'ailleurs dans le salon de Mme de Villeparisis l'absence de Mme Leroi si elle désolait la maîtresse de maison passait> **189:29.** <estampe du XVIIIe siècle. {189:30-189:32}

189:32. Il y avait, parmi les> **189:39.** <duchesse de Montmorency>

1146 (P. 189, note 1). <Montmorency... abbesse à [*blanc*])>

189:40. <était venu> **190:2.** <prochaines matinées. [189:41. <Fronde, enfin mon ancien camarade Bloch>] {190:2-192:15}

192:6. —Mon Dieu, mon cher monsieur, les ministres dit-elle à Bloch, une fois que j'avais pris une chaise, reprenant le fil d'une conversation que mon entrée avait interrompue, personne ne voulait les voir.

192:10. Si petite que> **192:14.** <disait le roi.

192:14. Mon grand-père s'inclina et écrivit le soir même à M. Decaze lui demandant de lui faire la grâce et l'honneur d'assister à son bal qui avait lieu la semaine suivante. Mais la veille du bal> {192:14-192:26}

192:26. <du bal on apprenait> **193:11.** <n'y fit attention. [192:28. <bal... Mais si monsieur, je me rappelle M. Molé, c'est* un homme> 192:31. <solennel et je me le rappelle très bien descendant>] {193:11-193:25}

193:26. Bloch lui coupa> **193:30.** < ne le sut pas.* Le visage maigre ponctué maintenant d'une barbiche, le nez équilibré et circonspect, le corps allongé dans une redingote, n'ayant qu'une seule main nue dans laquelle il tenait un gant peau de chien, comme un rouleau de papyrus [*cf.* 190:16], il avait l'air de quelque scribe assyrien peint en costume de cérémonie à la frise du palais de Darius.

193:31 to 193:35. (These lines do not figure in Grasset B, *but, because of the reply in the next passage, this must be an accidental omission.)*

193:36. —Ah! il vous a dit ça comme ça finit mal.* Il en a de bonnes! S'écria* Bloch en s'esclaffant> **195:30.** <immédiatement leur rame de papiers et feraient atteler pour huit heures. [193:43. <déjà, reprit Mme de Villeparisis laissant> 194:9. <lecteurs. Si le salon de Mme de Villeparisis se différenciait d'un salon> 194:17. <citées; et certaines relations élégantes qu'il n'avait pas n'y font pas faute> 194:22. <que puissent lui donner des mé-

moires est atteinte. 194:37. <souvenirs à l'aide. 195:3. <agréable et fuyant le ton>] {195:32-198:30}

198:31. —Monsieur, j'crois que> **199:5.** <s'était levé. {199:5-199:32}

199:33. —Ah! voilà> **199:40.** <de La Rochefoucauld.

199:42. Un jeune domestique entra portant> {199:42-200:3}

200:3. <portant une carte> **200:42.** <vient de famille. [200:25. <eux et qui après avoir poussé un léger soupir témoignait de la nullité absolue de l'impression> 200:29. <attestait le désœuvrement l'inertie>] {200:43-201:26}

201:27. —Ce que vous nous apprenez> **202:7.** <de Luynes. {202:8-202:27}

202:28. —Tenez, monsieur> **203:6.** <à vous offrir des sandwichs. [202:31. <les compliments. Profitant de ce que> 203:2. <je vais rendre la visite à ce monstre. On ne peut même pas s'en tirer par un carton sous prétexte>] {203:7-203:23}

203:23. <sandwichs. Comment c'est le frère!> **203:37.** <combien j'allais le blesser. [203:28. <me faire à l'idée>]

□**203:37.** <blesser. Or peut-être avais-je à cet âge l'intention de blesser, mais comme je ne souffrais pas moi-même de la blessure—à moins qu'on me la rendît, ce qui me stupéfiait et me donnait à réfléchir—le sentiment qui m'inspirait me semblait si inoffensif et si riant que je le croyais une forme plus ou moins secondaire de la bienveillance. Toujours est-il que M. Legrandin conclut (c'est le jugement qu'il formula de moi quelques jours plus tard) que j'étais un petit être foncièrement méchant et ne se plaisait qu'au mal des paroles que je lui adressai en m'approchant de lui:

—Hé bien, monsieur, voilà comme vous fuyez les salons; je vois qu'on peut vous y trouver tout de même.

204:1. —Vous pourriez commencer par me dire bonjour, me répondit-il d'un air furieux sans me donner la main. {204:3-204:24}

204:25. Naturellement quand on me persécute vingt fois de suite pour me faire venir quelque part continua-t-il à voix basse j'ai bien droit à ma liberté je ne peux pourtant pas agir comme un rustre.

204:29. Mme de Guermantes> **204:33.** <à l'entour du pouf> [209:30. <ajoutait à la personne physique de Mme de Guermantes, son Duché* qui>]

204:33. <pouf sur lequel elle s'était assise. J'étais étonné seulement que leur ressemblance ne fut* pas plus lisible sur son visage qui n'avait rien de végétal et où tout au plus le couperosé des joues—lesquelles auraient dû semblait-il être blasonnées par le nom de Guermantes—était l'effet, mais non l'image de longues chevauchées au grand air. Pourtant c'était bien elle> {204:40-205:11}

205:12. <elle que désignait> **206:18.** <couche de poussière. [205:27. <à un de ces «jours», à un> 205:32. <et donnent jour sur Paris à la fin de l'après-midi, plus que les hautes> 205:34. <victorias; celui dont était coiffé Mme de Guermantes était couvert de bleuets; et> 205:42. <vague, de la pointe de son ombrelle comme avec l'extrême antenne> 206:4. <soi-même, et qu'elle exprimait aussi par une moue de sa bouche serrée, son regard> 206:8. <connaît, qui est> 206:11. <du fauteuil de Beauvais> 206:13. <perspicacité et d'une désapprobation>] {206:19-209:19}

209:19. Pour que je n'eusse pas> **210:7.** <fraîcheur sylvestre. [209:21. <même si je ne l'avais pas aimée, il n'eut* pas plus suffi> 209:32. <dîner et sans prendre la peine d'indiquer qu'à ce moment-là ils sentaient dans ce nom> 209:40. <monde disait que> 210:4. <nullement des gens comme Bergotte qui pouvaient composer cette coterie.]

210:7. Même les propos les plus intelligents que Mme de Guermantes eut* pu tenir (dans le sens où je prenais le mot intelligent quand il s'agissait d'un philosophe ou d'un critique). Non* seulement n'eussent pas suffi mais aurait peut-être déçu plus encore mon attente d'une faculté si particulière, que si dans une conversation insignifiante la duchesse s'était contentée>

210:13. <contentée de parler> **211:7.** <grommellement indistinct. [210:18. —Je ne l'ai pas vu depuis au moins cinq jours, ton mari>] {211:9-212:21}

212:22. <indistinct. Le comte d'Argencourt chef* d'affaires de Belgique et petit-cousin par les lignes de Mme de Villeparisis, entre* en boitant> **213:23.** <personne ne l'entendit. [212:31.

<tout à fait le type> 213:3. <me demande le> 213:20. <Aristote au chapitre>] {213:24-213:39}

213:40. <entendit. Chacun s'était approché pour voir Mme de Villeparisis peindre. **215:20.** <ensanglanté l'histoire> [214:16. <Fronde avec quelque hésitation> 215:8. <monsieur Vallismère*, dit-elle>]

215:20. <ensanglanté l'histoire de France, avec un talent> {215:21-215:24}

215:25. <talent pareil et> **215:26.** <d'affaire. {215:27-215:32}

215:33. Bloch voulut faire> **216:42.** <des spectacles curieux. [216:6. <de Slimilliers) d'être> 216:41. <pantomime tout montés que>]

216:43. Bloch se leva pour partir et comme il n'avait pas été présenté aux personnes présentes, croyant qu'il devait cependant les saluer> {216:43-217:18}

217:19. <les saluer, par savoir-vivre> **217:39.** <à être séparés. [217:24. <parler de leur comédie et elle n'aurait pas voulu>] {217:39-219:32}

219:33. Bloch s'était montré> **219:39.** <à l'Ambassadeur. {219:40-220:13}

220:11. —Mais attendez un instant, je ne sais pas ce qu'il peut faire, dit Mme de Villeparisis. Elle sonna>

220:13. <sonna et quand> **221:8.** <dit Bloch> [220:25. <gouvernement car gardant tout de même sa hauteur de grande dame de l'aristocratie, elle restait en dehors et au-dessus des relations qu'il était obligé de cultiver, tout de même elle était> 220:42. <pour mon «foie», dit-il en riant d'un air satanique. 221:6. <de ne pas se connaître.]

□**221:8.** <Bloch confus et ravis*. Le jeune duc assis sur un canapé, près de la fenêtre causait avec M. d'Argencourt, l'œillet rose de sa boutonnière allait signifier qu'il était seulement lui-même une fleur animée. Et Bloch sentant s'ouvrir si vite devant lui un avenir où il prendrait comme compagnon de voyage le duc de Châtellerault se [*blanc*]. Et regardant dans la lumière blonde du couchant, M. de Châtellerault qui assis sur un canapé près de la fenêtre avait l'air, un énorme œillet rose à sa boutonnière, de figurer dans quelque tableau vivant une «fleur animée.»

Bloch voyait s'ouvrir si opinément devant lui un avenir où il aurait ce jeune compagnon de voyage, se demandait s'il n'était pas le jouet d'un songe d'une fin d'après-midi de printemps.

221:9. Le maître d'hôtel> **221:18.** <vraisemblance à cette comédie> [221:13. <prit au hasard un chapeau dans l'antichambre et vint>] {221:19-221:33}

221:18. <comédie à laquelle d'ailleurs elle coupa court en disant: «M. l'Ambassadeur [*cf.* 221:34], je voudrais vous faire connaître Monsieur. M. Bloch, M. le marquis de Norpois. Monsieur de Norpois noya> {221:36-222:2}

222:3. <noya son regard> **222:17.** <avec vous, je crois que vous vouliez lui parler de l'affaire Dreyfus.

Sans* plus se préoccuper si cela faisait plaisir à M. de Norpois qu'elle n'eût pensé>

222:20. <pensé à demander> **222:26.** <bien connu Bismarck? {222:26-223:22}

223:23. —J'ai entendu> **223:36.** <voir entrer son mari. {223:36-223:41}

223:41. Celui-ci promenait sur le grand nombre> **224:1.** <du soleil couchant> [223:43. <thé des regards>] {224:1-224:4}

224:4. <couchant, s'avançait> **224:24.** <petit tablier. [224:19. <homme.» Il ne fit de grandes démonstrations>] {224:25-224:35}

224:36. —Vraiment? elle a joué> **224:43.** <sa tante). [224:38. <bouquet de lys dans sa main et d'autres lys «sur»* sa robe (Mme de Guermantes mettait>] {225:1-226:26}

227:1. —Vous savez> **228:8.** <de plus ridicule. {227:9-227:12}

227:13. <ridicule. Je ne peux pas comprendre comment Robert> **228:7.** <personne ridicule> {228:9-228-28}

228:29. —Pourtant voyez Swann objecte* M. d'Argencourt> **228:41.** <encore merveilleusement. [228:34. <la même chose, protesta> 228:37. <elle était jolie> 228:40. <choses «ch» armantes, de>]

228:41. <merveilleusement. Oh! si c'est une ravissante personne. Ça ne m'a pas fait moins de chagrin que Charles l'ait épousée mais je comprends qu'on fît l'amour tandis que la de-

moiselle de Robert je vous assure qu'elle est à mourir de rire [*cf.* 229:12]. {229:3-229:16}

229:16. <rire. D'abord, imaginez-vous> **229:26.** <toute la pièce. [229:24. <oh! yoil*, yoil, quel>] {229:26-229:30}

229:31. —Ah! vous les connaissez les Sept Princesses? Tous mes compliments! moi je n'en connais> **229:39.** <Maeterlinck. Et elle est ignorante comme une carpe. C'est pour une pareille femme>

229:39. <femme que tous les matins> **230:8.** <m'en a toujours voulu. [229:41. <d'elle. Tels>] {230:8-230:20}

230:21. —D'abord la veille il y a* une espèce de répétition qui était une bien belle chose! dit ironiquement Mme de Guermantes. Imaginez qu'elle disait une chose et puis elle s'arrêtait ne disait plus rien, mais>

230:25. <mais je n'exagère pas> **230:38.** <pas de talent.

230:40. Tout le monde> **231:3.** —Allons, Monsieur Devallenères, dit-elle à l'archiviste selon une plaisanterie consacrée, faites la jeune fille. M. de Guermantes se redressa>

231:6. <redressa dans> **231:28.** <désagréable, nous dit-il d'un air de satisfaction.

—Il s'appelle M. Legrandin.

—Ah! non alors il y a erreur. Je connais des Grandin, sans le, des Grandin de l'Epervier, mais je ne connais pas Legrandin.

—Comment s'écria la duchesse avec indignation, mais c'est le frère de cette énorme Cambremer que vous avez eu>

231:42. <eu l'étrange idée> **232:30.** <troupeau de vaches. [232:2. <entrer à mon jour une personne que je ne connaissais pas et qui m'avait l'air d'une vache. 232:10. <stimulée pour* la contradiction (c'est ainsi> 232:16. <réussir son coup, comme> 232:26. <votre Gambremes* était>] {232:30-232:38}

232:30. Elle a aussi un peu du ventre de la Reine de Suède.

232:39. —Mais c'est très flatteur> **234:5.** <par un cygne. [233:2. <il tenait beaucoup cependant. 233:10. <d'affabilité pour son interlocuteur, des> 233:40. <Norpois. Ayant tâché de le faire parler des officiers dont le nom revenait souvent dans les journaux à ce moment-là excitaient* plus la curiosité>] {234:5-234:25}

234:25. <cygne. M. de Norpois lui dit:

—Il y en a deux dont j'ai entendu parler>

234:27. <parler autrefois> **234:29.** <grand cas le lieutenant-colonel Henry et le lieutenant-colonel Picquart.

—Mais ils pensent exactement le contraire s'écria Bloch. {234:31-234:39}

234:40. M. de Norpois ne répondit pas. **235:9.** <les juifs à Jérusalem> [235:5. <quand on l'a appris, cela> 235:8. <comme Gombaud qui>]

235:10. —Ah! oui, le prince de Guermantes est un anti-sémite à tous crins, interrompit M. d'Argencourt.

—Mais ma chère, répondit le duc, il ne s'agit pas de Gombaud, ni de Jérusalem, mais enfin, vous m'avouerez> {235:11-235:18}

235:21. <m'avouerez que si un des nôtres> **235:28.** <notre époque, mais enfin quand on s'appelle Saint-Loup, on n'est pas dreyfusard, que voulez-vous que je vous dise! {235:31-237:1}

236:36. <dise. Que voulez-vous avec l'esprit qui règne là c'est assez compréhensible.

237:1. —Vous ne saviez> **237:7.** <qu'on veut dire. {237:7-237:15}

237:16. —Ah! mentalité, j'en prends note, je le reservirai. Mentalité me plaît.

237:19. <plaît. Il y a comme cela> **237:36.** <ni du cercle Volney> [237:21. <talentueux. Puis je ne l'ai> 237:33. <jeter à leur tour des regards>]

237:37. <Volney, je ne suis que de l'Union et du Jockey).* (vous* n'êtes pas du Jockey, monsieur, demanda-t-il à l'historien qui rougissant encore davantage, répondit que non en balbutiant, moi qui ne dîne même pas chez M. Emile Olivier*, j'avoue que je ne connaissais pas mentalité. Je suis sûr que vous êtes dans mon cas d'Argencourt*.

—Vous savez pourquoi on ne peut pas montrer les preuves de la trahison de Dreyfus. Il paraît que c'est parce qu'il est l'amant de la femme du ministre de la Guerre.

238:5. —Ah! je croyais> **238:6.** <d'Argencourt. {238:6-238:24}

238:25. —Non, du ministre de la guerre> **238:34.** <quand on s'appelle Saint-Loup> [238:30. <de mon cousin Astolphe et que

je n'ai aucun préjugé de races, j'ai la prétention d'être un homme de mon époque, je me promènerais avec un nègre>]

238:34. <Saint-Loup, on n'est pas dreyfusard et surtout huit jours avant de se présenter au cercle, que voulez-vous que je vous dise! Non, c'est probablement>

238:40. <probablement sa petite> **239:16.** <dans notre famille. [239:14. <tribu de Lévy*, et je prétends qu'il n'y a jamais eu>] {239:16-240:11}

240:10. Bloch cherchait à pousser M. de Norpois sur le colonel Picquart.

Il est certain répondit M. de Norpois que sa déposition à la première audience a produit une impression singulièrement heureuse. Quand on a vu cet officier, bien pris> {240:14-240:22}

240:23. <pris dans le joli uniforme> **240:41.** <je dis la vérité». [240:32. <avait pu exciter alors cela a été sa confrontation avec l'archiviste Gribelin, quand on a vu ce vieux serviteur> 240:36. <quand on l'entendit dire d'un ton qui n'admettait pas de réplique>] {240:41-240:43}

241:1. <vérité». «Non, décidément> **241:25.** <circonstances secondaires. [241:8. Peut-être la raison pour laquelle il lui parlait comme s'ils avaient été d'accord venait de ce qu'il était> 241:15. <comme des modalités sans importance et qui ne méritent pas> 241:18. Peut-être parce que> {241:25-242:19}

242:19. <secondaires. Tout ce que Bloch put tirer de lui c'est que s'il était vrai que le Chef d'Etat-Major eut* fait faire une communication secrète à M. Rochefort il y avait évidemment là quelque chose de singulièrement regrettable.

—J'ai entendu dire ajouta-t-il que le Général Billot l'avait formellement désapprouvé. {242:24-242:30}

242:31. —Mais ces pièces> □**242:35.** <d'Orléans d'avoir serré dans ses bras le Capitaine Esterhazy:

—Je n'ai pas eu l'honneur de rencontrer M. le Duc de Chartres [*cf.* 243:14] depuis longtemps mais je doute qu'elle eut* été de son goût. «A vue de nez [*cf.* 244:39] le Colonel du Paty de Clam lui paraissent* un cerveau fumeux et dont le choix n'avait peut-être pas été heureux pour conduire cette chose délicate et qui exige tant de sang-froid et de discernement, une instruction. {242:36-243:2}

243:3. Bloch ne put arriver> **243:11.** <puissent invoquer. {243:12-243:28}

243:29. —Vous n'allez pas> **243:31.** <avec Bloch. {243:32-243:43}

244:1. —Non, monsieur> **244:35.** —Ah! je croyais le contraire> [244:4. <regard les deux jeunes gens et Bloch. 244:12. Mme de Villeparisis ne répondit> 244:17. <Royale parce qu'il était vraiment trop mal composé maintenant et qu'on y entrait comme dans>]

244:35. <contraire, dit Bloch qui crut Mme de Guermantes sincère.

Aux questions que Bloch posa à M. de Norpois sur les officiers dont le nom revenait le plus souvent à propos de l'affaire Dreyfus, celui-ci déclara qu'à «vue de nez» [*cf.* 242:31] le colonel du Paty de Clam lui faisait l'effet d'un cerveau un peu fumeux et qui n'avait peut-être pas été très heureusement choisi pour conduire une instruction. {245:1-246:43}

247:1. —Vous Monsieur, dit Bloch> **247:23.** <radicalement étrangers. [274:12. <il se tempéra>] {247:24-249:17}

249:18. —Vous parliez> **249:24.** <ajouta-t-il.

249:25. Vraiment? Heureusement qu'ils ne sont pas tous comme cela vos compatriotes. Je connais des belges* très aimables, vous, votre Roi qui est plein d'esprit>

249:30. <d'esprit, mes cousins> **250:5.** <la mère de Robert. [249:40. <cela a choqué*, moi je trouvais cela curieux. Mais les Sept Princesses! 250:2. <pour son* neveu>]

□**250:5.** <Robert. Legrandin se leva et garda longtemps la main que lui avait tendu* Mme de Villeparisis en lui parlant très vite, avec beaucoup de gestes, mais à voix si basse que je ne pus rien entendre de ce qu'il disait, comme c'était peut-être son but.

250:5. <but. Mme de Marsantes était considérée> **250:23.** <de cœur dur. [250:16. <pareils du visage> 250:18. <me semblaient avoir>]

1150 (P. 250, note 3). Quand... Mme de Marsantes une exception* très différente... enthousiasmait>

250:25. <enthousiasmait le faubourg> **250:40.** <tare de sottise> [250:27. <pénétrant m'inciterait pourtant>]

250:40. <sottise, une sainte sans aucune entrave de cette brutalité. On me dit plus tard, quand je racontai que je l'avais vue, que j'avais dû me rendre compte combien elle était ravissante. Mais en réalité je remarquai seulement ce jour-là qu'elle avait l'air triste. {250:41-253:43}

—Vous n'avez pas vu Robert, comme c'est samedi je pensais qu'il aurait pu passer vingt-quatre heures [*cf.* 253:42] à Paris et dans ce cas il serait sûrement venu vous voir dit Mme de Marsantes à Mme de Villeparisis. En réalité elle croyait que son fils n'aurait pas de permission, mais comme en tous cas elle croyait que s'il en avait eu une il ne serait pas venu chez sa tante, elle espérait>

254:4. <espérait, en ayant l'air> **254:13.** <sur le tapis. {254:13-254:18}

254:18. <tapis. Mais à ce moment-là la porte s'ouvrit de nouveau et Robert entra.

—Tiens quand on parle du loup dit Mme de Villeparisis.

—Du Saint-Loup rectifia Mme de Guermantes pendant que la porte se rouvrait pour laisser passer M. de Charlus.

Mme de Saint-Loup* qui tournait le dos à la porte, n'avait pas vu entrer son fils. Quand elle l'aperçut, la joie battit en cette mère véritablement>

254:24. <véritablement comme un coup> **255:13.** <très flattée. [254:41. <sur moi l'averse lumineuse et bleue de son regard, hésita>]

255:13. Elle se tut, mais Saint-Loup restait là. Je voyais dans le fond de la piece, à côté de M. d'Argencourt avec qui il causait, M. de Charlus.

△**269:39.** La houpette* de ses cheveux gris, son œil dont le sourcil était relevé par le monocle et qui souriant*, sa boutonnière de* fleurs rouges, formaient comme les trois sommets mobiles d'un triangle convulsif et saisissant. Je n'avais pas osé le saluer car il n'avait fait aucun signe, or bien qu'il ne fut* pas tourné de mon côté j'étais persuadé qu'il m'avait vu: tandis qu'il débitait quelque histoire à M. d'Argencourt, ses yeux errants* comme ceux d'un marchand de plein vent qui craint l'arrivée de la «Rousse» avaient certainement exploré chaque partie du salon et découvert toutes les personnes qui s'y trouvaient, M. de Châtellerault vint lui dire bonjour sans que rien ne décelât dans le visage de M. de Charlus qu'il avait aperçu le jeune duc, qu'au moment où celui-ci se trouvait devant lui. Dans les réunions un peu nombreuses comme était celle-ci, M. de Charlus laissait flotter d'une façon presque constante un sourire sans direction indéterminée* ni sans direction particulière et qui préexistant ainsi aux saluts des arrivants se trouvait aussi dépouillé de toute signification aimable. {270:18-270:22}

255:14. —Tiens, je fais> **256:18.** <qui l'attendait. [255:22. <Mme de Saint-Loup, vous> 255:33. <décision affectant d'ignorait* tout ce qui> 255:36. <donné ce beau canard qui tenait un sac de chocolat que tu aimais tant.] {256:19-256:21}

256:22. Or le nom du Prince gardait la vive attaque des premières syllabes, la naïveté>

256:25. <naïveté maniérée> **257:14.** <électeur palatin> [256:32. <grand'mère, jouant sur les pentes d'une montagne honorée> 256:37. <le nom qu'avant de l'avoir reconnu il me parut> 256:40. <à laquelle il adhère*, familier, terre à terre, pittoresque, léger, prochain savoureux et permis. Bien> 257:8. <ses titres, les noms qu'on>]

257:14. <palatin, fut* entré, car il était gros et court et disait «Matame», et les revenus>

257:15. <les revenus qu'il tirait> **257:26.** <qu'il lui conférait> [257:20. <une loge à l'Opéra et une aux Français. 257:22. <qu'il différait des>]

257:26. <conférait, me* montrait qu'il n'était pas français qu'en cherchant à être un peu trop parisien et n'avait plus>

257:26. <plus qu'une ambition> **259:24.** <pas cela qu'il voulait. [257:28. <l'Académie des Sciences Morales et Politiques. Et c'est pour cela qu'il était aujourd'hui chez Mme de Villeparisis. 257:33. <désir. Depuis des années il était rongé par cette ambition d'entrer à l'Institut, n'avait> 257:37. <Norpois, un des membres les plus influents de l'Académie disposait> 257:43. <amabilités, lui faire avoir des décorations> 258:9. <prince disait*: «je voudrais> 258:13. <tenu à se déranger parce qu'il> 258:29. Le Prince avait été Ambassadeur et avait tenu, pour> 258:33. <dire. Il savait que> 259:14. <une partie sans espoir.

Tant> 259:19. <se dessiner, des chances surgir, vous pouvez compter que je vous en aviserais.] {259:24-261:15}

261:16. L'hiver suivant> **263:11.** <amené à venir ce jour-là voir Mme de Villeparisis. [262:12. <monde; mais> 262:19. <Beaulieu dans la villa de la Grande Duchesse Jean. 262:31. <le salon de Mme de Villeparisis qui est> 262:32. Je lui transmettrai votre requête elle en sera>] {263:12-263:27}

263:28. Vous ne voulez pas> **263:43.** <sans me dire adieu. {263:43-268:38}

269:39. See after 255:13.

□**270:22.** Je me décidai à aller saluer M. de Charlus. Il devait très bien voir que je venais vers lui mais comme il n'en donnait aucun signe je commençais à regretter de ne pouvoir revenir sur mes pas. Au moment où je m'inclinai devant lui, je trouvai, distant de son corps dont il m'empêchait d'approcher de toute la longueur de son bras tendu, deux doigts veufs eut on* dit d'un anneau épiscopal dont il avait l'air d'offrir, pour qu'on la baisât, la place consacrée et dus me contenter devant l'interruption de son accueil constant anonyme* et épais de paraître avoir pénétré à son insu et par effraction dont il me laissait la responsabilité dans les permanences, la dispersion anonyme et vacante de son sourire. Saint-Loup qui était resté pour la tenir chambrée* à côté de moi se leva.

—Comme tu as l'air fatigué et agité, lui dit sa mère qui n'avait pas encore pu lui parler.

270:38. Et en effet> □**270:40.** <le fond. Car nos idées ont leur place. Il y en a qui sont situées très loin à l'extrême frontière de l'esprit, où notre attention cherche à les approcher, où* les distinguer sans d'habitude y parvenir. Et je doute que Saint-Loup est* jamais eu en lui ces idées-là. Mais il y en a d'autres, des idées douloureuses qui sont situées très loin aussi, à une grande profondeur du cœur et qui font si mal quand on les touche, qu'on les quitte aussitôt, pour y revenir un instant après. Telle était l'idée qu'il avait rompu avec sa maîtresse.

271:1. —Ça ne fait rien> **271:7.** <boutons d'or. [271:2. <son petit enfant. 271:3. <tendresse paraissait agacer Robert, Mme de Saint-Loup entraîna>] {271:8-273:21}

□**273:22.** J'aurais voulu avoir des renseignements sur tous les êtres qui approchaient Mme de Guermantes, comme on en souhaite sur les personnes qui sont représentées dans un roman qui nous passionne. A cause de cela j'étais aussi désireux de m'instruire sur Mme Leroi que Bloch sur du Paty de Clam, avec le manque de tact>

273:25. <tact des gens qui> **273:35.** <à ce que j'ai.

M. de Norpois était en train de dire au Prince de Faffenheim que les opinions révisionistes* d'un des candidats à l'Académie l'empêcheraient peut-être de passer. Mais Mme de Villeparisis l'interrompit éprouvant>] {273:36-274:8}

274:9. <éprouvant le besoin> **274:40.** <coloris de la fleur. [274:18. —Monsieur dit Mme de Villeparisis à M. de Norpois en riant, il y a> 274:35. <ordre, déclara M. de Norpois.] {274:41-275:28}

275:29. Robert m'appela> **275:31.** <te remercier {275:32-276:10}

276:10. —Mais je n'ai pas été gentil> **276:37.** <sur lequel elle croyait donc exercer un empire qui n'égalait pas et devait ménager le mien. J'aurais> [276:15. <notre imminent départ pour Balbec> 276:24. <d'elle; tout ce que j'avais pu souhaiter de plus, c'est> 276:28. <Balbec intacte et indéfiniment prolongée au lieu> 276:30. <moment Mme de Saint-Loup s'interrompait> 276:35. <avait de faire fâcher ce fils qu'elle n'avait pas encore vu, avec qui> {276:39-277:4}

277:5. J'aurais voulu tout le temps pouvoir l'assurer que Robert avait pour elle> **277:25.** <face de moi> [277:24. <causait, fit> {277:25-277:27}

277:28. <de moi et dans l'embrasure de la porte> **277:39.** <qu'instant. [277:35. <réaliser. Je dors tard, je suis peu>] {277:40-278:5}

278:5. Je lui dis qu'il fallait d'abord que je dise quelques mots à Saint-Loup.

—Allez. {278:6-278:24}

278:24. Pour tâcher de mettre quelque baume sur sa fierté que je croyais blessée je voulus chercher à excuser sa maîtresse. Je ne savais pas> **279:5.** <ce n'est pas vrai. [278:37. <collier, dit-il.]

279:5. <vrai. Car elle m'aime tant, que doit-elle se dire. Comme elle doit regretter, pauvre chérie, si tu savais elle a de telles délicatesses, je ne peux pas te dire, elle a souvent fait pour moi des choses adorables. A côté de cela, elle est très bruyante, c'est vrai. Mais ce qu'elle doit être>

279:9. <être malheureuse> **279:19.** <tout ce que je demande. [279:13. <torts. Pauvre chérie, c'est l'idée> 279:16. <se le représenter, oh! vois-tu, cela me déchire le cœur, je crois>]

279:19. Ecoute, je cours chez le bijoutier>

279:22. <bijoutier et après cela> **279:35.** <dès que je le saurai. [279:25. <hasard viens tout à l'heure chez elle>] {279:36-280:12}

280:12. Alors je vis le même battement d'ailes que Mme de Saint-Loup n'avait pu réprimer> **281:24.** <est trop tard. [281:2. <d'elle-même elle cessa> 281:8. <à Mme de Saint-Loup, mais>] {281:25-281:31}

281:32. Nous rentrâmes> **281:37.** <de l'orage.» {281:38-283:12}

283:13. —Il* ne me reproche qu'une chose, me dit tout bas Mme de Marsantes*, c'est> **283:21.** <vous êtes pressé [283:22-283:32]

283:33. —Mais non Madame répondis-je, d'ailleurs j'attends M. de Charlus avec qui je dois m'en aller.

283:35. Mme de Villeparisis entendit> **283:36.** <contrariée. {283:36-283:43}

284:1. —Vous devez> **284:2.** <dit-elle. {284:3-284:11}

284:11. —Ne l'attendez donc pas, me dit-elle> **284:13.** <vous a dit. Tenez, partez pendant qu'il a le dos tourné.

Mme de Villeparisis avait l'air de tenir à ce que je ne partisse pas avec M. de Charlus. Pourtant je n'étais guère pressé de retrouver Robert et sa maîtresse. Pourtant Mme de Villeparisis semblait tenir tellement à ce que je partisse, que pensant qu'elle avait peut-être à causer avec son neveu je pris congé d'elle. {284-19-284:35}

284:36. Dans l'escalier> **285:11.** <pour en décider. [284:42. <jusqu'à ce que j'ai* trouvé> 285:3. <trop si je les dirai. Certes> 285:8. <temps, des dérangements. Je me demande si>] {285:11-285:14}

285:14. <décider. Peut-être aussi n'avez-vous pas> **285:15.** <ce ne peut être que de l'ennui.

285:20. Je protestai> **285:33.** <en valût la peine. La question est de savoir si vous valez ou non la peine. {285:25-285:34}

285:36. —Je ne voudrais> **286:33.** <de la solitude et de l'ennui> [286:7. <prononcer au contraire sont> 286:8. <toucher et de me faire faire beaucoup pour vous. 286:10. < dessous avec moi et> 286:18. <tantôt il les> 286:22. —Ce n'est pas mon affaire, me dit-il> 286:29. J'étais frappé combien sa diction ressemblait à celle de Sawann* encore plus qu'à Balbec]. {286:33-287:4}

286:33. <l'ennui, que je vais vous la faire. Je n'aime pas beaucoup à parler de moi Monsieur. Mais enfin vous l'avez>

287:5. <l'avez peut-être appris> **287:24.** <certains événements eussent pris à ses yeux un aspect entièrement différent. [287:9. <dans un entretien que> 287:16. <d'expérience que je n'ai pas cru devoir utiliser personnellement mais qui> 287:22. <secrets qu'Henri Martin aurait donné des années de sa vie>] {287:25-291:19}

291:19.<différent. Ceci n'est rien. Ayant une formidable avance> □**291:33.** <qu'on pût rêver. J'ai un fils qui n'est pas, je ne dirai pas digne, mais capable de recevoir>

291:35. <recevoir l'héritage moral> **291:43.** <chaque jour.

292:1. A ce moment mon bras fut vivement déplacé par un choc, comme il arrive quand tenant un objet électrisé on a mis par mégarde sa main sur un bouton électrique. C'était> {292:1-292:3}

292:5. C'était M. de Charlus> **292:25.** Néanmoins je remarquai que M. d'Argencourt fut plus froid avec moi qu'il n'avait été chez Mme de Villeparisis, et dès lors, pendant fort longtemps>

292:30. <longtemps il en fut> **292:34.** <après une hésitation, il me tendit la main. [292:31. Il m'observait ce>]

292:36. —Je regrette cette rencontre me dit M. de Charlus. C'est un de ces hommes> {292:37-292:39}

292:39. <hommes incapables> **293:4.** <gens du monde. [292:41. <amitié, si elle doit se fondre un jour, en sera une et j'espère que vous me ferez l'honneur d'y tenir à l'abri> 293:1.

<par désœuvrement, par maladresse, par méchanceté>] {293:5-293:15}

293:15. Et c'est justement> **293:25.** <sans inconvénients. [293:20. <tantôt de vous voir>] {293:25-295:8}

295:9. Actuellement vous ne feriez que nuire à votre situation, déformant votre intelligence> **295:30.** <innocentes victimes. {295:30-295:40}

295:40. <victimes. Il n'est pas> **296:34.** <partit au grand trot.

NORTH CAROLINA STUDIES IN THE ROMANCE LANGUAGES AND LITERATURES

I.S.B.N. Prefix 0-8078-

Recent Titles

THE TEACHINGS OF SAINT LOUIS. A CRITICAL TEXT, by David O'Connell. 1972. (No. 116). *-916-2.*

HIGHER, HIDDEN ORDER: DESIGN AND MEANING IN THE ODES OF MALHERBE, by David Lee Rubin. 1972. (No. 117). *-917-0.*

JEAN DE LE MOTE "LE PARFAIT DU PAON," édition critique par Richard J. Carey. 1972. (No. 118). *-918-9.*

CAMUS' HELLENIC SOURCES, by Paul Archambault. 1972. (No. 119). *-919-7.*

FROM VULGAR LATIN TO OLD PROVENÇAL, by Frede Jensen. 1972. (No. 120). *-920-0.*

GOLDEN AGE DRAMA IN SPAIN: GENERAL CONSIDERATION AND UNUSUAL FEATURES, by Sturgis E. Leavitt. 1972. (No. 121). *-921-9.*

THE LEGEND OF THE "SIETE INFANTES DE LARA" (*Refundición toledana de la crónica de 1344* versión), study and edition by Thomas A. Lathrop. 1972. (No. 122). *-922-7.*

STRUCTURE AND IDEOLOGY IN BOIARDO'S "ORLANDO INNAMORATO," by Andrea di Tommaso. 1972. (No. 123). *-923-5.*

STUDIES IN HONOR OF ALFRED G. ENGSTROM, edited by Robert T. Cargo and Emmanuel J. Mickel, Jr. 1972. (No. 124). *-924-3.*

A CRITICAL EDITION WITH INTRODUCTION AND NOTES OF GIL VICENTE'S "FLORESTA DE ENGANOS," by Constantine Christopher Stathatos. 1972. (No. 125). *-925-1.*

LI ROMANS DE WITASSE LE MOINE. *Roman du treizième siècle.* Édité d'après le manuscrit, fonds français 1553, de la Bibliothèque Nationale, Paris, par Denis Joseph Conlon. 1972. (No. 126). *-926-X.*

EL CRONISTA PEDRO DE ESCAVIAS. *Una vida del Siglo XV*, por Juan Bautista Avalle-Arce. 1972. (No. 127). *-927-8.*

AN EDITION OF THE FIRST ITALIAN TRANSLATION OF THE "CELESTINA," by Kathleen V. Kish. 1973. (No. 128). *-928-6.*

MOLIÈRE MOCKED. THREE CONTEMPORARY HOSTILE COMEDIES: *Zélinde, Le portrait du peintre, Élomire Hypocondre*, by Frederick Wright Vogler. 1973. (No. 129). *-929-4.*

C.-A. SAINTE-BEUVE. *Chateaubriand et son groupe littéraire sous l'empire.* Index alphabétique et analytique établi par Lorin A. Uffenbeck. 1973. (No 130). *-930-8.*

THE ORIGINS OF THE BAROQUE CONCEPT OF "PEREGRINATIO," by Juergen Hahn. 1973. (No. 131). *-931-6.*

THE "AUTO SACRAMENTAL" AND THE PARABLE IN SPANISH GOLDEN AGE LITERATURE, by Donald Thaddeus Dietz. 1973. (No. 132). *-932-4.*

FRANCISCO DE OSUNA AND THE SPIRIT OF THE LETTER, by Laura Calvert. 1973. (No. 133). *-933-2.*

ITINERARIO DI AMORE: DIALETTICA DI AMORE E MORTE NELLA VITA NUOVA, by Margherita de Bonfils Templer. 1973. (No. 134). *-934-0.*

L'IMAGINATION POETIQUE CHEZ DU BARTAS: ELEMENTS DE SENSIBILITE BAROQUE DANS LA "CREATION DU MONDE," by Bruno Braunrot. 1973. (No. 135). *-934-0.*

ARTUS DESIRE: PRIEST AND PAMPHLETEER OF THE SIXTEENTH CENTURY, by Frank S. Giese. 1973. (No. 136). *-936-7.*

JARDIN DE NOBLES DONZELLAS, FRAY MARTIN DE CORDOBA, by Harriet Goldberg. 1974. (No. 137). *-937-5.*

When ordering please cite the *ISBN Prefix* plus the last four digits for each title.

Send orders to: University of North Carolina Press
Chapel Hill
North Carolina 27514
U. S. A.

NORTH CAROLINA STUDIES IN THE ROMANCE LANGUAGES AND LITERATURES

I.S.B.N. Prefix 0-8078-

Recent Titles

MYTHE ET PSYCHOLOGIE CHEZ MARIE DE FRANCE DANS "GUIGEMAR", par Antoinette Knapton. 1975. (No. 142). *-942-1.*

THE LYRIC POEMS OF JEHAN FROISSART: A CRITICAL EDITION, by Rob Roy McGregor, Jr. 1975. (No. 143). *-943-X.*

THE HISPANO-PORTUGUESE CANCIONERO OF THE HISPANIC SOCIETY OF AMERICA, by Arthur Askins. 1974. (No. 144). *-944-8.*

HISTORIA Y BIBLIOGRAFÍA DE LA CRÍTICA SOBRE EL "POEMA DE MÍO CID" (1750-1971), por Miguel Magnotta. 1976. (No. 145). *-945-6.*

LES ENCHANTEMENZ DE BRETAIGNE. AN EXTRACT FROM A THIRTEENTH CENTURY PROSE ROMANCE "LA SUITE DU MERLIN", edited by Patrick C. Smith. 1977. (No. 146). *-9146-0.*

THE DRAMATIC WORKS OF ÁLVARO CUBILLO DE ARAGÓN, by Shirley B. Whitaker. 1975. (No. 149). *-949-9.*

A CONCORDANCE TO THE "ROMAN DE LA ROSE" OF GUILLAUME DE LORRIS, by Joseph R. Danos. 1976. (No. 156). *0-88438-403-9.*

POETRY AND ANTIPOETRY: A STUDY OF SELECTED ASPECTS OF MAX JACOB'S POETIC STYLE, by Annette Thau. 1976. (No. 158). *-005-X.*

FRANCIS PETRARCH, SIX CENTURIES LATER, by Aldo Scaglione. 1975. (No. 159).

STYLE AND STRUCTURE IN GRACIÁN'S "EL CRITICÓN", by Marcia L. Welles, 1976. (No. 160). *-007-6.*

MOLIERE: TRADITIONS IN CRITICISM, by Laurence Romero. 1974 (Essays, No. 1). *-001-7.*

CHRÉTIEN'S JEWISH GRAIL. A NEW INVESTIGATION OF THE IMAGERY AND SIGNIFICANCE OF CHRÉTIEN DE TROYES'S GRAIL EPISODE BASED UPON MEDIEVAL HEBRAIC SOURCES, by Eugene J. Weinraub. 1976. (Essays, No. 2). *-002-5.*

STUDIES IN TIRSO, I, by Ruth Lee Kennedy. 1974. (Essays, No. 3). *-003-3.*

VOLTAIRE AND THE FRENCH ACADEMY, by Karlis Racevskis. 1975. (Essays, No. 4). *-004-1.*

THE NOVELS OF MME RICCOBONI, by Joan Hinde Stewart. 1976. (Essays, No. 8). *-008-4.*

FIRE AND ICE: THE POETRY OF XAVIER VILLAURRUTIA, by Merlin H. Forster. 1976. (Essays, No. 11). *-011-4.*

THE THEATER OF ARTHUR ADAMOV, by John J. McCann. 1975. (Essays, No. 13). *-013-0.*

AN ANATOMY OF POESIS: THE PROSE POEMS OF STÉPHANE MALLARMÉ, by Ursula Franklin. 1976. (Essays, No. 16). *-016-5.*

LAS MEMORIAS DE GONZALO FERNÁNDEZ DE OVIEDO, Vols. I and II, by Juan Bautista Avalle-Arce. 1974. (Texts, Textual Studies, and Translations, Nos. 1 and 2). *-401-2; 402-0.*

GIACOMO LEOPARDI: THE WAR OF THE MICE AND THE CRABS, translated, introduced and annotated by Ernesto G. Caserta. 1976. (Texts, Textual Studies, and Translations, No. 4). *-404-7.*

LUIS VÉLEZ DE GUEVARA: A CRITICAL BIBLIOGRAPHY, by Mary G. Hauer. 1975. (Texts, Textual Studies, and Translations, No. 5). *-405-5.*

UN TRÍPTICO DEL PERÚ VIRREINAL: "EL VIRREY AMAT, EL MARQUÉS DE SOTO FLORIDO Y LA PERRICHOLI". EL "DRAMA DE DOS PALANGANAS" Y SU CIRCUNSTANCIA, estudio preliminar, reedición y notas por Guillermo Lohmann Villena. 1976. (Texts, Textual Studies, and Translation, No. 15). *-415-2.*

LOS NARRADORES HISPANOAMERICANOS DE HOY, edited by Juan Bautista Avalle-Arce. 1973. (Symposia, No. 1). *-951-0.*

When ordering please cite the *ISBN Prefix* plus the last four digits for each title.

Send orders to: University of North Carolina Press
Chapel Hill
North Carolina 27514
U. S. A.

NORTH CAROLINA STUDIES IN THE ROMANCE LANGUAGES AND LITERATURES

I.S.B.N. Prefix 0-8078-

Recent Titles

ESTUDIOS DE LITERATURA HISPANOAMERICANA EN HONOR A JOSÉ J. ARROM, edited by Andrew P. Debicki and Enrique Pupo-Walker. 1975. (Symposia, No. 2). *-952-9.*

MEDIEVAL MANUSCRIPTS AND TEXTUAL CRITICISM, edited by Christopher Kleinhenz. 1976. (Symposia, No. 4). *-954-5.*

SAMUEL BECKETT. THE ART OF RHETORIC, edited by Edouard Morot-Sir, Howard Harper, and Dougald McMillan III. 1976. (Symposia, No. 5). *-955-3.*

DELIE. CONCORDANCE, by Jerry Nash. 1976. 2 Volumes. (No. 174).

FIGURES OF REPETITION IN THE OLD PROVENÇAL LYRIC: A STUDY IN THE STYLE OF THE TROUBADOURS, by Nathaniel B. Smith. 1976. (No. 176). *-9176-2.*

A CRITICAL EDITION OF LE REGIME TRESUTILE ET TRESPROUFITABLE POUR CONSERVER ET GARDER LA SANTE DU CORPS HUMAIN, by Patricia Willett Cummins. 1977. (No. 177).

THE DRAMA OF SELF IN GUILLAUME APOLLINAIRE'S "ALCOOLS", by Richard Howard Stamelman. 1976. (No. 178). *-9178-9.*

A CRITICAL EDITION OF "LA PASSION NOSTRE SEIGNEUR" FROM MANUSCRIPT 1131 FROM THE BIBLIOTHEQUE SAINTE-GENEVIEVE, PARIS, by Edward J. Gallagher. 1976. (No. 179). *-9179-7.*

A QUANTITATIVE AND COMPARATIVE STUDY OF THE VOCALISM OF THE LATIN INSCRIPTIONS OF NORTH AFRICA, BRITAIN, DALMATIA, AND THE BALKANS, by Stephen William Omeltchenko. 1977. (No. 180). *-9180-0.*

OCTAVIEN DE SAINT-GELAIS "LE SEJOUR D'HONNEUR", edited by Joseph A. James. 1977. (No. 181). *-9181-9.*

A STUDY OF NOMINAL INFLECTION IN LATIN INSCRIPTIONS, by Paul A. Gaeng. 1977. (No. 182). *-9182-7.*

THE LIFE AND WORKS OF LUIS CARLOS LÓPEZ, by Martha S. Bazik. 1977. (No. 183). *-9183-5.*

"THE CORT D'AMOR". A THIRTEENTH-CENTURY ALLEGORICAL ART OF LOVE, by Lowanne E. Jones. 1977. (No. 185). *-9185-1.*

PHYTONYMIC DERIVATIONAL SYSTEMS IN THE ROMANCE LANGUAGES: STUDIES IN THEIR ORIGIN AND DEVELOPMENT, by Walter E. Geiger. 1978. (No. 187). *-9187-8.*

LANGUAGE IN GIOVANNI VERGA'S EARLY NOVELS, by Nicholas Patruno. 1977. (No. 188). *-9188-6.*

BLAS DE OTERO EN SU POESÍA, by Moraima de Semprún Donahue. 1977. (No. 189). *-9189-4.*

LA ANATOMÍA DE "EL DIABLO COJUELO": DESLINDES DEL GÉNERO ANATOMÍSTICO, por C. George Peale. 1977. (No. 191). *-9191-6.*

RICHARD SANS PEUR, EDITED FROM "LE ROMANT DE RICHART" AND FROM GILLES CORROZET'S "RICHART SANS PAOUR", by Denis Joseph Conlon. 1977. (No. 192). *-9192-4.*

MARCEL PROUST'S GRASSET PROOFS. *Commentary and Variants,* by Douglas Alden. 1978. (No. 193). *-9193-2.*

MONTAIGNE AND FEMINISM, by Cecile Insdorf. 1977. (No. 194). *-9194-0.*

SANTIAGO F. PUGLIA, AN EARLY PHILADELPHIA PROPAGANDIST FOR SPANISH AMERICAN INDEPENDENCE, by Merle S. Simmons. 1977. (No. 195). *-9195-9.*

BAROQUE FICTION-MAKING. A STUDY OF GOMBERVILLE'S "POLEXANDRE", by Edward Baron Turk. 1978. (No. 196). *-9196-7.*

TWO AGAINST TIME. *A Study of the very present worlds of Paul Claudel and Charles Péguy,* by Joy Nachod Humes. 1978. (No. 200). *-9200-9.*

When ordering please cite the *ISBN Prefix* plus the last four digits for each title.

Send orders to: University of North Carolina Press
Chapel Hill
North Carolina 27514
U. S. A.

The Department of Romance Studies Digital Arts and Collaboration Lab at the University of North Carolina at Chapel Hill is proud to support the digitization of the North Carolina Studies in the Romance Languages and Literatures series.

www.ingramcontent.com/pod-product-compliance
Lightning Source LLC
Chambersburg PA
CBHW021413300426
44114CB00010B/479

* 9 7 8 0 8 0 7 8 9 1 9 3 3 *